THE AMERICAN
COUNTRY INN
and
BED & BREAKFAST
COOKBOOK

THE AMERICAN

COUNTRY INN
and
BED & BREAKFAST
COOKBOOK

Kitty and Lucian Maynard

❖ ❖ ❖

More than 1,700 crowd-pleasing
recipes from 500 American Inns

Julia M. Pitkin, Editor

RUTLEDGE HILL PRESS
Nashville, Tennessee

Published in Nashville, Tennessee, by Rutledge Hill Press, Inc., 513 Third Avenue South, Nashville, Tennessee 37210.

Typography: ProtoType Graphics, Inc., Nashville, Tennessee
Design: Harriette Bateman
Art: Tonya M. Pitkin

Library of Congress Cataloging-in-Publication Data

Maynard, Kitty, 1955–
   The American country inn and bed & breakfast cookbook.

   Includes indexes.
   1. Breakfasts.   2. Bed and breakfast accommodations
—United States—Directories.   I. Maynard, Lucian,
1952–   . II. Title.
TX733.M43   1987   641.5′0973   87–10105
ISBN 0–934395–50–0   (Hardcover)
ISBN 1–55853–064–9 (Paperback)

Manufactured in the United States of America
9 10 11 12 13 14 15 — 95 94 93 92 91 90

Dedication

To the country inns, bed and breakfast inns, innkeepers and chefs of America. They are truly this country's ambassadors of good company and great food.

Thanks

To Kelly, Barry and Nick for being three very patient and loving children.

Table of Contents

Preface

*T*he *American Country Inn and Bed & Breakfast Cookbook* is designed to give you an accurate picture of what each of these inns and bed and breakfasts offers its guests. It will also give you recipes for the finest in American cooking.

The book is organized alphabetically by state—for all fifty states and the District of Columbia—and by city within each state. Information about each inn is provided, usually describing the inn and the facilities it offers, as well as a brief sketch of nearby attractions. Address and telephone information is included, except in those rare instances where an inn prefers to be contacted by mail or where it does not have a telephone.

Recipes are printed with the inns that submitted them. For each inn, the recipes follow a sequence common in cookbooks: Breakfast Dishes; Jams, Jellies, and Butters; Appetizers; Beverages; Soups; Sauces; Salads and Dressings; Breads; Entrees; Vegetables; and Desserts.

The exhaustive index of foods beginning on page 485 indexes each recipe in alphabetical order, under its main ingredient or ingredients (such as Blueberries, Corn, Oranges, or Pork), and with its food category (such as Appetizers, Salads, or Entrees).

We do not wish to imply that these country inns and bed and breakfasts are the only good ones to visit. Time and space limitations prevented our including every inn we wanted to list. And we cannot guarantee that everyone visiting these inns will find them as special as we do. But we have taken care to provide you with a cookbook and guide that is as reliable as we can make it.

Introduction

In ever-increasing numbers Americans are searching for new and innovative ways to invest their "free" time. Whether planning a two-day weekend escape or an extended vacation, we want to be assured that our time and money are well spent and that our experience is memorable.

Our family is no exception. When we look for the perfect getaway, we keep both cost and character in mind; that is how we are accustomed to living. Character means a great deal to us; it marks the difference between the ordinary and the "special." Apparently many Americans feel as we do, for since the 1960s people have been turning to country inns and bed and breakfasts in increasing numbers.

For our family the answer to this search began almost by accident. We were driving to Kitty's parents' home and decided to take the more unconventional route through the Smoky Mountains via the Blue Ridge Parkway. There we found a scenic beauty that was beyond our expectations; as we drove we could feel the stress leaving us.

And then we saw a sign for a bed and breakfast home. It sounded good. It looked good. It turned out to be even better! We had found something new. In addition to a comfortable, clean room, we were blessed with the company of a good host and hostess and a relaxing "laid back" atmosphere.

Since that day fourteen years ago, each time we have traveled we have purposely chosen routes that would make it possible for us to stay in inns or bed and breakfast homes. How strange it seems now to realize that this practice of staying in homes while traveling has been the norm for as long as man can remember, but we found it almost by accident.

A bed and breakfast traditionally offers a comfortable night's lodging and a pleasant breakfast in a private home. Travelers who choose this type of accommodation prefer the personal contact and friendly warmth that a bed and breakfast provides. Bed and breakfasts come in many shapes and sizes, as well as in many price ranges. They range from cottages to historical mansions, from country inns to farm houses, from modern condominiums to boats moored at piers. They may or may not be very large, and they may or may not be filled with antiques.

However, a successful bed and breakfast does offer three essential ingredients: genuine hospitality, cleanliness, and a comfortable guest bedroom. A private bathroom for guests is very convenient, but it is common for guests to share a bathroom "down the hall." In this sense, staying at a bed and breakfast home reminds one of the days when we lived at home and stood in line to use the bath. It is amazing what kinds of conversations begin in the hall with fellow guests! And while you stand there, the smells of coffee, muffins, fresh bread, and tea welcome you to the new day. It is this warmth and congeniality that drew us to these establishments, as I suspect is true for most who choose to travel the bed and breakfast way.

A country inn provides many of these same wonderful experiences, but on a grander scale. Generally, a country inn is a larger establishment than a bed and breakfast. In many cases they not only serve breakfast and tea, but also have full service restaurants and lounges, and occasionally even gift shops. The foods they serve range from mouth-watering home-style cooking to ethnic or gourmet. Country inns generally offer more facilities, such as a recreational center, a ski resort, a swimming pool and sunbathing area, or even a complete health facility. It may even be an elegant night spot in the heart of a large city or a mansion in the middle of a lush plantation. Some have said that country inns are the Grand Dames of guest house facilities.

While *The American Country Inn and Bed & Breakfast Cookbook* is not a travel guide, it is a guide of sorts. Within these pages you can read about some of the most unique homes and inns in America. One of our goals in producing this book was to find and write about places that we consider offer something unique to their guests. We looked for the unusual. The discerning reader will quickly notice that a number of these inns are listed in the Registry of Historical Places. Visiting country inns and bed and breakfasts will acquaint guests with knowledge of the people, history, and culture of surrounding areas. These homes and inns are part of that history.

Being food aficionados ourselves, we were naturally drawn to the cuisine of the country inn and bed and breakfast establishments we visited. Kitty's own style is similar to those of the bed and breakfast and country inns included in this book; she likes to experiment. Sometimes that includes flaming a dish and setting off the fire alarm or adding sour cream to a muffin to change the flavor and texture.

We have found the chefs at the inns and beds and breakfasts to be a hearty and creative group. They range from chefs who are graduates of prominent culinary schools to creative housewives and mothers. At an inn or bed and breakfast, a chef can find experience, room to experiment, and creative expression through the art of cooking. These chefs and cooks obviously delight in creative experimentation in their kitchens.

Look carefully at the recipes in this book, for they range from gourmet to family style. These recipes are used and praised daily by guests. We call them "crowd pleasers." They are the most frequently requested recipes at the inns and homes. From the seafood of New England to the wholesome country cuisine of the South, from the whole grain breads of the Midwest, to the "health" foods of the West Coast, it all spells good cooking. You should not be afraid to try these recipes. If we can prepare them—and we have—so can you. The cuisine is both American and international.

This book can provide you with alternative ideas for your next vacation, getaway, or trip. Find a place to relax. Discover a delightful nook or cranny in America!

Where else can you leave your shoes outside the door to have them magically shined by morning? Where else can you "check out" a cat to stay in your room while you sleep? Where else can you pick out a teddy bear to sleep with at night, or find fresh flowers by the bedside each morning, or ride horses on the range or a sleigh through newfallen snow? Where else can you go on a hayride, or find a candy kiss on the pillow of your turned down bed, or awake to the aroma of great food?

So here it is—a book of over 500 inns and 180 recipes from the country inns and bed and breakfasts in each state. In it you will discover one of the most diverse and unique collections of recipes found anywhere.

It has been said that this is the year of the American chef and American cuisine. We couldn't agree more. This is the year for us—American food lovers—and *The American Country Inn and Bed & Breakfast Cookbook* is a supreme example of how we express our art—through our recipes.

Enjoy and experiment! We hope you have as much fun reading and preparing these dishes as we had in gathering them for you.

Kitty E. Maynard
Lucian Maynard

THE AMERICAN
COUNTRY INN
and
BED & BREAKFAST
COOKBOOK

Alabama

Bed N' Breakfast at Mentone Inn

Box 284
Mentone, Alabama 35984
(205) 634-4836

The Mentone Inn offers a touch of yesterday-today atop beautiful Lookout Mountain. Built in 1927, the inn has twelve rooms and one cottage. The day starts off with a good breakfast, and then guests may rest and relax in a pleasant quiet setting. There is a sun deck with hot tub, as well as table tennis and horseshoes for those wanting to use a little more energy. Arrangements can also be made for trail rides.

Cold English Pea Salad

1 16-ounce can English peas

❖   ❖   ❖

2 tablespoons chopped green
   peppers
2 tablespoons chopped celery
1 teaspoon chopped pimientos
1 teaspoon chopped onion
2 tablespoons diced sharp cheese
1 tablespoon pickle relish

❖   ❖   ❖

1 hard-cooked egg, diced
1½ teaspoons mayonnaise

Drain peas; in a salad bowl combine the next 6 ingredients and mix well. Add peas, egg and mayonnaise and mix gently. Chill.
   Serves 6.

Easy Tomato Aspic

2 3-ounce packages lemon gelatin
1½ cups boiling water
2 cups V-8 juice
½ cup chili sauce

In a medium saucepan, dissolve the gelatin in boiling water. Add remaining ingredients. Pour into a lightly oiled 9-inch square pan. Chill until firm. Cut into squares to serve. This is especially good with tuna salad.
   Serves 9.

Hot Chicken Salad

4 cups cold cooked chicken chunks
2 tablespoons lemon juice
¾ cup mayonnaise
1 teaspoon salt
½ teaspoon Accent
1 cup chopped celery
4 hard-cooked eggs, chopped
1 10¾-ounce can cream of chicken
   soup
1 teaspoon finely minced onion
2 pimientoes, finely minced

❖   ❖   ❖

1 cup grated New York sharp
   cheese
1½ cups crushed potato chips
⅔ cup finely chopped toasted
   almonds

In a large bowl, combine all ingredients except cheese, potato chips and almonds. Place salad in a 2-quart Pyrex oblong casserole. Top with cheese, potato chips and almonds. Refrigerate overnight. Bake in a 350° oven about 45 minutes.
   Serves 10 to 12.

Avocado Tortilla Treat

An after-school "specialty" for the kids to fix for themselves.

1 ripe avocado
½ cup shredded cheese
1 tablespoon minced onion
¼ cup chili sauce
Flour tortillas

Combine all ingredients except tortillas. Separate 4 to 5 tortillas (if frozen, microwave 30 seconds to thaw). Spread some of the avocado mixture down the center of each. Roll up tortillas. Arrange on a paper plate. Microwave uncovered about 15 seconds per tortilla.
   Makes 4 to 5 treats.

1

Chicken Rosemary

4 chicken breasts, split
½ cup margarine (1 stick), melted
½ cup all-purpose flour
Salt and pepper to taste
Rosemary leaves, crushed
Water

Dip each piece of chicken in melted margarine, roll in flour, salt and pepper well. Place in a shallow greased pan. Sprinkle lightly with rosemary leaves. Add a small amount of water to cover the bottom of the pan. Cover with foil and bake in a 350° oven for about an hour. Remove foil and place under the broiler for a few seconds to brown the chicken. Watch closely or the chicken will burn.

Serves 4.

Lemon Chicken

1 lemon
4 chicken breasts, split
½ cup all-purpose flour
1½ teaspoons salt
½ teaspoon paprika
4 tablespoons oil
2 tablespoons brown sugar
1 lemon, thinly sliced
1 cup chicken broth
Fresh mint

Grate the peel from the lemon. Cut the lemon in half and squeeze the juice over the pieces of chicken, rubbing the juice into the chicken. Shake the chicken in a paper bag with flour, salt and paprika. In a skillet, brown chicken slowly in the salad oil. Arrange in a casserole or baking pan. Sprinkle grated peel over the chicken, add the brown sugar and then cover with the thinly sliced lemon. Pour in the broth and place mint over the top. Cover and bake in a 350° oven until the chicken is tender, about 45 minutes. Remove mint before serving.

Serves 4.

Beets in Orange Sauce

2 16-ounce cans sliced beets, drained
1 6-ounce can frozen orange juice, undiluted
2 tablespoons sugar
1 tablespoon Accent
Dash salt
1 tablespoon grated lemon rind
⅓ stick butter or margarine
Juice of 2 lemons
1 tablespoon cornstarch
Water

Drain the beets and set aside. In a medium saucepan, heat orange juice, stir in sugar, Accent, salt, and lemon rind. Add butter and lemon juice, bring to a boil. Dissolve cornstarch in a little water, add to the orange sauce and stir until thickened. Pour the sauce over beets and heat. Don't overcook.

Serves 4.

Broccoli Casserole

2 10-ounce packages frozen chopped broccoli

❖ ❖ ❖

1 10½-ounce can cream of mushroom soup
1 cup mayonnaise
1 cup grated sharp cheese
1 medium onion, chopped
Salt and pepper to taste
2 eggs, well-beaten

❖ ❖ ❖

¼ cup margarine (½ stick), melted
½ an 8-ounce package herb stuffing mix

Thaw and drain the broccoli well; do not cook. In a mixing bowl, combine soup, mayonnaise, cheese, onion, salt and pepper. Add broccoli. Fold in beaten eggs. Place in a 2-quart oblong glass casserole dish. Combine margarine and stuffing mix, sprinkle on casserole. Bake in a 350° oven about 45 minutes.

Serves 10 to 12.

Rice-Asparagus Casserole

¼ cup margarine (½ stick)
½ cup slivered almonds
1 cup cooked rice
1 10¾-ounce can cream of mushroom soup
½ cup milk
1 15-ounce can asparagus
1 cup grated sharp cheese
1 cup Rice Krispies

Melt the margarine in a casserole dish. Add almonds and return to the oven to toast lightly. Add rice and mix well. Combine soup with milk and pour over rice mixture, but do not mix. Lay asparagus on top and gently press down into the soup. Top with cheese and with Rice Krispies. Bake in a 300° oven until bubbly.

Serves 4 to 6.

Sweet Potato Soufflé

1 1-pound can sweet potatoes
1 cup sugar
½ cup brown sugar, firmly packed
3 eggs
½ cup butter or margarine (1 stick)

❖ ❖ ❖

½ cup butter or margarine (1 stick)
3 cups corn flakes
1 cup chopped nuts

Mix the potatoes, sugar, brown sugar, eggs and 1 stick of margarine with an electric mixer. Pour into a casserole dish and heat in a 350° oven until thoroughly heated. Combine the other stick of margarine with corn flakes and nuts. Pour over potato mixture and return to the oven for a few minutes until bubbly.

Serves 4 to 6.

Tangy Mustard Cauliflower

A very impressive dish, with no fuss!

1 medium head cauliflower
2 tablespoons water

❖   ❖   ❖

½ cup mayonnaise or salad
dressing
1 teaspoon finely chopped onion
1 teaspoon prepared mustard

❖   ❖   ❖

½ cup shredded cheese

Place the cauliflower in a casserole dish. Add water and cover with a lid or plastic wrap. Microwave on high for 8 to 9 minutes, or until tender. Combine the mayonnaise, onion and mustard in a small mixing bowl. Spoon mustard sauce on top of the cauliflower; sprinkle with cheese. Microwave for 1 to 2 minutes to heat the topping and melt the cheese. Let stand for 2 minutes before serving.
Serves 6 to 8.

Vegetable Casserole

1 16-ounce can French-style green
beans, drained
1 15-ounce can shoe peg or whole
kernel corn, drained
1 8-ounce can sliced water
chestnuts, drained
½ cup chopped onion
1 10¾-ounce can cream of celery
soup, undiluted
1 8-ounce carton sour cream
½ cup grated cheese
35 Ritz crackers
½ cup margarine (1 stick), melted

Layer the green beans, corn, water chestnuts and onion in a casserole dish. Mix the soup and sour cream together, spread over top of the vegetables. Sprinkle cheese on top of the soup mixture. Crush Ritz crackers and mix with the melted margarine, spread over the top of the casserole. Bake in a 350° oven about 45 minutes, or until bubbly and lightly brown.
Serves 10 to 12.

Zucchini Bake

1 large zucchini
Salt and pepper
2 medium tomatoes
Parmesan cheese

Slice the zucchini into ½- to-1-inch thick slices. Place in a shallow round glass baking dish; salt and pepper to taste. Cover with waxed paper. Microwave on high for 5 minutes, until zucchini is partially cooked. Top with tomato slices, sprinkle with cheese. Cover; microwave 1½ to 2 minutes or until the tomato is heated. Cook all fresh vegetables on high to capture ultimate goodness, nutrition and tender-crispness.
Serves 4 to 6.

Bread Pudding

1 cup dark brown sugar, firmly
packed
3 slices bread, buttered
½ to ¾ cup raisins

❖   ❖   ❖

3 eggs
2 cups milk
⅛ teaspoon salt
1 teaspoon vanilla extract

❖   ❖   ❖

Cream

Sprinkle brown sugar over the bottom of a buttered Pyrex baking dish. Butter slices of bread and dice, sprinkle over the brown sugar. Add raisins. Beat eggs, milk, salt, and vanilla, pour over the bread. Do not stir. Place the baking dish over simmering water and bake in a 350° oven for 1 hour. The brown sugar will form a sauce. Serve warm with cream.
Serves 8.

Citrus Chiffon Pie

1 envelope (1 tablespoon)
unflavored gelatin
½ cup sugar
Dash salt

❖   ❖   ❖

4 egg yolks
⅓ cup lemon juice
½ cup orange juice
¼ cup cold water
½ teaspoon grated orange peel
½ teaspoon grated lemon peel

❖   ❖   ❖

4 egg whites
⅓ cup sugar
1 9-inch pie shell, baked and cooled

Blend gelatin, ½ cup sugar and a dash of salt in a saucepan. Beat the egg yolks, juices, and cold water. Stir into gelatin. Cook and stir over medium heat until the mixture comes to a boil and gelatin is dissolved. Remove from heat; stir in peel. Chill until partially set. Beat the egg whites until soft peaks form. Gradually add ⅓ cup sugar. Beat until stiff. Fold in the gelatin mixture. Pile into a cooled pastry shell. Chill. Garnish with whipped cream.
Serves 12.

Honey Apple Crisp

4 cups sliced apples
¼ cup sugar
1 tablespoon lemon juice
½ cup honey

❖   ❖   ❖

1 cup all-purpose flour
½ cup brown sugar, firmly packed
½ teaspoon salt
½ cup butter (1 stick)

Spread the apples in a 1½-quart baking dish. Sprinkle with granulated sugar and lemon juice. Pour honey over all. Mix the flour, brown sugar, and salt in a bowl and work in butter, making a crumbly mixture. Spread over the apples. Bake in a 375° oven for about 40 minutes, or until the apples are tender and the crust is crisp and brown.
Serves 4 to 6.

Ice Cream Pie

1 cup evaporated milk
1 6-ounce package chocolate chips
1 cup small marshmallows

❖   ❖   ❖

Vanilla wafers
1 quart vanilla ice cream
Crushed nuts (optional)

Combine the first 3 ingredients; cook and stir until thick. Cool. Line a buttered pie pan with whole vanilla wafers, crumbling a few to fill bare spots for better fit. Add vanilla ice cream. Top with the sauce and freeze. A few crushed nuts can be added.

Easy, but very good!

Serves 10.

Krafts' Korner

90 Carlile Drive
Mobile, Alabama 36619
(205) 666-6819

The innkeepers consider this to be their guests' home away from home. There is a lovely rose garden in the back yard of this contemporary home that is five miles from I-10 and near Bellingrath Gardens, called the "Charm Spot of the South." The home is on a quiet country street near a 200-acre field

Alabama Cornbread

1¼ cups self-rising yellow
    corn meal
1 cup sour cream (or yogurt)
1 cup cream-style corn
⅓ cup cooking oil
3 whole eggs, lightly salted
4 teaspoons sugar (optional)

Combine all ingredients; beat with a wooden spoon until the batter is smooth. Bake in a 400° oven in a 9x13-inch greased pan for 30 to 35 minutes, until golden brown. If thicker cornbread is desired, bake in a smaller pan.

Serves 16.

Apple-Carrot Quick Bread

1 cup unbleached flour
¾ cup whole wheat flour
1 teaspoon mace
1 teaspoon baking powder
½ teaspoon salt

    ❖   ❖

1½ cups (2 medium) apples,
    shredded
½ cup (1 medium) carrot, shredded
¼ cup butter or margarine (½
    stick)
½ teaspoon almond extract
1 teaspoon vanilla extract
2 eggs
½ cup honey
½ teaspoon liquid sweetener
½ cup coconut
½ cup chopped pecans

Sift the dry ingredients together several times, then combine all the ingredients in a large mixing bowl, and mix with a wooden spoon. Bake in a greased, floured, 9x5-inch loaf pan in a 350° oven until a toothpick inserted into the center comes out clean—at least 1 hour. Let the bread stand in the pan for 5 to 10 minutes, then remove and cool on a cake rack.

Makes 1 loaf or 16 servings.

Foolproof Biscuits

2 cups sifted self-rising flour
1 teaspoon baking powder
2 tablespoons sugar (or ½ teaspoon
    liquid sweetener)

    ❖   ❖   ❖

1 egg
Milk
5 tablespoons oil

In a mixing bowl, combine the dry ingredients. Beat the egg in a measuring cup, then add milk to measure ¾ cup. Add egg, milk, and oil all at once to dry ingredients, and stir with a large fork until the dough follows the fork around the bowl. Turn the dough out on a floured surface and knead gently for about a minute. Roll out the dough and cut 12 biscuits, place on an ungreased pan and brush the tops with melted butter or margarine before putting the biscuits in the oven. Bake in a 425° oven for 10 to 12 minutes.

Makes 12 biscuits.

Lemon Cake

1 18¼-ounce package lemon cake
    mix
1 3-ounce package lemon gelatin
4 eggs, well beaten
¾ cup water
¾ cup oil

   ❖   ❖   ❖

Grated rind from 2 lemons
¼ cup lemon juice
½ pound confectioners' sugar

In a mixing bowl, combine the cake mix and gelatin. Add the beaten eggs and water, beat well. Add the oil and beat until the dough is smooth and glossy. Bake in a greased, floured 9x13-inch pan in a 350° oven about 35 minutes.

Combine the grated rind and lemon juice, add confectioners' sugar to obtain correct consistency, so the glaze dribbles off a spoon. Poke holes in the cake with a large kitchen fork, and pour the glaze over the cake and into holes.

Serves 12.

Alaska

Heavenly View Bed and Breakfast

10740 Kasilof Boulevard
Anchorage, Alaska 99516
(907) 346-1130

Heavenly View Bed and Breakfast is probably one of the most popular homes in Anchorage, due to the enviable view of the city. The Home sits 1600 feet above sea level and has a commanding view of the entire Anchorage Bowl Area. Floor-to-ceiling plate glass windows cover the entire front of the living room offering a magnificent view of Cook Inlet, Mt. McKinley, Mt. Susitna, and the Alaska Range. The master bedroom has large windows overlooking the same scene. The gorgeous sunsets and breathtakingly beautiful sunrises make one want to sit and stare for hours on end, making it truly a peaceful and relaxing experience to stay at Heavenly View Bed and Breakfast.

Heavenly View

Alaskan Blueberry Coffee Cake

1½ cups all-purpose flour
¾ cup sugar
2½ teaspoons baking powder
1 teaspoon salt
¼ cup vegetable oil
¾ cup milk
1 egg
1½ cups fresh Alaskan blueberries
❖ ❖ ❖
⅓ cup all-purpose flour
½ cup brown sugar, firmly packed
½ teaspoon cinnamon (or more to taste)
¼ cup firm butter (½ stick)

In a medium mixing bowl, blend together 1½ cups flour, sugar, baking power, salt, oil, milk, egg, and 1 cup blueberries. Beat thoroughly for 30 seconds and spread in a greased round 9x1½-inch pan or an 8x8x2-inch pan. Combine ⅓ cup flour, brown sugar, cinnamon, and butter. Sprinkle over batter and top with the remaining berries. Bake in a 375° oven for 25 to 30 minutes, until done. Don't overbake. Serve warm with butter or honey.
    Serves 8.

5

Aurora Downtown Bed and Breakfast

302 Cowles
Fairbanks, Alaska 99701
(907) 452-3511

The Aurora Downtown Bed and Breakfast is for the interior Alaskan adventurer. At the Aurora guests find a unique blend of Alaskan and Southern hospitality. This home has been a working bed and breakfast since being a "pipeline" guest house. Old-fashioned breakfasts are served, complete with homemade sourdough specialties.

Sourdough Starter

1 ¼-ounce package active dry yeast
2½ cups warm water
2 cups all-purpose flour
1 tablespoon sugar

In a bowl, soften active dry yeast in ½ cup warm water (110°). Stir in 2 cups of warm water, flour, and sugar. Beat until smooth.

Cover with cheese cloth and set in warm place until bubbly, 5 to 10 days, stirring 2 to 3 times a day. (A warmer temperature speeds fermentation.) Store covered in the refrigerator.

Sourdough Waffles

Sourdough Starter
4 cups water
4 cups all-purpose flour
1 teaspoon sugar

❖ ❖ ❖

¼ cup sugar
½ cup oil
2 egg yolks

1 teaspoon salt
2 teaspoons baking soda
¼ cup warm water

❖ ❖ ❖

2 egg whites

The night before you plan to make waffles, take the starter out of the refrigerator and put it into a large bowl. Add water, flour, and sugar. Cover bowl with cheese cloth, set in a warm place overnight.

In the morning, take out 3 cups of the sourdough mixture. (Put leftover sourdough starter in a glass jar, cover with lid and put in refrigerator until ready to make waffles again.) To make the sourdough waffles add sugar, oil, egg yolks and salt. Dissolve soda in warm water, stir to dissolve. Set aside.

In a separate bowl beat egg whites until stiff. To sourdough mixture add the dissolved soda, then fold in the stiff egg whites. Cook in a preheated, oil-brushed waffle iron. Cooking the waffles at a little lower heat for a longer time helps crisp up the waffles.

Enjoy with your favorite syrup or berries!
Serves 12 to 16.

Fairbanks Bed and Breakfast

Post Office Box 74573
Fairbanks, Alaska 99707
(907) 452-4967

The Fairbanks Bed and Breakfast is a family-owned reservation and referral service. In the traditional English style of travel, they book travelers into private lodgings with families in the Fairbanks area. Guest rooms are friendly, comfortable, and clean.

Peach Crisp

1 29-ounce can sliced peaches and juice
1 18¼-ounce box yellow cake mix
½ cup melted butter or margarine
1 cup shredded coconut
1 cup chopped pecans

Place ingredients in the order listed in a 9x13-inch ungreased baking dish. Bake in a 325° oven for 55 minutes.
Serves 12.

The Glacier Bay Country Inn

Post Office Box 5
Gustavus, Alaska 99826
(907) 697-2288

The Glacier Bay Country Inn blends the comforts of old-fashioned country living with the rustic wilderness that is Alaska.

Less than a half hour by air from Juneau, Alaska's capital, Gustavus and the Glacier Bay Country Inn seem generations away—a place apart, where life passes at a different pace, slower, somehow richer. Set in a clearing surrounded by trees and a majestic mountain backdrop, the inn is in an idyllic setting that is further enhanced by the warm, personal attention given guests.

Coconut Butter Croissants

1 ¼-ounce package active dry yeast
½ cup warm water (105° to 110°)

❖ ❖ ❖

¼ cup butter (½ stick)
⅓ cup sugar

The Glacier Bay

double (about 30 minutes). Bake in a 400° oven for 10 to 12 minutes. Cool.

Combine confectioners' sugar, ½ teaspoon vanilla, and milk to make a glaze, drizzle over the croissants.

Makes 2 dozen.

Salmon Spread

2 15½-ounce cans salmon
1 8-ounce package cream cheese, softened
3 teaspoons grated onion
1 tablespoon lemon juice
¼ teaspoon salt
2 teaspoons Worcestershire sauce
¼ teaspoon liquid smoke
Pinch horseradish

In a large bowl, blend all together. Refrigerate. Good on sandwiches or crackers.

Makes 2 cups of spread.

1½ teaspoons salt
¼ teaspoon nutmeg
1 teaspoon grated orange peel
½ cup dry milk
¾ cup hot water
2 cups all-purpose flour

❖ ❖ ❖

2 eggs (reserve 1 yolk)
½ teaspoon vanilla extract

❖ ❖ ❖

2½ to 3 cups all-purpose flour

❖ ❖ ❖

¼ cup butter

❖ ❖ ❖

½ cup sugar
3 tablespoons butter
1 cup coconut
Reserved egg yolk

❖ ❖ ❖

1 cup confectioners' sugar
½ teaspoon vanilla extract
2 to 3 tablespoons milk

Dissolve yeast in warm water; set aside. In mixer combine ¼ cup butter, ⅓ cup sugar, salt, nutmeg, orange peel, dry milk, hot water, and 2 cups flour. Beat until well blended.

Setting one yolk aside, add remaining eggs, ½ teaspoon vanilla extract, and dissolved yeast to the flour mixture. Mix on low speed, then 3 minutes on medium speed.

Stir in and knead with 2½ to 3 cups flour. Place in a greased bowl, turn the dough to coat the surface. Let rise until double in bulk, about 1½ hours.

Divide the dough in half. Spread ¹⁄₈ cup of butter on each half to within 2 inches of the edges. Roll each half into a 14-inch square. On half of each square, spread ¹⁄₈ cup butter to within 2 inches of the edge. Fold in half, then in quarters; seal the edges. Cover and let rise for 15 minutes. (For extra flakiness, roll out, butter, fold and let rise again.)

Prepare the filling by beating together with a mixer ½ cup sugar, 3 tablespoons butter, coconut and the reserved egg yolk. Divide the dough in thirds.

Roll each third of dough into a 9-inch circle; cut into 8 wedges. Put a scant tablespoon of filling in the middle of each wedge. Starting at the wide end, roll up each wedge into a crescent shape.

Place the point side down on an ungreased baking sheet. Let rise until

Rhubarb Lemonade

3 cups rhubarb
3 cups water
1¼ cups sugar
½ cup lemon juice
1 .032-ounce package lemon-flavored drink mix
Ice cubes
1 16-ounce bottle lemon-lime carbonated drink

❖ ❖ ❖

Lemon slices
Whole strawberries
Mint leaves
Borage flowers

Bring rhubarb, water, sugar, lemon juice and drink mix to a boil. Cover and simmer for 10 minutes. Strain to remove pulp; chill. Just before serving, pour syrup over ice cubes; pour in carbonated beverage.

Garnish with lemon slices or pour in a punch bowl over an ice ring for open house, weddings, etc.

For an ice ring, arrange lemon slices vertically in round ring mold. Place the strawberries between lemon slices. Arrange mint leaves and borage flowers around top. Pour rhubarb lemonade over all and freeze until firm (overnight).

Makes about 5½ cups.

Overnight Coleslaw

1½ cups sugar
¾ cup vinegar
¾ cup vegetable oil
1 teaspoon celery seed

❖   ❖   ❖

1 medium head cabbage, thinly
    sliced
1 grated onion
1 grated carrot
Green pepper (optional)
Salt and pepper

In a small saucepan, boil together sugar, vinegar, vegetable oil and celery seed. Place layer of vegetables in a bowl, then pour hot dressing mixture over; repeat until all vegetables and dressing are used. Cover and store overnight in refrigerator. Will keep for several days.

Serves 6 to 8.

Chicken Pot Pie

2 cups all-purpose flour
1 teaspoon salt
¾ cup butter (1½ sticks), chilled
3 tablespoons solid white vegetable
    shortening
⅓ cup ice water

❖   ❖   ❖

1 3-pound whole broiler/fryer
    chicken
4 cups water
1 bay leaf
1 garlic clove, crushed

❖   ❖   ❖

½ cup dry sherry or vermouth (or
    ½ cup chicken broth)
1½ cups raw green beans, cut into
    1-inch lengths
1½ cups sliced raw carrots, ¼-inch
    thick
1 cup diced raw potato (peeled and
    cut into ½-inch cubes)
½ teaspoon dried basil

❖   ❖   ❖

½ cup sliced mushrooms
1 10-ounce package frozen peas

1 16-ounce can whole peeled
    tomatoes, drained and
    quartered

❖   ❖   ❖

4 tablespoons butter
4 tablespoons all-purpose flour

❖   ❖   ❖

1 cup heavy cream
2 egg yolks
Salt and pepper

Put 2 cups flour and 1 teaspoon salt into a large mixing bowl. Cut ¾ cup chilled butter into thin slices. Blend along with shortening into the flour, using a pastry blender or two knives. Blend until the mixture resembles coarse meal. Work quickly so the butter does not soften. Sprinkle the ice water evenly over the top. Mix rapidly with a fork. Gather into a ball and flatten it; wrap it in foil and refrigerate it for 3 hours or overnight.

Place the chicken, 4 cups water, bay leaf, and garlic in a Dutch oven or covered kettle; cover and bring to a boil. Reduce heat to a simmer and cook, covered, for 30 to 40 minutes or until done; when done, a leg will easily pull off. Place the chicken in a colander to drain until cool enough to handle. Strain the broth and place it over high heat; boil, uncovered, until it has reduced to 2 cups (2½ cups if substituting broth for sherry or vermouth). Add the sherry. Remove all meat from the chicken and cut into 1-inch pieces; set aside. Add to the broth the green beans, carrots, potato, and basil; cover and simmer for 12 to 15 minutes or until the vegetables are just tender. Add mushrooms, peas and tomatoes; cover and simmer 2 to 3 minutes. Place vegetables in colander over a bowl to drain; there should be 1½ cups liquid. Add water if necessary.

Melt ¼ cup butter in the Dutch oven; stir in 4 tablespoons flour with a whisk; cook briefly. Using whisk, stir in the 1½ cups of broth. Cook over low heat, stirring constantly, until the sauce is smooth and has thickened.

In a small bowl, beat the cream into the 2 egg yolks; beat the mixture into the sauce and remove it from the heat.

Add salt and pepper to taste. Fold in the reserved chicken pieces and vegetables. Cool to room temperature. Place in a 9-inch pie pan; roll out pastry and place over filling, fluting edges. Bake in a 425° oven for 35 to 40 minutes or until the pastry is crisp and golden brown and the filling is hot.

For a really special presentation, the pot pies can be made in flowerpots—the recipe will fill six 4x4-inch pots. Cut six 12-inch squares of foil. Turn one flowerpot upside down and place one square of foil over the bottom; shape the foil around the pot so it conforms to the outside shape. Remove the foil shape carefully. Turn the pot right side up and place the foil inside it. Be careful not to tear the foil. Trim away any excess foil at the top—the foil should just reach the top of the pot. Repeat for remaining pots. Brush each pot with vegetable oil. Spoon chicken pot pie filling into each to within ½-inch of top. Roll pastry to ⅛-inch thick. Cut into six 6-inch circles. Place one circle of dough over one filled flowerpot. Turn under overhanging edge and make decorative crimped edge all around. Cut 3 small steam holes into the center of the pastry.

Repeat for remaining pots.

Paint tops of each pie with egg yolk glaze (1 egg yolk mixed with 1 tablespoon cold water). Place pots on baking sheets. Bake in a 425° oven for 35 to 40 minutes.

Serves 6.

Salmon Marinade

½ cup butter (1 stick)
¼ cup Worcestershire sauce
¼ cup soy sauce
¼ cup chili sauce
2 tablespoons mustard
1 clove garlic

In a small saucepan, bring ingredients to a boil. Cool and let thicken. Do not refrigerate. Marinate salmon steaks in mixture for several hours; barbecue.

Makes approximately 1 cup of marinade.

Pickled Pea Pods

4 quarts edible pod peas

❖ ❖ ❖

**½ teaspoon crushed red peppers
(per jar)**
**½ teaspoon whole mustard seed
(per jar)**
½ teaspoon dill seed (per jar)
1 clove garlic (per jar)

❖ ❖ ❖

5 cups vinegar
5 cups water
½ cup salt

Wash the peas and place in 12 sterilized pint jars, dividing evenly. In each jar add the peppers, mustard seed, dill seed, and garlic.

In a saucepan combine the vinegar, water and salt and bring to a boil. Pour over the peas and spices in the jars. Seal. Process for 5 minutes in a boiling water bath.

Fills 12 pint jars.

Whole Wheat Carrot Cake

1 cup cooking oil
1 cup sugar
1 cup brown sugar, firmly packed
1 teaspoon vanilla extract
4 eggs

❖ ❖ ❖

2 cups whole wheat flour
1 teaspoon salt
⅓ cup nonfat dry milk
1 teaspoon baking soda
1 teaspoon baking powder
2 teaspoons cinnamon

❖ ❖ ❖

3 cups carrots, shredded
1 cup walnuts, chopped
Confectioners' sugar

In a medium mixer bowl, blend oil, sugar and brown sugar on low speed until mixed. Add vanilla, beat in eggs one at a time, blending well. In a separate bowl, stir together flour, salt, dry milk, soda, baking powder and cinnamon. Add to egg mixture until well blended. Stir in carrots and walnuts by hand.

Pour into greased and floured 10-inch tube or 12-cup fluted tube pan. Bake in a 350° oven for 50 to 60 minutes or until the cake tests done. Cool in pan; invert onto a serving plate. Sprinkle sifted confectioners' sugar on top.

Serves 12 to 16.

Gustavus Inn

Box 31
Gustavus, Alaska 99826
(907) 697-2254

The Gustavus Inn combines a traditional homestead atmosphere and a magnificent Alaskan setting with modern accommodations and convenient transportation. It is the perfect retreat from which to base a Glacier Bay adventure. The Gustavus Inn began in 1928 as a farm homestead for a nine-child family carving a home out of the Alaskan wilderness. Today, its attractive and comfortable accommodations retain the spirit of the early pioneers.

Anya's Mushroom Soup

"I followed an old Hungarian lady through the woods and watched her pick mushrooms. The good ones she placed carefully in the basket she carried over her arm and the poisonous ones were thrown angrily into the brush. 'Goot!' and it would be kept; 'No goot!', and it would be discarded. She knew no English and I knew no Hungarian, but we were good friends in the kitchen, and I wrote down everything she did as she made us mushroom soup for lunch."

2 tablespoons butter
2 tablespoons all-purpose flour
2 quarts water
**1 quart mushrooms, washed and
thinly-sliced**

❖ ❖ ❖

4 egg yolks
1 cup sour cream

❖ ❖ ❖

1 lemon

Make a roux by melting the butter and whisking in the flour; cook in a soup kettle over medium heat. Add water and mushrooms that have been washed and thinly sliced. Bring all to a boil, reduce heat so that it bubbles gently, and cook for 15 minutes. In a small bowl mix egg yolks with sour cream until blended. Pour some of the hot soup into the egg mixture and stir, add a little more soup and stir, then pour the contents of the small bowl carefully and slowly into the hot soup, stirring all the while to prevent curdling. Keep hot but do not boil. Just before serving, cut a lemon in half and squeeze the juice into the soup. Season to taste.

Serves 8.

Green Beans
with Sweet Mustard Sauce

2 tablespoons prepared mustard
2 tablespoons sugar
¼ cup butter (½ stick)
½ teaspoon salt
3 tablespoons cider vinegar
**2 tablespoons freshly-squeezed
lemon juice**

❖ ❖ ❖

**2 1-pound cans green beans,
drained**

Combine in a small saucepan the prepared mustard, sugar, butter, salt, cider vinegar and the lemon juice. Heat slowly until the butter has melted and all the ingredients are blended. Pour over the heated green beans and keep hot until serving time.

Serves 4 to 6.

Gustavus Inn

Poached Salmon

1 salmon
Peppercorns
Pinch of tarragon
Celery tops
2 sprigs parsley
½ lemon, sliced
1 small carrot, scraped
1 medium onion, thickly sliced
½ cup dry white wine
2 teaspoons salt

Select a cleaned and scaled fresh salmon that will fit into your fish boiler when the head and tail are removed. Rinse the fish inside and out with cold water, removing all traces of blood and slime. Fill the fish boiler one half full with cold water. Add several peppercorns, a pinch of tarragon, a handful of celery tops, two sprigs of parsley, the fresh lemon slices, one small carrot scraped and broken in half, sliced onion, dry white wine and salt. Bring to a boil and add the whole fish, including the head and the tail which have been cut off, if they will fit into the boiler. Bring to a boil and lower the heat so the water will simmer but not boil, and poach just until the fish flakes easily. Lift it out of the water and place

it on a heated platter. Trim away odd bits of celery, etc., so the fish looks whole and pretty. Garnish with parsley and present whole at the table.

To serve, draw the tip of a sharp knife along the median line, from head to tail cutting through to the backbone, and gently pull the skin back over each side exposing the flesh. Remove serving size pieces of fish from the exposed side. Pass the egg sauce. Serves 4.

Egg Sauce

3 tablespoons butter
3 tablespoons all-purpose flour
2 cups milk, scalded
Salt to taste
White pepper

❖ ❖ ❖

2 eggs, hard cooked
1 tablespoon capers, drained

Make a medium thick white sauce with butter and flour mixed together over low heat until well integrated and smooth. Add the scalded milk and salt to taste, and a few grindings of white pepper. Stir until thick and the floury

taste is gone. Chop the hard cooked eggs coarsely and stir into the cream sauce. Finely chop the capers and add to the sauce. Keep over hot water until serving time, but be careful not to cook it any more.

Makes 2 cups of sauce.

Roast Beef Blintzes

2 eggs
1 teaspoon salt
1 cup milk
1 cup all-purpose flour
Butter or margarine

❖ ❖ ❖

1 tablespoon butter
¼ cup finely chopped onion
½ pound cold ground roast beef
1 teaspoon salt
½ teaspoon pepper
¼ cup buckwheat groats
1 cup homemade beef stock or beef consommé

To make the crêpes, Place the eggs in a small bowl and beat well. Add salt and milk. Add flour gradually, stirring to make a smooth batter. Place a clean tea towel on the counter near the stove. Have ready a 7-inch skillet, a dish of butter or margarine, a quarter cup measure and a small folded piece of waxed paper. Using the waxed paper smear about a teaspoonful of butter over the bottom of the hot skillet. Using the quarter cup measure, pour two or three tablespoons of the batter into the skillet. Cook over high heat and work quickly. Tilt the skillet so that the batter covers the bottom. When the bottom of the crêpe is golden, flip it over and cook the other side. Use a small pancake turner for ease of flipping. When the second side is brown remove the completed crêpe to the towel to cool. Continue in this manner until the batter is used up. You should have about nine or ten thin crêpes. Set these aside while making the filling.

In a large skillet, melt one tablespoon of butter. When it sizzles, add onions. When the onions are limp, but have not taken on color, add cold ground roast beef (preferably rare), salt, pepper and buckwheat groats. Stir all together and cook for five minutes. Add homemade beef stock or beef consommé, cover and cook gently for 15 minutes. Set aside to cool.

When the filling is cool you may proceed with the rolling up. Have ready a buttered baking dish that can be brought to the table and will be big enough to hold all the blintzes in a single layer.

Take a cooled crêpe and, as if it were a clock face, at nine, twelve and three o'clock place a small bit of butter with a knife. Put a tablespoonful of the roast beef mixture at the six o'clock position and roll the crêpe away from you, folding over the ends and placing the rolled up blintz, seam side down in the baking dish. Continue in this manner until all the crêpes and meat mixture have been used up. At this point you may cover the pan closely with foil and refrigerate for several hours, or you may freeze the whole thing for several days, but not longer than two weeks.

When ready to serve, drizzle melted butter over the top of the blintzes and heat in a 400° oven for about 30 minutes, or until brown, bubbly and *very* hot. Serve at once with a side dish of sour cream.

Serves 6 to 8.

Grasshopper Pie

"This pie has been on the menu ever since we opened as a Country inn and still remains the most asked-for dessert. The beauty of this pie is that it can be frozen for several weeks and served directly from the freezer."

**1 cup chocolate wafer crumbs
1 tablespoon sugar
3 tablespoons shortening**

❖   ❖   ❖

**20 to 24 marshmallows
¼ cup milk**

❖   ❖   ❖

1 cup heavy cream

**2 tablespoons white crème de cacao
3 tablespoons green crème de menthe**

With a rolling pin, crush the chocolate wafers until finely crumbled. (If you put them in a plastic bag first the job is more quickly and neatly done.) Place the crumbs in a small bowl and add sugar and shortening. Working with a fork or pastry blender blend together until no trace of shortening remains. Press firmly onto the bottom and sides of a 9-inch pie pan. Bake in a 350° oven for 7 minutes, then let the crumb crust cool on a wire rack while preparing the filling.

In the top of a double boiler melt marshmallows with milk. When the marshmallows are all melted set the pot aside to cool slightly. In a small bowl whip the heavy cream until very stiff. When the marshmallow mixture is a little cooler add white crème de cacao and green crème de menthe (you may add more if desired). Stir well and fold into the whipped cream, scraping the sides with a rubber scraper. Pour into the waiting, cooled chocolate crumb pie crust. Place in the freezer and when it is frozen hard cover with plastic wrap and aluminum foil, folded tightly over the edges.

Serves 12.

The Brass Ring Bed and Breakfast

987 Hillfair Court
Homer, Alaska 99603
(907) 235-5450

The Brass Ring Bed and Breakfast is a traditional log home designed and built as a bed and breakfast guest-

house. It is located a short walk from the heart of Homer. Accommodations include five private bedrooms, two bathrooms, and laundry facilities. Guests will enjoy a large living room with hardwood floors, open beam ceiling, and cozy woodstove, or a secluded den for reading, television, and VCR. All rooms are lovingly furnished in antiques and traditional country style. For the comfort of all guests, no smoking is permitted in the house. A breakfast consisting of continental-style or hearty American-style is served at a time most convenient for each guest. Breakfast is served for guests only.

Oatmeal-Blueberry Muffins

1 egg

❖   ❖   ❖

**1 cup buttermilk
½ cup brown sugar, firmly packed
⅓ cup shortening**

❖   ❖   ❖

**1 cup quick-cooking oats
½ cup unbleached flour
½ cup whole wheat flour
1 teaspoon baking powder
½ teaspoon baking soda
1 teaspoon salt (optional)**

❖   ❖   ❖

1 cup fresh blueberries

Beat egg in a medium mixing bowl. Stir in buttermilk, brown sugar and shortening and beat well. Mix in oats, flours, baking powder, soda and salt until batter becomes lumpy. Stir in blueberries. Fill muffin cups ⅔ full. Bake in a 400° oven 20 to 25 minutes or until light brown. Immediately remove from the pan.

Makes 1 to 1½ dozen muffins.

Spinach Salad
with Mustard-Egg Dressing

**3 hard boiled eggs
1½ teaspoons prepared yellow mustard**

3 tablespoons cider vinegar
3 tablespoons sugar

❖ ❖ ❖

Spinach leaves, torn
⅓ cup warm bacon drippings

❖ ❖ ❖

4 slices bacon, cooked and
    crumbled
2 green onions, chopped

Separate hard boiled eggs into whites and yolks. Chop whites. Mix yolks with mustard, vinegar, and sugar until smooth to make dressing.

Combine spinach and egg dressing in a salad bowl, add warm bacon drippings and toss. Sprinkle chopped egg whites, crumbled bacon pieces and green onions over salad. Serve.

Serves 4 to 6.

Quick Delicious Halibut

1 large fillet of halibut
1 8-ounce jar ranch dressing

Place halibut in a baking dish and pour ranch dressing over the top to coat halibut. Bake in a 425° oven for 10 minutes per inch of fish. Serve immediately.

Serves 2 to 4, depending on the size of the halibut.

Salmon Steaks
with Dill Sauce

Butter
4 small salmon steaks or fillets
    (about 1 inch thick)
Salt and pepper
1 sprig fresh dill
½ cup dry white wine

❖ ❖ ❖

2 tablespoons minced shallots
2 tablespoons white wine vinegar
3 tablespoons dry white wine
2 tablespoons water

❖ ❖ ❖

2 tablespoons whipping cream

❖ ❖ ❖

Salt and pepper
1 cup cold, unsalted butter (2
    sticks), cubed

❖ ❖ ❖

4 tablespoons snipped fresh dill

Butter a baking dish and place the salmon in one layer. Salt and pepper the salmon. Add the sprig of dill and pour wine over top. Cover with foil and bake in a 425° oven about 15 minutes or until tender. Transfer to platter and keep warm. Prepare the sauce while salmon is baking.

In a small saucepan, combine shallots, vinegar, wine and water. Simmer over medium heat until the liquid is reduced to 2 tablespoons. Stir in cream and simmer over low heat until the mixture is again reduced to 2 tablespoons. Season with salt and pepper. Add butter cubes and whisk constantly.

Remove from heat as soon as the last butter cube is added. Stir in dill. Spoon a little sauce over the salmon, and serve the remaining sauce separately for dipping.

Serves 4.

The Brass Inn

Driftwood Inn

135 West Bunnell Avenue
Homer, Alaska 99603
(907) 235-8019

The Driftwood Inn is a family-owned and operated eighteen-room inn on the shores of beautiful Kachemak Bay in Homer, Alaska. This inn possesses a gorgeous view of the bay, mountains, glaciers, and marine life. A breathtaking view! Guests are greeted by a comfortable lobby with fireplace, as well as old-time Alaskan hospitality. Help is available in making arrangements for fishing, hunting, and viewing the magnificent Alaskan landscape.

Driftwood Inn Halibut Bake

2 eggs, separated
1 3-ounce package cream cheese
1 cup salad or olive oil
3 tablespoons tarragon vinegar
2 tablespoons lemon juice
1 tablespoon honey
1½ teaspoons salt
1 teaspoon dry mustard
Dash cayenne pepper

❖ ❖ ❖

1 rounded tablespoon chopped
   parsley
1 teaspoon minced garlic
1 teaspoon thyme
1 teaspoon celery salt
1 teaspoon lemon pepper
½ teaspoon turmeric

❖ ❖ ❖

3 to 4 pounds skinned halibut
   fillets

❖ ❖ ❖

2 pounds grated Cheddar or Jack
   cheese
1 bunch green onions, finely
   chopped
Paprika

Beat egg whites until stiff. Cream the cream cheese and the egg yolks, and beat together with egg whites. Add ¼ cup of oil. Beat in vinegar, lemon juice, honey, salt, dry mustard and cayenne pepper. Gradually beat in the remaining oil. This makes about 2 cups of mayonnaise mixture.

Mix together 2 cups of mayonnaise mixture, parsley, garlic, thyme, celery salt, lemon pepper and turmeric. Dip the bottom of the halibut fillets in the mayonnaise mixture and place on a rack in a foil-lined pan.

Fold into the remaining mayonnaise mixture the grated cheese and green onion. Cover fillets with the cheese mixture. Sprinkle with paprika and bake in a 350° oven for 25 minutes.

Any leftovers can be used in place of tuna for sandwiches or mixed in with leftover Wild Rice for a hot lunch delight. Any remaining cheese-mayonnaise mixture can be baked over broccoli, cauliflower, etc. or mixed into omelettes the next day.

Note from the Innkeeper: "My secret for skinning is to free meat from skin at 1 corner and then clamp skin to bread board with vice grips and then work fillet knife down fillet between meat and skin while raising meat to cut and separate. Leave fillets whole." Serves 6.

Wild Rice Mixture

1 cup wild rice
2 cups water
1 bunch green onions, chopped
1 teaspoon salt
1 cube vegetable bouillon

❖ ❖ ❖

1 10-ounce box frozen peas
2 tablespoons butter

Bring the first 5 ingredients to a boil; reduce heat and cook for 20 minutes.

Add peas and butter to the rice mixture and bring back to a boil, reduce heat and cook for an additional 15 to 20 minutes.
Serves 4.

Fireweed Lodge Riptide Outfitters

Post Office Box 116
Klawock, Alaska 99925
(907) 755-2930

Nestled in the mountains at the mouth of the Klawock River, the Fireweed is prepared to offer a multitude of services. The Prince of Wales Island offers black bear and Sitka blacktail deer for the big game hunters. Excellent fishing is close at hand or just outside the lodge. Guests may rent a skiff or charter a deep sea fishing trip through arrangements made through the lodge. Tour trips of the island are available to historic native Indian villages, totem poles, and scenic overlooks. After a full day, guests enjoy the comfortable rooms and meals, which are famous on the island and prepared family style.

Fireweed's Famous Bleu Cheese Dressing

2 cups mayonnaise
¼ pound bleu cheese

❖ ❖ ❖

½ teaspoon lemon juice
¼ cup finely diced onion
1/8 teaspoon salt
1/8 teaspoon pepper
½ teaspoon garlic powder

Heat the mayonnaise and bleu cheese over medium heat until the bleu cheese is broken down into small pieces. Remove from heat. Add the remaining ingredients and stir well. Chill and serve. Store in the refrigerator.
Makes 2 cups of dressing.

Fried Alaskan Sea Cucumbers

An appetizer of Alaskan excellence.

The sea cucumber is a rare treat. The white fillets from the skin are fried and served as an appetizer. The taste is very similar to that of fried clam strips.

Roll the white fillets of meat in a mixture of flour, cracker crumbs, and seasoned salt. Amounts vary according to taste. Be sure to lay the strips of meat out flat to coat them thoroughly. Fry the strips in a skillet in hot butter. The meat turns from clear to opaque when done (2 to 4 minutes on each side). Serve with tartar or cocktail sauce.

Banana Split Pie

1 14-ounce can sweetened condensed milk (reserve ¼ cup)
1 3½-ounce package instant vanilla pudding
¼ cup milk
1 teaspoon vanilla extract
2 cups whipped cream
1 baked pie shell

❖ ❖ ❖

¼ cup sweetened condensed milk
1 1-ounce square unsweetened chocolate
1 to 2 tablespoons milk

❖ ❖ ❖

Bananas
Maraschino cherries
Nuts

Mix the condensed milk, pudding, milk and vanilla extract in a bowl with a wire whisk until smooth. Fold in whipped cream. Spoon this mixture into the baked pie shell.

Combine reserved sweetened condensed milk and unsweetened chocolate in a small saucepan. Cook over medium heat until thickened. Remove from heat and blend in enough milk to make the fudge sauce thin enough to drizzle.

Decorate the top of the filling with bananas, maraschino cherries and nuts. Drizzle fudge topping over all. Chill for 3 hours.

Serves 8.

Baranof Museum— Erskine House

Post Office Box 61
Kodiak, Alaska 99615
(907) 486-5920

The Baranof Museum has something to interest visitors and Alaskans alike. The most impressive find is the Samovar collection, although other high quality hand-crafted items are found here. Descriptive information of inn facilities was not given for this publication but a wonderful collection of Russian recipes was shared with us.

Salmonberry Jelly

4 cups salmonberry juice
5 cups sugar
1 3-ounce bottle Certo pectin (or 1 1¾-ounce package Sure Jel)
Lemon juice (optional)

Prepare the juice by heating berries and mashing. Place in a jelly cloth or bag and strain. Measure the juice into a large saucepan, add sugar and mix well. Place over high heat, bring to a boil, stirring constantly. Add Certo, then allow to boil rapidly for one minute. Remove from heat, skim off foam. Pour into glasses and seal.

Fills 6 8-ounce jars.

Instant Russian Tea

18 ounces powdered orange drink
¾ cup instant lemon tea
¾ teaspoon cinnamon
¾ teaspoon nutmeg
Sugar to taste

Mix the ingredients thoroughly. To serve, add 1 teaspoon of mixture to a cup of boiling water.

Makes 3¾ cups of tea mix.

Russian Tea

1 quart boiling water
2 or 3 sticks cinnamon
12 whole cloves
1½ cups sugar

❖ ❖ ❖

3 tablespoons tea

❖ ❖ ❖

Juice of 4 oranges
Juice of 2 lemons
3 quarts boiling water

In a medium saucepan, boil the first 4 ingredients for about 15 minutes. Add tea and let steep. Strain. Pour into a 4-quart container and add juices and water, let stand overnight.

Or, omit the last 3 quarts water and store in the refrigerator. When ready for tea, add 3 parts water to 1 part tea as desired.

Makes about 4 quarts, or 30 servings.

Kulich

Kulich (pronounced koo-LEETCH) is characteristic of Old Russia's holiday breads. There are as many recipes for kulich as there are kulich bakers. In Kodiak, Alaska, the custom has become very widespread and almost everyone bakes this delicious, tender, moist and very rich bread. The heavy batter is generally baked in one or two pound coffee cans and allowed to rise well above the tops to form a dome-shaped top. It thus resembles the Russian Church spires.

This recipe is an original by Mrs. Katherine Chichenoff, who was the winner of the kulich contest held by the Baranof Museum during the Crab Festival.

2 to 3 packages yeast
½ cup lukewarm water
1 cup butter (2 sticks)
2½ cups sugar
8 eggs, well-beaten
2 teaspoons salt
1 teaspoon nutmeg
1½ teaspoons vanilla extract
1 teaspoon lemon extract
1 quart milk, lukewarm
15 to 16 cups all-purpose flour
¾ cup raisins (or currants)
1 cup almonds, peeled and halved

Dissolve the yeast in water. In a large mixing bowl, beat the butter and sugar, add eggs, beating well. Add salt, nutmeg, vanilla, and lemon extract. Beat well. Add the yeast mixture and warm milk. Stir in flour a little at a time until it thickens. Add raisins and almonds. Continue to add flour until you have a dough stiff enough to handle. On a lightly floured board, knead the dough until smooth and stretched. Place in a greased bowl and let rise. Punch down and knead a few times. Divide into six parts. Place in greased 2-pound coffee cans and let rise until double in bulk. Bake in a 375° oven about 45 minutes to 1 hour. If they become too dark while baking, cover with brown paper to keep from burning. May be glazed if desired.

Makes 2 large loaves.

Perok

1 2-pound package carrots, grated
1 medium green pepper, chopped
3 medium stalks celery, chopped
1 medium cabbage, shredded
1 large onion, chopped
1 large rutabaga, chopped
2 tablespoons butter
Water
Salt and pepper

❖ ❖ ❖

Pie crust for top and bottom of a 10x15x12-inch oblong pan
1 cup rice, cooked and rinsed
1 salmon, skinned, boned and filleted (salt salmon may be used)
4 or 5 hard-boiled eggs, chopped or sliced

In a large saucepan, simmer vegetables with one cube of butter in water to cover until soft, 10 to 15 minutes. Salt and pepper to taste.

Line an oblong pan with the pie crust, then place a thin layer of rice on the bottom. Add a layer of about half the cooked vegetables, then the filleted fish, a layer of eggs, and then the other half of the vegetables. Add a layer of rice and the top crust. Bake in a 350° oven approximately one hour.

Serves 12.

Russian Tea Cakes

¼ teaspoon salt
1 teaspoon vanilla extract
¾ cup finely-chopped walnuts
1 cup butter (2 sticks)
½ cup confectioners' sugar
2½ cups all-purpose flour
Confectioners' sugar

In a large mixing bowl, combine all ingredients; form into balls about one inch in diameter. Bake on a greased cookie sheet in a 400° oven about 14 to 17 minutes. While hot, roll in confectioners' sugar.

Makes 1½ to 2 dozen cakes.

1260 Inn

Mile 1260, Alaska Highway
Via Tok, Alaska 99780
(907) 778-2205

The 1260 Inn is decorated with Alaskan antiques. A collection of old photos, letters, newspapers, and memorabilia dating back to 1793 is available for viewing and the Sluice Box Saloon is an ideal place to visit with fellow travelers. Hundreds of lakes and rivers offer the best fishing in Alaska as well as opportunities for boating, hiking, and photography.

Beef-Barley Soup

2 pounds cut-up beef or round steak
Small amount of cooking oil
7 cups water
1 16-ounce can tomatoes
1 large onion, chopped
2 beef bouillon cubes

❖ ❖ ❖

1 cup chopped carrots
1 cup chopped celery
½ cup chopped green pepper
⅔ cup barley
Parsley
Salt and pepper to taste
1 teaspoon basil
½ teaspoon Worcestershire sauce

In a large skillet, brown the beef in oil. Stir in water, undrained tomatoes, onion, and bouillon cubes. Simmer for 1½ hours. Add carrots, celery, green pepper, barley, and seasonings. Simmer until the vegetables are tender.

Serves 6 to 8.

Cinnamon Rolls

2 cups milk
½ cup shortening

❖ ❖ ❖

½ cup sugar
2 teaspoons salt
3 cups all-purpose flour

❖ ❖ ❖

2 eggs
2 tablespoons yeast (softened in small amount of warm water)
3½ to 4½ cups all-purpose flour

Water
1 cup sugar
Cinnamon

In a small saucepan, heat the milk and shortening until melted. Pour into a large bowl and add sugar and salt. Add 3 cups of flour and beat into a smooth batter. Add eggs. Test the temperature of the batter (no hotter than 120 degrees). Add softened yeast. Stir in the remaining flour until you have a soft, slightly sticky dough. Cover with plastic wrap and let rise until double.

After the dough rises, flatten out into a rectangle on a greased counter. Dampen the top of the dough with a small amount of water. Sprinkle 1 cup of sugar over the dough. Sprinkle with cinnamon. Roll and cut into 12 large rolls. Place in a generously buttered pan and bake in a 375° oven for 25 to 30 minutes.

Makes 12 rolls.

Dinner Rolls

2 cups milk
¼ cup shortening

❖ ❖ ❖

¼ cup sugar
2 teaspoons salt
3 cups all-purpose flour

❖ ❖ ❖

2 eggs
2 tablespoons yeast (softened in small amount of warm water)
3½ to 4½ cups all-purpose flour

In a small saucepan, heat milk and shortening until melted. Pour into a large bowl and add sugar and salt. Add 3 cups of flour and beat into smooth batter. Add eggs. Test temperature of batter (no hotter than 120 degrees). Add softened yeast. Stir in remainder of flour until you have a soft, slightly sticky dough. Cover with plastic wrap and let rise until double. Punch down and shape into rolls. Place in a buttered pan. Let rise until double and bake in a 375° oven for 25 to 30 minutes.

Makes 24 rolls.

Arizona

The Dierker House Bed and Breakfast

423 West Cherry
Flagstaff, Arizona 86002
(602) 774-3249

The Dierker House Bed and Breakfast is a charming old house with spacious antique-filled rooms. Privacy and European comforts accompany an excellent continental breakfast.

"A Bucket" of Bran Muffins

    2 cups boiling water
    1 cup shortening
        ❖ ❖ ❖
    2 cups Nabisco 100% bran (40%
        bran can be used)
    4 cups Kellogg's Bran Buds
    2½ cups sugar
    4 eggs
    1 quart buttermilk
    5 cups all-purpose flour (may be
        part wheat)
    4 teaspoons baking soda
    1½ teaspoons salt

Mix the water and shortening and let stand. Add remaining ingredients, and stir all together. Can add raisins, nuts, currants, etc. Bake in muffin pans lined with baking cups in a 400° oven for 20 minutes.

Will keep 6 weeks in the refrigerator in a covered container.

Makes 4 to 6 dozen muffins.

Marjorie Ann Lindmark

Bed-N-Breakfast in Arizona
5995 East Orange Blossom Lane
Phoenix, Arizona 85018
(602) 994-3759

Bed and Breakfast at this tri-level home on the exclusive Arizona Country Club properties on Arizona Lake is a special treat for visitors who occupy its three guest rooms. The rooms throughout the home are light and sunny, and there is a sparkling swimming pool. A full breakfast is served every morning. Located near Scottsdale shops, this home is within easy access to all area attractions.

Scrambled Eggs

    2 tablespoons butter
    6 eggs
    ¼ cup milk

Place butter in a casserole or serving dish. Microwave on high (100%) until butter melts, about 30 seconds. Add eggs and milk and scramble with a fork. Microwave on high (100%) for about 1½ minutes.

Eggs will start to set around the edge of the dish. Break up cooked portions with fork; stir them to the center of the dish. Microwave another 1½ minutes, stirring once or twice more from outside to center.

Stop cooking while eggs still look moist, soft and slightly underdone. If cooked until they are as firm as you like, they will be overcooked and tough when served. Let stand 1 to 4 minutes. Stir again. If eggs are not firm enough, microwave a few seconds more.

Serves 4.

The Lodge on the Desert

306 North Alvernon Way
Post Office Box 42500
Tucson, Arizona 85733
(602) 325-3366

The Lodge on the Desert is a small American and European plan resort hotel providing the finest in food and accommodations to seventy guests in an atmosphere of quiet luxury for over 50 years. The feeling of Old Mexico

The Dierker House

Add almond extract.

Arrange the turkey on a platter and pour the sauce over. Sprinkle with slivered almonds. Serve at once.

Serves 4 to 6.

Banana Chantilly

3 egg whites
¾ cup sugar
½ teaspoon vanilla extract
¼ teaspoon vinegar

❖ ❖ ❖

1 cup mashed bananas
¼ teaspoon salt
1½ tablespoons lemon juice
1 cup whipping cream
Mint leaves
Red cherries

Beat egg whites until nearly stiff. Gradually add sugar, beating constantly. Add vanilla and vinegar. Beat until stiff and well blended. Divide the meringue in half. Spread each half over a 3x9-inch area of a baking sheet. Bake in a 275° oven for 40 to 45 minutes or until delicately browned. Remove from the oven. Cool.

Combine the banana pulp with salt and lemon juice. Whisk the whipping cream into the banana mixture. Place one baked meringue in a refrigerator tray and cover with filling. Top with the second meringue. Freeze about 3 hours. Slice into 6 to 8 portions and top each with mint leaves and a red cherry. This is a favorite Christmas dessert at the Lodge.

Serves 6 to 8.

and the flavor of the Southwest have been captured within the lodge with its unique architectural design.

Cream of Broccoli Soup

2 tablespoons butter
2 tablespoons all-purpose flour
½ teaspoon salt
Pepper to taste
1½ cups chicken broth
2 cups milk

❖ ❖ ❖

1 cup heavy cream
10 broccoli spears, cooked

In a saucepan, melt the butter. Stir in flour, salt and pepper until blended. Add chicken broth, stirring over medium heat until the mixture thickens. Add the milk and stir until smooth. Pour into a blender the cream and 6 broccoli spears, blend until smooth and add to the cooked mixture. Chop the remaining broccoli and add to the soup. Simmer for 5 minutes and serve.

Serves 6.

French-Fried Turkey

1½ cups all-purpose flour
2¼ teaspoons baking powder
¾ teaspoon salt
2 eggs
¾ cup milk
1½ tablespoons salad oil
Cooked turkey breast

❖ ❖ ❖

1 tablespoon butter or margarine
1 tablespoon all-purpose flour
1 cup milk
2 egg yolks, beaten
¼ teaspoon almond extract
Slivered almonds

In a mixing bowl, combine flour, baking powder, salt, eggs, milk and oil. Cut cooked turkey breast into 1½-inch pieces and dip into batter. Drain excess batter and drop into a deep fryer. Cook until golden brown.

To make the sauce, make a thin white sauce by melting butter and stirring in flour; gradually stir in milk and stir constantly until the mixture thickens and is smooth. Add egg yolks, continue to stir until the mixture thickens.

Arkansas

Bridgeford Cottage

#263 Spring Street
Eureka Springs, Arkansas 72632
(501) 253-7853

Bridgeford Cottage, nestled in the heart of Eureka Springs' historic residential district, is a Victorian delight. The gracious hospitality of that era has been carefully rekindled in this 1884 gingerbread house. Outside, shady porches invite guests to pull up a wicker chair, relax, and enjoy the unique panorama of Spring Street. Bridgeford Cottage is within walking of downtown Eureka Springs, but far enough away from its hustle and bustle to afford guests a peaceful, calm visit.

Mom's Apple Butter Bars

1 cup brown sugar, firmly packed
1½ cups all-purpose flour
¾ cup butter (1½ sticks)
1½ cups oatmeal
½ teaspoon baking soda
1 teaspoon vanilla extract
½ teaspoon salt

❖ ❖ ❖

Apple butter

In a mixing bowl, mix all ingredients except apple butter until crumbly. Spread half of the mixture in a 9x13-inch pan. Spread apple butter over crumbly mixture. Cover with the remaining mixture of crumbs. Bake in a 350° oven for 20 to 25 minutes. May be served with whipped cream.
Serves 8.

Pineapple Sheet Cake

2 cups all-purpose flour
2 cups sugar
2 teaspoons baking soda
2 teaspoons vanilla extract
2 eggs
1 16-ounce can crushed pineapple
½ cup chopped nuts

❖ ❖ ❖

1 8-ounce package cream cheese
2 cups confectioners' sugar
2 teaspoons vanilla extract
¼ cup margarine (½ stick)

In a large mixing bowl, mix together flour, sugar, baking soda, vanilla, eggs, pineapple, and nuts. Bake in a greased 10x15-inch sheet cake pan in a 350° oven for 20 to 25 minutes.
Combine the cream cheese, confectioners' sugar, vanilla and margarine; frost the cake while it is still warm.
Serves 16.

❖ ❖ ❖ ❖ ❖ ❖

The Heartstone Inn

35 Kingshighway
Eureka Springs, Arkansas 72632
(501) 253-8916

Described as "a pink and white confection," and voted one of the ten best new inns for 1985 by the National Inn Review, this restored two-story Victorian home, with wrap-around verandas, is conveniently located in the historical district. Each carefully restored room has a private bath, queen-size bed, antique furnishings, air conditioning, and cable television. A full gourmet breakfast consisting of such tantalizing delights as German Apple Baked Pancakes or Strawberry Blintzes (with all the trimmings, of course) is served in the breakfast room. Other refreshments are available throughout the day and evening in the cozy guest lounge or under umbrellas in the garden. The inn has ample off-street parking for guests, and the trolley stops a few feet from the front door.

Breakfast Vol-au-Vent

This dish has brought applause!

1 pound bulk pork sausage

❖ ❖ ❖

1 medium onion, chopped
1 cup celery, chopped
4 ounces mushrooms, sliced
1 to 2 tablespoons butter

❖ ❖ ❖

1 10¾-ounce can cream of
    mushroom soup
8 hard boiled eggs, sliced
1 tablespoon chopped pimiento
1 cup milk

❖ ❖ ❖

Seasoned salt and pepper to taste

❖ ❖ ❖

Tomato slices and parsley for
    garnish
8 puff pastry shells

Cook, crumble and drain the sausage, set aside. Sauté the onion, celery and mushrooms in butter. Add sausage, mushroom soup, pimiento and milk, stirring well over medium heat. Add seasoned salt and pepper to taste. Add the sliced eggs, stirring gently until mixture is heated through. Keep warm.

Bake pastry shells according to directions. Remove caps and reserve, scoop out the center. Place warm, prepared pastry shells in individual au gratin dishes. Spoon sausage-egg mixture into each pastry shell to overflowing. Replace pastry caps. Serve immediately, garnished with tomato slices and parsley sprigs.

Serves 8.

Mandarin Muffins

This recipe was created just for this publication—thanks, Iris Simantel!

1 11-ounce can Mandarin orange
    segments
1 tablespoon orange extract

❖ ❖ ❖

2 cups all-purpose flour
2 teaspoons baking powder
½ teaspoon baking soda
½ teaspoon salt
½ cup brown sugar, packed
¼ cup sugar

❖ ❖ ❖

1 egg, well-beaten
1 8-ounce carton sour cream
⅓ cup shortening, melted

❖ ❖ ❖

½ cup pecans

Drain orange segments, reserving liquid. Cut the segments into halves and place in a measuring cup, add orange extract and reserved liquid to make 8 ounces (1 cup). Set aside.

Combine flour, baking powder, soda, salt and sugars in a large bowl. In a separate bowl, combine egg, sour cream, orange mixture and melted shortening. Make a well in the center of dry ingredients. Add orange mixture and pecans. Stir just until moistened. Spoon into greased or lined muffin pans, filling ⅔ full. Bake in a 400° oven for 20 to 25 minutes.

Makes 1 to 1½ dozen muffins.

Delicious Creamy Zucchini Quiche

1 9½- to 10-inch unbaked pastry
    shell
2 tablespoons Dijon mustard

❖ ❖ ❖

3 cups grated zucchini
Salt

❖ ❖ ❖

8 large mushrooms, sliced
2 tablespoons butter

❖ ❖ ❖

2 cups grated Monterey Jack
    cheese
1 8-ounce package cream cheese
½ cup whipping cream
2 egg yolks
1 egg
Salt and pepper to taste

Spread the bottom of a pastry shell with mustard. Bake in a 450° oven for 10 minutes. Cool. Reduce oven heat to 350°. Place zucchini in colander, sprinkle with salt and drain 5 minutes. Sauté mushrooms in butter. Sprinkle one cup of Jack cheese in the bottom of the pastry shell. Spoon mushrooms on top. Squeeze zucchini to remove excess moisture. Place in the shell, sepa-

The Hearthstone Inn

rating and fluffing with fingers. Beat together cream cheese, cream, egg yolks and egg, season with salt and pepper. Place the pastry dish on a baking sheet and carefully pour in egg-cream mixture. Sprinkle the remaining Jack cheese on top.

Bake in a 350° oven for 45 minutes, until top is puffed and golden and a knife inserted in center comes out clean. Let stand 5 minutes before cutting. Very rich.

Serves 6.

Corn Cob Inn

Route 1, Box 183
Everton, Arkansas 72633
(501) 429-6545

This historical stone house sits beside Clear Creek in the Ozarks. The Corn Cob Inn originally was built as a general store for a mining community, then was used as a corn cob pipe factory, and now is a comfortable home located on eighteen acres. The Corn Cob Inn is a perfect place to relax; its three bedrooms share a bath. A country-style breakfast is served in the dining room or on the outdoor patio. Lunch and dinner are also available on request. A private beach offers fishing, swimming, and floating. The Corn Cob Inn is near many Ozark attractions.

Pasta Fagioli

1 cup dried lima beans
5 cups water

❖ ❖ ❖

1 medium onion, chopped
2 cloves garlic, minced
2 stalks celery, chopped
1 tablespoon oil

❖ ❖ ❖

1 14-ounce can stewed tomatoes
1 teaspoon salt
½ teaspoon pepper

½ teaspoon rosemary
1½ cups elbow macaroni

❖ ❖ ❖

¼ cup chopped fresh parsley
Freshly grated Parmesan cheese

Soak the beans overnight. Cook over medium heat for 1 hour. Sauté the onion, garlic, and celery in oil, and add to the beans. Add tomatoes and seasonings. Bring to a boil and add macaroni. Cook for 8 minutes, until the noodles are soft. Add parsley and serve with grated cheese sprinkled over each serving. Together with hot crusty homemade bread and a tossed salad, this makes a hearty meal.

Serves 6 to 8.

Spinach-Filled Lasagna

2 bunches spinach
¼ pound mushrooms, sliced and sautéed
1 cup ricotta or cottage cheese
¼ teaspoon nutmeg
Salt and pepper
8 cooked lasagna noodles

❖ ❖ ❖

2 cloves garlic, minced
½ cup onions, sautéed
1 green pepper, chopped and sautéed
2 cups tomato sauce
½ teaspoon basil
½ teaspoon oregano

❖ ❖ ❖

Grated Mozzarella cheese

Steam the spinach until limp; chop. Mix with sautéed mushrooms, ricotta, and seasonings. Coat each noodle with 2 to 3 tablespoons of this mixture, roll up, turn on its end so you can see the spiral and place each in a shallow baking pan.

Combine the remaining ingredients except Mozzarella and pour over the rolled up noodles. Sprinkle with grated cheese. Bake in a 350° oven for 20 minutes.

Serves 8.

Wild Persimmon Pudding

1 cup all-purpose flour
½ teaspoon cinnamon
½ teaspoon salt
¼ teaspoon baking soda
1 teaspoon baking powder

❖ ❖ ❖

1 cup sugar
1 egg
1½ cups milk
¼ cup margarine (½ stick), melted
¾ cup persimmon pulp

Sift the first five ingredients together. Combine sugar, egg, milk, margarine, and persimmon pulp. Slowly add the dry ingredients and blend together with an electric mixer. Pour into a well-greased 8x4-inch pan and bake in a 350° oven for 1 hour.

Serves 6 to 8.

Thomas Quinn Guest House

814 North B Street
Fort Smith, Arkansas 72901
(501) 782-0499

The Thomas Quinn Guest House is on the edge of Fort Smith's Historic District. The first story was built in 1863, with the second floor and Corinthian columns added in 1916. There are seven two-bedroom suites and two one-bedroom suites. All suites have a furnished compact kitchen with bar, living room, full private bath, satellite TV, and private phones. The Thomas Quinn House offers a large patio area complete with Jacuzzi and large fish pond. Complimentary coffee is provided in each suite with a continental breakfast across the street Monday through Friday. Horse-drawn carriage rides to local points of interest are available.

Thomas Quinn's Favorite Cake

The topping is baked in; stays moist for two or three days and freezes beautifully.

    1 cup butter (2 sticks)
    2 cups sugar
    1 very ripe banana (or 2 or 3)
    2 or 3 eggs
    1 teaspoon vanilla extract
            ❖ ❖ ❖
    Dash salt
    2 teaspoons baking powder
    2 teaspoons baking soda
    3 cups all-purpose flour
            ❖ ❖ ❖
    1 pint sour cream
            ❖ ❖ ❖
    ⅓ cup brown sugar, firmly packed
    1 tablespoon cinnamon
    1 cup chopped walnuts
    1 6-ounce package chocolate chips

In a mixing bowl, cream butter, sugar, bananas, eggs, and vanilla. If 3 bananas are used, add a third egg. Add dry ingredients, blend thoroughly. Add sour cream. Pour half the batter into a well-buttered 9x13-inch pan. Combine the remaining ingredients, sprinkle over batter. Pour the remaining batter over the filling, and sprinkle remaining filling on top. Any extra batter may be used for another cake baked in a round pan. Bake in a 350° oven for about 45 minutes. Delicious. Serves 16.

The Oak Tree Inn

Vinegar Hill
Highway 110 West
Heber Springs, Arkansas 72543
(501) 362-7731

The Oak Tree Inn welcomes guests to enjoy the beautiful scenery of Greers Ferry Lake and the friendly people of Heber Springs. The Inn has been designed to recapture the warmth and charm of a bygone era; each room is named for a citizen who contributed to the development of Cleburne County. The innkeeper invites travelers to enjoy the shade of the Arkansas oaks and partake of the character of The Oak Tree Inn.

Oak Tree Granola Muffins

    2 cups all-purpose flour
    2 cups oats
    1½ cups granola
    2 tablespoons baking powder
    2 teaspoons salt
    3 teaspoons cinnamon
    1 cup sugar
    1 cup raisins
            ❖ ❖ ❖
    2 cups water
    2 eggs
    ½ cup vegetable oil

Mix the dry ingredients and raisins, add water, eggs, and oil. Stir until moist. Pour into greased muffin cups. Bake in a 400° oven for 20 to 30 minutes.
    Makes about 2 dozen medium-sized muffins.

Dave's Hot Fudge

    2 cups instant dry milk
    1½ cups sugar
    ¾ cup cocoa
    2 teaspoons vanilla extract
    1 cup boiling water
    ½ cup margarine (1 stick), melted

Place the dry ingredients and vanilla in a blender. In a two-cup measuring cup, place water and margarine, bring to a boil in the microwave. Pour the hot mixture into the blender and turn on at the highest speed for 2 to 3 minutes. Store in the refrigerator.
    Makes 2 cups of hot fudge.

Fred's Piña Colada Dessert

    2 1¼-ounce packages whipped
        topping mix
            ❖ ❖ ❖
    1 cup browned coconut
            ❖ ❖ ❖
    2 8-ounce packages cream cheese,
        softened
    2 cups confectioners' sugar
    ½ cup piña colada mix
            ❖ ❖ ❖
    1 16-ounce can crushed pineapple,
        well-drained

Beat the whipped topping mix according to the directions on the package. Refrigerate.
    To brown the coconut, place under the broiler (or in a 350° oven for 10 to 15 minutes), stirring frequently and watching carefully to avoid burning.
    In a mixer bowl, beat the cream cheese, confectioners' sugar, and piña colada mix together. Add to the whipped topping and beat at high speed. Add the pineapple and coconut; mix. Chill.
    This can be served as a topping like whipped cream on a spice cake, or placed in a graham cracker crust and served as a pie.
    Serves 10.

California

The Guest House Bed and Breakfast Inn

120 Hart Lane
Arroyo Grande, California 93420
(805) 481-9304

The Guest House, situated in the charming old village of Arroyo Grande, was built in the 1850s by a sea captain from New England. Hosts Mark Miller and Jim Cunningham have kept the flavor of Old New England alive with many family heirlooms to create a mellow and inviting home. A crackling fire in the fireplace and easy chairs make the living room a haven for relaxation and easy conversation, adding to the enjoyment of afternoon wine and cheeses.

These recipes date back to the early 1800s and are from Mark Miller's great-grandmother's time in Vermont. They have been handed down from one generation to the next, but seldom have been put in writing.

Creamed Beef

**1 3-ounce jar dried beef, cut in
   strips**

**¼ cup butter (½ stick)
¼ cup all-purpose flour
1¼ cups milk
1 cup cream
1 8-ounce package cream cheese,
   cut into small cubes**

Melt butter in a heavy skillet, sauté the beef. Add flour and cook until golden brown, add milk, cream, and cream cheese all at once. Cook and stir until smooth and thickened. Serve on toast, hot biscuits or corn bread.

Makes 4 generous servings.

Creamed Eggs

**1 pint thick white sauce
6 slices toast, buttered
6 hard-boiled eggs
Parsley**

Put a layer of sauce on each piece of toast, part of the egg whites sliced thin and some of the yolks sieved. Repeat three times, ending with a layer of sauce. Place in a warm oven for 3 minutes. Garnish with parsley and serve. Serves 6.

Ham 'n' Eggs Ale Luxe

Sauté thinly sliced ham in butter, sprinkle lightly with brown sugar, place on toasted English muffin halves and top ham with a poached egg. Smother eggs with a rich white sauce to which you have added grated Swiss cheese and sherry. Garnish with pimiento and sliced ripe olives.

Squash Griddle Cakes

**2 cups all-purpose flour
1 teaspoon cream of tartar
1 teaspoon baking soda
2 tablespoons sugar
1 teaspoon salt**

❖ ❖ ❖

**2 eggs, well-beaten
2 cups milk**

❖ ❖ ❖

2 cups puréed squash

❖ ❖ ❖

Vermont maple syrup

Mix dry ingredients. Add the eggs and milk to squash and combine with the flour mixture. Beat until light and smooth. Makes a thin batter. Fry on greased griddle. Serve with Vermont maple syrup.

Makes about 20 4-inch cakes.

The Gull House

Post Office Box 1381
344 Whittley Avenue
Avalon, California 90704
(213) 510-2547

Guests enjoy Santa Catalina Island at the Gull House where the two deluxe suites have separate entrances, stereo, and color television. Guests enjoy the spa, small pool, and barbecue. Continental breakfast is served at guests' leisure under an Italian umbrella on the patio or in the morning room.

The Gull House

Low Calorie Blueberry Crêpes

½ cup fresh or frozen blueberries
1 teaspoon vanilla extract
1 .035-ounce envelope sugar
    substitute

   ❖   ❖   ❖

1 egg
¼ cup yogurt or buttermilk
1 slice of white bread
1 .035-ounce envelope sugar
    substitute
Pinch ground cardamom (optional)

   ❖   ❖   ❖

1 teaspoon butter or margarine

In a saucepan, combine the blueberries, vanilla and 1 envelope of sugar substitute. Barely cover with water. Over medium heat, bring to a slow boil and cook uncovered, stirring often, until the consistency of preserves. Remove from heat, cover and keep warm while making the crêpe.

In blender jar, combine egg, yogurt, bread torn in pieces, and the other envelope of sugar substitute; blend until smooth. Add up to ¼ teaspoon of cardamom to taste. Heat 10-inch non-stick skillet over low heat and pour in blender contents, tilting pan to spread evenly. Lift edges with rubber spatula; turn only when brown-flecked or pancake may tear. Cook other side, then spread fruit in center and roll up. Serve dotted with butter.

Makes 1 serving of 265 calories.

The Union Hotel

401 First Street
Benicia, California 94510
(707) 746-0100

Whitewashed and statuesque in three-story grandeur, The Union Hotel sits proudly on historic First Street as a reminder of Benicia's nineteenth century California heritage. The Union Hotel combines Victorian architecture, period furnishings, and contemporary comforts.

Cream Biscuits

4 cups all-purpose flour
2 tablespoons baking powder
1 teaspoon salt
½ cup good quality salted butter (1
    stick)
1 pint plus 1 tablespoon heavy
    cream

The Union Hotel

In a large mixing bowl, stir together flour, baking powder, and salt. Cut in butter until coarse, gradually pour in the heavy cream. Stir, then knead quickly to make a stiff dough. Do not overwork.

Roll out to ½-inch thickness and cut into squares of desired size. Bake in a 400° oven for 18 minutes and serve immediately.

Dough can be kept in the refrigerator for up to 6 hours after being cut. Do not attempt to freeze the dough.

Makes approximately 3 dozen biscuits.

Burbank/ Belair Bed and Breakfast

941 North Frederic
Burbank, California 91505
(818) 848-9227

Retired teacher / singer / musician / adventurer / world traveler / collector of exotic art, Harry Bell is the host of this convenient and comfortable two-story home. In quiet residential Burbank, it is only two miles from Universal and NBC Studios (tours), five miles from Hollywood, ten miles from downtown Los Angeles, and thirty miles from beaches and mountain resorts.

Banana Toast

Toast sourdough bread. Butter, and place sliced ripe bananas on top. Sprinkle sugar around the edges. In the center put various jams (apricot, etc.). Sprinkle cinnamon over all, and grill. When bubbly, add small marshmallows and nuts. Grated coconut may also be added.

Foothill House

3037 Foothill Boulevard
Calistoga, California 94515
(707) 942-6933

The Foothill House setting is distinguished by the wide variety of lovely old trees that surround it, keeping it comfortably shaded and cool. The inn offers views across the valley of wooded hills and Mount St. Helena. The Foothills' vicinity abounds with such wildlife as quail, hummingbirds, and hawks. Three cozy, yet spacious, suites are individually decorated with country antiques. The color scheme for each room complements the handmade quilt that adorns the queen-size four-poster bed.

Foothill House Oven-Baked Pancakes

½ cup milk
½ cup all-purpose flour
½ teaspoon baking soda
3 eggs

1 teaspoon sugar
Dash salt

❖ ❖ ❖

3 tablespoons butter
¼ cup sugar
1 teaspoon cinnamon
2 apples, peeled, cored and sliced
⅓ cup currants
⅓ cup chopped walnuts

❖ ❖ ❖

¼ cup sugar mixed with 1 teaspoon cinnamon
2 tablespoons butter
Whipped cream

In a small mixing bowl, mix the milk, flour, baking soda, eggs, sugar, and salt together until smooth; set aside. In a heated oven, melt butter in the bottom of a 9-inch skillet with an oven-proof handle. Mix in sugar and cinnamon. Sauté apples, currants, and walnuts in butter until soft, but not mushy. Pour batter over the apples. Bake in a 400° oven for 10 minutes. Remove from the oven, top with sugar/cinnamon mixture and dot with butter. Return the pan to the oven for 15 minutes. Serve immediately topped with whipped cream.

Note: This recipe can be made in individual, 4-inch baking dishes.

Variation: Instead of apples, currants, and walnuts, use 2 pears peeled, cored and sliced plus 1 cup of frozen or fresh cranberries and add 2 tablespoons of Grand Marnier before you finish sautéing.

Serves 4.

Foothill House Cheese Torte

4 8-ounce packages cream cheese, softened
½ cup butter, unsalted (1 stick)
2 cups fresh basil
⅔ cup freshly grated Parmesan cheese
2 teaspoons minced garlic
⅓ cup olive oil
1 cup pine nuts

Whip 3 packages of cream cheese with butter and set aside. Chop the basil in

food processor. Add Parmesan cheese, 1 package of cream cheese, garlic, olive oil and mix. Remove from the food processor, place in a mixing bowl and add pine nuts. Layer whipped cheese and basil mixture in ½-inch layers in serving dishes. At the Foothill House this is made in 5 1-cup cheese pots to serve to guests. You may line your dish with 2 layers of wet cheese cloth and unmold approximately ½ hour before serving. Garnish with a sprig of fresh basil.

Note from the innkeeper: Guests often inhale this—it's best not to force them to share with strangers!

Serves 5.

Foothill House "Hot-Hot" Artichoke Spread

⅔ cup freshly grated Parmesan cheese
⅔ cup mayonnaise
1 4½-ounce can diced green chiles
1 13½-ounce can artichoke hearts, chopped (not marinated)
1 teaspoon seasoned salt

Combine all ingredients in a casserole. Microwave on high for 3 minutes or heat in a 350° conventional oven for 20 minutes. Serve with thinly sliced French bread or crackers.

Makes approximately 1 cup of spread.

Foothill House Breakfast Drink

1 banana
1 cup plain yogurt
1 cup fresh orange juice, chilled
1 cup hulled strawberries
½ teaspoon vanilla extract
1 teaspoon clover honey
3 fresh mint sprigs

Blend all ingredients except mint in a blender. Pour into 3 large (10-ounce) wine glasses. Garnish with fresh mint.

Note: A teaspoon of Meloso sherry gives a nice "tang."

Serves 3.

Foothill House "Sweet Dreams"

Foothill House "Sweet Dreams" are left on the bedside table along with a decanter of Napa Valley sherry when turn-down service is done each night.

1 cup butter (2 sticks)
1½ cups brown sugar, firmly
    packed
1 egg

   ❖   ❖   ❖

2 cups unbleached flour
1 teaspoon baking soda
½ teaspoon salt
1 teaspoon cinnamon
1 teaspoon ginger

   ❖   ❖   ❖

1 cup chopped walnuts
1 12-ounce package chocolate chips
1 teaspoon vanilla extract
Confectioners' sugar

Cream the butter, add brown sugar and egg and beat well. Mix together the flour, baking soda, salt, cinnamon, and ginger and blend well. Combine with butter mixture. Fold in the walnuts, chocolate chips, and vanilla. Chill for several hours. Form the dough in 1-inch balls and roll them in the confectioners' sugar. Place on a cookie sheet and bake in a 375° oven for 8 to 10 minutes.

Makes 6 dozen.

Susan's Late Harvest Wine Cake

3 cups all-purpose flour
1 teaspoon baking powder
1 teaspoon baking soda
1 teaspoon salt
1 teaspoon cinnamon
1 teaspoon ground cloves

   ❖   ❖   ❖

3 eggs
1 cup butter (2 sticks), melted
1¾ cups sugar
1 cup Late Harvest wine
½ cup buttermilk
2 tablespoons Grand Marnier

   ❖   ❖   ❖

4 tablespoons grated orange rind
1 cup walnuts

Mix together flour, baking powder, soda, salt, cinnamon, and cloves, set aside. Beat eggs until frothy. Add and mix in remaining ingredients except orange rind and walnuts. Add wet to dry ingredients, mix well and add orange rind and walnuts. Pour into a bundt pan. Bake in a 350° oven for 50 minutes or until a cake tester inserted in the center comes out clean.

Serves 16.

The Cobblestone Inn

Post Office Box 3185
Carmel-by-the-Sea, California 93921
(408) 625-5222
Toll Free 1-800-AAA-INNS

The Cobblestone Inn invites guests to experience a unique country inn nestled romantically in the heart of Carmel-by-the-Sea. One of the oldest inns in the area, it presents an ideal vacation retreat setting and a quality weekend get-away for rest and relaxation. The English country garden atmosphere is enhanced by the personal attention given to each guest.

Kugelis

A giant hashbrown—Chef Sharon Miller's great-great-grandmother's recipe.

4 large potatoes
½ pound bacon, cooked and
    crumbled
1 onion, minced
3 eggs, beaten slightly
3 teaspoons salt
1 cup sour cream
¼ cup half and half

The Cobblestone Inn

Grate potatoes. Mix with the remaining ingredients. Bake in a 13x9x2-inch pan in a 400° oven for 20 minutes. Reduce heat to 350° and bake 50 minutes more or until potatoes are brown.

Serves 4.

Banana Nut Bread

¾ cup shortening
1½ cups sugar
4 eggs
1½ teaspoons vanilla extract
3 cups all-purpose flour
1½ teaspoons salt
1½ teaspoons baking soda
1 cup chopped nuts
5 large bananas, mashed

Cream the first three ingredients together and add vanilla. Add remaining ingredients and pour into 2 well-greased and floured loaf pans. Bake in a 350° oven for 1 hour.

Makes 2 loaves.

Broccoli or Any Vegie Strudel

2 shallots, chopped
3 heads broccoli, chopped
Mushrooms, if desired
2 cups butter (4 sticks)
1 pound Swiss cheese, grated
Salt and pepper
1 teaspoon paprika
4 tablespoons lemon juice
4 ounces almonds
6 eggs
Mixture of herbs (parsley, mint, dill, chives)
Dash cayenne pepper

❖   ❖   ❖

24 sheets of phyllo dough

Sauté the shallots, broccoli, and mushrooms in butter. Add the next 8 ingredients to make filling.

Working on a large piece of waxed paper, layer 6 sheets of phyllo (each brushed with melted butter).

Divide the vegetable mixture into fourths and place one portion on the layered sheets of phyllo, covering about half of the rectangle. Starting with the side with the filling, roll the phyllo in the same manner as a jelly roll. Repeat to make 4 rolls.

Place rolls seam side down on a baking sheet. Brush rolls with melted butter. Using a sharp knife, diagonally cut just halfway through the phyllo layers on each roll to make 1-inch-wide pieces.

Bake in a 375° oven for 20 to 30 minutes, until golden.

Serves 8.

Sharon's Chef Surprise

5 white potatoes, cooked until almost done, diced
3 to 5 hard-boiled eggs, diced
½ to ¾ pound mushrooms, sliced, sautéed
1 onion, chopped
2 cups shredded Cheddar cheese
½ cup chopped parsley
1 bunch green onions, chopped
2 tablespoons Dijon mustard
Salt and pepper
Basil to taste

❖   ❖   ❖

1 sheet puff pastry
1 egg, beaten

Potatoes and hard-boiled eggs can be done the day before and refrigerated. Mix all ingredients together in a quiche pan, and stretch puff pastry over top of pan. Seal with beaten egg. With leftover dough, make some kind of design and coat with egg. Place on top of the dough. Bake in a 400° oven for ½ hour or until pastry dough is golden brown.

Serves 8 to 10.

Happy Landing Inn

Post Office Box 2619
Carmel-by-the-Sea, California 93921
(408) 624-7917

The Happy Landing was built in 1925 as a family retreat. This early Comstock-designed Inn has evolved into one of Carmel's charming and romantic places to stay. Cathedral ceiling rooms with antiques open onto a beautiful central garden with gazebo, pond and flagstone paths.

Happy Landing Inn Pumpkin Bread

4 eggs
1 cup oil
⅔ cup water
2 cups pumpkin

❖   ❖   ❖

3⅓ cups all-purpose flour
3 cups sugar
2½ teaspoons salt
2 teaspoons baking soda
1 teaspoon baking powder
1 teaspoon cinnamon
1 teaspoon nutmeg

In a large mixing bowl combine eggs, oil, water, and pumpkin; mix well. Add remaining ingredients. Bake in two 9x5-inch pans in a 350° oven for 1 hour.

Makes 2 loaves.

The City Hotel

Main Street
Post Office Box 1870
Columbia, California 95310
(209) 532-1479

The City Hotel in Columbia continues to provide hospitality to wayfarers as was traditionally extended 100 years ago. Small and intimate, with nine lovely and luxuriously appointed guest rooms, the hotel appears to have been left behind intact as the gold miners left and the twentieth century dawned. The service is attentive, the atmosphere warm and personal, the food and drink most satisfying, and the lodging intimate.

Cream of Carrot Soup

1 leek, sliced
2 tablespoons butter
2 to 3 carrots, peeled and sliced
1 medium baking potato, cubed
3 quarts chicken stock (or canned chicken consommé)

❖ ❖ ❖

Butter and cream to taste
Salt and white pepper to taste
Shot of Sherry (optional)

Sauté the leek in butter in a soup pot or large saucepan, until translucent. Add the carrots, potato and stock; cover and bring to a boil. Simmer until the potato and carrots are tender. Place in a blender, reserving some of the liquid for later; blend until smooth. Strain. Pour the carrot purée back into the soup pot and add cream and butter, using the reserved liquid to correct the texture of the soup. Salt and pepper to taste. Add dry sherry if the soup needs to be sweetened.
Serves 4 to 6.

Broiled Pork Chops
with Orange and Honey Mustard Sauce

8 to 12 loin pork chops
Salt and pepper

❖ ❖ ❖

¾ cup dry white wine
3 tablespoons orange mustard
3 tablespoons orange blossom honey
½ cup butter (1 stick)

Charbroil the chops until half-cooked; season and place in a roasting pan; stacking them is alright. Cook until done in a 350° oven; remove and place the meat on a large heated serving tray. Add the wine, mustard, and honey to the roasting pan and reduce until thickened; whip in the butter and pour over the meat or serve on the side.
Serves 4 to 6.

City Hotel Chocolate Mousse

¼ cup sugar
⅓ cup water
1 6-ounce package semi-sweet chocolate chips
3 egg yolks

❖ ❖ ❖

1¾ cups whipping cream
1½ tablespoons confectioners' sugar

Boil the sugar and water. Place in a blender with chocolate chips; blend 20 seconds. Add the egg yolks; blend another 30 seconds. Whip the cream and add confectioners' sugar. Fold the melted chocolate and cream together and divide into serving glasses (large red wine glasses are nice). Chill for 2 hours. Serve with more sweet whipped cream and shaved milk chocolate to garnish. Powdered coffee or Kahlua may be added if desired.
Serves 6 to 8.

City Hotel's Christmas Plum Pudding

1 teaspoon baking soda
1 tablespoon warm water

❖ ❖ ❖

1 cup raisins
1 cup candied fruit
½ cup sliced citron
2 cups all-purpose flour

❖ ❖ ❖

4 eggs, beaten
1 cup sugar
1 teaspoon cloves
2 teaspoons cinamon
½ teaspoon nutmeg
1 teaspoon salt
1 cup milk
1 cup blanched almonds, chopped
2 cups bread crumbs
1 cup diced beef suet

Dissolve the soda in the warm water; set aside. Dredge the raisins, candied fruit, and citron in the flour; set aside. Reserve the remaining flour.
Place the eggs in a large mixing bowl. Add the sugar, spices, salt, and milk. Stir in the dredged fruits, chopped almonds, bread crumbs, and suet in that order, until all are combined. Stir in the reserved soda and flour, mixing well. Place into individual serving dishes. Set the dishes in a deep pan. Add an inch of water in the bottom of the pan; cover tightly. Bake in a 375° oven for 35 to 40 minutes. Serve the pudding with a sweet sauce of your choice.
Serves 12.

Fresh Mint Ice Cream

2 cups cream
¾ cup whole milk
½ cup sugar
¼ cup fresh chopped mint

❖ ❖ ❖

3 egg yolks, beaten

Combine the cream, whole milk, sugar, and mint in a 2-quart saucepan. Bring to a boil over medium heat, stirring constantly. Cover and set aside for 30 minutes to steep, allowing the mint to infuse the cream.

Strain the cream to remove the mint. Place the egg yolks in another 2-quart saucepan. Pour one cup of the hot cream mixture into the egg yolks; mix well with a whisk. Add the remaining cream mixture. Cook over low heat, whisking constantly until the mixture coats a wooden spoon, about 7 to 15 minutes. Strain again and chill for about 1 hour, then freeze in an ice cream maker according to the manufacturer's instructions. May be served with grated bittersweet chocolate on top.

Serves 6 to 8.

Lime Cheesecake
with Chocolate Crust

For best results, place the cream cheese in a mixing bowl to soften about 30 minutes before preparing the cheesecake.

1 box chocolate wafers
3 to 4 ounces clarified butter
 ❖ ❖ ❖
3 egg yolks
1 cup sugar
1 teaspoon vanilla extract
Juice of 3 limes
 ❖ ❖ ❖
3 8-ounce packages cream cheese, softened
 ❖ ❖ ❖
1 pint sour cream
¼ cup sugar
1 teaspoon vanilla extract

Place chocolate wafers in a double bag and use a rolling pin to crush into fine crumbs. Mix the crumbs with clarified butter in a springform pan to form crust.

Whip egg yolks and sugar to a light lemon color, and when they fall from the whisk in a ribbon, mix in vanilla and lime juice.

Whip the softened cream cheese in mixer until smooth, then slowly add the egg yolk and lime mixture. Pour into the crust and bake in a 300° oven for 25 to 35 minutes. Remove and cool.

Mix together remaining ingredients and pour onto cheesecake. Bake an additional 10 minutes.

Serves 20.

Furnace Creek Resort

Post Office Box 1
Death Valley, California 92328
(619) 786-2345

Furnace Creek Resort combines the elegance of the inn with the rustic charm of the ranch. The inn is an old California grande hotel, and the ranch is a rustic, charming throwback to the adventurous olden days. Both offer sumptuous cuisine, gracious comfort, and activities ranging from horseback riding, tennis, and golf to lounging by a naturally warm spring-fed pool.

Death Valley Date Nut Bread

2 cups chopped dates
 ❖ ❖ ❖
4 cups sifted all-purpose flour
1 cup brown sugar, firmly packed
1 cup sugar
1 cup chopped walnuts
½ cup butter (1 stick), softened
3 teaspoons salt
3 teaspoons baking soda

Soak the dates in hot water for 1 hour.

Blend all ingredients except the dates. Add 1 cup of dates and mix until smooth, add the remaining dates and mix well. Pour into 2 aluminum foil

loaf pans and bake in a 360° oven for approximately 1 hour.

Makes 2 2-pound loaves.

Rock Haus Bed and Breakfast Inn

410 15th Street
Del Mar, California 92014
(619) 481-3764

A private home, a place of worship, a gambling parlor, a hotel—the Rock Haus has been all of these and more. This early California bungalow-style house is a historical landmark that was built at the turn of the century. Guests may visit the wine cellar to help select a wine for the afternoon and can watch the spectacular sunset from the veranda or gather around the fireplace in the living room.

Pepper Jelly

1 cup red and green bell peppers
1 small jalapeno (optional)
1 small yellow pepper (optional)
1 small serano pepper, seeded (optional)
6½ cups sugar
1½ cups vinegar
1 6-ounce box fruit pectin (both packs)
Few drops green food coloring

Chop the peppers in a food processor. Wash the peppers in a strainer with cold water after chopping to make the jelly clear. In an enamel pot, bring the peppers, sugar, and vinegar to a full boil, boil for 2½ minutes. Add pectin and boil 1 minute longer. Turn the heat off and add 2 to 3 drops of food coloring. Remove from heat and skim the bubbles from the top with a slotted spoon. Pour the jelly into sterilized jars and seal. (Use paraffin if the jars are not self-sealing.)

Note from the innkeeper: This is served over cream cheese with a basket of crackers at "Wine Time," in the early evening.

Fills 6 8-ounce jars.

Blueberry Buckle

¼ **cup butter (½ stick), softened**
¾ **cup sugar**
1 egg
1½ **cups sifted all-purpose flour**
2 teaspoons baking powder
½ **teaspoon salt**
½ **cup milk**
2 cups blueberries, drained

❖ ❖ ❖

½ **cup sugar**
⅓ **cup all-purpose flour**
½ **teaspoon cinnamon**
¼ **cup butter (½ stick)**

In a mixing bowl, cream ¼ cup butter with ¾ cup sugar until light and airy. Blend in the egg. In another bowl, sift together 1½ cups flour, baking powder, and salt. Add the flour mixture alternately with milk to the creamed mixture. Gently fold in blueberries. Pour into a greased and floured 8x8-inch pan.

To make the topping, combine the remaining sugar, flour, and cinnamon. Cut in butter until the mixture resembles coarse meal. Sprinkle over batter in the pan. Bake in a 375° oven for 40 to 45 minutes. Place the pan on a rack to cool. Cut into squares and serve warm.

Serves 6.

Halbig's Hacienda

432 South Citrus Avenue
Escondido, California 92027
(619) 745-1296

Halbig's Hacienda is a large adobe ranch house sitting on a knoll overlooking the surrounding mountains. It offers spacious patios to enjoy the outdoors when dining or lounging. Three rooms are available for bed and breakfast.

Raisin and Walnut Bread

1 ¼-ounce package active dry yeast
1¼ **cups water (tepid)**
2 tablespoons butter, softened
1 tablespoon sugar
1 teaspoon salt
1¼ **cups coarsely chopped walnuts**
1¼ **cups raisins**
3½ **cups (approximately) whole wheat flour**

In a large bowl, dissolve yeast in ¼ cup of water, stirring in remaining water, butter, sugar, and salt. Stir in walnuts, raisins, and flour. Makes a firm dough.

Turn onto a floured board. Knead 10 minutes or until smooth and elastic. A little more flour can be added to prevent the dough from sticking. Form the dough into a ball. Place in a greased bowl and cover. Let rise in a warm place approximately 2 hours, until double.

Punch the dough down and divide in half. Form each half into a ball and place well apart on a greased cookie sheet. Cover, let rise again until double in size (45 to 60 minutes). Bake in a 400° oven for 25 to 30 minutes. Test with a cake tester for doneness. (Loaves can be covered with foil the last 10 minutes to prevent raisins from over-browning.) Remove to wire racks to cool completely. Will have a firm crust.

Makes 2 loaves.

The Gingerbread Mansion

400 Berding Street
Ferndale, California 95536
(707) 786-4000

Exquisitely turreted, carved, and gabled and colorfully landscaped with lush English gardens, The Gingerbread Mansion is a visual masterpiece! One of Northern California's most photographed buildings, this grand lady of the Victorian village also possesses a beautifully restored interior, where guests are welcomed to a world of warmth, elegance and charm as guests of The Gingerbread Mansion. A very special experience.

Gingerbread Mansion Glogg

For winter afternoons or evenings around the parlor fireplace this heated beverage will warm the spirits.

1 12-ounce can frozen undiluted cranberry juice
2 12-ounce cans frozen undiluted apple juice or cider
1 quart red wine (optional)
3 to 4 cups water (or more to taste)
10 whole cloves
5 cinnamon sticks
⅓ **cup sugar (or more to taste)**

❖ ❖ ❖

Orange slices or wedges (optional)
Raisins or whole almonds (optional)

Combine the ingredients in a Dutch oven or other large pot. Cover and allow to chill at least 6 hours (overnight is even better, for a full flavor). To serve, warm until hot enough to sip comfortably. Float orange slices on top for a nice serving effect, or for individual servings, add an orange wedge. Raisins and/or whole almonds may be added to each serving cup if desired.

Makes about 12½ cups.

Pumpkin Gingerbread

3 cups sugar
1 cup oil
4 eggs

❖ ❖ ❖

3½ cups all-purpose flour
2 teaspoons baking soda
1½ teaspoons salt
½ teaspoon baking powder

2 teaspoons ginger
1 teaspoon cinnamon
1 teaspoon nutmeg
1 teaspoon cloves
1 teaspoon allspice

❖ ❖ ❖

⅔ cup water

❖ ❖ ❖

1 1-pound can pumpkin

In a large mixing bowl, mix together sugar, oil, and egg. In a separate bowl, sift the dry ingredients and spices together. Add the sifted ingredients and water alternately to the creamed mixture. Beat in the pumpkin. Pour the batter into 2 greased 5x9-inch loaf pans. Bake in a 350° oven for 1 hour, or until done.

Makes 2 loaves.

The Gingerbread Mansion

Valerie's Sour Cream Banana Bread

"Sour cream makes this very moist and flavorful! We serve this for breakfast."

½ cup butter (1 stick)
1 cup sugar
2 eggs
1 teaspoon vanilla extract
1½ cups all-purpose flour
1 teaspoon baking soda
½ teaspoon salt
1 cup mashed bananas
½ cup nuts
½ cup sour cream

Cream the butter with the sugar. Add the eggs and vanilla. Add the dry ingredients; mix. Add the mashed bananas, nuts and sour cream. Bake in a greased loaf pan in a 350° oven for 1 hour.

Makes 1 loaf.

Gingerbread Mansion Lemon Delight

"This qualifies as the most lemony lemon cake ever. We serve it at tea time in the 4 parlors."

½ cup shortening
1 cup sugar
2 eggs, slightly beaten
1¼ cups sifted all-purpose flour
    (sift before measuring)
1 teaspoon baking powder
½ teaspoon salt
½ cup milk
½ cup finely chopped nuts
Grated peel of 1 lemon

❖ ❖ ❖

Juice of 1 lemon
¼ cup sugar

Cream the shortening with 1 cup of sugar; mix in the eggs. Sift the flour again with baking powder and salt. Alternately add the flour mixture and milk to the shortening mixture, stirring constantly. Mix in the nuts and lemon peel. Bake in a greased 5x9-inch loaf pan in a 350° oven for 1 hour. Remove from the oven, poke holes in the top with a fork. Combine the lemon juice with the ¼ cup sugar; pour over the cake.

The Pudding Creek Inn

700 North Main Street
Fort Bragg, California 95437
(707) 964-9529

The tiny northern coastal community, more recently known for its salmon fishing, was once renowned as the center of the world's sea otter pelt industry, run by Russian settlers. The inn is a 100-year-old redwood frame home built by one of those settlers. Many of the furnishings in the inn are leftovers from previous owners, including the home's original owner—a Russian count. It is rumored that he brought much royal jewelry when he fled his native land after falling in disfavor with the czar, but no jewelry has been found to date.

Cheese Fingers

2 8-ounce packages cream cheese, softened
½ cup sugar
4 egg yolks
1 teaspoon vanilla or almond extract

❖ ❖ ❖

1 16-ounce box phyllo dough
1 cup butter (2 sticks)

❖ ❖ ❖

Diced almonds

To make filling, blend in a mixing bowl the cream cheese and sugar. Add egg yolks and vanilla, beat until mixed.

Unwrap phyllo dough package and keep damp towel over dough so it does not dry out.

Melt butter. Take phyllo sheets and brush with butter, then fold top halves of sheets over. Brush again with butter. Put 2 teaspoons filling on long ends. Take wide end and fold ½-inch on each end. Starting at filling side roll into fingers. Brush with butter. Repeat with the remaining dough and filling. Place seam side down on an ungreased cookie sheet. Sprinkle with diced almonds if desired. Bake in a 375° oven for 10 to 15 minutes until brown.

Serves 15.

Starlight Sugar Crisps

The dough may be prepared up to four days in advance and stored in the refrigerator, and baked as needed.

1 ¼-ounce package active dry yeast
¼ cup warm water

❖ ❖ ❖

3½ cups sifted all-purpose flour
1½ teaspoons salt
½ cup butter or margarine (1 stick)
½ cup shortening
2 eggs, beaten
½ cup sour cream
1 teaspoon vanilla extract

❖ ❖ ❖

1½ cups sugar
2 teaspoons vanilla extract

In a cup, soften yeast in warm water. In a mixing bowl, sift flour with salt. Cut in the butter and shortening until particles are fine. Blend in eggs, sour cream, 1 teaspoon vanilla, and yeast. Mix well. Cover and chill at least 2 hours.

Combine sugar and 2 teaspoons vanilla. Sprinkle ½ cup on rolling surface. Roll out half of the dough on the vanilla-sugar mixture to a 16x8-inch shape. Sprinkle with about 1 table-spoon vanilla-sugar mixture. Fold one end of the dough over the center then fold over the other end to make 3 layers. Turn the ¼ turn, repeat rolling and folding and sprinkling. Roll out to 16x8 inches, cut into strips. Twist each strip 2 to 3 times. Place on ungreased cookie sheets. Repeat process with remaining dough and vanilla-sugar mixture. Bake in a 375° oven for 15 to 20 minutes or until golden brown.

Makes about 60 crisps.

The Historic American River Inn

Post Office Box 43
Georgetown, California 95634
(916) 333-4499

Rediscover the gold rush era at The American River Inn in its heritage and hospitality. Guests may cool off in a beautiful mountain pool or relax in the spa. Amidst choice antiques, award-winning local wines are served in the parlor each evening. Some may choose a day of bicycling amid the colorful breathtaking daffodils, iris, and brilliant yellow-gold scotch broom. The nearby American River provides the adventure of white-water rafting.

Lemon Date Pecan Muffins

½ cup brown sugar, firmly packed
6 tablespoons unsalted butter
5 tablespoons lemon juice
¼ cup honey

❖ ❖ ❖

½ cup sour cream
1 egg
1 tablespoon grated lemon peel

 ❖   ❖   ❖

1¾ cups all-purpose flour
1½ teaspoons baking powder
½ teaspoon baking soda
¾ teaspoon salt

 ❖   ❖   ❖

1 cup chopped dates
1 cup chopped pecans
¼ cup hot water

In a saucepan heat the brown sugar, butter, lemon juice, and honey until hot and blended. In a medium mixing bowl, whisk the sour cream, egg, and lemon peel. Whisk in the brown sugar mixture. Combine the flour, baking powder, baking soda, and salt in another bowl. Add to the liquid ingredients and stir. Add the dates, pecans and hot water and stir until blended. Bake in 14 buttered muffin cups in a 400° oven for 20 minutes.

Makes 14 muffins.

The Campbell Ranch Inn

1475 Canyon Road
Geyserville, California 95441
(707) 857-3476

The spectacular view from Mary Jane and Jerry's hilltop home is the highlight of their ranch. The beautiful rolling vineyards and the abundance of flowers in Mary Jane's garden provide a photographer's dream. During warm weather, breakfast is served on the terrace so guests can enjoy the view while dining on a scrumptious meal. What distinguishes the Campbell Ranch from the traditional bed and breakfast inn are the professional tennis court, the 20'x40' swimming pool, and the hot tub spa.

Campbell Ranch Egg Puff

½ cup margarine (1 stick)
1 pound fresh mushrooms, diced

 ❖   ❖   ❖

1 pound Monterey Jack cheese, shredded

 ❖   ❖   ❖

10 extra-large eggs
1 pint cottage cheese, creamed
½ cup all-purpose flour
1 teaspoon baking powder
½ teaspoon salt

In a large frying pan melt the margarine. Set aside to cool. Peel mushrooms and dice into small pieces. Place mushrooms into the cooled margarine and stir until completely coated.

In a large mixer bowl beat eggs until blended. Add remaining ingredients and mushrooms. Pour into a well-greased 9x13-inch dish and bake in a 350° oven for approximately 45 minutes or until a knife inserted in the center comes out clean.

Serve immediately while it is pretty and puffy. This will serve 10 people for brunch if a large fruit salad and rolls are added. This is also wonderful for company because it can be made the night before, refrigerated, and then baked just before serving. (Allow extra baking time if it has been chilled.)

Serves 10.

Sour Cream Coffee Cake

¾ cup dried bread crumbs
½ cup all-purpose flour
½ cup butter or margarine (1 stick)
⅓ cup sugar
1½ teaspoons cinnamon
½ teaspoon nutmeg
1 cup ground walnuts

 ❖   ❖   ❖

¾ cup butter or margarine (1½ sticks)
1½ cups sugar
3 extra large eggs
1½ cups sour cream
1½ teaspoons baking powder
1½ teaspoons baking soda
1½ teaspoons vanilla extract
3 cups all-purpose flour

In a small mixer bowl beat together at low speed the bread crumbs, ½ cup flour, ½ cup butter, ⅓ cup sugar, cinnamon, and nutmeg until well blended. Stir in walnuts with a fork. Set aside.

In a large mixer bowl beat ¾ cup butter and 1½ cups sugar until light and fluffy. Add the remaining ingredients, scraping the bowl often. Beat at

The Historic American River Inn

medium speed for 3 minutes. Spread ⅓ of the batter into a greased 10-inch tube pan. Sprinkle with ⅓ of the crumb filling. Repeat twice. Bake in a 350° oven for 50 to 60 minutes, until the cake is done. Test with a knife or long stick. Do not overbake.

This freezes beautifully, either whole or in individual servings wrapped in foil.

Serves 16.

Roast Chicken with Herbs

    2 whole chickens or 1 large turkey
    7 cloves garlic
    2 bay leaves

        ❖   ❖   ❖

    6 tablespoons margarine
    1½ teaspoons salt
    1 teaspoon pepper
    ½ teaspoon thyme leaves
    ½ teaspoon rubbed sage
    ½ teaspoon oregano
    ½ teaspoon marjoram
    ½ teaspoon dry basil

Rinse and dry the chickens or turkey. Rub the skin with a clove of the garlic. Stuff the cavity with the bay leaves and garlic cloves. In a saucepan melt the margarine and add the remaining ingredients. Place 1 tablespoon of butter-herb mixture in each cavity. Place the chickens on a foil-lined pan. Baste the chickens with the remaining herb mixture. Bake in a 350° oven for 1½ hours or until tender.

Serves 12.

French-Fried Onion Rings

    1½ cups all-purpose flour
    1½ cups beer

        ❖   ❖   ❖

    6 large onions
    3 cups oil

Three hours before you plan to fry the onions, combine the flour and beer.

Mix well; let stand at room temperature. Peel and slice the onions, separating to form rings. Heat the oil in a large frying pan. Dip each ring separately in the flour and beer mixture. Drop into hot oil and fry until golden brown, turning once. Remove to drain on paper towels and keep in a warm oven until ready to serve.

These freeze beautifully. After draining on paper towels, place on cookie sheets and freeze in a single layer until very hard. Put into airtight containers to seal. To serve, place in a single layer on a cookie sheet and bake in a 400° oven for 5 to 6 minutes. Salt lightly before serving.

Serves 8 to 10.

St. Orres

Post Office Box 523
Gualala, California 95445
(707) 884-3303

Perched on the rise above a sheltered, sandy cove, the inn welcomes guests to St. Orres. Marked by the influence of early Russian settlers, its architecture intrigues and invites. The sparkling colors of its many gardens and the play of light from stained glass windows weave a tapestry of color and texture that can only be described as magical.

Chilled Strawberry Soup

    3 cups strawberry purée, strained
    1 cup heavy cream or half and half
    ½ cup plain yogurt
    Sugar to sweeten
    Triple Sec to taste

In a blender, combine purée, cream, and yogurt. Add sugar and Triple Sec to taste. Chill.

Serves 8.

Escargot Stuffed Mushroom Caps

    24 escargot
    White wine
    ¼ cup Panchetta (Italian bacon),
        cooked and finely chopped
    24 large mushroom caps

        ❖   ❖   ❖

    4 cups sweet butter (8 sticks)
    ⅔ cup peeled and chopped garlic
    ½ cup chopped parsley
    2 tablespoons Dijon mustard
    ⅓ cup blanched and finely chopped
        hazelnuts or almonds
    1 tablespoon salt
    2 teaspoons white pepper
    2 tablespoons Panchetta, cooked
        and finely chopped
    Dash Worcestershire sauce

        ❖   ❖   ❖

    Toasted round croutons

Simmer escargot in white wine for 30 seconds, drain and set aside. Divide the Panchetta among the mushrooms caps, top with the escargot. Combine the remaining ingredients except croutons and cover each escargot with some of this mixture. Bake in ovenproof individual serving dishes in a 500° oven for 10 minutes or until mushrooms are cooked and the butter is bubbling. Top each with a toasted crouton.

Serves 6.

Roasted Quail
Stuffed with Leeks and Breadcrumbs, Served with Madeira and Panchetta Sauce

    8 fresh quail

        ❖   ❖   ❖

    6 leeks, trimmed and finely diced
    6 onions, peeled and finely diced
    6 celery stalks, finely diced
    4 tablespoons sweet butter

        ❖   ❖   ❖

    3 cups breadcrumbs
    Chicken stock (to moisten
        breadcrumbs)
    Pinch fresh chopped thyme
    Pinch nutmeg

Salt and pepper to taste
Peanut oil

❖   ❖   ❖

2 shallots, peeled and finely
    chopped
½ cup Madeira
4 tablespoons Panchetta, blanched,
    browned and cut in ¼-inch
    cubes
8 mushroom caps, quartered
2 cups demiglace
2 cups cream

❖   ❖   ❖

Salt and pepper to taste

Remove the breast bones from the quail, rinse and dry. Sauté leeks, onions, and celery in sweet butter until tender, drain. Combine breadcrumbs, chicken stock, thyme, nutmeg, salt, and pepper. Add to the cooked vegetables and allow to cool before dressing the quail.

Secure the neck opening of the quail with toothpicks. Stuff through the vent with 2 tablespoons of stuffing. Secure the vent with a toothpick and cross the quail's legs, using extra toothpicks if necessary. Heat a large frying pan coated with peanut oil. Lightly salt and pepper each bird and place the breast side down in the pan. Brown on all sides and transfer to a warm ovenproof pan. Bake in a 350° oven to finish cooking. While the quail cooks, make the Madeira and Panchetta Sauce in the pan used to brown the quail.

Deglaze the original pan, adding Madeira and shallots. Burn off the alcohol. Add the panchetta, mushrooms, demiglace, and cream. Boil until reduced by one half. Season and serve over quail.

Note: To make the demiglace, reduce 4 cups of beef or veal stock to 2 cups.

Serves 4.

Terrine of Smoked Salmon

1 envelope (1 tablespoon) gelatin
½ cup water

1½ cups fish velouté
1½ pounds smoked salmon
1 cup heavy cream, whipped to soft
    peaks
6 tablespoons snipped chives

Soften gelatin in water. In a small saucepan heat velouté to boiling and add gelatin mixture to dissolve. Remove from heat and set aside. Process the smoked salmon in a food processor fitted with a metal blade. Add the velouté and gelatin mixture, and process until smooth. Strain the mixture by pushing it through a coarse sieve. Fold in the whipped cream and chives. Refrigerate for 15 minutes. Line a loaf pan with plastic wrap and fill with the mousse. Cover the top and refrigerate until set.

Garnish each slice of terrine with sliced smoked salmon and golden caviar if desired.

Serves 6 to 8.

Parsnip Soup

2 cups chopped onion
1 cup chopped celery
4 tablespoons sweet butter
12 parsnips, peeled and chopped
4 cups chicken stock, homemade
Salt
Pepper
Nutmeg

In a large saucepan, sauté the onion and celery in sweet butter until tender. Add the parsnips and chicken stock. Simmer until the parsnips are tender. Purée the soup in a blender and strain. Thin the soup to desired consistency with chicken stock or heavy cream. Add salt, pepper, and nutmeg to taste.

Serves 4 to 6.

Custard Potatoes

2 tablespoons sweet butter, melted
1 tablespoon peeled and chopped
    garlic
6 large potatoes, peeled and sliced
    thin

❖   ❖   ❖

1 quart heavy cream (or half and
    half)
8 eggs
Salt and white pepper
Pinch nutmeg
Grated Parmesan cheese

Rub the bottom of a 9x9-inch baking dish with melted butter and garlic. Arrange potatoes in dish.

Whisk heavy cream and eggs together. Season, adding extra salt to compensate for the potatoes. Pour the mixture over potatoes in the pan. Top with grated Parmesan cheese.

Bake in a 350° oven for 40 minutes or until potatoes are tender and custard is set.

Serves 16.

Blackberry Tart

This recipe makes two 10-inch tart shells. You can make both shells at once and freeze one, or freeze half of the uncooked dough.

5 cups all-purpose flour
¾ cup sugar
1 tablespoon grated lemon peel
1½ cups sweet butter, cold and cut
    into small pieces
3 egg yolks

❖   ❖   ❖

4 ounces cream cheese, softened
½ cup confectioners' sugar
2 cups heavy cream
¼ teaspoon almond extract
1 teaspoon vanilla extract

Combine the flour, sugar, and lemon peel. Cut in butter until the mixture resembles coarse meal. Add egg yolks and blend until the dough holds together. Pat the dough into 2 balls and chill. Roll out the dough and fit into 2 well-greased 10-inch tart pan(s) with removable bottoms. Prick the bottom of shells with a fork and bake in a 300° oven for 30 minutes. Cool shells before removing from the pan.

Thoroughly cream together cream cheese, confectioners' sugar and a few tablespoons of the cream. Gradually add the remaining cream and extracts, whipping to stiff peaks. Spread evenly into a cooled tart shell. Top the tart with blackberries, or other seasonal fruit. Cut fruit used on tarts should always be glazed with a fruit glaze.

Makes 2 10-inch tarts.

The Heirloom

Post Office Box 322
214 Shakeley Lane
Ione, California 95640
(209) 274-4468

Built about 1863 and hidden away in the historic Gold Country is a treasure called the Heirloom. Comfortable twin, double, queen, or king-size beds, private or shared baths, cozy fireplaces, and balconies overlooking the spacious old "English romantic garden" are offered to guests.

Heirloom Cheese Soufflé

    3 tablespoons butter, melted
    4 tablespoons all-purpose flour
    ¼ teaspoon salt
    1 cup milk
    1 cup grated sharp Cheddar cheese
            ❖ ❖ ❖
    ¹/₈ teaspoon cayenne pepper
    ¾ teaspoon dry mustard
    1½ teaspoons sugar
    2 teaspoons water
            ❖ ❖ ❖
    3 egg yolks
    3 egg whites

Melt the butter over medium heat. Stir in flour and salt to make a paste. Add the milk and stir until smooth and thickened. Add the Cheddar cheese and stir until melted. In a separate bowl mix cayenne, mustard, sugar, and water. Add to the cheese sauce; remove from heat. Add a little of the sauce to the egg yolks to warm them before adding to the sauce. Beat the

egg whites until they are stiff enough to hold peaks. Fold the sauce into the whites. Pour into an ungreased 1-quart soufflé dish. Set the dish in a 1½-inch bath of lukewarm water. Bake in a 350° oven for 40 minutes. Serve immediately.

Serves 4 to 6.

Hot Cross Buns

    ½ cup butter (1 stick)
    1 cup water
    1 tablespoon sugar
    1 teaspoon salt
    1 cup all-purpose flour
            ❖ ❖ ❖
    4 eggs
    ½ to 1 cup candied fruit and
        raisins
            ❖ ❖ ❖
    Confectioners' sugar icing

Combine butter, water, sugar, and salt in a saucepan over medium heat. Stir in flour. Beat with a wooden spoon until mixture forms a ball. Remove from heat; then add eggs one at a time, beating well after each to maintain a smooth consistency. Stir in candied fruit. Shape into balls and place on a buttered baking sheet. Bake in a 375° oven for 30 minutes. Frost with confectioners' sugar icing in a cross on each bun.

Makes 12 buns.

Baked Pears

    1 Anjou pear
    Butter
    1 tablespoon sugar
    2 tablespoons cream

Peel each pear, halve, remove seeds. Generously butter baking dish just large enough to hold pears. Sprinkle dish with half of the sugar. Place pears cut side down.

Sprinkle with remaining sugar. Bake in a 375° oven about 20 minutes. Remove from oven. Pour cream over

pears. Return to oven 15 minutes; then serve pears hot or warm.

Serves 2.

The Gate House

1330 Jackson Gate Road
Jackson, California 95642
(209) 223-3500

The Gate House is a charming turn-of-the-century Victorian inn offering its guests three rooms, a two-room suite, or a private summer house all with private baths. Each evokes the past, with lace curtains, handmade afghans, brass or Early American queen-size beds, and Victorian furnishings to complete the comfortable decor. Guests may relax on the wide porches, picnic on the lovely grounds, or enjoy the swimming pool on warm summer days.

Gate House Unbeatable Cream Tomato Soup

    ¼ cup butter (½ stick)
    1 tablespoon olive oil
    1 yellow onion, thinly sliced
    4 ripe tomatoes, coarsely chopped
    6½ ounces tomato paste
    4 tablespoons all-purpose flour
    2½ cups clear chicken broth
    ½ teaspoon sugar
    Salt, if necessary
    Ground white pepper
    1 cup heavy cream

Heat the butter and oil in a heavy saucepan. Add the onion and sauté 5 minutes. Stir in tomatoes and paste. Cook for 2 to 3 minutes. Sprinkle with flour and mix well with a wooden spoon. Add broth, sugar, salt, and pepper; simmer 15 minutes. Pour into a blender and blend at high speed a few seconds, pour back into the saucepan and add cream. Bring to a boil. Reduce heat and simmer 3 minutes. Serve immediately.

Serves 6.

Marinated Mushroom Dressing

This dressing should be prepared at least 3 days prior to serving.

**2 pounds medium white
     mushrooms, sliced
2 cups olive oil
1 cup red wine vinegar
4 teaspoons salt
2 teaspoons pepper
8 cloves garlic, finely chopped
2 teaspoons Accent**

Combine all ingredients in a large bowl; cover. Refrigerate for 3 days. Stir occasionally. Remove from the refrigerator several hours before serving. Stir well.

Makes 10 to 12 servings.

Bed and Breakfast International

151 Ardmore Road
Kensington, California 94707
(415) 525-4569

Bed and Breakfast International has been arranging reservations in private homes offering comfortable rooms and a complete breakfast since 1978. Hosts share hospitality, not just a rented room. The homes are located in good neighborhoods, ranging from apartments in the city center to spacious homes in residential neighborhoods. Accommodations available include a houseboat in a marina, a penthouse overlooking the city, or a house set on a bluff with a view of the sun setting over the Pacific Ocean.

There is a two-night minimum stay.

Locations of homes with Bed and Breakfast International include San Francisco (and all Bay Area cities), northern coast and Napa Valley wine country, Sacramento, Gold Country, Lake Tahoe mountain region, central coast as well as the Los Angeles area and the southern coast as far as San Diego.

Alicia's Chicken Wings
in Basic Soy Sauce

**1 cup dark soy sauce
1 cup thin soy sauce
1 cup sugar
3 dried chili pepers
4 slices ginger root
4 cloves garlic, split
5 flowerets star anise
½ cup peanut oil**

❖   ❖   ❖

1 to 2 pounds chicken wings

❖   ❖   ❖

**Green onions
Cherry tomatoes
Jicama, thinly sliced
Daikon radishes
Lemon juice**

In a saucepan combine the first 8 ingredients. Simmer for 15 minutes. This sauce may be stored in the refrigerator for months.

Cut off the tips of the chicken wings and reserve for stock. Bring the Basic Soy Sauce to a rolling boil and drop in the chicken wings. Cover and turn off the heat, or simmer very low for 15 minutes. Store in the refrigerator. Serve for breakfast, lunch or high tea.

May be served with lightly steamed vegetables of the season (asparagus, snow peas, etc.). Garnish with green onions, cherry tomatoes, oranges, thin slices of jicama, and daikon radishes sprinkled with lemon juice.

Serves 2 to 4.

The Carriage House

Chopped Liver

1 chicken or duck liver
3 tablespoons soy sauce
1 small onion, chopped and sautéed
1 hard-boiled egg, chopped
1 tablespoon butter, softened

Simmer the liver in the soy sauce until pink. Transfer to a food processor with the onion and pulse. Add the chopped egg and butter; pulse. The butter will stiffen when the mixture is chilled.
Serves 1.

The Carriage House

1322 Catalina Street
Laguna Beach, California 92651
(714) 494-8945

The Carriage House is a charming old New Orleans-style bed and breakfast inn just several houses away from the beautiful beaches of the Pacific Ocean. One of Laguna Beach's designated historical landmarks, the colonial-style Carriage House is situated in the heart of the village within pleasant walking distance to shops and galleries.

Coconut Coffeecake

Do not let the cheese soup scare you away, this is delicious.

1 18¼-ounce box yellow cake mix
1 11-ounce can condensed Cheddar cheese soup
½ cup water
2 eggs
1 tablespoon grated lemon rind

 ❖ ❖ ❖

1 cup shredded coconut
½ cup crushed pineapple, drained
½ cup chopped nuts

 ❖ ❖ ❖

3 tablespoons butter, softened
½ cup unsifted all-purpose flour
¼ cup brown sugar, firmly packed
½ cup shredded coconut

In a large mixing bowl combine the cake mix, soup, water, eggs, and lemon rind. Beat until blended. Stir in 1 cup of coconut, pineapple, and nuts. Spread the batter evenly in a greased and floured 9x13-inch pan. In another bowl, cut butter into the flour until crumbly. Stir in sugar and the remaining coconut. Sprinkle over the batter. Bake in a 350° oven for 50 minutes or until done.
Serves 18 to 24, depending on the cut.

Easy Strudel

1 cup margarine (2 sticks)
2 cups sifted all-purpose flour
2 tablespoons water
2 tablespoons white vinegar
3 egg yolks

 ❖ ❖ ❖

6 apples, pared and diced
1 cup raisins
1 cup finely chopped nuts
½ cup sugar
2 tablespoons cinnamon

 ❖ ❖ ❖

¾ cup confectioners' sugar
1 tablespoon cream
½ teaspoon almond extract

Mix the margarine, flour, water, vinegar, and egg yolks; refrigerate.
Prepare the filling by combining apples, raisins, nuts, sugar, and cinnamon.
Separate the dough into two balls, roll each ball (as thin as possible) into a rectangle and spread with half the filling. Roll up jelly roll-style.
Bake on a lightly greased cookie sheet in a 350° oven for 20 minutes or until brown.
Combine confectioners' sugar, cream, and almond extract for icing, if desired.
Makes 2 strudels.

Bluebelle House Bed 'n' Breakfast

263 South State Highway 173
Post Office Box 2177
Lake Arrowhead, California 92352
(714) 336-3292

Guests step into a mountain home, Bluebelle House, where they may sit by the big rock fireplace on wintry days and forget worldly cares. Enjoy the deck or nap in the hammock during the mountain summer days. Casual elegance is the theme here.

Bluebelle House Bran Muffins

5 teaspoons baking soda
2 cups boiling water

 ❖ ❖ ❖

1 cup margarine (2 sticks)
2 cups sugar
4 eggs

 ❖ ❖ ❖

1 quart buttermilk
2½ cups all-purpose flour
2½ cups whole wheat flour
1 tablespoon salt

 ❖ ❖ ❖

2 cups 40% bran
4 cups 100% bran
2 cups chopped dates or raisins
2 cups chopped walnuts

Add baking soda to boiling water. Let cool. In a large mixing bowl, cream margarine and sugar; add eggs. Blend well. Stir in buttermilk, flours, and salt. Add soda water mixture. Combine brans, dates, and walnuts, and add to the first mixture. Fill greased muffin pans greased ⅔ full. Bake in a 400°

Bluebelle House

monds, raisins, and coconut. Optional ingredients may be added in addition to or in place of almonds, raisins, and coconut.

One of the most important steps is the stirring before baking.

Serves 6 to 8.

Whitegate Inn Waffles

4 cups all-purpose flour
2⅔ cups whole wheat flour
2 tablespoons baking powder
1 tablespoon baking soda
2 tablespoons cinnamon

❖ ❖ ❖

12 eggs
4 tablespoons sugar
5 cups buttermilk
1 cup oil
2 tablespoons vanilla extract

❖ ❖ ❖

1⅔ cups chopped walnuts

Mix flours, baking powder, soda, and cinnamon thoroughly. In a separate bowl beat eggs, blend in sugar, add buttermilk, oil, and vanilla. Add the flour mixture and mix lightly. Add walnuts. Sometimes a little more buttermilk is necessary to thin out batter. Cook as directed for waffle iron.

Diced apples are a nice addition mixed into the batter or sliced bananas placed on the batter just before closing the lid of the waffle iron.

This batter may be frozen, just add a little oil and baking powder before use after defrosting.

Serves 12.

Apricot Nut Butter

Margarine may be used instead of butter in this recipe, but the egg should be eliminated if margarine is used.

1 egg
½ cup confectioners' sugar
4 cups butter (8 sticks)
1 pound dried apricots, ground
1½ cups ground nuts

oven for 20 to 25 minutes. Recipe may be halved.

Makes approximately 24 muffins.

Whitegate Inn

Post Office Box 150
499 Howard Street
Mendocino, California 95460
(707) 937-4892

The Whitegate Inn sits behind a white picket fence amidst an English garden. Great cypress trees bend close to shelter the old house, built in 1880. The feeling of comfort and welcome, even wellness, is strong at the Whitegate Inn. Down comforters, lace-edged sheets, crystal, china, and silver are part of the special touches of this inn. The house abounds with antiques, from the old Hamilton pump organ to original light fixtures throughout.

Patricia's Granola

½ cup salted, roasted sunflower
**   seeds**
5 cups oatmeal
⅓ cup oil
⅓ cup honey
¼ cup brown sugar, firmly packed
1 teaspoon vanilla extract
Pinch cinnamon (or more if
**   desired)**

❖ ❖ ❖

½ cup toasted diced almonds
½ cup raisins
¼ cup shaved, lightly-toasted
**   coconut**

❖ ❖ ❖

½ cup diced dried apricots
**   (optional)**
½ cup currants (optional)
½ cup diced dried apples (optional)
½ cup diced walnuts (optional)

Stir the sunflower seeds, oatmeal, oil, honey, brown sugar, vanilla, and cinnamon together until completely blended (this may take 5 or more minutes). Spread in a jelly roll pan and bake in a 350° oven for 30 minutes, stirring frequently. Cool and add al-

In a food processor or mixer beat the egg, add sugar, then butter, scrape sides, mix until well blended. Add the apricots, then walnuts, mix until well blended. This freezes well.

Apricots grind nicely in food processor after they have been frozen.

Makes 4 cups of butter.

Strawberry Butter

1 cup strawberries
2 cups butter or margarine (4 sticks)
⅓ cup confectioners' sugar

Blend all ingredients in a food processor or mixing bowl until light pink in color.

Note: This freezes well and can be used right from the freezer.

Makes 2½ cups of butter.

Whitegate Inn Carrot Bread

3 eggs
2 cups sugar
1 cup oil
3 tablespoons vanilla extract
2 cups grated carrots
3½ cups all-purpose flour
1½ cups whole wheat flour
1 teaspoon baking powder
1 teaspoon baking soda
1 teaspoon cinnamon
1 teaspoon salt
1 8-ounce can crushed pineapple, undrained
1 cup chopped walnuts

Grease and flour 2 9x5-inch loaf pans. Beat eggs fluffy, add sugar, oil, and vanilla and blend well. Add carrots. Sift together flours, baking powder, baking soda, cinnamon, and salt; add to egg mixture, blend well. Stir in pineapple and walnuts and mix well. Bake in a 350° oven for 1 hour and allow to cool in pans.

Note: ½ cup of raisins may be added if desired.

Makes 2 loaves.

Green Gables

104 Fifth Street
Monterey, California 93950
(408) 375-2095

The Green Gables, built in 1888, is situated at the corner of 5th Street and Ocean View Boulevard in Pacific Grove, California. It is an excellent example of Queen Anne Victorian architecture in a fairy tale setting by the sea. The special touches at Green Gables provide for each guest's comfort. Each room is elegantly appointed with antiques of burnished wood, soft quilts, fresh fruit, and garden flowers. Most rooms have excellent ocean views, and six have working fireplaces.

Potpourri

1 cup cracked orange peel (well dried)
⅓ cup cracked cinnamon stick
⅓ cup whole cloves
⅓ cup whole allspice

Mix well and place in a small glass jar in your kitchen. A teaspoon or two in a pan of water simmering on the back burner will create a delightful fragrance throughout your house and return a nice scented moisture to the air. If desired, substitute grapefruit, lemon or lime peel for ½ the orange peel. Bay leaves can be crushed into the mixture and a little anise and rosemary added. A vegetable peeler works well to remove peel from the fruit.

Cheese Strudel

Chef Janet Beilman's personal creation.

15 slices French bread, buttered
1 cup chopped green onions
4 cups cheese (Cheddar or Swiss)
❖ ❖ ❖

6 eggs, beaten with whisk
1 teaspoon Dijon mustard
2½ cups milk
½ teaspoon salt
❖ ❖ ❖

Bread crumbs
½ cup Parmesan cheese

In a large baking dish, using half of the specified amount at a time, place in layers the bread, onions, and cheese. Combine the eggs, mustard, milk, and salt, and pour this over the layers. Top with a mixture of bread crumbs and Parmesan cheese. Let stand for ½ hour. Bake in a 350° oven for 1 hour.

Serves 6 to 8.

Spinach Frittata

½ cup chopped green onions
2 tablespoons olive oil
10 eggs
½ cup milk
3 cups fresh spinach
½ cup mushrooms

In a frying pan with an ovenproof handle, sauté onions until transparent. Beat the eggs and milk. Add to the onions. Press the spinach and mushrooms into the egg mixture in the pan. Cook on medium heat for 5 minutes. Bake in a 325° oven for 15 minutes.

Serves 6.

Melt-in-a-Moment Cookies

1 cup butter (2 sticks), softened
½ cup confectioners' sugar
⅔ cup cornstarch
1 cup all-purpose flour
❖ ❖ ❖

¼ cup butter (½ stick)
1 pound confectioners' sugar
Juice and grated rind of ½ lemon

Cream 1 cup butter and ½ cup confectioners' sugar. Add cornstarch and flour, drop by teaspoonfuls onto an ungreased baking sheet. Bake in a 325° oven for 10 minutes. Do not brown.

Combine the remaining ingredients and frost the cookies when they have cooled.

Makes 1 dozen cookies.

Petite Cherry Cheesecakes

2 8-ounce packages cream cheese,
   softened
¾ cup sugar
2 eggs
1 tablespoon lemon juice
1 teaspoon vanilla extract
24 vanilla wafers

❖   ❖   ❖

1 21-ounce can cherry pie filling

Beat the cream cheese, sugar, eggs, lemon juice, and vanilla until light and fluffy. Line small muffin pans with paper baking cups and place a vanilla wafer in the bottom of each cup. Fill the cups ⅔ full with cream cheese mixture. Bake in a 375° oven for 15 to 20 minutes or until set. Top each with about 1 tablespoon pie filling. Chill.

Makes 2 dozen.

Dunbar House, 1880

271 Jones Street
Murphys, California 95247
(209) 728-2897

Dunbar House will seem familiar to fans of the TV series "Seven Brides for Seven Brothers" because it was filmed here. Now it is an inviting bed and breakfast inn that makes a perfect base of operations for exploring the old town of Murphys, one of the best preserved and least changed of the early mining towns of Calaveras County and the Mother Lode.

Dunbar House was built in 1880 and is a lovely example of Italianate style, with wide porches and beautiful gardens.

Buttermilk Poppy Seed Cake

1 cup butter or margarine (2
   sticks), softened
1½ cups sugar
3 eggs
½ teaspoon vanilla extract

❖   ❖   ❖

2½ cups all-purpose flour
3 teaspoons baking powder
1 teaspoon cinnamon
½ teaspoon salt

❖   ❖   ❖

1 cup buttermilk
⅓ cup poppy seeds
1½ teaspoons grated lemon peel

❖   ❖   ❖

Confectioners' sugar

In a large mixing bowl beat together the butter and sugar. Beat in eggs and vanilla. In a separate bowl combine the flour, baking powder, cinnamon, and salt. Mix into the creamed mixture alternately with buttermilk. Stir in poppy seeds and lemon peel. Turn into a greased and floured 9-cup tube mold or bundt pan. Bake in a 350° oven 50 minutes or until a toothpick inserted in the center comes out clean. Cool 10 minutes; then remove from the pan onto a rack to cool completely. Dust the top with sifted confectioners' sugar.

Serves 10 to 12.

Pumpkin Apple Cake

½ cup margarine or butter (1 stick)
1½ cups sugar
2 eggs
1 teaspoon vanilla extract
2 medium apples, pared and diced
   (1½ cups)

1 cup canned pumpkin
2 cups all-purpose flour
1 teaspoon baking powder
¾ teaspoon baking soda
½ teaspoon salt
½ teaspoon cinnamon
¼ teaspoon nutmeg
¼ teaspoon cloves
¼ teaspoon ginger
2 teaspoons grated orange rind
   (optional)

❖   ❖   ❖

Confectioners' sugar

In a large mixing bowl cream the butter or margarine; beat in sugar. Add the eggs, one at a time. Stir in vanilla, apples, and pumpkin. Blend in dry ingredients and orange rind. Turn into a greased and floured 9-inch bundt or angel cake pan. Bake in a 350° oven for 55 to 60 minutes. Cool in the pan for 10 minutes, then turn out on a rack to cool. Sprinkle with confectioners' sugar when cool.

Serves 16.

The Old World Inn Bed and Breakfast

1301 Jefferson Street
Napa, California 94559
(707) 257-0112

The historic Old World Inn was built in 1906 by local contractor E. W. Doughty for his private town residence. The home is an eclectic combination of architectural styles detailed with wood shingles, wide shady porches, clinker brick, and leaded and bevelled glass. The inn is furnished throughout with painted Victorian and antique furniture accentuated by an abundance of indoor plants and flowers.

Desperately Healthy Pancakes

For the food processor.

½ cup soy flour
½ cup whole wheat flour
½ cup unbleached all-purpose flour
2 tablespoons wheat germ
2 tablespoons powdered milk
2 tablespoons unprocessed bran
1 tablespoon baking powder
½ teaspoon baking soda
¼ teaspoon salt
Grated peel of 1 orange

❖ ❖ ❖

2 eggs, separated
½ cup plain yogurt
¼ cup oil
1 tablespoon molasses
1 tablespoon honey
1½ cups orange juice

Combine the first 10 ingredients. Reserve the egg whites and add the egg yolks and the remaining ingredients to the flour mixture in a food processor, blend well. Beat the egg whites until stiff; fold into the pancake mixture. Cook on a 300° griddle, for 2½ minutes on one side and 1 minute on the other.

Makes about 36 3-inch cakes.

Orange Pancake Syrup

2 tablespoons water
¾ cup brown sugar, firmly packed
½ cup orange juice concentrate

❖ ❖ ❖

½ cup butter (1 stick)
1 teaspoon maple flavoring or 2 tablespoons maple syrup
4 tablespoons grated orange peel

❖ ❖ ❖

½ cup honey

In a small saucepan, boil together the water, sugar, and orange juice. In the food processor bowl blend together the butter, flavoring, and orange peel. Add the orange mixture and the honey. Blend well.

Makes 1 cup of syrup.

Dill Mushrooms

For the food processor.

24 large mushrooms (1½-inch)
3 scallions (1-ounce), cut into 2-inch pieces
3 tablespoons butter
½ teaspoon salt
⅛ teaspoon white pepper
¾ ounce grated Parmesan cheese
2 tablespoons diced dill
6 ounces cream cheese

Remove stems from 18 mushrooms, reserve. Cut remaining mushrooms (with stems), in quarters, and finely chop with the metal blade in a food processor for 25 pulses, reserve. Finely chop scallions, reserve. In a small sauté pan melt the butter, add the chopped mushrooms and cook until done, about 4 minutes. Add scallions and cook 30 seconds to wilt. Season with salt and pepper, reserve. With the metal blade process the Parmesan and dill until fine. Add the cream cheese and process until smooth. Add mushroom and scallion mixture, pulse 5 times. Cover and chill until firm, about 30 minutes.

Fill each mushroom cap with the mushroom and cheese mixture and place on a greased cookie sheet. Broil at 400° for about 4 minutes, until slightly bubbly, then bake in a 300° oven for 4 to 5 minutes. Mushrooms should be firm. Serve immediately.

Makes 18 stuffed mushrooms.

Chocolate Layer Cake

2 cups sugar
½ cup margarine (1 stick)
½ cup mayonnaise
½ cup oil
2 eggs
½ cup cocoa
1 cup buttermilk
½ teaspoon salt
2 teaspoons vanilla extract
2 teaspoons baking soda
2¾ cups all-purpose flour
1 cup boiling water

Cream together the sugar and margarine, add the mayonnaise and oil, beat thoroughly. Add eggs, beat. Add cocoa and mix slowly while adding buttermilk. Add salt, vanilla, baking soda, and flour, mix in boiling water. Fill 3 greased 8-inch layer cake tins equally. Bake in a 325° oven for 35 minutes or until done. Remove from pans and cool. Wrap in plastic wrap and freeze until ready to use.

Serves 12.

Chocolate Frosting

1½ pounds confectioners' sugar
¼ teaspoon salt
3 heaped tablespoons cocoa powder

❖ ❖ ❖

½ cup margarine (1 stick)
4 ounces baking chocolate
½ cup water
2 tablespoons instant coffee
2 teaspoons vanilla extract

Sift together the sugar, salt, and cocoa powder. Melt the margarine and chocolate in a double boiler. Combine the water, coffee, and vanilla, bring to a boil. Stir the boiling coffee into the sugar mixture, then add the chocolate mixture. Beat thoroughly. Store the frosting in 2x2-inch plastic containers. When needed, heat in a double boiler. Take 1 layer cake out of the freezer and split it in half. Working quickly, use half the frosting to fill the cake and half for the top. Decorate with walnuts. Place on a service dish and cover for about 24 hours.

Frosts 1 cake.

Rum Truffles

9 ounces chocolate
1½ tablespoons half and half
3 eggs
3 tablespoons rum
3 tablespoons butter
Powdered chocolate

Melt the chocolate and half and half in a pan over very low heat. Remove from heat. Add eggs, butter, and rum. Blend the mixture until thick (in a food processor at least 5 minutes). Refrigerate. When cool, form into ¾-inch balls and toss in powdered chocolate—not cocoa.

If not eaten first, these freeze well. Makes 1 dozen truffles.

Red Castle Inn

109 Prospect Street
Nevada City, California 95959
(916) 265-5135

Staying at the Red Castle Inn is a truly unique experience, providing the authentic feel of a glamorous past pre-

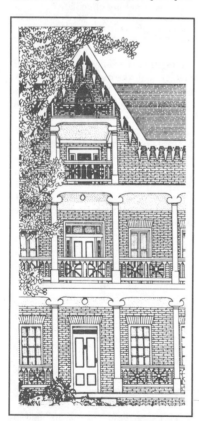

Red Castle Inn

served in a warm and comfortable atmosphere. Built in 1860 as a family home by Judge John Williams, a mine owner who crossed the plains in 1849, the four-story brick mansion is one of only two genuine Gothic revival houses on the West Coast.

Raisin Pumpkin Bread

**1 cup sugar
1 cup canned pumpkin
2 eggs, unbeaten
½ cup brown sugar, firmly packed
½ cup oil**

❖ ❖ ❖

**2 cups sifted all-purpose flour
1 teaspoon baking soda
½ teaspoon salt
½ teaspoon cinnamon
½ teaspoon nutmeg
¼ teaspoon ginger
½ teaspoon baking powder**

❖ ❖ ❖

**1 cup raisins
½ cup nuts
¼ cup water**

In a large mixing bowl combine sugar, pumpkin, eggs, brown sugar, and oil, beat until well blended. Sift together the flour, baking soda, salt, cinnamon, nutmeg, ginger, and baking powder. Combine with the liquid mixture, mixing well. Fold in raisins, nuts, and water, turn into a well-oiled loaf pan. Bake in a 350° oven for 65 to 75 minutes. Cool in the pan 5 minutes, then turn out to cool thoroughly.

Tastes best if made several days in advance.

Serves 16.

Petticoat Tails

**6 tablespoons sugar
2½ cups sifted all-purpose flour
1 cup butter (2 sticks), softened**

Blend sugar with flour, cut in butter with a pastry blender until the mixture holds together somewhat. Using a

fork, pat into a round cake pan. Chill overnight.

Using a table knife score into 16 wedges and bake in a 300° oven until slightly golden, about 20 to 25 minutes. Store in an airtight container.

Serves 16.

The Olema Inn

10,000 Sir Francis Drake Boulevard
Olema, California 94950
(415) 663-8441

The Olema Inn graces the entryway to the Point Reyes National Seashore. The drive up the California coast takes potential diners by small towns and cafes with typical menus. The stop at the Olema Inn is anything but typical, however. Lofty ceilings and book-lined shelves are the background for a constantly changing art exhibit. The Olema offers full-service inn facilities, as well as dining facilities.

Sweetwater Oyster Stew

From the kitchen of Micheal Golstein.

**24 Sweetwater (Hog Island) oysters
in the shell
3 cups half and half
Salt and freshly ground white
pepper**

❖ ❖ ❖

**½ cup sweet butter (1 stick)
1 tablespoon paprika
Pinch cayenne pepper
Pinch salt**

❖ ❖ ❖

1 teaspoon finely chopped chives

Open the oysters, placing liquid in a saucepan. Add half and half and heat to a simmer. Add oysters and gently cook until edges curl. Do not overcook.

While oysters cook, prepare red pepper butter by combining butter, paprika, cayenne pepper, and salt.

When oysters are done, season with salt and freshly ground white pepper (more subtle than black). Pour into preheated bowls. Garnish with softened red pepper butter and chopped chives. Serves 4.

Baked Shiitake Mushroom Caps
Stuffed with Goat Cheese and Herbs

8 ounces goat cheese, softened
1 clove garlic, finely chopped
2 tablespoons fines herbes
(chopped parsley, chives,
tarragon)
Fresh ground pepper
8 large fresh Shiitake mushrooms,
cleaned
Melted butter

Mix the goat cheese with garlic, fines herbes, and ground pepper. Remove stems from the mushrooms and stuff caps with cheese and place on a baking pan. Brush with melted butter and place in a 400° oven for approximately 10 minutes, until the cheese melts.
Serves 4.

The Gosby House Inn

643 Lighthouse Avenue
Pacific Grove, California 93950
(408) 375-1287

The Gosby House, built in 1887, is an example of Queen Anne-style, with the rounded corner tower, varied sur-face textures, and bay windows. The Victorian atmosphere has been retained. An open-hearth fireplace entices visitors to gather to enjoy afternoon tea, sherry, fresh fruits, and hors d'oeuvres.

Country Sausage Pie

2 pounds Italian sausage
2 apples, peeled and cored
½ cup raisins
❖ ❖ ❖
1 teaspoon anise
1½ pounds baked potatoes, cooled
1 onion, chopped
1 teaspoon sage
¼ teaspoon cinnamon
Salt and pepper to taste
❖ ❖ ❖
One layer puff pastry
1 egg
2 tablespoons cream (or milk)

Over medium heat lightly brown the sausage with apples and raisins until ¾ of the sausage is gray (to render fat) but still barely pink. Drain fat. Mix with the next 6 ingredients. Fill a quiche pan. Lay puff pastry on top. Brush with egg wash made with 1 egg and 2 table-spoons cream. Bake in a 450° oven for 30 to 40 minutes (if potatoes were chilled bake 40 minutes).
Serves 8.

Rosie's Eggs Mexicana—Chili Casserole

5 eggs
2 tablespoons butter, melted
¼ cup flour
½ teaspoon baking powder
1 8-ounce carton cottage cheese
2 cups shredded Monterey Jack
cheese
1 4-ounce can chopped green
chiles, drained
❖ ❖ ❖

1 tomato, sliced
❖ ❖ ❖
Sour cream
Salsa

Combine the eggs, butter, flour, and baking powder. Mix well. Stir in cheeses and chiles. Pour into well-greased quiche pan. Bake in a 400° oven for 10 minutes. Slice a tomato and place on top. Return to oven. Reduce temperature to 350°, bake another 20 minutes. Serve with sour cream and salsa.
Serves 4 to 6.

Dried Fruit Sour Cream Coffee Cake

¾ cup margarine (1½ sticks)
1½ cups sugar
2 eggs
1 teaspoon vanilla extract
2 teaspoons baking powder
½ teaspoon baking soda
½ teaspoon salt
2¼ cups all-purpose flour
1 cup sour cream
¼ cup chopped walnuts
¼ cup dried chopped dates
¼ cup chopped prunes
¼ cup dried chopped apricots
❖ ❖ ❖
½ teaspoon cinnamon
2 tablespoons sugar

Grease and flour a 10-inch tube pan. Cream together the margarine and sugar. Add the eggs and beat until light. Mix in vanilla, baking powder, baking soda, salt, and half of the flour. Add sour cream and beat until smooth. Beat in the remaining flour. Stir in walnuts and fruit. Spread the batter in the pan. Combine cinnamon and sugar and sprinkle over the batter. Bake in a 350° oven for 45 minutes.
Serves 16.

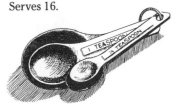

The Gosby House Inn

top. Pour fruit dressing over the entire fruit bowl. Sprinkle shredded coconut and chopped walnuts over dressing. Sprinkle boiled raisins over the entire fruit bowl. Serve the fruit bowl with hot, flaky croissants, juice, and coffee.

Serves 4 or more, depending on the amounts of fruit.

Historic Combellack Blair House

3059 Cedar Ravine
Placerville, California 95667
(916) 622-3764

The Combellack Blair House, built in 1895, is an outstanding example of the Queen Anne-style house typical of the late Victorian period. When new, it was acclaimed as elaborate, artistic, and a handsome addition to the community. The house is a feast to the eye, beginning at the front gate where the white picket fence and gently sloping front lawn frame bay windows with original stained glass panels. Once inside, a free standing spiral staircase leads to the third floor cupola. The house is the only Bed and Breakfast in the El Dorado county area listed in The National Register of Historic Places.

Frittata

This Italian vegetable omelet can be made with your favorite vegetables. Listed below are suggestions for a good combination, but you can vary the kinds and amounts to suit your own taste. For this reason, amounts are not given for most of the vegetables.

**3 tablespoons olive oil
1 medium onion, chopped
1 clove garlic, minced
Celery**

Crown Bed and Breakfast Inn

530 South Marengo Avenue
Pasadena, California 91101
(818) 792-4031

Crown Bed and Breakfast Inn is conveniently located in the beautiful South Marengo historical district in downtown Pasadena. Built in 1905 by craftsman-designer Louis B. Easton, the Crown Bed and Breakfast Inn offers a comfortable and relaxing atmosphere for the weary traveler, business person, or tourist.

Fruit Bowl with Dressing

**Fruit-flavored yogurt (raspberry
  and strawberry are very good)
1 pint sour cream
Half and half (for flavor and
  consistency)
Shredded coconut
Chopped walnuts
Boiled raisins**

❖ ❖ ❖

Seasonal fruit

Combine all ingredients except fruit to your own preferred consistency. Mix well.

Cut several different seasonal fruits (apples, melons, kiwi, strawberries, and peaches) and mix together in a large bowl. Place seedless grapes on

Bell pepper
Mushrooms
Zucchini
Swiss chard or spinach
1 teaspoon Italian herbs
Tomatoes
Salt and pepper
Red or white wine
5 eggs
Milk
Grated cheese

Pour the oil in a frying pan. Sauté the onions and garlic until transparent. Add celery and bell pepper, mushrooms, zucchini, swiss chard or spinach, herbs, and tomatoes, sauté a few minutes after the addition of each, and until all the liquid is gone but do not burn. Season with salt and pepper. Add wine, cooking until the wine has evaporated; remove from heat.

Beat the eggs with a little milk. Add the vegetable mixture to the eggs, stir a little, and pour into a greased shallow ovenproof casserole. Add grated cheese to the top of the eggs and bake in a 350° oven for about 25 minutes. Place under the broiler a few minutes to brown the top slightly.

Makes 4 to 6 servings.

Chocolate Coated Cherry-ettes

2¼ cups all-purpose flour
¾ cup confectioners' sugar
½ teaspoon salt
1 cup margarine or butter, softened
1½ teaspoons vanilla extract
1 teaspoon almond extract
½ cup chopped maraschino
    cherries, drained
¼ cup chopped pecans and walnuts

❖ ❖ ❖

2 cups confectioners' sugar
3 tablespoons margarine or butter,
    softened
2 tablespoons unsweetened cocoa
2 to 4 tablespoons milk or half and
    half
½ teaspoon vanilla extract

In a large bowl, combine the flour, ¾ cup confectioners' sugar, salt, 1 cup margarine, 1 teaspoon vanilla, and almond extract. Mix well. Stir in the

cherries and pecans. Shape into ¾-inch balls. Place 2 inches apart on ungreased cookie sheets. Bake in a 350° oven for 15 to 18 minutes or until light golden brown around edges. Cool.

In a small bowl, combine the remaining ingredients until smooth. Generously frost the cooled cookies.

Makes about 54 cookies.

Ginger Creams

½ cup sugar
½ cup hot water
½ cup dark molasses
¼ cup butter (½ stick)
1 egg

❖ ❖ ❖

2 cups all-purpose flour
1 teaspoon baking soda
½ teaspoon salt
½ teaspoon ginger
½ teaspoon cinnamon
½ teaspoon nutmeg
½ teaspoon cloves

❖ ❖ ❖

2 cups confectioners' sugar
2 tablespoons butter, softened
3 tablespoons milk
½ teaspoon vanilla extract

In a separate bowl combine the flour, soda, salt, ginger, cinnamon, nutmeg, and cloves, add to the cookie ingredients until well blended. Drop by rounded teaspoons 2 inches apart onto a prepared cookie sheet. Bake in a 375° oven for 10 to 15 minutes. Combine the confectioners' sugar, softened butter, milk, and vanilla, frost the cookies.

Makes 1 dozen cookies.

The James Blair House

2985 Clay Street
Placerville, California 95667
(916) 626-6136

The James Blair House is a bed and breakfast inn filled with historic elegance in the Mother Lode. Built by James B. Blair in 1901, this historic Queen Anne-style home is a pleasure

The James Blair House

to see. The Blair family of Placerville was involved in the development of the lumber industry in this region. The James Blair House is one of Placerville's finest existing old Victorians. It has such unique features as a three-story turret, stained glass windows, a conservatory with a sky light, beautiful interior woodwork, and a clinker brick fireplace.

Creamy Scrambled Eggs

2 tablespoons butter or margarine
½ cup finely chopped shallots
⅓ cup whipping cream
1 3-ounce package cream cheese, cut into small pieces
5 eggs
Salt and pepper
Chopped parsley (optional)

In a large frying pan, melt the butter over low heat. Add shallots and stir until limp. Add the cream and cream cheese; stir until the cream cheese melts. In a bowl, lightly beat the eggs with salt and pepper to taste. Pour the egg mixture into the pan, gently stirring to blend with the cream mixture. Cook just until the eggs are softly set. Transfer to warm plates. Sprinkle eggs with parsley.

Makes 3 to 4 servings.

Sesame-Date Muffins

¼ cup sesame seeds
❖ ❖ ❖
1½ cups whole wheat pastry flour
¾ cup cornmeal
1 tablespoon baking powder
½ teaspoon salt
❖ ❖ ❖
2 eggs, beaten
¼ cup safflower oil
2 tablespoons each malt syrup and honey (or ¼ cup of either)
1 cup water or milk
❖ ❖ ❖
½ cup chopped dates

Toast sesame seeds by stirring constantly in a dry pan over medium heat for about 1 minute until they just begin to pop; remove from heat immediately. In a large mixing bowl mix the flours, cornmeal, baking powder, salt, and sesame seeds. In another bowl mix the eggs, oil, sweetener, and liquid. Add dates and mix again. Combine liquid mixture with the dry ingredients and pour batter into lightly-oiled muffin cups. Bake in a 375° oven for 20 to 25 minutes until a toothpick inserted comes out dry. Remove from cups and let cool a bit before serving.

Makes 12 muffins.

Poached Pears
with Raspberry Sauce

6 firm ripe pears
4 cups cold water
¼ cup lemon juice
❖ ❖ ❖
1 cup fresh or frozen unsweetened raspberries
½ cup fresh orange juice
2 tablespoons fresh lime juice
⅓ cup sifted confectioners' sugar

Peel pears, leaving stems. Cut thin slice off bottom of each so it will stand upright. Place pears in a large saucepan; add cold water and lemon juice. Bring to a boil; reduce heat and simmer, covered, for 10 to 15 minutes. Drain. Place in baking dish, cover. Chill 3 hours or overnight.

For Raspberry Sauce, place raspberries, orange juice, lime juice, and confectioners' sugar in blender container. Blend on high speed for 1 minute. Strain to remove seeds, if desired.

To serve, place pears in serving dishes; pour Raspberry Sauce over pears.

Makes 6 servings.

The Wine Country Inn

1152 Lodi Lane
St. Helena, California 94574
(707) 963-7077

Perched on a knoll, overlooking manicured vineyards and nearby hills, the Wine Country Inn offers twenty-five individually decorated guest rooms. All rooms are decorated with antique furnishings and lovely, fresh colors reflecting the seasonal moods of the Napa Valley. Each room has its own private bathroom, but no television or telephone. The agricultural beauty of the valley contrasts with the rugged, tree-covered hills surrounding it. Century old stone bridges, pump houses, barns, and rock buildings afford artists and photographers with a wide variety of subjects. Within a short distance of the Wine Country Inn are tennis courts, hot air balloon rides, mineral baths, several Robert Louis Stevenson sites, antique shops, and over fifteen excellent restaurants serving luncheon and dinner.

Creamy Fruit Topping

1 cup sour cream
1 cup plain yogurt
1 tablespoon sugar
2 teaspoons vanilla extract
¼ teaspoon nutmeg

Combine all ingredients until smooth and creamy. A wire whisk is ideal for mixing. Serve spooned over fruit. Especially good on bananas, garnished with sliced almonds or a strawberry.

Makes 2 cups of topping.

The Wine Country Inn

Poached Pears

¼ cup lemon juice
1 cup water
8 pears
Apple juice
¼ cup grenadine
Sprinkle cinnamon

Combine the lemon juice and water. Quarter, core and peel the pears, dipping them in the lemon juice mixture as you go to prevent browning. Place them in a crock pot and cover with apple juice. Add the grenadine and a sprinkle of cinnamon. Cook on the low setting for about 1½ hours, or until tender.

Serves 8.

Marge's Baked Apples

12 Rome Beauty apples
Sprinkle cinnamon and cloves
2 tablespoons butter

1 cup chopped walnuts
¾ cup brown sugar, firmly packed
Apple juice

❖ ❖ ❖

Milk or cream

Core each apple and slice off the top. Puncture the bottom several times with a fork. Into each apple place a sprinkle of cinnamon and cloves, ½ teaspoon of butter and as many chopped walnuts as it will hold, as well as 1 tablespoon of brown sugar. Top with chopped walnuts. Place the apples into a baking pan with about ¾ of an inch of apple juice. Bake in a 150° oven, basting occasionally for about 1 to 1½ hours.

Best served fresh from the oven with milk or cream. May be re-heated in the oven or a microwave. Serve each apple with a little of the juice they baked in as a sauce.

Makes 12 baked apples.

The Inn at Union Square

440 Post Street
San Francisco, California 94102
(415) 397-3510

Experience this European haven of a hideaway. Snuggled in the heart of San Francisco's Union Square, the inn is only a cablecar ride from such famous sites as Nob Hill and Ghiradelli Square. Small and elegant, each floor of the inn has its own elegant lobby where guests enjoy an afternoon tea and hors d'oeuvres created by chefs Glenda Sweigart and Scott Buchman.

California Shrimp Spread

The avocados and shrimp make it authentically Californian.

½ cup mayonnaise
1 tablespoon lemon juice
2 tablespoons curry powder
1 tablespoon Dijon mustard
¼ teaspoon ground nutmeg

❖ ❖ ❖

2 large ripe avocados, peeled,
  pitted and cut into small pieces
2 tablespoons lemon juice

❖ ❖ ❖

3 4½-ounce cans tiny shrimp,
  drained
½ cup finely chopped celery
½ cup finely chopped onion
½ cup chopped fresh parsley

❖ ❖ ❖

Pita breads, cut into quarters
Assorted crackers

Mix the mayonnaise, 1 tablespoon lemon juice, curry powder, mustard, and nutmeg in a small bowl. Cover and chill at least 1 hour to blend flavors.

Toss avocados with 2 tablespoons lemon juice in a large bowl.

To serve, add shrimp, celery, onion, and parsley to avocados. Pour mayonnaise over and toss to mix. Spoon into pita quarters and/or serve with crackers.

Makes about 3 cups.

Peanut Chile Sauce

¼ cup peanut butter
½ teaspoon sesame oil
½ cup light soy sauce
1 tablespoon lemon juice
2 tablespoons vinegar
1 large clove garlic, minced
1 teaspoon diced chiles
4 sprigs cilantro, lightly chopped

Place all ingredients in small mixing bowl and whisk until well blended.

Makes about 1 cup of sauce.

Woodib
(China Butterfly)

1 pound fresh snow peas
2 red bell peppers
2 yellow bell peppers
16 slices bacon
Soy sauce

Blanch the snow peas. Cut bell peppers into strips; fry the bacon for 2 minutes and drain on paper towels. Take 2 snow peas, 1 red and 1 yellow pepper strip, wrap with a slice of bacon and secure with a toothpick. Repeat with the remaining ingredients. Bake in a 350° oven for 15 to 20 minutes, basting once with soy sauce.

Serves 4 to 6.

Honey Lemon Soaked Cake

½ cup butter (1 stick)
½ cup sugar
2 eggs
¾ cup honey

❖ ❖ ❖

2½ cups all-purpose flour
2 teaspoons baking powder
1 teaspoon salt
½ teaspoon baking soda

❖ ❖ ❖

½ cup milk

❖ ❖ ❖

¼ cup honey
½ cup fresh lemon juice

❖ ❖ ❖

Confectioners' sugar

In a mixing bowl cream the butter and sugar. Add eggs one at a time, beating well after each egg. Blend in ¾ cup honey.

Mix together the flour, baking powder, salt, and baking soda. Add to the creamed mixture alternately with milk. Beat until well blended.

Pour into a greased and floured 6-cup tube pan. Bake in a 350° oven for 45 to 50 minutes. Cool in the pan 10 minutes. Remove from the pan onto a cooling rack with waxed paper underneath.

Pierce the warm cake with a long-tined fork. Warm ¼ cup honey in a small saucepan, combine with lemon juice and spoon over the cake. Cool completely and sprinkle with confectioners' sugar before serving.

Serves 16.

Shortbread

2 cups butter (4 sticks)
½ cup sugar
½ cup confectioners' sugar
½ teaspoon vanilla extract
½ teaspoon cinnamon
½ teaspoon baking powder
½ teaspoon salt
4 cups all-purpose flour

Soften the butter. Place the butter and both sugars in a food processor and blend well, then add all remaining ingredients except the flour and blend well again. Finally add 1 cup of flour at a time, blending well each time. Remove from the food processor bowl and spread evenly in a baking pan. Bake in a 350° oven for 20 to 25 minutes.

Makes 3 dozen cookies.

Petite Auberge

863 Bush Street
San Francisco, California 94108
(415) 928-6000

Upon entering Petite Auberge, guests are transported immediately into the romantic comfort of a French country inn. An antique carousel horse, burnished woods, and fresh cut flowers provide a warm reception and a comfortably elegant room awaits as well. Its tastefully appointed rooms serve as a relaxing haven away from the hustle and bustle of the city. Turn down service and a flower on the pillow are but a few of the amenities found at Petite Auberge.

French Toast

50 eggs
2 teaspoons vanilla extract
2 quarts whipping cream
2 cups honey
2 teaspoons nutmeg
4 loaves sweet French bread, sliced

Mix the first five ingredients. Soak the sliced French bread in the egg mixture. Bake in a 400° oven for 15 minutes or until brown. Make about 15 slices at a time. After baking for 5 minutes, brush the toast with melted butter.

Serves 16.

Musli
(Swiss Oatmeal)

6 cups oats
12 to 16 cups whipping cream
1 cup brown sugar, firmly packed
1 teaspoon cinnamon

1 apple, unpeeled and chopped
1 banana, chopped
2 cups raisins
1 cup chopped walnuts

Mix all together, reserving some raisins, walnuts, and apple for garnish, and refrigerate overnight. The mixture might get thick. Add cream to desired consistency. Garnish with raisins, walnuts, and apple slices.

Serves 12.

Bagna Cuda
(Hot Creamy Dip)

2 cups heavy cream
3 tablespoons butter
1 garlic clove, minced
1 teaspoon thyme leaves
1/8 teaspoon pepper
1 2-ounce can anchovy fillets,
drained and mashed
1 teaspoon salt
1 teaspoon oregano leaves
1 teaspoon fresh chopped basil

In a 2-quart sauce pan over medium heat, boil the cream and reduce to about 1⅓ cups. Stir often. Remove from heat. In hot butter, sauté garlic for 1 minute. Stir in remaining ingredients until smooth. Pour into 1-quart candle warmed dish or fondue pot. Serve with an assortment of prepared vegetables and breadsticks.

Serves 20.

"An Original" Quiche Italiano

2 cups sliced pepperoni
2 bell peppers, chopped
1 onion, chopped
2 cups chopped mushrooms
2 cups grated Mozzarella
2 quarts whipping cream
2 teaspoons salt
2 teaspoons white pepper
1 teaspoon oregano
2 teaspoons basil

❖ ❖ ❖

30 eggs, beaten slightly
2 tomatoes, cut in wedges

Chop and mix all ingredients except eggs and tomatoes. Fill 5 quiche pans. Pour eggs over. Garnish with tomato wedges. Bake in a 350° oven for 40 minutes.

Makes 5 quiches.

Petite Auberge

Potato Corn Gratin

An original and such a favorite that these large quantities are required.

**16 pounds potatoes, peeled and
  sliced
8 cups grated corn (32 ears)
Salt and white pepper to taste
4 cups butter (8 sticks), cut in small
  pieces
4 quarts buttermilk**

❖ ❖ ❖

**5 tablespoons plus 1 teaspoon
  chopped green onions**

Layer the potatoes and corn, salt, pepper, and butter. Repeat. Pour buttermilk over the layers. Bake in a 375° oven until milk is absorbed (1 to 1½ hours). Sprinkle with green onions.
Serves 16.

The White Swan Inn

845 Bush Street
San Francisco, California 94108
(415) 775-1755

Blending the serenity of an English garden inn with the graceful sophistication of cosmopolitan San Francisco, The White Swan Inn proudly invites the most discriminating traveler to share the superior accommodations and personal service. Guests are welcomed to enjoy the plush warmth of a romantic garden retreat accented with curved bay windows, fresh flowers, cozy quilts, handsome antiques, comfortable chairs, and fresh fruit. All rooms are tastefully appointed in rich, warm woods.

Four Sisters Carrot Cake

**2 cups all-purpose flour
2 teaspoons baking soda
½ teaspoon salt
2 teaspoons cinnamon**

❖ ❖ ❖

**3 eggs
¾ cup oil
¾ cup buttermilk
1 cup brown sugar, firmly packed
1 cup sugar
2 teaspoons vanilla extract**

❖ ❖ ❖

**1 8-ounce can crushed pineapple,
  drained
2 cups grated carrots
1 3½-ounce can coconut
2 cups chopped nuts**

❖ ❖ ❖

**1 cup sugar
½ teaspoon baking soda
½ cup buttermilk
½ cup butter
1 teaspoon corn syrup
1 teaspoon vanilla extract**

Sift flour, 2 teaspoons baking soda, salt, and cinnamon. Set aside. In a large mixing bowl, beat eggs. Add oil, ¾ cup buttermilk, 1 cup brown sugar, 1 cup sugar, and 2 teaspoons vanilla, mix well. Add in the dry ingredients, blending thoroughly. Mix in the pineapple, carrots, coconut and nuts. Pour into a greased and floured 13x9x2½-inch pan. Bake in a 350° oven for 55 minutes.

To make frosting, using a large saucepan, mix together 1 cup sugar, ½ teaspoon baking soda, ½ cup buttermilk, butter, and corn syrup. Boil for 5 minutes. Remove from heat and add 1 teaspoon vanilla. Pour over the hot cake.
Serves 16.

Blue Quail Inn Bed and Breakfast

1908 Bath Street
Santa Barbara, California 93101
(805) 687-2300

The Blue Quail Inn and cottages welcome guests to relax and enjoy their visit in Santa Barbara. Each guest room and guest cottage is uniquely decorated with antiques and is filled with country charm. Following a leisurely, delicious continental breakfast each morning, guests may spend the rest of the day experiencing beautiful Santa Barbara.

❖ ❖ ❖ ❖ ❖

Blue Quail Inn Popovers

**1 cup milk
1 cup all-purpose flour
2 eggs
½ teaspoon salt
1 tablespoon oil**

Combine all ingredients in a small mixing bowl and whip until smooth with a wire whisk. Grease hot pans with shortening. Fill with batter to the top. Bake in a 425° oven for 15 to 20 minutes. Lower heat and finish baking at 375° for 15 to 20 minutes.

Serve hot with butter and preserves. Enjoy at breakfast.

Makes 6 popovers.

The Glenborough Inn

1327 Bath Street
Santa Barbara, California 93101
(805) 966-0589

Nestled on the California Riviera in the inviting seacoast town of Santa Barbara between mountains and shore, The Glenborough Inn is a stroll from quaint shops, world class restaurants, and a thriving arts community. A romantic's dream, this cozy inn's specialties include a gourmet breakfast served in guests' rooms on the secluded flower-filled grounds. The inn also boasts a privately used garden hot tub and fireplace suites with canopy beds.

Moma's Egg Casserole

Prepare this recipe the night before, and refrigerate until ready to bake.

  8 slices heavy bread, cut or
      pressed to fit heavy pan
  1 tablespoon crushed oregano
      leaves
  1 teaspoon garlic salt
  1 4-ounce can chopped green chiles
  3 cups shredded sharp Cheddar
      cheese
  3 cups shredded Jack cheese
          ❖ ❖ ❖
  7 eggs
  2 cups water
  ¾ cup dry milk
          ❖ ❖ ❖
  1 avocado
  ¾ cup sour cream

In a 9x13-inch greased pan layer the first six ingredients in the order listed. Place eggs, water, and dry milk in a blender, blend very briefly and pour over the cheese. Chill overnight.

Bake in a 325° oven for 50 minutes or until barely set.

Top each serving with a slice of avocado and a dollop of sour cream.

Serves 8 to 10.

Chile Relleno Casserole

  1 27-ounce can whole green chiles,
      rinsed, opened and seeded
  1 pound sharp Cheddar cheese,
      shredded
  4 green onions, chopped
  5 fresh tomatoes, chopped
          ❖ ❖ ❖
  1 cup all-purpose flour
  ¾ cup dry milk
  9 eggs
  2½ cups water
          ❖ ❖ ❖
  ¾ pound Jack cheese, shredded

Layer chiles, Cheddar, onions, and tomatoes in casserole dishes (either 1 8x8-inch, 1 9x13-inch, or 2 7x11-inch), making 2 to 3 layers ending with cheese. In a blender, mix the flour, dry milk, eggs, and water. Pour over the layers. Top with Jack cheese. Bake in a 350° oven for 45 minutes until set and lightly browned. Serve hot.

Serves 16 plus.

Huevos Rancheros

The sauce may be made up to a week ahead of time. The remainder is assembled on the day of serving, as much as a couple of hours in advance.

  2 tablespoons margarine
  1 onion, chopped
  1 green pepper, chopped
  1 clove garlic, minced
          ❖ ❖ ❖

  2 tablespoons all-purpose flour
          ❖ ❖ ❖
  1 28-ounce can tomatoes, slightly
      drained, chopped into chunks
  1 teaspoon oregano
  ½ teaspoon pepper
  1½ teaspoons salt
  ½ teaspoon hot sauce (or Tabasco)
      to taste
  3 tablespoons canned green chiles,
      chopped
  1 teaspoon chili powder
  1 teaspoon Worcestershire sauce
  ½ teaspoon Accent
          ❖ ❖ ❖
  1½ to 2 cups sauce (ingredients
      listed above)
  12 to 16 eggs
  1 to 2 tablespoons sliced black
      olives
  3 to 4 cups shredded Cheddar
      cheese

To make sauce melt margarine in large skillet; sauté onion, pepper and garlic until tender. Remove from heat and stir in flour. Return to heat and stir until well mixed. Add the next 9 ingredients and simmer at least 30 minutes.

On the day of serving, in 12 to 16 individual greased ramekins, or casseroles, layer 2 tablespoons of sauce, 1 egg, ½ teaspoon of black olives, and ¼ cup of Cheddar cheese. Bake in a 350° oven for 15 minutes until the egg is slightly set and bubbly. Serve hot.

Serves 12 to 16.

Nachos Con Huevos

This recipe is for 1 serving. Increase according to the number of servings needed.

  1 cup tortilla strips
  2 tablespoons refried beans at
      room temperature
  1 egg, scrambled
  1 tablespoon salsa
  1⅓ cups shredded Cheddar cheese
  Sour cream

Layer the ingredients except sour cream in the order listed on a 5 to 6-

inch ovenproof plate. Bake in a 325° oven for 15 minutes or until cheese is well melted.

Top with a dollop of sour cream and serve immediately.

Bon Huelos

In hot oil, fry quickly a flour tortilla turning to brown both sides. Dust with cinnamon sugar.

Serves 1.

Ocean View House Bed and Breakfast

Post Office Box 20065
Santa Barbara, California 93102
(805) 966-6659

Enjoy the comfort of a private home in a quiet neighborhood. A continental breakfast is served on a patio, where one can view sailboats and the Channel Islands.

Crab Hors d'Oeuvres

½ cup margarine (1 stick)
1 4-ounce jar Old English cheese
1 6-ounce can crab
4 green onions, chopped
Dash cayenne pepper
5 English muffins
Paprika

Cream the margarine and cheese. Add drained crab, chopped onions, and cayenne. Split muffins in half, spread with crab mixture, and cut each into 6 wedges. Freeze on a cookie sheet.

Store in plastic bags and use as needed. To use, broil until slightly brown, sprinkle with paprika, and serve warm.

Makes 60 hors d'oeuvres.

The Old Yacht Club Inn

431 Corona Del Mar
Santa Barbara, California 93103
(805) 962-1277

For turn-of-the-century charm by the sea, The Old Yacht Club Inn is unique. Situated just half a block from the beach, the inn was built in 1912 as a private home and opened as Santa Barbara's first bed and breakfast inn in 1980. Today the home has been furnished with period pieces, European antiques and Oriental rugs, creating the warm, "homey" atmosphere of another era. Downstairs, guests are invited to relax and mingle in front of the big brick fireplace with a glass of wine or a cup of tea. Upstairs, four large, sunny guest rooms and two full baths have been decorated with an old-fashioned, personal touch. Window seats and balconies provide cozy sitting areas in the larger Castellamare and Portofino rooms.

Next door to the Old Yacht Club Inn, the Hitchcock House offers four guest rooms, each with its own private entry. Each room is named after one of the innkeepers' family and contains family photos, mementos, and furnishings. Dining is a memorable experience. Guests awaken to the smell of freshly-brewed coffee, accompanied by juice, fruit, baked breads, and delicious omelets. Five-course gourmet dinners are served in the candlelit dining room, usually during the weekend.

The Old Yacht Club

Spinach Salad
with Balsamic Vinaigrette

1 large shallot, finely chopped
⅓ cup balsamic vinegar
1 cup olive oil
1 teaspoon Dijon mustard
½ teaspoon salt
½ teaspoon freshly ground pepper

❖ ❖ ❖

1 bunch spinach, washed and stems
    removed
¼ pound bean sprouts
¼ pound pine nuts
¼ pound bay scallops
1 clove garlic, minced
1 tablespoon butter

In a large cup or jar, mix together the chopped shallot, vinegar, olive oil, mustard, salt, and pepper. Stir to blend well. Chill 2 to 3 hours before using.

Makes approximately 1½ cups of Balsamic Vinaigrette dressing.

In a large salad bowl, mix the spinach, sprouts, and pine nuts. Melt butter in a skillet, add scallops and garlic. Cook over high heat for 3 to 5 minutes until the scallops are opaque and firm. Remove to a plate to cool. Add cooled scallops to the spinach mixture. Pour Balsamic Vinaigrette dressing over and mix well. Serve on individual plates.

Serves 4 to 6.

Baked Fish
with Beurre Blanc Sauce

2 pounds salmon fillet or petrale
    sole or any firm white fish
2 tablespoons butter, melted
Lemon pepper
Dried tarragon or dill

❖ ❖ ❖

2 shallots, finely diced
1 cup white wine
1 tablespoon tarragon wine vinegar
1 cup crème fraiche or whipping
    cream
2 cubes (4 tablespoons) unsalted
    butter
2 tablespoons fresh tarragon or
    fresh dill

Cut the fish into 5-ounce slices. If using salmon remove rib bones with tweezers. Place the fish in a flat baking dish. Brush with melted butter. Season with lemon pepper and dried tarragon or dill, depending on which herb you are using in the sauce. Butter one side of parchment paper cut large enough to cover the baking dish. Place buttered side down, loosely covering the dish. Bake in a 350° oven for 15 to 20 minutes or until fish flakes with a fork. Do not overcook. Meanwhile prepare the sauce.

Place the shallots in a saucepan with wine and vinegar. Boil over medium heat until the liquid is reduced to 1 tablespoon or less. Add creme fraiche and reduce by half. Cut the cold butter into tablespoon-size slices. Whisk butter into the cream 1 tablespoon at a time, allowing each slice to melt into the sauce. Continue until all butter is incorporated into the sauce. Add fresh tarragon or dill (use ½ teaspoon dried if necessary). Keep the heat very low or the butter will melt out of the sauce. Shallots may be strained out if a smooth sauce is desired. Remove the fish to serving plates and cover with sauce. Serve at once.

Note: If the fish is cooked before you are ready to serve, turn the oven off and prop the door open 2 to 3 inches. Fish will stay hot but will not overcook.

Serves 6.

Artichokes Athena

1 package frozen artichoke hearts
½ cup butter (1 stick)
4 ounces cream cheese
½ teaspoon Nature's Seasonings

❖ ❖ ❖

1 package phyllo dough

❖ ❖ ❖

2 tablespoons grated Romano
    cheese

Cook artichoke hearts with 2 tablespoons butter in a covered skillet over low to medium heat, 10 to 15 minutes. Do not brown. Turn the heat off. Add the cream cheese. Cover and set aside until the cheese is soft. Stir to mix with the artichoke hearts. Add seasoning.

Thaw the phyllo, leave wrapped. This takes at least an hour at room temperature. Melt the remaining butter. Place 4 sheets of phyllo (double thickness) on a flat surface. Brush with ½ of the butter. Place ½ mixture in center of each double sheet. Fold sides and one end. Then roll up lengthwise to make two 4x4-inch packets. Brush with remaining butter. Bake in a 350° oven for 20 to 25 minutes until the phyllo is browned. Sprinkle with grated cheese. Return to the oven until the cheese melts. Cut each packet in 3 pieces. Serve hot.

Serves 4 to 6.

Carrot Vichyssoise

4 large carrots, peeled and cut into
    4 pieces
1 medium onion, peeled and cut
    into 4 pieces
2 potatoes, peeled and cut into 4
    pieces
4 cups chicken broth
1 teaspoon salt
2 cups whipping cream
½ teaspoon white pepper
⅛ teaspoon cayenne pepper
Fresh mint leaves

Place the carrots, onion and potatoes in a food processor and process on and off until the vegetables are finely diced. Place the vegetables in a large, heavy Dutch oven. Pour in chicken broth and salt. Bring to a boil and cook over medium heat for 25 minutes. Drain the vegetables and pour the broth into a large bowl. Return the vegetables to the processor and purée until smooth. Add the vegetables to the broth. Whisk in cream and stir well to mix. Add pepper. Taste and adjust seasoning. Chill well. Serve with minced fresh mint leaves sprinkled on top.

Serves 6 to 8.

Chocolate Cheesecake

1 cup finely chopped almonds
2 tablespoons sugar
3 tablespoons melted butter

❖ ❖ ❖

5 ounces semi-sweet chocolate
5 ounces milk chocolate
2 tablespoons butter
⅓ cup Amaretto

❖ ❖ ❖

2 8-ounce packages cream cheese
2 large eggs
⅓ cup sugar
1 cup sour cream

❖ ❖ ❖

½ cup whipping cream
1 package frozen raspberries
2 tablespoons Amaretto

Place the almonds in the bottom of a 9-inch springform pan. Sprinkle sugar over the nuts. Pour in melted butter. Use a fork to mix nuts, sugar and butter. Press crust into bottom of pan. Bake in a 350° oven for 15 to 20 minutes, until crust is lightly browned. Remove from the oven and lower the oven temperature to 325°.

Put chocolates, butter and ⅓ cup Amaretto in the top of a double boiler. Cook over hot water until the chocolate is melted and can be stirred with a wire whisk. Cut the cream cheese into 8 pieces and place in work bowl of a food processor fitted with the steel blade. Process on and off until the cream cheese is softened. Add the eggs and process to mix. Add sugar and process 5 to 10 seconds. Scrape down the sides of the bowl. Add sour cream. Process lightly. With the motor running, pour the melted chocolate mixture in the feed tube. Process 10 to 15 seconds. Scrape the sides and bottom of the work bowl. Process another 5 seconds. Pour the mixture into a pre-cooked crust in a springform pan. Bake in a 325° oven for 45 minutes. Turn the oven off and prop the door open 3 to 4 inches. Allow the cheesecake to sit in the oven for two hours. Remove and cool to room temperature

before serving. Refrigerate to store up to one week. This freezes well too.

To serve, use the processor to whip the cream until stiff. Spread over the top of the cheesecake.

Purée the frozen raspberries. If desired, run through a food mill to remove seeds. Add 2 tablespoons Amaretto. Cut the cheesecake into 16 pieces and place on individual plates. Place 1 tablespoon of whipped cream on top. Pour 1 to 2 tablespoons of raspberry sauce over each serving.

Serves 20.

Sunflower House

243 Third Street
Solvang, California 93463
(805) 688-4492

As guests cross the bridge over the meandering creek to the house, they seem to step back in time. Nestled amid the soft, rolling foothills of the lush, historic Santa Ynez Valley, sits the Christensen family's unique "bed and breakfast" in the quaint Danish community of Solvang. The fragrance of flowers among the mature oak trees and the adobe with its tiled roof and floor remind one of the best of California's early history.

Sunflower House Muffins

For the microwave. Prepare this recipe the night before serving, and keep in the refrigerator. It may be prepared and refrigerated up to six weeks before use.

1 cup boiling water

1 cup bran

❖ ❖ ❖

½ cup butter (1 stick)
1 cup sugar
2 eggs
2 cups buttermilk

❖ ❖ ❖

2½ cups all-purpose flour
2½ teaspoons baking soda
¼ teaspoon salt

❖ ❖ ❖

2 cups All Bran
1 cup raisins
1 cup nuts

Combine the boiling water and bran and set aside. Cream the butter and sugar. Add to the bran mixture. Mix thoroughly. Add the eggs and buttermilk, mix thoroughly. Sift the flour, soda and salt. Blend into mixture. Add the All-Bran, raisins and nuts. This can be stored in the refrigerator up to six weeks. Use when needed. This mixture should be chilled in refrigerator overnight before baking. Bake in the microwave; six muffins for 3 minutes on high, or 1 muffin for 30 seconds on high.

Makes about 4 dozen muffins.

Donna's Hot Apple Cider

2 quarts apple cider
8 whole cloves
8 whole allspice
1 cinnamon stick

Simmer all ingredients in a covered pan for 10 minutes. Strain and pour into cups.

Makes 8 cups.

Jameson's: A Bed and Breakfast Inn

22157 Feather River Drive
Sonora, California 95370
(209) 532-1248

Jameson's is located in the Mother Lode, or Gold Rush Country. This enormous home has a rustic ski-lodge atmosphere. It is nestled among huge rocks and tall pines and oaks and is surrounded by a wrap-around deck. Jameson's offers seclusion and comfort to their guests.

Jameson's Cranberry Frappé

On those hot summer mornings when a leisurely breakfast on the deck is in order, try this for a starter.

1 cup frozen vanilla yogurt
1 cup cranberry juice

Place in blender and blend 10 seconds. Serve at once in champagne glasses. Special!
Serves 4.

Jameson's Mayer Lemon Bread

The Mayer lemon, often grown in gardens in California, is milder than the usual ones found in stores, but either may be used.

½ cup shortening
1 cup sugar
2 eggs, slightly beaten

1¼ cups all-purpose flour
1 teaspoon baking powder
½ teaspoon salt
½ cup milk
½ cup nuts, chopped fine
Grated rind of 1 Mayer lemon
¼ cup sugar
Juice of 1 Mayer lemon

Cream the shortening and sugar; mix in eggs. Sift the flour, baking powder and salt together. Alternately add the flour mixture and the milk to shortening mixture, stirring constantly. Mix in the nuts and lemon rind.

Bake in a greased 5x9-inch loaf pan in a 350° oven for 1 hour. Combine ¼ cup sugar with the lemon juice and pour over the top of the loaf when it comes from the oven (poke a few holes in the bread top with a toothpick so the lemon-sugar mixture is better integrated in the bread—the glaze is great!)
Makes 1 loaf.

Pecan-Raisin Stuffed Apples

6 large firm baking apples

    ❖ ❖ ❖

2 tablespoons raisins
2 tablespoons chopped pecans
3 tablespoons brown sugar
2 tablespoons sweet butter
1 teaspoon cinnamon

    ❖ ❖ ❖

½ cup apple juice

    ❖ ❖ ❖

1 tablespoon chopped preserved ginger (optional)

Core the apples. Do not pierce the bottom of the apples (cut a small slice off the bottom of the apple so they stand upright). Make several vertical cuts through the peel at the top (so you can stuff them easily). Mix all ingredients except the apple juice; stuff the apples and place in a baking pan. Pour the apple juice in the pan, bake in a 350° oven for 30 to 40 minutes. Baste from time to time with the sauce that forms in the pan. Serve warm topped with

frozen vanilla yogurt (or ice cream). Pour a little sauce from the pan over the frozen topping. You can sprinkle with chopped preserved ginger if desired.
Serves 6.

Pineapple Boats

Another "best seller" for summer pleasure.

Cut a whole pineapple in fourths; core and cube fruit. Refill with strawberries, the cubed pineapple, tiny scoops of cantaloupe and tiny scoops of frozen lemon custard yogurt.
Serves 4.

Sutter Creek Inn

Post Office Box 385
75 Main Street
Sutter Creek, California 95685
(209) 267-5606

The Sutter Creek Inn is a lovely country inn built over one hundred years ago. It is the oldest bed and breakfast inn west of the Mississippi. It is centrally located in the Mother Lode, two and one-half hours from the Bay area. Each room is decorated uniquely and with flair; many have fireplaces, patios, and secret gardens. Others are furnished with canopied beds and claw feet bathtubs; some have swinging beds that hang from the ceiling on chains. Lovely gardens surround the inn, providing the perfect setting for relaxing in the hammocks or playing croquet on the lush green lawns.

Sutter Creek Inn

Chilean Eggs a la Way

A lovely dish full of wonderful flavors to serve at breakfast or lunch.

2 cups all-purpose flour
1 teaspoon baking powder
½ teaspoon garlic salt
2 cups cottage cheese
1 pound shredded Monterey Jack cheese
½ cup butter, melted
2 cups diced green chiles
10 eggs, beaten

Beat all ingredients together and bake in a 9x13-inch dish or pan in a 350° oven until eggs set.
Serves 10.

Pineapple Nut Bread

¾ cup brown sugar
3 tablespoons oil
2 eggs, beaten

❖ ❖ ❖

1 8½-ounce can crushed pineapple with juice
½ cup raisins

❖ ❖ ❖

1 cup all-purpose flour
¾ cup whole wheat flour
2 teaspoons baking powder
½ teaspoon salt
¼ teaspoon baking soda
1 cup chopped walnuts

❖ ❖ ❖

2 tablespoons sugar
½ teaspoon cinnamon

Combine brown sugar, oil and beaten eggs. Mix well, add pineapple, and raisins. Add in flours, baking powder, salt, soda and walnuts. Mix well and pour into a greased 9x5x3-inch loaf pan. Bake in a 350° oven for 30 to 40 minutes. Sprinkle a mixture of sugar and cinnamon on top of the hot baked bread.
Makes 1 loaf.

Individual Swiss Soufflés a la Spanish Sutter

Included is a recipe for a sauce to be poured over the baked soufflé.

Butter
Salt
4 teaspoons fine bread crumbs

❖ ❖ ❖

3 tablespoons butter
3 tablespoons minced green onions
3 tablespoons all-purpose flour
1 cup milk
4 egg yolks
½ cup Monterey Jack cheese, grated
½ cup Swiss cheese, grated
Salt and pepper to taste

❖ ❖ ❖

4 egg whites
¼ teaspoon cream of tartar

❖ ❖ ❖

1 teaspoon chopped green pepper
2 sticks celery, chopped
1 small onion, chopped
1 small clove garlic, minced
3 small tomatoes, chopped
Pinch sugar
Salt and pepper to taste

Butter and salt 4 small soufflé dishes and sprinkle with crumbs.
Sauté onions in 3 tablespoons of butter. Stir in flour, then the milk and continue to stir slowly until the mixture thickens and is smooth.
Transfer the hot mixture to a bowl and add egg yolks slowly, stirring thoroughly. Then add cheeses and salt and pepper.
In a separate bowl beat whites until soft peaks form, then add cream of tartar and beat until stiff. Fold ⅓ of the egg whites into the egg yolk mixture. Then gently fold in the rest of the egg whites and pour into soufflé dishes. Bake in a 425° oven for about 20 minutes.
Sauté the pepper, celery, onion and garlic until soft. Add tomatoes, cook and stir 5 minutes. Add sugar and season to taste. Pour over the soufflés.
Serves 4.

Creamy Potato Puff

This is especially good at breakfast.

4 cups hot mashed potatoes
1 8-ounce package cream cheese
1 egg, beaten

❖ ❖ ❖

¼ cup finely chopped onion
¼ cup chopped pimento
1 teaspoon salt
White pepper

In a large mixing bowl combine cream cheese and potatoes, then add remaining ingredients. Bake in a 1 quart casserole in a 350° oven for 45 minutes. Serve hot with 3 large scoops of butter over the top.

Serves 8.

Mayfield House

Post Office Box 5999
236 Grove Street
Tahoe City, California 95730
(916) 583-1001

Built in 1932 by Norman Mayfield, Lake Tahoe's pioneer contractor, the Mayfield House is one of the finest examples of Old Tahoe architecture. Completely refurbished in 1979, it is now a fine bed and breakfast inn, boasting six bedrooms, each with down comforters and down pillows, lots of books to enjoy, and fresh flowers. In every room is a cozy nook where guests can enjoy a quiet breakfast, if they desire. A large living room with fireplace is available to all for comfort and enjoyment, and the breakfast dining room is a place to make new friends.

Sweet Potato Muffins

½ cup butter (1 stick)
1 cup sugar

❖ ❖ ❖

1¼ cup canned yams
2 eggs

❖ ❖ ❖

1½ cups all-purpose flour
2 teaspoons baking powder
1 teaspoon cinnamon
¼ teaspoon nutmeg
¼ teaspoon salt

❖ ❖ ❖

1 cup milk

❖ ❖ ❖

½ cup chopped nuts
½ cup chopped raisins

Have all ingredients at room temperature. Cream the butter, sugar and yams until smooth. Add eggs, blend well. Sift flour, baking powder and spices together. Add alternately with milk to egg batter. Do not overmix. Fold in nuts and raisins last. Bake in greased muffin cups in a 375° oven for 25 minutes.

Makes 2 dozen.

Colorado

Snow Queen Lodge

124 East Cooper Street
Aspen, Colorado 81611
(303) 925-8455
(303) 925-9973

The Snow Queen is a quaint Victorian lodge built during the 1890s. The lodge is small and cozy, offering a variety of rooms, some with private bath facilities. Accommodations range from a private twin to a dormitory-style room for four people. A Continental breakfast is served. The Snow Queen specializes in a friendly, congenial atmosphere with Western hospitality and inexpensive rates.

German Coffee Cake

½ cup butter (1 stick)
1 cup sugar
  ❖ ❖ ❖
2 eggs
1 cup sour cream
1 teaspoon vanilla extract
1 teaspoon baking soda
1 teaspoon baking powder
½ teaspoon salt
2 cups all-purpose flour
  ❖ ❖ ❖

¼ cup sugar
½ cup chopped nuts
1 teaspoon cinnamon

Cream butter and 1 cup sugar thoroughly. Add eggs, sour cream, vanilla, soda, baking powder, salt, and flour, beat well. Pour into a 13x9-inch greased pan. Combine ¼ cup sugar, nuts and cinnamon to make the topping. Sprinkle on the topping and marbleize by lightly stirring the topping into the batter. Bake in a 350° oven for 35 to 40 minutes.
  Serve with coffee or hot chocolate. Serves 10.

The Briar Rose Bed and Breakfast Inn

2151 Arapahoe Avenue
Boulder, Colorado 80302
(303) 442-3007

The Briar Rose Bed and Breakfast is a beautiful English country-style inn. All guest rooms are comfortable and attractive, with antique furniture, fresh fruit and flowers, handmade feather comforters, and good books. Guests find candies on their pillows at bedtime and a decanter of sherry is always in the dining room.

Cucumber Sandwiches

The Briar Rose has a high tea the last Sunday of each month. It features chamber music and refreshments from 4 P.M. to 6 P.M. Besides tea, French pastries, scones, and cucumber sandwiches are served.

Cucumbers, very thinly-sliced
Whole wheat bread, crusts
  removed
  ❖ ❖ ❖
2 6-ounce bottles horseradish, very
  well drained
1 pint whipping cream, whipped

Serve cucumber slices on crustless whole wheat bread. Combine horseradish with whipped cream, and serve on the cucumber sandwiches.

Lemon Curd

12 eggs
  ❖ ❖ ❖
Juice of 6 lemons
1 cup butter (2 sticks)
3 cups sugar
1 tablespoon lemon rind

In a large mixer bowl beat eggs for 5 minutes. Add lemon juice, butter, sugar and lemon rind. Place in a double boiler over simmering water and stir continuously until thick.

Shortbread Cookies

These are dangerously good.

1 cup confectioners' sugar
2 cups butter (4 sticks), room temperature

❖ ❖ ❖

4 cups all-purpose flour
Pinch salt
Pinch baking powder

Cream sugar and butter together. Sift in the flour and other ingredients. Form into balls the size of a quarter, and place on an ungreased cookie sheet. Bake in a 350° oven for 15 to 20 minutes. Watch carefully.

Makes 60 cookies.

The Briar Rose

Sheets Bed and Breakfast

577 High Street
Denver, Colorado 80218
(303) 329-6170

This beautiful year-round bed and breakfast is the ultimate in gracious living in the Mile High City. Its four tastefully decorated rooms each have private bathrooms. A fine breakfast is served, as well as afternoon tea if desired. Other enjoyments for guests include a sitting room, a piano, and bicycles.

Buttermilk Pancakes

1 egg

❖ ❖ ❖

1¼ cups buttermilk
2 tablespoons oil

❖ ❖ ❖

1 cup all-purpose flour

1 teaspoon sugar
2 teaspoons baking powder
½ teaspoon baking soda
½ teaspoon salt

In a small mixing bowl, beat the egg with a fork. Beat in buttermilk and oil. Set aside. In a large mixing bowl, combine the flour, sugar, baking powder, soda and salt. Add egg mixture to dry ingredients. Stir the mixture until blended but slightly lumpy. Lightly grease a griddle or heavy skillet. Pour ¼ cup of batter for each pancake.

Top the pancakes with large blueberries, bananas, two very large scoops of gourmet ice cream.

Makes 8 or 9 4-inch pancakes.

Macadamia Nut and Maple Syrup Bread

2 cups all-purpose flour
1 teaspoon baking powder
1 teaspoon baking soda
1 teaspoon coarse salt

❖ ❖ ❖

1 egg

❖ ❖ ❖

⅓ cup maple syrup
¾ cup buttermilk
3 tablespoons butter, melted

❖ ❖ ❖

1 cup roughly chopped macadamia nuts

Sift the flour, baking powder, soda, and salt in a medium mixing bowl. Blend in egg. Mix thoroughly. Add maple syrup, buttermilk and butter. Mix until blended. Stir in nuts. Pour batter into a 9-inch loaf pan. Bake in a 350° oven for 50 minutes. Let rest several hours before slicing.

Makes 1 loaf.

Strater Hotel

Post Office Drawer E
Durango, Colorado 81302
(303) 247-4431

The Strater Hotel, established in 1887, is the historic landmark of Durango, a quaint mountain town nestled in the Animas Valley high atop the southern reaches of the Rockies. The Strater Hotel has served as a civilized refuge for travelers from throughout the world.

Fresh Rocky Mountain trout, caught in the cold clear rivers of the valley, has long been a favorite at the Strater with both the locals and the thousands of tourists who flock here yearly. Trout Columbian is the Strater's signature item and was created by the hotel's chef in honor of the Columbian Room, named for one of the Strater's historic annexes. The recipe blends the delicate flavor of fresh rainbow trout with tender new spinach mousse and subtle seasonings. Notice that the recipe calls for no added salt, relying on the blending of natural ingredients for its flavor balance.

Trout Columbian

10 ounces fresh spinach
1 small onion, chopped
4 ounces salt pork
Pinch thyme
4 drops Worcestershire sauce
¼ teaspoon cayenne pepper
2 cloves garlic
Pinch tarragon

❖ ❖ ❖

1 tablespoon bacon grease
1 tablespoon Cognac
1½ teaspoons sherry
1½ teaspoons Pernod

❖ ❖ ❖

4 fresh trout, cleaned and boned
 (10 ounces after cleaning)
4 ounces Hollandaise sauce
¼ ounce salmon roe
¼ cup clarified butter

In a blender, purée the spinach, onion, salt pork, thyme, Worcestershire, cayenne, garlic and tarragon until smooth. Heat the bacon grease in a sauté pan and add the Cognac, sherry, and Pernod. Add the spinach purée, cook until the moisture is absorbed.

Open the trout flat, skin side down. Cover half the inside with 2 ounces of spinach mousse. Fold the fish over to close the cavity. Place butter in the bottom of a shallow baking dish. Bake in a 375° oven until the fish feel springy to the touch. Remove from the baking dish and place on a plate. Use 1 ounce of Hollandaise to make a diagonal strip 1 inch wide across the front ⅓ of the fish, behind the head. Place salmon eggs over the strip of Hollandaise.

Serves 4.

Elizabeth Street Guest House for Bed and Breakfast

202 East Elizabeth Street
Fort Collins, Colorado 80524
(303) 493-BEDS

Elizabeth Street Guest House is a beautifully restored American four-square brick home. It is lovingly furnished with family antiques, plants, old quilts, and handmade items. The leaded windows and oak woodwork are special features.

Baking Powder Drop Biscuits

Easy, fast, and terrific with homemade jams and apple butter.

2 cups all-purpose flour
3 teaspoons baking powder
1 teaspoon salt
1 teaspoon sugar

❖ ❖ ❖

¾ cup milk
⅓ cup corn oil
1 beaten egg (optional)

Blend the flour, baking powder, salt and sugar. Combine the remaining ingredients and pour over the dry ingredients. Stir together lightly. Drop by spoonfuls onto a buttered cookie sheet. Bake in a 450° oven for 12 to 15 minutes.

Makes 12 to 14 biscuits.

Elizabeth Street Guest House

Breakfast Dish

12 eggs
½ pound bacon
1 8-ounce carton sour cream
1 cup shredded Cheddar cheese

Soft scramble the eggs with a little milk. Dice and fry the bacon. Place a layer of eggs in the bottom of a casserole dish. Spread with sour cream. Layer the bacon over the sour cream and top with cheese. Bake in a 350° oven for 20 minutes. This can be made the day before and baked in the morning. Rich and yummy!
Serves 6 to 8.

Chile Cheese Puff

Make this hot or mild according to your preference. Use a 4-ounce can of diced green chiles for mild; a 7-ounce can for hot. Can be baked in a pie crust as a Mexican quiche.

5 eggs
½ teaspoon baking powder
¼ cup flour
¼ teaspoon salt
1 cup creamed small curd cottage cheese
½ pound grated Monterey Jack (or a mixture of Cheddar and Jack)
¼ cup butter, melted
1 can diced green chiles

Beat the eggs until light and lemon colored. Add the baking powder, flour, salt, cottage cheese, cheese, and melted butter. Stir in the chiles. Pour into a well-buttered 8-inch or 9-inch baking dish. Bake in a 350° oven for 45 to 60 minutes until the top is lightly browned and the center is firm. Serve with tomato salsa on the side and garnish with sour cream and chives. This can be made the night before and partially cooked for about 30 minutes. Finish cooking the next morning.
Serves 4 to 6.

❖ ❖ ❖ ❖ ❖ ❖

The Outlook Lodge

Post Office Box 5
Green Mountain Falls, Colorado 80819
(303) 684-2303

Pine and spruce trees surround this 1889 structure. Green Mountain Falls is a heavily-wooded little vale with a fishing lake that has a gazebo in the center. Its claim to historical fame comes from being the parsonage for the "Little Brown Church in the Wildwood." Both church and parsonage were built in 1889, and many of the furnishings are the original pieces.

Aloha Bread

⅓ cup butter or margarine, softened
⅔ cup sugar
❖ ❖ ❖
2 eggs
❖ ❖ ❖
3 tablespoons milk
1 teaspoon lemon juice
❖ ❖ ❖
2 cups all-purpose flour
1 teaspoon baking powder
½ teaspoon baking soda
½ teaspoon salt
❖ ❖ ❖
½ cup mashed bananas
½ cup crushed pineapple with juice
❖ ❖ ❖
1 cup toasted coconut
1 cup chopped macadamia nuts

Cream the butter and sugar, beat in eggs one at a time. Add milk and lemon juice. Sift the flour with baking powder, soda and salt, add to the creamed mixture with bananas and pineapple. Fold in coconut and nuts. Pour into 2 small loaf pans or 1 large loaf pan. Bake in a 350° oven for about 1 hour.
Makes 1 large or 2 small loaves.

Genevieve's Cardamom Bread

2 eggs
1⅓ cups sugar
½ cup oil
2⅓ cups flour
1 teaspoon cloves
1 teaspoon cardamom
1 teaspoon soda
1 cup buttermilk

In a large mixing bowl beat the eggs and sugar together. Add the oil; beat well. Sift the dry ingredients together; add alternately with the buttermilk. Pour into a greased, floured loaf pan. Bake in a 350° oven for about 1 hour.
Makes 1 loaf.

Strawberry Bread

3 cups all-purpose flour
1 teaspoon baking soda
1 teaspoon salt
1 tablespoon cinnamon
2 cups sugar
❖ ❖ ❖
4 eggs, beaten
2 cups frozen strawberries, thawed
1½ cups cooking oil
❖ ❖ ❖
1¼ cups chopped pecans

Sift the dry ingredients together. Combine the eggs, strawberries, and oil and add to the dry ingredients. Add pecans. Bake in a 325° oven for about 1 hour.
Makes 4 small or 2 large loaves.

Waunita Hot Springs Ranch

8007 County Road 887
Department 7
Gunnison, Colorado 81230
(303) 641-1266

This 24-year-old home has shared warm western hospitality with families, couples, and singles looking for a wholesome, no-alcohol, vacation atmosphere. It is secluded amidst beautiful scenery, colorful history, and delightful weather; yet it is easily accessible from Gunnison (thirty minutes) and Colorado Springs (three hours). Activities are as endless as the memories. They include trail rides that go from flowered meadows to snowridged mountain tops, and riding instructions are available. Also available are campfire cookouts, fishing, scenic 4x4 trips, river rafting, golf, hay rides, musical shows, and square dancing. Supervised children's activities are provided and a unique crystal clear pool fed by natural hot springs is on the grounds. Accommodations are very comfortable and clean, and all have private baths. Meals are delicious and plentiful.

Apple Fritters

These are cooked at a weekly campfire cookout.

2 cups grated apples
2 tablespoons milk
2 eggs
1 tablespoon margarine, melted
1 cup all-purpose flour
3 tablespoons sugar
1 teaspoon baking powder
½ teaspoon salt
¼ teaspoon cinnamon
Dash nutmeg

❖ ❖ ❖

Confectioners' sugar

Mix all ingredients together. If the batter is too thin, more flour may be added. Drop by teaspoonfuls into hot oil (about 3 inches deep). Drain and shake in confectioner's sugar.
Serves 6.

Syrup for Hot Cakes or Ice Cream

2 cups brown sugar
1 cup white corn syrup

❖ ❖ ❖

1 egg
½ cup milk or cream

Bring brown sugar and corn syrup to a boil. Slowly add the egg and milk, bring to a boil again. Serve hot.
Makes 2½ cups of syrup.

Bar-B-Q Sauce

Good with beef, pork or chicken.

4 teaspoons chili powder
½ cup margarine (1 stick)
¾ cup catsup
¼ cup lemon juice

1 teaspoon coarse black pepper
¾ cup brown sugar
¼ cup white vinegar
4 teaspoons Worcestershire sauce

Combine all ingredients in a saucepan and bring to a boil.
Makes 2¾ cups of sauce.

Cowboy Cookies

These are sent along on weekly, all-day rides.

2¼ cups shortening
2 cups sugar
2½ cups brown sugar
5 eggs
2 teaspoons vanilla extract
¾ cup chunky peanut butter

❖ ❖ ❖

4½ cups all-purpose flour
2 teaspoons baking soda
1 teaspoon baking powder
1 teaspoon salt

❖ ❖ ❖

3 cups rolled oats
2½ cups bran flakes or other cereal
2 cups chocolate chips
1 cup chopped walnuts

Cream together shortening, sugar, and brown sugar. Add the eggs, vanilla, and peanut butter. Sift together the flour, baking soda, baking powder and salt; add to the creamed mixture. Add oats, bran flakes, chocolate chips and walnuts; mix well. Drop by rounded ⅛-cupfuls onto a greased cookie sheet. Bake in a 350° oven until the edges turn brown and centers still look chewy.
Makes 3½ to 4 dozen cookies.

Connecticut

Riverwind Country Inn and Antiques

209 Main Street, Route 9A
Deep River, Connecticut 06417
(203) 526-2014

Riverwind Country Inn and Antiques is a blend of New England charm and Southern hospitality. The restored 1850 home is centrally located among the Connecticut River Valley's finest theatres, historical sites, and recreational and dining facilities. The inn is furnished with country antiques and includes an antique shop in the converted summer kitchen. All rooms have a private bath, and guests are invited to enjoy a complimentary continental breakfast in the ambiance of early Americana.

Riverwind Biscuits

The biscuits, which are cut in the shape of little pigs, are served with Smithfield ham each morning. The result is a true "ham biscuit"!

½ cup shortening
2 cups self-rising flour
¾ cup milk

Cut the shortening into the flour, then add milk. The dough will be sticky. Turn out onto a floured board and knead at least 6 times, adding flour each time. Roll out and cut into shapes. Bake on an ungreased cookie sheet in a 450° oven for 8 to 12 minutes.
   Makes 1½ dozen biscuits.

RIVERWIND

Tollgate Hill Inn and Restaurant

Route 202
Litchfield, Connecticut 06759
(203) 482-6116

Find stylish slumber at the Tollgate Hill Inn. A true country inn experience will be enjoyed here. There are no televisions or telephones. A light breakfast of freshly squeezed orange juice, fruit breads and muffins, and coffee is served in each room. All rooms feature double beds and have private baths.

Tollgate Hill Shellfish Pie

2 tablespoons unsalted butter (¼ stick)
3 tablespoons finely chopped shallots
1 pound mushrooms, thinly sliced
⅓ cup dry sherry
2 tablespoons all-purpose flour
2 cups whipping cream
¼ teaspoon paprika

❖   ❖   ❖

1 egg yolk, room temperature
Salt and freshly ground pepper
16 small cherrystone clams, shelled
½ pound crabmeat
½ pound uncooked medium shrimp, peeled and deveined
½ pound bay scallops
½ pound lobster meat
½ pound puff pastry
1 egg, beaten to blend (glaze)

Melt the butter in a large heavy saucepan over medium heat. Add the shallots and sauté until slightly softened, about 3 minutes. Add the mushrooms and sauté until slightly softened, about 3 minutes. Stir in the sherry. Cook until reduced by half. Reduce heat to medium-low, add flour and stir 3 minutes. Blend in the cream and paprika. Increase heat and boil gently until the sauce is very thick.

Whisk ¼ cup sauce into the yolk. Whisk back into the saucepan. Season generously with salt and pepper. Pat the shellfish dry. Stir into the sauce. Divide the mixture among 8 small or 4 larger ramekins, or pour into a 1-quart baking dish; do not fill to the top. Roll the pastry out on a lightly floured surface to a thickness of ¹/₈ to ¼ inch. Cover the ramekins or dish with pastry, pinching edges to seal. Brush with glaze. Bake in a 425° oven until the pastry is puffed and golden brown, about 15 minutes. Serve pie immediately.

Makes 8 appetizers or 4 main-course servings.

Manor House: The Inn at Norfolk

Manor House

Post Office Box 447, Maple Avenue
Norfolk, Connecticut 06058
(203) 542-5690

The Manor House is an elegant and romantic Victorian bed and breakfast inn. Guests are surrounded by Old World refinement while they enjoy baronial living and breakfast rooms with Tiffany and leaded glass windows. A six-foot fireplace in the foyer invites relaxing moments for quiet or conversation, and a handsomely carved and cherry-panelled staircase leads to the antique-decorated guest rooms.

Orange Waffles

2 cups sifted all-purpose flour
3 teaspoons baking powder
2 tablespoons sugar
½ teaspoon salt

❖ ❖ ❖

4 eggs, lightly beaten
4 tablespoons melted butter
1 cup milk
3 tablespoons grated orange rind

Sift together the dry ingredients, set aside. Combine eggs, milk and butter; add orange rind. Add the sifted dry ingredients, ½ of the total amount at a time. Beat well after each addition until the batter is smooth. Pour about ¾ to 1 cup of batter at a time onto a preheated waffle iron, following manufacturer's directions. Bake until the waffles are golden brown.

Serves 8.

Rhubarb Coffee Cake

1½ cups brown sugar, firmly packed
⅔ cup vegetable oil

1 egg
1 teaspoon vanilla extract

❖ ❖ ❖

2½ cups sifted all-purpose flour
1 teaspoon salt
1 teaspoon baking soda

❖ ❖ ❖

1 cup milk

❖ ❖ ❖

1½ cups chopped rhubarb
½ cup sliced almonds

❖ ❖ ❖

½ cup sugar
1 tablespoon butter
¼ cup sliced almonds

Grease and flour 2 9x1½-inch pans. Mix brown sugar, oil, egg and vanilla. Combine flour, salt and baking soda. Add to the egg mixture alternately with milk. Stir in rhubarb and ½ cup almonds. Pour into pans. Mix sugar, butter and ¼ cup almonds; sprinkle on batter. Bake in a 350° oven for 40 to 45 minutes.

Serves 12 to 16.

Lemon-Chive Sauce

⅓ cup butter
2 tablespoons finely chopped
    chives
1 tablespoon lemon juice
1 teaspoon grated lemon peel
½ teaspoon salt
Dash pepper

In a small saucepan melt the butter. Add remaining ingredients, beating thoroughly. Serve sauce hot over poached eggs on English muffins.

Makes about ½ cup.

The Old Lyme Inn

Lyme Street
Old Lyme, Connecticut 06371
(203) 434-2600

The warm exterior of a fine old nineteenth century home, typifying New England's charming colonial residences, welcomes travelers and diners alike to the elegance of The Old Lyme Inn. Situated on the main street in Old Lyme's historical district, the inn represents the classic traditions of excellence in dining and lodging that is the very heart of a small Connecticut town.

Built in the 1850s, the inn remained a working farm of some 300 acres and a private residence for 100 years. After several grim years as a down-on-its-heels restaurant, it has been restored to its former grandeur. The original ornate iron fence, tree-shaded lawn, and banistered front porch greet each guest. Once inside, the curly maple staircase, hand-painted murals, and antique furnishings remind one of the grace of America's past and the warmth and promise of its future.

Duck Ravioli
with Lingonberry Sauce

3 egg yolks
1 whole egg
2 tablespoons water
1 teaspoon olive oil
½ teaspoon salt
1¾ cups all-purpose flour

❖ ❖ ❖

1 4- to 5-pound duck
½ teaspoon salt
¼ teaspoon nutmeg
1 ounce Madeira wine
¼ teaspoon black pepper
1 egg
½ cup raisins
¼ cup chopped parsley
1 egg, beaten

❖ ❖ ❖

3 tablespoons shallots, finely diced
1 cup burgundy
2 cups concentrated veal stock
½ cup lingonberry preserves
¼ cup watercress, roughly chopped

Combine the egg yolks, egg, water, olive oil, salt, and flour in a mixer bowl with a paddle. Mix on low until the dough forms a ball (approximately 1 minute). Remove paddle and replace with dough hook or knead by hand for 10 minutes. Let the dough rest, covered, in the refrigerator a minimum of 2 hours.

For the stuffing, remove the breasts and legs from the duck. Remove all bones, skin and fat, discard. Dice the breast meat into ¼-inch cubes, set aside. In a food processor, finely grind the leg meat. Add the salt, nutmeg, Madeira, pepper, 1 egg, raisins and parsley, process to blend. Remove to a bowl and fold in diced breast meat.

Remove the dough from the refrigerator and roll it into thin sheets using a pasta machine or rolling pin. Brush one sheet with a beaten egg. Place a rounded teaspoon of stuffing every 1½ inches on dough. Place a second sheet over the stuffing and press down between stuffing. Cut out the ravioli.

Ravioli may be kept in the refrigerator, covered, for one day or frozen on a cookie sheet and then bagged. Frozen, they will keep for a month.

To cook, bring salted water to a boil, add ravioli and simmer 5 minutes.

The Old Lyme Inn

For the sauce, place the shallots and burgundy in a saucepan and reduce until almost dry. Add the veal stock and lingonberry preserves, reduce to 1½ cups. Add the watercress to the sauce and spoon over the hot ravioli.

Makes 3 to 4 dozen ravioli.

Stuffed Pork Loin
with Hazelnut and Frangelica Sauce

1 10- to 12-ounce pork tenderloin
2 pounds center-cut pork loin, closely trimmed
1 tablespoon shallots, finely diced
1 teaspoon black pepper
¼ cup parsley, chopped
1 egg white

❖   ❖   ❖

2 tablespoons shallots, finely diced
½ cup brandy
4 cups chicken stock
2 cups concentrated veal stock
3 ounces Frangelica
⅛ teaspoon ginger
½ cup hazelnuts, toasted
½ cup sweet butter (1 stick)

❖   ❖   ❖

2 pears
½ cup port wine
½ cup Chablis

Preheat a meat smoker for 15 minutes. Take the pork tenderloin directly from the refrigerator and place it in the smoker for 30 minutes. Remove and place in a 350° oven to bring to an internal temperature of 150°. Set aside to cool.

Insert a long, pointed slicing knife into the center of one end of the center-cut pork loin. Push the knife directly down the center of the loin to exit in the center of the other end. Do not cut through the sides of the loin. The cut should be approximately 1½ inches wide.

Combine 1 tablespoon shallots, pepper, parsley and the egg white. Open one end of the loin and fill with the shallot mixture. Place the smoked tenderloin between 2 long-handled kitchen utensils and guide the tenderloin into the loin using the handles.

Hold the tenderloin and remove the handles, secure with string. Sear the roast in hot oil. Roast in a 350° oven to an internal temperature of 140°.

For the Frangelica sauce, place 2 tablespoons shallots and brandy in a saucepan and reduce to almost dry. Add chicken and veal stocks and reduce to 1½ cups. Add Frangelica, ginger and hazelnuts, stir and remove from heat.

Peel and core the pears, cut into ¼-inch cubes. Poach ½ of the pear cubes in port wine and the other ½ in Chablis. Let each cool in its own poaching liquor.

To serve, bring the Frangelica sauce to a simmer. Remove from heat and whisk in small pieces of butter until all the butter is incorporated. Place slices of pork on each plate and top with sauce. Sprinkle heavily with heated, poached pears.

Serves 6.

Raspberry Cheese Japonaise

6 ounces toasted almonds
4 ounces toasted hazelnuts
4 tablespoons cornstarch
1½ cups sugar
9 egg whites

❖   ❖   ❖

18 ounces cream cheese, room temperature
¾ cup sugar
4 eggs, room temperature
3 ounces Chambord
¾ teaspoon vanilla extract

❖   ❖   ❖

½ pound cream cheese, room temperature
1 cup sweet butter (2 sticks), room temperature
3 tablespoons sour cream
1 teaspoon vanilla extract
5 ounces semisweet chocolate, melted
12 ounces raspberries, fresh or frozen

In a food processor, finely grind together the nuts, cornstarch, and ½ cup of the sugar. In a separate bowl whip

the egg whites with ½ cup sugar to soft peaks. Gently fold in the remaining ½ cup sugar and the nut mixture. Line a cookie sheet with buttered parchment paper and pipe and fill in 2 9-inch circles using a ½-inch round pastry tip. Pipe the remaining meringue into as many strips as possible. Bake in a 275° oven for approximately 1 hour. Remove and let dry. These can be made a day ahead.

In a mixing bowl, combine cream cheese and sugar, blend until smooth. Add eggs one at a time, scraping down the sides of the bowl twice. Add Chambord and vanilla extract and mix. Pour the batter into a buttered and floured 9-inch cake pan and place in the oven on a cookie sheet containing a small amount of water. Bake in a 350° oven for approximately 30 minutes, until a skewer comes out clean. Turn the oven off and let the cheesecake cool in the oven for 15 minutes with the door slightly open. Place the cheesecake in the refrigerator a minimum of one hour before assembling.

For the frosting, place the cream cheese and sweet butter in a food processor and process until smooth. Add the sour cream and vanilla and mix. Pour in melted chocolate and mix. Divide the chocolate frosting into 2 equal batches. Reserve 17 of the nicest raspberries for decoration and fold remaining berries into one batch of frosting. If the frosting is too thin to pipe, place in the refrigerator for a few minutes.

To assemble, begin with one meringue circle, and cover with ½ of the raspberry and chocolate frosting. Place the cheesecake on top, and top with the remaining raspberry and chocolate frosting. Place the remaining meringue circle on top. Frost the entire outside of the cake with the plain chocolate frosting. With a knife, mark the top for 16 slices. Cut the meringue strips into lengths equal to the height of the cake. Press the meringue strips against the sides of the cake. Pipe a border around the edge of the cake with a star tip, and pipe rosettes on each slice and one directly in the

center of the cake. Top each rosette with a raspberry. Let the cake sit a minimum of two hours before serving.
Serves 16.

The Mayflower Inn and Restaurant

Route 47
Washington, Connecticut 06793
(203) 868-0515

An 1894 colonial home, the Mayflower has been operating as an inn for over sixty years. It sits on thirty glorious wooded acres filled with wildlife and tranquility. The favorite pastimes here are strolling, reading, sipping wine, and good conversation. Rooms are not equipped with telephones and televisions, but the inn does boast a restaurant with excellent food, along with a cocktail parlor, piano music, crafts for sale, and an art gallery. Guests enjoy outdoor dining in the Summer and crackling fires in the Winter.

Mayflower's Tomato Soup

2 pounds onion, finely chopped
1½ cup vegetable oil
1 cup sugar

❖ ❖ ❖

6 cups tomato purée
¼ cup fresh lemon juice
2 cloves garlic, chopped
1 teaspoon allspice
3 bay leaves
Salt and pepper to taste

❖ ❖ ❖

2½ cups heavy cream

The Mayflower Inn and Restaurant

Sauté the onion in oil, add sugar and cook until caramelized (light gold). Add remaining ingredients except cream, mix well and simmer for 45 minutes. Add cream, heat, but do not boil, and serve.

The soup is quite thick but can be thinned with chicken stock.

Makes about 12 cups.

Mayflower's Baked Stuffed Shrimp with Crabmeat

24 large raw shrimp

❖ ❖ ❖

2 cups butter (4 sticks)
1 cup carrots, diced
1 cup onion, diced
1 cup celery, diced
1 cup green peppers, diced

❖ ❖ ❖

½ cup Parmesan cheese
2 cloves garlic, finely chopped

1 pound crabmeat, shredded
Salt and pepper to taste

❖ ❖ ❖

Bread crumbs

Remove the shells from shrimp with exception of the last tail section; butterfly and devein.

Prepare the stuffing by sautéing finely diced vegetables in butter for 10 minutes—they should still be *al dente;* add Parmesan, garlic, crabmeat, salt, and pepper, and sauté for an additional 5 minutes. Add enough bread crumbs to make a semi-firm stuffing.

Place shrimp on baking sheet, add stuffing to top of shrimp, and pack down firmly. Place the baking sheet in a pre-heated 400° oven and bake until firm to the touch.

Serves 6.

Mayflower's Zitronen Mousse

2 teaspoons gelatin
2 teaspoons white wine
⅓ cup lemon juice
1½ tablespoons grated lemon rind

❖ ❖ ❖

3 eggs, separated
⅓ cup sugar
1 cup heavy cream
Pinch salt

In a small bowl, sprinkle the gelatin over white wine to soften for 5 minutes; add lemon juice and rind and stir the mixture over hot water until the gelatin dissolves. Let the mixture cool but not set. In another bowl, beat the 3 egg yolks with 3 tablespoons of sugar until the mixture forms ribbons when the beater is lifted. Pour in the gelatin mixture in a stream, stirring constantly. In another bowl, beat the egg whites with a pinch of salt until they hold soft peaks. Combine whipped heavy cream with the egg yolk mixture and fold in ¼ of the meringue. Add the cream mixture to the remaining meringue and fold together gently until they are combined. Chill at least 2 hours.

Delaware

The Savannah Inn: Bed and Breakfast

330 Savannah Road
Lewes, Delaware 19958
(302) 645-5592

The Savannah Inn is situated in the town of Lewes, the first town in the first state, in a quiet and relaxing environment near major ocean resorts. Comfortable bedrooms with double beds await guests, and a large screened and glass porch offer comfort for sitting. Breakfast is served European style; the cuisine is vegetarian. The menu includes bran muffins or other homemade breads with jams, granola, fresh fruit, juices, and a variety of hot beverages. The Savannah Inn is open only during the Summer season.

Fresh Fruit Breakfast Cup

1 fresh pineapple, peeled, cored, and cut into chunks
1 pink grapefruit, peeled and sectioned
1 large (or 2 small) cantaloupe, in balls
1 honeydew melon, in balls
2 kiwi fruit, peeled and sliced in rounds
Large bunch of red seedless grapes
4 bananas, sliced in rounds
2 large peaches, peeled and sliced

Combine all fruit, preparing bananas and peaches last. No sugar or dressing is needed.

NOTE: Other fruit may be substituted or added as you like. Try to keep a variety of colors for eye appeal. Purple plums are a nice addition if they are not too sour.

Serves 15.

Granola

6 cups rolled oats
2 cups shredded coconut
1 cup wheat germ
1 cup chopped nuts (almonds or pecans)
1 cup hulled sunflower seeds
1 cup sesame seeds
❖ ❖ ❖
½ cup vegetable oil
¾ cup honey
2 teaspoons vanilla extract

Combine the dry ingredients. Ratio of dry ingredients to wet should be 8 to 1. For the quantity of dry ingredients listed above, combine and heat in a saucepan the oil, honey and vanilla.

Stir wet ingredients into dry and spread onto two greased cookie sheets. Bake in a 250° oven 20 to 30 minutes, stirring occasionally. Cool completely. Store in an airtight container.

Optional ingredients: grated toasted soybeans, bran, brown sugar, raisins and chopped dates.

Savannah Inn Bran Muffins

4 cups bran cereal
1½ cups boiling water
❖ ❖ ❖
2 cups 100% bran cereal
1 quart buttermilk
❖ ❖ ❖
1 cup shortening
2½ cups sugar
4 eggs
❖ ❖ ❖
1½ cups all-purpose flour
5 teaspoons baking soda
2 teaspoons salt
❖ ❖ ❖
3½ cups sifted whole wheat flour
❖ ❖ ❖
1 cup raisins

Place 4 cups of bran cereal in boiling water to soak a few minutes. Soak 2 cups 100% bran cereal in the buttermilk. While these mixtures soak, using a mixer or food processor, cream together shortening, sugar and eggs, and then combine with buttermilk mixture.

Sift together the flour, soda and salt; then add to buttermilk mixture. Stir into this the whole wheat flour.

Now add the 4 cups of bran cereal that has been soaking and the raisins. Stir to blend.

The Savanah Inn

been in operation for more than fifty years. The eighteen rooms, all with private baths and air conditioning, are in two houses and an additional small building to the rear of each. While the decor might be termed "early American attic," some very nice antiques are included. The inn is one and one-half blocks from the beach, which is the main attraction. Breakfast and dinner, which are served in the restaurant, are included in the summer rates; and the restaurant is open to the public. During the rest of the year, the rates include breakfast only.

Delaware Soft Top Rolls

½ cup shortening
1 cup hot mashed potatoes
2 teaspoons salt
⅔ cup sugar
1 ¼-ounce package active dry yeast
1 pint lukewarm milk (110 to 115°)
2 eggs
6 cups all-purpose flour

Mix the shortening with the potatoes, salt, and sugar. Dissolve the yeast in milk; add to the potato mixture. Beat the eggs in a mixing bowl. Pour in the potato mixture and stir well with a spoon. Add enough flour to make a soft dough. Rub the surface with melted fat. Leave in a warm place until double in bulk, about 3 hours. Use hands to form rolls, each about the size of a pullet egg; place in large greased muffin pans. Let rise until doubled. Bake in a 450° oven for 10 minutes.

Makes 5 dozen rolls.

This batter keeps well in the refrigerator for up to a week.

To bake, fill well-greased muffin cups ¾ full of batter and bake in 400° oven 20 to 25 minutes. Cool in pan 2 minutes before removing.

Makes 5 dozen muffins.

Apricot Roll

1 6-ounce package dried apricots
2 to 3 tablespoons sugar

❖ ❖ ❖

½ cup chopped pecans
Juice of ½ lemon

❖ ❖ ❖

1½ cups self-rising flour
1 tablespoon sugar
⅓ to ½ cup milk

❖ ❖ ❖

Whipped cream (optional)

Soak apricots in water overnight. Simmer in a little water and add sugar to taste. Blend in a blender or food processor. To make the filling, add pecans and lemon juice to the blended fruit.

To make pastry, combine the flour, sugar and enough milk to make a stiff biscuit dough, mixing gently until just combined. Turn out onto a floured board. Turn the dough over to flour both sides. Roll out the dough thinly on a floured board to form a large rectangle. Place filling along the center to within 1½ inches of edges. Fold the sides of dough over the center. Fold up the ends to seal and place on greased cookie sheet.

Bake in a 375° oven for 15 to 20 minutes, until brown. Serve warm.

Note: This makes a delicious dessert with whipped cream. Also, it is great for a holiday breakfast or brunch.

Serves 2.

The Corner Cupboard Inn

50 Park Avenue
Rehoboth Beach, Delaware 19971
(302) 227-8553

The Corner Cupboard Inn, "The inn that was in before inns were in," has

Crab Imperial

1 pound crab meat (carefully
**   picked over for shells)**
½ cup finely chopped green pepper
½ cup chopped pimiento
2 slices crustless white bread
2 eggs, beaten
1 cup mayonnaise
Dash Worcestershire sauce

^{1}/8 teaspoon cayenne pepper
1 teaspoon dry mustard
1 tablespoon mustard
¼ teaspoon salt
Juice of ½ lemon

❖ ❖ ❖

Mayonnaise
Paprika

Combine in a mixing bowl the crab meat, green pepper, and pimiento. Crumble the slices of bread and add to the mixture. Add the eggs, mayonnaise, Worcestershire, cayenne, mustards, salt, and lemon juice, mix gently. Place in a buttered 1½-quart casserole dish or 6 ramekins. Top with mayonnaise and a pinch of paprika. Bake in a 400° oven for 15 to 20 minutes, until lightly brown. Serve at once.
Serves 6.

Beef Stroganoff
for Fifty People

18 to 20 pounds of top round
4 pounds mushrooms
2 pounds shallots (or spring onions)
Butter
Olive oil

❖ ❖ ❖

1 6-ounce tomato paste (or ketchup)
½ to 1 teaspoon Tabasco sauce
¼ cup Worcestershire sauce
2 tablespoons tarragon
3 quarts sour cream
1½ to 2 cups Sherry
Salt and pepper to taste

Prepare the top round by cutting it into cubes or thin strips. Cut the large mushrooms in half; chop the shallots. In a large heavy frypan sauté the mushrooms and shallots in an equal mixture of butter and olive oil. Cook until tender; do not brown. Sear the top round in a hot pan. Brown only; do not cook. Combine the two mixtures in a large pan over low heat.

To the meat mixture add tomato paste, Tabasco, Worcestershire, tarragon, sour cream, and Sherry. (Add more sour cream or Sherry to adjust the consistency.) Heat through but do not boil, it will curdle. Add salt and

pepper to taste. Adjust the other seasonings as necessary.
Serves 50.

Pecan Pie

1 cup pecans
1 unbaked 9-inch pie shell
½ cup brown sugar, firmly packed
1 cup dark corn syrup
1 tablespoon butter
1 teaspoon vanilla extract
4 eggs, whipped lightly

Place the pecans in the bottom of the pie shell. Combine the sugar, corn syrup, butter, and vanilla. Then add the eggs; mix thoroughly. Bake in a 350° oven about 30 minutes or until the filling is set. Must be watched.
Serves 6 to 8.

Sour Cream Raisin Pie

2 eggs, slightly beaten
1 cup sugar
1 cup sour cream
1 tablespoon all-purpose flour
⅛ teaspoon salt
½ teaspoon cinnamon
½ teaspoon nutmeg
1 cup seedless raisins, chopped
½ cup chopped walnut meats (optional)
1 unbaked 9-inch pie shell

❖ ❖ ❖

2 egg whites
3 tablespoons sugar

In a mixing bowl beat together the 2 eggs and 1 cup of sugar; gradually stir in the sour cream. In a separate bowl mix together the flour, salt, and spices; stir into the raisins and nuts. Add to the egg mixture. Pour into the pie shell. Bake in a 450° oven for 10 minutes, then lower the temperature to 350° and bake for 15 to 20 minutes longer.

While the pie bakes prepare the meringue. Beat the 2 egg whites until foamy. Gradually add 3 tablespoons of sugar, beating until stiff. Remove the

pie from the oven when the baking time is finished. Add the meringue and bake an additional 10 minutes.
Serves 6 to 8.

Small Wonder Bed and Breakfast

Post Office Box 25254
Wilmington, Delaware 19899
(302) 764-0789

At Small Wonder Bed and Breakfast, guests enjoy their stay in a modified Cape Cod home, decorated traditionally in wedgewood blue with mauve and white highlights. Inn entertainment includes Small Wonder's Baldwin piano or organ, stereo, television, books, shuffleboard, table games, rebounder, exercise gym, and an exhibit of original paintings by Delaware artist Lloyd W. Kline.

Hot Apple Cereal

4 cups skim milk
½ cup brown sugar or 8 packages Nutrasweet
2 teaspoons margarine
½ teaspoon salt
½ teaspoon cinnamon
2 cups rolled oats
2 cups peeled and chopped apples
1 cup walnuts
1 cup raisins
1 cup wheat germ

Combine the milk, brown sugar, margarine, salt and cinnamon. Scald. Combine the remaining ingredients in a greased 2 quart casserole. Cover.

Bake in a 350° oven for 45 minutes or microwave 10 minutes at full power. Stir several times.
Serves 6 to 8.

District of Columbia

Adams Inn Bed and Breakfast

1744 Lanier Place, Northwest
Washington, D.C. 20009
(202) 745-3600

Adams Inn specializes in hospitable and comfortable surroundings in a personal atmosphere. The rooms are furnished homestyle. Some rooms have a private bath; the rest have a wash basin in the room and share a bath. Guests may relax and socialize in the sitting parlor. A continental breakfast is served in the spacious dining room.

The Adams Inn is just two miles north of the White House in the city's most interesting and diverse neighborhood. The inn is within walking distance of the three major convention hotels: the Shoreham, the Washington Hilton, and the Washington–Sheraton. Many of Washington's top rated restaurants are only a block or two away, and boutiques, antiques and international shops abound.

Nancy's Ham Quiche

1 8-inch deep dish pie shell
½ cup diced ham
½ pound Swiss cheese, diced
4 eggs
½ teaspoon salt
½ teaspoon pepper
1 cup milk

❖ ❖ ❖

Nutmeg (optional)

Chill the pie shell. Sprinkle ham on the bottom of the shell. Put the remaining ingredients except nutmeg in blender; blend until fine. Pour over the ham. Bake in a 375° oven for about 40 minutes, until the crust is browned and the custard is set. Can be sprinkled with nutmeg if desired.
Serves 6.

Petros a la Douglas

2 15-ounce cans chili (with or without beans)
1 8-ounce package Fritos
1 cup (4 ounces) grated Cheddar cheese
4 cups chopped lettuce
1 medium tomato, chopped
Sour cream

Heat the chili. Arrange the Fritos on 5 or 6 plates. Divide the chili over the Fritos; then sprinkle with cheese, lettuce, chopped tomato, and top with a dollop of sour cream.
Serves 5 or 6.

Honey Gingered Chicken

3 cups oil
1 chicken, cut in serving pieces
⅓ cup lemon juice
2 teaspoons cornstarch
2 teaspoons soy sauce
½ teaspoon five spice powder
1 cup white wine
1½ teaspoons grated fresh ginger
6 green onions, chopped
3 tablespoons honey

❖ ❖ ❖

Cooked rice

In a large frypan heat oil and fry the chicken pieces until brown and fork tender. Drain the chicken on paper towels. Drain the oil from the frypan. Place the lemon juice, cornstarch, soy sauce, five spice powder, and white wine in the frypan; cook until smooth and well blended. Add ginger and green onions; cook about 2 minutes. Add honey; cook 1 minute. Place the chicken back into the sauce for about 3 minutes. Serve on rice.
Serves 4.

Scottish Oat Cakes

4 cups rolled oats
¾ cup all-purpose flour
1½ teaspoons baking powder
½ cup butter (1 stick)
2 to 3 tablespoons milk

Process the oats in a food processor until fine. Combine with the remaining ingredients to form a stiff dough; let rest for 30 minutes. Roll out to ¼-inch thickness on a floured surface. Cut into circles.

Bake in a 400° oven for 4 to 8 minutes or until golden. Serve with butter and honey.

Makes about 3 dozen cakes.

Sybille's English Trifle

1 sponge cake
Raspberry preserves
1 29-ounce can fruit salad
⅓ cup Sherry

❖ ❖ ❖

1 3-ounce package vanilla pudding
    mix

❖ ❖ ❖

½ cup whipping cream (whipped)

Cut the sponge cake in half and spread with preserves. Layer both halves in the bottom of a glass bowl. Drain the juice from the can of fruit salad and combine with the Sherry; pour over the cake and let it soak. Layer the drained fruit over the top.

  Prepare the pudding according to label directions; let cool. Spread over the fruit and chill until set. Garnish with whipped cream. May be decorated with fruit or slivered almonds.
    Serves 12.

Fantastic Frosted Fattening Brownies

1 cup margarine (2 sticks)
½ cup cocoa
2 cups sugar
1½ cups all-purpose flour
Pinch salt
4 eggs
½ cup nuts
1 teaspoon vanilla extract

❖ ❖ ❖

¼ cup margarine (½ stick)
⅓ cup cocoa
⅓ cup milk
1 teaspoon vanilla extract
1 pound confectioners' sugar

❖ ❖ ❖

4½ cups miniature marshmallows

Place 1 cup of margarine and ½ cup of cocoa in a saucepan. Heat over low heat until the margarine melts. Place 2 cups of sugar, the flour, salt, and eggs in a mixing bowl. Stir in the cocoa mixture. Add the nuts and vanilla, mix well. Pour into a greased jelly roll pan. Bake in a 350° oven for 20 minutes.

  While the brownies are baking make the frosting. Place ¼ cup of margarine, ⅓ cup cocoa, and milk in a saucepan. Heat over low heat until the margarine melts. Add the vanilla and confectioners' sugar. Beat until smooth.

  When the brownies have finished baking, remove from the oven and turn off the heat. Spread the marshmallows over the top of the brownies and place the pan back into the oven for 2 minutes. Remove from the oven again and swirl the frosting around over the marshmallows. Cut into 2 x 1-inch bars.

  Makes 42 bars.

Florida

Hotel Place St. Michel

Restaurant St. Michel
162 Alcazar Avenue
Coral Gables, Florida 33134
(305) 444-1666 Hotel
(305) 446-7183 Charcuterie
(305) 446-6572 Restaurant

Hotel Place St. Michel is a small, charming European style inn unexpectedly nestled in a tropical setting. The building is remembered by some as the historical Sevilla Hotel, built in 1926 and host to discriminating travelers of that era. Awareness of this architectural heritage has guided the management in restoring the hotel to its original character. The result is a small hotel that each guest deserves to know. Within the building are a thirty-room hotel, an outstanding French restaurant, and a gathering of fine shops, including the Charcuterie St. Michel, which features elegant cuisine-to-go. The hotel is an active part of Coral Gables, just minutes from galleries, theatres, museums, golf courses, tennis courts, sparkling beaches, Miami International Airport, Coconut Grove on Biscayne Bay, and Downtown Miami.

Chicken and Shrimp St. Michel

½ cup butter (1 stick)
2 shallots, chopped
4 mushrooms, chopped
4 chicken breast halves
8 jumbo shrimps
6 tablespoons Brandy
6 tablespoons heavy cream
Salt and pepper to taste
½ bunch marjoram, chopped

Melt the butter in a frypan; sauté the shallots and mushrooms. Add the chicken breasts and shrimps. Pour in the Brandy and flambé. Add the cream, salt, pepper, and marjoram. Remove the chicken breasts and shrimps, place on a serving platter and keep warm. Continue to cook the sauce over low heat until reduced and of a creamy consistency; pour over the chicken breasts and shrimps. Serve very hot.
Serves 4.

Entrecôte Marchand de Vin

10 tablespoons butter
6 8-ounce sirloin steaks

❖ ❖ ❖

8 shallots, chopped
1 teaspoon flour
Salt and pepper to taste
½ bunch marjoran, chopped
1½ cups red wine
½ cup beef stock

Melt the butter in a large frypan. Sauté the sirloin to desired tenderness; remove and place in a warming dish.

Using the same frypan, sauté the shallots for 3 minutes. Stir in the flour; then add the salt, pepper, marjoram, and wine. Turn the heat to high and flambé the wine to eliminate the alcohol. Then add the stock; cook over low heat 3 minutes. Pour the sauce over the meat and serve.
Serves 6.

Red Snapper
with Green Pepper Corn Sauce

4 red snapper fillets, skinned and
    boned
½ cup butter (1 stick)

❖ ❖ ❖

¼ cup fish stock
¾ cup heavy cream
6 tarragon leaves
3 ounces green pepper corn
Salt to taste

Coat the fillets with flour. Melt the butter in a large frypan. Sauté the fillets, turning carefully with a spatula to avoid breaking them. When nicely browned, add the stock, cream, tarragon leaves, green pepper corn, and salt. Cook over low heat until reduced or place in a 350° oven for 10 minutes.
Serves 4.

73

Veal Provencale

3 tomatoes
6 tablespoons olive oil
3 scallions, chopped
8 veal scallopini
Salt and pepper
6 tablespoons dry white wine
½ bunch basil

Chop the tomatoes after removing the skin and seeds. Set aside. Heat the oil in a frypan. Sauté the scallions and scallopini. Then add the salt, pepper, tomatoes, wine, and basil. Cover the pan and cook over low heat until reduced, about 5 minutes.

Serves 6.

Velouté of Asparagus

6 tablespoons butter
5 scallions, chopped
1 pound asparagus tips

❖   ❖   ❖

½ cup wine
¾ cup heavy cream
Salt and pepper to taste
½ teaspoon nutmeg
⅔ cup water

❖   ❖   ❖

Croutons

In a large saucepan melt the butter, sauté the scallions and asparagus for 2 minutes. Add the wine, cream, salt, pepper, nutmeg, and water. Cook for 5 minutes. Place in a blender, process until very thin. Serve very hot, garnished with croutons.

Serves 6.

Lemon Bay Bed and Breakfast

Post Office Box 422
Englewood, Florida 33533
(813) 474-7571

The Lemon Bay Bed and Breakfast is a casual arrangement with a maximum of two nights' stay. Its one room has its own bathroom, double bed, cot, and closet with a carpeted floor and full view of the enormous Canary Island. A full breakfast is served. Guests who enjoy fishing are encouraged to fish from the dock.

Mabel's Corncakes

1⅓ cups buttermilk
1 tablespoon oil
1 teaspoon baking soda
1 egg
1 teaspoon salt
¾ cup corn meal
¼ cup flour

Combine the ingredients and mix well. Drop by heaping tablespoons onto a hot griddle. Cook until golden on each side.

These are served with homemade jam and Vermont maple syrup.

Serves 2 to 4.

Eaton Lodge

511 Eaton Street
Key West, Florida 33040
(305) 294-3800

A hundred years ago, 511 Eaton Street was built to the highest standards as a private residence. It is now listed as an architectually important building. Each room in the lodge has its individual character, "Victorian" but tropical and airy. The many handsome details, such as paneled walls and polished wood floors, have been enhanced by discreet modernization and the use of fabrics and rugs from England. The original coachhouse, tucked into the lush rear garden, has been attractively adapted to provide guest rooms with verandahs and studio apartments with patios. Paddle ceiling fans throughout continue the airy theme. Each room has dual windows, allowing Eaton Lodge to take full advantage of the famous Key West breeze.

Housekeeper's Applesauce Cake

2 cups all-purpose flour
1 cup sugar
1 teaspoon cinnamon
½ teaspoon mace or nutmeg
¼ teaspoon cloves
2 teaspoons baking soda
1 cup raisins
1 cup pecans
1½ cups applesauce (1 1-pound can)
1 teaspoon salt

❖   ❖   ❖

½ cup margarine (1 stick)

Combine all of the ingredients except margarine in a bowl. Melt the margarine in a baking pan, and pour over the other ingredients. Mix well. Pour into a 9 x 9 x 2-inch pan or an 11 x 7 x 2-inch pan, and bake in a 350° oven for 45 to 50 minutes.

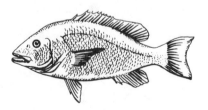

Chalet Suzanne Restaurant and Country Inn

Post Office Drawer A C
Lake Wales, Florida 33859-9003
(813) 676-6011

Chalet Suzanne Restaurant and Country Inn

The experience begins as guests wind their way along a country road and come upon this very special creation. The Hinshaw family has been making guests welcome for over fifty years, whether they come by car or by a plane landing at the private airstrip on the grounds. The inn has thirty rooms, nestled on a charming seventy-acre estate beautifully landscaped with palm trees leaning with the breeze. The guestrooms are warm, delightfully different, and provide privacy for all.

Shrimp Suzanne with Dill

½ cup sour cream
½ cup mayonnaise
½ cup peeled grated cucumber, seeded
⅓ cup minced onion
1½ tablespoons fresh chopped dill
1½ teaspoons lemon juice
Garlic to taste
Salt and pepper
8 drops Tabasco sauce
¼ teaspoon caraway seed

❖ ❖ ❖

1 pound shrimp (25 to 30 count), cooked, peeled, and cleaned
Bibb lettuce

Combine the first ten ingredients together to make a sauce. Stir in shrimp. Mix well and chill. Serve on a bed of Bibb lettuce, either as individual servings or in a lettuce-lined bowl.
Serves 4 to 6.

Stuffed Eggplants

6 medium eggplants

❖ ❖ ❖

4 bell peppers
4 medium onions
½ cup celery
3 cloves garlic
1 pound small shrimp
1 pound white lump crab meat
½ cup parsley
Bread crumbs
Salt and pepper to taste
Paprika

Boil the eggplants until soft; then remove the pulp. Save eggplant shells. Sauté bell peppers, onion, celery and garlic until limp, then add the eggplant meat. Simmer on medium heat until most of the water is cooked out, then add the shrimp. Cook for another 20 minutes, then put all of this in another bowl. Fold in crab meat and parsley. Let cool a little, then add enough bread crumbs for the mixture to hold together, add salt and pepper to taste, and stuff the shells. Add a few bread crumbs, paprika, and butter on top. Bake in a 350° oven until done.
Serves 12.

Hopp-Inn Guest House

Bed & Breakfast Inc. of the Florida Keys
5 Man-O-War Drive
Marathon, Florida 33050
(305) 743-4118

The Hopp-Inn Guest House is on the ocean in Marathon, the heart of the Florida keys. It has three guest rooms, each with its private bath and a private entrance. Rooms are decorated with bamboo and tropical plants. The surroundings are tropical, with hibiscus, palm trees, poinsettias, banana trees, and many varieties of cactus. A full American breakfast of sausage or bacon, eggs or french toast, and/or cereal and muffins is served. The Inn also has two guest apartments, both with an ocean view. These apartments are furnished with a king-sized bed in the master bedroom and have a separate living room/kitchen combination. Activities available include fishing, snorkeling, scuba diving, visiting Key West, John Pennykamp State Park, Bahia Honda State Park, The Dolphin Research Center, and The Theatre of the Sea in Islamorada.

Cherry Omelet

1 17-ounce can dark pitted cherries
  (or frozen)
2 teaspoons cornstarch (or enough
  to thicken cherry mixture)

❖ ❖ ❖

6 eggs
2 tablespoons milk
Dash salt and pepper
Margarine

In a small saucepan combine the cornstarch and cherries. Cook over low
heat, stirring often, until the mixture
thickens, about 4 to 5 minutes.

In a medium bowl, beat the eggs,
milk, salt and pepper. In a 10-inch skillet or omelet pan, melt margarine over
medium heat tilting pan to cover the
bottom. Pour the egg mixture into the
skillet; reduce heat to allow the uncooked egg to flow to the bottom of the
pan, tilting as necessary. Cook until
the mixture is set (top will remain
moist). Place some of the cherry mixture on half the omelet, fold in half, and
place some on top as a garnish.
Serves 4.

Key Lime Muffins

Key limes are a favorite of the Florida
Keys.

2 cups sifted all-purpose flour
1 cup sugar
3 teaspoons baking powder
½ teaspoon salt

❖ ❖ ❖

¼ cup milk
2 eggs lightly beaten
¼ cup vegetable oil
1 teaspoon grated lime rind
¼ cup lime juice

Sift together the flour, sugar, baking
powder and salt into a large bowl.
Combine the milk, eggs, oil, rind and
juice. Add all at once to the flour mixture, stir lightly with a fork just until
moist (batter will be lumpy). Spoon
into greased muffin cups, filling each
¾ full. Bake in a 400° oven for 20 minutes or until golden. Remove muffins

from pan to wire rack. Serve warm
with butter if you wish, and/or orange
marmalade.
Makes 12 muffins.

Christmas Baked Apples

6 apples
1 5¼-ounce package cinnamon
  imperials
2 cups water
Whipped cream topping

Core apples and cut a 1-inch strip
around top to prevent splitting. Place
apples in an 8-inch square baking dish.
In a small pan simmer slowly the cinnamon candies and water, stirring often to prevent the candies from
sticking to the bottom of the pan.
When thickened, fill apples with
candy syrup, place in a 350° oven and
baste often so they become red in
color. Serve with whipped topping.
Serves 6.

Lemon Fruit Dip

8 ounces lemon yogurt
8 ounces sour cream
1 tablespoon honey
¼ teaspoon lemon juice

In a small bowl, combine yogurt, sour
cream, honey and lemon juice, blend
well. Cover and refrigerate 1 or 2
hours or overnight. Serve with fresh
fruit, such as strawberries, bananas,
white seedless grapes or melon
wedges.
Makes 2½ cups of dip.

Key Lime Cream Cheese Pie

4 egg yolks
1 14-ounce can condensed milk
½ cup Key lime juice

1 8-ounce package cream cheese,
  softened
1 9-inch pie shell or graham
  cracker crust
Whipped cream topping

Combine egg yolks, condensed milk
and lime juice. When cream cheese is
very soft, fold into milk mixture. Place
in pie shell and refrigerate overnight.
Serve with whipped cream topping.
Serves 6.

Casa De Solana

21 Aviles Street
St. Augustine, Florida 32084
(904) 824-3555

Casa De Solana is a lovingly renovated colonial home in the heart of St.
Augustine's historical area, within
walking distance of restaurants, museums, and quaint shops. All four
antique-filled guest accommodations
are suites, some with fireplaces, some
with balconies that overlook the beautiful garden, and others with a breathtaking view of the Matanzas Bay. All
have private baths. Tariff includes a full
breakfast served in the formal guest
dining room, morning newspaper,
chocolates, decanter of sherry, and the
use of bicycles for touring the ever-
inviting city of St. Augustine.

Lost Bread

"This breakfast recipe was given to the
Casa De Solana several years ago by a
Sarasota client who had become in-
tensely interested in New Orleans cui-
sine. Its name, 'Lost Bread,' refers to
the fact that it was a way to use stale
bread. He said he did not know of any
New Orleans restaurants that now
serve it. We once saw a reference to
'Lost Bread' in a culinary article on
New Orleans but it was described as
French toast.

"The real secret of this recipe seems to be that the frying process caramelizes the strawberry preserves. We have tried other kinds of preserves but none seemed to taste as good as strawberry."

Per serving:

**2 slices French bread (1½ to 2
    inches thick)
Strawberry preserves**

❖ ❖ ❖

**2 eggs
2 tablespoons half and half
Dash vanilla extract**

❖ ❖ ❖

Confectioners' sugar

Cut the crust off the bottom side of the bread and then cut a pocket in the bottom. Fill the pocket with a heaping tablespoon of strawberry preserves and press the pocket closed. Beat eggs, half and half, and vanilla. Soak bread in egg mixture for a minute or so. In a deep fry pan (we use a Chinese wok) heat cooking oil (enough to completely cover the slice of bread) so that when you lay the filled slice of bread in it, it will brown quickly. As soon as it is brown on one side, turn over and brown on the other. Drain on paper towels and sprinkle with confectioners' sugar. If you are preparing for a large number, keep warm in oven and sprinkle with sugar just before serving.

Serves 1.

Arroz Con Langostinos
Rice with Shrimp

"This recipe was given to us by our brother-in-law, Edmund (Ted) Blackwell. He related the following story.

"One day he had some leftover chicken broth and he had planned to have shrimp for dinner. So he went into the kitchen before his wife came home from work and started adding a pinch of this and a can of that, and by the time she arrived he had dinner prepared except for a salad, which she made. They were so pleased with the flavor that he later invited us over for dinner and made the same dish. We in turn enjoyed it so much we asked him for the recipe. Now that was the hard part of it, because this recipe was all in his head, but we all had a fun-filled afternoon going through a make-believe preparation of this dish in order to get the ingredients. We later talked about other seafoods that could be used instead of shrimp, such as lobster, scallops or mussels, or one could make this dish using chicken. It is a complete meal within itself. A green tossed salad with a light creamy dressing compliments this dish, but is not needed."

2 pounds shrimp

❖ ❖ ❖

**2 14½-ounce cans chicken stock
½ cup chopped celery tops
1 clove garlic, minced
2 medium tomatoes, chopped
¼ teaspoon coriander
½ teaspoon turmeric
¼ teaspoon cumin
2 bay leaves
Pinch seasoned pepper
½ teaspoon Seafood seasoning**

❖ ❖ ❖

**¼ cup olive oil
4 green onions (reserve green tops)
1 bell pepper, chopped
1½ cups white rice, cooked
1 3-ounce can mushrooms, drained
1 2-ounce jar pimiento
½ cup olives**

❖ ❖ ❖

**Pinch turmeric
1 8½-ounce can English peas
Salt and pepper to taste**

Peel the shrimp and put peelings in a large saucepan; add the two cans of chicken stock with celery tops, minced garlic, and chopped tomatoes, and add coriander, turmeric, cumin, bay leaves, seasoned pepper, and Seafood seasoning. Bring to a boil and let simmer on low heat while preparing in a large frying pan ¼ cup olive oil, green onions, and bell pepper. Cook slowly until done. Add rice, stir and allow the rice to become clear looking. Strain the broth and add into the rice mixture. Add mushrooms, pimiento, and olives. Add the shrimp (leaving some of the shrimp whole and with the tail on for decoration) which have been cut up in large chunks. Add a pinch of

Casa De Solana

turmeric for color, English peas, and salt and pepper to taste. Cook on low temperature for about 30 minutes. Sprinkle some chopped green onion tops over the dish when done.

Serves 6.

The St. Francis Inn

279 St. George Street
St. Augustine, Florida 32084
(904) 824-6068

The St. Francis Inn has been a part of St. Augustine's history for almost 200 years, and today it is a classic example of Old World architecture and charm. The inn is situated in the heart of the historic section of the oldest city on the North American continent. The Spanish style entrance faces a courtyard and garden containing lush banana trees, bougainvillea, jasmine, and other tropical flowers and shrubs. A patio and balcony overlook the courtyard garden. The main shopping area, post office, and churches are all within a short walking distance of the inn. Those who choose to reside here enjoy a convenient location, historical atmosphere, and quiet comfort: the perfect residence, whether for a short visit or an extended stay.

Citrus Muffins

1¾ cups sifted all-purpose flour
3 tablespoons sugar
2½ teaspoons baking powder
½ teaspoon salt
❖ ❖ ❖
1 egg
¾ cup milk
⅓ cup unsalted butter, melted
1 tablespoon grated orange rind
1 tablespoon grated lime rind
❖ ❖ ❖

¼ cup unsalted butter (½ stick)
Sugar

Sift together the flour, 3 tablespoons sugar, baking powder, and salt. Beat eggs, milk, ⅓ cup butter (melted); stir in the rinds. Pour into the flour mixture. Stir until the ingredients are moistened. Do not overstir. Fill greased muffin cups ⅔ full. Bake in a 400° oven for 20 minutes. (Brush with melted butter, dip in sugar . . . optional.)

Makes 12 to 15 muffins.

Orange Butter

1 tablespoon minced orange peel
½ cup unsalted butter (1 stick)
1 8-ounce package cream cheese
1 orange, sectioned and chopped
2 tablespoons honey

Whip the orange peel, butter, and cream cheese. Stir in orange pieces and honey. Refrigerate at least 2 hours.

Makes the equivalent of 1 pound of butter.

Ozark Pudding

2 eggs
1½ cups sugar
6 tablespoons sifted all-purpose flour
2½ teaspoons baking powder
¼ teaspoon salt
2 teaspoons vanilla extract
❖ ❖ ❖
1 apple, pared and diced
1 cup chopped walnuts

Beat the eggs with sugar. Mix in the flour, baking powder, and salt. Add vanilla and stir well. Blend in apple and walnuts. Pour into a greased 9x13-inch pan.

Bake in a 350° oven for 20 to 25 minutes. Cool. May be served plain, with fresh cream poured over the top, or with ice cream.

Serves 12.

Konakai Motel

1539 Periwinkle Way
Sanibel Island, Florida 33957

The Konakai Motel, on beautiful Sanibel Island, has twelve guest rooms. The decor is tropical, depicting an old Hawaiian garden. A large swimming pool for guests is on the premises.

Broccoli Chicken Casserole

2 10-ounce packages frozen chopped broccoli
2 10¾ cans cream of chicken soup (or 2½ cups thickened chicken or turkey broth)
2 cups diced cooked chicken (or turkey)
1 8-ounce package seasoned poultry stuffing

Cook the broccoli in a large saucepan with boiling salted water until tender. Drain and layer in the bottom of a shallow 12 x 7½-inch baking dish.

Heat the soup and combine with the chicken. Layer over the broccoli.

Prepare the stuffing according to package directions. Place 3 cups of the prepared stuffing over the top of the casserole. Bake in a 350° oven for 30 minutes.

Serves 8.

Georgia

The De Loffre House

812 Broadway
Columbus, Georgia 31901
(404) 324-1144

The De Loffre House is an 1863 townhouse, elegantly restored and modernized, where guests may enjoy Victorian charm and the gracious hospitality of the South. Five luxurious guest rooms, some with original fireplaces, have been attractively decorated and furnished with antiques. To add to the comfort and convenience, each room is provided with a complimentary bowl of fruit and decanter of wine, as well as private bath, phone, and television. Complimentary continental breakfast is served in the handsomely appointed candlelit dining room between 8 and 10 A.M., with newspapers, antique china, and homemade sweet breads.

Date Nut Bread

1 cup chopped dates
2 teaspoons baking soda
2 cups boiling water

❖ ❖ ❖

2 tablespoons butter
1 cup brown sugar, firmly packed
1 cup granulated sugar

2 eggs

❖ ❖ ❖

4 cups sifted all-purpose flour
1 teaspoon salt

❖ ❖ ❖

2 teaspoons vanilla extract
1½ cups chopped nuts

Combine dates, baking soda, and boiling water; let cool. In a large bowl, cream together butter, sugars, and eggs. Add flour and salt. Add date mixture, vanilla, and nuts. Bake in 5 12-ounce (no. 2) cans in a 350° oven for 1 hour.

Makes 5 loaves.

The Smith House

202 South Chestatee Street
Dahlonega, Georgia 30533
(404) 864-3566

The story of the Smith House goes back to 1884, when Captain Hall purchased an acre of land east of the town square and began to excavate the land in order to build. When his son discovered a rich vein of gold ore, the city officials would not allow him to mine for gold just one block from the public square. After losing his lawsuit against the city, Hall build his house on top of the vein.

In 1922 Henry and Bessie Smith purchased the property and turned their home into an inn with seven rooms for travelers. Today the Smith House is composed of three establishments: a family-style restaurant, a country inn, and an authentic gift shop. Guests experience true southern hospitality and some of the finest food the South has to offer. The seven rooms have grown to fifteen.

Squash Casserole

3 pounds squash
2 medium onions, chopped
2 medium carrots, grated
1 cup sour cream
2 10¾-ounce cans cream of chicken soup
1 8-ounce package seasoned poultry stuffing
½ cup butter (1 stick), melted

Cook the squash, onions and carrots in salted water until tender. Drain and add sour cream and soup. Mix the stuffing with butter. Alternate layers of the squash mixture with the buttered stuffing, ending with stuffing on top. Bake in a 350° oven for 30 minutes.

Serves 6 to 8.

Rice and Chicken Casserole

1 10¾-ounce can cream of mushroom soup
1 soup can milk
¾ cup uncooked regular rice
1 4-ounce can mushroom stems and pieces

1 1¼-ounce package dry onion
    soup mix

❖   ❖   ❖

4 chicken breast halves

Combine the mushroom soup and milk in a mixing bowl; reserve ½ cup of the mixture. To the remaining soup mixture add the rice, mushrooms with liquid, and ½ the onion soup mix. Pour into an ungreased 12 x 7-inch baking dish. Place the chicken breasts on top. Pour the reserved soup mixture over the chicken breasts; sprinkle with remaining onion soup mix. Cover with aluminum foil. Bake in a 350° oven for 1 hour. Uncover and bake 15 minutes.
    Serves 4.

Worley Homestead

410 West Main Street
Dahlonega, Georgia 30533
(404) 864-7002

Worley Homestead has seven bedrooms, each with a private bath. Three guestrooms have fireplaces, as do the parlor and dining room. The home is furnished with antiques and the gracious staff wear period costumes. Every effort is made for guests to have the feeling of going back in time, but with modern conveniences. Adjoining the homestead is a two bedroom, one bath cottage of a later vintage, also furnished with antiques. The private parlor, dining nook, kitchen, and canopied master bed make Chestnut Cottage perfect for honeymooners. Breakfast at the main house is included. Breakfast is served from 8 to 10 each morning in the dining room and features foods that would have been served in the late 1800s. It is included in the cost of the room.

Cheesy Egg Casserole

6 eggs
½ cup all-purpose flour
1 teaspoon baking powder
⅛ teaspoon salt
1 cup milk

❖   ❖   ❖

8 ounces cottage cheese
1 3-ounce package cream cheese,
    cubed

❖   ❖   ❖

2 tablespoons butter
1 pound Monterey Jack Cheese,
    cubed

In a large bowl, beat the eggs. Add flour, baking powder, salt, and milk, beating until smooth. Beat in the cottage cheese. Stir in the cubed cream cheese and cubed Monterey Jack cheese. Pour into a well-greased and floured 2-quart baking dish. Dot with butter. Bake in a 350° oven for 45 minutes.
    Serves 6.

Ginger Snap Cookies

1½ cups margarine (3 sticks)
2 cups brown sugar, firmly packed
2 eggs
½ cup molasses
4 cups all-purpose flour
½ teaspoon salt
4 teaspoons baking soda
2 teaspoons cloves
2 teaspoons ginger
2 teaspoons cinnamon

❖   ❖   ❖

Sugar

Combine all ingredients except the sugar, form into small balls. Roll balls of dough in the sugar. Bake in a 350° oven for 10 minutes.
    Makes 3½ to 4 dozen.

❖ ❖ ❖ ❖ ❖ ❖

The Stovall House

Route 1, Box 103-A
Sautée, Georgia 30571
(404) 878-3355

The Stovall House, built in 1837, is a Victorian eclectic farmhouse transformed to an inn in 1983. Situated on twenty-eight acres in a valley, the porches and rooms afford the guests views of mountains in all directions. The five guest rooms have private baths and are decorated with family antiques and handiworked stenciling, draperies, net-darned curtains and needlework, which instill the guests with a feeling of being at home. The fifty-seat restaurant provides an intimate, but casual, atmosphere in which patrons can enjoy the unique menu featuring homegrown vegetables and herbs. A country experience to take home.

Cheese Muffins

2 cups all-purpose flour
1 tablespoon baking powder
2 tablespoons sugar
⅛ teaspoon garlic salt
Dash pepper
1 egg
1 cup milk
¼ cup oil
1 cup grated Cheddar cheese

Combine all of the ingredients and bake in greased muffin cups in a 350° oven for 15 minutes.
    Makes 12 to 15 muffins.

Chicken Tetrazzini in Phyllo

4 tablespoons butter
½ cup all-purpose flour

2 cups milk
1 cup chicken stock
3 tablespoons white wine
Dash salt
1 clove garlic
¼ cup Parmesan cheese
3½ cups diced chicken

❖ ❖ ❖

Butter
1 16-ounce box phyllo dough

Make a roux with butter and flour; slowly add milk and whisk until smooth. Add the stock, wine, and seasonings, and mix in chicken.

Lay a sheet of phyllo on a flat surface, brush with melted butter and cover with a second sheet. Spoon 3 heaping tablespoons of chicken mixture on one end of sheets; fold in sides and roll up, burrito style. Continue in this manner, using up the phyllo and filling. Place on a greased baking sheet, brush with butter and bake in a 350° oven for 15 to 20 minutes, until lightly browned.

Serves 6.

Zucchini-Ricotta Casserole

1 small onion, diced
½ pound zucchini, chopped
½ teaspoon butter
3 tablespoons all-purpose flour
Dash salt and pepper
½ teaspoon basil

❖ ❖ ❖

3 eggs
1 pound Ricotta
½ cup grated Cheddar cheese
Dash nutmeg

Sauté the onion and zucchini in butter, stir in flour, and add salt, pepper, and basil. Remove from heat, add the remaining ingredients and mix well. Bake in a 1½ quart casserole dish in a 375° oven for 40 to 45 minutes.

Serves 4 to 6.

Dutch-Apple Pie

¾ cup brown sugar, firmly packed
2 tablespoons all-purpose flour
½ teaspoon nutmeg
½ teaspoon cinnamon
¾ cup raisins
5 cups fresh or canned apples

❖ ❖ ❖

1 9-inch pie shell

❖ ❖ ❖

1 cup all-purpose flour
½ cup margarine (1 stick)
½ cup sugar

Stir together brown sugar, 2 tablespoons flour, nutmeg, cinnamon, raisins, and apples. Pour into a 9-inch pie shell. With pastry cutter, mix together 1 cup flour, margarine, and sugar till crumbly. Sprinkle over pie. Bake in a 400° oven for 45 minutes.

Serves 6.

The Liberty Inn—1834

128 West Liberty Street
Savannah, Georgia 31401
(912) 233-1007

Welcome to history. Each guest is welcomed in the Liberty-Dent parlor of 1834. Here all are invited to enjoy Peach Schnapps or Harvey's Bristol Cream Sherry on the afternoon of arrival. In this room a Savannah mayor celebrated his triumph in 1840, and local gentry presented calling cards to a young Philadelphia bride of the 1850s. On a more somber occasion, condo-

The Liberty Inn—1834

lences were offered to the Cohen family after their son was killed during the Civil War. Original fireplaces, exposed beams, and interior brick walls have been preserved. Each suite is decorated in Savannah's Tabby White and is comfortably furnished with period pieces and antiques. Such conveniences as modern baths, kitchenettes, and laundry facilities, plus color cablevision and private phones, have been tastefully integrated.

Liberty Inn English Tea Biscuits

These delicious little biscuits may be stored for 3 months in an airtight container. They are great when heated and served with butter and marmalades, "dunked" in hot or cold beverages, served with hors d'oeuvres, salads, soups, spreads, or just nibbled. In Merry Olde England, they would soak the biscuits for 4 to 5 days in cold milk, then remove them to serve with melted butter for breakfast. Small wonder the Colonists brought this recipe from the "Olde Country"!

1 cup butter (2 sticks), softened
2 cups sugar
3 eggs
¾ cup sour cream
1 cup finely chopped pecans
1 teaspoon baking soda
1 teaspoon vanilla extract
¼ teaspoon salt
3 to 4 cups all-purpose flour

Cream the butter and sugar and add the eggs. Stir in the sour cream, pecans, baking soda, vanilla, and salt. Add the flour gradually, using just enough to make a biscuit-type dough. Roll the dough out to ¼-inch thickness, and cut into rounds with a biscuit cutter, preferably a small one. Bake in a 425° oven for 15 to 20 minutes, or until browned.

Makes 3 to 4 dozen biscuits.

Morel House

117 West Perry Street
Savannah, Georgia 31401
(912) 234-4088

The Morel House is a four-story, wooden frame house built in 1818, overlooking Orleans Square. It is situated in the heart of the Downtown Historic District and within walking distances of River Street, churches, shops, museums, and the civic center. There is also a ground floor-level apartment. Savannah is a walking city, so bring some comfortable shoes and walk, walk, walk.

Crab Pie

1 9-inch frozen deep-dish pie shell
❖ ❖ ❖
½ cup mayonnaise
⅓ cup chopped bell pepper
⅓ cup chopped onion
2 tablespoons all-purpose flour
½ teaspoon salt
6 ounces Swiss cheese, grated
2½ cups crab meat
1½ teaspoons Worcestershire sauce
1½ teaspoons mustard

Thaw the pie shell for 20 minutes. Prick the bottom with a fork and bake in a 350° oven for 7 to 10 minutes. Combine the remaining ingredients and pour into pie shell and bake in a 350° oven for 40 to 50 minutes or until the top is lightly browned.

Makes 1 pie; a double recipe makes 3 pies.

Hot Crab

2 tablespoons butter
2 tablespoons all-purpose flour
1 pint half and half
1 teaspoon paprika
1 tablespoon lemon juice
2 tablespoons ketchup

2 tablespoons sherry
Dash cayenne pepper
❖ ❖ ❖
1 14-ounce can artichokes, drained
❖ ❖ ❖
1 pound crab or 1½ pounds shrimp (or a combination of both)
❖ ❖ ❖
1 cup grated American cheese
Bread crumbs

Make sauce by melting butter in a small saucepan over medium heat and stirring in flour until smooth. Mix in half and half, paprika, lemon juice, ketchup, sherry, and cayenne pepper. Continue cooking and stir occasionally until sauce has thickened and is smooth. Set aside.

Slice (or quarter) artichokes. In a casserole dish, alternate layers of seafood, artichokes and sauce until used. Sprinkle grated cheese and a small amount of bread crumbs on top. Bake in a 350° oven for 15 to 30 minutes or until it bubbles.

Serves 4 to 6.

17 Hundred 90 Inn

307 East President Street
Savannah, Georgia 31401
(912) 236-7122

The 17 Hundred 90 Inn is located on the corner of Lincoln and President Streets in the heart of Savannah's historical district. This fourteen-room inn and restaurant has the characteristic second floor entrance. Once inside, antique furnishings and paintings, as well as reproductions of period fabrics, complement the feel of Savannah. Guest rooms are graced with fresh flowers and a complimentary bottle of wine. Twelve of the fourteen rooms have fireplaces. Before retiring, guests indicate the hour in which they prefer to have a continental breakfast served in their room. Old-time Southern hospitality is combined with a European flair.

Fruit Soup

1½ cups watermelon
1½ cups cantaloupe
1 cup strawberries
1 banana
½ teaspoon lemon juice
Apple juice

Purée all fruits in a blender. Add apple juice or artificial sweetener as desired. Chill and garnish with a sprig of mint leaves.

Makes about 4½ cups of soup.

Key Lime Pie

10 tablespoons margarine
¼ cup sugar
1 egg
1 cup all-purpose flour
Pinch salt

❖ ❖ ❖

3 eggs
7 ounces condensed milk
2 tablespoons lime juice
Green food coloring (optional)

Cream the margarine and sugar together. Add 1 egg and mix well. Gradually fold in flour and salt. Mix lightly until smooth. Allow the dough to rest. Roll out on a floured board and place in a flan pan and cook. Allow to cool.

Separate remaining eggs and whip egg whites until stiff. In a separate bowl, whip egg yolks, milk, lime juice, and food coloring if desired for lime effect. Fold the whites into this mixture. Place in the cooled flan pastry shell and freeze for 1 hour.

Serves 8 to 10.

The Culpepper House Bed and Breakfast

Broad at Morgan, Post Office Box 462
Senoia, Georgia 30276
(404) 599-8182

The Culpepper House displays many features that were popular during the Victorian period, including matching gingerbread trim on porches and interior staircases, curved wall, stained glass in the stairwell, and pocket sliding doors leading to the parlor. The house is furnished with period furniture, collectibles, and comfortable whimsey. The hostess will prepare some suggestions of activities that should make a stay in "your home away from home" a satisfying adventure.

Orange Balls

Serve with early coffee as an eye opener.

½ cup butter or margarine (1 stick), softened
1 1-pound box confectioners' sugar
1 7¼-ounce box vanilla wafers, crushed
1 6-ounce can frozen orange juice concentrate
1 cup chopped pecans

❖ ❖ ❖

1 12-ounce package shredded coconut

Combine the butter, sugar, wafer crumbs, and orange juice concentrate. Add pecans and mix well. This will make a very stiff mix. Chill in the refrigerator for 5 minutes. Roll into ¾-inch balls; roll the balls in coconut.

Refrigerate until ready to serve. Freezes well also. About 1½ hours before use, set out on the kitchen counter to thaw.

Makes about 4 dozen balls.

Quick Graham Biscuits

2 cups Bisquick
4 tablespoons whole wheat flour
1 teaspoon baking powder
2 tablespoons butter or vegetable oil
½ cup milk (more if needed)

Combine the dry ingredients, cut in butter or oil. Starting with ½ cup milk, add until the dough is moist. Knead as little as possible. Roll out on a floured board and cut with a biscuit cutter. Bake in a 450° oven about 5 to 10 minutes. Enjoy with homemade jellies and jams.

Makes about 2 dozen biscuits.

Zucchini Bread

3 eggs
1 cup oil
2½ cups sugar
2 cups grated zucchini
2½ teaspoons vanilla extract

❖ ❖ ❖

3 cups all-purpose flour
1 teaspoon salt
½ teaspoon baking powder
3 teaspoons cinnamon

❖ ❖ ❖

½ cup chopped nuts

Beat eggs in a large bowl. Add oil, sugar, zucchini, and vanilla. Combine dry ingredients. Add to egg mixture; blend well. Stir in nuts. Pour into 2 greased loaf pans. Bake in a 350° oven for 1 hour.

Makes 2 loaves.

Hawaii

Poipu Plantation

1792 Pe'e Road
Route 1, Box 119
Koloa, Kauai, Hawaii 96756
(808) 742-7038
(808) 822-7771

Centuries of tides and tradewinds have created the beautiful white sand beaches of Poipu, the most appealing resort area on Kauai. Guests of Poipu Plantation will find quiet and seclusion, with exciting ocean and mountain views from each private lanai—1 bedroom, full kitchen, living/dining room, 2 ceiling fans, and tropical decor. Poipu Plantation is a short distance from hotels, restaurants, shopping, a championship golf course, tennis courts, and beach parks. Tropical fish and shells are abundant on nearby beaches and coves. Swimming, snorkeling and diving are good year-round.

Another way to visit and stay in Hawaii is through Bed and Breakfast Hawaii for accommodations in private homes. The bed may be in an extra room, in a family room usually, with a private bath, an apartment with a separate entrance, or a free-standing cottage elsewhere on the host's property. Homes are available on the islands of Oahu, Hawaii, Maui, Kauai, Nolokai, and Lanai. Write to Post Office Box 449, Kapaa, HI 96746. Call—Kauai phone: (808) 822-7771; or Oahu phone: (808) 536-8421.

No-Knead Whole Wheat Bread

4 teaspoons active dry yeast
⅔ cup warm water
2 teaspoons honey

❖ ❖ ❖

5 cups whole wheat flour

❖ ❖ ❖

3 tablespoons molasses
⅔ cup warm water
½ tablespoon butter

❖ ❖ ❖

½ cup bran
1½ teaspoons salt
⅓ cup wheat germ
⅔ cup warm water

❖ ❖ ❖

⅓ cup sesame seeds

Sprinkle yeast over ⅔ cup water. Add the honey. Set aside. Warm the whole wheat flour in a 250° oven for 20 minutes. Combine the molasses with ⅔ cup lukewarm water and butter. Combine the yeast mixture with the molasses mixture. Stir this into the warmed flour, add bran, salt, wheat germ, and lukewarm water. Mix well, the dough will be sticky. Divide into 3 loaf pans. Sprinkle with sesame seeds, let rise to top of pan. Bake in a 400° oven for 30 to 40 minutes.

Makes 3 loaves.

Quick and Easy Banana Bread

2 eggs
3 to 4 bananas, mashed
¼ cup oil
½ cup honey
1 teaspoon lemon juice
2 cups whole wheat flour
1 teaspoon baking soda
½ teaspoon salt
1 cup chopped nuts
1 cup raisins

Combine all ingredients and bake in a 375° oven for approximately 45 minutes.

Makes 1 loaf.

Papaya Seed Dressing

½ cup sugar
1 teaspoon salt
1½ teaspoons dry mustard
1 cup red wine vinegar
2 cups salad oil
2 tablespoons papaya seeds
½ cup Macadamia nuts
½ onion, grated

In a blender mix sugar, salt, mustard, and vinegar. Add the oil gradually; pour into a serving bowl. Blend in papaya seeds, Macadamia nuts, and onion. Stir well.

Makes about 4¾ cups of dressing.

The Coconut Inn

Post Office Box 10517
Napili, Maui, Hawaii 96761
Toll Free: 1-800-367-8006
In Hawaii: 669-5712

The Coconut Inn is a forty-one-unit property in the Napili Bay area of Maui. It is Hawaii's first country inn. Situated just south of Kapalua, the inn is tucked in by the pineapple fields—with the beautiful West Maui Mountains as a backdrop. Yet, it is but a short stroll to the beaches of Napili Bay. Tennis and golf at Kapalua is a short four-minute drive. The property features studio, one bedroom, and several loft units, all furnished with fully-equipped, full-sized kitchens and ample storage. Amenities include an oversized heated spa, a swimming pool, and a lushly landscaped stream and lagoon. A complimentary continental breakfast is served poolside each morning. Breakfast treats include fresh island fruits, coffee, juices, and breakfast breads baked on the property.

The Coconut Inn

Banana Bread

The Coconut Inn's most popular bread is the Banana Bread that uses bananas that are grown right on the property and are often seen hanging to ripen in front of the breakfast room.

1 cup butter (2 sticks)
4 cups sugar
4 eggs

❖ ❖ ❖

2 teaspoons salt
2 teaspoons baking soda
8 cups all-purpose flour

❖ ❖ ❖

12 ripe bananas

❖ ❖ ❖

2 cups finely chopped nuts

Cream the butter, sugar, and eggs. Sift together the salt, baking soda, and flour, then in a separate bowl mash the 12 ripe bananas. If bananas are not ripe enough the bread will be very dry. Add bananas to the creamed mixture and stir thoroughly. Mix in the flour and the finely chopped nuts. Pour the mixture into 4 well-greased bread pans and bake in a 350° oven for 1 hour. Enjoy!

Makes 4 loaves.

Idaho

Deep Creek Lodge, Restaurant and Motel

Route 1 Deep Creek
Bonners Ferry, Idaho 83805
(208) 267-2373

Deep Creek is nestled in a lovely little valley with a creek running through it, and the surrounding hillsides are covered with gorgeous pines. This is a family-oriented, twelve-room country inn, with a heated pool, hiking and biking trails, cross country skiing, and twenty-nine very beautiful acres for camping, tenting, and RV hookups. A restaurant, cafe, lounge, sun deck, and great fishing are available for guests. A gorgeous crab apple tree on the property is the source of the crab apple liqueur that is served to guests when it is available.

Crab Apple Liqueur

1 pound red crab apples
    (approximately) per quart jar
1 cup sugar per quart jar
2 cups vodka (approximately) per
    quart jar

Wash and remove the stems from the ripe red crab apples. Cut into quarters. Pack into quart jars up to an inch from the top. Add 1 cup of sugar to each jar. Pour the vodka over the apples and sugar until it just reaches the surface. Seal the jars. Place the sealed jars on their sides in a cool storage room. Turn once a day for 25 to 28 days. Then strain the liquid through a sieve and again through a fine strainer. When you are satisfied with its clarity, bottle in clean gin or vodka bottles. For a clearer drink, you may want to decant it after a few days. Do not throw away the pulp, but put it back into the jars, and carefully pour off the remaining liquid. Eventually when there is very little settling out, you can discard the pulp.

Cricket on the Hearth

1521 Lakeside Avenue
Coeur D'Alene, Idaho 83814
(208) 664-6926

Cricket on the Hearth was chosen as this comfortable older home's name because it has long been a symbol of hospitality and good fortune. Guests are greeted at the door with a warm "welcome home," and the charm of a bygone era takes over from there.

Guests can choose to be alone in their rooms, to socialize in the living room with its gallery of paintings and baby grand piano, or to join the fun in the game room equipped with a pool table, assorted games, and a bar ("bring your own"). The three guest rooms each have their own decor and personality. Depending upon the whims of weather and the hostesses, breakfast may be served in the dining room, in the game room, on the deck, or even at an umbrella table in the garden.

Apple Filling for Crêpes

Crêpes
    ❖ ❖ ❖
5 to 6 Granny Smith apples (tart
    apples)
2 tablespoons butter
½ cup brown sugar, firmly packed
½ teaspoon grated ginger root
Grated rind of 1 orange
¼ cup raisins
¼ cup chopped walnuts
Sour cream

Make crêpes from your favorite recipe and keep warm wrapped in a tea towel.

Peel and slice the apples. Melt the butter in a large skillet. Add apples and cook over medium heat, covered, until tender. When almost done, add the sugar (to taste according to tartness of apples), grated ginger root, orange rind, raisins and chopped walnuts. When the sugar is melted and the apples are glazed, fill the crêpes and roll up. Serve with sour cream.

Makes 12 crêpes.

Cranberry Muffins

1 cup ground fresh cranberries
½ cup sugar

❖ ❖ ❖

¼ cup sugar
¼ cup shortening
1 egg

❖ ❖ ❖

2 cups sifted all-purpose flour
½ teaspoon salt
¾ teaspoon baking soda

❖ ❖ ❖

¾ cup sour milk
1 teaspoon grated orange rind

❖ ❖ ❖

½ cup sugar
½ teaspoon cinnamon

Mix the cranberries with ½ cup sugar. Cream ¼ cup sugar with the shortening. Beat in the egg. Sift together the flour, salt, and baking soda, and add to the creamed mixture with cranberries. Add the sour milk and orange rind. Stir just enough to mix. Spoon the batter into greased and floured muffin tins. Mix together ½ cup sugar and cinnamon. Sprinkle over each muffin. Bake in a 400° oven for 20 to 25 minutes.

Makes about 18 muffins.

Greenbriar Bed and Breakfast Inn

315 Wallace
Coeur D'Alene, Idaho 83814
(208) 667-9660

The Greenbriar Inn is a 1908 brick house that is on the National Historic Register. It boasts winding mahogany staircases, original high ceilings and woodwork. Elegant simplicity and comfort, antiques, and down comforters on each bed are the rule. Breakfast is a four-course gourmet delight. A hot tub, TV room, and library are there for entertainment, and guests can even saunter to the dinner-dance boat that departs each evening during warm weather.

Almond Egg Puffs

½ cup margarine (1 stick)
1 cup boiling water
1 cup all-purpose flour
4 eggs

❖ ❖ ❖

12 eggs
¾ cup cream
Pinch thyme
Swiss cheese
Shaved almonds

Melt the margarine in the boiling water. Remove from heat and add the flour all at once. Stir until well blended. Add eggs, one at a time, stirring after each addition until well-blended. Drop on a greased baking pan and bake in a 450° oven for 5 minutes, then reduce to 350° for 25 minutes until golden brown. Slice in half.

Makes 10 to 12 large puffs.

For the filling, whip together eggs, cream, and a pinch of thyme to taste. Scramble the eggs on medium heat until light and fluffy. Slice off the tops of the puffs; fill the puffs with eggs, then add Swiss cheese. Place caps on puffs and top with grated Swiss cheese. Put in the oven or microwave briefly to melt the cheese topping. Just before serving, top with shaved almonds.

Serves 6.

Apple-Raisin-Nut Tart

½ cup margarine (1 stick)
2 cups all-purpose flour

¾ cup sugar
1 egg

❖ ❖ ❖

4 cups finely chopped apples
½ cup sugar
3 tablespoons lemon juice
2 teaspoons cinnamon
½ cup raisins
1½ cup nuts

❖ ❖ ❖

3 tablespoons raspberry or apricot
jam, or marmalade
3 tablespoons honey
1 tablespoon brandy

In a mixing bowl cut the margarine into the flour and sugar. Add the egg and mix well. Roll out on a floured board into 2 circles that would fit the bottom of a 10-inch springform pan. Place 1 circle in the bottom of the pan.

Combine the apples, sugar, lemon juice, cinnamon, raisins, and nuts, pour into the springform pan. Top with the remaining pastry circle, patting around the edges to meet the pan. Bake in a 400° oven for 35 minutes. Combine the jam, honey, and brandy, and pour over the tart when cool.

Serves 12 to 16.

Cherry-Berry Coffee Cake

1 8-ounce package cream cheese,
softened
½ cup margarine (1 stick)
1½ cups sugar
2 eggs
1 teaspoon almond extract
1 teaspoon baking powder
½ teaspoon baking soda
¼ cup milk
1⅓ cups all-purpose flour

❖ ❖ ❖

1 16-ounce can pitted cherries
1 cup frozen cranberries
1 cup sugar

❖ ❖ ❖

Nuts
Sugar
Cinnamon

In a medium mixing bowl, cream together the cream cheese, margarine, and sugar. Add eggs, almond extract, baking powder, baking soda, and milk. Beat in the flour. Divide the mixture in half, spreading half over the bottom of a greased and floured glass 9x12-inch baking dish.

In a saucepan, combine the cherries and cranberries. Cook until the cranberries pop. Remove from heat and add the sugar. Allow to cool. Pour the filling over the batter in the baking dish, and then cover with the remaining batter, dropping small amounts from a spoon. Cover with nuts and sprinkle sugar and cinnamon over all. Bake in a 350° oven for 45 to 50 minutes.

Serves 12 to 16.

Jack-in-the-Puff

Puff pastry squares (6x6, frozen or substitute croissants)

❖ ❖ ❖

4 eggs
¼ cup chives (or finely chopped green onion)
1 3-ounce package cream cheese, cubed
Pinch oregano

❖ ❖ ❖

Grated Jack cheese
Chopped walnuts

Bake the puff pastry until light brown and set aside after cutting in half.

For the filling, whip together eggs, chives, cream cheese, and oregano. Scramble in a frying pan until light and fluffy. Put the eggs in the pastry and generously add grated Jack cheese. Replace top and sprinkle with chopped walnuts.

Serves 2.

Everyday Apple Drink

Combine apple juice with cranberry-raspberry ice cubes. Beautiful and yummy.

You can substitute pineapple juice or orange juice for the apple juice.

Honeymooners Gentle Awakening

½ cup pineapple juice
3 cranberry-raspberry ice cubes
½ cup champagne

Combine all ingredients in a glass; serve.

Serves 1.

Banana Pumpkin Bread

3 to 4 bananas
1 cup cooked pumpkin
3 eggs
1½ cups sugar
1 cup oil
5 cups all-purpose flour
1 tablespoon baking soda
2 teaspoons cinnamon
½ teaspoon ground cloves
2 cups chopped walnuts

❖ ❖ ❖

1 8-ounce package cream cheese, softened
½ cup sugar
2 teaspoons orange or lemon extract

Purée bananas and pumpkin, add eggs and sugar, mix well. Add oil. Stir in flour, baking soda, cinnamon, cloves, and walnuts, mixing until just blended. Pour into 3 greased loaf pans. Bake in a 350° oven for 50 to 60 minutes.

In a small mixing bowl, blend together the cream cheese, sugar, and extract. Place in a pastry bag. Make little rosettes on the serving plate so your guests can choose the amount they desire to use on their bread.

Makes 3 loaves.

Green Chile Timbale

3 tablespoons chopped mild green chiles
¼ cup cottage cheese
8 slices bacon, chopped
1 cup grated Swiss cheese

❖ ❖ ❖

4 eggs
1 cup milk
2 teaspoons paprika
Dash onion salt
2 tablespoons Parmesan cheese

❖ ❖ ❖

2 tablespoons butter
2 tablespoons all-purpose flour
1 cup milk
½ to ¾ cup Swiss cheese

❖ ❖ ❖

Paprika
Green pepper, diced (optional)

In 4 greased 8-ounce custard cups, place about 2 teaspoons chiles, 1 tablespoon cottage cheese, ¼ of the bacon, and ¼ cup Swiss cheese.

In a separate bowl, blend with a wire whisk the eggs, 1 cup milk, paprika, onion salt, and Parmesan cheese. Bake in a 350° oven for 30 minutes or until firm, or microwave for approximately 10 minutes until done.

For the topping, melt the butter, add flour and stir rapidly. Add 1 cup milk to make a roux, or white sauce. Add the Swiss cheese and stir until melted.

Invert the custard out of the custard cups onto serving plates and pour the topping over each. It is important that the custard be well done or it will not hold its shape when the sauce is poured over it. Sprinkle paprika on top and garnish with green pepper if desired.

Serves 4.

Maryanne's on O'Gara Bay

HCR 1, Box 43E
Harrison, Idaho 83833
(208) 245-2537
(208) 689-3630
Bed and Breakfast Association of North
Idaho

Maryanne's offers a serene, secluded, country setting where the traveler can take a quiet walk in the woods, beachcomb along the shore of Lake Coeur D'Alene, or just sit on the big rock that overlooks the bay. Its three rooms have different views of the lake and woods, each with a special quilt on the bed, lovingly handmade by grandma. A Continental breakfast is served each morning with fresh fruit and berries in season from the garden and orchard. Swimming, boating, and hiking are offered in the Summer.

Frosty Fruit Slush

4 cups sugar
6 cups water
1 46-ounce can pineapple juice
2 12-ounce cans frozen orange
    juice, undiluted
1 12-ounce can frozen lemonade,
    undiluted
5 bananas, mashed
Lemon-lime soft drink

Bring the sugar and water to a full rolling boil. Cool for 10 minutes. Mix with the remainder of ingredients, pour into 5 1-quart freezer containers or several ice cube trays. Freeze. When ready to serve, fill glasses half full of lemon-lime flavored soft drink, add a generous scoop of the mixture and several ice cubes. Serve with a sprig of mint and a colorful straw.
    Makes 5 quarts.

Quick and Delicious Salad

2 10-ounce packages frozen peas
1 pound drained, crisply fried
    bacon pieces
1 cup sour cream
1 cup diced celery
1 cup diced onion

Mix together and chill. Serve in a lettuce lined bowl; garnish with herb-flavored croutons.
    Serves 6.

Crab-Stuffed Avocado

1 can crab meat
½ cup finely chopped celery
2 tablespoons mayonnaise
1 tablespoon chili sauce
2 tablespoons lemon juice

    ❖ ❖ ❖

3 or 4 avocados
2 tablespoons lemon juice

Mix the crab meat, celery, mayonnaise, chili sauce, and 2 tablespoons lemon juice. Split the avocados, remove the pits, sprinkle avocado halves with 2 tablespoons lemon juice and stuff with the crab meat mixture. For a spicier dish, use salsa in the place of chili sauce. Serve on lettuce-lined plates with crackers and fresh fruit.
    Serves 6 to 8.

Tea Cakes

1 cup butter (2 sticks), room
    temperature
6 heaping tablespoons
    confectioners' sugar
2 cups all-purpose flour
1 teaspoon vanilla extract
1 cup finely chopped walnuts
Confectioners' sugar

Cream butter with sugar. Add flour, vanilla, and walnuts. Roll into walnut-sized balls and bake on an ungreased cookie sheet in a 350° oven for about 12 minutes. Cool on a rack and sprinkle with confectioners' sugar. These will melt in your mouth.
    Makes 3 to 4 dozen tea cakes.

Indian Creek Guest Ranch

Route 2, Box 105
North Fork, Idaho 83466
Call Salmon operator and ask for 24F-211

Visitors to the Indian Creek Guest Ranch truly are able to relax in the woods. The guest ranch is small, with a main lodge and three cabins. Its cozy, comfortable cabins each have a private bath and shower. All meals are home-cooked and delicious—prime rib, steaks, chicken, home-baked bread, biscuits, muffins—it is all good. The ranch is surrounded by Forest Service land and borders the Idaho primitive area. There are many activities for the guest who wants to be busy, and those who so desire can be busy doing nothing at all.

Basic Roll Recipe

1⅓ cups milk
⅓ cup sugar
1½ teaspoons salt
½ cup oil
2 ¼-ounce packages active dry
    yeast
½ cup warm water (105° to 115°)
2 eggs, beaten
7 cups all-purpose flour
    (approximately)

In a saucepan combine the milk, sugar, salt, and oil, heat until warm or lukewarm. Mix the yeast with the warm water and set aside for 5 minutes. Stir in the milk mixture and the beaten eggs. Add 4 cups of flour. On a floured board knead the dough, adding additional flour. Knead 10 minutes, let rise. Punch down and shape into rolls, let rolls rise until doubled in bulk. Bake in a 400° oven for 25 minutes.

Makes approximately 3 dozen.

Chicken Rice

1½ cups chopped onion
2 cups diced celery
2 tablespoons butter

❖ ❖ ❖

1 10¾-ounce can mushroom soup
¾ cup long grain rice, uncooked
1 10½-ounce can chicken rice soup
1½ cups water
½ teaspoon poultry seasoning
1 6¾-ounce can chicken chunks

❖ ❖ ❖

1 4-ounce can mushrooms
Salt

❖ ❖ ❖

1 cup almonds, walnuts, or cashews

Sauté the onion and celery in butter, simmering until transparent. Add the mushroom soup, rice, chicken rice soup, water, poultry seasoning, and chicken. Add the mushrooms and juice. Salt to taste. Mix together and bake in a 350° oven for 2 hours. Remove from the oven 20 minutes before done and add almonds, walnuts, or cashews. (The juice of the canned chicken can be used as part of the water.)

Serves 8.

Spaghetti Sauce

1 pound ground round or lean hamburger
1 cup chopped onions
1 cup diced celery
⅓ cup shortening

❖ ❖ ❖

2 cups water
1 15-ounce can tomato sauce
1 4-ounce can mushrooms
4 tablespoons Worcestershire sauce
1 14-ounce bottle ketchup
Garlic

Brown the hamburger, onions, and celery in the shortening. Add the remaining ingredients and cook slowly for 4 hours.

Serves 4 to 6.

Key Hotel

Box 23
Pierce, Idaho 83546
(208) 464-2487

This seven-room hotel reminds one of a scene from *The Last Picture Show*. With its community kitchen, the Key Hotel is not elegant or Victorian, but it is inexpensive. Room rates are ten dollars per person. Fishing, hunting, camping, skiing, and snowmobiling are available in town.

"Pluckets" Bread

½ cup margarine
1 cup brown sugar, firmly packed
2 teaspoons cinnamon
3 10-ounce cans biscuits (any kind), cut in 4 sections

Melt margarine, sugar, and cinnamon together. Pour over biscuits that have been placed in a greased bundt pan. Bake in a 400° oven for 20 minutes. Delicious, none is ever left over.

Serves 8 to 10.

Knoll Hus at Round Lake

Post Office Box 572
St. Maries, Idaho 83861
(208) 245-4137

Knoll Hus is on a small wooded hillside above Round Lake, eight miles from St. Maries, Idaho. The hostess and her husband are of Swedish ancestry, and their background is reflected in the furnishings of this charming cabin, as well as their nearby home. In addition to the Swedish ambience of this bed and breakfast, the traveler is treated to a panoramic view of the lake, the St. Joe River as it winds its way to Coeur D'Alene Lake, and the many water birds and other forms of wildlife that make their homes along the banks and shores. Knoll Hus is the perfect weekend away from everyday pressures. Swimming and boating, hiking and bicycling are offered in the Summer and plans are underway to offer cross-country skiing, ice skating, and sleigh rides during the Winter season.

All the recipes are Swedish and have been handed down through the family of the innkeeper for generations. All are simple and simply delicious.

Apple Cake (Swedish)

10 apples
1 cup butter (2 sticks)
1 16-ounce package brown sugar
2 cups all-purpose flour
2 teaspoons nutmeg

Peel the apples and slice them into an 8x10-inch pan. Mix butter, sugar, flour, and nutmeg together. Pour the mixture over the apples. Bake in a 375° oven for 45 minutes. Very simple and good.

Serves 8 to 9.

Fläsk Pan Kakka

1 1-pound package bacon (optional)
6 eggs
1½ cups sifted all-purpose flour
2 teaspoons salt
3 cups milk

Fry the bacon, reserving the grease. Beat the eggs, and add the flour and salt alternately with the milk in a blender. Pour the grease into 2 9x13-inch pans. Break the bacon into bite-sized pieces and divide between the pans, then pour in batter on top of the bacon. The batter will be thin. Bake in a pre-heated 500° oven for 15 minutes, reduce heat to 400° and continue baking 15 minutes longer, until golden brown. The batter will puff up into mountains and usually fall after it is removed from the oven. Serve with warm syrup and lingonberries. For variety try sausage instead of bacon, or try blueberries or peaches rather than the lingonberries. When not using bacon, grease pans well.

Serves 8 to 12.

Weimerbrod Rolls

2 ¼-ounce packages active dry
    yeast
¼ cup water

❖ ❖ ❖

1 cup cold milk
1 egg, beaten
2½ tablespoons sugar
½ teaspoon salt
1 teaspoon ground cardamom seed
½ cup oil
3 cups all-purpose flour

❖ ❖ ❖

¼ cup butter

Mix yeast in ¼ cup warm water. In a large mixing bowl, combine the milk, egg, sugar, salt, cardamom, and oil. Add the yeast mixture and the flour. Knead on a board, roll out and spread with ¼ cup butter. Roll out and fold up three times. Shape into spiral-shaped rolls. Let rise for 2 hours. Bake in a 400° oven for 15 to 20 minutes, not too long, until slightly brown.

Makes approximately 2 dozen rolls.

Pine Tree Inn

177 King Street
Wallace, Idaho 83873
(208) 752-4391

The Pine Tree Inn is in a picturesque and historic mining town, "the silver capital of the world." The inn is set away from traffic, with Placer Creek running through the back yard, and is nestled among the hillside pines. Guests can picnic, fish, or just relax in the fresh cool mountain air in the secluded back yard. There are four guest rooms, with cable TV, kitchen and laundry facilities, a picnic table, and barbecue equipment.

Knoll Hus at Round Lake

Strata

12 slices bread, remove crust and
    cut into cubes

❖ ❖ ❖

1½ cups diced ham
1 cup diced green pepper
⅓ cup finely minced onion
¾ cup grated Cheddar cheese
¾ cup grated Jack cheese

❖ ❖ ❖

7 eggs
1 teaspoon salt
3 teaspoons dry mustard
3 cups milk

Grease a 9x13-inch pan and place bread on the bottom. Combine the ham, green pepper, onion, and cheeses, pour over the bread. Mix together the remaining ingredients and pour over the strata. Let sit overnight in the refrigerator. In the morning bake in a 325° oven for 1 hour.

Serves 6 to 8.

Huckleberry Cheesecake

1½ cups graham cracker crumbs
¼ cup confectioners' sugar
½ cup butter (1 stick), melted

❖ ❖ ❖

2 8-ounce packages cream cheese,
    softened
3 eggs
1 teaspoon vanilla extract
1 cup sugar

❖ ❖ ❖

1 quart huckleberries
1 cup sugar
3 tablespoons cornstarch

Mix together the graham cracker crumbs, sugar, and butter, and line a pie pan with mixture.

Combine the cream cheese, eggs, vanilla, and sugar, mix well and pour into crust. Bake in a 350° oven for 50 minutes. Cool.

In a medium saucepan, cook the huckleberries, sugar, and cornstarch until thick. Allow to cool and serve over cheesecake.

Serves 12 to 16.

Alpine Village

Post Office Box 34
Yellow Pine, Idaho 83677
(208) 382-4336

The Alpine Village is nestled in Idaho's unspoiled mountain wilderness. It is attractively situated in a park-like setting with two rustic gazebos, trees, flowers, shrubs, and lawn bordering the circular drive. Deer and other wildlife are frequent visitors near the lodge. This is a year-round resort with completely furnished "A" frame cabins. All that is needed is a change of clothing and a tooth brush. Each cabin will accommodate up to five guests. The lodge has a restaurant and dining area.

Cabbage Patch Soup

2 pounds hamburger
1 cup chopped celery
1 cup chopped onion
1 gallon can diced tomatoes
1 6-ounce can mushrooms
1 gallon can kidney or chili beans
1½ or 2 small heads cabbage, chopped
Dash Tabasco (optional)

Brown the hamburger. Add the remaining ingredients and cook until the vegetables are tender.

Makes approximately 36 to 40 cups.

Beer Bread

3 cups self-rising flour
¾ cup brown sugar, firmly packed
1 teaspoon cinnamon
1 12-ounce can beer
½ cup raisins (optional)
½ cup chopped walnuts (optional)

In a large mixing bowl, combine all ingredients. Pour into a greased loaf pan and bake in a 350° oven for 45 minutes.

Makes 1 loaf of sweet bread.

Green Bean Casserole

1 gallon can green beans (pour most of water out)
1 10¾-ounce can cream of mushroom soup
1 8-ounce can sliced water chestnuts, drained
1 6-ounce can mushrooms, drained

❖ ❖ ❖

1 3-ounce can deep fried onions

Combine all ingredients and heat thoroughly (microwave is great). Add canned deep fried onions sprinkled on top and reheat about 1 minute.

Serves 12 to 16.

Illinois

Bed and Breakfast-Chicago, Inc.

P.O. Box 14088
Chicago, Illinois 60614-0088
(312) 951-0085

Guests of Bed and Breakfast-Chicago find accommodations they never knew existed. Among the possibilities are a 56th-floor mid-town apartment, garden court apartments, or a coach house in the middle of Historic Old Town. A call to Mary Shaw, owner, will bring information on how 54 bed and breakfasts in the area can provide accommodations for the discerning traveler.

Great Raspberry Muffins

1½ cups all-purpose flour
¼ cup sugar
¼ cup brown sugar, firmly packed
2 teaspoons baking powder
¼ teaspoon salt
1 teaspoon ground cinnamon
1 egg, slightly beaten
½ cup butter, melted
½ cup milk

1¼ cups fresh or frozen raspberries (if frozen do not thaw)

❖ ❖ ❖

½ cup chopped nuts (pecan or walnuts)
½ cup brown sugar, firmly packed
¼ cup all-purpose flour
1 teaspoon cinnamon
2 teaspoons grated lemon zest
3 tablespoons melted butter

Combine the first 6 ingredients in a medium mixing bowl. Make a well in the center and add the egg, ¹/₂ cup melted butter, and milk. Stir with a wooden bowl just until the dry ingredients are combined, do not overmix. Gently and quickly stir in the raspberries and lemon zest. Fill muffin cups that have been lined with papers ¾ full. For the topping combine the nuts, brown sugar, flour, cinnamon and lemon zest in a small bowl. Add the butter and combine. Sprinkle evenly over the top of each muffin. Bake in a 350° oven for 20 to 25 minutes until firm.
Makes 12 muffins.

Elsa's German Syrup

2 cups brown sugar, firmly packed
1 cup light corn syrup
½ cup crème fraiche
1 egg

Combine the first 3 ingredients and boil for 3 minutes. Beat the cream and egg together, then beat into the hot syrup. Great on pancakes and waffles.
Makes 3 cups syrup.

Burton House— A Bed and Breakfast Inn

1454 North Dearborn Parkway
Chicago, Illinois 60610
(312) 787-9015

Hospitality is the byword of the Burton House, and guests are greeted by the innkeeper in the spacious entrance gallery, a part of the first floor grand lobby. The house and its family are historically significant to Chicago and the nation. Built in 1877 by Joseph Bullock, it is listed on the National Register of Historic Places. The original decor and furnishings in the large, sunny rooms bespeak a truly gracious Chicago landmark. There is an eclectic blend of art, antiques, objects d'art, and carpets, with a 100-year-old Steinway to surprise and please guests. Each bedroom has its own private bath, marble fireplace, parquet floor, and gilded ceiling, to enhance comfort and provide the individuality one would expect.

93

Burton House

Burton House Gingerbread

2½ cups all-purpose flour
1 cup sugar
½ cup butter (1 stick), softened
1 cup non-sulphured molasses
2 whole eggs
2 teaspoons ground ginger
2 teaspoons ground cinnamon
1 cup boiling water

❖ ❖ ❖

1 teaspoon baking soda
Water

Combine the flour, sugar, butter, molasses, eggs, spices, and boiling water in a large mixing bowl, stir well. Dissolve the soda in a little water and stir in last. Pour into a greased and floured 13x9x2-inch baking pan. Bake in a 350° oven for 45 minutes, or until done, when a tester comes out clean.

When cool, cut into squares and serve. The flavor is even better if the gingerbread is not served until the next day. Great with mulled cider in winter and with lemonade in summer.

Serves 12 to 16.

Burton House Oatmeal Macaroons

1 tablespoon butter
1 cup sugar

❖ ❖ ❖

2 eggs
2 cups quick-cooking rolled oats
1½ teaspoons baking powder
¼ teaspoon salt
1½ teaspoons vanilla extract

Cream together the butter and sugar. Separate the eggs and beat the whites until stiff. Beat the yolks separately. Add to the creamed mixture along with the remaining ingredients. Drop by tablespoonfuls onto greased cookie sheets and bake in a 325° oven for 15 to 20 minutes.

Makes about 3 dozen macaroons.

The Tremont Hotel

100 East Chestnut Street
Chicago, Illinois 60611
In Chicago: (312) 751-1900
Outside Illinois: (800) 621-8133

The Tremont Hotel, which provides the luxury of a superb location in the heart of Chicago, offers the discerning traveler a very special experience. Its ideal location puts guests close to the central business district, within steps of North Michigan Avenue and Water Tower Place, and it has been recognized by *Architectural Digest* as "one of the leading small hotels in the United States." Rooms are decorated in the style of a traditional English Country Manor, emphasizing comfort and luxury. "Crickets" is the four-star restaurant that provides guests the best in dining pleasure.

Senegalese Soup

2 tablespoons butter
1 small onion, coarsely chopped
1 carrot, coarsely chopped
1 stalk celery, coarsely chopped

❖ ❖ ❖

1 heaping teaspoon curry powder
3 small cinnamon sticks
2 bay leaves
1 teaspoon whole cloves
5 cups strong chicken broth
1 tablespoon tomato purée
2 heaping tablespoons almond
    paste
1 tablespoon red currant jelly

❖ ❖ ❖

3 tablespoons butter
3 tablespoons all-purpose flour
Salt and freshly ground white
    pepper

❖ ❖ ❖

2 cups heavy cream
Toasted coconut

Melt 2 tablespoons of butter in a heavy saucepan. Add the onion, carrot, and celery. Cook over moderate heat, stirring occasionally, until the vegetables have taken on a little color. Stir in the curry powder until well blended. Add cinnamon sticks, bay leaves, cloves, broth, tomato purée, almond paste, and jelly. Mix well, bring to a boil, and simmer for 1 hour. Skim off any foam that rises to the surface. Knead the remaining butter together with the flour. Add this (called beurre manié) bit by bit to the soup, stirring until well blended. Cook for 5 to 6 minutes, or until the soup has thickened slightly. Strain, season to taste, cool, and refrigerate. Just before serving blend in the cream. Serve in well-chilled soup cups with a sprinkling of toasted coconut on top.

Serves 6 to 8.

Shrimp Sauté Vin Blanc

2 pounds jumbo shrimp
2 tablespoons clarified butter
(or regular butter)
4 medium shallots, chopped
½ cup dry white wine
2 cups whipping cream
1 tablespoon chopped parsley

In a sauté pan, sauté the shrimp in butter for 4 minutes on high heat. Drain off the butter and add the shallots. Sauté 30 seconds with the shrimp; remove the shrimp and put aside. Using the same pan, simmer and reduce white wine by one half. Add the cream; reduce by one third. Put the shrimp back in and boil ½ minute. Add the chopped parsley. Serve hot with French bread.

Serves 4.

Veal Cricket

For each serving use:

6 ounces veal scallops (2 3-ounce pieces)
1 tablespoon clarified butter

❖ ❖ ❖

2 tablespoons Mushroom Duxelle
4 tablespoons Mornay sauce

❖ ❖ ❖

2 tablespoons demiglace
1 watercress leaf
1 broccoli floweret
1 cherry tomato

Sauté the veal lightly in the clarified butter for 2 minutes on each side. Place the scallops on dinner plates, spread Mushroom Duxelle over the veal. Top with the Mornay sauce and brown under the broiler. Add the demiglace sauce around the edges, and garnish with watercress, a broccoli flowerette, and a cherry tomato.

Serves 2.

Mushroom Duxelle

½ medium onion, chopped
1 tablespoon clarified butter
1 pound mushrooms, chopped
1 tablespoon Bechamel

Sauté the chopped onion in the clarified butter. Add the mushrooms. Sauté and cook until the liquid is gone. Add the Bechamel. Bring to a boil. Set aside.

Hot Cabbage a la Riems

1 egg yolk
2 tablespoons Dijon mustard
1 shallot, finely chopped
5 tablespoons red vinegar
10 tablespoons olive oil
Salt
Pepper, freshly ground to taste

❖ ❖ ❖

1 cabbage, finely shredded
2 tablespoons demiglace or brown sauce
2 tablespoons butter

To make the vinaigrette dressing, whisk together the egg yolk and mustard. Add the shallot, red vinegar, olive oil, salt, and pepper, and whisk until well blended.

In a casserole, mix the shredded cabbage with 1 cup of vinaigrette dressing and demiglace. Place the casserole in a 500° oven for 2 minutes. Separately, melt the butter until the color is light brown.

Take the casserole from the oven and pour the butter over the cabbage mixture.

To serve, allow the excess liquid to drain, portioning from the top of the casserole. Cabbage should be al dente.

Serves 1.

Hot Apple Tarts

Puff pastry dough (buy from specialty store)
2 tablespoons butter
1 sheet parchment paper

❖ ❖ ❖

½ cup butter (1 stick), softened
⅓ cup sugar
1 egg
Drop vanilla extract
½ cup ground almonds

❖ ❖ ❖

2 apples
½ cup butter (1 stick), melted
3 tablespoons sugar

❖ ❖ ❖

½ cup sugar
½ cup water
½ cup cream

Roll out the puff pastry dough to a square shape. Cut circles 4 inches in diameter using a butter plate (use 2 tablespoons of butter to grease the plate). Set the 4-inch rounds in a baking pan lined with parchment paper. Place the pan in the refrigerator.

To make the almond cream, mix the soft butter with ⅓ cup of sugar. Cream together. Slowly add 1 egg, a drop of vanilla, and the ground almonds, mix well. (Can be made a day before.) Spread the almond cream in the center ½ inch away from the border of dough. Peel and thinly slice the apples. Arrange in a circle in the center of each round of dough. Combine the melted butter and 3 tablespoons of sugar. Pour the mixture over the apple slices. Bake in a 425° oven. In a heavy saucepan over low heat melt ½ cup of sugar. Stir constantly until it is dark colored. Remove from heat and cool. Very slowly add ½ cup of water. Return to low heat and stir; add the cream and bring to a boil. Serve on the side with the hot apple tarts.

This may be made the day before serving.

Serves 4.

The Comfort Guest House

1000 Third Street
Galena, Illinois 61036
(815) 777-3062

The Comfort Guest House in historic Galena, an authentically restored riverfront town, was built in 1856 by William H. Snyder. It is a leisurely four-block stroll from a downtown brimming with antique shops, galleries, museums, parks, restaurants, and unlimited tranquility. At day's end one can take in the dance of the fireflies from the old porch swing or meander to an antique-furnished room to snuggle under a hand-tied quilt for a peaceful night's rest.

Rhubarb Muffins

1¼ cups brown sugar, firmly packed
1 egg
½ cup oil
2 teaspoons vanilla extract
1 cup buttermilk
1½ cups diced rhubarb

❖   ❖   ❖

2½ cups all-purpose flour
1 teaspoon baking soda
1 teaspoon baking powder
½ teaspoon salt

❖   ❖   ❖

1 tablespoon butter, melted
⅓ cup sugar
2 teaspoons cinnamon

In a bowl, combine the brown sugar, egg, oil, vanilla, and buttermilk. Add the rhubarb. In a separate bowl, stir together the flour, soda, baking powder, and salt. Add the dry ingredients to the wet batter. Stir until just blended. Use muffin papers and fill each ⅔ full. Sprinkle with a mixture of butter, sugar, and cinnamon and bake in a 400° oven for 20 to 25 minutes.

Makes 14 muffins.

Chocolate Chip Banana Muffins

½ cup butter (1 stick)
¾ cup sugar
2 eggs
1 teaspoon vanilla extract
1 cup mashed ripe bananas

❖   ❖   ❖

2 cups all-purpose flour
1 teaspoon baking soda
1 teaspoon salt
¾ cup semi-sweet chocolate chips

Cream together the butter and sugar in a large bowl. Add the eggs one at a time, beating after each. Add the vanilla and mashed bananas.

In a separate bowl, combine the flour, soda, salt, and chocolate chips. Add to the creamed mixture and stir until just blended; the batter will be lumpy. Pour into greased muffin tins and bake in a 350° oven for 25 minutes.

Makes 12 muffins.

The DeSoto House

230 South Main Street
Galena, Illinois 61036
(815) 777-9208

The DeSoto House has hosted many famous men and women. These guests include Mark Twain, Ralph Waldo Emerson, Susan B. Anthony, Horace Greeley, sculptor Lorado Taft, and a total of seven United States presidents, besides Abraham Lincoln and Ulysses S. Grant.

Times have changed, and so has the DeSoto House. In past years modernization took the form of whitewashing walls, repapering hallways, and even replacing communal bathrooms with private baths adjoining guest rooms. Then in 1880 the massive roof was raised on jacks, and the fourth and fifth floors were dismantled. But the most important changes have been very recent. The facilities now include five quiet, comfortable meeting rooms and fifty-five individually appointed guest rooms, as well as specialty shops, indoor parking, and a variety of other conveniences all under one roof. While the physical structure has changed, the philosophy of the DeSoto House has been continuous for over 135 years: each guest receives personalized attention in the manner of the grand hotel. Luxury, service, and hospitality are of the utmost importance.

Pain au Chocolat

A Continental breakfast pastry.

1½ tablespoons sugar
1 ⅝-ounce cake yeast
1 cup milk, warm
3½ cups sifted all-purpose flour
1 teaspoon salt
2½ tablespoons butter, softened

❖   ❖   ❖

1 cup butter (2 sticks)

❖   ❖   ❖

2 eggs

❖   ❖   ❖

Chocolate chips

Dissolve the sugar and yeast in the warm milk and let stand until the yeast starts to swell and bubble. Add the flour, salt, and butter in that order and mix to a smooth dough. Let the dough rest in the refrigerator for 30 minutes.

Wrap 1 cup of butter in plastic wrap and pound it until soft and pliable. Roll the dough out to a rectangle ½-inch thick and place the butter over half the dough. Fold the dough over to seal the butter in. Roll out to a large rectangle ½-inch thick and fold in thirds like a letter. Let the dough rest for 30 minutes in the refrigerator. Repeat rolling, folding and resting the dough twice, and let the dough rest for 2 hours.

Roll the dough out ¼-inch thick. Cut into 4x3-inch rectangles. Beat the eggs and brush each rectangle with egg. Sprinkle chocolate chips on the center of each rectangle and fold the pastry in thirds like a letter, enclosing the chocolate in pastry. Place on a cookie sheet. Bake in a 350° oven for 10 to 15 minutes.

Serves 6 to 8.

Grand Marnier Gugelhopf

⅞ cup butter, softened
1 cup sifted confectioners' sugar
❖ ❖ ❖
5 egg yolks, large
❖ ❖ ❖
1 tablespoon vanilla extract
½ teaspoon lemon extract
❖ ❖ ❖
2 cups sifted all-purpose flour
½ teaspoon baking powder
❖ ❖ ❖
⅛ cup Grand Marnier orange
  liqueur
½ cup milk
❖ ❖ ❖
4 egg whites, large
½ cup sugar
❖ ❖ ❖
Confectioners' sugar

Grease and flour 1 9- or 10-inch tube cake mold or Gugelhopf form. Cream together the butter and sugar. Whip in the egg yolks until light and fluffy. Mix in the vanilla and extracts. Sift the flour and baking powder together and set aside. Mix the liquids together and set aside.

In another bowl, whip the egg whites to soft peaks, add the sugar gradually and whip to a stiff peak me-

ringue. Add the dry ingredients alternately with the liquids to the butter mixture. Fold the meringue into the mixture and turn into the cake form. Bake in a 350° oven for 1 to 1½ hours. Cool 15 minutes in the form. Turn out and cool on a rack. Dust with confectioners' sugar when cool.

Serves 8 to 10.

Cranberry Sorbet

1 12-ounce package cranberries
1½ cups sugar
1 cup orange juice
6 12-ounce cans lemon-lime soda
  (or 1 2-liter bottle)

Boil the berries, sugar, and orange juice until all the berries have popped. Place in the refrigerator until cold. Mix the soda in until all of the cranberry sauce is dissolved. Process in an ice cream churn until frozen. Store in the freezer until hard.

Serves 16.

The Mansion of Golconda

Post Office Box 339
Golconda, Illinois 62938
(618) 683-4400

The Mansion of Golconda was built in 1894 and has been an inn since 1928. In 1981 the downstairs dining rooms were refurbished, the kitchen modernized for restaurant service, and the outside landscaping completed. The restaurant has been rated as one of the ten best restaurants in the tri-state area. The entire town of Golconda, a river town established in 1830, is listed on the National Register of Historical Places. It also is situated in the heart of Shawnee National Forest, an area of such splendid beauty that it is known as the Illinois Ozarks. The inn has four beautiful Victorian rooms. A full breakfast is served every morning.

The Mansion of Golconda

Italian Dressing

1 clove garlic, peeled and finely
   chopped
4 cups salad oil
2 cups wine vinegar
2 cups cider vinegar
6 tablespoons oregano
3 tablespoons basil
3 tablespoons salt
3 tablespoons coarsely ground
   black pepper
¾ cup brown sugar, firmly packed
1 cup Parmesan cheese

Blend all the ingredients and store in a
covered container. It tastes better the
longer it is stored.
   Makes 1 gallon.

Chicken with Prosciutto and Cheese

Another variation on a classic.

4 boneless chicken breasts
1 cup Italian Dressing

❖ ❖ ❖

4 slices Prosciutto (other ham can
   be substituted)
4 slices Mozzarella cheese

❖ ❖ ❖

Béarnaise sauce

Marinate the chicken breasts in Italian
dressing at least 4 hours. Place between 2 sheets of waxed paper, and
pound thin. Fold the Prosciutto and
cheese and place inside each chicken
breast. Bake in a 350° oven for 35 minutes. Serve with a spoonful of Bearnaise over top, on a bed of rice.
   Serves 4.

Fettuccine with Two Cheeses and Cream

3 cups cooked fettuccine noodles
½ cup butter (1 stick), melted

½ cup heavy cream
½ cup shredded Mozzarella cheese

❖ ❖ ❖

1 teaspoon finely chopped fresh
   parsley

❖ ❖ ❖

¼ cup grated Parmesan cheese

Arrange the fettuccine on 4 plates.
Combine the melted butter, cream,
and Mozzarella cheese and cook over
low heat until the cheese melts and the
cream bubbles and thickens. Add the
parsley, stir and pour over the noodles.
Sprinkle with Parmesan cheese and
serve promptly.
   This recipe is a variation on the classic Fettuccine Alfredo. The Mansion of
Golconda uses homemade egg noodles. Microwave briefly to make it
steam and serve the dish as an appetizer.
   Serves 4.

Liver Diablo

Liver Diablo should be spicy and hot.
Customers say this is the best preparation of liver *ever*.
   In the summer, the Mansion grows
its own basil, and usually substitutes 1
tablespoon chopped fresh basil for the
dried spice.

6 ripe tomatoes, cored and finely
   chopped
1 cup Burgundy
½ cup finely chopped onion
½ cup tomato paste
¼ cup sugar
½ cup Parmesan cheese
½ teaspoon oregano
½ teaspoon basil
½ teaspoon garlic powder, or 1
   teaspoon finely chopped garlic
½ teaspoon allspice
1 teaspoon paprika
1 teaspoon cayenne pepper
1 teaspoon white pepper
Salt to taste

❖ ❖ ❖

3 pounds beef liver
Seasoned flour
3 tablespoons margarine
3 tablespoons vegetable oil

❖ ❖ ❖

1 green pepper, cored, seeded and
   sliced into strips
1 large onion, sliced into wedges

In a large saucepan combine the tomatoes, Burgundy, onion, tomato paste,
sugar, cheese, and seasonings. Cook
over low heat for about 15 minutes; adjust the seasonings to taste. This sauce
keeps several days in the refrigerator.
   Lightly dredge the liver slices in seasoned flour. In a skillet combine the
margarine and oil. Fry the liver to the
desired degree of doneness, about 4
minutes on each side. Remove the liver
to a heated plate, keep warm. Sauté
the pepper and onion slices in the skillet to tender-crisp, about 4 to 5 minutes. Add the tomato sauce, and heat
through. Pour over the liver and serve.
   Serves 6 to 8.

Double Fudge Hazelnut Pie

"We usually top this with whipped
cream, but that really is not necessary.
The calorie count on this is astronomi-
cal, but for some reason, no one
cares!"

½ cup sugar
½ cup cocoa
3 eggs, slightly beaten
1¼ cups light corn syrup
½ cup heavy cream
½ cup hazelnut liquor
½ cup butter (1 stick), melted
¾ cup hazelnuts, halved
1 cup chocolate chips (mini chips
   are best)
1 9-inch unbaked pie shell, edges
   crimped high

Mix the sugar and cocoa thoroughly,
add to the eggs. Add the corn syrup,
cream, hazelnut liqueur, and melted
butter. Mix well by hand. Add the hazelnuts and chocolate chips, mix and
pour into the pie shell. Bake for 45 to
50 minutes in a 350° oven until the filling is set. It will puff up slightly and
cracks will form around the edges. As
the pie cools, it will settle. The texture
is similar to a wet brownie, but the
taste is of scrumptious fudge.
   Serves 6 to 8.

Indiana

Sherman House Century Old Inn and Restaurant

35 South Main Street
Batesville, Indiana 47006
(812) 934-2407

The Sherman House is one of the oldest buildings and a significant landmark in its community, having opened its door to guests during the War Between the States. It was given its present name to commemorate General Sherman's "march to the sea." Later owners retained the name and added historical significance by collecting the priceless prints of the Sherman era that hang in the lounge.

The following recipes are from chef Joseph R. Shook.

Cream of Cauliflower Soup

2 large heads cauliflower

❖ ❖ ❖

¼ cup chopped onions
1 small stalk celery, minced
½ cup butter (1 stick)

⅓ cup all-purpose flour

❖ ❖ ❖

8 cups chicken stock

❖ ❖ ❖

4 cups rich milk or cream (1 quart)

❖ ❖ ❖

Salt and paprika to taste
Grating of nutmeg

❖ ❖ ❖

Grated Cheddar cheese (optional)

Prepare heads of cauliflower by steaming or poaching until very tender. Drain, reserving liquid and about ⅓ of the florets of each head. Put the remainder through a food mill, food processor, or blender until finely minced. Set aside.

Sauté onions and celery in ½ cup butter, cooking until tender. Stir in flour to make a roux, remove from heat when flour is golden.

In a large saucepan, or steamer pot, combine reserved cauliflower liquid, minced cauliflower, onions, celery, roux, chicken stock, and cook until slightly thickened.

Cool slightly, then add rich milk or cream, the florets, and the seasonings. Heat through and serve immediately.

Note: May be made au gratin simply by adding grated cheese on top of each hot bowl of soup just before serving.

Makes 12 cups.

Deep-Fried Biscuits

4 cups scalded milk, cooled to lukewarm
1 ¼-ounce package active dry yeast
3 cups all-purpose flour

❖ ❖ ❖

½ cup lard, melted and cooled
¼ cup sugar
2 teaspoons salt
2 cups all-purpose flour

In a large bowl, add the milk in a stream to the yeast and stir until yeast is dissolved. Beat in 3 cups of the flour and let batter rise, covered, in a warm place for 1 hour. Then beat in the lard, sugar, salt, and remaining 2 cups of flour. Beat the dough until it leaves the sides of the bowl and let it rise, covered, in a warm place for 1 hour.

Roll out the dough ½-inch thick on a lightly floured surface, and with a floured 2-inch biscuit cutter, cut out rounds. Fry the rounds in batches in deep, hot oil (350°), turning them until they are golden brown. Transfer biscuits to paper towels to drain and serve hot. Especially good served with apple butter.

Makes 24 biscuits.

Individual Beef Wellingtons

4 6-ounce beef tenderloins, trimmed
Salt and pepper to taste
Meat tenderizer to taste

❖ ❖ ❖

2 shallots, finely chopped
8 ounces fresh mushrooms, finely
   chopped
1 tablespoon Burgundy

❖ ❖ ❖

4 ounces chicken or goose liver
   pâté

❖ ❖ ❖

4 puff pastries, cut into 6 to 8-inch
   squares
Egg yolk, beaten as needed

Season the meat with salt, pepper, and
meat tenderizer, sear lightly on each
side keeping the meat very rare (with a
cold center). Set aside. Sauté the shallots and fresh mushrooms until tender,
add the Burgundy and let the mixture
reduce to a paste-like form.

On the top of each tenderloin fillet
spread the chicken or goose liver pâté,
then on top of the pâté spread evenly
the mushroom and shallot mixture.

Roll each puff pastry out until it is 8
to 10 inches square and wrap each
fillet. Decorate by scoring the top or
using decorative cut-outs. Brush with
the beaten egg yolk. Bake in a 350°
oven for approximately 20 minutes or
until golden.

Makes 4 individual servings.

Quail for Six

12 slices bacon
6 quail
2 juniper berries, crushed
2 tablespoons Sherry
Salt and freshly ground pepper
   (coarse), to taste

❖ ❖ ❖

2 pints beef stock
2 pints chicken stock

❖ ❖ ❖

¼ cup half and half
1 tablespoon cornstarch
Chopped fresh parsley

Dice the bacon and place in a casserole that will hold the quails snugly.
Place the quails in the casserole in a
single layer and sprinkle the crushed
juniper berries over the quails. Add the
Sherry and season the quails with salt

and pepper. Cover the casserole, place
in a 350° oven and bake for 30 minutes
or until the quails are tender.

Pour the beef stock together with
the chicken stock into a 1½-quart
saucepan while the quails are baking
and bring to a boil until reduced to approximately 1¼ cups of stock. After
removing quails from the oven strain
the casserole liquid into the stock in
the saucepan and remove the excess
fat from the top. Place the saucepan
back over medium heat and thicken
by adding half and half cream and dissolved cornstarch, add to the saucepan
and bring to a boil stirring constantly.
Pour the sauce over the quails and
sprinkle with parsley.

Serves 6.

Stewed Rabbit Chinon

1 parsley stalk
1 bay leaf
2 sprigs thyme
1 sprig marjoram (optional)

❖ ❖ ❖

1 rabbit, disjointed
Salt and pepper to taste
All-purpose flour
½ cup bacon drippings

❖ ❖ ❖

1 cup red wine
1½ cups beef broth
1 large onion, quartered
3 cloves garlic

❖ ❖ ❖

¼ cup butter (½ stick)
12 tiny whole onions

❖ ❖ ❖

3 tablespoons cornstarch
2 tablespoons Bovril or Kitchen
   Bouquet

❖ ❖ ❖

Duchess potatoes

To make Bouquet Garni (used to season rabbit while baking), combine
parsley, bay leaf, thyme, and marjoram in a small double cheesecloth and
tie securely with a string. Set aside for
later use.

Season the rabbit pieces with salt
and pepper, then dredge with flour.
Heat the bacon drippings in a frying
pan, then add the rabbit pieces and
brown on all sides. Remove the rabbit
and place in a baking dish. Add the
wine, broth, Bouquet Garni (made pre-
viously), the large onion, and garlic
cloves, then cover. Bake in a preheated 350° oven for 1 hour and 30
minutes or until the rabbit is tender.

While the rabbit is baking, melt the
butter in a heavy saucepan. Add the
tiny whole onions and sauté over medium heat until golden, stirring constantly. Add a small amount of water,
then cover and simmer until onions
are tender, stirring carefully several
times. Remove the rabbit pieces from
the baking dish and place them on a
serving platter. Remove the onions
from the saucepan, using a slotted
spoon, and place over the rabbit. Keep
warm.

Discard the Bouquet Garni, onion,
and garlic cloves, then pour the pan
juices from the baking dish into the
saucepan. Combine a small amount of
the juices with the cornstarch to make
a smooth paste, then stir the paste into
the pan juices. Bring to a boil, stirring
constantly. Reduce the heat and cook
until the wine sauce is smooth and
thick. Stir in the Kitchen Bouquet and
season to taste. Pour the sauce over the
onions and rabbit. To add a little something extra, pipe a border of duchess
potatoes around the edge of the serving platter, brown lightly, and serve
immediately.

Serves 4 to 6.

The Dunes Shore Inn

Post Office Box 807
Lakeshore County Road
Beverly Shores, Indiana 46301
(219) 879-9029

The Dunes Shore Inn is situated in the Indiana dunes, only a short walk from Lake Michigan. Set in an area of natural beauty to offer a stopping-off place for exploring the many attractions in the area, it was formerly a summer hotel but has recently reopened. The comfortable single and/or double rooms, newly redecorated, share a bath "down the hall." The main lounge is used for serving the complimentary Continental breakfast; it is also an ideal place for spending time with new and old friends. Each floor has its own lounge for reading, writing, or relaxing.

The Dunes Shore Simple Winter Breakfast

Oatmeal with raisins, apples, nuts, brown sugar—proportions to suit taste/texture. Serve with butter and cream.

Special Preserves

Gooseberries with chopped orange including skin, sugar to taste. Combine and cook. Serve as a sauce over ice cream, on rolls or bread, in cereal.

The Bauer House—A Bed and Breakfast

4595 North Maple Grove Road
Bloomington, Indiana 47401
(812) 336-4383

The Bauer House, surrounded by an old stone wall, offers two rooms in the 120-year-old brick building. A country breakfast including bacon, eggs, toast, coffee, or tea is served. Each room is furnished with a double bed and cots can be arranged for additional persons. The bathroom facilities are shared by the two guest rooms.

Oatmeal Raisin Muffins

1 egg
½ cup vegetable oil
¾ cup milk

❖ ❖ ❖

1 cup all-purpose flour
1 cup oatmeal
½ cup brown sugar, firmly packed
3 teaspoons baking powder
1 teaspoon salt
½ teaspoon nutmeg
½ teaspoon cinnamon
½ cup raisins

Grease the bottoms of a muffin pan. Beat the egg, stir in the oil and milk. Stir in the remaining ingredients all at once until the flour is moistened. Fill the muffin cups ¾ full. Bake in a 400° oven for 20 minutes.

Makes 1 dozen muffins.

The Hoosier Hospitality Bed and Breakfast

1480 Southdowns
Bloomington, Indiana 47401
(812) 339-1491

Hoosier Hospitality is set in the rolling hills of southern Indiana. The house is a large Cape Cod capable of accommodating two couples easily. One room has a queen-sized bed, and the other has a double bed; the rooms share a bathroom. On busy weekends, such as homecoming or parents' weekend at Indiana University, two other rooms are opened. Every day a different gourmet breakfast is served.

Eggs Poached in White Wine

1 tablespoon butter
¼ cup dry white wine or vermouth
2 eggs
Grated Parmesan cheese

❖ ❖ ❖

2 English muffin halves (or 2 pieces toast)

❖ ❖ ❖

1 teaspoon all-purpose flour
2 tablespoons sour cream
White pepper
Salt to taste

In a small omelet pan melt the butter and add the white wine; slip in the eggs. Sprinkle grated Parmesan generously over each egg. Cook over low heat until the whites are firm (covering the pan speeds up this process). Lift out the eggs onto slices of buttered or toasted English muffins or toast.

Add to the liquid in the pan the flour, sour cream, white pepper, and salt.

Stir over moderate heat until the sauce bubbles and thickens, about 1 minute. Pour over the eggs and serve immediately.

It takes about 15 minutes to make this dish.

Serves 2.

Overnight Cinnamon Coffeecake

1 package frozen dinner rolls
1 3½-ounce package instant butterscotch pudding
1 cup brown sugar, firmly packed
2 tablespoons cinnamon
½ cup butter (1 stick), melted
½ cup pecans

Layer in a greased bundt cake pan in the following order: frozen rolls, powdered pudding, brown sugar, cinnamon, melted butter, and pecans. Cover the pan with foil topped with a clean towel and allow to sit overnight.

Bake in a 350° oven for 30 minutes. Serves 8 to 10.

Brigadoon Bed and Breakfast Inn

1201 East Second Street
Evansville, Indiana 47713
(812) 422-9635
(812) 425-1696

The Brigadoon, an 1892 white frame house with Victorian gingerbread porch and picket fence, has large rooms decorated with gentle colors and antique furniture. Four guest rooms are available, two with private baths. The rooms have private vanities as well. The house is near the downtown and riverfront. A full breakfast is included with the night's stay. Every day a different main dish, perhaps a soufflé or quiche, is served, along with homemade breads, jams, and apple butter.

Oatmeal Raisin Rolls

3 cups water
2½ cups old-fashioned oats
2 cups raisins

❖ ❖ ❖

¾ cup warm water
½ cup honey
⅓ cup molasses
¼ cup plus 3 tablespoons butter
3 tablespoons yeast
1 tablespoon plus 2 teaspoons salt

❖ ❖ ❖

1 teaspoon cinnamon
6 to 8 cups all-purpose flour

Boil 3 cups of water, pour over the oats and raisins. Cover and let sit until warm. Combine ¾ cup of warm water, the honey, molasses, butter, and yeast. Let stand until the yeast bubbles up. Add the salt and oats. Add the cinnamon and flour until stiff enough to knead. Knead 10 to 12 minutes. The dough will remain fairly soft and sticky but should hold shape when standing alone and sound slightly drum-like when slapped hard. Place the dough in an oiled bowl, and cover with a wet towel. Let rise in a warm place for 45 minutes. Form into 1½- to 2-inch balls, let rise until 75% larger. Bake in a 350° oven for 12 to 20 minutes until medium dark brown.

Makes approximately 3½ to 4 dozen rolls.

The Candlewyck Inn Bed and Breakfast

331 West Washington Boulevard
Fort Wayne, Indiana 46802
(219) 424-2643

The Candlewyck Inn is a fine example of a California-style bungalow. Built and designed in 1914 by Paul Kinder, a local contractor, Candlewyck Inn's beauty is evident in the lovely beveled glass and stained glass windows located throughout. The oak-beamed ceilings in the parlor and dining room add to the charm of this home, which is listed on the National Historical Register. Five quaint bedrooms with shared baths are available; all are furnished with antiques and brass. Wood floors, and handsome wallcoverings and accessories add the finishing touches to this beautiful inn.

Apple Muffins

1½ cups all-purpose flour
½ cup sugar
2 teaspoons baking powder
½ teaspoon salt
½ teaspoon cinnamon

❖ ❖ ❖

¼ cup soft shortening
1 egg
½ cup milk
1 cup finely chopped apple

❖ ❖ ❖

⅓ cup brown sugar, firmly packed
⅓ cup broken nuts
½ teaspoon cinnamon

Combine in a bowl the flour, sugar, baking powder, salt, and cinnamon. Blend the shortening, egg, milk, and apple. Add to the dry ingredients and stir just until ingredients are blended. Fill greased muffin pans ¾ full. Top with the brown sugar, nuts, and cinnamon. Bake in a 400° oven for 25 to 30 minutes.

Makes 1 dozen muffins.

Fresh Peach Muffins

1 cup whole wheat flour
1 cup all-purpose flour
1½ teaspoons baking powder
½ teaspoon baking soda
½ teaspoon ground cinnamon

❖   ❖   ❖

1 egg
⅔ cup brown sugar, lightly packed
¾ cup buttermilk
¼ cup corn oil
½ teaspoon almond extract

❖   ❖   ❖

1 cup diced fresh peaches

Spray a muffin pan with a non-stick spray. Set aside.

In a medium bowl, combine the flours, baking powder, soda, and cinnamon. Mix well.

In a large bowl, beat the egg lightly. Stir in the brown sugar, buttermilk, oil, and almond extract. Blend well. Add the flour mixture and gently fold together until the dry ingredients are moistened. Gently fold in the peaches. Fill muffin cups ¾ full. Bake in a 375° oven for 20 to 25 minutes or until toothpick inserted in center comes out clean. Serve warm.

Makes 1 dozen muffins.

Strawberry Nut Muffins

¾ cup whole wheat flour
¾ cup all-purpose flour
½ teaspoon baking powder
½ teaspoon baking soda
½ teaspoon ground cinnamon
½ cup chopped pecans

❖   ❖   ❖

1 egg
½ cup brown sugar, firmly packed
1 cup buttermilk
¼ cup corn oil
1 teaspoon vanilla extract

❖   ❖   ❖

1 cup coarsely chopped
strawberries

The Candlewyck Inn

Spray a muffin pan with a non-stick spray, set aside. In a medium bowl, combine the flours, baking powder, soda, cinnamon, and pecans. Mix well. In a large bowl, beat the egg lightly. Stir in the brown sugar, buttermilk, oil, and vanilla. Blend well. Add the flour mixture and gently fold together until the dry ingredients are moistened. Gently fold in the strawberries. Fill muffins cups ¾ full. Bake in a 375° oven for 20 to 25 minutes or until toothpick inserted in center comes out clean. Serve warm.

Makes 1 dozen muffins.

Fresh Blueberry Banana Bread

1 cup blueberries

❖   ❖   ❖

1¾ cups all-purpose flour
2 teaspoons baking powder
¼ teaspoon baking soda
½ teaspoon salt

❖   ❖   ❖

⅓ cup margarine
⅔ cup sugar
2 eggs
1 cup mashed banana

Toss the washed and drained blueberries with 2 tablespoons of the flour. Sift the flour, baking powder, soda, and salt together. Set aside. Cream the margarine and gradually beat in the sugar until fluffy. Beat in the eggs, one at a time. Add the flour mixture alternately with the mashed banana, stirring until blended. Stir in the blueberries. Bake in a greased loaf pan in a 350° oven for 50 to 60 minutes.

Makes 1 loaf.

Poppy Seed Cheese Bread

This is a quick recipe.

3¾ cups Bisquick mix
1¼ cups shredded sharp cheese

1 tablespoon poppy seeds
1 egg, beaten
1½ cups milk

Combine the Bisquick, cheese, and poppy seeds; add the egg and milk. Mix just to blend. Beat vigorously for 1 minute. Turn into a well-greased 9x5x3-inch loaf pan. Sprinkle with poppy seeds. Bake in a 350° oven for 50 to 60 minutes. Remove from the pan; cool.

Makes 1 loaf.

Mushroom Scramble

The microwave produces very tender scrambled eggs. This main dish is surprisingly low in calories, only about 200 per serving.

¾ cup chopped celery
¼ cup chopped onion
1 cup chopped fresh mushrooms
8 eggs
¼ cup grated Parmesan cheese
½ teaspoon salt

In a 1½-quart dish mix the celery and onion. Cook for 2 minutes on high. Top with mushrooms. Beat together the eggs, cheese, and salt. Pour over the vegetables and cover with plastic wrap. Cook 3 minutes on high. Using a rubber spatula or wooden spoon, break up the cooked portions and push toward the center. Cook 2 to 3 minutes more, breaking up the mixture once or twice until thickened, but before the eggs reach desired doneness. Stir again, cover, and let stand 2 to 3 minutes to finish cooking.

Serves 4.

The Old Hoosier House

Route 2, Box 299-1
Knightstown, Indiana 46148
(317) 345-2969

The Old Hoosier House is a Georgian-style, two-story all-brick house built between 1836 and 1840. It has been added to, subtracted from, and modernized somewhat; but it retains its original exterior appearance, with a few modern innovations such as the popular sun deck. The high-ceilinged rooms give a spacious feeling, and the tall, arched windows and curved staircase reflect the age of the house. One of the four large bedrooms, known as the "Travelers Room," overlooks the main entrance hall with its curved stairs but has its own private staircase. Tasteful modern touches include bathroom and kitchen areas. A butler's pantry, used as an intimate breakfast room, provides a view of the pond and golf course adjoining the property. A complete laundry room is available for guests. The deck is a favorite spot to relax, watch the golfers, to read, or to sip tea.

Chicken Wellington

A pastry supper loaf.

6 cups cut-up cooked chicken
3 tablespoons chopped pimiento
1½ teaspoon salt
⅛ teaspoon pepper
1 teaspoon Worcestershire sauce
6 tablespoons butter
6 tablespoons all-purpose flour
1 cup chicken stock

❖ ❖ ❖

1 egg
2 frozen pie shells, thawed

❖ ❖ ❖

¼ cup butter (½ stick)
2 cups sliced mushroom caps

2 teaspoons grated onion
4 tablespoons all-purpose flour
1 teaspoon salt
¼ teaspoon pepper
2 cups milk (or 1 cup milk and 1 cup chicken stock)

Combine the chicken, pimiento, salt, pepper, and Worcestershire sauce, set aside. In a saucepan, melt butter; add flour and mix until smooth. Gradually add the stock and continue to cook, stirring constantly until very thick. Add just enough of the stock mixture to hold the meat mixture together. Shape into a loaf on a shallow pan and chill at least 3 hours.

Place 1 pie shell in a large oblong pan. Rolling may be necessary to fit the oblong pan. Add all of the chicken mixture. Cover with the other pie shell. Seal all the edges. Decorate as desired. Chill thoroughly; brush with egg diluted with a little water. Bake in a 425° oven for 1 hour or until brown.

In a saucepan melt the ¼ cup of butter, sauté the mushroom caps and onion in the butter; remove the mushrooms and onion and set aside. Add 4 tablespoons of flour, the salt, and pepper, and stir until combined. Add the milk and stir constantly until thick and bubbly over medium or medium-low heat. Place in a serving bowl to be served with Chicken Wellington as desired.

Serves 8.

The Cliff House

122 Fairmount Drive
Madison, Indiana 47250
(812) 265-5272

This outstanding Victorian home was built in 1885 on a bluff high above the mighty Ohio River. The mansion has a widow's walk where guests can relax and watch the river roll by. Most of the rooms have canopy beds, and a candlelight breakfast is served each morning. The town of Madison has been called "the nineteenth century Williamsburg of America."

The Cliff House

Poppy Seed Cake

2 cups sugar
1½ cups oil
4 eggs
1 teaspoon vanilla extract

❖ ❖ ❖

3 cups all-purpose flour
¾ teaspoon salt
1½ teaspoons baking soda
1 12-ounce can evaporated milk
1 2½-ounce can or package poppy
   seeds
1 3-ounce package walnuts
   (or pecans)

Combine in a large bowl the sugar, oil, eggs, and vanilla. Add in all the remaining ingredients and mix well.

Bake in a 350° oven for 1 hour and 10 minutes in a bundt pan or 3 small pans.

Clifty Inn

Clifty Falls State Park
Box 387
Madison, Indiana 47250
(812) 265-4135

Clifty Inn is open all year with accommodations to meet any need.

Many guests say the scenic beauty of Clifty Falls State Park, overlooking the Ohio River, is unequalled in the United States and is comparable to that of the Swiss Alps. The view overlooking the river and the city of Madison is spectacular, while the seventy-foot falls in Clifty Creek is a never-failing attraction. Trails wind through the great canyon and along the sides of precipitous vine-and-fern-covered cliffs, giving access to wooded ravines and smaller waterfalls.

Orange Eggnog Punch

1 quart sherbet (raspberry, orange,
   or lime)

❖ ❖ ❖

2 cups orange juice
2 cups pineapple juice

❖ ❖ ❖

1 quart dairy eggnog

❖ ❖ ❖

1 cup sherbet

In a mixing bowl, beat the sherbet until smooth. Add orange and pineapple juices and blend thoroughly. Gradually add the eggnog. Pour into a punch bowl. Float small scoops of sherbet on the top.

Marinated Salad

This salad is best when prepared the day before serving.

2 16-ounce cans French-style green
   beans
1 16-ounce can small peas
1 16-ounce can corn
1 green pepper, finely chopped
1 small onion, finely chopped
2 cups finely chopped celery
1 2-ounce jar chopped pimientos

❖ ❖ ❖

1 cup sugar
1 teaspoon salt
¼ cup oil
½ cup vinegar
⅛ cup water

In a large bowl, combine green beans, peas, corn, green pepper, onion, celery, and pimientos.

Make dressing in a separate bowl by combining sugar, salt, oil, vinegar, and water. Mix thoroughly, until all the sugar is dissolved. Pour over the salad, cover, and refrigerate overnight for the best flavor.

Serves 8 to 10.

Spanish Cauliflower

1 head cauliflower

❖ ❖ ❖

¼ cup butter (½ stick), melted
1 tablespoon sugar
½ teaspoon salt
½ teaspoon pepper
1 cup cracker crumbs
½ cup diced green pepper
1 16-ounce can tomatoes, chopped
1 medium onion, chopped
1½ cups shredded Cheddar cheese

Wash the cauliflower and remove the leaves. Break into florets. Cook for 5 minutes in salted water. Drain. In a large mixing bowl, combine the butter, sugar, salt, pepper, and cracker crumbs. Stir in the green pepper, tomatoes, onion, 1¼ cups cheese, and hot drained cauliflower. Pour into a 2-quart casserole. Sprinkle with the remaining cheese. Bake in a 350° oven for 1 hour. Serve hot.

Serves 8 to 10.

Corn Pudding

½ cup margarine (1 stick)
2 eggs, beaten
1 16-ounce can corn
1 16-ounce can cream-style corn
1 8-ounce container sour cream
1 8½-ounce box Jiffy cornbread
   mix

In a mixing bowl, combine margarine, eggs, cans of corn, and sour cream. Add the cornbread mix and stir well. Pour into a long, shallow baking dish. Bake in a 350° oven for 45 minutes.

Serves 8.

The Thorpe House

Clayborne Street
Just One Square North of Canal Foot
   Bridge
Metamora, Indiana 47030
(317) 647-5425
(317) 932-2365

In Old Metamora the steam engine still brings passenger cars, the horses still pull the canal boat, and the grist mill still grinds corn meal. After a relaxing evening and peaceful night in the hospitable country rooms, guests of The Thorpe House will awaken to the aroma of a farm-fresh breakfast. Black raspberry pie, hot breads and muffins, specialty jellies, and home cooked meals all are standard fare.

Wake-Up Casserole

2 cups seasoned croutons
1 cup shredded Cheddar cheese
1 4-ounce can mushroom pieces,
   drained
1½ pounds bulk country fresh
   sausage, crumbled
½ cup chopped onion
6 eggs
2 cups milk
½ teaspoon salt
½ teaspoon pepper
½ teaspoon dry mustard

❖ ❖ ❖

1 10¾-ounce can cream of
   mushroom soup
½ cup milk

Place croutons in greased 13x9x2-inch pan. Top with cheese and mushrooms. Brown sausage and onion. Drain and spread over cheese. Beat eggs with 2 cups milk and seasonings; pour over sausage. Cover and refrigerate overnight. (May be frozen at this point.) Mix soup with ½ cup milk and spread on top before you bake. Bake in a 325° oven for 60 minutes.

Note from the innkeeper: Not even a night owl can sleep through this wonderful smell coming from the kitchen!
Serves 8.

Lottie's Beet Jelly

4 cups beet juice (strained)
½ cup lemon juice
1 1¾-ounce box Sure-Jel

❖ ❖ ❖

6 cups sugar

Bring to a boil the beet and lemon juices, and Sure-Jel, stirring constantly. Add the sugar and bring to a rolling boil. Boil 3 minutes. Pour into prepared hot jars and cover at once.
Fills 4 8-ounce jars.

Amy Rose's Molasses Cookies

¾ cup shortening (part butter)

❖ ❖ ❖

1 cup sugar
¼ cup molasses
1 egg

❖ ❖ ❖

1 teaspoon cinnamon
2 teaspoons baking soda
2 cups sifted all-purpose flour
½ teaspoon cloves
½ teaspoon ginger
½ teaspoon salt

❖ ❖ ❖

Confectioners' sugar

In a saucepan, melt the shortening. When cooled, add the sugar, molasses, and egg; beat well. Sift together the dry ingredients and add to the first mixture. Mix well. Chill thoroughly.

Form into 1-inch balls and roll in sugar. Place 2 inches apart on a greased cookie sheet. Bake in a 375° oven for 8 to 10 minutes.
Makes about 4 dozen cookies.

Peanut Butter Pie

3 eggs
1 cup light corn syrup
1 cup sugar
½ cup peanut butter
½ teaspoon vanilla extract

❖ ❖ ❖

1 10-inch unbaked pie shell
Semi-sweet chocolate
Whipped cream (optional)

In a large bowl, whisk eggs slightly. Whisk in the next 4 ingredients, and beat until well blended. Pour into prepared pie shell. Bake in a 400° oven for 15 minutes, then reduce temperature to 350° and bake for 30 minutes.

When pie is cooled, shave some chocolate curls on top. Delicious with whipped cream, or without.
Serves 6.

Spring Mill Inn

Spring Mill State Park
Rural Route 2, Post Office Box 68
Mitchell, Indiana 47446
(812) 849-4081

Spring Mill Inn is a modern facility in Spring Mill State Park. All rates are on the European plan. All rooms are air-conditioned, have a private bath, and also are equipped with color television and a telephone. The appeal of this inn is its surroundings and Hoosier hospitality. Spring Mill State Park is unique among Indiana parks because of its underground caves and 1200 acres of forests, in which camping facilities, trails for hiking and two swimming pools are available. Reconstruction of the Pioneer Village began in 1932, and since then several historic buildings have been rebuilt and furnished. In the spring the roads and trails are lined with gorgeous white dogwood, and in the fall colorful maple trees make the park roads tunnels of gold.

Spring Mill Corn Muffins

½ cup shortening
¼ cup sugar

❖ ❖ ❖

1 egg, beaten
1 cup milk

❖ ❖ ❖

½ cup all-purpose flour
1½ cups cornmeal
¼ teaspoon baking powder
1 teaspoon baking soda
½ teaspoon salt

Cream the shortening with the sugar, add the egg and milk. Combine the dry ingredients and add to the liquid mixture. Stir until smooth. Fill greased muffin cups ¾ full. Bake in a 400° oven for 25 minutes.

Makes 1 dozen muffins.

Corn Meal Pie

½ cup butter (1 stick)
1 cup sugar
½ cup brown sugar, firmly packed

❖ ❖ ❖

3 eggs, beaten
1¼ teaspoon vanilla extract
½ cup milk
½ cup yellow corn meal

❖ ❖ ❖

1 9-inch pie shell
½ cup almonds

Cream the butter and sugars. Add the eggs, vanilla, milk, and corn meal, and mix well. Pour into an unbaked pie shell and sprinkle almonds on top. Bake in 350° over for 45 minutes.

Serves 6.

The Old Franklin House

704 East Washington Street
Muncie, Indiana 47305
(317) 286-0277

The Old Franklin House provides relaxation in comfortable Victorian surroundings. An elegant, restored colonial-revival home built in the 1890s, the house contains period antiques throughout its rooms. Breakfast includes orange juice, coffee or tea, omelet, and toast made from homemade bread with butter, jelly, and apple butter.

Apple Coffee Cake

¼ cup milk
¼ cup sugar
½ teaspoon salt
⅓ cup vegetable shortening

❖ ❖ ❖

1 ¼-ounce package active dry yeast
¼ cup warm water (110° to 115°)

❖ ❖ ❖

2 eggs, beaten
2¼ cups sifted all-purpose flour

❖ ❖ ❖

3 medium cooking apples

❖ ❖ ❖

½ cup light brown sugar, firmly packed
½ teaspoon cinnamon
¼ teaspoon cloves
¼ teaspoon allspice

❖ ❖ ❖

¼ cup butter or margarine
(½ stick)

Combine the milk, sugar, salt, and shortening in a saucepan. Heat just until the shortening is melted; cool to lukewarm. Sprinkle the yeast into very warm water in a large bowl. Add the lukewarm milk mixture, eggs and 1 cup of the flour; beat until

smooth. Add just enough of the remaining flour to make a soft dough.

Turn out on a lightly floured surface; knead until the dough is smooth and elastic, about 5 minutes, using only as much flour as needed to keep the dough from sticking. Place in a large greased bowl; turn to bring the greased side up. Cover. Let rise in a warm place away from drafts, 1 to 1½ hours, or until double in bulk. Punch the dough down, knead a few times; let rest 5 minutes.

Press the dough evenly into a greased 9x13-inch baking pan. Cover with a towel; let rise in a warm place, away from drafts, 30 minutes or until dough is almost doubled in bulk.

Pare, quarter, and core the apples; cut into very thin slices. Mix the brown sugar, cinnamon, cloves, and allspice in a small bowl. Melt the butter or margarine in a small saucepan. Arrange the apple slices over dough in an overlapping pattern. Sprinkle with the sugar mixture; drizzle with butter. Bake in a 375° oven for 25 to 30 minutes, or until a wooden pick inserted in center comes out clean. Remove from the oven. Cool the coffee cake in the pan on a wire rack at least 30 minutes before cutting.

Serves 10.

Dill Bread

This wonderful tasting casserole bread does not have to be kneaded.

1 ¼-ounce package active dry yeast
1 cup warm water

❖ ❖ ❖

1 tablespoon minced onion
2 teaspoons dill seed (or weed)
1 teaspoon salt
1 egg
¼ teaspoon baking soda
½ cup butter or margarine (1 stick), or corn oil
2 tablespoons honey

❖ ❖ ❖

1 cup small curd cottage cheese, heated to lukewarm
5 cups all-purpose flour

Dissolve the yeast in the water in a large bowl and set aside. Mix the remaining ingredients, except the cottage cheese and flour, in another large bowl. Stir the cottage cheese into the yeast mixture and add the flour. Combine the flour mixture with the dill mixture and beat or mix vigorously until the dough is sticky-heavy. Cover with a clean cloth and put in a warm place for nearly 1 hour. Punch and stir the dough down. Spoon into a deep casserole, cover again, and let rise until doubled in bulk. Bake in a 350° oven for about 1 hour. Brush the top with butter, remove from the dish. Enjoy.

Makes 1 loaf.

Mayor Wilhelm's Villa

428 North Fifth Street
Vincennes, Indiana 47591
(812) 882-9487

Amidst nostalgic dwellings and historic landmarks stands the home of a Vincennes Former Mayor. This charming structure, built in 1887 for Mayor Wilhelm, is embellished with treasures of the past, including beautiful fireplaces and elaborate woodwork. To-day his home is a bed and breakfast facility that combines the charms of yesterday with the luxuries of today. Modern air conditioning and heating systems make for a comfortable stay, and guests can sit by a crackling fire in the sitting room, watch cable television, read, or visit.

Snackin' Granola Bars

3½ cups oats (quick or old-
    fashioned, uncooked)
1 cup raisins
1 cup chopped nuts
⅔ cup butter, melted
⅓ cup honey, molasses, or corn
    syrup
1 egg, beaten
½ teaspoon vanilla extract
½ teaspoon salt
½ cup brown sugar, firmly packed

Toss the oats with the remaining ingredients and mix well. Press firmly into a well-greased 15½x10½-inch jelly roll pan. Bake in a 350° oven for 20 minutes. Cool. Cut into bars.

Makes 10 to 12 bars.

Peach Preserves
For the Microwave

4 large peaches, peeled and cut in
    pieces (4 cups)

6 cups sugar
¼ cup lemon juice

❖ ❖ ❖

1 3-ounce package liquid fruit
    pectin

In a 3-quart glass casserole mix the peaches, sugar, and lemon juice. Cover with plastic wrap. Cook in the microwave for 14 minutes on high or until the sugar is dissolved and the peaches are soft. Stir every 3 minutes. Boil for 1 minute. Remove from the oven and stir in the liquid pectin. Let stand uncovered for 10 minutes. Stir. Pour the preserves into hot sterilized jars and cover. Allow to cool. Store in the refrigerator.

Fills 6 8-ounce jars.

Hot Apple Cider

2 quarts apple cider
3 cups cranberry juice
4 cinnamon sticks
2 teaspoons whole cloves

❖ ❖ ❖

Lemon slices
Cloves

Bring the first four ingredients to a boil. Simmer for 5 minutes. Pour into mugs and garnish with lemon slices studded with cloves.

Serves 12.

Iowa

The Redstone Inn

Post Office Box 3257
Fifth and Bluff
Dubuque, Iowa 52001
(319) 582-1894

Built in 1894, the Redstone is the only remaining mansion of the three built by A. A. Cooper, one of early Iowa's leading industrialists. Guests register in an oak-paneled reception area where stained glass reflects shades of mauve, burgundy, deep blue, and green used as the color scheme throughout the inn. A Continental breakfast and afternoon tea are served on fine linens in an intimate dining room as the hues of the stained glass play off the decorative ceramic tiles of the fireplace. Wine, champagne, and premium beers and liquors are served in the ornate parlor where gilded cherubs look down on the mansion's original gas chandelier and part of the $180,000 collection of antique furnishings. Like all of the Redstone's antiques, these elegant period pieces are from within a 150-mile radius of Dubuque.

Throughout the Redstone one encounters the best of the old and the new. Some rooms feature original, working fireplaces of marble or oak; and while all bathrooms are modern, the tilework is reminiscent of the Victorian era. Listed on the National Register of Historic Places, the inn is surrounded by three of the city's five historical preservation districts.

Cooper Eggs Benedict

¾ cup butter (1½ sticks)
¾ cup all-purpose flour
6 cups milk

❖ ❖ ❖

1 pound ham
1 cup grated Cheddar cheese

❖ ❖ ❖

8 eggs, hard-boiled
1 pound asparagus, blanched
Salt and pepper to taste
1 tablespoon cooking Sherry
   (optional)

❖ ❖ ❖

8 3-inch squares corn bread

Make white sauce in a medium saucepan over moderate heat by melting the butter, blending in the flour, then adding the milk, stirring constantly until thick and smooth.

Cut the ham into chunks and add with the cheese to the white sauce. Heat on low heat to blend the flavors.

Cut cooled eggs into quarters. Prepare asparagus by cutting into 1-inch pieces. Before serving, add eggs and asparagus, seasonings, and Sherry if used, to the sauce. Stir very gently.

To serve, place a piece of warm corn bread on each plate and pour 1 cup of sauce over it.

This has been served at the Redstone for special breakfast parties. Serve with fresh fruit and small sweet rolls.

Makes 8 servings.

Chicken Cordon Bleu

4 whole chicken breasts

❖ ❖ ❖

8 slices cooked ham
8 slices Swiss cheese
3 tablespoons minced parsley
Pepper to taste
1 egg, beaten
½ cup Italian bread crumbs
¼ cup butter (½ stick)

❖ ❖ ❖

1 10¾-ounce can Cheddar cheese
   soup
8 ounces sour cream
⅓ cup dry Sherry

Split, bone, and skin the chicken pieces. Place each chicken breast half

The Redstone Inn

on a sheet of waxed paper. Using a meat mallet, flatten to ¼-inch thick. Place 1 slice each of ham and cheese in the center of each piece. Sprinkle evenly with parsley and pepper. Roll up each chicken breast lengthwise and secure with a wooden pick. Dip each piece into beaten egg and coat well with the crumbs.

In a heavy skillet, melt the butter, brown the chicken pieces, and place in a 12x8-inch baking dish, reserving the drippings.

To the drippings, add the cheese soup, sour cream, and Sherry. Stir well and pour over the chicken. Bake uncovered in a 350° oven for 40 to 45 minutes.

This is a very popular entree at the Redstone's catered dinners. It was the hit of the show at the Dubuque tasting party.

Makes 8 servings.

Mincemeat Tea Biscuits

1 9-ounce package mincemeat
3 tablespoons water

❖ ❖ ❖

½ cup butter (1 stick), softened
⅓ cup shortening
1½ cups sugar
3 eggs, well beaten
1½ cups all-purpose flour

❖ ❖ ❖

1½ cups all-purpose flour
1 cup chopped walnuts
1 teaspoon baking soda
½ teaspoon nutmeg

Place the mincemeat in a small bowl, add the water, blend and set aside. In a large mixing bowl, cream the butter and shortening with the sugar. Add the eggs and beat well. Add 1½ cups of flour to the butter mixture and blend to smooth the batter. Stir in the mincemeat. Mix the remaining 1½ cups flour with the walnuts, soda, and nutmeg. Add to the batter and blend. Drop by spoonfuls onto a greased and floured baking sheet. Bake in a 375° oven until firm, about 10 minutes.

These are served at the Redstone's English afternoon tea.
Makes 36 biscuits.

Chocolate Ladyfinger Cake

4 eggs, separated
2 bars German's sweet chocolate
2 teaspoons vanilla extract
1 9.6-ounce carton whipped topping
3 packages ladyfingers
½ pint whipping cream, whipped
1 cup finely chopped English walnuts

Beat the egg yolks until they are a lemon color. In a separate bowl, beat the egg whites until stiff peaks form.

Melt the chocolate bars in the microwave or over hot water in the top of a double boiler. Remove from the heat and beat egg yolks into chocolate, add the vanilla and mix well. Fold the mixture into the stiffly beaten egg whites.

When the mixture is cool, fold in ½ the carton of whipped topping and then the walnuts.

Using a 9 or 10-inch springform pan, line bottom and sides with the ladyfingers, placing the rounded side against the sides of the pan. Pour ½ of the chocolate mixture over the ladyfingers. Then add another layer of ladyfingers and the other half of the chocolate mixture.

Fold the whipped cream and the remaining whipped topping together and smooth onto the top of the cake. It will just fill to the top of the standing ladyfingers. Refrigerate for 24 hours, covered.

To serve, place the cake on a pretty cake stand and remove the sides from the pan.

Cake can be decorated if you desire. Tie a pretty satin ribbon around the cake so that it looks like the ribbon is holding the cake together. Garnish with silk flowers and greens in the winter. In the summer, fresh strawberries make a nice garnish.

This dessert is served at the Redstone during afternoon tea and for special catered dinners.

Old-Fashioned Lemon Curd Tart Filling

3 whole eggs
3 egg yolks
1 cup sugar
½ cup fresh lemon juice
¼ cup butter (½ stick), cut into pieces

In a glass dish, beat together the whole eggs, the yolks, sugar, and lemon juice. Beat well and then add butter. Place in the microwave and cook on high for 3 1½-minute intervals, removing the dish and beating well after each 1½-minute interval. Should be silky smooth and thickened. Cover with plastic wrap and refrigerate.

This tart filling is used for the Redstone's English tea plate and is also good as a pie filling, topped with whipped cream.

Makes approximately 2 cups.

1909 home nestled in the peaceful Danish town of Elk Horn, seven miles north of I–80, in the heart of the largest Danish settlement in the United States. No more charming lodging could be found that offers so much to the traveller. The rooms contain the most comfortable furnishings available. The Ortgies, who own this inn, chose the name, "The Travelling Companion" from one of Hans Christian Andersen's fairy tales and each guest room is named after a different fairy tale. The complimentary breakfast, served in the privacy of one's room, includes hot coffee or tea and various items such as quiche, strata, or Danish pastry.

Danish Kringle

In addition to the ingredients listed below, have ready a filling of your choice. This could be jam, chopped apples, raisins or chopped dates, or some special family favorite.

1 ¼-ounce package active dry yeast
¼ cup warm milk
1 cup butter or margarine (2 sticks)
2¼ cups all-purpose flour
½ teaspoon salt
2 tablespoons sugar
2 eggs, beaten

❖ ❖ ❖

½ cup butter (1 stick), melted
½ cup sugar
Filling
Vanilla extract

❖ ❖ ❖

2 eggs whites, beaten slightly

❖ ❖ ❖

Confectioners' sugar icing
Nuts

Dissolve the yeast in the warm milk. Mix 1 cup of margarine, flour, and salt as you would for a pie crust. Add the yeast and 2 tablespoons sugar. Add as much beaten egg as you need to absorb the flour mixture. Turn onto a floured board and knead until smooth.

Divide into 2 or 3 parts and roll into oblong strips. Spread ½ cup melted butter mixed with ½ cup sugar onto the strips. Then add the desired fruit fillings, which have a little vanilla added. Fold over and brush with the egg whites. Let rise for 2 hours.

Bake in a 375° oven for 20 minutes. Frost with a confectioners' sugar icing and top with nuts.

Serves 8 to 10.

Frozen Fruit Cup

1 6-ounce can frozen orange juice, thawed
1 6-ounce can frozen lemonade, thawed
⅔ cup sugar
4 bananas, mashed
1 16-ounce can crushed pineapple (not drained)
1 pint ginger ale
1 10-ounce package frozen strawberries, thawed

In a large pitcher, stir together all the ingredients. Pour into individual freezer-proof cups and freeze. Remove from the freezer ½ hour before serving for partial defrosting.

Serves 6 to 8.

The Hannah Marie Country Inn

Route One
Spencer, Iowa 51301
(712) 262-1286

The Hannah Marie has retained the original character of its ninety-five-year-old farm house. Restored to its first luster, its simplicity reflects the gentle style of long ago days. The marks of many years of living make this house a home: dents in the original doors, sloping ceilings, turn-of-the-century plaster, authentic stairway, and old house noises. Guests are pampered in the Victorian manner; the porch swing and rocking chairs, as well as heirloom table linens, are part of the atmosphere.

Carrot Muffins

¼ cup corn oil
½ cup honey

❖ ❖ ❖

½ cup milk
2 large eggs (room temperature)
1 tablespoon finely grated orange rind

❖ ❖ ❖

1 cup whole wheat flour
¾ cup unbleached flour
¼ cup soy flour
1 tablespoon baking powder

❖ ❖ ❖

1 cup grated carrots
1 cup raisins

In a large mixing bowl, blend together oil and honey. Stir in the milk, eggs, and orange rind, beating well.

In another bowl combine, but do not sift, the flours and baking powder. Stir in the liquid mixture just until dry ingredients are moist.

Stir in the carrots and raisins. Spoon into lightly greased muffin tins. Bake in a 425° oven for 15 to 20 minutes. Let stand for 5 minutes before removing from the tins. Delicious served warm with butter or cream cheese.

Makes 12 regular-size muffins.

Gingerbread Muffins

1 egg
½ cup corn oil
¾ cup molasses
½ cup rice syrup
1¼ cups buttermilk

❖ ❖ ❖

1¼ cups plus 1 tablespoon whole
   wheat flour
1¼ cups plus 1 tablespoon
   unbleached flour
6 tablespoons soy flour
1½ teaspoons ground ginger
1 teaspoon ground cinnamon
½ teaspoon ground cloves

❖ ❖ ❖

1 tablespoon finely chopped
   candied ginger
½ cup raisins

Beat the egg and stir in the corn oil.
Add the molasses, rice syrup, and buttermilk, set aside. In a large mixing
bowl, combine the dry ingredients,
then add the ginger and raisins. Pour
the liquid mixture into the dry mixture. Do not overmix. Pour into prepared muffin cups. Bake in a 425°
oven for 15 to 20 minutes. Let stand 5
minutes before removing from cups.
  Makes 12 muffins.

Elizabeth's Applesauce Cookies

These good-for-you goodies, made
with whole grain flours and rice syrup
sweetener found at health food stores,
are served with a cream cheese filling
between two cookies.

1 cup whole wheat flour
¾ cup unbleached flour
¼ cup soy flour
1 teaspoon baking soda
½ teaspoon cinnamon
½ teaspoon cloves
½ teaspoon nutmeg

❖ ❖ ❖

1 egg (room temperature)
½ cup corn oil
1 cup rice syrup

❖ ❖ ❖

1 cup applesauce
¼ cup finely chopped nuts

❖ ❖ ❖

4 ounces cream cheese, softened
2 to 3 tablespoons marmalade or
   berry preserves

Blend together in a large bowl the
flours, the soda, and the spices. Set
aside.
  In a large mixing bowl, beat the egg.
Slowly beat in the oil, then the rice
syrup. Alternately add the applesauce
and flour mixture to the liquids. Last
add the nuts.
  Drop by teaspoonfuls onto lightly
greased cookie sheets. Bake in a 375°
oven for 8 to 10 minutes.
  Make a filling by beating well the
cream cheese and marmalade or preserves and spread between cookies.
  Makes 3 to 4 dozen cookies.

Punch Cup Cookies

14 tablespoons (7 ounces) unsalted
   butter, softened
½ cup confectioners' sugar
1 teaspoon vanilla extract
2 teaspoons lemon juice
2½ cups unbleached flour

In a large mixing bowl, beat butter until light, then beat in confectioners'
sugar. Add the vanilla and lemon juice.

Mix in the flour until the dough is
smooth and stiff. Roll out the dough.
For a design, you can press the design-
cut bottom of a punch cup into the
dough, cutting around it. Place onto a
cookie sheet. Bake in a 450° oven for 8
to 10 minutes, until barely light
brown—do not overbake. Place on a
wire rack to cool.
  These store nicely in a tin until
served.
  Makes 2½ dozen cookies.

Autumn Apple Pie

4 tart green apples (medium size)
¼ cup cranberry sauce
¼ cup raisins
1 cup rice syrup*
2 tablespoons Sherry
2½ tablespoons tapioca
1 teaspoon nutmeg

❖ ❖ ❖

Pastry for 1 9-inch 2-crust pie

Peel, core, and thinly slice the apples.
Cut the cranberry sauce into very
small pieces and combine with the apples, raisins, rice syrup, wine, tapioca,
and nutmeg.
  Line pie tin with pastry, add filling,
and cover with top pastry which has
been slit several times to allow steam
to escape.
  Bake in a 450° oven for 10 minutes.
Reduce temperature to 375° and bake
about 45 minutes longer or until the
crust is golden brown.
  Delicious served with cheese.
  *Vary the amount of rice syrup de-
pending on the sweetness of the apples. Rice syrup is a very mild
sweetener, available at health food
stores.
  Serves 6.

Kansas

Bed and Breakfast Kansas City

Post Office Box 14781
Lenexa, Kansas 66215
(913) 888-3636

This bed and breakfast ranch home is located on a quiet street in an exclusive suburb of Kansas City. Beautifully decorated, it has one upstairs guest room with a private bath. Guests staying here are just five minutes away from some of the best shops and restaurants in the area. The hostess is a gourmet cook, and the host is an engineer who collects sports cars as a hobby.

Bonnie's Breakfast

**6 hard-cooked eggs
1 10¾-ounce can mushroom soup
½ cup mayonnaise
½ cup milk
1 teaspoon chives**
❖ ❖ ❖
**6 slices bacon, cooked and
crumbled**

Put all ingredients except bacon in a 1-quart casserole. Chill overnight.

Bake 20 to 25 minutes. Top with the bacon. Bake 5 minutes longer. Serve on toasted English muffins.
Serves 4.

Kimble Cliff

6782 Anderson Ave.
Manhattan, Kansas 66502
(913) 539-3816

Kimble Cliff, otherwise known as Cedar Knoll Farm, was built in 1894 of stone quarried nearby, hand fashioned, and decorated. It is a rural bed and breakfast facility with ten rooms and a full attic. The home is well-endowed with antiques collected by the owner, who also owns and operates an antique business. A Continental breakfast is served each morning, with the added plus of two or more varieties of coffee cake or sweet rolls and fruit.

Peanut Butter Muffins

**1¾ cup all-purpose flour
½ cup sugar
1 tablespoon baking powder**
❖ ❖ ❖
**¾ cup milk
½ cup peanut butter (crunchy is
great)**

**⅓ cup salad oil
1 egg**
❖ ❖ ❖
½ cup raisins

In a large mixing bowl, mix together the flour, sugar, and baking powder. In a separate bowl, beat together the milk, peanut butter, oil, and egg until smooth. Add the milk mixture to the flour and add the raisins. Fill muffin cups ⅔ full. Bake in a 400° oven for 15 minutes.
Makes 12 muffins.

Frozen Fruit Slush

**1¼ cups sugar
2 cups hot water
1 12-ounce can frozen orange juice
   concentrate
6 bananas, sliced
1 8-ounce can crushed pineapple
16 ounces frozen sliced
   strawberries**

Dissolve sugar in the hot water. Add the orange juice, bananas, pineapple, and strawberries. Freeze. Remove from the freezer about 2 hours before serving.
Serves 6 to 8.

Norwegian Fruit Soup

This is good for the winter season when fresh fruits are hard to get.

1 29-ounce can pear halves
1 29-ounce can sliced peaches

❖ ❖ ❖

1½ cups raisins
¼ cup water
½ teaspoon cornstarch
3 tablespoons brown sugar, firmly
 packed
½ teaspoon salt
½ teaspoon grated lemon peel
¼ teaspoon ground allspice
⅛ teaspoon ground cloves
¼ teaspoon cinnamon

Drain the pears and peaches, reserving 1½ cups of syrup. Cut the pears into chunks.

In a 4-quart saucepan over high heat combine the raisins, water mixed with the cornstarch, brown sugar, salt, cornstarch, lemon peel, allspice, cloves, cinnamon, and reserved fruit syrup. Bring to a boil, reduce heat to low, cover and simmer for 10 minutes. Add the pears and peaches. Serve hot or chilled.

Makes 8 cups.

Kimble Cliff

Norwegian Honey Cake

4 cups all-purpose flour
1 teaspoon baking soda
½ teaspoon ground cloves
½ teaspoon cinnamon

❖ ❖ ❖

3 eggs
2⅓ cups sugar
1½ cups sour cream
2 tablespoons honey
1 cup raisins
3 tablespoons grated orange rind

❖ ❖ ❖

Confectioners' sugar

Sift together the flour, soda, cloves, and cinnamon. Beat eggs and sugar until fluffy. Beat in sour cream and honey. Stir in the flour mixture until blended. Then add raisins and orange rind. Pour into a greased and floured 10-inch tube pan. Bake in a 325° oven for 1 hour and 15 minutes. Cool in the pan for 5 minutes, then turn out to cool completely. Sprinkle with confectioners' sugar, if desired.

Serves 12.

Kentucky

The Old Talbott Tavern

107 West Stephen Foster
Bardstown, Kentucky 40004
(502) 348-3494

Settlers first began arriving in Bardstown about 1775, and in 1782 it was incorporated as a town under the laws of Virginia, of which Kentucky was then a part. The first permanent building erected was a stone, all-purpose public house on the town square, now known as the Talbott Tavern. To this day the tavern still stands as the oldest western stagecoach stop in America. It was licensed when Patrick Henry was Governor of Virginia. The original outside stone wall is a rare example of Flemish bond stone construction in which each stone was faced by over two hundred hand-chiseled marks.

Many famous historical characters have visited the inn, including King Louis Philippe of France, Jesse James, Abraham Lincoln, Daniel Boone, George Rogers Clark, John J. Audubon, Theodore O'Hara, and General George Patton. Today's travelers use seven bedrooms furnished with antiques but with all modern conveniences.

Corn Fritters

2 cups self-rising flour
¼ teaspoon sugar
1 egg
¼ cup whole kernel corn
Milk to moisten

❖ ❖ ❖

Confectioners' sugar

Mix all ingredients together and drop by tablespoonfuls into a 325° deep fryer. Cook until golden brown, roll in confectioners' sugar and serve warm.
Serves 12.

Chess Pies

This recipe makes 2 pies.

½ cup margarine (1 stick)
2½ cups sugar
2 tablespoons self-rising flour
Dash salt
4 eggs
1½ teaspoons vanilla extract
1 cup milk

❖ ❖ ❖

2 unbaked 9-inch pie shells

Cream together the margarine and sugar. Gradually add the flour, salt, and eggs; add vanilla and milk, beating only until ingredients are mixed.

Divide mixture equally between pie shells. Bake in a 375° oven for 1 hour and 25 minutes.
Serves 12.

Old Talbott Tavern Pie

¾ cup sugar
½ cup all-purpose flour
¼ teaspoon salt
1¼ cups water

❖ ❖ ❖

2 egg yolks, slightly beaten

❖ ❖ ❖

½ cup orange juice
2 tablespoons lemon juice
1 tablespoon grated orange rind

❖ ❖ ❖

1 pie shell, baked
Meringue or whipped topping

Combine sugar, flour, and salt in the top of a double boiler over simmering water, stir in water, stirring until smooth. Remove and stir over direct heat for 5 minutes. Add the yolks and place over the simmering water; cook 5 minutes longer, stirring constantly. Remove from heat and add the fruit juices and rind. Chill thoroughly. Pour into a baked pie shell. Cover with meringue or whipped topping.
Serves 6.

The Boone Tavern Hotel

CPO 2345
Berea, Kentucky 40404
(606) 986-9358
(606) 986-9559

The fifty-seven guest rooms of the Boone Tavern are filled with elegant handmade furniture, yet they all have modern conveniences. In this inn are blended the quality and tradition of southern hospitality with the youthful vigor of a college town. The staff is made up mostly of Berea College Students. No tipping allowed.

Boone Tavern Spoonbread

2½ cups milk
2 tablespoons butter
1¾ teaspoons baking powder
1 teaspoon salt
⅔ cup white cornmeal
❖ ❖ ❖
3 eggs, well beaten

In a heavy kettle, heat the milk to scalding. Add the cornmeal, stirring constantly. Remove from heat and cool.

Pour the milk mixture into a mixing bowl and begin mixing. Add the butter, baking powder and salt; mix well. Add the eggs and mix well. Pour into a greased casserole. Bake in a 375° oven for about 45 minutes. Spoon from the baking dish and serve with butter.

Serves 4 to 6.

Log Cabin Bed and Breakfast

350 North Broadway
Georgetown, Kentucky 40324
(502) 863-3514

Guests can enjoy the best of times in a rustic restored Kentucky log cabin (circa 1809). A shake shingle roof and chinked logs on the outside surround a completely modern interior. The living room is dominated by a huge fieldstone fireplace, and the master bedroom and bath are on the ground floor. A loft bedroom sleeps an additional two people. The dining and kitchen wing is equipped with all new appliances. Closet space was a forethought, and there is more than ample room for any traveler.

Blueberry Coffee Cake

1 cup butter (2 sticks)
1 cup sugar
2 eggs
1 8-ounce carton sour cream
1 teaspoon vanilla extract
2 cups all-purpose flour
1 teaspoon baking powder
1 teaspoon baking soda
❖ ❖ ❖
1 21-ounce can blueberry pie filling
❖ ❖ ❖
¼ cup all-purpose flour
¼ cup sugar
½ cup pecans
3 tablespoons butter

Cream 1 cup of butter, gradually add 1 cup of sugar, beating until light and fluffy. Add eggs one at a time. Beat well after each addition. Stir in the sour cream and vanilla. Combine 2 cups of flour, baking powder, and soda; gradually add to the creamed mixture,

beating well after each addition. Spread ½ of the batter in a greased 13x9-inch pan. Over this spread the pie filling, then the remaining batter.

Make the topping by combining ¼ cup of flour and ¼ cup of sugar. Cut in 3 tablespoons of butter until the mixture resembles coarse meal. Mix in the pecans and sprinkle over cake batter. Bake in a 375° oven for 45 minutes.

Serves 16.

Pecan Balls

Make 5 or 6 balls of ice cream and roll in chopped pecans to completely cover. Wrap each ball in waxed paper, seal securely, and freeze. Serve with hot fudge or caramel sauce.

For hot fudge sauce, melt ½ cup butter (1 stick) and 3 1-ounce squares of chocolate. Add 3 cups of sugar. Add 1 can of evaporated milk and mix over low heat until the sugar is melted. Serve over ice cream.

For caramel sauce, combine in a saucepan ⅓ cup of melted butter, 1 cup of firmly packed brown sugar, 2 tablespoons of dark Karo syrup and ⅓ cup of heavy cream. Bring to a boil to dissolve the sugar. Cool before serving over ice cream.

Makes 20 to 30 servings.

The Old Stone Inn

Route 5
Simpsonville, Kentucky 40065
(502) 722-8882

Simpsonville lies between Lexington and Louisville, in the heart of the fabulously beautiful bluegrass country that is characterized by white-fenced pastures as elegantly manicured as the best of parks. Here the aristocracy of horse breeders lives and raises some of the world's prize horses. Many of the stock farms are open to the public, and the thoroughbreds are well worth seeing. The visitor to this region will find a tempting luncheon or dinner at the Old Stone Inn, a handsome house built before the War Between the States and once a rest station for stagecoach travelers. Decorated in early American style, the inn is more like a home than a restaurant. The Old Stone Inn serves superb food in keeping with the spirit of its decor.

The Old Stone Inn

Scalloped Zucchini

4 large zucchini, sliced ½-inch thick
4 hard-cooked eggs, chopped
1 10¾-ounce can Cheddar cheese soup
⅓ cup heavy cream
½ cup grated sharp Cheddar cheese
¼ cup flavored dry bread crumbs

Layer zucchini and eggs alternately in a greased 8-inch square pan, ending with eggs. Mix the soup and cream; spoon evenly over the casserole. Sprinkle the top with cheese and bread crumbs. Bake in a preheated 350° oven for 40 to 45 minutes, or until zucchini is easily pierced with a fork and the top of the casserole is lightly browned.

Serves 6.

Stuffed Eggplant

1 large eggplant
½ cup water
½ teaspoon salt

❖ ❖ ❖

¼ cup chopped onion
1 tablespoon butter
1 10½-ounce can cream of mushroom soup
1 teaspoon Worcestershire sauce
1 cup fine butter-type cracker crumbs (about 24)
1 tablespoon chopped parsley
1½ cups water

Slice off one side of the eggplant. Remove pulp to within ½ inch of skin. Dice the pulp and place in a saucepan. Add water and salt. Simmer until the eggplant is tender. Drain. Sauté the onion in butter until golden brown. Stir onion, mushroom soup, Worcestershire sauce, and all of the cracker crumbs except 2 tablespoons into the eggplant pulp. Fill the eggplant shell with the mixture. Place the eggplant in a shallow baking pan. Sprinkle the top with reserved crumbs and parsley. Pour water into the baking pan. Bake in a preheated 375° oven for 1 hour or until piping hot.

Serves 4.

Louisiana

Asphodel Plantation

Route 2, Box 89
Jackson, Louisiana 70748
(504) 654-6868

Asphodel Plantation is set in its antebellum splendor, with hosts who have not forgotten southern hospitality and are prepared to serve traditional regional meals. Its many rooms reflect a romantic past: the main dining room, the small dining room, the parlor, the gallery (a wrap-around porch overlooking the pool, terrace, and woods), the terrace, and the lobby. Each guest room has a personality all its own.

Corn Crab Soup

1 bunch green onions, chopped
½ cup all-purpose flour
½ cup butter (1 stick)
½ gallon water
Whole crabs (approximately ½
  dozen)
3 cups milk (optional)
1 pound white crab meat
1 17-ounce can white cream-style
  corn
Salt and pepper to taste

In a large pot, sauté the chopped green onions in flour and butter until the onions are limp. Add the water and whole crabs. Stir over medium heat for 5 to 10 minutes. Add the milk, crab meat, cream-style corn, and salt and pepper to taste. Reduce heat and simmer 20 to 25 minutes.

Serves approximately 10.

The Asphodel Bread

"This is the bread that came about because I was too lazy to go through all the kneading, turning, and twisting that it takes to really make bread. Besides, I always think of it too late. So here is a fast easy bread that turns out to be pretty good!"

5 cups biscuit mix
4 tablespoons sugar
½ teaspoon salt
2 cups warm milk
2 tablespoons (or envelopes) yeast
4 eggs
¼ teaspoon cream of tartar

Sift into a very large bowl the biscuit mix, sugar and salt. Soften the yeast in milk. Make sure the milk is only warm—too much heat will kill the yeast. Beat the eggs with a pinch of cream of tartar until thoroughly blended. Combine the milk and eggs and pour into the dry ingredients. This

Asphodel Plantation

118

is a heavy, sticky mixture, so be sure to stir until it is well mixed. Set aside in a warm place covered with a damp dishtowel, or sealed with plastic wrap. (A yeast mixture rises best at about 80 degrees.)

When doubled in bulk, punch down and place in a greased loaf pan. Again let rise to doubled in size before baking in a 350° oven for approximately 20 minutes. Serve very hot.

The bread freezes quite well. Remember to allow it to completely thaw before reheating, otherwise you may be serving a beautifully heated exterior with a nasty frozen inside.

Makes 1 loaf.

The Columns

3811 Saint Charles Avenue
New Orleans, Louisiana 70115
(504) 899-9308

The Columns Hotel is in the heart of the city's finest residential section, the fashionable, historic garden district on Saint Charles Avenue. Built in 1883 by a wealthy tobacco merchant, The Columns remained a private residence until 1915, when it became an exclusive boarding house. In the 1940s it began its illustrious career as one of the finest small hotels in New Orleans. The Saint Charles streetcar passes in front of the hotel and transports its passengers within minutes of the famous old French Quarter, Canal Street, the business district, parks, universities, and elegant shopping.

A glorious Victorian lounge and beautiful dining room are part of the hotel's assets. Restored period rooms are available for receptions and conferences. The Columns Hotel, with its carved mahogany stairwell, magnificent stained glass panels, skylights, and windows, allows guests to sample those gentler, Victorian days of New Orleans in the 1880s. The Victorian Lounge is among the top 100 bars in

the nation, and The Columns Hotel is listed on the National Register of Historic Places. The inn has eighteen rooms, Continental breakfast, and newspaper for the guest. The accommodations are for two persons per room.

Alligator Chili Piquante

2 pounds alligator meat, diced
4 tablespoons chili powder
2 large onions, chopped
1 stalk celery, chopped
2 green peppers, chopped
⅓ cup oil

❖ ❖ ❖

1 teaspoon fresh minced garlic
1 teaspoon salt
1 teaspoon Italian seasoning (thyme, oregano, basil, and rosemary)
2 bay leaves
1 teaspoon red pepper (cayenne)
½ teaspoon black pepper
1 8-ounce can tomato sauce
1 8-ounce can chili sauce

Combine the alligator meat, chili powder, onions, celery, and green peppers. Sauté in the oil until the vegetables are translucent. Add the remaining ingredients and simmer for 1 hour and 30 minutes.

Serves 8.

Shrimp Scampi Renee

2 cloves garlic, minced
1 stalk shallots, minced
1 cup butter (2 sticks)

❖ ❖ ❖

½ cup water
½ teaspoon chicken base
2 teaspoons cornstarch
¼ cup water

❖ ❖ ❖

12 large shrimps, peeled
½ cup all-purpose flour
4 eggs, beaten

❖ ❖ ❖

1 cup vegetable oil

❖ ❖ ❖

½ teaspoon Worcestershire sauce
¼ teaspoon Tabasco
Juice of ½ lemon

❖ ❖ ❖

Hot cooked rice
Chopped scallops

Combine the garlic, shallots, and butter; set aside.

Bring ½ cup of water to a boil, add the chicken base. Combine the cornstarch and ¼ cup of water, and add to the boiling water.

Dust the shrimp with flour and soak in the beaten eggs for 2 minutes. In a 6-inch sauté pan, heat the oil to 350°. Add the shrimp and sauté until golden brown on both sides. Set aside for 5 minutes.

Drain the oil from the pan. Add the shallot mixture and the chicken base mixture. Add the Worcestershire, Tabasco, and lemon juice; simmer for 3 minutes. Add the shrimp and serve over rice; garnish with chopped shallots.

Serves 3.

Eggplant St. Claire

4 eggplant halves, peeled and hollowed
All-purpose flour
1 egg, beaten
Bread crumbs

❖ ❖ ❖

¼ cup crab meat
1 tablespoon whipping cream
Pinch seafood seasoning (sage, rosemary, and thyme)
Pinch garlic
⅔ cup parsley, chopped

❖ ❖ ❖

1 pint heavy cream
1 pint oyster water
Chablis to taste
Chicken base to taste
Garlic to taste
Pinch thyme
¼ cup chopped green onions
1 teaspoon Worcestershire sauce

❖ ❖ ❖

3 tablespoons cornstarch

❖ ❖ ❖

Parsley for garnish
8 oysters
4 shrimps, peeled

Preheat a deep-fryer to 320 degrees.

Dredge the eggplant halves in flour, coat with the egg, and roll in bread crumbs. Deep fry for 5 minutes, 2½ minutes on each side.

In a saucepan, combine the crab meat, whipping cream, seasonings and parsley; heat until hot. Bring the heavy cream and oyster water to a boil. Add the white wine, chicken base, garlic, thyme, green onions and Worcestershire sauce. In a separate bowl, add water to the cornstarch until thickened. Stir the cornstarch liquid into the oyster sauce. Stir until thickened, remove from heat. Place the eggplant on individual plates. Fill each with hot crab filling and top with the oyster sauce. Sprinkle with chopped parsley. Place 2 oysters and 1 shrimp on each plate.

Serves 4.

Torte Diane

¾ cup butter (1½ sticks)
7 1-ounce squares white chocolate
3 egg yolks
¾ cup sugar
1 cup all-purpose flour
¾ cup finely chopped pecans
¼ cup Bourbon
3 egg whites, whipped stiff

❖ ❖ ❖

1 tablespoon instant coffee
½ cup Crème de Cacao
1 cup butter, room temperature
2 cups confectioners' sugar

❖ ❖ ❖

1 tablespoon instant coffee
¼ cup Crème de Cacao
1 6-ounce envelope instant
    Chocolate mousse
1½ cups cold milk

❖ ❖ ❖

3 cups toasted sliced almonds
¼ cup cocoa powder

Melt the butter, add the white chocolate and heat until melted. Cool to room temperature, add the egg yolks and sugar, and cream together. Add the flour, nuts and bourbon. Mix well. Fold in the beaten egg whites. Pour into 2 greased and lined 9-inch springform pans. Bake in a 375°

oven for 15 to 30 minutes until firm to touch. Let rest for 10 minutes; turn out onto a rack to cool.

For the buttercream, dissolve 1 tablespoon instant coffee in ½ cup Creme de Cacao. Cream together the butter and sugar; add the Creme de Cacao mixture. Add enough confectioners' sugar to make a spreadable icing consistency.

For the mocha mousse, dissolve the instant coffee in ¼ cup Creme de Cacao. Combine the instant mousse and the milk; add the Creme de Cacao mixture. Whip until the mixture is a firm spreading consistency.

Place 1 layer of torte on waxed paper or a serving plate. Cover with a layer of buttercream. Cover the top with a layer of mocha mousse to within ¼ inch of the edge. Cover with the remaining layer. Chill in the refrigerator for 15 minutes. Cover with a layer of buttercream. Cover the sides with toasted almonds. Add the cocoa to the remaining buttercream to make the color darker. Mark slices on top of the cake. Pipe design on the individual slices with contrasting buttercream. Chill until firm.

Serves 16.

The Frenchmen—A Hotel

417 Frenchmen Street
New Orleans, Louisiana 70116
Outside of Louisiana: (800) 831-1781
(504) 948-2166

The Frenchmen Hotel combines two classical 1860s Creole townhouses standing across from the old U.S. Mint and the French Market in the Vieux Carré. It has recently been renovated to provide the charming atmosphere

of old New Orleans with the amenities of today. The tariff includes an antique-furnished, individually decorated and climate-controlled room, a private bath, a color television, direct dial phone, and the famous "Frenchmen" breakfast served compliments "de la maison." It features a full American style breakfast with a menu that changes daily. The tropical patio features a swimming pool and a heated spa. The concierge is on duty twenty-four hours a day, and a licensed tour guide is available at no charge to assist in the daily planning. The Frenchmen offers the French Quarter at its doorstep. All of the historical homes, quaint shops, Jackson Square, the Mississippi River, bars, nightclubs, and restaurants are all within easy walking distance of the hotel.

Southern Casserole

1 cup quick grits
4 cups water
1 teaspoon salt
½ cup butter (1 stick)
1 cup sharp Cheddar cheese,
    grated
6 eggs
1¼ cups bacon, finely chopped
½ cup half-and-half

Cook the grits with water and salt according to package directions. Add butter and cheese; cook over low heat until the butter and cheese have melted. Cool slightly. Stir in 2 beaten eggs. Pour in a 2-quart casserole and set aside. Fry the bacon until crisp. Crumble and sprinkle over the grits, reserving ½ cup of bacon crumbs. Beat 4 eggs and milk. Pour the egg mixture over bacon and grits. Bake in a 350° oven for 50 minutes. Sprinkle the top with the remaining bacon crumbs. Serve hot.

Serves 6 to 8.

Hotel Maison De Ville and The Audubon Cottages

727 Rue Toulouse
New Orleans, Louisiana 70130
(504) 561-5858

Hotel Maison De Ville is an enchanting, two-story hotel with wooden balconies pre-dating the more common wrought iron decoration of its neighbors. Guests choose from three delightful accommodations: the high-ceiling rooms in the main house, furnished with antiques, majestic four-poster beds, marble basins, period paintings and old brass fittings; the slave quarters in the rear, which are less formal, but equally comfortable, with wood white-painted ceilings, brick walls, and fireplaces; and just a block away, the seven Audubon Cottages, a cluster of small romantic houses behind a stucco wall, each with its own courtyard but all surrounding a common swimming pool. The Audubon Cottages are among the oldest in the Quarter. Here the feeling is country: exposed beam-and-plank ceilings, brick walls and wood, slate or terra cotta floors with period antiques and rare Audubon prints. All rooms have refrigerators fully stocked with a selection of wines, liquors, mixers, and so forth.

This is no ordinary hotel. The concierge is there to serve guests' needs, shoes left outside bedroom doors greet the dawn polished, and every morning each guest is brought a silver tray with freshly-squeezed orange juice, croissants, a pot of coffee, and the *Times-Picayune*. Guests may have tea or sherry, may sip a Sazerac where it was born, every evening in the courtyard, or may enjoy the finest cuisine at the Bistro at Maison De Ville. . . . A remarkable blend of true French bistro fare is blended with the Cajun and Creole influences of New Orleans.

Duck with Cranberry Mushroom Stuffing

1 tablespoon minced shallots
1 tablespoon butter
1 tablespoon chopped pecans
1 tablespoon chopped walnuts
1 cup chopped fresh mushrooms
2 tablespoons Port wine
1 tablespoon minced parsley
¼ teaspoon thyme leaves
¼ teaspoon sage leaves
¼ teaspoon poultry seasoning
⅓ cup (½ slice) finely diced whole wheat bread

❖ ❖ ❖

1 cup fresh or frozen cranberries
1 tablespoon butter
2 tablespoons sugar
Salt and pepper

❖ ❖ ❖

1 3- to 4-pound duck, cut up
Salt and pepper

❖ ❖ ❖

Vodka
Bottled duck sauce

To prepare the stuffing, in a skillet over medium heat, sauté the shallots in 1 tablespoon of butter until translucent. Add the pecans and walnuts. Sauté 3 minutes, stirring frequently. Add the mushrooms; stir until mixed. Remove from heat and add the wine, seasonings and bread.

In a saucepan over medium heat, cook the cranberries in the remaining 1 tablespoon of butter until tender; stir frequently. Stir in the sugar. Combine with the mushroom mixture. Season to taste with salt and pepper. There should be about 1 cup of stuffing.

Rinse the duck pieces in cold running water; drain and pat dry. Sprinkle with salt and pepper. Fill each leg with stuffing; secure with poultry pins or toothpicks. Place the duck pieces on a rack in a shallow roasting pan. Roast 20 to 25 minutes or until the duck is tender and done, basting occasionally. If a deeper brown is desired on the duck skin, place the duck pieces under a hot broiler for 2 to 5 minutes.

When ready to serve, blend the vodka to taste with duck sauce; spoon some onto each serving plate. Slice the stuffed, boneless section of each duck leg; arrange in a fan shape on each plate along with a breast half.

Note: Have the butcher quarter the duck, removing bones completely from each breast half; leave the wing bones intact. Remove the thigh bone from each leg, leaving the lower leg bone intact.

Serves 2.

Eggplant Caviar and Tapenade

1 large eggplant
¼ to ½ small onion
¼ teaspoon garlic
½ tomato, peeled and seeded
4 tablespoons olive oil
Juice of ½ lemon
2 tablespoons parsley
Salt and pepper
Fresh basil (optional)

❖ ❖ ❖

4 ounces Greek olives, pitted
2 fillets anchovies
1 tablespoon capers
2 teaspoons Dijon mustard
2 ounces olive oil

❖ ❖ ❖

French bread, toasted (optional)
Garlic croutons (optional)

Prick the eggplant several times with a fork. Either in a hot oven, on a flat stove top, a grill or right in the flame of a burner, roast the eggplant until the skin starts to blacken, the juices turn syrupy and the pulp feels completely soft. (For roasting in the oven, place a tray or sheet of foil on the shelf beneath the eggplant, but don't put the eggplant on a tray—this seems to change the flavor.) When cool enough to handle, peel the eggplant and roughly chop the pulp. Add the finely chopped onion, minced garlic, tomato, olive oil, lemon juice, chopped parsley, salt and pepper to taste, and a bit of chopped fresh basil (optional). Add more olive oil or lemon if desired.

For the tapenade, put the olives, anchovies, capers, and mustard in a blender or food processor and pulse on and off until finely chopped. Slowly add in the olive oil and 1 tablespoon water.

Serve in crocks or ramekins with toasted French bread or garlic croutons.

Serves 4 to 6.

St. Charles Guest House Bed and Breakfast

1748 Prytania Street
New Orleans, Louisiana 70130
(504) 523-6556

The St. Charles Guest House, found in New Orleans's historical Lower Garden District, features European-style accommodations that are simple, cozy, and affordable. Rooms are equipped with either private or shared baths. A complimentary Continental breakfast is served, and a charming pool and patio area offers maximum enjoyment of the semitropical climate. Guests have only a ten-minute trolley ride to the French Quarter or to the downtown area. Sightseeing tours are available from the lobby.

Bed and Breakfast Banana Fritters

"Did you know that New Orleans' climate is temperate enough to grow bananas? At the St. Charles Guest House our little pool and patio are surrounded by a thicket of banana trees that grow real bananas. Even though they freeze at the first frost (usually late December or early January) and have to be cut way back, they come out even bigger starting in early spring. Our guests from other parts of the country and Europe are particularly entranced by this, so the recipe below is called Bed and Breakfast Banana Fritters."

1 large egg
½ cup milk
1 cup self-rising flour
3 tablespoons sugar
¾ cup mashed ripe bananas

Beat the egg and milk together. Add to this mixture the flour and sugar which has been sifted together. Blend in the mashed bananas. Drop by small teaspoonfuls into medium hot oil. Turn with slotted spoon when brown. Drain on a paper towel and dust with confectioners' sugar. Make sure the oil is not too hot as the fritters will not cook on the inside before getting too brown.

St. Chuck Poolside Chicken Jambalaya

"Our little guest house has hosted many interesting groups, from dance troupes to international choirs, and even foreign journalists visiting the 'real' USA. We often honor their visit with a simple meal by the pool, one which gives them a taste of our unique cuisine. This dish is good because, for one, it's good, and two, it's inexpensive to make for a crowd. It's particularly good cooked in advance and allowed to 'mellow' for a day in the refrigera-

tor. It's also quite simple and affordable—like our hotel!"

1 large chicken fryer, cut up
2 quarts water
2 teaspoons salt

❖ ❖ ❖

3 cups uncooked "converted" rice
2 bay leaves

❖ ❖ ❖

2 pounds smoked sausage
1 large white onion, chopped
1 large green pepper, chopped
2 cloves garlic, minced
1 cup coarsely chopped celery
½ teaspoon hot sauce (optional)
2 bay leaves
¼ teaspoon cayenne or red pepper (optional)

❖ ❖ ❖

1 15-ounce can tomato sauce
1 10-ounce can rotel tomatoes

❖ ❖ ❖

½ cup chopped green onions

Boil the chicken pieces in a large pot with water and salt. When tender, remove the chicken, reserving the stock. Tear the meat, discarding the skin, into bite-sized pieces.

Cook the rice in 7 cups of the reserved stock seasoned with 2 bay leaves.

While the rice cooks, cut the sausage into bite-size pieces and sauté with the onion, green pepper, garlic, celery, hot sauce, 2 bay leaves and cayenne pepper. Cook until tender, skim off the fat and add the tomato sauce and tomatoes. Combine with the rice, and the chicken pieces. Let the mixture sit for a while for flavors to mingle. When ready to serve, add raw chopped green onions.

Serve with hot crispy bread and a good green salad with vinagrette dressing.

Dennis Hilton's Mardi Gras Red Beans and Rice

1 pound red kidney beans (dried)
8 to 10 cups water

❖ ❖ ❖

1½ pounds hot or smoked sausage,
    cut into bite size pieces
1 white onion, chopped
1 large clove garlic, minced
2 tablespoons chopped parsley
2 stalks celery, chopped
2 or 3 bay leaves
Salt to taste
½ cup real butter (1 stick)

❖   ❖   ❖

Hot cooked rice
Chopped raw green onions

Rinse and sort the beans to remove hard ones, or rocks. Cover with water and begin to cook over low heat. In a skillet, sauté the sausage with vegetables and seasonings until tender. Skim and discard the fat and add the meat mixture to the beans. Cook over low to medium heat for 1½ to 2 hours, adding salt as necessary. When the beans are tender (add water if they become too dry or thick), take out one cup, mash and return to the pot, to make the mixture creamy. Before serving, add a stick of butter. Serve over fluffy rice and top with chopped raw green onions, for a delicious touch.

Makes 6 generous servings.

Joanne's Peanut Butter Ice Cream Pie

1 large cooked pie crust, either
    pastry or cookie crumb
½ gallon vanilla ice cream (cheap
    will do)
½ cup creamy peanut butter

Combine softened ice cream with peanut butter until blended. Place in prepared shell, being careful not to break up crust. Re-freeze at least eight hours, preferably overnight. You may serve this plain, or with whipped cream, chopped nuts, fudge sauce, or any combination thereof.

Serves 6.

Chocolate Bread Pudding a La Grand Hotel

4 cups stale bread, torn into small
    pieces
4 cups milk
1 cup sugar
4 1-ounce squares melted
    unsweetened chocolate
4 eggs
2 teaspoons vanilla extract
½ cup raisins (optional)
½ cup chopped pecans or coconut
    (optional)

Soak the bread in the milk until it's absorbed. In a separate bowl, beat eggs, vanilla, sugar and melted chocolate until well blended. Add to the bread mixture, along with the raisins, pecans, etc. Pour in a buttered baking dish; place this in large pan of water and bake in a 350° oven for 45 to 60 minutes, until set. This is good alone, or served with a vanilla sauce.

Serves 4.

Pointe Coupee Bed and Breakfast

Post Office Box 386
New Roads, Louisiana 70760
(504) 638-6254

Pointe Coupee Bed and Breakfast consists of three restored homes and a lakeside cottage: the Bondy House, circa 1902, at 304 Court Street; the Claiborne House, circa 1835, at 405 Richey Street; the Hebert House, circa 1902, at 401 Richey Street, and Matt's House on False River at 504 East Main Street. All are in downtown New Roads, which face False River and are flanked by historic Saint Mary's Catholic Church.

Pointe Coupee

My Bread Recipe

1 ¼-ounce package active dry yeast
2 cups warm water (110°)
4 cups all-purpose flour (white)

❖ ❖ ❖

½ cup butter (1 stick)
½ cup hot water
½ cup molasses or cane syrup
4 cups whole wheat flour

Dissolve the yeast in warm water. Add the all-purpose flour and beat until smooth, the consistency of pancake batter. Cover and let it sit in a warm place (82°) until bubbly.

Melt the butter in the hot water, add the molasses and cool the mixture to lukewarm. Mix with the batter. Add the whole wheat flour to make a stiff dough. Knead into a ball and place in a greased bowl to rise until doubled.

Lightly grease two loaf pans. Divide the dough in half, knead the portions, shape into loaves, and place in the pans. Place the pans on the lower rack of a cold oven; let the dough rise at least above the pan lip. When doubled in bulk turn the oven on to bake at 325° for at least 30 minutes or until hollow-sounding when thumped. Let the loaves cool and turn out on a wire rack.

Makes 2 loaves.

Glencoe Plantation

Post Office Box 178
Wilson, Louisiana 70789
(504) 629-5387

Nestled in the rolling hills of the Felicianas' fabled plantation country, Glencoe Plantation fits most people's fantasy of what a mansion should be. The home, which is open for tours, overnight accommodations, weddings, and receptions, is a treasure of authentic Victorian embellishments. From its wide, welcoming gingerbread-bedecked galleries to its formal oak-paneled living foyer, double parlors, and interesting diagonally-paneled dining room, Glencoe is a home made for entertaining. Guests may enjoy facilities for swimming, playing tennis, fishing, strolling through century-old lanes, jogging on country roads, or relaxing in one of the comfortable rocking chairs or porch swings on the galleries.

Glencoe Baked Onions

6 whole onions
6 tablespoons Italian salad dressing
Romano cheese

Peel the onions. Slice ends evenly. Score each onion six times in a cross-like fashion leaving the outer ring intact. Place onions in aluminum foil squares that have been coated with a spray vegetable shortening. Place one tablespoon salad dressing over each onion. Sprinkle with Romano cheese.

Breast of Chicken
with Apricot Glaze

2 teaspoons seasoned salt
1 teaspoon garlic powder
6 chicken breasts
½ cup butter (1 stick)
1 cup apricot syrup or apricot
  preserves

Sprinkle seasoned salt and garlic powder over chicken. Melt butter and pour over chicken. Cover with aluminum foil and bake in a 350° oven for 45 minutes or until tender. Drain excess fat and juice. Pour the apricot syrup over the chicken and bake uncovered for 15 minutes.

Serves 6.

Wrap each onion in foil like a tulip. Bake in a 350° oven for 1 hour.

Serves 6.

Roast Potatoes Westerfield

Potatoes
Vegetable oil
Creole seasoning

Wash, peel and slice baking potatoes as for thick French fries. Lightly coat an ovenproof dish or pan with oil and add potatoes in single layer. Sprinkle liberally with seasoning. Bake in a preheated 350° oven until potatoes are browned and crispy, about 30 minutes.

Baked Apples
in Tuaca Sauce

1 cup water
1 cup sugar
1 teaspoon cinnamon (or to taste)
½ cup rum
4 to 5 ounces Tuaca liqueur

❖ ❖ ❖

4 apples
Butter

In a large saucepan, combine the water, sugar, cinnamon, and rum. Heat to boiling, stirring constantly until the sugar is dissolved. Remove from heat and cool to lukewarm. Add the Tuaca. Stir well and store in the refrigerator. The sauce thickens as it cools.

Makes about 2 cups of sauce.

Peel the apples and core to within ½ inch of the bottoms. Place in an ovenproof dish and baste with the Tuaca sauce. Dot with butter and bake in a preheated 375° oven for 40 to 60 minutes, or until the apples are tender but not mushy. Baste again with Tuaca sauce right before the apples are done.

Serves 4.

Maine

Katie's Ketch

Post Office Box 105
Bailey Island, Maine 04003

"**W**e were ready to sell our home with so many unused rooms when we read about bed and breakfast. We knew it was for us," say Albert and Katie, grandparents of five. Albert, a semi-retired lobsterman, can tell guests about his colorful military background and his lobstering experiences or recount tales of his family that has fished off the Grand Banks since the 1600s. Katie's plants decorate the house inside and out with a cascade of colors. In July bunches of sweet peas add splashes of color and a sweet fragrance to the house. Being native islanders, Katie and Albert know all the interesting spots within walking distance from the house. Two doubles and a single bedroom are offered for guests, and all rooms are furnished with family heirlooms and feature a panoramic view of the Atlantic Ocean.

Frittata

An upside-down omelet with an Italian name.

> **3 tablespoons butter**
>   ❖   ❖   ❖

½ cup chopped onion
½ cup chopped green pepper
2 medium potatoes, peeled and
     cubed ¼-inch
   ❖   ❖   ❖

1 7-ounce can Spam, cubed ¼-inch
10 pitted black olives, chopped
   ❖   ❖   ❖

6 eggs
2 tablespoons water
¼ teaspoon pepper

In a 10-inch omelet pan or skillet melt 2 tablespoons of butter over medium heat. Add the onion, green pepper and potatoes; cook over medium heat, stirring occasionally, until vegetables are crispy tender (5 to 7 minutes). Add Spam and olives; continue cooking until meat is heated through. Loosen sautéed ingredients from the bottom of the pan; add the remaining 1 tablespoon butter. Tilt the pan to cover the bottom with butter. In a small bowl mix eggs, water and pepper; pour over the Spam mixture. Cover. Cook over low heat for 12 to 15 minutes or until the egg mixture is set on top; with a pancake turner, loosen the edges and bottom; invert onto a serving platter.
   Serves 6.

Corn Pancakes

1½ cups all-purpose flour
¾ teaspoon baking soda
½ teaspoon salt
2 tablespoons sugar
   ❖   ❖   ❖

2 eggs
1 17-ounce can whole kernel corn,
     drained

1½ teaspoons cream
1 tablespoon oil
   ❖   ❖   ❖

Milk

In a large bowl mix dry ingredients together. In a smaller bowl, beat the eggs, add corn, cream, and liquid shortening. Stir into the flour mixture just until mixed. If the batter is too thick, add a little milk. Pour spoonfuls of batter onto a heated greased pan. Cook until the top is covered with bubbles. Turn pancakes and brown the other side.
   Makes 10 to 15 pancakes.

The Lady and the Loon

Post Office Box #98
Bailey Island, Maine 04003
(207) 833-6871

The Lady and the Loon has one room available as a bed and breakfast facility. Guests enjoy the privacy of a separate entrance and private bath in one of Bailey Island's original inns, as well as the luxury of a queen-size bed covered with a handmade quilt. Mornings begin with home-brewed coffee, steeped tea or milk, orange juice, and homemade muffins. Breakfast is served in the room if desired, or may be enjoyed at the picnic table on the backyard bluff overlooking Ragged Island or with the family around the kitchen table. Guests may walk the private stairs to the beach, at their own risk, to bask on a large rock and observe the marine environment, or to simply explore one of Maine's tidepools.

The Lady's Poppy-Orange Muffins

½ cup sugar
1 tablespoon poppy seed
1½ cups biscuit mix
¾ cup chopped raisins
1 egg, beaten
¾ cup buttermilk
1 teaspoon vanilla extract
1 tablespoon grated orange peel
    (or more to taste)

Combine the sugar, poppy seeds and biscuit mix. Cut in or add the remaining ingredients. Stir. Fill the greased muffin pan cups ¾ full. Bake in a 400° oven for 20 minutes.

Makes 8 good-sized muffins.

tion of quality coffee and teas, and much more. Situated on a tree-lined acre of ground in a historical residential district, the inn charmingly combines the convenience of an in-town location with an out-of-town atmosphere. Here guests enjoy quiet privacy while living within easy walking distance of fine shops, restaurants, the municipal pier, and Bar Island. The splendors of Acadia National Park are only minutes away by car, bicycle, or on foot.

Lemon Loaf

½ cup shortening
1 cup sugar
2 eggs

❖ ❖ ❖

1½ cups all-purpose flour
½ teaspoon salt
1 teaspoon baking powder
Grated rind of 1 lemon

❖ ❖ ❖

½ cup milk
Juice of half a lemon

❖ ❖ ❖

Juice of half a lemon
¼ cup sugar

Cream the shortening and 1 cup of sugar, then add the eggs, one at a time, beating well each time until the mixture is light and fluffy. Sift the dry ingredients over this. Stir in lemon rind. Add the milk and juice of half a lemon. Beat together until well-blended. Bake in a greased loaf pan in a 350° oven for 50 to 60 minutes, until the top is golden brown. Remove from the oven. Mix the juice of half a lemon and ¼ cup sugar and spread over the top of the hot loaf. Let cool 10 minutes, then remove from the pan. Cool well before slicing.

Thornhedge Inn

47 Mount Desert Street
Bar Harbor, Maine 04609
(207) 288-5398

Thornhedge, a Victorian mansion, was built for Lewis Augustas Roberts in 1900. Mr. Roberts, a publisher, was

Manor House Inn

West Street
Bar Harbor, Maine 04609
(207) 288-3759

All of the Manor House Inn's charming guest rooms and spacious suites have private baths and authentic turn-of-the-century decor. Guests enjoy the gardens, veranda, public rooms, and Victorian fireplaces. Each morning features a superb Continental-plus breakfast that includes fresh native blueberry muffins, home-baked breads, in-season fruits, a fine selec-

Manor House Inn

the head of Roberts Brothers, one of the two largest and most successful publishing companies in Boston after the Civil War. The other was Little, Brown and Company, which bought Roberts Brothers in 1898. The home has been improved with all the modern conveniences without disturbing the original intent of Mr. Roberts's design. Added to the mansion is a Victorian dollhouse and dolls from the 1890s.

Thornhedge also has a three-story Victorian house with six guest rooms and two public rooms, situated directly behind Thornhedge. The public rooms feature menus of local restaurants, historic and tourist information, and a dollhouse replica of a Bar Harbor "cottage."

Grane's Fairhaven Inn

North Bath Road
Bath, Maine 04530
(207) 443-4391

Fairhaven is the Maine experience, an inn for all seasons and for all reasons. Nestled into a hillside overlooking the wide Kennebec River, this charming old country inn is surrounded by lush green lawns and bountiful woods and meadows. The Fairhaven welcomes guests for a night or two or for a vacation of a week or more to enjoy the atmosphere of old Maine.

Blueberry Molasses Cake

1 cup sugar
1 cup oil
4 eggs
2 cups molasses

❖ ❖ ❖

4 cups all-purpose flour
2 teaspoons salt
2 teaspoons cinnamon
1 teaspoon ginger
1 teaspoon allspice
½ teaspoon cloves

❖ ❖ ❖

2 teaspoons baking soda
1 cup hot water

❖ ❖ ❖

3 cups frozen or fresh blueberries

In a large bowl whip together the sugar, oil, eggs, and molasses. In a separate bowl, sift together the dry ingredients. Add to the molasses mixture alternately with baking soda dissolved in hot water. Add the blueberries and pour into a greased 12x16-inch sheet pan. Bake in a 325° oven for 1 hour or until the cake tests done.

Serves 12 to 16.

Easy Pita Spread

½ cup sour cream
¼ cup salad dressing
½ cup grated Parmesan cheese
½ teaspoon garlic powder
2 teaspoons oregano
½ teaspoon pepper
1 teaspoon chopped basil

❖ ❖ ❖

Pita bread

Combine all the ingredients except the bread, mix. Cut pita bread into 1½-inch triangles, spread with mix and broil until brown and bubbly on top. Serve at once. Refrigerates well for 1 week.

Makes approximately 2 cups of spread.

Grane's Shrub

First course for breakfast. Easy and so delicious.

1 banana
4 ounces crushed pineapple
½ apple, unpeeled

4 strawberries (or any other fruit you have)
3 cups orange juice

In a blender, purée the fruit. Add the orange juice and blend. Pour into wine glasses and garnish with fruit sherbet.

Serves 6.

Tipsy French Toast

6 eggs
¼ cup Triple Sec
¼ cup light cream
3 tablespoons pure maple syrup
1 tablespoon grated orange rind
¼ cup fresh orange juice
Pinch salt

❖ ❖ ❖

French bread
Salad oil
Grated nutmeg
Butter
Maple syrup

Whisk together the eggs, Triple Sec, cream, syrup, rind, juice, and salt. Slice the French bread thin. Dip slices into the egg mixture and brown in oil on a hot griddle. Sprinkle with nutmeg, butter, and maple syrup.

Serves 6.

Sweet and Tangy Chicken

6 chicken breasts, boned and skinned
Butter

❖ ❖ ❖

¾ cup sour cream
2 tablespoons honey
2 tablespoons Dijon mustard
Salt and pepper

In a heavy ovenproof skillet sauté the chicken in butter until brown on both sides. Place in the skillet breast side up. Bake in a 350° oven for 30 minutes. Place chicken on a hot platter.

Add sour cream to the skillet and scrape the skillet. Add the honey and

Dijon mustard. Serve hot over the chicken. Salt and pepper to taste.
Serves 6.

Northport House Bed and Breakfast

City One, Mounted Route
United States Route 1
Belfast, Maine 04915
(207) 338-1422

This restored Victorian house (circa 1873) is in a coastal community near Camden and Searsport. At one time it was an overnight stop on the Portland/Bar Harbor Road. In the morning guests enjoy a breakfast of muffins, breads, and cereal, along with fresh fruit, cheese, coffee, and tea served in the large common room or on the deck. The eight guest rooms are spacious and tastefully decorated, featuring period pieces reflecting traditional New England charm. Rooms are available with queen, double, or twin beds. Each of the six bathrooms has both tub and shower. Two of the rooms have full kitchens.

Raisin Biscuit Rhapsody

Found by JoAnn Sasto.

3 cups sifted all-purpose flour
3 teaspoons double-acting baking powder
2 tablespoons sugar
1 teaspoon salt
½ teaspoon baking soda
❖ ❖ ❖
½ cup shortening
❖ ❖ ❖

1 cup buttermilk
¼ cup dark seedless raisins
❖ ❖ ❖
1 egg white, slightly beaten
❖ ❖ ❖
Butter
Jam

Sift together flour, baking powder, sugar, salt and baking soda into a bowl. Cut in shortening until it resembles coarse meal. Add buttermilk and raisins and stir until well blended. Divide dough into 3 parts. On a floured surface, roll each part into a circle about ⅓ inch thick. Cut each into 5 wedges, place on an ungreased baking sheet. Brush the tops with the egg white. Bake in a 425° oven for 12 to 15 minutes. Serve warm with butter and/or jam.
Can be frozen after baking.
Makes 15 biscuits.

Blueberry Nut Muffins

½ cup milk
¼ cup fresh lemon juice
¾ cup margarine (1½ sticks)
1¼ cups sugar
3 eggs
2 cups all-purpose flour
½ cup wheat flour
2 teaspoons baking powder
1 teaspoon salt
¾ cup chopped pecans
2 teaspoons lemon rind, grated
1 cup blueberries

Mix milk with lemon juice. Cream together the margarine and sugar in a large bowl. Add eggs. Combine the dry ingredients and add to the creamed mixture alternately with the milk. Stir in pecans, rind and blueberries. Fill greased muffin pans ⅔ full. Bake in a 350° oven for 30 to 40 minutes. Cool for 5 minutes. Remove.
Makes 18 to 22.

The Chapman Inn

On the Bethel Common
Post Office Box 206
Bethel, Maine 04217
(207) 824-2657

The Chapman Inn, dating back to 1865, faces the village green in the center of the beautiful town of Bethel. Guests can rest comfortably in the large, sunny rooms, eat a hearty, healthy breakfast, and enjoy convenient access to fine shops, restaurants, sightseeing, and recreation for all ages. Activities available include Alpine and cross-country skiing, swimming, golfing, boating and fishing, canoeing, hiking, and rock hunting, as well as touring the rugged beauty of the area or walking in Bethel's historic district. Two saunas and a gameroom are on the premises. A private beach four miles from the inn on Songo Pond is perfect for swimming.

Blueberry Pancakes

1 egg
1 cup buttermilk
1 tablespoon oil
1 tablespoon honey
❖ ❖ ❖
1 cup whole wheat pastry flour
2 teaspoons baking powder
½ teaspoon baking soda
❖ ❖ ❖
½ cup fresh or thawed blueberries, drained

Mix together the egg, buttermilk, oil and honey. In a separate bowl combine the dry ingredients, then add the blueberries. Combine both mixtures until blended. Use ¼ cup of batter for each cake. Cook on a hot griddle at 400°.
Serves 2 to 4.

Fruit Jams

**8 cups mashed fruit (strawberries,
   blueberries, blackberries,
   raspberries, peaches)**
1 cup honey
2 cups finely ground dried apples

Combine all and cook in a stainless steel pot. Bring to a boil and stir occasionally. Let boil for approximately 10 minutes. Sterilize ½ pint jars in boiling water bath, then fill to within ¼ inch of top. Seal and return to the boiling water bath for 15 to 20 minutes. Allow to cool on a rack; store without rings in a cool dark place. Jams tend to be loose, not like traditional pectin jam, but they are great.

Makes 8 8-ounce jars.

Fruit Salad

Use a variety of fresh fruits cut into small pieces. Soak overnight with a mixture of fruit jam and juice. Add nuts for variety.

Favorite combinations are: banana, apple, pear, grapefruit (divided into sections), seedless red grapes, strawberries or blueberries and walnuts.

Note from the Innkeeper: "I mix in some of my homemade blackberry jam and allow it to sit overnight in the refrigerator. Delicious!"

Arcady Down East

South Street
Blue Hill, Maine 04614
(207) 374-5576

Guests of Arcady Down East enjoy New England hospitality in an atmosphere of Victorian graciousness. They may choose from a variety of room accommodations, from "Juan Carlos," a master suite with fireplace, sitting area, and private bath, to a secluded, cozy room with its own turret, perhaps inhabited by a resident ghost! Fireplaces and spacious, relaxing areas abound, with game room, library, and sunny porches available.

Fare includes a home-baked, Continental breakfast served in the old, formal dining room or on the sunny porch with a view of the pleasant natural beauty of the area. Bicycles are available.

Strata Ade

**8 slices whole wheat bread
   (homemade type), cubed**
**1½ cups sharp Cheddar cheese,
   grated**
1 cup chopped ham
Pepper to taste
**4 apples, sliced and rolled in
   cinnamon sugar**

❖ ❖ ❖

8 eggs
2 cups milk
½ teaspoon dry mustard
Worcestershire sauce to taste
¼ cup butter (½ stick), melted

Layer in order half of the bread, half of the cheese, all of the ham (sprinkled generously with fresh pepper), all of the apple slices, the remaining bread cubes, and the remaining cheese.

In a blender combine the remaining ingredients except butter. Pour over the casserole, top with melted butter

Arcady Down East

and refrigerate overnight. Bake uncovered in a 350° oven for 45 to 60 minutes or until firm to the touch.

Serves 6 to 8.

Arcady Cheese Grits

1 teaspoon salt
4 cups boiling water
1 cup old-fashioned grits

❖ ❖ ❖

2 eggs, beaten
½ cup butter
1 10-ounce package sharp Cheddar cheese, grated
1 small clove garlic, minced
Fresh ground pepper to taste

In a saucepan add the salt to the boiling water and add the grits. Cook until the grits are done.

To the cooked grits add the eggs, butter, cheese, garlic, and pepper, and pour into a casserole or soufflé dish. Bake in a 350° oven for 45 to 60 minutes or until brown.

Note: If using white Cheddar, sprinkle paprika over the grits before baking.

Serves 6 to 8.

Michael's Crêpes

1 10-ounce package frozen chopped spinach
1 cup cottage cheese with chives
3 eggs
1 cup Swiss cheese, grated
½ cup walnuts, toasted in butter
Fresh dillweed
Nutmeg
Salt and pepper to taste

❖ ❖ ❖

8 crêpes

❖ ❖ ❖

1 cup sour cream
Parmesan cheese
Paprika

In a food processor with a steel blade combine the spinach, cottage cheese, eggs, Swiss cheese, walnuts, and seasonings. Fill the crêpes with the spinach mixture, reserving a small amount and roll the crêpes up. Place in a buttered pan and cover, refrigerate overnight. To the reserved spinach mixture add the sour cream and process just until mixed. Refrigerate separately.

The next morning, remove from the refrigerator 20 to 30 minutes before baking. Bake in a 350° oven for 15 minutes. Place the sauce on top and sprinkle with Parmesan cheese and paprika. Bake uncovered for 15 to 20 minutes or until light brown and heated through.

Serves 6 to 8.

Blueberry Cobbler

½ cup sugar
1 tablespoon cornstarch
2 tablespoons water
4 cups Maine blueberries

❖ ❖ ❖

1 cup baking mix
½ cup milk
1 tablespoon melted butter

Combine the sugar, cornstarch and water. In a 1½-quart casserole place the blueberries, and pour the sugar mixture over all. Bake in a 350° oven until bubbly.

Combine the baking mix, milk and melted butter. Drop by tablespoonfuls onto the hot berries and bake in a 425° oven for 15 minutes or until the topping is brown (like biscuits).

Serves 6.

Kenniston Hill Inn

Route 27
Boothbay, Maine 04537
(207) 633-2159

Kenniston Hill Inn perpetuates the name of the original owner, a member of a prominent Boothbay family. This 200-year-old house has been transformed into a cozy, inviting bed and breakfast home with rooms comfortably and tastefully decorated. Each room has its own personality; most have a queen or king bed, private bath, and fireplace. A bountiful family breakfast is served in the dining area overlooking gardens and fields, or by a roaring fire on a cool morning. Because the host was a chef/restaurateur in Vermont before opening the inn, tantalizing specialties are always on the menu. A public golf course borders the property, and cycles are available. The harbor is but minutes down the road, as are a dinner theater, shops, galleries, cruise boats, and the ferry to Monhegan Island. Children over ten are allowed, but no pets.

Ellen's Blueberry Delight

3 cups fresh blueberries
1 cup sour cream
1 teaspoon vanilla extract
1 cup brown sugar, firmly packed

Place the blueberries in a 9-inch glass pie pan or other shallow ovenproof dish. In a small bowl, combine the sour cream and vanilla. Pour over the fruit. Sprinkle evenly with brown sugar. Broil until the sugar caramelizes. Watch carefully because the sugar needs to melt but not burn. Cover and refrigerate several hours before serving.

Note: This recipe can be made with seedless green grapes, peaches or strawberries.

Serves 4 to 6.

Peaches and Cream French Toast

6 slices French or Italian bread cut diagonally ¾-inch thick

❖ ❖ ❖

Kenniston Hill Inn

or relax, plus marked walking trails. The trails provide excellent cross-country skiing in winter. This is a small working farm with horses, sheep, goats, geese, ducks, and chickens. Guests will eat farm-fresh eggs and maybe some just-made herbed Chèvre cheese. Cotswolds, a rare breed of sheep, are raised on the farm. Guests can watch fleece from the flock being spun or woven on most evenings. A country breakfast is served in a sunny breakfast room overlooking an old-fashioned English perennial garden.

Granola
with Fresh Fruit and Swedish Cream

"I put the granola into a glass bowl, add fresh fruit (strawberries, blueberries, melon balls, kiwi, apple, nectarine, etc.), spoon the Swedish Cream on top and add a mint leaf fresh from the herb garden."

6 cups uncooked rolled oats
1 cup honey
1 cup oil or margarine
1 cup wheat germ
½ ounce vanilla extract
Raisins
Chopped nuts

❖ ❖ ❖

1 ¼-ounce envelope unflavored gelatin
½ cup hot water
2½ cups whipping cream
½ cup sugar
2 cups sour cream

Mix together the oats, honey, oil, wheat germ, vanilla, raisins, and nuts. Bake on cookie sheets in a 325° oven for 20 minutes until golden. Stir frequently while baking. Cool thoroughly.

Dissolve the unflavored gelatin in the hot water in a small saucepan. Add the whipping cream and warm but do not boil. Dissolve the sugar in the cream mixture. Fold in the sour cream. Chill until congealed.

Serves 12 to 16.

---

3 eggs
1 cup light cream
2 tablespoons peach preserves
½ teaspoon nutmeg
3 tablespoons melted butter
3 cups fresh, peeled, sliced peaches
Confectioners' sugar

Arrange bread in a single layer in a baking pan. Combine eggs, cream, peach preserves and nutmeg. Beat until smooth and pour over the bread. Turn the slices to coat evenly. Cover and refrigerate overnight. To cook, melt the butter in a skillet or grill. Sauté the bread slices until golden brown, about 5 minutes on each side. Top with fresh peaches and sprinkle with confectioners' sugar.

Serves 4.

Sausage and Egg Casserole

24 sausages
20 eggs
1 10¾-ounce can Cheddar cheese soup
1 pint small curd cottage cheese
Paprika

Steam the sausages and drain, cut into 1-inch pieces and layer the bottom of a 9x13-inch baking pan. On top of the stove scramble the eggs until lightly done. Spoon over the sausage mixture. Warm the soup, add the cottage cheese and mix. Pour over the egg mixture. Poke with a fork and sprinkle with paprika. Cover and bake in a 350° oven for 1 hour. Can be prepared 1 day in advance.

Serves 12.

Middlefield Farm

Upper Round Pond Road
Post Office Box 4
Bristol Mills, Maine 04539
(207) 529-5439

This elegant Federal house circa 1800 is set on 180 acres of woods and fields and has a ten-acre lake. Huge shade trees line the drive, and the grounds have many cool, private places to read

Center Lovell Inn

Route 5
Center Lovell, Maine 04016
(207) 925-1575

The Center Lovell Inn boasts ten guest rooms, two cozy parlors, and a gracious wrap-around porch for dining and relaxing. It has been restored according to a philosophy that says, "We are all caretakers of our world." The beautifully prepared gourmet dishes are served in front of the huge fireplace in its small, homey dining room.

Marinated Mushroom Antipasto

Antipasto is a marvelous start to a meal as it allows the hostess to prepare well in advance and to sit down to enjoy her guests as well as the appetizer.

Use cheeses, salami, pickles, olives, anchovies, and breadsticks to accompany marinated vegetables.

3 tablespoons oil
3 cloves garlic, minced
1 pound mushrooms (cleaned in
 warm salt water)
1 bay leaf
2 cloves
4 peppercorns
½ cup white wine
1 tablespoon lemon juice
Salt and pepper to taste

In a saucepan heat the oil over medium heat. Brown the garlic, add the mushrooms, bay leaf, cloves, and peppercorns. Sauté for about 3 minutes, stirring constantly. Add the wine, lemon juice, and seasonings, cover and simmer about 10 minutes. Re-

move to a glass bowl and chill overnight before serving.

Serves 6 to 8.

Stuffed Celery Antipasto

Celery can be stuffed with ½ of an 8-ounce package of cream cheese blended with one 2-ounce tin of anchovies and ½ of the package of cream cheese mixed with chopped green olives and pimientos (½ cup).

Marinated Carrot Antipasto

1 pound tender young carrots
¾ cup dry white wine
¾ cup white wine vinegar
4 cups water
6 tablespoons oil
2 cloves garlic
Small bunch parsley
1 teaspoon sugar
1 teaspoon salt
Pinch pepper

 ❖ ❖ ❖

1 teaspoon chopped basil
1 teaspoon spicy mustard

Wash and scrape the carrots, cut into strips. In an enamel saucepan combine the carrots, wine, vinegar, water, oil, garlic, parsley, sugar, salt, and pepper. Bring to a boil over moderate heat and cook about 10 minutes. Remove from heat and allow to cool.

Remove the carrots and boil the marinade to reduce to about 2 cups. Place the carrots in a serving dish, pour the marinade over them; sprinkle with basil, mix in the mustard and chill.

Variation: To make Marinated Onion Antipasto, use 1 pound of small white onions. Peel and cook as directed for Marinated Carrots.

Serves 4 to 6.

Green Split Pea Soup

This recipe uses the leftover Apple-Prune Stuffing, bones, skin, joints, and scrap meat from the Roast Suckling Pig. Allow the peas to soak overnight before preparing the soup.

2 pounds split peas
2 gallons water

 ❖ ❖ ❖

2 gallons water

 ❖ ❖ ❖

Center Lovell Inn

Apple-Prune Stuffing leftovers
Roast Suckling Pig leftovers
1 large Spanish onion
3 carrots, cut up
3 ribs celery, cut up
Parsley

❖   ❖   ❖

Croutons

Soak the peas overnight in 2 gallons of water.

Drain the peas and add 2 gallons of fresh water. Add the leftover stuffing and any bones, skin, joints, and scrap meat available, as well as the onion, carrots, celery and parsley. Simmer for 3 to 4 hours. Skim off the surface of the soup occasionally while cooking. Strain through a food mill.

Serve with croutons made from buttered bread cut into small squares and toasted in a 400° oven until golden brown.

Serves 16.

Roast Suckling Pig

1 10 to 15-pound pig
1 tablespoon salt
1 teaspoon ground pepper
¾ teaspoon thyme
2 tablespoons spicy mustard
Apple-Prune stuffing

❖   ❖   ❖

2 cherries
1 small shiny red apple
Fresh parsley

❖   ❖   ❖

3 tablespoons Sherry

Wash the pig thoroughly and dry. Mix together the salt, pepper, and thyme. Rub mustard liberally over the inside cavity of the pig and sprinkle with the spices. Fill the cavity with the stuffing and skewer the opening closed. Place a tightly rolled ball of aluminum foil in the mouth and cover the ears and tail with foil. Place the pig on aluminum foil in a deep roasting pan (probably will need to go on a diagonal) with the back legs folded forward and the front legs folded back at the knee joint.

Roast in a 350° oven for 3½ to 4 hours. When serving, place the pig on a hot platter—toothpick cherries for eyes, a red apple in the mouth, and ring with fresh parsley.

Drippings can go into a pan, skim the fat, add the Sherry and serve as a sauce.

Serves 8 to 12.

Apple-Prune Stuffing

½ pound slivered almonds
1½ pounds prunes, pitted
3 pounds apples, peeled and quartered
Salt and pepper
¼ cup butter (½ stick), melted
½ cup Sherry

Combine the ingredients in a mixing bowl and stir well. Stuff the Roast Suckling Pig.

Serves 8 to 12.

Zuppa Inglese
Italian Rum Cake

5 egg yolks
Grated rind of ½ lemon
1½ tablespoons lemon juice
½ cup sugar

❖   ❖   ❖

1 cup sifted all-purpose flour
¼ teaspoon salt

❖   ❖   ❖

5 egg whites
½ cup sugar

❖   ❖   ❖

2 tablespoons butter
¼ cup cornstarch
¾ cup sugar
½ teaspoon salt
2 cups milk
2 egg yolks, slightly beaten
1 teaspoon vanilla extract

❖   ❖   ❖

2 1-ounce squares chocolate, melted

❖   ❖   ❖

Dark Rum
Sliced fruit or preserves
Whipped cream

In a mixing bowl beat 5 egg yolks, gradually adding the lemon rind, juice, and ½ cup of sugar.

Sift together the flour and ¼ teaspoon of salt. Fold the flour into the egg yolks ¼ cup at a time until it is all folded in.

In a separate bowl beat the egg whites until foamy. Gradually add ½ cup of sugar and beat until the egg whites are stiff. Spread the egg whites over the egg yolk mixture and gently fold together.

Bake in a 12x16-inch pan in a 350° oven for approximately 15 minutes. The top will be golden and spring back to a gentle touch. Allow to cool in the pan, and cut into 4 layers.

For the custard filling, in a saucepan melt the butter and blend in the cornstarch, ¾ cup of sugar, and ½ teaspoon of salt. Gradually add the milk and heat to boiling. Stir in the slightly beaten egg yolks and cook 2 minutes, stirring constantly. Add the vanilla, cool slightly. Divide in half and add the chocolate to one half.

Place one layer of the sponge cake on a serving tray and sprinkle with rum. Spread the sponge cake with chocolate custard and sprinkle liberally with rum. Add a layer of sponge cake, place sliced fruit or preserves over the layer, and douse with rum. Add another layer of sponge cake, sprinkle with rum, spread with vanilla custard and sprinkle again with rum. Top with the last layer of cake and sprinkle with rum. Cover with plastic wrap and allow to set overnight.

Before serving, cover with whipped cream. If soupy, eat with a spoon.

Serves 8 to 12.

High Meadows

Route 101
Eliot, Maine 03903
(207) 439-0590

Perched on the side of a hill, this colonial house was built in 1736 by Elliott Frost, a merchant ship builder and captain. Today it has all the modern conveniences, while retaining the charm of the past in a relaxed country setting. On the route to the mountains and lake regions for fall foliage tours, it is slightly over one hour away from the best ski areas. Guests can snuggle up to an open fire in the evening and can enjoy breakfast in the warm and friendly country kitchen. Cross country skiing in the surrounding area is also available.

Roquefort (Bleu) Cheese Soup

¼ cup butter (½ stick)
¼ cup minced celery and/or green pepper
½ cup all-purpose flour
1 14-ounce can chicken broth
4 ounces Roquefort or bleu cheese, broken up
1 cup light cream
1 cup milk
2 ounces Sherry
Chives or croutons for garnish

Melt the butter in a heavy skillet and sauté the vegetables until soft. Add flour, stir and cook over low heat a few minutes. Add the chicken broth and stir 2 minutes to prevent lumps. Add the broken up cheese and stir until smooth. Add cream and milk and heat to serving temperature. Add Sherry just before serving. Garnish with chives or croutons.
Serves 6.

Oven Fish Chowder

2 cups sliced carrots
2 cups raw cubed potatoes
2 cups sliced onions
1 teaspoon dill weed
2 whole cloves
1 small bay leaf
1 clove garlic
¼ cup butter (½ stick)
2 cups boiling water

❖   ❖   ❖

2 pounds fish fillets (haddock, cod, pollack or any firm fish)
½ cup dry vermouth

❖   ❖   ❖

1 cup light cream
Parsley

In a 6-quart ovenproof Dutch oven or large crock pot, combine carrots, potatoes, onions, dill, cloves, bay leaf, garlic, butter, and boiling water; cover tightly. Bake in a 375° oven for 40 minutes, or in the crock pot until the vegetables are tender. Cut the fish into 1½-inch pieces; add the fish and the wine. Cover and return to the oven until the fish is done, about 20 minutes. Test with a fork to see if the fish is tender. Add the cream. Garnish with parsley.
Serves 8.

Lemon Squares

½ cup margarine or butter (1 stick)
1 cup all-purpose flour
¼ cup confectioners' sugar

❖   ❖   ❖

1 cup sugar
2 eggs, beaten
2 tablespoons lemon juice
2 tablespoons all-purpose flour
½ teaspoon baking powder

❖   ❖   ❖

Confectioners' sugar

Combine the butter, 1 cup flour, and confectioners' sugar. Pat into an 8-inch pie pan. Bake in a 350° oven for 15 minutes.
Mix together the sugar, eggs, lemon juice, 2 tablespoons flour, and baking powder; pour over the crust. Bake in a 350° oven for 25 minutes. Sprinkle

with confectioners' sugar when cool.
Serves 6.

The Inn at Cold Stream Pond

Lakeside Lodging and Art Gallery
Post Office Box 76
Enfield, Maine 04433
(207) 732-3595

Guests of The Inn at Cold Stream Pond enjoy getting off the beaten path to travel picturesque backroads and to enjoy local festivals. The Pond is a seven-mile-long secluded lake that offers fishing, boating, canoeing, swimming, and even islands to explore. For land lovers, there are horseshoes, croquet, and volleyball; golf facilities and state parks are nearby. A rock herb garden and wildflowers have been planted in the yard to attract birds, making for a lovely paradise indeed.

Herb Bread

Slice day old French bread into 1-inch pieces. Make a spread of butter and freshly snipped herbs to taste (any combination seems to work, i.e., parsley, chives, thyme, oregano, basil, tarragon, etc.) and thickly coat bread. Sprinkle the tops with Parmesan cheese and broil or bake until brown and crusty.
Serves 8 to 12, depending on the size of the French bread slices.

Lemon Ice Cream

1½ pints whipping cream
1½ pints half and half
1 cup sugar
1 teaspoon vanilla extract
¼ teaspoon salt

**Juice and grated rind of 1 large or
2 small lemons**

Combine all ingredients; pour into an ice cream maker. Use ice cream makers' directions concerning the method of freezing. Keep in the freezer overnight before serving.

Serves 14 (makes about 2 quarts).

The Oxford House Inn

105 Main Street
Fryeburg, Maine 04037
(207) 935-3442

The Oxford House Inn, built as a family home in 1913, was converted in 1985 into a five-room inn and restaurant. The style is Edwardian, with beautiful cypress woodwork throughout the building. Country wallpaper and leaded glass bookcases and cupboards catch the eye. The guest rooms are large, comfortable, and tastefully decorated with antiques and old-fashioned furniture. The inn provides a dramatic view of the Saco River valley and the White Mountains of New Hampshire. Outdoor activities available nearby include hiking, fishing, canoeing, cross-country skiing, and downhill skiing in the winter.

Sunflower Seed Dressing
for Fresh Green Salads

1 cup lemon juice
1 tablespoon Pommery mustard
¼ cup honey
1 teaspoon salt
½ teaspoon white pepper
1 cup sunflower seeds
4 cups salad oil

Combine all the above ingredients except the oil in a mixer and mix well. In a stream, slowly add 4 cups of salad oil while mixing.

Makes 6 cups.

Crab Chowder

½ pound salt pork or bacon
2 large onions
3 stalks celery
½ carrot
1 tablespoon dried tarragon
1 tablespoon lobster, crab, or shrimp paste

❖ ❖ ❖

3 pounds potatoes, peeled and diced
2 pounds fresh Maine crab meat

❖ ❖ ❖

1 pint heavy cream
Salt and pepper
Hot sauce to taste

With the fine blade of a meat grinder, grind the pork, onions, celery and carrot into a stock pot. Add the tarragon and lobster paste. Simmer over medium heat until tender but not brown.

Cover the potatoes with cold water and slowly boil until slightly underdone. Add the potatoes and their water to the vegetable mixture. Bring to a slow boil. Add the crab meat and bring to a boil and remove from heat.

Just before serving, return to a boil and add the cream. Add salt, pepper and hot sauce to taste.

Serves 8.

Turkey Waldorf

Flour for dredging turkey
Salt and pepper
1 pound turkey cutlets

❖ ❖ ❖

¾ cup clarified butter (1½ sticks), or vegetable oil
½ cup Applejack or apple brandy
1 pint whipping cream
4 Granny Smith apples, peeled and sliced
½ cup walnut halves

Season the flour with salt and pepper. Slightly pound the turkey cutlets with a mallet or the side of a cleaver. Heat the butter in a sauté pan just until it begins to smoke. Dredge the turkey in the seasoned flour and sauté quickly until tender, but not crisp. Pour off the butter and keep the turkey warm over low heat. Add the Applejack, cream, apples and walnuts. Simmer until the liquid is reduced enough to coat the back of a spoon.

Serves 4.

Dark Zucchini Bread

3 eggs
1 cup sugar
1 cup vegetable oil
2 cups peeled grated zucchini
1 cup molasses
⅛ cup Kitchen Bouquet
3 teaspoons vanilla extract

❖ ❖ ❖

3½ cups all-purpose flour
1 teaspoon salt
1 teaspoon baking soda
¼ teaspoon baking powder
3 teaspoons cinnamon

❖ ❖ ❖

1 cup raisins
¾ cup chopped walnuts

Beat the eggs, add the sugar, oil, zucchini, molasses, Kitchen Bouquet and vanilla; mix well. Combine the dry ingredients and stir into the egg mixture with a spoon. Add the raisins and walnuts. Bake in 2 loaf pans in a 350° oven for 1 hour and 10 minutes.

Makes 2 loaves.

Greenville Inn

Norris Street
Greenville, Maine 04441
(207) 695-2206

The inn was built in 1895 by a wealthy lumbering family. It took ten years for ships' carpenters from the coast to complete the inn's cherry, mahogany, and oak paneling, and other unusual embellishments.

A spruce tree is painted on the leaded glass window on the landing of the stairway. Six fireplaces are ornamented with mosaics and carved mantels, and a marble shower offers hot and cold needle spray, as well as a regular shower. Two of the inn's ten rooms have working marble-tiled fireplaces; one is accented with intriguing black iron clown andirons. Many of the bedrooms have private adjoining baths, some with nostalgic pull-chains.

Greenville Inn

Shrimp with Garlic Sauce

½ cup butter (1 stick)
¼ cup vegetable oil
2 cloves garlic, minced
2 bay leaves
½ teaspoon oregano
Salt and pepper
Red pepper flakes
Dash lemon juice
1 pound shrimp

Melt the butter in a 3-quart pot. Remove from heat. Add oil, garlic, bay leaves, oregano, salt and pepper, red pepper flakes, lemon juice and shrimp. Toss well. Set aside for 30 minutes, stirring occasionally. Place the pot over low heat and allow to come to a gentle bubble. Stir. Cover and cook the shrimp for five minutes or until they turn pink. Spoon into serving dishes. Divide pan juices between the servings. Serve immediately.
Serves 2.

Honey-Orange Glazed Chicken

½ cup orange juice
1 tablespoon honey

❖   ❖   ❖

2 teaspoons butter
1 tablespoon minced apple
1 tablespoon minced shallots

❖   ❖   ❖

1 ounce minced ham
Pinch cinnamon
1 tablespoon chopped walnuts
1 tablespoon currants
⅛ teaspoon orange zest
Salt and pepper to taste
2 tablespoons softened cream cheese
2 boned, half chicken breasts with skin

Combine the orange juice and honey in a saucepan, heat until reduced to 3 tablespoons. In a separate saucepan, melt 2 teaspoons butter and sauté the apples and shallots until the shallots are translucent. Combine with the next 7 ingredients. Make a pocket under the skin of each chicken breast and stuff half the mixture under the skin of each breast. Place the chicken in a buttered baking dish, tucking under the skin to secure the filling. Bake in a 400° oven for 10 minutes, brush with the prepared honey glaze and bake for another 10 minutes.
Serves 2.

The Inn on South Street

Post Office Box 478A, South Street
Kennebunkport, Maine 04046
(207) 967-4639
(207) 967-5151

The Inn on South Street is situated on a quiet, tree-lined street in the historic village area within easy walking distance to shops, restaurants, and

beaches. The Inn is open year round, except for three weeks in January. The decor of this nineteenth century Greek Revival home is strongly reminiscent of Kennebunkport's maritime past, particularly its connection with nineteenth century China. The oriental flavor is evident upon entering the foyer, which is dominated by an elaborately carved shrine door. Three spacious rooms with private baths are available for guests. Breakfast is intentionally special. Homebaked breads, soufflé, omelets with fruit sauces or filled pastries or blintzes, juice, and fresh fruit in season are all common breakfast items. Hot coffee is available at seven AM, and afternoon tea, wine, hot cider, or lemonade is served daily. The garden offers a secluded area for rest and relaxation.

Eva's Cheese Blintzes

"Blintzes are a favorite with guests. These make an easy breakfast because all the real work is done ahead of time."

3 eggs
1½ cups milk
1¼ cups all-purpose flour
Pinch salt

❖   ❖   ❖

1 pound Ricotta cheese
1 egg
3 tablespoons sugar or to taste
½ teaspoon cinnamon
1 tablespoon grated lemon rind

❖   ❖   ❖

Fruit sauce
Sour cream

To make crêpes combine in a blender 3 eggs, milk, flour, and salt. Set aside for 30 minutes. When ready, pour a small amount of batter at a time into a pan with heated oil, brown one side only.

Combine the cheese, egg, sugar, cinnamon, and lemon rind. Mix until smooth. Place 1 rounded tablespoon of cheese mixture in the center of each crêpe. Fold each crêpe like an envelope. Place the crêpes close together on a buttered pie pan. Cover with foil. The crêpes may be frozen. When ready to serve, warm in the oven on a low setting. Arrange on a heated platter, spoon on some fruit sauce (blueberry, strawberry or blackberry) and garnish with a dab of sour cream. Serve with extra fruit sauce and sour cream.

Makes 12 blintzes.

Eggs and Mushrooms in Tarragon Cream

14 eggs, hard-boiled
2 pounds mushrooms
6 tablespoons butter

❖ ❖ ❖

¼ cup butter (½ stick)
5 tablespoons all-purpose flour
1½ cups hot chicken broth
1½ cups cream
3 egg yolks, beaten
2 tablespoons crushed dried
  tarragon

❖ ❖ ❖

Parsley
Toast points

Cut the eggs in half lengthwise. Sauté the mushrooms in 6 tablespoons of butter. Set aside and keep warm.

In a saucepan, melt ¼ cup of butter. Add the flour and stir for 1 minute. Add the chicken broth to the butter and flour, stir continuously. Add the cream. Stir and cook until slightly thick. Add the egg yolks and stir, but do not boil. Add tarragon.

Arrange the eggs and mushrooms in the sauce in a large ovenproof dish. Garnish with chopped parsley or sprigs of fresh tarragon. Serve with toast points. This dish can be kept warm on a heating tray.

Serves 8.

Orange Soufflé-Omelet
with Strawberries

Up to an hour ahead, separate the eggs, assemble the sauce ingredients, and prepare the berries. Beat the eggs just before baking. Have your guests seated when you bring this dish to the table.

9 large eggs, separated
9 tablespoons sugar

❖ ❖ ❖

9 egg yolks
¼ cup orange juice
3 tablespoons all-purpose flour

❖ ❖ ❖

6 tablespoons butter
½ cup orange juice
2 tablespoons sugar

❖ ❖ ❖

2 tablespoons butter
2 tablespoons sugar
½ cup orange juice
4 cups sliced strawberries

In a large bowl, beat the egg whites until foamy, add 9 tablespoons of sugar and beat until the whites hold stiff peaks. Do not overbeat.

In a separate bowl, beat together the egg yolks, ¼ cup of orange juice and flour until well mixed. Gently fold into the egg whites.

In a 10- to 12-inch oval baking dish melt 6 tablespoons of butter. Add ½ cup of orange juice and 2 tablespoons of sugar, remove from heat when bubbly. Gently slide large spoonfuls of egg mixture into the hot sauce. Bake in a 350° oven for 13 to 15 minutes, until the center jiggles only slightly.

In a 10- to 12-inch frying pan, melt 2 tablespoons of butter. Stir in 2 tablespoons of sugar and ½ cup of orange juice. When bubbling stir in the sliced strawberries. Just warm, do not cook. Serve over the soufflé.

Serves 12.

Summer Minted Lemonade

1 cup fresh mint leaves, crushed
3 cups boiling water
1 12-ounce can frozen lemonade
1 can water
Ice
Mint leaves for garnish

Steep the mint in boiling water for 1 hour. Mix all the ingredients except the mint together in a large pitcher. Serve in a glass pitcher with ice and garnish with mint leaves.

Serves 8 to 12.

Kylemere House 1818

South Street
Box 1333
Kennebunkport, Maine 04046
(207) 967-2780

The Kylemere House was built in 1818 by the Daniel Walker family, a branch of one of the first four families in the port. In 1895 the well-known Maine artist and architect Abbot Graves purchased the house and used the barn as his studio. He named the house "Crosstrees" for the two maple trees planted on both sides of the front door. Today only one remains, shading the house in the Summer and bursting with brilliant colors in the Fall. Kylemere is a quiet, relaxing haven, just a few minutes walk from the ocean, shops, and good restaurants. In the winter guests are only two hours from skiing.

The newly decorated rooms are warm and inviting, with soft colors and coordinated bedding that enhance the charm and setting of this comfortable home. A leisurely breakfast prepared by hosts Bill and Mary is served in the formal dining room overlooking the garden. The fare may include fresh juice and fruit, quiche, egg specialties, homemade bread, muffins, and other favorites of the family.

Brunch Eggs

2 cups grated American cheese
¼ cup butter (½ stick)

❖ ❖ ❖

1 cup half and half
½ teaspoon salt
2 teaspoons dry mustard
¼ teaspoon pepper

❖ ❖ ❖

10 eggs, slightly beaten
Parsley sprig

Sprinkle the cheese on the bottom of a 9x13-inch dish, dot with butter. Combine the half and half, salt, dry mustard, and pepper, pour half over the cheese. Pour the eggs over the cheese, then pour the remaining cream over the eggs. Place the parsley sprig on top. Bake in a 325° oven for 45 minutes.
Serves 8 to 10.

Sausage

1 pound ground pork (about 20% fat)
1 teaspoon salt
¼ teaspoon black pepper
½ teaspoon sage
⅛ teaspoon mace
¼ teaspoon ginger
⅓ teaspoon cardamom
⅛ teaspoon dill
1 tablespoon maple syrup

Combine all the ingredients until well-blended. Form patties or roll up.
Makes 1 pound of sausage.

Lobster Quiche

½ cup finely chopped onion
1 tablespoon butter
Pie shell, partially baked

❖ ❖ ❖

¼ cup Parmesan cheese
8 large mushrooms, sliced
1 pound lobster or crab
¾ pound Swiss or Gruyère cheese, sliced

❖ ❖ ❖

7 eggs, lightly beaten
2 cups heavy cream
1 tablespoon all-purpose flour
½ teaspoon salt
Dash cayenne pepper
Dash nutmeg

Sauté the onion in butter until transparent. Sprinkle the onion in the bottom of the pie shell, adding Parmesan cheese, mushrooms, lobster or crab and cover with slices of Swiss cheese. Mix the eggs with the cream, flour, salt, cayenne and nutmeg. Pour over the lobster mixture. Bake in a 450° oven for 10 minutes. Reduce to 325° for 15 to 20 minutes or until the custard is set and golden.
Serves 6.

Hot Fruit Compote
served with Sour Cream

1 12-ounce can orange juice concentrate, thawed
2½ tablespoons cornstarch

❖ ❖ ❖

2 pounds apples, peeled, sliced, cooked until tender
2 large bananas, sliced
1 cup pineapple chunks
1 cup cooked apricots, drained
1 cup Bing cherries, pitted

❖ ❖ ❖

¼ cup white wine

Make a paste with the orange juice and cornstarch. In a buttered casserole, layer the fruit alternating with the orange juice paste, ending with cherries on top. Pour the wine over all. Cover and bake in a 350° oven for 1 hour.
Serves 10.

Old Fort Inn

Post Office Box 759 A
Kennebunkport, Maine 04046
(207) 967-5353

The Old Fort Inn is a luxurious adult resort nestled in a secluded setting, combining yesterday's charm with today's conveniences. This intimate lodge, in a converted barn built about 1880, is filled with antiques including many early pine and oak pieces, complementing its huge beams, weathered pine wall boards, and a massive brick fireplace. Guest rooms are in a quaint turn-of-the-century carriage house made of brick and stone. Each colorful and beautifully decorated room has electric heat, wall-to-wall carpeting, and a complete, fully equipped kitchen unit. A Continental breakfast is included. Breads are baked daily at the inn.

Cranberry Almond Bread

1½ teaspoons baking powder
1½ teaspoons baking soda
2½ cups all-purpose flour
½ teaspoon salt

❖ ❖ ❖

1 cup butter (2 sticks)
1½ cup sugar

❖ ❖ ❖

3 eggs
1½ cups sour cream
1 teaspoon almond extract

❖ ❖ ❖

1 16-ounce can whole cranberry sauce

❖ ❖ ❖

½ cup chopped almonds

Combine the baking powder, soda, flour and salt. Cream together the butter and sugar. Add the eggs and dry ingredients alternately with the sour cream. Add the almond extract. Alternate layers of batter and cranberry sauce in loaf pans. Sprinkle with almonds and bake in a 350° oven for 1 hour.

Port Gallery Inn

Post Office Box 1367
Kennebunkport, Maine 04046
(207) 967-3728

Port Gallery Inn was a wedding gift in 1891 to Captain Titcomb, builder of the largest ships on the Kennebunk River. The inn is one of only a few Victorian houses in the area, and the attempt has been made to recapture that spirit in the inn's decor. Featured on the first floor of the inn is a marine art gallery including paintings by Lawrence E. Donnison of England. Mr. Donnison, in addition to recreating seafaring scenes of a bygone era, also produced a series of canvasses of Kennebunkport in the early 1800s. Some of the amenities include private bathrooms, cable color television, queen and double size beds, and a Continental breakfast.

Holiday Wreath

**2 8-ounce packages cream cheese
½ cup mayonnaise
⅓ cup Parmesan cheese
10 slices bacon, crisply cooked and crumbled
¼ cup spring onions (including the green stalks), diced
Pimientos
Fresh parsley**

Combine the cream cheese and mayonnaise. Add all the remaining ingredients except pimientos and parsley. Mix well. Chill in the refrigerator. Place a drinking (medium or small size) glass in the middle of a plate. Drop teaspoonfuls of chilled ingredients around the glass forming a ring or wreath. Decorate with parsley sprigs and pimientos alternately. Chill again.

Serves 6 to 8.

Lobster Spread

**2 ¼-ounce envelopes unflavored gelatin
½ cup water
2 tablespoons real lemon juice
1 pint sour cream
1 12-ounce bottle chili sauce
2 tablespoons horseradish
1½ cups (8 ounces) cooked lobster meat or shrimp**

In a medium saucepan sprinkle the unflavored gelatin over the water and lemon juice. Let stand one minute, then stir over low heat until the gelatin is completely dissolved, about 5 minutes. With a wire whisk or rotary beater, blend in the sour cream, chili sauce and horseradish. When this is done, fold in the lobster meat or shrimp. Turn into a 3½ cup lobster mold and chill until firm. Turn out onto a platter surrounded with parsley sprigs or other garnishes. Serve with assorted crackers.

Makes about 3 to 3½ cups of spread.

Lobster Newberg

**3 tablespoons butter
1½ pounds lobster meat**

❖ ❖ ❖

**1 tablespoon all-purpose flour
1 cup heavy cream
1 4-ounce jar mushrooms**

❖ ❖ ❖

**Salt to taste
Paprika
Sherry to taste**

❖ ❖ ❖

2 tablespoons grated Parmesan cheese

Melt the butter in a large heavy saucepan over medium heat. Add the lobster and cook for about 5 minutes. Add the flour, cream and mushrooms; sauté for 5 minutes. Season with salt and paprika. Add the Sherry. Place the mixture in a baking pan and sprinkle with Parmesan cheese. Bake in a 450° oven until browned, or broil for a deeper color.

Serve over cooked rice or in puff pastry shells.

Serves 4 to 5.

Due East: A Natural Environment Saltwater Farm

Bailey's Mistake
Lubec, Maine 04652
(207) 733-2413

Due East enjoys the finest summer climate in the nation, as reported by the National Weather Service. A paradise for nature lovers, artists, and photographers, Due East is a haven for those seeking rest and relaxation in an environment free from pollution, chemicals, and commercialism. Guests are invited to share the comfort of the farmhouse built about 1800 that has sitting-sleeping rooms overlooking the sea. The regular, unbroken rhythm of the mighty Atlantic waves lull guests to sleep and gently wakes them to the first sunrise in the continental United States. Lodging at the inn includes a hearty farm-style breakfast.

Mushroom Bread

**¼ cup margarine (1 stick)
½ pound mushrooms, finely chopped**

1 cup finely chopped onion

❖ ❖ ❖

2 cups milk
3 tablespoons molasses
4 teaspoons salt
¼ teaspoon pepper

❖ ❖ ❖

½ cup warm water
2 ¼-ounce packages active dry
   yeast

❖ ❖ ❖

1 egg
1 cup wheat germ
8 cups unsifted all-purpose flour

Melt the margarine over low heat. Add mushrooms and onion and sauté until the onion is tender and the liquid has evaporated. Cool. Scald the milk; stir in the molasses, salt and pepper. Cool to lukewarm. Measure warm water in a large warm bowl. Sprinkle in the yeast; stir until dissolved. Add the lukewarm milk mixture, mushroom mixture, egg, wheat germ, and 2 cups of flour. Beat until smooth. Stir in enough additional flour to make a stiff dough. Knead until smooth. Let rise until doubled in size. Shape into 3 or 4 loaves. Let rise again until double. Bake in a 350° oven until the loaves sound hollow when tapped, about 50 minutes.

Makes 3 or 4 loaves.

Stuffed Clams

Due East clams are dug daily at Due East.

½ medium onion, chopped
1 cup butter (2 sticks)

❖ ❖ ❖

1 pint minced clams with juice
1 cup evaporated milk
1 tablespoon Worcestershire sauce
Salt and pepper to taste
Sage to taste
½ teaspoon Accent

❖ ❖ ❖

¼ pound grated sharp cheese
4 ounces bread stuffing
¾ cup all-purpose flour
Paprika

In a medium saucepan, sauté the onions in butter. Add the clams and juice, milk, and spices and cook until hot. Add the cheese and stir until dissolved. Add the stuffing and flour, mix and heat. Fill clam shells and sprinkle with paprika. Bake in a 350° oven for 10 minutes. These freeze well.

Makes 8 filled clam shells.

Lobster Pie

1 pound lobster meat
½ pound mushrooms, thinly sliced
½ cup scallions
2 tablespoons butter

❖ ❖ ❖

2 tablespoons butter
3 tablespoons all-purpose flour
1 cup light cream

❖ ❖ ❖

⅓ cup grated Swiss cheese
½ cup cooking sherry

❖ ❖ ❖

⅔ cup bread crumbs

Cut the lobster into bite-sized pieces. Sauté mushrooms and scallions in 2 tablespoons butter. Make a white sauce by melting 2 tablespoons butter, stirring in flour, adding the cream and heating until thickened. To the white sauce stir in grated cheese over low heat until melted. Add wine, lobster, mushrooms, and scallions. Pour into 4 individual casseroles and sprinkle with bread crumbs and melted butter. Bake in a 350° oven for 15 minutes.

Serves 4.

Peaches and Cream Pie

1 9-inch pie shell, baked and
   chilled
5 to 6 ripe peaches, peeled and
   halved

❖ ❖ ❖

1 cup light cream
1 teaspoon vanilla extract
2 eggs
⅓ cup sugar

❖ ❖ ❖

2 tablespoons butter
Whipped cream (optional)

Arrange peach halves, pitted side up, in baked shell. Combine cream, vanilla, eggs and ¼ sugar, beat until well blended. Pour around peaches in shell. Dot the tops of the peaches with butter; sprinkle with the remaining sugar. Bake in a 350° oven for 1 hour, until the crust is golden brown and the filling is set. Serve with whipped cream if desired.

Serves 6.

Bayside Inn

Route 1
Milbridge, Maine 04658
(207) 546-7852

The Bayside Inn is a stately Victorian building in a coastal village with a view of beautiful Narraguagus Bay. The house was built in the 1900s by the Sawyer family (one of the oldest in Milbridge) and was owned by Captain Sawyer and his family until 1964, when it was bought by its present owners. The Sawyers owned the local shipyard, and the house was built by ships' carpenters when they were not working on boats. Some of the inn's most beautiful features are fireplaces with Italian tile, a grand stairway carved from Japanese rosewood, and oak wainscoting.

Maine Blueberry Muffins

¼ cup butter (½ stick), softened
1 cup sugar (scant)
1 egg

❖ ❖ ❖

¼ teaspoon cinnamon
¼ teaspoon nutmeg
½ teaspoon vanilla extract

❖ ❖ ❖

1⅓ cup all-purpose flour
2 teaspoons baking powder

½ teaspoon salt

❖ ❖ ❖

½ cup milk
½ cup plain yogurt

❖ ❖ ❖

1 cup wild Maine blueberries

Cream the butter and sugar well. Add the egg. Add the spices and vanilla. Add the dry ingredients alternately with milk and yogurt. Do not over-beat. Carefully fold in the blueberries. Spoon into greased muffin tins. Bake in a 350° oven for 20 to 30 minutes.
Makes 12 muffins.

Sand Tarts

1 cup butter (2 sticks), softened
2 cups sugar
3 eggs
1 teaspoon vanilla extract
4 cups all-purpose flour
½ teaspoon baking soda
Jelly

Cream the butter until light. Gradually add the sugar. Add the eggs one at a time, beating well after each addition. Beat in vanilla. Beat in half of the flour and baking soda with a mixer. Add the rest of the flour and hand mix until well-blended. Drop dough by well rounded teaspoonfuls on greased cookie sheets. Indent the middle and fill with jelly. Bake in a 350° oven for 10 to 12 minutes.
Makes 2 dozen tarts.

The Newcastle Inn

Newcastle, Maine 04553
(207) 563-5685

The Newcastle Inn has been in opera-tion for over sixty years in the pictur-esque twin towns of Damariscotta and Newcastle, which are joined together by the Damariscotta River. The two villages have everything people think of when New England is mentioned. The inn has twenty sleeping rooms and features an outstanding breakfast. It also boasts antiques, stenciled floors, American bald eagles, spectacular views, and music by Vivaldi.

Broccoli Cheese Scrambled Eggs

4 eggs, beaten
2 tablespoons milk
Salt and pepper to taste
1 tablespoon margarine
½ cup Cheddar cheese
¼ cup broccoli, cooked

Mix the eggs with the milk, salt, and pepper. In a frying pan, melt the mar-garine and add the eggs. Add the cheese and broccoli, scramble. Serve hot.
Serves 2.

Norridgewock Colonial Inn

RFD #1, Box 1190
Norridgewock, Maine 04957
(207) 634-3470

The Norridgewock Colonial Inn, in a small, friendly New England village, provides a pleasant place from which to visit the New England area. Guest rooms are large and warmly deco-rated, with private baths. A full break-fast is served daily. The Norridgewock is located near Colby and Thomas Col-lege and skiing, fishing, hunting, and scenic areas.

Blueberry Pancakes

Simple and great. Use your favorite pancake recipe and add fresh blueber-ries after the batter has been placed in the frying pan. For some reason it adds a much better flavor than adding ber-ries in the batter.

Bed and Breakfast Omelet

Make your favorite recipe for scram-bled eggs. Sauté green pepper, onion and chopped mushrooms. Remove from the pan. Pour the egg mixture in the pan, cook slowly and turn. Place green pepper, onions, mushrooms, chopped ham on half of the egg and cover with shredded Cheddar cheese. Fold the egg over and sprinkle with more shredded cheese and paprika. Cover until the cheese melts.
Serves 1.

Sea Chambers— The Sea Bell

37 Shore Road
Ogunquit, Maine 03907
(207) 646-9311

The Sea Bell, at 33 Shore Road, was built about 1800 and is now a part of the Sea Chambers Motor Lodge. Until recently it had been operated by the same family for 145 years who at one time catered to sea captains, who moored their schooners at the river's edge and walked up what is now

Wharf Lane. This section of the river, now bordered by the footpath to the public beach, was once dotted by fishing shacks and cottages. The feeling of yesterday is recaptured when the complimentary Continental breakfast is served in the charming surroundings of The Sea Bell. All the muffins, coffee cakes, and sweet breads are baked on the premises from old family recipes.

Fine lodging at the edge of the SEA

Lee Trotzky's Butter Muffins

¾ cup butter (1½ sticks), softened
1½ cups sugar

❖   ❖   ❖

2 eggs

❖   ❖   ❖

½ teaspoon salt
2 teaspoons baking powder
2 cups all-purpose flour

❖   ❖   ❖

1 cup milk
1 teaspoon vanilla extract

Cream together the butter and sugar. Add the eggs and mix well.

In a separate bowl sift together the salt, baking powder and flour. Add the dry ingredients to the creamed mixture alternately with the milk and vanilla. Bake in a 350° oven for 20 minutes for small muffins, 25 minutes for large muffins. Great served warm!

Makes 12 muffins.

Lemon Tea Bread

¾ cup margarine (1½ sticks)
2 cups sugar
Grated rind of 2 lemons
4 eggs

❖   ❖   ❖

3 cups all-purpose flour
2 teaspoons baking powder
½ teaspoon salt
1 cup milk

❖   ❖   ❖

Juice of 2 lemons
½ cup sugar

Cream the margarine and 2 cups of sugar with lemon rind. Add the eggs and beat well. Add dry ingredients alternating with milk. Squeeze about 1 tablespoon of juice from the lemon into batter for better flavor. Bake in greased loaf pans in a 325° oven for 1 hour. Mix ½ cup of sugar and juice from the remaining lemons. Pour over the bread while hot, then cool completely on a wire rack.

Makes 2 loaves.

Daryl's Peanut Butter Bread

2½ cups all-purpose flour
4 teaspoons baking powder
½ teaspoon salt

❖   ❖   ❖

¾ cup peanut butter
½ cup sugar
1 teaspoon vanilla extract
1 egg

❖   ❖   ❖

1¾ cups milk

Sift together the dry ingredients. In a separate bowl, beat the peanut butter, sugar, and vanilla until well combined, add the egg. Gradually add the milk and stir until well blended, then add the flour mixture. Bake in a greased 9x5-inch loaf pan in a 350° oven for 1 hour then let cool 10 minutes.

Makes one loaf.

Seafair Inn

24 Shore Road
Post Office Box 1221
Ogunquit, Maine 03907
(207) 646-2181

The Seafair Inn, family owned and operated, has nineteen rooms decorated in period antiques. Making the inn's guests feel comfortable and at home is a specialty of the family. A homemade Continental breakfast is served in the dining room and also in the enclosed sun porch in the summer. Afternoon tea is served daily in the living room and on the front porch. During the winter months, guests can be found sipping tea around a warm, inviting fire in the living room. The inn is centrally located in the small village of Ogunquit, across the street from the beach and just a short walk to shops and restaurants.

Coffee Praline Muffins

The secret to never-fail muffins is two things: always be sure the oven is thoroughly heated, and never overmix the batter. Only mix enough to dampen the dry ingredients, and forget the lumps.

1¾ cups all-purpose flour
⅓ cup light brown sugar
3 teaspoons baking powder
¼ teaspoon salt
½ cup chopped pecans

❖   ❖   ❖

1 egg
¾ cup milk
2 tablespoons instant coffee
1 teaspoon vanilla extract

❖   ❖   ❖

½ cup melted butter

❖   ❖   ❖

1 tablespoon sugar
2 tablespoons pecans

In a large bowl combine the flour, brown sugar, baking powder, salt and pecans. In a small bowl combine the egg, milk, instant coffee and vanilla. With a whisk beat the liquid until the instant coffee is dissolved. Mix the egg mixture and melted butter into the dry ingredients. Hand mix the batter just until the dry ingredients are moistened. Pour the batter into greased muffin tins and sprinkle the tops with sugar and pecans. Bake in a 375° oven for 18 to 20 minutes.

Makes 8 to 12 muffins.

Blueberry Gingerbread

½ cup butter (1 stick)
1 cup sugar
1 egg

❖   ❖   ❖

2 cups all-purpose flour
½ teaspoon ground ginger
1 teaspoon cinnamon
½ teaspoon salt
1 teaspoon baking soda
1 cup buttermilk
3 tablespoons molasses
1 cup blueberries
3 tablespoons sugar

Cream the butter and sugar. Add the egg, mix well. Sift together flour, ginger, cinnamon and salt. Dissolve the baking soda in the buttermilk and add to the creamed mixture. Add the flour mixture; blend well. Add the molasses and then add the blueberries and stir until mixed well. Pour the batter into a greased and floured 9-inch square pan. (May be put in small loaf pans—will fill 2 small loaf pans.) Sprinkle 3 tablespoons of sugar over the batter. Bake in a 350° oven for 50 to 60 minutes.

This is at its best when served warm.

Serves 12.

Orange Pecan Bread

"We like to serve Orange Pecan Bread in the winter months, mainly because the Florida oranges are at their best, but also because the flavors in the bread help to warm your insides when it's cold outside."

Seafair Inn

½ cup butter (1 stick)
¾ cup sugar
2 eggs, separated
Grated rind of 1 large orange
½ cup fresh orange juice
1½ cups all-purpose flour
1½ teaspoons baking powder
¼ teaspoon baking soda
Pinch salt
1 cup chopped pecans

Cream the butter and sugar. Beat the egg yolks and orange rind. Add the orange juice and stir in the dry ingredients. Mix in the pecans. Beat the egg whites until stiff. Fold into the batter. Grease 1 loaf pan or 3 mini-loaf pans. Bake in a 350° oven for 50 minutes.

Makes 1 loaf.

Chocolate-Almond Filled Butter Cookies

These cookies are offered at afternoon tea.

1 cup plus 2 tablespoons all-purpose flour
3 tablespoons plus 1½ teaspoons sugar
¼ teaspoon salt
6 tablespoons unsalted butter
1 egg yolk
½ teaspoon vanilla extract
⅛ teaspoon almond extract

❖   ❖   ❖

2 cups ground almonds
½ cup unsalted butter (1 stick), softened
6 tablespoons sugar
3 tablespoons dark rum
2 eggs
½ teaspoon almond extract
½ teaspoon vanilla extract

❖   ❖   ❖

4 tablespoons almond paste
6 tablespoons whipping cream
5 ounces semi-sweet chocolate
3 tablespoons unsalted butter, softened
3 tablespoons Amaretto liqueur
¼ teaspoon vanilla extract

❖   ❖   ❖

Confectioners' sugar

In a mixing bowl combine the flour, sugar and salt. With a pastry blender, cut in the 6 tablespoons butter until the mixture resembles coarse meal. Add the egg yolk, ½ teaspoon vanilla, and ⅛ teaspoon almond extract and blend with the pastry blender until the dough holds together. Wrap in plastic wrap and freeze for 30 minutes.

Heavily grease 1¾x¾-inch tartlet pans. Press the dough into cups to a depth of ⅛-inch, prick with a fork and chill 10 minutes. Place on an oven rack set in the lowest position. Bake in a 350° oven for 15 minutes. Remove from pan immediately and place on a wire rack to cool.

To make almond paste, in a small bowl whisk together the almonds, ½ cup butter, 6 tablespoons sugar, dark rum, eggs, ½ teaspoon each almond and vanilla extracts.

In a heavy medium saucepan stir together over low heat the almond paste, whipping cream, and chocolate, stirring until the chocolate is melted. Add the 3 tablespoons of unsalted butter. Stir in the Amaretto and ¼ teaspoon vanilla extract. Transfer to a small bowl and refrigerate covered for 30 minutes.

Spoon into a pastry bag with a number 5 or number 6 star tip and pipe the filling into the baked cookie cups. Chill for 30 minutes, and sprinkle with confectioners' sugar prior to serving.

Makes 1 dozen cookies.

Clifford Tea Cookies

"This recipe has been in our family as long as I can remember. It was always traditionally made at Christmas time with several other special cookies. Today we share this recipe with our guest at tea time."

    1 cup butter (2 sticks)
    2 cups brown sugar, firmly packed
    2 eggs
    1 teaspoon baking soda

½ teaspoon salt
1 cup chopped walnuts
3½ cups all-purpose flour

In a large bowl cream the butter and sugar. Add the eggs and stir in the flour, soda, salt and nuts. Cover the bowl with plastic wrap and refrigerate overnight. (It may be kept in the refrigerator up to 2 weeks.) The next day roll out the dough until thin (These cookies taste much better when rolled thin). Cut with a cookie cutter and bake in a preheated 375° oven for 10 to 15 minutes, or until lightly golden.

Makes 2 dozen cookies.

The Copper Light

Bed and Breakfast by the Sea
Box 67
Port Clyde, Maine 04855
(207) 372-8510

The Copper Light offers its guests quiet, private surroundings, forests for strolling, shores for beachcombing, a lighthouse to photograph, a General Store for browsing, good local eateries, and a nearby sandy beach for guests who enjoy ocean swimming. The Monhegan Ferry is minutes away. The homestead is on the water, overlooking the harbor and beyond to Marshall Point Lighthouse. To the rear of the house is a field, and beyond that acres and acres of forest. The house is surrounded by gardens and includes a living room, library, dining room, and a large stone terrace overlooking the home port for lobster fishermen. The protected harbor often hosts the windjammer fleet and sailing vessels of all shapes and sizes in summer. The Copper Light is quiet, comfortable, caring, and relaxed. Two guest rooms are available.

Melt-In-Your-Mouth Blueberry Cake

    2 egg whites
    ¼ cup sugar
        ❖ ❖ ❖
    ½ cup butter
    Salt
    1 teaspoon vanilla extract
    ¾ cup sugar
    2 egg yolks
        ❖ ❖ ❖
    1½ cups sifted all-purpose flour
    1 teaspoon baking powder
    ⅓ cup milk
    1½ cups blueberries
    Sugar

Beat the egg whites until stiff. Add ¼ cup sugar. In a separate bowl, cream the butter, add salt and vanilla. Add the remaining sugar and egg yolks. Beat until light and fluffy. Sift together the flour and baking powder, add alternately with the milk to the creamed mixture. Fold in the egg white mixture and the blueberries. Grease an 8x8-inch pan. Pour in the batter and sprinkle the top with granulated sugar. Bake in a 350° oven for 50 minutes. (Place the pan in the upper ⅓ of the oven.)

Serves 9.

Mill Pond House

Box 640
Tenants Harbor, Maine 04860
(207) 372-6209

Mill Pond House is an old, white house with a beautiful view of the ocean. Three rooms are available for guests; two have a shared bath and the third has a private bath. A sitting room for guests is on the same floor. A Continental breakfast is served daily. The

Mill Pond House is near a public beach, tennis, library, stores, a post office, and gift shops.

Blueberry Muffins

3 cups all-purpose flour
1 cup sugar
4 teaspoons baking powder
1 teaspoon salt

❖ ❖ ❖

2 eggs, lightly beaten
½ cup oil
1 cup milk

❖ ❖ ❖

1½ cups blueberries

Mix flour, sugar, baking powder and salt in a bowl. Combine the eggs and oil, add the milk and stir into the dry ingredients until just moistened. Stir the berries into the mixture. Spoon into greased muffin pans to ½ full. Bake in a 400° oven for 20 minutes.

Makes 14 large muffins.

The Captains House 1840

122 Main Street
Thomaston, Maine 04861
(207) 354-6738

Once the home of two Thomaston sea captains, Captains House is now a Bed and Breakfast establishment that is open year round. Thomaston is the gateway to the fishing villages of Tenants Harbor, Port Clyde, Cushing, and Friendship.

Blueberry Muffins

2 cups all-purpose flour
¼ cup sugar
3 tablespoons baking powder
Pinch salt

❖ ❖ ❖

1 cup milk
¼ cup oil
1 egg

❖ ❖ ❖

1 cup blueberries

Grease muffin tins. Sift the dry ingredients, beat milk, oil and egg together. Drain blueberries (if frozen) and toss in the flour mixture. Lightly combine dry and wet ingredients. Fill cups ¾ full and bake in a 375° oven for 20 minutes. Have ready the melted butter in a pan wide enough to dip the hot muffins. Put the sugar in a saucer. Dip hot muffins in the butter, then twirl in sugar. Serve.

Makes 8 to 12 muffins.

Broad Bay Inn and Gallery

Post Office Box 607
Main Street
Waldoboro, Maine 04572
(207) 832-6668

Old Broad Bay Inn is in the charming coastal village of Waldoboro within walking distance of general stores, the post office and the Waldo Theatre. Built in classic colonial style, it has airy, sunny rooms, comfortable beds (some with Victorian furnishings and canopy beds), attractive grounds, and a large deck for afternoon tea or sherry. Sumptuous homemade breakfasts are included with room rates. Candlelight dinners on Saturday night are available with prior arrangements. The inn is centrally located on the Maine coast.

Carrot Soup

1 pound peeled sliced carrots
1 pound tomatoes (use canned if
    not in season)
2 large onions, chopped
1 clove garlic, chopped

2 tablespoons chopped parsley
2 teaspoons salt
Pepper to taste

❖ ❖ ❖

½ cup cream
¼ cup butter (½ stick)

In a large saucepan combine the carrots, tomatoes, onions, garlic clove, parsley, salt, and pepper. Cover with water. Bring to a boil. Cover the saucepan and simmer for 1 hour. Process through a food mill or a blender. If the mixture is too thick, add water. Return to a boil. Add the cream and butter. Serve.

For Halloween, place in a cleaned-out pumpkin and heat in a warm oven for about 5 minutes. The children will love it.

Serves 6 to 8.

Carrot-Ginger Cream Soup
with a Hint of Orange

½ cup unsalted butter (1 stick)
2½ pounds carrots, cut up
1 cup onions, chopped

❖ ❖ ❖

4 cups chicken stock
3 cups whipping cream
½ cup orange juice
⅓ cup dry Sherry
1 teaspoon fresh ginger
1 teaspoon fresh tarragon leaves
Salt and white pepper

Melt the butter in a heavy 4-quart pan over low heat. Add carrots and onions, cook for 15 minutes. Stir. Increase heat to medium. Stir in remaining ingredients except the salt and pepper. Simmer for about 25 minutes. Transfer to a food processor and purée until smooth. Season with salt and pepper. Serve immediately.

Serves 6 to 8.

Leek and Potato Soup

3 or 4 leeks
4 medium potatoes
Salt and pepper
½ pint heavy cream
2 tablespoons butter

Peel and wash the leeks very carefully and cut into small pieces. Peel and cut the potatoes in small squares. Place in a pan and cover with water, adding salt and pepper to taste. Bring to a boil and simmer for at least 30 minutes. Mash part of the potatoes and return to the pan to thicken the soup. Remove from the heat, add the cream and butter and serve right away. C'est si bon!
   Serves 4.

Old Broad Bay Inn

Curried Chicken Salad

This should be prepared the day before serving and refrigerated overnight.

2 cups mayonnaise
2 tablespoons lemon juice
2½ tablespoons soy sauce
1 rounded tablespoon curry powder
1 tablespoon onion juice (mincing some onions will do)
1 to 2 tablespoons chopped chutney
3 cups diced white chicken or turkey meat
1½ cups chopped celery
1 8-ounce can water chestnuts, well drained and sliced
2 cups seedless white grapes
1 1-pound can pineapple chunks, well drained
½ cup slivered almonds, toasted

Combine all the ingredients except the almonds. Place in the refrigerator and chill overnight. When ready to serve, sprinkle with almonds.
   Serves 6.

The Roaring Lion

Post Office Box 756
75 Main Street
Waldoboro, Maine 04572
(207) 832-4038

The Roaring Lion is a country Victorian bed and breakfast facility that is open all year round. Located just off Route 1 in the village of Waldoboro, The Roaring Lion was built in 1905 and features classic oak woodwork, tin ceilings, two fireplaces, and a screened porch. A visit to The Roaring Lion provides guests a quiet atmosphere conducive to rest and refreshment. Four rooms are available, one with a private bath. A full breakfast is served featuring homemade breads, muffins, coffeecakes, jam, and jellies. Special dishes, such as "lion eggs," are featured.

Sourdough Pancakes

1 cup sourdough starter
1 egg, separated
1 tablespoon oil
All-purpose flour
1 tablespoon sugar
½ teaspoon baking soda
½ teaspoon salt

Combine the sourdough starter, egg yolk and oil, add enough flour for a thin batter. Beat the egg white until fluffy and fold into the batter. Bake on a hot griddle.
   Serves 4.

Mrs. Boyd's Coffee Cake

¼ cup butter (½ stick)
⅓ cup sugar
1 egg
1 teaspoon vanilla extract
1 cup all-purpose flour

1½ teaspoons baking powder
Pinch salt
⅓ cup milk
⅓ cup jelly

❖ ❖ ❖

2 tablespoons butter
2 tablespoons sugar
½ teaspoon cinnamon
¼ cup all-purpose flour

Cream together ¼ cup butter and ⅓ cup sugar. Add the egg, vanilla, flour, baking powder, salt and milk. Pour the batter into a well-greased 8-inch layer pan, dot with jelly.

Combine 2 tablespoons butter, 2 tablespoons sugar, cinnamon, and ¼ cup flour to make a crumbly mixture, sprinkle over the batter. Bake in a 375° oven for 30 minutes.

Serves 8 to 10.

Crab Fondue Casserole

3 tablespoons mayonnaise
1 tablespoon prepared mustard
Dash chives
8 ounces Maine crabmeat
1 cup chopped celery
Salt and paprika to taste
6 or 8 slices of bread
Sliced Swiss or American cheese

❖ ❖ ❖

2 eggs, well-beaten
1 cup milk
Dash Worcestershire sauce

Combine the mayonnaise, mustard and chives. Add the crabmeat, celery, salt and paprika; spread between slices of bread and then cut in half. Layer in a greased casserole with slices of cheese between the layers.

Combine the eggs, milk, and Worcestershire sauce and pour over the bread layers. Cover and bake in a 325° oven for 40 minutes. Good cold, too.

Serves 4 to 6.

Spaghetti Squash Italian Casserole

1 medium spaghetti squash
18 ounces spaghetti sauce
½ pound Mozzarrella cheese, thinly sliced
Butter
Parmesan cheese
Paprika

Wash the squash and place in a pot of boiling water. Boil until the skin loosens and a fork easily pokes into the squash through the skin. Remove from the pot and cool to handling temperature. Remove the skin and use a fork to separate the squash into strings.

Heavily butter a casserole and place a layer of spaghetti squash about ½-inch thick in the bottom. Cover with sauce and then a layer of sliced mozzarella cheese. Place a few pats of butter on each layer. Repeat layers until the casserole is filled. Bake in a 300° oven for about 30 minutes or until the casserole bubbles. Remove from the oven and sprinkle the Parmesan cheese over the top. Return to the oven for 5 minutes. Just before serving, sprinkle the top with paprika for color and an added touch of flavor.

Serves 8.

Bill's Clam Cakes

Minced clams
Italian-style bread crumbs
1 egg
Minced onion (optional)
Salt and pepper

Mince fresh "hen" clams (found on the Maine coast in early spring). Mix with bread crumbs in equal portions. Add the egg, onion, salt to taste and plenty of pepper. Roll into golf ball-sized cakes. Drop into deep hot fat and cook until a golden crust is formed. Serve hot.

The Stacked Arms

RFD #2, Box 420
Wiscasset, Maine 04578
(207) 882-5436

The Stacked Arms Bed and Breakfast has five bedrooms available for guests, four with shared baths and one with twin-sized beds and a private bath. Each bedroom has been decorated in its own color scheme and style. A large, light and airy dining room with individual tables and family style dining table are available. The Stacked Arms also has a large lounge with a floor-to-ceiling bookcase filled with a variety of reading material. Seven acres of land surround the house, and a path goes to the top of a hill that overlooks Wiscasset Harbor and part of the village. Guests may prefer to relax in the shade of a spreading pine or oak tree where there is always a breeze, or stroll through the grounds where there are many different trees and flowers to admire.

Sourdough Starter

¼ cup milk
¼ cup warm water
2 teaspoons salad oil
1 ¼-ounce package active dry yeast
½ cup warm water
2 teaspoons sugar
1¼ teaspoons salt
2⅓ cups sifted all-purpose flour

Combine the milk, ¼ cup water and oil, bring to a boil; cook to lukewarm. Sprinkle the yeast on ½ cup warm water; stir until dissolved; add with sugar and salt to the cooled milk mixture. Stir the liquid into the flour just enough to blend thoroughly. Cover; let stand in a warm place for 12 to 18 hours to sour.

Sourdough Blueberry Pancakes

1 cup Sourdough Starter
2 cups all-purpose flour
Milk (just enough to make a batter)
Pinch salt
2 eggs
3 tablespoons oil or melted fat
1 tablespoon baking soda
Water
½ cup sugar

Mix all ingredients in a glass bowl big enough so it can rise without running over, and let it sit overnight in a warm room. As soon as the starter looks like a sponge, it is ready. Place one cup in the refrigerator for future use. (Just keep adding to this starter each time you make bread or whatever and you can keep your starter going for years and years.) To the remainder (about 2 cups of sponge) add eggs, melted fat or oil, soda moistened with water and sugar (you may even use dietetic sweetener). This can be mixed with a fork, spoon or electric mixer into a smooth batter. Pour enough batter onto the griddle for the size pancake you want, sprinkle with blueberries (either fresh or canned, preferably fresh) and brown to a golden turn. Then live it up!
Serves 6.

Quiche

5 eggs
2 cups evaporated milk
¾ teaspoon salt
Dash nutmeg
Pinch sugar
Dash cayenne pepper
Dash black pepper
   ❖   ❖   ❖
12 strips bacon, crisply fried
Large unbaked pie shell
1⅓ cups grated Cheddar cheese

Beat the eggs, milk, and seasonings together. Sprinkle crumbled bacon into the pie shell and cover with grated cheese. Pour the milk-egg mixture over all. Bake in a 300° oven for 25 to 30 minutes or until the quiche has puffed and browned. Allow 15 minutes for cooling.
Serves 5.

The Lilac Inn

Ridge Road
Box 1325
York Beach, Maine 03910
(207) 363-3930

The Lilac Inn is actually two houses. The Victorian house (1890) has beautiful bays, some with ocean views, a center staircase, gingerbread, and a doll house tied together in the Laura Ashley manner. The Cape Cod house (1800s) has wide floor boards, a unique staircase, early door latches, and a wide porch for inhaling the salty ocean breezes. In the summer guests can swim and picnic on the beautiful beaches, as well as look at the lovely old buildings, visit the animal farm, and play the golf courses. In the fall the beaches are uncrowded and the sunset is unforgettable. In winter guests can snuggle by the stove in the common room and delve into the collection of Victoriana and books on New England.

Pull-Apart Coffee Cake

1 loaf frozen white bread dough
Butter
Cinnamon
Sugar
Confectioners' glaze

Thaw one loaf of frozen white bread dough. Roll individual balls of dough into melted butter, then a cinnamon and sugar mixture. Place in a greased cake pan in a warm place. Allow to rise and double or triple in size. Bake in a 350° oven for 10 to 15 minutes. Drizzle with confectioners' glaze made with a drop of almond extract and coconut added to the usual recipe.
Serves 8 to 12.

Tomatoes Eisenhower

Ripe tomatoes
Brown sugar
Diced onion
Pinch curry powder
Grated Swiss or Cheddar cheese

Slice tomatoes. Place on a cookie sheet. Drizzle with brown sugar and a teaspoon of diced onion. Top the onion with a pinch of curry powder. Finish with grated cheese. Place in the oven or under the broiler until bubbly.
Great as a side dish and is something to do with all those fall tomatoes.

The Wild Rose of York

78 Long Sands Road
York, Maine 03909
(207) 363-2532

The Wild Rose of York is a new replica of an 1814 captain's house. Boasting fireplaces in most rooms, its cozy decor includes braided rugs, four poster and high back beds, wallpapers with tiny flowers, and, in one room, stenciling that matches a handmade green, white, and red quilt. Rooms are named for wildflowers. Breakfast and tea are served on the large porch, which is also a great place to sun, play cards, have cookouts, or relax and read a good book. The house sits high on a hill with a view of the rolling lawn where children can sled in winter. The Wild Rose is open all year.

Dutch Puff

2 cups all-purpose flour
½ teaspoon salt
4 tablespoons sugar
½ teaspoon cinnamon

❖ ❖ ❖

2 cups milk
6 eggs, beaten well

❖ ❖ ❖

4 tablespoons melted butter
1 large apple, chopped
Maple syrup
Lemon juice

Grease well a 6x10-inch pan. Mix flour, salt, sugar and cinnamon. Add milk to eggs. Combine flour and liquid, blend until smooth. Add butter and beat hard for 2 minutes, add the apple. Pour into the pan and bake in a 450° oven for 20 minutes. Reduce heat to 350° and bake 30 minutes more (or less). Puncture tops of the bumps to let steam out and bake 2 more minutes. Serve hot with maple syrup mixed with lemon. Slice into squares.

Serves 9 to 10.

Pfannkuchen
German Crêpes

3 eggs, beaten
1 teaspoon sugar
½ teaspoon vanilla extract
Pinch salt
1 cup milk

❖ ❖ ❖

1 cup all-purpose flour
2 tablespoons melted butter

❖ ❖ ❖

Peaches or apples
Cinnamon
Sugar

Blend the eggs, sugar, vanilla, salt and milk. Beat in the flour with a whisk, and then beat in the melted butter. The consistency of the batter should be that of heavy cream. In a very hot frying pan with a small amount of cooking oil, pour in about 2 to 3 tablespoons of batter and quickly tilt the pan so the batter spreads evenly over the bottom. As soon as the top is dry turn the crêpe over. Repeat until all the batter is used.

For the filling, make a compote of peaches or apples or mixed fruit beaten with cinnamon and sugar, and fill the crêpes.

Makes 12 crêpes.

Maryland

The Inn at Mitchell House

RFD #2, Box 329
Tolchester Estates
Chestertown, Maryland 21620
(301) 778-6500

Nestled on ten rolling acres, surrounded by woods and stream, and overlooking a pond, this historic, eighteenth century manor house with 7 fireplaces offers a touch of tranquility to those who yearn for a retreat from the mundane. The five bedrooms, authentically furnished with period antique appointments, greet guests with warmth and invite them to take a restful step back in time.

Peach-Raspberry Breakfast Cake

2 cups all-purpose flour
1 tablespoon baking powder
½ teaspoon salt
2 tablespoons sugar
⅓ cup shortening
1 egg
1 cup milk

❖ ❖ ❖

¼ cup melted butter
¼ cup brown sugar, firmly packed
¼ teaspoon cinnamon
¼ teaspoon nutmeg

2 cups fresh, frozen or canned peaches, thinly sliced
⅓ cup sour cream
½ cup red raspberry preserves

To make the batter sift together the flour, baking powder, salt and sugar in a large bowl. Cut in the shortening. Beat the egg with the milk; add to the flour mixture. Stir lightly, just until mixed. Set aside.

Combine the melted butter, brown sugar, cinnamon and nutmeg; spread over the bottom of a 9-inch square baking pan. Arrange the peach slices in four rows. Spoon half of the batter over the peaches and smooth. Combine the sour cream and the red raspberry preserves. Pour over batter. Drop spoonfuls of remaining batter over preserves mixture and smooth.

Bake in a preheated 350° oven for 50 minutes. Cool 15 minutes on a wire rack. Invert cake over a plate. Remove pan; cut into 16 pieces. Serve warm.

Variation: For Apple-Strawberry Breakfast Cake, substitute 2 cups of thinly sliced Golden Delicious apples

The Inn at Mitchell House

for the peaches and ½ cup of strawberry preserves in place of the red raspberry preserves. Follow the same directions.

Serves 16.

French Toast a la Caroll

6 eggs
⅔ cup orange juice
⅓ cup orange liqueur
⅓ cup milk
¼ teaspoon vanilla extract
¼ teaspoon salt
Rind of one orange, finely grated
8 slices French bread, ¾-inch thick

❖ ❖ ❖

Butter
3 tablespoons confectioners' sugar
Orange slices
Maple syrup

Beat the eggs in a large bowl. Add the orange juice, orange liqueur, milk, sugar, vanilla, salt, and orange rind and mix well. Dip the bread into the egg mixture, turning to coat all surfaces. Place in a baking dish in a single layer. Pour any remaining egg mixture over the top. Cover and refrigerate overnight, turning occasionally. Bring to room temperature before cooking.

Melt the butter in a large skillet over medium heat. Add the slices and cook until browned on both sides. Arrange on a platter, sprinkle with confectioners' sugar, and garnish with orange slices. Serve with maple syrup.

Serves 6 to 8.

Whole Wheat and Honey Bagels

Sounds complicated, but it's not! After enjoying one, you will never eat a store-bought bagel again.

2 cups bread flour (all-purpose flour can be used)
2 cups whole wheat flour
¼ cup lukewarm water (105° to 115°)
1 ¼-ounce package active dry yeast
2 teaspoons honey

❖ ❖ ❖

3 tablespoons plus 1 teaspoon honey
¼ cup oil
2 eggs
½ cup lukewarm water
1¾ teaspoons salt

❖ ❖ ❖

2 quarts water
1½ tablespoons sugar

❖ ❖ ❖

1 egg, beaten
Pinch salt
Poppy seeds (optional)

Sift both types of flour in a large bowl. Make a well in the center. Pour in ¼ cup lukewarm water. Sprinkle the yeast on top and add 2 teaspoons honey. Let stand until the yeast is foamy (10 to 15 minutes). Add the remaining honey, oil, 2 eggs, ½ cup water, and 1¾ teaspoons salt. Mix with a wooden spoon until the ingredients form a dough. When the mixing becomes difficult, continue mixing by hand. Knead the dough vigorously on a work surface until smooth and no longer sticky. Place the dough in a clean oiled bowl, cover with a damp cloth, and let rise in a warm place for 45 minutes. Punch down. Cover with a damp cloth and refrigerate overnight.

Allow the dough to return to room temperature. Knead the dough again lightly. Roll it into a thick log and cut into 12 pieces with a floured knife. To shape the bagels, roll each piece of dough to a smooth ball by holding it under your cupped palm on an unfloured surface and rolling it over and over. Flatten the ball slightly. Make a hole by flouring your index finger and pushing it through the center. Twirl the round of dough around your finger to stretch the hole. Gently pull the edges to even out the shape. Cover and let rise on a floured board for 15 minutes.

To simmer the bagels, bring the water and sugar to a boil. Add four bagels at a time and simmer over medium heat for one minute. Turn and simmer another minute. If the holes begin to close, force them open with the handle of a wooden spoon. With a slotted spoon, transfer to a paper towel.

Make an egg glaze by combining the egg and a pinch of salt, beating with a wire whisk. Place the bagels on two greased baking sheets. Brush with egg glaze and top with poppy seeds. Bake in a 400° oven for about 20 minutes, or until browned.

Makes 12 to 16 bagels.

Honey Cheese Spread

1 8-ounce package cream cheese, softened
½ teaspoon lemon rind
⅓ cup honey

Blend all the ingredients. Serve with bagels or other hot breads.

Makes 1 cup.

Dover Roast Potatoes

12 medium-sized potatoes
1 quart vegetable oil (approximately)
Salt

Place peeled potatoes in a large pan, cover with water and boil for 20 minutes. Drain well and allow to dry.

Place enough oil in a roasting pan to come halfway up on the potatoes when they are placed in the pan. Place the pan in a preheated 450° oven and allow to get very hot. Place the potatoes in the hot oil very carefully with a spoon. Roast the potatoes for 45 minutes, turning every 15 minutes until brown. Salt the potatoes when they are removed from the fat. The potatoes can be kept in a warm oven for a while after being removed from the oil.

Serves 12.

Mitchell House Sweet Potatoes

4 large sweet potatoes
½ cup orange liqueur
¼ teaspoon salt
½ cup brown sugar
½ cup pecans, chopped
2 eggs, beaten
½ cup butter (1 stick), melted

❖ ❖ ❖

¼ cup pecans

Cook and mash the sweet potatoes. Whip all the ingredients together, reserving the ¼ cup pecans. Fold into a buttered 2-quart ovenproof glass dish and top with the remaining pecans. Bake in a 325° oven until golden, about 30 minutes.

Serves 4.

Bed and Breakfast at Tran Crossing

121 East Patrick Street
Frederick, Maryland 21701
(301) 663-8449

Tran Crossing is a guest house standing beside the Old National Pike, the gateway through the Cumberland

Mountains for covered wagons heading west. Today the house stands within the heart of Frederick's historic district, a short distance from Maryland's oldest business and around the corner from Kemp Hall, where state legislators narrowly resisted secession from the Union. For more modern-day enthusiasts, antique, craft, and specialty stores are within strolling distance, as are good restaurants sure to please a variety of tastes and palates. Guests enjoy the serenity of the garden as they sip morning coffee or relax from sightseeing.

Jim-Dandy Muffins

1⅔ cups sifted all-purpose flour
2 tablespoons baking powder
1 tablespoon salt

❖   ❖   ❖

⅔ cup sugar
1 egg
⅓ cup salad oil
⅔ cup milk
⅓ cup crushed pineapple, drained

Sift into a mixing bowl the flour, baking powder, and salt. Add the sugar, egg, salad oil, milk, and pineapple. Mix until all the flour is moistened. The batter will be lumpy. Fill greased muffin tins ½ full. Bake in a 400° oven for 20 minutes to 25 minutes.

Makes 12 large muffins.

Turning Point Inn

3406 Urbana Pike
Frederick, Maryland 21701
(301) 874-2421

The Turning Point Inn is an imposing Victorian home with Georgian colonial features that sits back on almost four acres of spacious tree-studded lawn. Built by Dr. Benjamin Perry (a physician and gentleman farmer) in 1910, the home was a much admired residence. The inn has four beautiful bedrooms with antiques, reproductions, many personal touches, and private baths. Room fees include a fruit basket, Sherry, and a full country breakfast. The inn's living room is warm and gracious in tones of cream, mauve and French blue, with a fireplace and fine paintings and prints. The two elegant, intimate dining rooms are furnished with Queen Anne furnishings and oil paintings; a porch area is also available for dining. Lunch and dinner are served daily except Mondays. Dinner is a pre-selected menu of soup, salad, entree, and dessert served by candlelight and soft music.

Turning Point Fruit Glaze

For duck or Cornish hens.

2 teaspoons cornstarch
¼ cup sugar
2 tablespoons lemon juice
1 cup strawberry preserves
   (½ pint)
½ cup red wine vinegar
1 teaspoon Worcestershire sauce
¾ teaspoon allspice
½ teaspoon nutmeg
½ teaspoon cinnamon
½ cup red wine

❖   ❖   ❖

Oranges or strawberries
Fresh green watercress

Combine the cornstarch and sugar, stir in the lemon juice to make a smooth paste. Add in the preserves, vinegar, Worcestershire sauce, spices, and wine. Cook over medium heat until thickened. Brush over the duck or Cornish hens and if more sauce is desired serve a small portion in a sauceboat. Garnish attractively with oranges or strawberries in season and watercress.

Serves 2 to 4.

Broccoli Soup

2 pounds broccoli, chopped

❖   ❖   ❖

3 stalks celery, chopped fine
1 large onion, chopped fine
1 cup butter (2 sticks)
¼ cup flour
1 12-ounce can evaporated milk
3 cups chicken broth
½ cup whipping cream
Dash nutmeg
Salt and pepper to taste

❖   ❖   ❖

Sprinkle of grated carrot
Chopped parsley

In a large saucepan cook the broccoli in water, drain and set aside. In the same pan sauté the celery and onion; stir in the flour, mixing until well blended. Combine the milk, chicken broth, and broccoli. Working with a portion at a time, pulverize this mixture in the blender.

Return the mixture to the saucepan, simmer until thickened and add cream, nutmeg, salt, and pepper. Serve with a sprinkle of grated carrots and chopped parsley.

Serves 4.

Crab Leora

1 pound lump crab meat (we use
   jumbo lump)
¼ cup Sherry
2 tablespoons fresh lemon juice
Salt and pepper to taste
½ cup medium white sauce
Grated Parmesan cheese

❖   ❖   ❖

Slice of lemon
Sprig of dill or burnet
2 jumbo shrimp

Pick the crab meat carefully, without breaking up the crab meat too much. Add the Sherry, lemon juice, salt, and pepper to the white sauce and mix gently with crab meat. Mound in a lovely buttered scallop shell, or a large clam shell found at the beach. Top with the Parmesan cheese and bake in a 350° oven until golden brown. Garnish with a slice of lemon and a sprig of

dill or burnet. Place pan sautéed or boiled shrimp on either side of the shell. This is nice served with rice pilaf and broccoli, carrot, mushroom, green pepper, onion vegetable or any combination of vegetables that are colorful.
Serves 2.

Scalloped Oysters

1 pint select oysters
½ cup oyster liquor
1½ cups mixed bread and cracker crumbs
1 teaspoon salt
¼ teaspoon pepper
⅓ cup melted butter
½ cup light or regular cream
Worcestershire sauce
Dash of mace (optional)
Grated Parmesan cheese

❖ ❖ ❖

1 lemon slice
½ cherry tomato
2 small sprigs watercress

Pick over the oysters to remove any bits of shell; drain and reserve the oyster liquor. Combine the crumbs, salt, and pepper with the melted butter and stir with a fork until mixed. Place a light layer of crumbs in a greased baking dish and cover with half of the oysters and half of the liquor. Add half of the cream and a few drops of Worcestershire sauce. Add another layer of crumbs, oysters, liquor, cream and Worcestershire. Top with crumbs and mace and sprinkle generously with Parmesan. Bake in a 350° oven for 30 minutes or until golden brown. Garnish with a lemon slice and cherry tomato half on two small sprigs of watercress or parsley. This may be served as an entree or a nice accompaniment with roast turkey or chicken.
Serves 4.

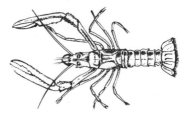

The Strawberry Inn

Box 237, 17 Main Street
New Market, Maryland 21774
(301) 865-3318

The Strawberry Inn has five guest rooms and offers the only overnight accommodations in New Market. Each room is furnished differently with period pieces, and each has a modern tiled bath. All rooms are air-conditioned. The inn is completely restored and is known for its gracious hospitality. A Continental breakfast is served in the morning on butler's trays outside guests' doors at the time requested.

Crab Dip

1 pound crab meat
2 8-ounce packages cream cheese
1 cup sour cream
4 tablespoons mayonnaise
Juice of ½ lemon
3 teaspoons Worcestershire sauce
½ teaspoon hot sauce
½ teaspoon garlic salt
½ cup sharp Cheddar cheese

❖ ❖ ❖

½ cup Cheddar cheese

Combine the ingredients except ½ cup Cheddar cheese, sprinkle the Cheddar on top. Bake in an ovenproof dish in a 325° oven for 30 minutes. Best served with plain crackers or over rice as main dish. If it has been frozen before baking, baking time should be increased. May be garnished with parsley flakes for color.
Serves 16 to 20.

Soldiers Bread

Begin preparations the night before you plan to bake this bread.

1½ cups raisins
2 cups hot water
2 tablespoons butter
2 teaspoons soda

❖ ❖ ❖

2 cups sugar
2 eggs, well beaten
1 teaspoon cinnamon
4 cups all-purpose flour
1 teaspoon vanilla extract
1 cup chopped nuts

Mix the raisins, hot water, butter, and soda; cover and let stand overnight.
The next morning, add to this mixture the remaining ingredients. Pour into 3 greased and floured 1-pound coffee cans, filling each ½ full. Bake in a 350° oven for 1 hour.
Serves 12 to 16.

Hot Fruit

1 1-pound can sliced pineapple
1 1-pound can peach halves
1 1-pound can apricot halves
1 1-pound can black bing cherries, pitted
1 15-ounce jar apple rings

❖ ❖ ❖

¼ cup butter
½ cup brown sugar
1 cup crumbled macaroons
1 cup Sherry

Drain the fruits, cut the pineapple slices in half. Arrange the fruits in alternate layers in a casserole dish.
In the top of a double boiler, mix the butter, sugar, macaroons and Sherry. Cook until slightly thickened. Pour over the fruit. Cover and chill overnight in the refrigerator. Before serving heat in a 350° oven until hot, 20 to 25 minutes. Uncover to heat, but recover to keep hot after baking, until ready to be served.
Serves 8.

The Oxford Inn

Box 447
Oxford, Maryland 21654
(301) 226-5220

Across the Chesapeake Bay is The Oxford Inn with three available bedrooms. Meals, including a Continental breakfast, are served with a flair. In its Pope's Tavern note the windows artistically sandblasted to display the forms of two ships that were America's Cup winners.

Oyster Stew

This is a traditional Eastern shore stew. Seasonings can be adjusted to taste but the technique in this is very important.

    12 large freshly shucked oysters
        with their liquor
    ½ cup butter (1 stick)
    1½ teaspoons dried parsley
    1 teaspoon Old Bay seasoning
    ½ teaspoon black pepper (adjusted
        to taste)
    ½ teaspoon Worcestershire sauce
    12 ounces half and half cream
        (1½ cups)

Sauté the oysters with the butter in a small sauté pan with all the seasonings. Stir the oysters just once, cook until the oysters curl on the sides. Add the half and half all at once, and do not stir. Bring to a slight boil so that the half and half separates. Turn off the heat. Divide the oysters between two bowls and pour the cream sauce over them. Serve with oyster crackers.
    Serves 2.

Vinaigrette Dressing

To be used with Crab Roma.

    1 pint 100% olive oil
    1 pint red wine vinegar
    2 teaspoons salt
    2 teaspoons black pepper
    2 teaspoons chopped garlic in oil
        (or 3 large cloves, fresh)
    ¾ cup chopped parsley

Mix all the ingredients well and put in a jar or some other storage vessel. Allow to stand and age one day for the best flavor. Shake well before serving.
    Makes 4 cups.

Crab Roma

This is a cold pasta salad that is just right for a hot summer day. Serve with Vinaigrette Dressing, prepared the day before use.

    3 ounces cooked, cooled fettuccine
            ❖   ❖   ❖
    ½ cucumber
    6 medium mushrooms
    2 scallions, including greens
    ½ medium green pepper
    1 medium tomato
    2 hard-boiled eggs
            ❖   ❖   ❖
    ½ cup Vinaigrette Dressing
            ❖   ❖   ❖
    ½ cup lump crab meat, picked over,
        leaving lumps

Cook the fettuccine according to the package directions. Rinse well in cold water and refrigerate or let it stand on ice, making sure that you drain it well before serving.
    Peel the cucumber; slice cucumber and mushrooms. Chop the scallions, green pepper, tomato, and eggs; place in a large salad bowl along with the pasta. Mix well and add dressing. Fold in the crab meat. Serve with cole slaw.
    Serves 2 to 4.

Crab Cakes

    ½ cup mayonnaise
    1 large egg
    1 teaspoon spike or Old Bay
        seasoning
    1 teaspoon pepper
    1 teaspoon fresh lemon juice
    1 teaspoon Worcestershire sauce
    1 teaspoon garlic powder
            ❖   ❖   ❖
    1 pound Maryland lump crab meat
    2 slices white bread
            ❖   ❖   ❖
    ½ cup butter (1 stick)

Make dressing by combining the mayonnaise, egg, seasonings, lemon juice, Worcestershire sauce, and garlic powder. Do not overmix. Leaving the lumps in the crab meat, fold into the dressing.
    Break slices of bread into crumbs, mix gently into the crab mixture. Make into 6 cakes. In a large sauté pan, fry the cakes in the butter. Cook until browned on both sides and thoroughly heated, about 15 to 20 minutes, turning once.
    Serves 4.

Shrimp and Pasta

Sautéed shrimps with fettuccine in an Alfredo-type sauce made with fresh Parmesan cheese make this really special.

    ⅓ cup clarified butter
    14 large shrimps, peeled and
        deveined
    2 teaspoons fresh or dried parsley
    1 teaspoon black pepper
            ❖   ❖   ❖
    ¼ cup dry white wine
            ❖   ❖   ❖
    5 ounces fettuccine, cooked to box
        directions
    ½ cup half and half
    1 cup freshly grated Parmesan
        cheese

Heat the butter in a medium or large sauté pan, add the shrimps, parsley, and pepper, cook until the shrimps are done, but don't overcook. Remove from the pan, then deglaze the pan with white wine over low heat. Add the fettuccine and shrimps, and stir. Add half and half, stir again and then toss with Parmesan cheese. Serve immediately.
    Serves 4.

The Robert Morris Inn

Box 70
On the Tred Avon
Oxford, Maryland 21654
(301) 226-5111

It has been said that the Robert Morris Inn is one of the most relaxed places on the eastern shore of Maryland. Situated by the scenic Tred Avon River, it offers quiet walks along the beach, peaceful spots to read a book, breathtaking sunsets, and good eastern shore food.

The Robert Morris Inn

Crab and Shrimp Soup

1 cup water
½ cup chopped onions
½ teaspoon seafood seasoning
½ teaspoon thyme leaves, crushed
½ teaspoon marjoram leaves, crushed
Dash white pepper

❖   ❖   ❖

1 pound shrimp, shelled, deveined and cut up

❖   ❖   ❖

2 10¾-ounce cans cream of chicken soup
1 soup can of milk
¼ pound fresh or frozen Maryland crab meat
2 tablespoons Chablis or other dry white wine

In a 2-quart saucepan, combine water, onions and seasonings; heat to boiling. Reduce heat to low. Cover; simmer 10 minutes. Add shrimp; simmer 10 minutes more. Stir in soup, milk, crab meat and wine; heat. Ladle into soup bowls.

Makes 4 servings or 5½ cups.

The Inn at Antietam

220 East Main Street
Post Office Box 119
Sharpsburg, Maryland 21782
(301) 432-6601

The Inn at Antietam is a classic turn-of-the-century Victorian house with a wrap-around porch that provides views of Antietam National Battlefield, the village of Sharpsburg, and the lovely Blue Ridge Mountains. Each of the four guest rooms is decorated individually with period furniture. Guests enjoy the plant-filled sunroom, the spacious parlor, and the warmth of the large fireplace in the country room that creates a mood of warmth, friendliness, and comfort.

Breakfast Casserole

12 slices white bread
4 cups ground ham (or chopped)
½ cup grated sharp Cheddar cheese
5 eggs
2 cups milk
1 teaspoon prepared mustard

❖   ❖   ❖

1 10¾-ounce can mushroom soup
1 cup sour cream
1 cup grated sharp Cheddar cheese
1 3-ounce can sliced mushrooms

Trim the crust from the bread and butter slices. Place 6 of the slices with the buttered side down in a 9x13-inch baking dish. Using half of the ham, make a layer over the bread followed with a layer of ½ the cheese. Add the remaining bread slices, buttered side up and finish layering the ham and cheese.

Beat together the eggs, milk, and mustard, pour over the layers. Refrigerate overnight.

Bake in a 325° oven for 40 minutes. While it is baking, make the sauce by combining the soup, sour cream, remaining cheese and mushrooms. Remove the casserole from the oven, add the sauce over the top and finish baking for 20 minutes.

Serves 8.

Buttery Cinnamon Skillet Apples

4 medium cooking apples

❖ ❖ ❖

⅓ cup butter
½ to ¾ cup sugar
2 tablespoons cornstarch
1½ cups water
¼ to ½ teaspoon cinnamon

Peel, core, and cut the apples in half.

Make a sauce by melting the butter in a 10-inch skillet over medium heat; stir in the sugar and cornstarch. Mix well and add the remaining ingredients.

Add the apples to the sauce, cover and cook over medium heat. Occasionally spoon the sauce over the apples as they cook.

Cook 12 to 15 minutes, until the apples are fork tender and sauce is thickened. To serve, place 2 apple halves in each dessert dish and ladle ½ cup sauce over each serving.

Makes 4 servings.

Dutch Apple Roll

6 apples

❖ ❖ ❖

2 cups all-purpose flour
1 teaspoon salt
2 teaspoons baking powder
¾ cup shortening
½ cup milk
Sugar
Cinnamon

❖ ❖ ❖

2 cups sugar
2 cups water
¼ teaspoon cinnamon
¼ cup butter

Prepare the apples by peeling, coring, and chopping them. Set aside.

Sift together the flour, salt, and baking powder. Cut in the shortening, add milk. Roll out on a floured board to ¼-inch thickness. Sprinkle chopped apples over the dough. Add sprinkles of sugar and cinnamon. Roll up as a jelly roll, cut in slices, and arrange in a baking pan. (Roll of dough may be wrapped in foil and frozen, to be sliced and baked later.)

Make syrup by dissolving 2 cups of sugar in the water and boil in a saucepan. Add ¼ teaspoon of cinnamon and butter and boil until slightly thickened.

Pour syrup over the apple roll slices and bake in a 375° oven for 25 to 35 minutes. Serve warm with whipping cream.

Serves 8 to 12.

Massachusetts

Cobbs Cove

Post Office Box 208
Route 6A
Barnstable Village Cape Cod
Barnstable, Massachusetts 02630
(617) 362-9356

This colonial-timbered manor on a site in use since 1643 commands a 360-degree view overlooking Barnstable Village, the harbor and the ocean. Centrally located on Route 6A, it is convenient to Hyannis and its airport. Cobbs Cove offers six spacious suites providing gracious accommodations for couples who enjoy an intimate atmosphere. Each room includes a full bath with a whirlpool tub, a dressing room, and a picture window view. The tradition of Cobbs Cove is in the old-time manner of good food and conversation to warm the heart and delight the spirit. Guests share the unspoiled, historical north shore of Cape Cod, a pleasure in all seasons. They may walk the winding paths and then return to a warm winter's fire or the peaceful garden patio.

Alsatian Potato Puffs

2 pounds potatoes

❖ ❖ ❖

2 tablespoons all-purpose flour
2 eggs, beaten
1 clove garlic, crushed
2 tablespoons parsley, finely
   chopped
1 tablespoon butter, melted
Salt, pepper, nutmeg to taste

❖ ❖ ❖

Dash paprika

Peel, boil, and mash the potatoes. Blend the flour, eggs, garlic, parsley, and melted butter into the potatoes. Add salt, pepper, and nutmeg to taste. Mix well and place large tablespoons of the mixture (not quite touching) in a buttered baking dish. Bake in a 325° oven for about 12 minutes. Sprinkle with paprika. Run under broiler to brown.

Serves 4.

Onion Soup

Be aware that this is a single serving recipe, but it can be expanded to serve as many as you like. You can serve it in individual casseroles or in one large casserole. The innkeeper also notes, "This is just a bit different."

1 onion, chopped fine
3 cloves garlic, minced
1 tablespoon butter

❖ ❖ ❖

½ teaspoon sugar
½ teaspoon nutmeg
1 cup chicken stock

❖ ❖ ❖

Dash Sherry
Square of toasted French bread
Grated Parmesan cheese.

Sauté the onion and garlic in the butter until translucent. Add the sugar and nutmeg. Add stock and bring to a boil. Simmer 30 to 40 minutes. At serving time add a dash of Sherry, top with a square of toasted French bread and grated Parmesan cheese.

Serves 1.

Fruit Tarte

5 large ripe pears or apples
1 tablespoon lemon juice

❖ ❖ ❖

10 tablespoons all-purpose flour
¾ teaspoon baking powder
6 tablespoons sugar
¼ cup vegetable oil
½ cup milk
2 eggs
½ teaspoon vanilla extract
Pinch salt

❖ ❖ ❖

¼ cup butter
Sugar to sprinkle
¼ cup slivered almonds (optional)

❖ ❖ ❖

Whipped cream or ice cream

Peel, core, and slice the fruit (peel may be left on apples for added color). Sprinkle with the lemon juice, turning gently to mix with all the fruit.

Mix the batter by combining in a large mixing bowl the flour, baking powder, sugar, oil, milk, eggs, vanilla, and salt in that order. Pour into a buttered 10-inch shallow cake pan. Arrange the fruit slices on the top. Dot with the butter and sprinkle with sugar. Sprinkle almonds on top if desired. Bake in a 400° oven about 50 minutes or until golden brown and puffy. Serve warm with whipped cream or ice cream.

Serves 5.

The Thomas Huckins House

2701 Olde King's Highway (Route 6A)
Barnstable Village, Cape Cod
Box 515
Barnstable, Massachusetts 02630
(617) 362-6379

A stay at the Thomas Huckins House is a visit into America's past. Built by a descendant of one of the first settlers of Barnstable (founded in 1639), the house has been carefully restored to its original condition. It contains three cooking fireplaces, one with a twelve-foot opening, another with a beehive oven; other features include wide board floors and paneling, eighteenth century doors with their original blacksmith-made hinges and latches, built-in chimney and barrelback cupboards, and small pane windows with some of the original glass. Furnished with antiques, the house has an eighteenth century atmosphere with all the modern conveniences.

Banana Pancakes

2 cups all-purpose flour
2 tablespoons sugar
1 teaspoon baking soda
½ teaspoon salt
2 eggs, unbeaten
2 cups buttermilk
2 tablespoons oil
2 bananas, mashed

Sift together the dry ingredients. Add the eggs one at a time, buttermilk and oil and stir until just mixed. Stir in the bananas. Fry on a griddle in butter over medium heat until dry around edges (they are thick so it takes a while). Turn briefly. Serve with New England maple syrup.

Serves 4.

Cape Cod Cranberry Muffins

1 cup cranberries (fresh)
¼ cup sugar

❖   ❖   ❖

2 cups all-purpose flour
¼ cup sugar
3 teaspoons baking powder
½ teaspoon salt

❖   ❖   ❖

1 egg, beaten
¾ cup milk
¼ cup margarine or butter, melted

Cut the cranberries in half and combine with ¼ cup sugar. Set aside.

Sift together the flour, remaining sugar, baking powder, and salt.

In a separate bowl, combine the egg, milk, and margarine. Add all at once to the dry ingredients and stir just until mixed. Stir in the cranberries. Pour into greased muffin cups and bake in a 400° oven for 25 minutes.

Makes 12 muffins.

The Old Cape House

108 Old Main Street
Bass River, Massachusetts 02664
(617) 398-1068

The Old Cape House, located on historic Old Main Street, was built in the early 1800s by the Bakers, a farming and seafaring family who owned most of the land in Bass River. The inn is a fine example of the Greek Revival architecture of the nineteenth century and is eligible for the National Register of Historic Places. In keeping with the English motif, the guest rooms are named after London streets. All suites and guest rooms feature beamed ceilings and are comfortably furnished in New England style with handmade quilts for the cooler evenings. Breakfast is served in the colonial dining room, featuring a sumptuous table of homemade muffins, coffee cakes, breads, cereals, fresh fruits, and homemade preserves with lots of good conversation.

Rhubarb Bread

This recipe evolved from a very plentiful supply of rhubarb last summer and served with Rhubarb Ginger Preserve is delicious.

2¼ cups sifted all-purpose flour
1 cup whole wheat flour
2 teaspoons baking soda
1 teaspoon baking powder
1 teaspoon salt
2 teaspoons ground cinnamon
½ teaspoon ground nutmeg
½ teaspoon ground allspice

❖   ❖   ❖

3 eggs
1 cup vegetable oil
1½ cups dark or light brown sugar
2 teaspoons vanilla extract

❖   ❖   ❖

2½ cups diced rhubarb (1 pound
fresh)
½ cup chopped walnuts

Grease 2 loaf pans. Combine the dry
ingredients. Beat the eggs, oil, brown
sugar, and vanilla in a large bowl until
smooth and fluffy. Stir in the dry ingredients and mix until just moistened.
Stir in the rhubarb and walnuts. Spoon
into the prepared pans.

Bake in a 350° oven for 50 minutes
or until a tester inserted in the center
comes out clean. Cool in pans 10 minutes and turn out on racks to cool. Dust
with confectioners' sugar if you wish.

Makes 2 loaves.

Apple Raisin Bread

3 cups chopped unpeeled apples
3 cups all-purpose flour
2½ cups sugar
1¼ cups vegetable oil
4 eggs, beaten
1 tablespoon vanilla extract
2 teaspoons cinnamon
1 teaspoon ground cloves
1½ teaspoons baking soda
½ teaspoon baking powder
½ cup raisins
½ cup chopped nuts

Beat all the ingredients together until
well moistened and blended, pour into
2 greased loaf pans. Bake in a 325°
oven for approximately 1 hour or until
a tester comes out clean. Cool for 10
minutes and remove from pans. Cool
completely before slicing.

Makes 2 loaves.

Cape Cod Cranberry Nut Bread

2½ cups all-purpose flour
1 cup buttermilk
½ cup sugar
½ cup brown sugar, firmly packed
¼ cup oil or shortening
2 eggs
3 teaspoons baking powder

½ teaspoon baking soda
½ cup chopped walnuts
½ cup fresh or frozen cranberries
Grated rind and juice of one lemon

Beat all the ingredients together until
well-moistened, and pour into a
greased loaf pan. Bake in a 350° oven
until a tester inserted in the center
comes out clean, approximately 60 to
65 minutes. Cool for 10 minutes and
remove from the pan.

Store at least 8 hours before slicing,
and serve with Cranberry Butter.

Makes 1 loaf.

Keeping Bread

"This is a very old English recipe, orig-
inating in the Middlesex area of Southern England. The rule is not to cut the
bread for at least three days after baking. It is usually served sliced thin and
spread with butter and jams and preserves."

6 cups all-purpose flour
2 tablespoons baking powder
½ cup sugar
½ teaspoon salt
1 cup raisins

❖ ❖ ❖

2 eggs
1½ cups milk
½ cup treacle or dark Karo syrup

Mix together the dry ingredients and
add the raisins. Beat together the eggs,
milk and syrup and add to the flour
mixture. Mix all ingredients thoroughly. Pour into 2 well-greased loaf
pans and bake in a preheated 350°
oven for 1¼ to 1½ hours. Cool on a
rack. Wrap tightly in foil and keep for
three days.

Makes 2 loaves.

Cranberry Butter

1 cup fresh or frozen cranberries
(thawed if frozen)
1½ cups sugar or 1 cup honey
½ cup unsalted butter (1 stick)
1 tablespoon lemon juice

Purée the cranberries in a blender
with the sugar until smooth. Add the
butter and lemon juice and blend for 1
minute. Place the mixture in a saucepan and heat until the butter has
melted. Place in a serving dish and
chill in the refrigerator until firm.
Serve with cranberry bread, cranberry muffins, toast or pancakes.

Makes 2 cups.

Rhubarb Ginger Preserve

2 pounds oranges
2 cups water
2 tablespoons chopped ginger root
2 pounds rhubarb
6 cups sugar

Grate the rind of the oranges and reserve. Cut away the pith with a sharp
knife and cut the oranges into pieces.
Wash and slice the rhubarb and place
in large pan with the oranges, orange
peel, water, and chopped ginger and
boil until the setting point is reached.
Remove the scum and pour into prepared jars.

Makes about 5 pounds.

English Toad in the Hole

A very delicious brunch recipe.

1½ cups all-purpose flour
2 teaspoons baking powder
½ teaspoon salt
3 tablespoons vegetable oil
2 eggs
1 to 1¼ cups milk

❖ ❖ ❖

12 small link sausages

Combine the first 6 ingredients until
well-blended. Place the sausage in a
large rectangular pan and pour the
pancake batter over the top. Bake in a
350° oven for approximately 45 minutes until golden brown. Serve hot
with maple syrup and apple butter.

Serves 6 to 8.

Chocolate Chip Muffins

"This recipe is a much requested feature of our breakfasts. We have had guests ask for it several mornings in succession."

1½ cups all-purpose flour
2½ teaspoons baking powder
1 egg, beaten
1 cup sugar
1 cup chocolate chips
½ cup vegetable oil
Milk to mix

In a mixing bowl, mix all ingredients until the batter is smooth. Pour into a greased 12-cup muffin pan. Bake in a 350° oven for 15 to 20 minutes until golden brown. Serve warm.
Makes 12 muffins.

Spicy Bran Scones

1 cup whole bran cereal
½ cup buttermilk or sour milk
1 egg, beaten
1 egg white
3 tablespoons butter, melted

❖ ❖ ❖

3 cups packaged biscuit mix
½ cup sugar
1 teaspoon cinnamon

❖ ❖ ❖

1 egg yolk
1 tablespoon milk
1 tablespoon sugar

In a mixing bowl combine the cereal and buttermilk and let stand for 3 minutes until the milk is absorbed. Stir in the egg, egg white, and butter. Set aside. In a separate bowl stir together the biscuit mix, sugar, and cinnamon. Make a well in the center and add the bran/egg mixture. Mix until the dough clings together. Turn out on a floured board and knead gently for 10 to 15 strokes until smooth and well-blended. Divide the dough in half. On a large greased baking sheet pat each half into a circle. Cut each circle into eight

wedges. Stir together the egg yolk, milk, and sugar, brush over the tops of the circles. Bake in a 425° oven for 12 to 14 minutes until golden brown. Serve warm.
Serves 16.

Sweet Potato-Chocolate Nut Cake

4 ounces semi-sweet chocolate, melted
1 teaspoon vanilla extract

❖ ❖ ❖

3 cups all-purpose flour
1½ cups sugar
2 teaspoons baking powder
2 teaspoons baking soda
2 teaspoons cinnamon
½ teaspoon ground ginger
¼ teaspoon ground cloves
½ teaspoon ground nutmeg

❖ ❖ ❖

2 cups mashed cooked sweet potatoes
1½ cups oil
4 eggs
1 cup chopped nuts

Butter and lightly flour a 10-inch tube pan. Mix the melted chocolate together with the vanilla. Sift together the dry ingredients and set aside. In a large bowl beat the sweet potatoes and oil together, add the eggs one by one until well blended. Slowly add the dry ingredients and mix well. Stir in the nuts. Place ⅓ of the mixture in another bowl and stir in the chocolate mixture. Alternate batters in the tube pan, as with a marble cake. With a knife cut through the layers and swirl together. Bake in a 350° oven for 1 to 1¼ hours or until the sides have shrunk away from the pan, and a tester comes out clean. Let cool for 10 minutes and remove from the pan and cool on a rack.
Serves 12 to 15.

Stonehedge

Berlin, Massachusetts 01503
(617) 838-2574

Stonehedge is a historical Massachusetts home surrounded by old stone walls in a country setting. The guest suite in this 1735 farmhouse consists of a bedroom with twin beds, a sitting room, and a private bath. A swimming pool and tennis court are on the grounds. Stonehedge is in the village of Berlin, two miles from Route 495, an easy ride from Boston, Lexington, and Concord.

Coffee Ring

1 ¼-ounce package active dry yeast
2 cups warm water

❖ ❖ ❖

7 cups all-purpose flour
1 teaspoon salt
½ cup sugar
½ cup dry milk

❖ ❖ ❖

1 egg
3 tablespoons oil

❖ ❖ ❖

Butter
¼ cup sugar
1 teaspoon cinnamon
¼ cup raisins
¼ cup nuts

Dissolve the yeast in the warm water. Set aside. Combine the flour, salt, ½ cup of sugar, and dry milk.
In a large mixing bowl beat the egg, add the oil. Add in the yeast mixture and the dry ingredients. Mix together until dough forms a ball that pulls from the side of the bowl. Cover and set aside until double in bulk. Divide the dough into 4 parts. Roll each out like a pie crust. Spread with butter. Sprinkle each with the sugar and cinnamon and raisins. Roll like a jelly roll. Place in a circle on a 10-inch greased pie plate. Slash with kitchen shears about every

inch. Turn each cut, filling side up. Decorate with the nuts. Let rise until double in bulk. Bake in a 375° oven for 20 minutes. Cool and frost as desired.

Serves 16.

Inn of the Golden Ox

1360 Main Street
Route 6A and Tubman Road
Brewster, Massachusetts 02631
(617) 896-3111

On a hill overlooking Cape Cod Bay, the Inn of the Golden Ox is a blend of New England tradition and Old World charm. The building is 150 years old, and the inn has been in operation for more than a century. With its distinctive architectural style, it has been decorated to reflect the cozy warmth of Yankee hospitality. Nestled among stately beech and apple trees and surrounded by traditional privet hedge, the inn is among the most charming on the Cape. Its classic clapboard appearance has been a welcome sight to many a weary traveler.

Buttermilk Biscuits

2 cups sifted all-purpose flour
2 teaspoons baking powder
½ teaspoon baking soda
1 teaspoon salt
½ teaspoon sugar (optional)
⅓ cup butter
¾ cup buttermilk

In a bowl, sift together the dry ingredients; cut in butter with a pastry blender until the mixture resembles coarse meal. Add the buttermilk and mix until the dry ingredients are moistened. Turn onto a floured board and knead 6 to 10 times. Roll to ¾-inch thickness and cut with a lightly floured biscuit cutter. Place on an ungreased baking sheet and bake in a 450° oven for about 15 minutes, or until golden.

Makes 18 biscuits.

Country Corn Chowder

½ pound bacon or fatback, diced
❖ ❖ ❖
1 large Spanish onion, diced
1 cup diced celery
❖ ❖ ❖
½ cup all-purpose flour
❖ ❖ ❖
2 quarts chicken stock, chilled
❖ ❖ ❖
2 cups diced potatoes
½ teaspoon thyme
1 bay leaf
½ teaspoon marjoram
4 sprigs parsley
6 peppercorns, crushed
1 clove garlic
6 ears sweet corn
❖ ❖ ❖
2 cups half and half
Salt and pepper to taste
❖ ❖ ❖
Butter

In a 4-quart stock pot sauté bacon or fatback until the fat is rendered. With a slotted spoon remove the bacon or fatback and discard it, leaving rendered the fat in the stock pot.

Add the onions and celery to the fat and sauté until transparent but do not brown. Add the flour and continue cooking over low heat for 10 minutes but do not brown. Add the chicken stock and bring to a boil, stirring until no lumps remain.

Reduce to a simmer and add the potatoes. Tie the thyme, bay leaf, marjoram, parsley, peppercorns, and garlic in cheesecloth and add to the simmering soup.

Cut the corn off the cob with a sharp knife, being careful not to cut into the cob. Add the corn to the soup. Continue simmering the soup until the potatoes are tender.

Add the half and half and return to a simmer. Season with salt and pepper. Ladle into soup bowls and garnish with a dollop of butter.

Makes 8 to 10 servings.

Striped Bass
with Two Sauces

4 cups fish stock
½ cup white wine
1 small onion, sliced
1 bay leaf
2 sprigs parsley
1 2-pound striped bass fillet, boneless and skinless
❖ ❖ ❖
½ cup white wine
2 tablespoons chopped shallots
6 white peppercorns
½ cup heavy cream or crème fraiche
1 cup unsalted butter (2 sticks), chilled and cut into pieces
1 tablespoon lemon juice
❖ ❖ ❖
½ cup raspberry vinegar
2 tablespoons chopped shallots
6 black peppercorns
½ cup heavy cream, or crème fraiche
1 cup unsalted butter (2 sticks), chilled and cut into pieces
2 tablespoons raspberry couills for finish
❖ ❖ ❖
20 fresh raspberries

In a sautior or fish poacher combine the stock, wine, onion, bay leaf, and parsley. While the stock is still cool, cut the bass into 4 equal portions and add to the stock. Bring to a point just below simmer (or 140°), and poach the fillets, at this point for 8 to 10 minutes or until the fillets are just opaque.

For sauce Beurre Blanc, in a saucepan combine the white wine, shallots and white peppercorns and reduce by ⅔. Add the cream and reduce by ½. Reduce heat and add the cold butter piece by piece (do not add a piece until the prior piece is fully melted). Strain and adjust the flavor with fresh lemon juice.

For sauce Beurre Rouge, in a separate saucepan combine the raspberry vinegar, shallots, and black peppercorns; reduce by ⅔. Add the cream and reduce by ½. Reduce heat and add the cold butter piece by piece, adding each piece after the prior piece is fully melted. This sauce can be adjusted with fresh raspberry couills (fresh raspberries forced through a fine sieve) for more color and raspberry flavor.

On 4 large plates, place 2 ounces of sauce Beurre Blanc. Place a bass fillet in the center of each plate and coat with 2 ounces of sauce Beurre Rouge. Arrange 5 raspberries around each fillet and serve at once.

Serves 4.

Chocolate Kahlua Cheesecake

¼ cup butter (½ stick), sweet unsalted
½ cup sugar
1½ cups all-purpose flour
Grated rind of 1 lemon

❖ ❖ ❖

4 8-ounce packages cream cheese, softened
1⅓ cups sugar
5 whole eggs
2 egg yolks
1 cup heavy cream
1 tablespoon vanilla extract
¼ cup Kahlua

❖ ❖ ❖

2 1-ounce squares semi-sweet chocolate

With a mixer, cream the butter and sugar. Add the flour and lemon rind and mix for 2 minutes, or until thoroughly blended. Remove from the mixer, roll the dough into a ball, cover with plastic wrap and refrigerate for 1 hour.

After 1 hour, roll out the dough to ⅛-inch thickness and place in the bottom of a cake pan. Bake in a 375° oven for 10 minutes or until golden brown. Set aside to cool.

To make cheesecake filling, in a large bowl cream together the cream

cheese and sugar, making sure there are no lumps. Add the eggs, egg yolks, and cream and continue to mix until smooth. Add the vanilla and Kahlua, mix thoroughly. Pour the mixture onto the crust when cooled.

In a double boiler, melt the chocolate. Then drizzle the chocolate over the cheesecake mixture in a thin stream. With a paring knife swirl the chocolate through the mixture. Bake in a 275° oven for 2 hours, or until set. Turn off the oven and allow the cake to remain in the oven for 1 hour. Remove and refrigerate.

Serves 12.

Deerfield Inn

The Street
Deerfield, Massachusetts 01342
(413) 774-5587

Deerfield Inn, a one-hundred-year-old inn in Old New England style, has twenty-three guest rooms, all with private bathroom facilities. Furnished with many antiques, the inn boasts two lounges, a fine restaurant, a coffee shop, and a private dining room for groups. While the Deerfield has two attractive parlors, the Beehive is the more popular. Chris Opalenik is Executive Chef of this inn.

Veal Orloff

4 ounces veal medallion
Olive oil
Sautéed mushrooms
Sautéed shallots

❖ ❖ ❖

White wine
1 ounce veal velouté
Grated Gruyère cheese

Sauté the veal lightly in olive oil for 1 minute on each side. Place on a heated serving dish and cover with sautéed mushrooms and shallots.

Deglaze the pan with white wine, add the veal velouté and heat until simmering. Cover the veal, shallots, and mushrooms with sauce. Sprinkle with Gruyère and place under the broiler until melted. Serve immediately.

Serves 1.

Veal Gran Mere

4 ounces veal medallions
Olive oil

❖ ❖ ❖

2 pieces bacon
⅛ cup sliced onion
¼ cup mushrooms
White wine
1 ounce veal velouté
Lemon juice
Heavy cream
Chopped parsley

Sauté the veal medallions in olive oil for 1 minute on each side. Remove from the pan and place on a heated serving platter.

Sauté the bacon, onion, and mushroom in the same pan. Flambé with white wine, add the veal velouté, lemon juice, heavy cream, and chopped parsley, pour over the veal. Serve immediately.

Serves 1.

Lobster Christophe

4 1¼-pound fresh lobsters
1 gallon cold water
1 small onion, finely chopped
2 stalks celery, finely chopped
1 carrot, finely chopped
1 bay leaf
1 teaspoon thyme
1 teaspoon basil
1 teaspoon fennel seed
4 cloves garlic

❖ ❖ ❖

¼ cup heavy cream
2 tablespoons tomato paste
2 teaspoons fancy paprika
3 ounces roux
Salt and pepper

❖ ❖ ❖

3 ounces (6 tablespoons) vegetable oil

Deerfield Inn

¼ teaspoon salt
¼ teaspoon white pepper
4 tablespoons Dijon mustard
¹⁄₈ cup chopped fresh parsley
¹⁄₈ cup heavy cream

In a 20-inch skillet sauté the shallots in the oil. Add the wine and butter and bring to a simmer. Place the salmon in the skillet, and cook until done throughout. Carefully remove to a hot serving platter.

Reduce the remaining liquid by ⅓ and add the salt, pepper, mustard, parsley, and cream. Stir and cook for 2 minutes. Pour into a sauce boat. Spoon some of the sauce over the salmon and serve immediately with the remainder of the sauce on the side.

Serves 4 to 6.

Sole Lollar

Salt
8 3- to 4-ounce fresh Yellowtail sole fillets

❖ ❖ ❖

12 ounces fresh Snow Crab meat
4 teaspoons capers
2 tablespoons fresh chopped Italian parsley
1 teaspoon salt
¼ teaspoon white pepper
¼ cup Russian dressing

❖ ❖ ❖

1 tablespoon clarified butter
1 teaspoon fresh lemon juice
1 teaspoon dry white wine

❖ ❖ ❖

2 egg yolks
⅓ ounce dry white wine
¹⁄₈ teaspoon Dijon mustard
½ cup clarified butter (1 stick)
Salt and white pepper to taste

Salt the sole fillets lightly, and pat dry with a paper towel. Place the fillets in pairs, skin side up, in a lightly buttered casserole.

Chop the crab meat medium fine and combine with the capers, parsley, salt, white pepper, and Russian dressing, mix thoroughly. Place ¼ cup of stuffing in each pair of the sole fillets. Roll the sole around the stuffing to fit neatly in the casserole. Add the clarified butter, lemon juice, and white

1 pound fresh bay scallops
½ pound fresh mushrooms, sliced
2 pounds fresh stemless spinach
3 ounces Pernod
4 ounces fresh chopped parsley
1 cup heavy cream
Salt and pepper to taste

❖ ❖ ❖

½ cup fresh grated bread crumbs
8 ounces grated Gruyère cheese
Watercress for garnish

Boil the lobster in the cold water with the chopped onion, celery, and carrot, bay leaf, thyme, basil, fennel seed, and garlic. Cook until the lobsters are almost done, about 5 to 6 minutes after the stock boils. Reserve the liquid for the Lobster Newberg sauce. Let the lobsters cool on a tilted dish, reserving all the liquid. Strain the stock through a fine cheesecloth and place the liquid over medium heat to reduce to 1 pint.

Carefully remove all meat from the claws and joints. With a serrated knife slice from the top back of the tail toward the top back of the body and remove a thin slice of tail shell. Remove the tail meat and cut into 4 pieces crosswise. Place the tail meat with the claw and leg meat. Drain the lobster bodies of excess liquid and place each on a separate 12-inch oval platter for service.

For the Lobster Newberg sauce, add to the reduced lobster stock ¼ cup of cream, the tomato paste, paprika, and

the roux. Whisk until smooth and adjust the seasoning with salt and pepper. Continue the reduction until needed.

Heat the oil in a large skillet and sauté the scallops, mushrooms, and spinach until the scallops are just tender. Add the lobster meat and turn the heat to high. Flambé with the Pernod. Add the parsley, 1 pint of Newberg sauce, and 1 cup of cream. Simmer for 5 minutes over low heat. Season with salt and pepper.

Divide the lobster and scallops between the four lobster shells, evenly stuffing the meat into the back of the shells. Divide the mushrooms, spinach and sauce over and around the four lobsters. Sprinkle bread crumbs and Gruyère cheese over each lobster and place under a hot broiler until the cheese melts. Garnish with watercress and serve immediately.

Serves 4.

Salmon Dijonnaise

¼ cup minced shallots
2 tablespoons oil
½ cup dry white wine
½ cup clarified butter (1 stick)
6 4-ounce fillets fresh boneless salmon

❖ ❖ ❖

wine to the casserole. Bake in a 375° oven for 20 minutes or until firm. Remove and serve immediately with Sauce Hollandaise or any of your favorite sauces for seafood.

For Sauce Hollandaise whisk the egg yolks, wine, and mustard together in a stainless bowl over simmering hot water until the whisk leaves lines in the thickened egg mixture. Remove from heat and add the butter slowly. Continue whisking and add a pinch of salt and white pepper.

Serves 8.

Brandied Raisin Custard Bread Pudding

Bread, cut into ½-inch cubes
Milk
1⅓ ounces raisins
2½ ounces Brandy
Grated rind of ⅙ orange

❖ ❖ ❖

1¼ cups half and half
2 eggs
2 egg yolks
3⅓ ounces sugar
⅙ teaspoon vanilla extract
⅙ teaspoon cinnamon
⅙ teaspoon nutmeg
⅙ teaspoon mace

Butter a 9x12-inch baking dish. Place a water bath in a 350° oven when starting preparation.

Cut enough bread into cubes to fill the 9x12-inch baking dish. Add enough milk to soften the bread thoroughly.

In a saucepan simmer the raisins in Brandy until the Brandy evaporates. Add a little water to replump the raisins.

Sprinkle the grated orange rind over the bread, and scatter the raisins over the rind and bread.

Mix together the remaining ingredients and toss thoroughly with the bread mixture. Cover with buttered parchment. Bake in the hot water bath in a 350° oven for 1 hour and 15 minutes.

Serves 16.

Queen Mother's Cake

Fine dry bread crumbs
6 ounces sweet or semi-sweet
**   chocolate, coarsely cut or**
**   broken**
¾ cup butter (1½ sticks)
¾ cup sugar
6 egg yolks
1¼ cups finely ground almonds
⅛ teaspoon salt
6 egg whites

❖ ❖ ❖

½ cup heavy cream
2 teaspoons instant coffee
8 ounces sweet or semi-sweet
**   chocolate, coarsely cut or**
**   broken**

Butter a 9x2½-inch springform pan and line the bottom with wax paper or liner paper. Butter the paper and dust lightly with fine dry bread crumbs.

In the top of a small double boiler melt the chocolate. Remove from heat and set aside to cool slightly.

In the small bowl of an electric mixer cream the butter. Add the sugar and beat at a moderately high speed for 2 to 3 minutes. Add the egg yolks one at a time, beating until each addition is thoroughly blended. Beat in the chocolate. On the lowest speed, beat in the almonds, scraping the bowl with a rubber spatula as necessary to keep the mixture smooth. Transfer to a large mixing bowl.

In a large mixer bowl beat the salt with the egg whites until they hold a definite shape, or are stiff but not dry. Stir a large spoonful of the whites into

the chocolate, and then in three additions, fold in the balance. Turn into the springform pan. If necessary, level the top by rotating the pan briskly from side to side.

Bake in a 375° oven for 20 minutes. Reduce the oven temperature to 350° and bake for an additional 50 minutes. (The total baking time is 1 hour and 10 minutes). Do not overbake. The cake should remain soft in the center. Wet and slightly wring out a folded towel and place it on a smooth surface. Remove the springform from the oven and place it directly on the wet towel. Let stand 20 minutes. Remove sides of springform. Place a rack over the cake and carefully invert. Remove the bottom of the form and the lining. Cover with another rack and invert again to cool right side up. The cake will be about 1¾ inches high. When the cake is completely cool place four strips of wax paper around the edges of a cake plate. Gently transfer to the plate, bottom up. The cake may rise and crack unevenly during baking, but it will level almost completely while cooling.

Scald the cream in a heavy saucepan over moderate heat until it begins to form small bubbles around the edge or a skin on top. Add the instant coffee and whisk until dissolved. Add the chocolate. After 1 minute remove from the heat and stir with a wire whisk until the chocolate is melted and the mixture is smooth. Transfer to a small bowl or place the bottom of the saucepan in cold water to stop the cooking. Let the mixture stand at room temperature for 15 minutes or more, stirring occasionally until it reaches room temperature. Stir (do not beat) and pour over the top of the cake. Use a long narrow metal spatula to smooth the top, letting a bit of the icing run down the sides. Use a small metal spatula to smooth the sides. After about 5 minutes remove the wax paper strips, pulling each one out by a narrow end before the icing hardens.

If a turntable or Lazy Susan is available, use to ice the cake.

Serves 16.

The Over Look Inn

Route 6
Eastham, Cape Cod, Massachusetts 02642
(617) 255-1886

The Over Look Inn is a restored Victorian sea captain's house in the heart of historic Eastham, the oldest town on Cape Cod. Surrounded by one and one-half acres of tree-filled grounds, the inn's eight bedrooms with private baths retain their original charm and are furnished in the Victorian manner: queen-size brass beds, claw-foot bathtubs, wicker, and lace. Guests enjoy tea in the parlor and can play cards or relax with a good book in the gracious "Churchill" library overlooking the spacious front gardens.

Breakfast Sausage Casserole

½ cup butter (1 stick)
1 pound pork sausage, ground
6 slices white or wheat bread, cubed
2 teaspoons dried basil
1 teaspoon dried dill
½ cup shredded Cheddar cheese
6 eggs
2 cups milk

Melt the butter in small pan and pour into a 9x13-inch baking pan. Brown the sausage in a skillet and set aside. Layer half the cubed bread in the buttered baking pan and sprinkle with half the basil, dill and cheese. Then layer the remaining bread cubes, herbs and cheese. Sprinkle the browned sausage meat over all. Beat the eggs well and add the milk. Pour over the contents of the baking pan. Bake in a 350° oven for ½ hour or until set. Cut into squares and serve.
Serves 6 to 8.

Crab Muffins

1 6-ounce can crab meat
1 cup shredded Cheddar cheese
1 tablespoon mayonnaise
2 English muffins

Mix the crab meat, Cheddar and mayonnaise until well combined. Arrange the English muffins on a baking sheet and broil until the sides are slightly browned. Remove from the oven and divide the crab mixture evenly among the 4 muffin halves. Broil about 4 inches from the heat until the cheese is melted and very lightly browned, 3 to 5 minutes.
Serves 2.

Eggs Olivier

2 cups shredded Cheddar cheese
1 4½-ounce can black olives, chopped
½ sweet green pepper, chopped
1 onion, chopped
4 hard-boiled eggs, chopped
2 tablespoons tomato ketchup
2 teaspoons prepared mustard
4 English muffins, split

Mix the cheese, olives, green pepper, onion, eggs, ketchup and mustard until well combined. Arrange the English muffins on a baking sheet and broil until the cut sides are slightly browned. Remove from the oven and divide the egg mixture evenly among the 8 muffin halves. Broil about 4 inches from the heat until the cheese is melted and lightly browned, about 3 to 5 minutes.
Serves 4.

Scottish Kedgeree

A breakfast dish.

1 cup rice
4 eggs, hard-boiled
1 pound smoked cod
2 tablespoons butter
1 onion, diced

❖   ❖   ❖

Parsley
Indian Mango chutney

Boil the rice to the tenderness desired. Shell and chop the eggs into pieces. Cook the fish in boiling water until it flakes easily. Melt the butter in a saucepan, add the onion, rice and flaked fish. Mix lightly and simmer for 10 minutes. Add the chopped eggs. Cover and heat from a minute or two. Serve garnished with parsley and Indian Mango chutney.
Serves 6.

Country Breakfast

6 slices bacon, diced
4 cups cooked potatoes, cubed
½ cup chopped green pepper
2 tablespoons chopped onion
6 eggs
1 cup shredded Cheddar cheese

Cook the bacon in a skillet until crisp; remove from the skillet and pour off the excess fat. Add the potatoes, green pepper and onion to the skillet. Cook until lightly browned. Break the eggs over the potato mixture. Cover and cook until the eggs reach the desired firmness. Sprinkle with cheese and bacon. Cover and heat until the cheese is melted.
Serves 6.

The Nauset House Inn

Beach Road
Post Office Box 774
East Orleans, Massachusetts 02643
(617) 255-2195

The Nauset House Inn is a place where the gentle amenities of life are still observed. It is a quiet place removed from the cares of the workaday world, where sea and shore, orchard and field all combine to create a perfect setting for tranquil relaxation. Family-owned and operated, The Nauset House Inn, near one of the world's great ocean beaches is also close to all those things for which Cape Cod is famous: quaint antique and craft shops, sophisticated restaurants and remarkable art galleries, scenic paths, and remote places for sunning, swimming, and picnicking.

The Inn has fourteen cozy guest rooms (most with private bath), old-fashioned country breakfasts, and, among other surprises, a unique turn-of-the-century conservatory filled with plants and flowers and comfortable wicker furniture. Most important is the inn's warm and intimate atmosphere that is sure to delight and make the time spent there truly memorable.

French Toast, D.J.'s Style

1 loaf Italian bread

❖ ❖ ❖

4 eggs
2 cups milk
2 tablespoons vanilla extract
1 teaspoon nutmeg

❖ ❖ ❖

Corn oil
Maple syrup

Remove the crusts from the bread and cut into 1-inch thick slices. Place on a rimmed baking sheet. Beat together the remaining ingredients and pour over the bread. Let stand until all the liquid is absorbed. The bread should be saturated; if not, make more liquid. Turn the slices a few times while soaking. Deep fry in corn oil a few minutes on each side until golden brown and puffy. Serve immediately with maple syrup.
Serves 4.

Pumpkin Muffins

2²/₃ cups self-rising flour
¼ cup sugar
¾ cup light brown sugar, firmly
    packed
1 teaspoon baking soda
1 teaspoon cinnamon
1 teaspoon nutmeg
½ teaspoon salt

❖ ❖ ❖

½ cup butter (1 stick), softened

❖ ❖ ❖

1 cup golden raisins
¾ cup buttermilk
1 15-ounce can pumpkin purée
2 eggs, lightly beaten

In a food processor mix together in a food processor the flour, sugar, brown sugar, baking soda, spices, and salt. Add butter and mix until it resembles coarse meal. Add raisins, buttermilk, pumpkin purée, and eggs, mix until moist.

Divide the batter between 2 greased and floured muffin tins. Bake in a 400° oven for 18 minutes or until done.
Makes 24 muffins.

Flat Top Orange Date Muffins

Rind of 1 orange

❖ ❖ ❖

1 orange, quartered, pith removed
½ cup orange juice
½ cup unsalted butter (1 stick),
    softened
1 large egg, slighly beaten
½ cup chopped pitted dates

❖ ❖ ❖

1½ cups all-purpose flour
1 teaspoon baking soda
Dash salt
¾ cup sugar
1 teaspoon baking powder

Chop the orange rind in a food processor. Add the orange quarters, juice, butter, egg, and dates, and chop. Set aside.

Sift into a large mixing bowl the flour, soda, salt, sugar, and baking powder. Add the orange mixture to the

dry ingredients. Stir only until the dry ingredients are moistened. The batter will be lumpy. Divide the batter equally into 18 greased muffin tins. Bake in a 400° oven for 15 to 20 minutes.
Makes 18 muffins.

Ham Roll

12 tablespoons grated cheese,
    Swiss or Cheddar
12 ham slices, approximately 4x6
    inches
1 cup pineapple juice
¼ cup brown sugar, firmly packed

Roll 1 tablespoon of cheese into each ham slice, like a jelly roll. Place in a greased shallow baking dish. Pour the juice over them and sprinkle with sugar.

Bake in a 350° oven for 15 minutes or until hot and the cheese is melted.
Serves 6.

Hearty Sausage Pie

¾ pound sausage

❖ ❖ ❖

3 eggs
½ cup mayonnaise
½ cup milk
1 teaspoon onion, finely grated
½ teaspoon Dijon mustard
¼ teaspoon salt
¼ teaspoon seasoned pepper
    (optional)

❖ ❖ ❖

2 cups Cheddar cheese, grated
Pastry for 1 9-inch 1-crust pie

Cook, drain, and crumble the sausage. Set aside.

Mix together the eggs, mayonnaise, milk, onion, mustard, and seasonings. Add the cooked sausage and the cheese. Pour into the pie crust. Bake in a 350° oven for 1 hour.
Makes 6 servings.

Strawberry Frosty

½ cup frozen sliced strawberries
1 cup orange juice
1 tablespoon Grenadine
2 ice cubes

Place all the ingredients in a blender and mix well at high speed. Serve immediately.
    Serves 2.

The Governor Bradford Inn

128 Main Street
Edgartown, Massachusetts 02539
(617) 627-9510

The Governor Bradford Inn is a restored mid-nineteenth-century great house on Main Street in Edgartown on Martha's Vineyard Island. All the tastefully decorated rooms have private baths, ceiling fans, and king-size or twin brass beds. Suites are also available. At the Governor Bradford guests awaken to a leisurely breakfast of juices, tea or coffee, and fresh muffins and breads in the cheery breakfast room. The day can be filled with a short stroll to shops, restaurants, museums, and the harbor, or bicycling to nearby unsullied beaches. In the afternoon guests may enjoy tea or cocktails in the common room, sun porch, or garden. A bar is also available.

Governor Bradford's Christmas Braid

2½ cups all-purpose flour
2 ¼-ounce packages active dry yeast

❖ ❖ ❖

1¼ cups milk
⅔ cup brown sugar, firmly packed
6 tablespoons butter
1 teaspoon salt

❖ ❖ ❖

2 eggs
1 egg white
1 teaspoon crushed anise seed
2¼ cups all-purpose flour
1½ cups raisins

❖ ❖ ❖

1 beaten egg yolk

Combine 2½ cups of the flour with the yeast. Heat milk, brown sugar, butter, and salt till warm. Stir constantly. Add to the flour mixture, add the eggs, egg white and anise seed. Beat at low speed with electric mixer for ½ minute, then beat 3 minutes on high speed. Stir in as much of the remaining 2¼ cups of flour as possible with a spoon. Stir in the raisins. Knead the dough on a floured surface until dough is smooth and elastic. Shape into a ball and place in a greased bowl, turn once. Cover and let rise 1½ hours. Punch down. Divide the dough in half. Cover, let rest 10 minutes. Set half of the dough aside. Divide the remaining half of the dough in half. Cut one piece into thirds, roll each third into an 18-inch rope. Braid loosely. Place on greased sheet. Divide the other piece in quarters. Roll 3 of these quarters to 14 inch ropes. Braid. Place atop the first braid. Cut the remaining quarter in thirds.

The Governor Bradford Inn

Roll each third into a 12-inch rope. Braid. Place atop the second braid. Tuck the ends under. Repeat the directions with the remaining half of the dough. Cover, let rise 30 minutes. Brush the loaves with the beaten egg yolk. Bake in a 350° oven for 25 minutes. Cool on a wire rack.

Serves 16.

Dunscroft Inn

24 Pilgrim Road
Harwich Port, Massachusetts 02646
(617) 432-0810

Dunscroft Inn, in a quiet, exclusive, residential area off the main street of Harwich Port, is only 300 feet from a beautiful, private sandy beach. All rooms have private baths and are heated and tastefully decorated. A Continental breakfast is included in the room rate. The patio may be enjoyed for sunning, along with the spacious screened porch, which is newly enclosed for year-round comfort. Dunscroft is within walking distance of nine restaurants that provide everything from informal to fine dining, a shopping center, a movie theater, and quaint shops. Here guests can explore picturesque Cape Cod, visit antique shops, play golf, swim, bask in the sun, or relax. It's all here at Dunscroft.

English Muffin Bread

3 cups flour (preferably
    unbleached)
2 ¼-ounce packages active dry
    yeast
1 tablespoon sugar
2 teaspoons salt
¼ teaspoon baking soda

❖ ❖ ❖

2 cups milk
½ cup water

❖ ❖ ❖

3 cups flour (preferably
    unbleached)
Cornmeal

Combine 3 cups of flour, yeast, sugar, salt and soda. Heat the liquids until very warm. Add to the dry mixture. Beat well. Stir in the rest of flour to make a stiff batter. Spoon into 2 8½x4½-inch pans that have been greased and sprinkled with cornmeal. Sprinkle the tops with cornmeal. Cover and let rise in a warm spot for 45 minutes. Bake in a 400° oven for 25 minutes. Remove from the pans immediately and cool on a rack. This bread freezes very well.

Makes 2 loaves.

Orange Pecan Bread

½ cup sweet butter (1 stick),
    softened
¾ cup sugar
2 egg yolks
Grated rind of 1 large or 2 small
    oranges
1½ cups unbleached all-purpose
    flour
1½ teaspoons baking powder
¼ teaspoon baking soda
Pinch salt
½ cup fresh orange juice
1 cup shelled pecans, chopped
2 egg whites

❖ ❖ ❖

½ cup fresh orange juice
¼ cup sugar

Cream the butter, adding the sugar gradually, beating with an electric mixer until light. Beat in the egg yolks one at a time, and the grated orange rind. Sift the flour with the baking powder, baking soda and salt and add to the batter alternately with ½ cup orange juice, beginning and ending with the flour. Gently mix in the pecans. Beat the egg whites until stiff and fold carefully into the batter. Pour the batter into greased 8½x4½-inch loaf pan

and bake in a 350° oven for 50 to 60 minutes.

To make the glaze combine the orange juice and sugar in a small saucepan and simmer gently for 5 minutes, stirring occasionally until a light syrup forms. Spoon the glaze over the bread as soon as the bread is removed from the oven. Cool in the pan on a wire rack.

Makes 1 loaf.

The Inn on Bank Street

88 Bank Street
Harwich Port, Massachusetts 02646
(617) 432-3206

The Inn on Bank Street is a Bed and Breakfast facility in the center of Harwich Port on Cape Cod, a five-minute walk from the ocean and also close to restaurants, stores, galleries, and antique shops. Its six sunny guest rooms have private entrances; all have private baths. A peaceful atmosphere prevails, with gulls the only sound heard in the mornings. The cozy living room and library with piano, television, and fireplace are for guests' enjoyment. A leisurely breakfast is served on the sunporch: fresh-ground coffee, fruit, juice, granola, homemade bread, or muffins (served with cheerful stories and jokes).

Snackin' Granola Bars

Great for breakfast, too.

3½ cups oats (quick or old
    fashioned, uncooked)
1 cup raisins
1 cup chopped nuts

⅔ cup sweet butter, melted
½ cup brown sugar, firmly packed
⅓ cup honey or molasses
1 egg, beaten
½ teaspoon vanilla extract

Toast the oats in an ungreased large shallow baking pan in a 350° oven for 15 to 20 minutes. Combine the toasted oats with the remaining ingredients and mix well. Press firmly into a well greased 15½x10½-inch jelly roll pan. Bake in a preheated 350° oven for about 20 minutes. Cool and cut into bars.

Makes 8 bars.

Corn Muffins
Filled with Strawberry Jam

3¾ cups all-purpose flour
1¼ cups yellow cornmeal
5 teaspoons baking powder
½ cup sugar
1 teaspoon salt
2 eggs
½ cup vegetable oil
⅛ teaspoon nutmeg
1½ cups buttermilk
About ⅓ cup strawberry jam

Grease a 12 cup muffin pan. With an electric mixer combine the flour, cornmeal, baking powder, sugar, and salt, then add the eggs, oil, and nutmeg. Put the mixer on medium speed and pour in the buttermilk.

Fill the muffin cups very full, then fill the center of each muffin with a teaspoon of jam and press the jam into the middle of the batter. Place the muffin pan on a baking sheet and bake in the middle of a preheated 400° oven for 30 minutes. Leave in the pan for a few minutes to cool.

Makes 12 large muffins.

Strawberry Nut Bread

20 ounces frozen strawberries, thawed, reserve liquid (if mixture looks dry, add some liquid)

4 extra large eggs
1 cup vegetable oil
❖ ❖ ❖
3 cups all-purpose flour
2 cups sugar (can mix brown and white)
3 teaspoons cinnamon
1 teaspoon baking soda
1 teaspoon salt
❖ ❖ ❖
1 cup chopped walnuts
¾ cup raisins

Combine and stir the strawberries, eggs and oil. Sift the dry ingredients together. Add the wet ingredients to the dry and stir to blend. Stir in the nuts and raisins. Pour into a large, greased and floured tube pan. Bake in a 350° oven for 1 to 1¼ hours or until a tester comes out clean. Cool on a rack. Cut the bread when it is cool—the following day is fine.

Makes 20 generous slices.

The Cornell House

Main Street
Lenox, Massachusetts 01240
(413) 637-0562

In the heart of Lenox, just beyond the famous Church on the Hill, lies The Cornell House, a warm and friendly inn recently authentically renovated to the Victorian age. A stay at the Cornell House is an enjoyable one. Its nine spacious bedrooms have private baths, antique furnishings, and some working fireplaces that guests can enjoy on nippy New England evenings, regardless of the season. For those travelers who are more economy-minded or who want to experience the old days, the Carriage House has twelve guest rooms with shared baths. After a good night's rest, a Continental breakfast is served in the expanded dining facility or outdoors on the new deck.

Sour Cream Corn Muffins

Compliments of Aunt Polly.

1¼ cups all-purpose flour
¾ cup corn meal
3 teaspoons baking powder
½ teaspoon salt
¼ cup sugar
❖ ❖ ❖
½ teaspoon soda
1 cup sour cream
1 egg, beaten
Buttermilk (if needed)

Mix together the flour, corn meal, baking powder, salt, and sugar. In a separate bowl add soda to the sour cream and stir until frothy, add egg and mix well. Add in the dry ingredients, stir until just mixed well. Add buttermilk if more liquid is needed.

Fill greased muffin tins ⅔ full. Bake in a 350° oven for 25 minutes or until nicely brown.

Makes 12 muffins.

Honey of an Oat Banana Bread

Compliments of Aunt Polly.

⅔ cup sugar
⅓ cup shortening
2 eggs
⅓ cup milk
1½ teaspoons vanilla extract
⅔ cup oats
⅓ cup honey
2 medium bananas, mashed
1¼ teaspoons baking powder
½ teaspoon baking soda
1¾ cups all-purpose flour
¼ cup nuts (optional)

In mixing bowl beat sugar and shortening together. Add eggs, milk, vanilla, oats, honey, bananas, baking powder, and baking soda. Combine thoroughly then add flour and fold in nuts. Turn into lightly greased 8x4x2-

The Cornell House

The Carlisle House Inn

26 North Water Street
Nantucket, Massachusetts 02554
(617) 228-0720

This beautiful 220-year-old sea captain's home has been carefully restored with great attention to detail. It now boasts working fireplaces, authentic pine flooring, antiques, private baths, cozy rooms, and canopy beds. A complimentary Continental breakfast is served on the veranda which features white wicker furniture.

inch loaf pan. Bake in a 350° oven for 1 hour or until a tester inserted in center comes out clean.

Serves 16.

Marmalade Nut Bread

2½ cups all-purpose flour
1 teaspoon salt
⅓ cup sugar
3½ teaspoons baking powder
1 cup chopped nuts

❖   ❖   ❖

1 egg
1 cup orange marmalade
1 cup orange juice
3 tablespoons oil

Thoroughly stir together the flour, salt, sugar and baking powder. Add nuts and stir to coat evenly.

In a medium bowl, beat the egg, slightly stir in the marmalade, juice and oil. Add the flour mixture, stirring only until dry ingredients are moistened. Divide evenly between 2 8x4x2-inch loaf pans. Bake in a 350° oven for 1 hour. Cool in the pans for 10 minutes, then remove from the pans.

Makes 2 loaves.

Poppy Seed Bread

Compliments of Aunt Polly.

1¼ cups sugar
1¼ cups oil
1 cup evaporated milk
3 eggs
¼ cup milk
2½ cups all-purpose flour
2¼ teaspoons baking powder
⅛ teaspoon salt
¼ cup poppy seeds
1¼ teaspoons vanilla extract

Combine the sugar, oil, evaporated milk, eggs, and milk with a mixer until well blended. Sift the flour, baking powder, and salt together. Add to the egg mixture and beat at low speed. Add the poppy seeds and vanilla. Beat until smooth. Pour into 2 9x5-inch loaf pans. Bake in a 350° oven for about 50 minutes or until golden brown.

Makes 2 loaves.

Carlisle Chili Con Queso

1 16-ounce jar Cheez Whiz
1 6-ounce can chopped green chiles
1 pound ground beef, browned and drained
1 can Mexican beans, liquid and all

Warm everything together and serve with large corn chips or unsalted crackers.

Makes 3 cups.

Suzanne's No Peek Stew

2 pounds stewing beef
2 10¾-ounce cans mushroom soup
1½ cups mushrooms (button)
1 1¼-ounce envelope onion soup mix
½ cup red wine

❖   ❖   ❖

Egg noodles

Combine the beef, mushroom soup, mushrooms, onion soup mix, and wine in a 2½-quart casserole. Cover and

bake in a 325° oven for 3 hours.
Serve over egg noodles.
Serves 8.

Wicket's Wedgies

(Wicket is the resident springer spaniel.)

> 1 cup chopped ripe olives
> ½ cup thinly sliced onions
> 1½ cups shredded sharp Cheddar cheese
> ½ cup mayonnaise
> ½ teaspoon salt
> ½ teaspoon curry powder

Combine the ingredients and spread on toasted English muffin bread, broil until the cheese melts, then cut into wedges.
This is loved by the dog and guests as well.
Serve on 8 English muffins.

The Carriage House

Five Ray's Court
Nantucket, Massachusetts 02554
(617) 228-0326

Visitors to the Carriage House enjoy convenient access to shops, galleries, theater, and fine restaurants in Nantucket. The inn's seven guest rooms are individually appointed and are furnished with queen, double, or twin beds; each provides the convenience of a private bath with shower. A sheltered patio offers a congenial setting for a Continental breakfast, relaxation, and conversation. Color cable television, games, and a variety of books on Nantucket are available in the common room. Tennis, boating, and beautiful unspoiled beaches are nearby.

Morning Glory Muffins

These muffins are best when the batter is made up the night before and baked fresh at breakfast.

> 2½ cups sugar
> 4 cups all-purpose flour
> 4 teaspoons cinnamon
> 4 teaspoons baking soda
> 1 teaspoon salt
>
> ❖ ❖ ❖
>
> 1 cup shredded coconut
> 1 cup raisins
> 4 cups shredded carrots
> 2 apples, shredded
> 1 cup pecans
>
> ❖ ❖ ❖
>
> 6 eggs, lightly beaten
> 2 cups vegetable oil
> 1 teaspoon vanilla extract

Mix together into a large bowl the sugar, flour, cinnamon, baking soda, and salt. Add the coconut, raisins, carrots, apples, and pecans and stir well. Add the eggs, oil, and vanilla, stirring only until blended (not beaten).
Spoon into greased muffin tins and bake in a preheated 375° oven for 20 minutes.
Makes 16 to 20 muffins.

The Four Chimneys

38 Orange Street
Nantucket Island, Massachusetts 02554
(617) 228-1912

In the heart of Nantucket Island's unique historic district, The Four

Chimneys is on famed Orange Street, where 126 sea captains built their mansions, and is just a short picturesque walk from cobblestoned Main Street. Six original "master rooms" have been authentically restored and furnished with period antiques, canopy beds, and oriental rugs. Each of these traditional four-square rooms has its original fireplace, and one has its own porch.

Beef and Pecan Spread

> ½ cup chopped unsalted pecans
> ½ teaspoon butter
> 8 ounces chipped beef
> 1 8-ounce package cream cheese, softened
> 2 tablespoons milk
> ¼ cup chopped green pepper
> 2 teaspoons onion flakes
> ½ teaspoon garlic salt
> ½ cup sour cream

Sauté the pecans in butter until warm. Set aside. Using scissors, cut the chipped beef into small pieces; blend with the rest of the ingredients in a food processor. Place in a glass pie pan and sprinkle with pecan topping. Bake in a 350° oven until bubbly, about 20 minutes.
Serves 10 to 12.

Dill Dip

> 1 cup mayonnaise
> 1 cup sour cream
> 2 tablespoons minced onion
> 2 to 3 teaspoons seasoned salt
> 2 tablespoons chopped fresh dill
> Dry mustard
>
> ❖ ❖ ❖
>
> Lemon juice

Combine the ingredients except lemon juice, mix well and refrigerate. Season with lemon juice. Serve with chips or raw vegetables.
Note: Buy a whole loaf of unsliced dark bread. Cut out a hole in the cen-

ter, place the dip in the hole. Use torn-out pieces of bread to dip along with vegetables.

Makes 2 cups.

Pear-Cheese Melts

1 16-ounce can pear halves, drained and chopped
¼ pound Stilton cheese, crumbled
2 ounces cream cheese, softened
¾ cup coarsely chopped walnuts
1 loaf French or Italian bread, thinly sliced

Preheat broiler. Combine pears, cheeses and walnuts. Place the bread on cookie sheet. Toast on both sides. Spread the pear-cheese mixture on toast. Bake in a 400° oven until bubbly. Makes about 2 dozen.

Cranberry Crisp

1 cup sugar
¾ cup all-purpose flour
⅓ cup butter, softened
1 16-ounce can whole cranberry sauce

Using a pastry blender, combine the sugar, flour, and butter. Pour the cranberry sauce into a well-buttered baking pan and cover with the pastry mix. Bake in a 350° oven for 30 to 40 minutes, watching carefully. Cut into 9 pieces.

Rhubarb Crisp

3 cups rhubarb, cut in 1-inch pieces
¾ cup sugar
1 egg, well-beaten
¼ teaspoon mace
❖ ❖ ❖
¼ cup butter (½ stick)
⅓ cup brown sugar, firmly packed
⅔ cup all-purpose flour

Mix together the rhubarb, sugar, egg, and mace, place in a 9-inch pie plate.

Combine the butter, brown sugar and flour, and cover the rhubarb mix-

ture. Bake in a 350° oven for 30 minutes. Cut into 9 pieces.

The Farmhouse at Nauset Beach

163 Beach Road
Orleans, Massachusetts 02653
(617) 255-6654

The Farmhouse at Nauset Beach is a nineteenth-century farmhouse that has been carefully restored and furnished. Guests enjoy a blend of country life in a seashore setting. Some rooms have an ocean view, and it is just a short walk to the Nauset Beach. The innkeeper, Don Standish, is a tenth generation Standish who enjoys chatting with guests about his ancestors and showing them the Standish Bible.

Chocolate Chip Sour Cream Coffee Cake

½ cup shortening
1 cup sugar
2 eggs
1 cup sour cream
2 cups all-purpose flour
1 teaspoon baking powder
½ teaspoon salt
❖ ❖ ❖
½ cup sugar
1 teaspoon cinnamon
1 6-ounce package chocolate chips
½ cup chopped nuts

To make the batter cream the shortening and 1 cup sugar. Add the eggs one at a time, then sour cream. Sift to-

gether the flour, baking powder, and salt. Add to the egg mixture. Set aside.

To make the filling, combine in a separate bowl the ½ cup of sugar, cinnamon, chocolate chips, and nuts.

Spoon half the batter into a greased and floured tube pan. Then spread half the filling over the batter in a swirling motion. With a table knife cut through the batter. Add the rest of the batter, then the rest of the filling. Again cut through the batter. Bake in a 350° oven for 45 minutes.

Serves 16.

Sausage and Egg Casserole

1 pound bulk pork sausage
❖ ❖ ❖
6 eggs
2 cups milk
1 teaspoon salt
1 teaspoon dry mustard
❖ ❖ ❖
2 slices bread, cubed
❖ ❖ ❖
1 cup grated Cheddar cheese

Brown the sausage and drain. Beat the eggs with milk, salt, and mustard. Layer the bread cubes in the bottom of a buttered 9x13-inch casserole dish. Crumble the sausage over the bread and top with the cheese. Pour the egg mixture over all. Refrigerate overnight. Bake in a 350° oven for 30 to 40 minutes.

Note: When using a glass casserole, bake in a 325° oven for 45 to 60 minutes.

Serves 4.

Punch

This punch requires an ice mold, which should be made in advance. It may be fancy if desired. Measure the amount of water needed to fill the mold you wish to use. Allow the water to stand for about 15 minutes, stirring 4 or 5 times to break any air bubbles and prevent cloudiness in the ice. If you wish to add fruit, mint leaves, or other decorative items in your mold, then build gradually, freezing a layer at a time, and place the items in the middle layers.

> 1 quart apple juice
> 1 quart cranberry juice
> 7 10-ounce bottles 7-Up
> ❖ ❖ ❖
> Ice mold

Combine the juices in a large punch bowl. Add the ice mold. Slowly pour in the bottles of 7-Up.
Makes 30 to 40 cups.

Aunt Mary's Salad

> 3 29-ounce cans fruit cocktail (or 2 cans fruit salad and 1 can peaches)
> ❖ ❖ ❖
> ½ pint whipping cream
> 1 tablespoon confectioners' sugar
> 2 or 3 heaping tablespoons mayonnaise
> ❖ ❖ ❖
> Red cherries for garnish

Drain the fruit. Whip the cream and add the sugar. Fold in the mayonnaise and add the fruit. Mix well and garnish with red cherries. (Red and green cherries may be used for the holidays.)
Serves 8.

Winterwood at Petersham

North Main Street
Petersham, Massachusetts 01366
(617) 724-8885

Just off the Common in the historical district of Petersham is Winterwood, a

lovely Greek-Revival mansion that was built as a summer home in 1842 and is now on the National Register of Historic Homes. Radiating a hospitable, congenial atmosphere, it is a good place to relax, enjoy a good book, or perhaps indulge in a luxurious bubble-bath. Service is the theme, and every effort is made to make the guest as comfortable and as pampered as possible.

A lovely staircase leads overnight guests to their accommodations on the second floor, where there are five guest rooms, one a two-room suite with twin fireplaces. Each bedchamber is furnished with antiques. All have maintained their distinctive personalities and include a private bath. Most have working fireplaces.

New England Clam Chowder

> ¼ pound salt pork, cut into small cubes
> 2 cups finely chopped onion
> 3 cups diced raw potatoes
> ½ teaspoon dried thyme
> 2 cups water
> 4 cups finely chopped raw clams with their liquid
> 4 cups milk
> 2 tablespoons butter
> Salt and pepper to taste

Place the salt pork cubes in a kettle and cook until rendered of fat. Add the onion and cook, stirring until the onion is wilted. Add the diced potatoes, thyme and water and cook until the potatoes are tender, about 10 minutes. Add the remaining ingredients and cook about 10 minutes longer.
Serves 10.

Brandy Alexander Pie

> 1 ¼-ounce envelope unflavored gelatin
> ½ cup cold water

> ⅓ cup sugar
> ⅛ teaspoon salt
> 3 egg yolks
> ❖ ❖ ❖
> ¼ cup Cognac
> ¼ cup Crème de Cacao
> ❖ ❖ ❖
> 3 egg whites
> ⅓ cup sugar
> 1 cup heavy cream, whipped
> ❖ ❖ ❖
> 1 graham cracker crust
> 1 cup heavy cream, whipped

In a saucepan, sprinkle the gelatin over the cold water. Add ⅓ cup of sugar, the salt, and the egg yolks. Stir to blend. Over low heat, stir until the gelatin dissolves and the mixture thickens. Do not boil. Remove from heat and stir in the Cognac and Crème de Cacao. Chill until the mixture starts to mound slightly.

Beat the egg whites until stiff. Gradually beat the remaining sugar into the egg whites and fold into the thickened mixture. Fold in one cup of the whipped cream. Turn into the crust and chill for several hours. Garnish with the remaining whipped cream.
Serves 6.

Eden Pines Inn

Eden Road
Rockport, Massachusetts 01966
(617) 546-2505
(617) 443-2604 (off season)

Eden Pines Inn is directly on the ocean, one mile from the quaint, picturesque town of Rockport. Built around the turn of the century, it has been an inn for nearly forty-five years. It has six bedrooms, all with private baths, decorated in pale, restful shades. All have sitting areas, and some have private decks overlooking the ocean. The scene of Thacher's Island and Loblolly Cove is especially delightful in the morning when the lobstermen haul their traps. A large brick deck ablaze with red geraniums frames the view. Breakfast is served on the enclosed porch overlooking the ocean. Provisions are made for enjoying coffee and tea throughout the day and drinks before dinner. During cooler weather, a large granite fireplace that graces the comfortably appointed living room is lighted.

Sour Cream Coffee Cake

½ cup butter (1 stick)
1 cup sugar
2 eggs
2 cups sifted all-purpose flour
1 teaspoon baking soda
1 teaspoon baking powder
1 cup sour cream
1 teaspoon vanilla extract

❖ ❖ ❖

4 tablespoons sugar
2 teaspoons cinnamon
½ cup chopped nuts

❖ ❖ ❖

3 tablespoons melted butter

Cream together the butter and 1 cup of sugar. Add the eggs one at a time, beat well. Add the dry ingredients alternately with the sour cream. Beat well. Add the vanilla. Pour half of the batter in a greased 10-inch tube pan.

In a separate bowl combine 4 tablespoons of sugar, the cinnamon, and the chopped nuts to make the topping. Sprinkle half over the batter in the tube pan, and pour the remaining batter in the pan. Pour 3 tablespoons melted butter over the batter, and sprinkle the remaining topping over the butter. Bake in a 350° oven for 50 to 55 minutes.

Serves 12 to 16.

The Inn on Cove Hill

37 Mount Pleasant Street
Rockport, Massachusetts 01966
(617) 546-2701

Rockport is a small New England seaport town with stately colonial homes, a dramatic rocky coastline, and white picket fences festooned with pastel beach roses. Behind one of those fences is The Inn on Cove Hill, a gracious Federal-style home, just one block from one of the most picturesque harbors in New England. The inn was built in 1791 from the proceeds of pirates' gold found at nearby Gully Point. Many of the decorative and architectural features of this authentic colonial home have been carefully preserved or restored, providing guests the opportunity to stay in one of the few truly historical inns of Rockport.

Berry Muffins

If you find that your muffins are failing, we have conspired to leave out one essential ingredient from each of the recipes; that is umbrella tables in the summer and breakfast in bed in the winter. For access to both, come see us.

Blueberries, blackberries, or canned whole cranberry sauce work equally great in this recipe.

1¾ cups all-purpose flour
2 tablespoons sugar
1 teaspoon baking powder
¼ teaspoon baking soda
¼ teaspoon salt

❖ ❖ ❖

1 egg, well beaten
¾ cup buttermilk or sour milk
⅓ cup salad oil
1 cup berries

❖ ❖ ❖

Sugar

Sift together dry ingredients into a mixing bowl. Combine the remaining ingredients except sugar and stir into the dry ingredients, stirring just until moist. Pour into a greased muffin tin. Sprinkle sugar over the tops of the batter. Bake in a 400° oven for 20 to 25 minutes.

Makes 9 large or 12 small muffins.

Oatmeal Muffins

1 cup all-purpose flour
1 teaspoon baking powder
1 teaspoon salt
½ teaspoon baking soda
½ teaspoon cinnamon

❖ ❖ ❖

1 egg, well beaten
1 cup buttermilk (or sour milk)
1 cup oatmeal
½ cup brown sugar
⅓ cup melted shortening

Combine the flour, baking powder, salt, soda, and cinnamon in a mixing bowl. In a separate bowl mix together the egg, buttermilk, oatmeal, brown sugar, and shortening. Stir into the flour mixture just until moistened. Pour into greased muffin cups. Bake in a 400° oven for 20 to 25 minutes.

Makes 9 large or 12 small muffins.

Orange Buttermilk Muffins

³/₈ cup shortening (6 tablespoons)
½ cup sugar
1 egg

❖ ❖ ❖

2 cups all-purpose flour
1 teaspoon baking soda
¹/₈ teaspoon salt

❖ ❖ ❖

½ orange (including peel)
1 cup buttermilk or yogurt

Cream the shortening and sugar together, add egg and mix well. Set aside.

In a separate bowl mix together the flour, soda, and salt. Chop the orange half in a blender with the buttermilk or yogurt. Add alternately the flour mixture and the orange mixture to the sugar mixture, stirring only until the ingredients are moistened. Pour into greased muffin cups and bake in a 400° oven for 20 to 25 minutes.

Makes 9 large or 12 small muffins.

Moist Bran Muffins

1 cup buttermilk
¼ fresh lemon (including rind)

❖ ❖ ❖

1½ cups bran
⅓ cup oil
1 egg
⅔ cup brown sugar, firmly packed
½ teaspoon vanilla extract
½ cup raisins and/or dates

❖ ❖ ❖

1 cup all-purpose flour
1 teaspoon soda
1 teaspoon baking powder
½ teaspoon salt

Process the buttermilk and lemon in the blender until the lemon is finely chopped. Combine this with the bran, oil, egg, brown sugar, vanilla, raisins, and dates if used.

Combine the flour, soda, baking powder, and salt. Stir in the wet ingredients, mixing only until ingredients are moistened. Pour into greased muf-

fin cups. Bake in a 400° oven for 20 to 25 minutes.

Makes 9 large or 12 small muffins.

Banana Muffins

³/₈ cup shortening (6 tablespoons)
½ cup sugar
2 eggs
1 cup mashed ripe bananas
3 tablespoons milk

❖ ❖ ❖

2 cups all-purpose flour
2 teaspoons baking powder
1 teaspoon baking soda
½ teaspoon salt

Cream shortening and sugar together, add eggs, bananas, and milk.

In a separate bowl mix together the flour, baking powder, soda, and salt. Stir in the banana mixture, mixing only until dry ingredients are moist. Pour into a greased muffin pan. Bake in a 400° oven for 20 to 25 minutes.

Makes 9 large or 12 small muffins.

Captain Ezra Nye Guest House

152 Main Street
Sandwich, Massachusetts 02563
(617) 888-6142

This restored captain's house is situated in the heart of historical Sandwich village. Open year round, it provides comfortable rooms, most with private baths, and breakfast, which is served in the dining room between eight and ten each morning and includes fresh fruit and homemade pastries. Earlier breakfasts may be arranged upon request. Guests are invited to watch television or play the

piano in the parlor, enjoy a cup of tea, or choose from an assortment of games and books in the cozy den. The Captain Ezra Nye Guest House is within walking distance of the Thornton Burgess Doll and Glass Museums, Hoxie House, Heritage Plantation, Cape Cod Scenic Railroad, Dexter Grist Mill on Shawme Pond, public tennis courts, beaches, fine restaurants, churches, and antique and artisan shops.

Cranberry Nut Muffins

2 eggs
1 cup milk
½ cup oil

❖ ❖ ❖

3 cups all-purpose flour
1 cup sugar
4 teaspoons baking powder
1 teaspoon salt

❖ ❖ ❖

2 cups cranberries
¾ cup chopped nuts

In a mixing bowl combine the eggs, milk, and oil.

In a separate bowl sift together the dry ingredients, and mix into the egg mixture until just moistened. Add the cranberries and the chopped nuts. Bake in a well-greased muffin pan in a 400° oven for 20 minutes.

Makes 20 muffins.

Peach Muffins

4 cups all-purpose flour
1 cup sugar
8 teaspoons baking powder
1½ teaspoons salt

❖ ❖ ❖

2 eggs
2 cups milk
½ cup oil

❖ ❖ ❖

2 cups chopped fresh peaches
Sugar

Sift together the flour, sugar, baking powder, and salt.

In a separate bowl combine the eggs, milk, and oil. Add the dry ingredients and mix until just moistened. Add the peaches. Pour into a well-greased muffin pan and sprinkle with sugar. Bake in a 400° oven for 20 minutes.

Makes 2 dozen muffins.

The Dan'l Webster Inn

149 Main Street
Sandwich, Massachusetts 02563
(617) 888-3622

The innkeepers at The Dan'l Webster Inn extend to all their guests the hospitality of this proud old inn, be it for a happy refresher in the tavern, an evening of merriment by the hearth, or an elegant dinner in the eighteenth century Webster Room, which displays glass artifacts on loan from the Sandwich Glass Museum. The latchstring is always out to welcome guests to the inn, truly a memorable experience.

Creamed Butternut and Apple Soup

**5 pounds butternut squash, peeled
    and diced
1½ pounds apples, quartered
1 1-inch cinnamon stick
¹/₂ gallon chicken stock**

❖ ❖ ❖

**1½ cups unsalted butter (3 sticks)
¹/₃ cup pure maple syrup
½ teaspoon ginger
½ teaspoon salt
½ teaspoon nutmeg**

❖ ❖ ❖

1 pint light cream, hot

The Dan'l Webster Inn

Steam the butternut, apples, cinnamon and chicken stock together until the squash is soft. Run through a food mill and return to the pot. Add the remaining ingredients except cream and simmer fifteen minutes. Add the cream, strain, and serve.

Serves 8.

Fillet of Sole Webster

**2 cups butter (4 sticks), softened
½ cup parsley
½ cup white wine
¼ cup lemon juice
2 tablespoons minced shallots**

❖ ❖ ❖

**6 5- to 6-ounce fillets grey sole
1 cup light cream
All-purpose flour
Clarified butter
4 artichoke bottoms, sliced
3 ounces shrimp
3 ounces button mushrooms,
    blanched
2 tablespoons slivered, blanched
    almonds
1 tablespoon fresh tarragon**

To prepare the lemon butter, combine the softened butter, parsley, wine, lemon juice, and shallots; set aside.

Soak the fillets in the light cream for 5 minutes. Drain off the excess and dredge with flour. Shake off the excess flour and sauté flesh side down in hot clarified butter until golden brown. (This should be done very quickly so it is important that the butter is very hot.) Turn the fillets and sauté for 30 seconds. Remove to a serving plate.

Sauté the artichoke bottoms, shrimp, mushrooms, almonds, and tarragon in the lemon butter until hot. Spoon over the fillets and serve.

Serves 6.

Historic Merrell Tavern Inn

Main Street, Route 102
South Lee, Massachusetts 01260
(413) 243-1794

The authenticity and charm of this inn is enhanced by the natural beauty of its quaint New England setting. The Historic Merrell Tavern Inn is less than a mile from Norman Rockwell's beloved Stockbridge, in the heart of the beautiful Berkshire region.

Built about 1800, it retains its antique woodwork, fixtures, and original colonial bar, one of the few remaining in America. Rooms are furnished with a canopy or four-poster bed and antiques collected by the innkeepers over the past twenty-five years. Guests may roam the grounds, with the old stone walls and foundations, or stroll down to the shore of the Housatonic River, which borders the inn's property. Guests are able to rest, relax, and take advantage of the many cultural and natural pleasures which the area provides.

Chef's Omelet

Prepare two omelets and fill each with a slice of ham. In a separate pan grill ripe tomato slices in butter—enough to cover the finished omelet. Cover the omelet with grilled tomato slices and Hollandaise sauce. Garnish with ribbons of pimento or paprika. Serve with toast and slices of warm cornbread.

Serves 2.

Pampered Ramekin

Prepare a Bechamel sauce with a small amount of nutmeg added. Keep warm in an oven. Sauté enough sliced mushrooms to add a quarter cup for each serving. Trim two slices of bread, toast and butter. Place in the bottom of an individual ramekin so the edges protrude the ramekin and press slightly to create an indentation. Fill the indentation with two slices of ham (or chunks of chicken breast), add the sautéed mushroom slices and the Bechamel sauce. Garnish with half a sautéed mushroom and parsley or watercress. This can be served with a slice of cornbread.

Serves 2.

The Red Lion Inn

Stockbridge, Massachusetts 01262
(413) 298-5545

In a lovely Berkshire Hills town that once was an Indian village, on a street that once was a stagecoach road, the gracious old Red Lion Inn bids its guests a warm welcome. Here one enters a world of courtesy and hospitality amidst the charm of Staffordshire china, colonial pewter, eighteenth century furniture, and almost every contemporary comfort one might want. Guests may dine on traditional New England fare, or on Continental specialties with vintage wines; and they sleep in spacious rooms overlooking Historic Stockbridge and the rolling Berkshires.

Stockbridge and the Berkshires are rich in fall foliage, golf courses, ski areas, and woodland trails. Within easy strolling distance of The Red Lion are antique shops, boutiques, galleries, and museums. A bit farther away are the Berkshire Theater Festival, the Tanglewood summer concerts, the Jacob's Pillow Dance Festival, and Chesterwood. And all around is the beautiful Berkshire countryside.

Veal Oscar

4 5-ounce slices of veal
All-purpose flour
Salt and pepper to taste
Butter

❖   ❖   ❖

¼ cup crab meat
12 asparagus spears

❖   ❖   ❖

Hollandaise sauce

Pound the veal thin, or have your butcher do it. Dredge the veal in flour and season with salt and pepper to taste, and sauté in butter.

Remove the veal to a serving platter, place some of the crab meat on each piece of veal, and top each serving with 3 asparagus spears. Serve with Hollandaise sauce.

Makes 4 servings.

Chocolate Chip Pie

¾ cup butter (1½ sticks), softened
1 1-pound box light brown sugar
3 eggs

The Red Lion Inn

1 teaspoon vanilla extract
2⅔ cups all-purpose flour
2½ tablespoons baking powder
½ tablespoon salt
1 8-ounce package chocolate chips
1 cup chopped nuts

Cream the butter and sugar, add eggs and vanilla, beat well. Stir in the flour, baking powder, salt, chocolate chips, and chopped nuts. Bake in a pie pan in a 350° oven for 35 minutes. After baking top with melted butter.

Serves 6.

Indian Pudding

2½ cups milk
¼ cup butter (½ stick)
½ cup milk
½ cup cornmeal
½ cup molasses
¼ cup sugar
1 cup chopped apples
½ cup raisins
4½ teaspoons cinnamon
1½ teaspoons ginger
½ teaspoon salt
1 egg
1 cup milk

Combine 2½ cups milk with butter and scald. Combine ½ cup milk and the cornmeal, add to the scalded milk and butter. Cook 20 minutes, stirring slowly so the mixture does not burn. Add the molasses, sugar, apples, and raisins. Stir in the cinnamon, ginger, salt, and egg. Cook 5 more minutes. Pour into a well-greased shallow pan. Pour the remaining cup of milk over this. Bake in a 325° oven for 1½ hours or until the pudding is set. Top with ice cream or whipped cream.

Makes 8 to 10 servings.

Publick House On the Common

Post Office Box 187
Sturbridge, Massachusetts 01566
(617) 347-3313

The Publick House is three minutes and two centuries from I–91 and the Massachusetts Turnpike. Publick House Historic Inn serves hearty Yankee breakfasts, lunches, dinners, and suppers every day of the year, and the guest rooms are indulgently comfortable.

Pumpkin Muffins

2 cups sugar
½ cup vegetable oil
3 eggs
1½ cups canned pumpkin
½ cup water

❖ ❖ ❖

3 cups all-purpose flour
1½ teaspoons baking powder
1 teaspoon baking soda
1 teaspoon salt
½ teaspoon cloves
¾ teaspoon cinnamon
½ teaspoon nutmeg

❖ ❖ ❖

1½ cups raisins
1 cup walnuts

Place the sugar, vegetable oil, eggs, pumpkin and water in a bowl and mix. Sift together the flour, baking powder, baking soda, salt and spices. Add to the first mixture and mix. Add the raisins and walnuts. Let stand one hour at room temperature. Place in greased muffin tins. Bake in a preheated 400° oven for approximately 15 minutes.

Makes 2 dozen.

Publick House Individual Lobster Pie

¼ cup melted butter
4 tablespoons all-purpose flour
2 cups milk

❖ ❖ ❖

1 pound lobster meat
¼ cup butter (½ stick)
½ teaspoon paprika
⅓ cup Sherry
Pinch cayenne pepper
1 teaspoon salt

❖ ❖ ❖

4 egg yolks
1 pint light cream

❖ ❖ ❖

¾ cup grated fresh bread crumbs
¾ teaspoon paprika
3 tablespoons crushed potato chips
1 tablespoon Parmesan cheese
5 teaspoons melted butter

Combine ¼ cup of melted butter with the flour in a saucepan. Cook over low heat, do not brown. Add hot milk and cook 15 minutes stirring often. Strain. In a separate saucepan sauté the lobster meat in ¼ cup butter and paprika. Add ¼ cup of Sherry and cook for another 3 minutes. Add the cayenne pepper, salt and the thin cream sauce. Beat the egg yolks with the light cream. Blend 4 tablespoons of the lobster sauce into the egg yolks, then stir this back into the whole mixture. Stir until the mixture bubbles and thickens. Remove from the heat and stir in the remaining Sherry. Spoon the mixture into casseroles, making sure to distribute the lobster meat evenly. Combine the bread crumbs, ¾ teaspoon paprika, potato chips, Parmesan cheese, and 5 teaspoons melted butter. Sprinkle over the casseroles. Bake in a 400° oven until brown.

Serves 4.

Old-Fashioned Chicken Pie
with Brown Gravy

1 5-pound chicken
Onion
Celery
Carrot
Salt and pepper

❖ ❖ ❖

6 cups chicken stock
6 tablespoons margarine
6 tablespoons all-purpose flour
2 tablespoons Chablis
Salt and pepper
Kitchen Bouquet

❖ ❖ ❖

3 cups all-purpose flour
1½ cups shortening
1 teaspoon salt

Boil the chicken until tender with the onion, celery, carrot, salt, and pepper. Remove the chicken and cut into large pieces.

To make the gravy, bring 6 cups of chicken stock to a boil. In a small saucepan, melt the margarine and add 6 tablespoons of flour, stir. Add to the chicken stock and cook until the stock is thickened. Add the Chablis and season with salt and pepper, darken with Kitchen Bouquet.

Place the chicken in a 9x12x2-inch baking dish and pour the gravy over the chicken.

Make a pastry by mixing together 3 cups of flour, the shortening, and the salt, adding enough milk to make a dough. Roll out on a floured surface, and place the dough over the chicken and gravy.

Bake in a 375° oven until the chicken and gravy are sizzling and the pastry is nicely browned. Six individual casseroles may be used in place of 1 large baking dish.

Serves 6.

Bed and Breakfast at Wood Farm

40 Worchester Road
Townsend, Massachusetts 01469
(617) 597-5019

Enjoy a truly delightful stay in this restored Cape Cod home that was built in 1716 and has retained the warmth and charm of bygone days. Bedrooms are in an ell extension where the sun comes in on three sides, making the rooms light and cheerful. A quaint sitting room is a good place for visiting with other travelers, and the main keeping room with its open hearth fireplace is the setting for many evening conversations. Guests can tour the resident sheep farm, wander through the wooded trails, or sit by the pond to enjoy the waterfall and brook as they wind to the Squannacook River. Hiking and cross-country ski trails are nearby. In addition to the standard Bed and Breakfast schedule, the inn features several "country weekends" each Fall which includes the addition of a hearth-prepared meal on Saturday evening. Guests are invited to help prepare dinner in the beehive oven and eight-inch open hearth fireplace, including such eighteenth-century dishes as roast turkey and puddings.

Soufflé Pancakes

6 eggs, separated
⅓ cup pancake or buttermilk biscuit mix
⅓ cup sour cream
½ teaspoon salt

Beat the egg yolks until thick. Carefully blend in the pancake mix, sour cream and salt. Mix well until smooth. Beat the egg whites until slightly stiff, but not watery, and fold into the mixture. Drop by ¼ cups onto hot, greased griddle. Cook until golden brown on both sides. Serve with Vermont maple syrup.

Makes 4 servings.

Four Cheese Herb Quiche

½ cup Swiss cheese
½ cup Cheddar cheese
½ cup Mozzarella cheese
Prepared quiche or pie pastry shell
½ cup Ricotta cheese
5 eggs
1 cup light cream
1 teaspoon dried dill
1 teaspoon dried parsley
1 teaspoon dried onion, finely ground
1 teaspoon of favorite garden herb (chive, marjoram, etc.)
½ teaspoon of dried thyme

Finely shred the Swiss, Cheddar, and Mozzarella cheese. Mix together and place in a pie shell. Blend the remaining items in a blender on high for 2 minutes. Pour over the cheese mixture. Bake in a 400° oven for 1 hour or until the top is light brown and firm. Serve with a fresh fruit complement.

Makes 4 to 6 servings.

Sunday Morning Waffles

2 cups lukewarm milk
1 ¼-ounce package active dry yeast
4 egg yolks
2½ cups all-purpose flour (white works best)
½ teaspoon salt
1 tablespoon sugar
1 teaspoon cinnamon
½ teaspoon nutmeg
1 teaspoon vanilla extract
½ cup melted butter (1 stick)
4 egg whites

Pour the milk into a large mixing bowl, sprinkle the yeast over the top. Stir well to dissolve, making certain that no lumps remain. Beat egg yolks and add to cooled yeast mixture. Combine the flour, salt, sugar, cinnamon, and nutmeg; add to mixture. Add the vanilla. Stir in the melted butter. Combine completely. Beat the egg whites until stiff; fold into the batter.

Let the mixture stand in a warm place for 1 hour or until double in size. Using a Belgian waffle iron, fill the tray with about 1½ cups of mixture. Cook until golden brown. Serve with syrup or cream and fresh fruit.

Makes 6 servings.

Captain Dexter House

100 Main Street
Post Office Box 2457
Vineyard Haven, Massachusetts 02568
(617) 693-6564

Situated on the resort island of Martha's Vineyard, the Captain Dexter House is an 1843 sea captain's home, restored to reflect the charm and elegance of that period. It is beautifully furnished with fine period antiques, fireplaces, and canopied beds.

Cran-Apple Muffins

½ cup whole cranberry sauce
½ teaspoon shredded orange peel
1½ cups all-purpose flour
½ cup sugar
1 teaspoon cinnamon
½ teaspoon baking soda
¼ teaspoon baking powder
¼ teaspoon salt
1 egg, beaten
1 cup peeled shredded apple
⅓ cup milk
⅓ cup oil
½ cup sifted confectioners' sugar
2 to 3 teaspoons orange juice

Combine the cranberry sauce and orange peel. Set aside. Combine the flour, sugar, cinnamon, baking soda, baking powder, and salt. Make a well in the center. In a separate bowl, combine egg, apple, milk and oil. Add the egg mixture all at once to the dry ingredients. Stir until moistened. Fill greased muffin tins to ½ full. Make a well in the center of each with the back of a spoon. Spoon 2 teaspoons cranberry filling into each well. Bake in a 375° oven for 18 to 20 minutes.

Combine the sugar and juice. Drizzle over the warm muffins.

Makes 12 muffins.

The Inn at Duck Creeke

Box 364
East Main Street
Wellfleet, Massachusetts 02667
(617) 349-9333

The five-acre Inn at Duck Creeke complex sits between a tidal marsh and its own duck pond. The sea captain's home, built in the early 1800s, and the Saltworks House, moved from near the harbor, have twenty-six guest rooms, each individually decorated with period furniture. The inn has two screened porches and a veranda, and the grounds are a haven for bird life. On Main Street, a short walk to the village of Wellfleet, the inn is close to the bay, the ocean beaches, the National Seashore Park, the Audubon Sanctuary, and the harbor and marina. The well-known Sweet Seasons Restaurant and the Tavern Room Restaurant and Lounge are just across the drive, each with an interesting atmosphere and menu. From an unusual bar made of a collection of doors and nautical charts and a cozy fireplace in The Tavern, to the serene and sophisticated dining room of Sweet Seasons, a gracious blend of history and hospitality makes for a memorable visit.

Iced Mocha Espresso

This is a perfect way to end a meal, and can even serve as the dessert when served with thin wafer or pirouette cookies.

Small ices cubes
2 ounces chilled espresso
2 ounces heavy cream
1 ounce Kahlua
1 ounce Creme de Cacao

Combine all the ingredients in a large goblet or tall iced tea glass. Stir to mix. Top the glass with whipped cream and decorate with a twist of lemon peel and a whole coffee bean or shake of cinnamon.

Serves 1.

Chilled Strawberry and Burgundy Soup

A perfect summer soup which is sometimes ordered as dessert on hot July nights.

3 pints strawberries, washed and hulled
1 cup water
½ cup sugar
¼ cup all-purpose flour
2 cups Burgundy
2 cups orange juice
3 cups sour cream
1 cup milk or light cream
❖ ❖ ❖
Sliced strawberries
Mint leaves

Quarter the strawberries and cook in the water for 10 minutes. In a separate saucepan combine the sugar and flour. Stir in the wine and orange juice. Stir or whisk until the mixture boils, approximately 10 minutes. Add to the strawberries and cool, then purée in a blender and add the sour cream and milk. Chill. Served garnished with sliced strawberries and mint leaves.

Serves 6.

Seasons Shrimp with Rice

3 tablespoons butter
16 large shrimps, peeled and deveined
1 clove garlic, minced
1 tablespoon chopped fresh parsley
½ teaspoon freshly ground black pepper
1 to 2 ounces Ouzo (100 proof)
2 large tomatoes, chopped coarsely
¾ cup crumbled Feta cheese

❖ ❖ ❖

Hot cooked rice

Melt the butter in a sauté pan. Add the shrimp. Cook gently, keeping the pan moving during cooking. Add the garlic, parsley, and black pepper. Pour the Ouzo over the shrimp and flame. When the flame subsides, add the tomatoes and crumbled Feta. Cook until the cheese begins to melt.

To serve, arrange the shrimp tails up around a mound of rice and pour the sauce over the shrimp.

Note: Top the rice with leaves of kale and a tomato rose for a lovely presentation.

Serves 4.

Poached Haddock
with Leeks and Mussels

This is perfect for a bountiful platter presentation.

½ cup julienne-cut celery (1½x¼-inches)
½ cup julienne-cut carrots (1½x¼-inches)
½ cup julienne-cut zucchini (1½x¼-inches)

❖ ❖ ❖

1 cup water (reserved from cooking vegetables)
1 cup dry white wine
½ cup leeks or scallions, finely sliced
4 dozen mussels

❖ ❖ ❖

2 pounds haddock or cod

❖ ❖ ❖

½ cup heavy cream
¼ teaspoon nutmeg
Salt and pepper to taste
2 tablespoons chopped fresh parsley
¼ cup butter (½ stick)

In a large saucepan cook the julienne vegetables in water to cover until tender but still firm. Drain and reserve 1 cup of water. Set the vegetables aside. Bring the water, wine, and chopped leeks to a simmer. Scrub and debeard the mussels, add to the leeks, cover and steam. Continue to steam for 5 minutes after the mussels have opened. Remove about half from their shells and reserve the rest, keeping warm for garnish.

Strain the liquid from steaming the mussels into a large skillet and add the fish. Cover and gently simmer for 8 to 10 minutes, until the fish flakes easily. Transfer to an ovenproof platter and keep warm. Reduce the liquid quickly to ½ cup. Add the cream, seasonings, and butter in small pieces, whisking constantly. Add the shelled mussels and parsley and heat through. Pour the sauce over the fish, top with the julienne of vegetables, and garnish with the remaining mussels.

Serves 6.

The Elms: Bed and Breakfast

495 West Falmouth Highway
(On Route 28A)
West Falmouth, Massachusetts 02574
(617) 540-7232

The Elms is a lovely Victorian house built in the 1800s, featuring nine double rooms, seven with private baths. Many antiques adorn this home, and rooms are furnished in French, Victorian, and Queen Anne styles. Only one-fourth mile from the beach, it is also close to theaters, restaurants, the Woods Hole Oceanographic Institution, and the ferry for Martha's Vineyard and Nantucket islands. A gourmet breakfast is served daily in the library, or on the deck, weather permitting. Sherry and hors d'oeuvres are served each afternoon. The grounds are nicely landscaped; fresh flowers are in every room. The inn is open year round.

Artichoke Heart Squares

A delightful hors d'oeuvre.

2 6-ounce jars marinated artichoke hearts
1 small onion, finely chopped
1 clove garlic, minced
4 eggs
¼ cup dry bread crumbs
¼ cup salt
⅛ teaspoon pepper
⅛ teaspoon oregano
⅛ teaspoon hot sauce
½ pound shredded Cheddar cheese
2 tablespoons minced parsley

Drain the juice from 1 jar of artichoke hearts into a frying pan. Discard the juice from the second jar. Chop the artichokes and set aside. Sauté the onion and garlic in the artichoke liquid until the onion is transparent. Beat the eggs in a small bowl until frothy, add bread crumbs, salt, pepper, oregano and hot sauce. Stir in the Cheddar cheese, parsley, chopped artichokes and onion mixture. Turn into a buttered 7x11-inch pan and bake in a 350° oven for 30 minutes. Let cool and then cut into 1-inch squares. Serve cold or reheat in the oven before serving.

Makes 40 squares.

Chocolate Trifle

1 1-pound chocolate cake
1 cup Kahlua
1 12-ounce bag brickle
1 6-ounce package chocolate
    instant pudding mix, prepared
1 pint whipping cream, whipped
1 7½-ounce package slivered
    almonds
Cherries

Break half of the chocolate cake into the bottom of a glass bowl. Pour half of the Kahlua over the cake. Sprinkle half of the bag of brickle next. Then spread half of the instant chocolate pudding (made as directed on the package). Spread half of the whipped cream next. Repeat the steps and top off with the slivered almonds and cherries.

Serves 10 to 12.

Sunny Pines Bed and Breakfast Inn

77 Main Street, Box 667
West Harwich, Massachusetts 02671
(617) 432-9628

This turn-of-the-century Victorian home has been host to visitors for almost half of its life, providing a warm, friendly atmosphere for many generations of Cape Cod visitors. Its history is rich in tales of the sea, up to its present "Captain," who has sailed the world for twenty years researching the ocean floor with a famous oceanographic institution on the Cape. Warm hospitality is featured with a breakfast that includes a mixed grill, eggs, juice, coffee, tea, and Irish soda bread made from an old family recipe, served with homemade jams and jellies. Sunny Pines has six bedrooms with private baths. The decor is Victorian with a comfortable ambiance.

Seafood Omelet for Two

6 eggs
½ cup milk
2 tablespoons Parmesan cheese

❖ ❖ ❖

¼ cup grated Cheddar or Swiss
    cheese
3 slices white American cheese

❖ ❖ ❖

½ cup tender cooked shrimp,
    scallops, or crab meat
3 teaspoons sour cream (optional)

Place the eggs, milk, and Parmesan cheese in the blender, blend on high for 30 seconds. Pour into a heated, buttered omelet pan.

Add the grated cheese and the cheese slices. Cover loosely with aluminum foil and cook slowly. The omelet will puff up like a soufflé. Add the seafood filling and sour cream if desired. Fold out onto a platter and serve.

Other optional fillings may include broccoli and cheese, mushrooms, or spinach soufflé.

Eggs Sunny Pines

6 egg yolks
¼ cup lemon juice
Salt and pepper to taste
1 cup butter (2 sticks), melted

❖ ❖ ❖

1 English muffin
2 cooked sausage patties
2 poached eggs
Cranberry marmalade

Make Hollandaise sauce by blending 6 egg yolks, juice, salt, and pepper at high speed while adding hot melted butter very slowly.

Split and grill the English muffin. On each half place a sausage patty, a poached egg, Hollandaise sauce, and a dollop of cranberry marmalade.

Any remaining Hollandaise sauce will freeze well.

Serves 1.

Sunny Pines Irish Soda Bread

6½ cups all-purpose flour
1 cup sugar
2 tablespoons baking powder
2 teaspoons baking soda
2 teaspoons salt
4 eggs
4 cups buttermilk
4 tablespoons melted butter

❖ ❖ ❖

2 cups raisins or 1 cup raisins and
    1 cup currants
2 tablespoons caraway seed

Mix together very well the flour, sugar, baking powder, soda, salt, eggs, buttermilk, and butter. (Mixing well takes the place of kneading.) Add the raisins and currants if used, and caraway seeds. Divide among 4 large loaf pans or 8 small loaf pans. Bake in a 350° oven for 45 minutes or until hollow when tapped and a tester comes out clean.

Makes 4 loaves.

Michigan

The Bridge Street Inn Bed and Breakfast

113 Michigan Avenue
Charlevoix, Michigan 49720
(616) 547-6606

The Bridge Street Inn is housed in a three-story, colonial-revival home in the summer resort town of Charlevoix. It rests on a hill, affording beautiful views of Lake Michigan, Round Lake, Lake Charlevoix, the Drawbridge, and the downtown shopping area. Within walking distance are sandy beaches, specialty and gift shops, boating, restaurants, and art galleries. The nine guest rooms have warm, wooden floors covered by old floral rugs, antique furnishings, and comfortable beds to provide both charm and comfort. Breakfast and coffee are served in the dining room where French doors lead to a sitting area, promising a lazy meal on a warm summer's morning. The dining room is also the spot to find a refreshing glass of iced tea when temperatures soar.

Bridge Street Pancake

3 eggs
3 tablespoons almond filling

❖ ❖ ❖

½ cup all-purpose flour
½ teaspoon salt

❖ ❖ ❖

½ cup milk
2 tablespoons butter, melted

❖ ❖ ❖

½ cup sliced almonds
2 tablespoons butter, melted
¼ cup sugar
2 tablespoons butter, melted

Whisk together the eggs and the almond filling with a fork or wire whisk. Sift the flour, measure, and sift again with the salt. Add to the beaten egg mixture in four additions, beating after each just until the mixture is smooth. Add the milk, ¼ cup at a time, slightly beating after each addition. Add the melted butter to the batter.

Butter the bottom and sides of a 9-inch cast iron skillet with 2 tablespoons butter. Pour the batter into the skillet and bake in a preheated 450° oven for 15 minutes. Quickly sprinkle the pancake with the almonds, drizzle with the remaining 2 tablespoons melted butter, and sprinkle with sugar. Bake an additional 5 minutes. Slip onto a heated plate and serve at once.

Makes 2 to 4 servings.

Sour Cream-Cinnamon Breakfast Cake

4 eggs
½ cup sugar
¾ cup oil
1 package yellow cake mix
1 cup sour cream
¾ cup chopped nuts

❖ ❖ ❖

¼ cup dark brown sugar
1 tablespoon cinnamon

Beat the eggs until thick and fluffy. Add the sugar and oil and beat again. Blend in the cake mix, sour cream, and nuts. Pour ½ of the batter into a well-greased bundt pan. Mix together the brown sugar and cinnamon and sprinkle over the batter. Swirl in lightly with a knife. Pour the remaining batter on top. Bake in preheated 350° oven for 45 to 60 minutes.

Serves 12.

Hotel St. Regis

3071 West Grand Boulevard
Detroit, Michigan 48202
(313) 873-3000
TELEX: 23-5500
(800) 223-5560 (Toll Free)

Guests can relax and enjoy the charm of the unobtrusive service of a small Old World hotel. The European-trained staff—from the hotelier to the valets, from the concierge to the chef de cuisine—attend to all needs. Each of the 117 rooms has been designed for comfort, with separate lounging, sleeping, and dressing areas. The lounge, reminiscent of European cafés, is alive with activity of afternoon tea and cocktails and piano music late in the evening. The Restaurant St. Regis changes its atmosphere several times daily: from a bright 7:00 A.M. setting serving freshly baked croissants, to a busy luncheon haven for midtown's business community, to the intimate French cuisine prepared by the Cordon Bleu-trained chef for dinner.

❖ ❖ ❖ ❖ ❖ ❖

Basil Dressing

2 eggs (extra large)
1 cup basil leaves, tightly packed
3 tablespoons shallots, finely
   minced
3 tablespoons basil or red wine
   vinegar
¾ cup olive oil
6 grinds pepper

Boil the eggs for 3 to 4 minutes so that the yolks are still soft and runny but the whites are firm enough to mince. Rinse the basil and remove the leaves from the stems. Pack the basil to measure 1 cup. Shell the eggs and scoop the yolks into a processor or blender. Add the shallots, vinegar and basil leaves. Process to finely mince the basil. Add ¼ cup of the oil and process 2 to 3 minutes until the ingredients are smooth. Feed in the remaining oil slowly with the machine running. Season with pepper. Dressing will be thick, creamy and pale green. Pour dressing into a bowl. Mince the egg whites and fold gently into the dressing.

Makes 1½ cups of dressing.

Rack of Lamb

Have your butcher remove the chine for ease in carving and trim the bone ends to about 3 inches from the eye of the meat. (The chine is the large piece of bone which runs the length of the rack perpendicular to the rib bones.)

1 lamb rack (8 ribs)
2 tablespoons finely minced fresh
   herbs
1 tablespoon chopped shallots
8 grinds of pepper
1 tablespoon oil
1 clove garlic (optional)

❖ ❖ ❖

2 tablespoons white wine
½ cup veal or chicken demiglace
½ teaspoon finely minced fresh
   herbs
Salt (optional) and freshly ground
   pepper

Strip the fat layer from the top side of the rack by hand. There is meat in this piece. You can trim it out and freeze to use in ground or diced lamb dishes.

With a boning knife, remove the small, flat shoulder plate. Starting ½ inch from the eye of the meat, scrape all the fat and meat off the rib bones. This is called Frenching or French trimming. Trim out the heavy yellow-colored muscle sinew at the thick end of the meat. Lightly score the back of the meat in a criss-cross pattern. Combine herbs, shallots, garlic, pepper and oil and rub into all surfaces of the lamb rack. Let the meat sit at room temperature for 45 minutes or in the refrigerator for 2 to 3 hours.

To roast, preheat oven to the highest heat, 550 degrees. Allow at least 25 minutes for preheating to assure the correct heat buildup in the oven. Put the lamb in a roasting pan that is just large enough to hold it. It is important that the pan has low sides no more than 1 inch tall for correct heat circulation. Roast the rack 22 to 25 minutes for pink (rare).

The rack should stand 10 minutes before carving. During this time, add wine to roasting pan and boil for one minute to deglaze. Add the demiglace

and bring to a boil, scraping up any brown bits clinging to the pan. Boil briefly to reduce to sauce consistency. Strain the sauce into a clean small pot. Season and add herbs.

Serves 4.

Fillet of Lamb en Croute

Oil
1 6-ounce fillet of lamb mignon
Salt
Pepper
Garlic

❖ ❖ ❖

4 ounces puff pastry
1 ounce Duxelles
2 ounces flageolets
3 ounces asparagus tips
1 egg, slightly beaten
¼ pint lamb jus

Heat the oil in a frying pan and quickly cook the lamb, seasoned with salt, pepper, and garlic, until brown on both sides. Do not cook completely, just seal the meat.

Let the lamb cool. Roll out the puff pastry fairly thin into an 8-inch square, place the duxelles, flageolets, and asparagus tips in the center, the mignon of lamb on top and fold the pastry around the lamb so that it is completely sealed. Brush with the egg and bake in a 400° oven for 20 minutes. Serve with the lamb jus.

Serves 1.

Stuffed Flounder Fillets

6 flounder fillets
2 tablespoons lemon juice
Salt to taste

❖ ❖ ❖

2 tablespoons finely chopped
   shallots
4 tablespoons diced green onions
½ cup butter (1 stick)
Flour
½ cup light cream

❖ ❖ ❖

5 ounces king crab
½ cup dry white wine
White pepper to taste
Tabasco sauce to taste
½ cup fresh bread crumbs
2 eggs, beaten

❖   ❖   ❖

½ cup all-purpose flour
2 eggs, lightly beaten
Fresh bread crumbs
½ cup clarified butter (1 stick)

❖   ❖   ❖

Wine
Shallots
Herbs
Brown stock

Marinate the fillets for 1 hour in the lemon juice and salt. Sauté the shallots and green onion in ½ cup butter until tender. Add enough flour (about 2 tablespoons) to make a cream roux. Cook for a few minutes and add the cream. After bringing to a boil, reduce to a simmer, add the crab, wine and seasonings. Remove from heat and add ½ cup bread crumbs and 2 eggs. The filling should be firm yet spreadable. Spread on the fish and roll in a spiral. Coat the rolls in flour, the beaten eggs and bread crumbs. Brown in clarified butter. Bake in a 350° oven for 20 to 25 minutes. Let set for 10 to 15 minutes.

In a saucepan combine the wine, shallots and herbs. Reduce by half, and add the brown stock. Serve with the flounder fillets.

Serves 6.

Stuffed Pork Loin

2 green peppers
2 red peppers

❖   ❖   ❖

1 6- to 7-pound pork loin
Fresh ground pepper
2 tablespoons finely diced shallots
3 cloves garlic
Minced parsley
Fresh herbs
1 tablespoon olive oil
1 tablespoon butter

❖   ❖   ❖

1 cup white wine
1 quart veal stock

Place peppers several at a time on a long fork and char evenly over a gas flame or put on a rack under the broiler, turning and watching carefully. Rub off the blackened skin of the peppers by hand. Cut the peppers in half, remove the core and seeds and rinse quickly under running water. Open the pepper halves out flat and press between 2 layers of paper towels to remove all excess moisture.

Remove the meat from the bone. Cut the small pork tenderloin piece away from the main loin, trimming all excess fat and sinew, and set aside. Lay the pork loin fat side down on a cutting board. Cut into the meat at an angle without actually cutting completely through. Fold back the meat and gently pound out until almost double in size. Season the loin with ground pepper. Cut the peppers into 2-inch strips and place on the meat lengthwise. Gently place the shallots, garlic, parsley and herbs over the pepper. Place the small tenderloin piece in the center of the pepper and herb mixture. Roll up the meat and tie with a string to hold in place. In a large skillet over medium high heat, heat the olive oil and butter until lightly foaming. Place the pork loin fat side down in the lightly foaming oil and butter, turning gently until brown on all sides and both ends. Remove the pork loin to a roasting pan. In the skillet used for browning, deglaze with white wine. Add the veal stock and bring to a boil. Pour over the pork loin, cover and place in the center of a preheated 350° oven for 50 minutes. Uncover and cook for 40 additional minutes, basting every 10 to 15 minutes. Remove from the oven and place the pork loin on a platter to cool for 10 minutes.

To serve, slice the pork loin into medium thick slices and place on a warm serving platter. Reduce pan juices about 40% and pour over the slices before serving.

Serves 16.

❖ ❖ ❖ ❖ ❖ ❖

Sautéed Fillet of Salmon
with Chive Sauce

2 7-ounce salmon fillets
1½ tablespoons butter
½ teaspoon olive oil
Salt
Freshly ground pepper

❖   ❖   ❖

1 tablespoon finely minced shallots
2 medium mushrooms, peeled and
    thinly sliced
2 tablespoons dry white wine
1 cup salmon essence
2 teaspoons lemon juice
⅓ cup heavy cream
1 tablespoon snipped fresh chives

❖   ❖   ❖

Chives for garnish

Remove any small bones from the salmon fillets. In a 10-inch sauté pan over medium heat, heat the butter and oil. When melted swirl the pan to blend and raise heat to medium high. When fats are just starting to foam and have the faintest color, add the fillets, skin side up and lower the heat to medium. Sauté without turning for 1½ minutes, then sharply shake the pan to loosen the fillets (they usually stick). Carefully turn them and lightly season the cooked side with salt and pepper. Sauté on the other side 1½ minutes, then sharply shake the pan again to loosen fillets. Season the second side. Use some fat from the pan to coat the bottom of an ovenproof dish and place it in the oven to warm. Place the fillets in the warm dish. Place the fish in the oven for about 3 minutes while completing the sauce. Add the shallots and mushrooms to the sauté pan, stir to coat with fat and cook over medium heat ½ minute. Add the wine, turn the heat to high and boil rapidly to reduce to a glaze that just coats the pan but is not colored. Add the salmon essence, lemon juice and cream. Bring to a boil and whisk together. Boil rapidly 1 to 2 minutes to reduce to a sauce consistency. Strain into a small saucepan and stir in the chives; season if necessary.

Keep warm over low heat.

Remove the fillets from oven. Pour a shallow pool of sauce about 6 inches in diameter in the base of warmed dinner plates. Place a fillet in center and coat part of it with remaining sauce. Garnish salmon with additional snipped chives or 2 to 3 whole chive spears laid diagonally across the top of each fillet.

Note: There is a reason for only partly covering the fillets with sauce. When completely covered, it is not apparent whether the fish was sautéed, poached or baked. You went to the trouble to sauté it, so let it show!

Serves 2.

The House on the Hill

Box 206, Lake Street
Ellsworth, Michigan 49729
(616) 588-6304

The House on the Hill is a renovated 100-year-old farmhouse with three guest rooms. All the rooms overlook a beautiful lake, as does the Victorian porch. A full family-style breakfast is served daily. Two gourmet restaurants are within walking distance.

The House on the Hill

Nine Bean Soup

To make Soup Mix, buy 9 kinds of dried beans. Mix together and store in pint jars.

2 cups Nine Bean Soup Mix (1 pint)

❖ ❖ ❖

1 pound diced ham
1 large onion, chopped
2 cloves of garlic, minced
½ teaspoon salt
1 can of tomatoes with hot chili
     peppers
1 can tomatoes, undrained
6 cups water
2 beef bouillon cubes
1 teaspoon Worcestershire sauce
1 teaspoon seasoned salt
1 teaspoon bouquet garni
Pinch of soda

Wash the beans. Place in a Dutch oven, cover with water and soak overnight. The next morning, drain, add all the remaining ingredients and simmer about 3 hours or until tender, stirring occasionally.

Makes 8 cups.

Pumpkin Layer Cake and Frosting

2 cups sugar
4 eggs, well beaten

1 cup corn oil
2 cups cooked pumpkin

❖ ❖ ❖

2 cups all-purpose flour
2 teaspoons baking powder
2 teaspoons soda
1 teaspoon salt
1 teaspoon allspice
1 teaspoon cinnamon

❖ ❖ ❖

¾ cup sugar
1½ cups brown sugar, firmly
     packed
3 teaspoons all-purpose flour
1½ cups milk

❖ ❖ ❖

3 tablespoons butter
¾ cup chopped pecans
1½ cups flaked coconut
1½ teaspoons vanilla extract

Using an electric mixer, combine the sugar, eggs, oil, and pumpkin; mix well. Combine the flour, baking powder, soda, salt, and spices; add to the pumpkin mixture and beat for 1 minute at medium speed. Pour into 3 greased and floured 8-inch or 9-inch cake pans. Bake in a 325° oven for 25 to 30 minutes, or until done. Cool 10 minutes, then remove from the pans. Cool completely.

To make frosting, combine in a medium saucepan the sugar, brown sugar, flour, and milk. Cook over medium heat, stirring constantly, until thickened (225° on a candy thermometer). Add the butter and stir until it is melted. Stir in the pecans, coconut, and vanilla. Spread the frosting between the layers and on top.

Note: Cake slices best when it has been chilled.

Serves 12.

The Old Holland Inn

133 West 11th Street
Holland, Michigan 49423
(616) 396-6601

The Old Holland Inn offers accommodations in a Victorian atmosphere. The entrance hall with its original oak staircase reflects the warmth and charm of the 1900s, and the living room is graced by the stained glass windows and a hand-crafted copper and oak fireplace. Each large Victorian bedroom has been furnished with charming Michigan antiques and decorated for comfort and appeal. House guests are invited to the dining room for a hearty Continental breakfast. The back yard has been landscaped with a large array of flowers, herbs, and shrubs, and the recently built deck is available for guests to lounge and breakfast on during warm summer mornings.

Blueberry Corn Muffins

¾ cup yellow cornmeal
1 cup all-purpose flour
½ teaspoon salt
2 teaspoons baking powder

❖ ❖ ❖

1 egg plus 1 egg white
½ cup buttermilk
½ cup melted sweet butter (1 stick)

❖ ❖ ❖

1½ cups fresh or frozen
    blueberries

Mix the dry ingredients together, then add eggs, buttermilk, and melted butter. Do not overbeat, use approximately 50 strokes. Fold in the blueberries and turn into 6 greased muffin cups, filling almost completely

(crown will be large) or for smaller muffins fill ½ way and use 12 tins. Bake in a 400° oven for 20 to 25 minutes.
    Makes 12 muffins.

Whole Wheat Apple Nut Oatmeal Muffins

1 cup all-purpose flour
¾ cup whole wheat flour
2 teaspoons baking powder
1 teaspoon baking soda
1 cup old-fashioned oatmeal
½ cup raisins
½ cup nuts
1 cup coarse grated apples

❖ ❖ ❖

1 jumbo egg
1 jumbo egg white
1 cup apple juice
2 tablespoons apple juice
    concentrate, thawed
3 tablespoons melted butter

❖ ❖ ❖

2 tablespoons sugar
1 tablespoon brown sugar
½ teaspoon cinnamon

❖ ❖ ❖

1 tablespoon melted butter
1 cup coarse grated apples
1 cup crunch granola

In a large bowl combine the flours, baking powder, soda, and oatmeal, mixing well. Add the raisins, nuts, and 1 cup of grated apples to the flour mixture, mixing until well combined. Set aside.
    Beat the eggs until frothy, blend in the apple juice, and apple juice concentrate. Beat in 3 tablespoons melted butter. Pour into the dry mixture, stirring just until moist. Pour into a greased muffin tin.
    Combine the sugar, brown sugar, and cinnamon; set aside.
    Add the remaining tablespoon of melted butter to the remaining grated apples; blend thoroughly. Quickly add the granola and blend. Sprinkle this mixture over the tops of the muffin

batter. Then sprinkle the sugar mixture over this. Bake in a 400° oven for 25 to 30 minutes. Cool on a wire rack.
    Makes 12 muffins.

Chilled Pineapple Peach Soup

1½ pounds peaches
½ of a fresh pineapple

❖ ❖ ❖

1 cup fresh orange juice
1 cup pineapple juice
2 cups plain yogurt
½ cup dry white wine
1 tablespoon fresh lemon juice

❖ ❖ ❖

Lime slices
Mint leaves

Prepare the peaches by peeling, pitting, and slicing them. Purée the peaches and pineapple in a food processor until smooth. Add the juices, yogurt, and wine and blend well. Pass the soup through a fine strainer. Serve chilled, garnished with thin slices of lime and mint leaves.
    Serves 8.

Poppy Seed Orange Date-Nut Bread

1 cup warm orange juice
1½ cups warm water
1 1¼-ounce package active dry
    yeast
6 tablespoons honey
2 cups whole wheat flour

❖ ❖ ❖

2 tablespoons oil
3 tablespoons poppy seeds
3 tablespoons oats (optional)
Juice of 1 orange
1 tablespoon grated orange rind
½ cup chopped dates
½ cup chopped nuts

❖ ❖ ❖

3½ to 4 cups whole wheat flour

Mix together the orange juice, water, yeast, honey and 2 cups of flour, let this sit until bubbly, about 30 minutes.

Mix in the remaining ingredients and knead well, adding flour, as needed, to make a soft spongy dough. Let the dough rise in a covered oiled bowl until double in size, about 30 minutes.

Shape into two loaves and let rise again in oiled floured pans. Bake at 400° for about 35 minutes.

Makes 2 loaves.

Poached Pears in Cranberry-Apple Juice

6 ripe pears
2 cups cranberry-apple juice
½ cup water
1 cinnamon stick

❖ ❖ ❖

Mint sprigs
Lemon wedges

Wash and pare the pears, leave the stems on.

In a heavy saucepan combine the pears, cranberry-apple juice, water, and cinnamon stick. Bring to a boil uncovered. Reduce the heat and simmer until the pears are tender, 20 to 30 minutes. Remove the pears from heat. Carefully lift the pears to a bowl. Remove and discard the cinnamon stick. Bring the juice to boil, reduce the heat and simmer uncovered 20 minutes. Juice should measure 1½ cups liquid. Pour over the pears and refrigerate until well chilled, turning occasionally. Serve garnished with mint sprigs and lemon wedges.

Serves 6 to 12.

The Parsonage 1908 Bed and Breakfast

6 East 24th
Holland, Michigan 49423
(616) 396-1316

The Parsonage is a true European-style bed and breakfast home. Built in 1908 as a church parsonage, it has been a private residence since the 1970s. Situated in a quiet, residential neighborhood, it glows with the warmth of rich oak woodwork, antique furnishings, leaded glass windows, two cozy sitting rooms, and a summer porch for guests' enjoyment. The parsonage has four charming bedrooms from which to choose. A complimentary Continental breakfast is served in the formal dining room or on the outdoor garden patio. Holland is on the shores of Lake Michigan and beautiful Lake Macatawa.

Pomander Balls

Choose ripe healthy fruit. Though oranges are most frequently used, grapefruits, apples, pears, and limes can also be used. Stick the fruit full of whole dried cloves (approximately 2 ounces). Use an ordinary pin to fasten a pretty velvet ribbon to the center and hang the pomander to dry.

Chaffin Farms Bed and Breakfast

3239 West Street, Charles Road
Ithaca, Michigan 48847
(517) 463-4081

The Chaffin Farms is a turn-of-the-century farm house furnished with antiques, situated on a 600-acre working farm with tours available. The beds are comfortable in the three rooms with two baths. A country breakfast is served in the keeping room, with a fireplace glowing nearby. Bicycles are available for guests' pleasure. Antique shopping and restaurants are in three nearby towns.

Blueberry Muffins

1 egg, beaten
1 cup buttermilk
¼ cup salad oil

❖ ❖ ❖

2 cups all-purpose flour
¼ cup sugar
2 teaspoons baking powder
½ teaspoon soda
1 teaspoon salt

❖ ❖ ❖

1 cup fresh blueberries

Combine the egg, buttermilk, and oil. Mix together the dry ingredients; stir in buttermilk mixture until just moistened. Then fold in the blueberries. Pour into a greased muffin tin. Bake in a 400° oven for 20 to 25 minutes.

Makes 12 muffins.

Morning Glory Inn

8709 Old Channel Trail
Montague, Michigan 49437
(616) 894-8237

Morning Glory Inn, a turn-of-the-century house, sits on a hilltop with a view of White Lake. It has three guest bedrooms and offers a hearty Continental breakfast. Furnished with antiques, the inn has high ceilings and wooden floors, a parlor for games, chatting, and relaxing; a quiet window seat on the landing, and a fifty-foot-long wrap-around porch. The one-and-a-half bathrooms are shared (one has a beautiful clawfoot tub) and the bubble bath is furnished.

A five-minute walk will take guests to the Montague boat launching area, restaurants, grocery stores, marinas, and the largest weathervane in the world. It is but a five minute drive to Lake Michigan, the lighthouse, golf courses, and Whitehall, with its unique stores. Montague is an all-season area; fishing, swimming, boating, hunting, snowmobiling, cross country skiing are available to guests, depending on the season.

Bananas Calvin

6 ounces coconut

❖　❖　❖

½ cup mayonnaise
¼ cup sweet cream
2 tablespoons sugar

❖　❖　❖

4 bananas

Toast the coconut in a 300° oven until golden brown.

Blend the mayonnaise, cream, and sugar with a whisk.

Cut the bananas in half and dip into the mayonnaise mixture, then roll in the toasted coconut. Arrange on a serving plate, cover with plastic wrap, and refrigerate for 30 minutes.

Makes a delightful dessert on hot summer days or it is good as a fancy breakfast fruit to serve guests.

Serves 4.

Magic Bars

1½ cups of corn flakes cereal, crumbled
3 tablespoons sugar
½ cup margarine (1 stick), melted
1 12-ounce package semi-sweet chocolate morsels
1⅓ cups flaked coconut
1 cup chopped walnuts
1 14-ounce can sweetened condensed milk

Combine the corn flake crumbs, sugar, and margarine into a 13x9-inch pan. Mix thoroughly. With the back of a spoon press mixture firmly into the bottom of the pan. Sprinkle the chocolate morsels, coconut and walnuts evenly on crust. Pour condensed milk evenly over walnuts. Bake in a 350° oven for 25 minutes until lightly browned around edge. Cool and cut into bars.

Makes 12 bars.

The Mayflower Bed and Breakfast Hotel

Main and Ann Arbor Trail
Plymouth, Michigan 48170
(313) 453-1620

The family-operated Mayflower Bed and Breakfast Hotel is a Michigan landmark. This 100-room English style inn features a full complimentary breakfast for overnight guests, elegant but comfortable surroundings, and a reputation for good food and hospitality. Situated in the heart of beautiful Plymouth, the Mayflower is within walking distance of 150 charming shops. Kellogg Park, with its brick walks and lovely shade trees—the center of this colonial New England-style town—is directly across the street from the hotel. This town square is the site for many of Plymouth's events and festivals, including band concerts, street dances, art fairs, the popular fall

The Mayflower

festival, farmer's market, and the renowned Plymouth ice sculpture spectacular in January.

The two recipes listed below are a small sampling of the fare present at the first Thanksgiving table, December 13, 1621. Pilgrim women learned a completely new style of cooking that first year and one can imagine why with no source of gathered foods, meats, and staples other than their virgin land.

Plymouth Succotash

Very tasty is the Plymouth Succotash, said by tradition to have been part of the feast at the first Thanksgiving.

A fowl and a piece of corned beef, freshly corned and not too salty, were cooked together. A large white turnip and eight large potatoes sliced in 1-inch slices were added, then six quarts of hulled corn and finally, to thicken it, the sifted mush from a quart of cooked dry white beans. Hulled corn was the dried corn kernels, boiled in lye water until the hulls loosened. It was then put in cold water and the hulls rubbed off by hand. It was boiled in fresh water until it was soft and floury.

This food, as well as Bean Porridge, was poured into bowls with a loop of tow string laid over the rim, and left to freeze. Then, by putting the bowls in hot water, the Succotash could be slipped out for use. The belief was that the food was much better when nine days old. So, you see, frozen foods are nothing new.

Squash Bread

Squash bread is seldom seen nowadays, but is well worth making. To one cup of sifted squash, add two tablespoonfuls of sugar, one teaspoonful of salt, one and a half cupfuls of scalded milk, and a tablespoonful of butter.

When cool, add half a yeast cake and flour enough to knead fifteen minutes. When risen, knead again, shape into loaves, and bake, when light.

The Homestead

9279 Macon Road
Saline, Michigan 48176
(313) 429-9625

The Homestead Bed and Breakfast is a place for all seasons. There are woods, valleys, meadows, a river, and the silence found only in the country. Built as a family farmhouse in 1851, The Homestead has served as a home for generations. Filled with antiques, many having belonged to the original owners, the home provides a mixture of relaxed country comfort and Victorian elegance. Fifty acres of land produce fields of spectacular wildflowers in spring and in winter provide excellent cross country skiing. Long ago, Indians camped here as they salted their fish so walks along the river and through the fields still produce many arrowheads.

The six spacious bedrooms are furnished with antiques; handmade throw pillows grace the beds. Each room has a sitting area for reading or conversation. A full breakfast is served through 9:00 A.M. on weekdays, and 10:00 A.M., weekends. Fresh ground coffee is ready on a "help yourself" basis in the kitchen after 7:00 A.M., and a buffet breakfast is available for late risers.

Fruit Soup

Serve with Swedish Pancakes.

> 1 to 2 cups water
> 1 pound fruit
> ½ to 1 cup red wine
> ¼ cup sugar

½ teaspoon grated orange rind
3 tablespoons arrowroot or cornstarch

Reserve ¼ cup of the water; combine the fruit, water, wine, sugar, and rind. Dissolve the arrowroot or cornstarch with the reserved water and add to the mixture. Cook for 5 to 10 minutes. Serve warm or cold.

Makes 4 cups of soup.

Dilled Eggs

Beat ½ to 1 dozen eggs. Add fresh or dried dill weed, granulated garlic, and fresh pepper to taste. Softly scramble. Great!

Serves 6.

Manhattan Clam Chowder Eggs

Beat the desired number of eggs. Add canned, condensed Manhattan clam chowder to taste. Softly scramble. Also great!

Popovers

Serve with Dilled Eggs or Manhattan Clam Chowder Eggs.

> 2 eggs
> 1 cup milk
> 1 cup all-purpose flour
> ¼ teaspoon salt

Beat the eggs, add milk, then the flour and salt. Pour into well greased, deep muffin or popover pans, filling ⅔ full. Bake in a preheated 400° oven for 25 to 35 minutes, depending on the size of the cups in the pan. Don't peek for the first 25 minutes or the popovers will collapse!

Makes 12 popovers.

Seascape Bed and Breakfast

20009 Breton
Spring Lake, Michigan 49456
(616) 842-8409

The word *Seascape* evokes thoughts of majestic sunsets, seagulls swooping over sparkling water, seaport harbors with their quaint old lighthouses, and sugar sand beaches cultivated with sea oats. All this and more is the view guests enjoy every day at Seascape. Seascape is an all-season inn that offers a kaleidoscope of scenes with the changing of the seasons. Guests rekindle the half-forgotten pleasures of hospitality and feel as if they are staying with friends.

Bran Muffins

    1 15-ounce box raisin and bran
      cereal
    3 cups sugar
    5 cups all-purpose flour
    5 teaspoons soda
    2 teaspoons salt
    2 tablespoons cinnamon
    1 tablespoon nutmeg
    4 eggs, beaten
    1 quart buttermilk
    1 cup oil or melted shortening
            ❖ ❖ ❖
    ½ cup blueberries, chopped nuts,
      dates, or raisins (optional)

In a very large bowl, mix the dry ingredients. Add the eggs, milk, and oil. Mix well. Add the blueberries, nuts, dates, or extra raisins if desired. Fill the greased muffin cups ¾ full. Bake in a 400° oven for 20 minutes. Save the extra batter in a covered container in the refrigerator, with the date marked on it. The batter will keep for 6 weeks.
    Makes 4 dozen.

Pumpkin Bread

    3½ cups all-purpose flour
    2 teaspoons soda
    1 teaspoon salt
    ½ teaspoon baking powder
    3 cups sugar
    1 teaspoon cinnamon
    1 teaspoon pumpkin pie spice
            ❖ ❖ ❖
    1 cup cooking oil
    4 eggs
    1 16-ounce can pumpkin
    ½ cup chopped walnuts
    ¼ cup water

In a large mixing bowl combine the flour, soda, salt, baking powder, sugar, cinnamon, and pumpkin pie spice. In a separate bowl, mix by hand the oil, eggs, pumpkin, walnuts, and water. Combine with the dry ingredients. Bake in a loaf pan in a 350° oven for 1 hour.
    Makes 1 loaf.

Warwickshire Inn

5037 Barney Road
Traverse City, Michigan 49684
(616) 946-7176

The Warwickshire Inn is an antique-filled country farm house built about 1900 atop a long hill that gives a panoramic view of Traverse City and East and West bays. Traverse City's first bed and breakfast home, it is situated two miles west of town in a location easily accessible to Devonshire Antiques, ski resorts, and cross country skiing, downtown, shopping, and beaches. All the Warwickshire's rooms are spacious and comfortable.

Bananas Foster

    1 large banana
    3 tablespoons brown sugar
    2 tablespoons butter
    1 tablespoon lemon juice
    ¼ teaspoon cinnamon
    2 tablespoons banana liqueur
    2 tablespoons rum (150 proof)

Peel the banana and split in half lengthwise. Sauté in sugar and butter until tender. Sprinkle with the lemon juice and dust with cinnamon. Add the banana liqueur and rum and set aflame, basting the banana until the flame dies out. Serve over vanilla ice cream.
    Serves 2.

Apple Pancakes

    3 sweet apples
    2 eggs
    2 cups milk
    2 cups biscuit mix

Peel and core the apples and thinly slice. Beat the eggs, stir the eggs and milk into the biscuit mix. Add the apples. Cook on a buttered griddle.
    Serve with cider syrup.
    Serves 6.

Cider Syrup

    2 cups apple cider (or tangy apple
      juice)
    1 cup sugar
    ½ teaspoon grated lemon rind

Add sugar to cider and simmer 10 minutes, add lemon rind and simmer a little longer. Serve apple pancakes with melted butter and the syrup.

Minnesota

Thayer Hotel

Highway 55
Annandale, Minnesota 55302
(612) 274-3371

Filled with the charm of yesteryear and country comfort and charm, the Thayer Hotel has been in operation since 1895. The pressed tin walls and ceilings and Victorian-era millwork complement the many original pieces of furniture and authentic antiques and enhance the turn-of-the-century ambiance. The in-house bakery products tempt guests with sumptuous pastries, from apple pie to petit fours. Accommodations include ten regular-size rooms, three suites, and 1 bridal suite. All rooms include a European-style breakfast.

Clam Chowder

½ cup chopped mushrooms
1 cup chopped celery
1 cup chopped onion
½ cup chopped green pepper
¼ cup butter (½ stick)
❖ ❖ ❖
1 quart boiling water
1 cup finely diced carrots
2 cups diced potatoes
❖ ❖ ❖
2 tablespoons butter
2 tablespoons all-purpose flour
1 gallon milk
❖ ❖ ❖

2 6½-ounce cans chopped clams,
     including juice
1 tablespoon chopped pimientos

In a large heavy saucepan, sauté mushrooms, celery, onion, and green pepper in ¼ cup of butter. When cooked add water, carrots, and potatoes. Simmer for 20 minutes, or until the vegetables are tender.

While the vegetables are simmering, make a thin white sauce by melting 2 tablespoons of butter in a saucepan over medium heat. Stir in the flour and mix well. Mix in the milk and stir occasionally until thickened. Set aside.

When the vegetables are tender, add the clams with their juice, the pimientos, and the white sauce. Cook 10 minutes longer. Serve piping hot.

Serves 8 to 12.

Fitger's Inn and Restaurant

Historic Inns of America
600 E. Superior Street
Duluth, Minnesota 55802
(218) 722-8826

Fitger's Inn and Restaurant is housed in the old Fitger's Brewery, some of whose buildings date back to the 1800s and were constructed by immigrant stone masons from native bluestone.

The renovation (finished in 1984) created a complex of thirty shops, a multimedia theater, specialty restaurants, and the 48-room Fitger's Inn. On the shore of Lake Superior, its rooms offer a splendid view of shipping activity and the ever-changing personality of this great inland sea.

The food served at Fitger's Inn captures the flavor of the region. Fresh Lake Superior trout is the summer favorite, followed closely by almond-breaded walleye. The brewery tradition lingers in such favorites as the homemade beer barrel rye bread and the medallions of pork tenderloin with mushroom beer sauce.

Pumpkin Muffins

1½ cups all-purpose flour
½ cup sugar
2 teaspoons baking powder
½ teaspoon salt
½ teaspoon cinnamon
½ teaspoon nutmeg
½ cup milk
½ cup canned pumpkin
¼ cup butter margarine blend
     (½ stick), melted
1 egg
❖ ❖ ❖
1 tablespoon sugar

Mix all ingredients except for the 1 tablespoon sugar. Mix until blended. Do not overmix. Pour the batter into a greased muffin pan. Sprinkle the sugar over the batter in each cup. Bake in a 400° oven for 18 to 20 minutes.

Yields 12 muffins.

Mother's Cream of Chicken-Wild Rice Soup

½ cup wild rice
1½ cups water

❖ ❖ ❖

¼ cup butter (½ stick)
3 large cloves garlic, minced
1 medium onion, chopped
2 carrots, finely diced
6 stalks asparagus, finely diced

❖ ❖ ❖

½ cup all-purpose flour

❖ ❖ ❖

5 cups chicken stock
½ teaspoon thyme
1 bay leaf
¼ teaspoon nutmeg
Minced parsley
Minced chives
Salt and pepper to taste

❖ ❖ ❖

2 cups milk
2 cups half and half

In a covered pan cook the wild rice with water. In a large saucepan melt the butter, sauté the garlic and onion until tender. Add the carrots and asparagus; cook until tender. Mix in the flour and cook over low heat for approximately 10 minutes, stirring frequently. Pour in the chicken stock, using a wire whisk to blend until smooth. Add the seasonings. Slowly add the milk and half and half. Simmer for 20 minutes. Fold in the prepared rice and serve.

Makes 8 servings or about 9 cups.

Dilled Salmon Custard Pie

1½ cups chopped green onions
2 medium onions, diced
2 tablespoons margarine
Dash pepper
1 tablespoon seasoned salt

❖ ❖ ❖

Pastry for 3 10-inch 1-crust pies
2 cups shredded Swiss cheese
1 15½-ounce can salmon

❖ ❖ ❖

15 eggs
1 quart half and half

❖ ❖ ❖

1 tablespoon dill weed

Sauté the onions in the margarine. Add the pepper and seasoned salt and cook until the vegetables are tender. Drain off the excess margarine.

Line 3 10-inch pie plates with pastry. Sprinkle each pie shell with ⅓ cup of cheese. Cover the cheese with the vegetables. Drain, flake, and remove the cartilage from the salmon and layer on top of the vegetables. Layer the remaining cheese on top of the salmon. Beat the eggs and the half and half together and pour into each pie shell until the filling reaches the top of the pie shell. Sprinkle the dill weed on top of each pie. Bake in a 300° oven until the custard is set and is a light brown.

Each pie serves 6.

Medallions of Pork
in Mushroom Beer Sauce

2 pork tenderloins, trimmed of
    silver skin
½ cup all-purpose flour
2 tablespoons butter-margarine
    blend

❖ ❖ ❖

½ cup chopped green onions
2 garlic cloves, minced
1 cup sliced mushrooms
½ teaspoon dried thyme
Salt and pepper to taste
Fresh minced parsley

❖ ❖ ❖

1 cup beer

❖ ❖ ❖

½ cup half and half

Cut each tenderloin into three pieces. Pound each piece until flat. Lightly bread the medallions with flour. Sauté in the butter blend. When browned on the first side, turn and add the vegetables and seasonings. Drain off the excess butter. Add the beer and simmer until the pork is cooked through and the vegetables are tender. Add the half and half and simmer until all the ingredients are blended.

Serves 3.

Fitger's Inn

Basswood Hill's Farm

Route 1
Cannon Falls, Minnesota 55009
(507) 778-3259

Cannon Falls calls itself "Minnesota's best kept secret" but those who find this small town in the beautiful Sogn Valley will discover it is home to artists, woodcarvers, potters, and numerous craftpersons and has many fine shops and restaurants. Basswood Hill's Farm lies six miles from town and is forty-five minutes from Minneapolis/St. Paul. This large country estate, with many wildflowers on the grounds, is home to deer, grouse, and other wildlife that are fascinating to see. Bedrooms are decorated with handmade quilts and crocheted pieces.

Virginia's Breakfast Bake

2 8-ounce cans crescent rolls
1 6¾-ounce can chunked ham
1 15-ounce can asparagus spears, drained
1 11-ounce can Cheddar cheese soup

Roll out 1 can of crescent roll dough make a bottom pastry and place in an 8x8-inch pan. Place in layers the ham, asparagus, and soup. Roll out the other can of roll dough to make a top pastry, place on top of the pan and pinch around the edges. Prick holes in the crust to allow the steam to escape. Bake in a 350° oven for 30 to 45 minutes.
Serves 4 to 6 people.

Grandma's French Toast

Loaf French bread, day old
1 cup milk
2 tablespoons sugar
1 teaspoon vanilla extract
½ teaspoon grated lemon rind
¼ teaspoon ground nutmeg
1 tablespoon butter
1 tablespoon oil
3 eggs
Pinch salt

Cut the bread into 8 ¾-inch thick slices. Combine the milk, sugar, vanilla, rind, and nutmeg. Soak the bread in the mixture about 10 minutes until all the moisture is absorbed. Heat the butter and oil in a skillet or griddle over moderate heat. Beat the eggs and salt. Dip each bread slice in the egg mixture. Cook uncovered until golden brown.
Serves 4.

❖ ❖ ❖ ❖ ❖ ❖

Banana Tea Bread

1¾ cups sifted all-purpose flour
2 teaspoons baking powder
¼ teaspoon baking soda
½ teaspoon salt
❖ ❖ ❖
⅓ cup shortening
⅔ cup sugar
2 eggs, beaten
❖ ❖ ❖
1 cup mashed bananas
(2 to 3 ripe bananas)

Sift the flour, baking powder, soda and salt. Cream the shortening, add the sugar gradually and beat well. Add the eggs and beat until light and fluffy. Add the flour mixture alternately with the bananas. Pour the batter into a well-greased loaf pan. Bake in a 350° oven for 55 minutes or until a toothpick inserted in the center of the bread comes out clean.
Makes 1 loaf.

Chocolate Syrup Cake

½ cup butter (1 stick)
1 cup sugar
4 eggs, beaten
1 cup all-purpose flour
1 teaspoon baking powder
½ teaspoon salt
1 teaspoon vanilla extract
1 16-ounce can chocolate syrup
❖ ❖ ❖
Fudge frosting (optional)

Cream the butter and sugar together. Beat in the eggs. Stir in the flour, baking powder, and salt; then the vanilla and chocolate syrup. The batter will be thin. Pour into a greased 9x13-inch pan. Bake in a 350° oven for 30 to 35 minutes. Add fudge frosting if desired.
Serves 8.

Bluff Creek Inn

1161 Bluff Creek Drive
Chaska, Minnesota 55318
(612) 445-2735

Bluff Creek Inn is a historical Victorian folk home in the Minnesota River Valley. Built on a land grant from Abraham Lincoln to Joseph Vagel, a German immigrant, the inn offers nineteenth century hospitality in a country bed and breakfast setting. It is ten minutes from Canterbury Downs, Murphy's Landing, Chanhassen Dinner Theater, Minnesota Landscape Arboretum, the Renaissance Festival, and the "494" strip. It has five guest rooms, two with private baths. Three of the rooms have "water closets" and share a Victorian bathing room.

Creamy Ham Sauce

Prepare the ham sauce the day before serving. On the serving day prepare a dozen popovers. While they are baking scramble the eggs.

To serve, fill the popovers with eggs and cover with ham sauce.

½ pound sliced mushrooms
2 tablespoons butter

❖ ❖ ❖

¼ cup butter (½ stick)
¼ teaspoon dry mustard
¼ teaspoon thyme
3 tablespoons flour
1½ cups milk
2½ cups shredded Cheddar cheese
¼ cup dry Sherry
1 8½-ounce can artichokes, drained
2 to 3 cups cubed cooked ham
Salt to taste

Sauté the mushrooms in 2 tablespoons of butter until the liquid evaporates. Add the remaining butter, mustard, and thyme. When the butter melts add the flour and cook until bubbly. Gradually stir in the milk and continue to stir until it thickens. Add the cheese, sherry, artichokes, ham, and salt.

When the sauce has cooled, refrigerate until shortly before serving time. Allow time for reheating.

Serves 12.

Yorkshire Eggs

2 tablespoons butter
2 tablespoons all-purpose flour
1 8-ounce carton sour cream

❖ ❖ ❖

24 eggs
Salt and pepper to taste

Melt the butter in a small pan. Stir in the flour and cook until bubbly. Blend in the sour cream. Cook until bubbly and smooth. Remove the pan from the heat.

Beat together the eggs, salt, and pepper. Scramble in a large skillet and then stir in the sour cream mixture. May be kept warm for as long as one hour.

Serves 12.

Bluff Creek Inn

Jane's Caramel Sauce

1 1-pound bag dark brown sugar
1 pint whipping cream
2 cups butter (4 sticks)

❖ ❖ ❖

Rum or brandy

Combine the sugar, cream, and butter in a saucepan; bring to a slow boil. Cook until the sugar is completely dissolved. A little rum or brandy may be added for extra flavor, if desired.

Serve over waffles, French toast, sautéed bananas, etc.

Makes 2 cups of sauce.

Summer Fruit Dressing

½ cup sugar
1 teaspoon all-purpose flour
1 egg yolk

2½ tablespoons lemon juice
½ cup frozen pineapple juice
concentrate

❖ ❖ ❖

1 cup heavy cream, whipped

In a small saucepan over low heat stir together the sugar, flour, and egg yolk until smooth. Add the lemon juice and pineapple juice concentrate. Cook until thick, stirring occasionally. Cool. Fold in the whipped cream. Serve over fruit.

Makes 1½ cups of dressing.

Blueberry Grunt

4 to 5 pint boxes blueberries
1 tablespoon lemon juice
¾ cup sugar
1 tablespoon cornstarch
1 teaspoon cinnamon

❖ ❖ ❖

1 cup all-purpose flour
2 tablespoons sugar
1 teaspoon baking powder
½ teaspoon baking soda
Pinch salt

2 tablespoons butter, melted
½ cup buttermilk (or as needed)

❖   ❖   ❖

Cream or ice cream

Place the blueberries in a large saucepan. Sprinkle the lemon juice over the berries and stir. Add the sugar, cornstarch, and cinnamon, then cover the berries with water and bring to a gentle boil.

Make dumplings by combining the flour, sugar, baking powder, soda, and salt. Stir in the butter, then the buttermilk to form a soft dough. Drop by spoonfuls into the boiling blueberry mixture. Cover the pan tightly and allow the dumplings to simmer on low for 15 minutes without lifting the lid.

Serve with cream or top with ice cream.

Serves 6 to 8.

Apple Slump

Bread crumbs
1 cup brown sugar, firmly packed
1 tablespoon cinnamon
½ teaspoon nutmeg
5 medium apples, peeled and
    chopped
1 pint cream
8 eggs

Make a layer of bread crumbs in a 9x13-inch pan. Add the brown sugar, cinnamon, and nutmeg to the chopped apples and layer over the bread crumbs. Beat together the cream and eggs and pour over the top. Bake uncovered in a 375° oven for 30 minutes. Cover with foil and bake for 20 minutes more.

Serves 16.

East Bay Hotel

Grand Marais, Minnesota 55604
(218) 387-2800

The East Bay Hotel was built in the very early 1900s, when it was known as the Lake Side Hotel. The old hotel has been carefully restored, retaining its character while modernizing it to today's expectations of comfort. Some of the twenty guest rooms have private baths and each room has its own style of decor. The hotel overlooks Lake Superior at the start of the Boundry Waters Canoe Area and is near cross-country ski trails.

Swedish North Superior Herring Fishcakes

5 pounds fresh Lake Superior
    herring fillets, skinned
    and finely ground
½ cup melted butter
1 teaspoon nutmeg
4 tablespoons cornstarch
1 large onion, grated

❖   ❖   ❖

5 eggs
2 cups milk
3 12-ounce cans evaporated milk
4 to 5 tablespoons salt

❖   ❖   ❖

Oil

❖   ❖   ❖

White sauce or tartar sauce
    (optional)
Lemon wedges

Combine the herring, butter, nutmeg, cornstarch, and onion; mix thoroughly. Add 1 egg and 1 cup milk and beat very hard; continue to add the eggs, then gradually add the remaining milk, evaporated milk, and salt. Beat until the batter is very smooth,

then form into cakes about two inches in diameter.

In a fry pan pour oil in ½-inch deep, heat to 375° (do not get oil too hot). Fry until golden on one side, then turn and cook on the other side. Drain on paper towels.

Serve hot or cold, with white sauce or tartar sauce on the side. Garnish with a lemon wedge. May be served with a Swedish raisin rye bread.

Serves 10.

Apple Rum Dum

½ cup shortening (scant)
2 cups brown sugar, firmly packed
2 eggs

❖   ❖   ❖

2 cups all-purpose flour
2 teaspoons cinnamon
½ teaspoon salt

❖   ❖   ❖

2 teaspoons baking soda
2 tablespoons water

❖   ❖   ❖

½ cup chopped nuts
4 cups raw peeled apples,
    thickly-sliced
½ cup raisins

❖   ❖   ❖

½ cup butter (1 stick)
1 cup brown sugar, firmly packed
½ cup half and half
1 teaspoon rum flavoring

With a mixer cream together the shortening, 2 cups brown sugar, and eggs. Sift together the flour, cinnamon, and salt, add to the creamed mixture. Dissolve the soda in water and stir into the batter. Add the nuts, apples, and raisins; mix well and pour into a greased and floured 9x13-inch pan. Bake in a 350° oven for 30 minutes.

To make the rum sauce combine in a medium saucepan the butter, 1 cup brown sugar, and half and half. Stir well and cook until the mixture comes to a boil. Remove from the heat and stir in the rum flavoring.

Serve the pieces of cake with rum sauce spooned over them.

Serves 16.

The Rahilly House

304 South Oak Street
Lake City, Minnesota 55041
(612) 345-4664

The charm of this luxurious 1868 home is neatly wrapped in old-fashioned comfort. Featured are seven guest rooms, six fireplaces, antiques, quilts, and stained glass windows. Included in the room rate is a full country fresh breakfast. The commercial kitchen allows accommodations for groups.

The Rahilly House

Wholesome Pancakes

2 egg yolks
½ teaspoon salt
1 cup milk
1 tablespoon honey
1 cup whole wheat flour

❖ ❖ ❖

1 cup shredded carrots
½ cup chopped walnuts

❖ ❖ ❖

2 egg whites

Mix together the egg yolks, salt, milk, honey and flour. Blend well. Add the carrots and walnuts. In a separate bowl beat the egg whites until stiff.

Fold into the carrot mixture. Cook on a hot griddle.
  Serve with cinnamon syrup.
  Serves 4.

Cinnamon Syrup

½ cup sugar
1 tablespoon cornstarch
1 teaspoon cinnamon

❖ ❖ ❖

1 cup apple cider
1 tablespoon lemon juice

❖ ❖ ❖

2 tablespoons butter

In a small saucepan, combine the sugar, cornstarch, and cinnamon. Blend well; stir in the apple cider and lemon juice. Cook over medium heat until thickened. Remove from the heat, stir in the butter.
  Serve on pancakes, French toast, etc.
  Makes approximately 1½ cups of syrup.

The Pine Edge Inn

308 First Street Southeast
Little Falls, Minnesota 56345
(612) 632-6681

Caramel Walnut Pie

3 eggs
½ cup sugar
1 cup light corn syrup
½ cup milk
½ teaspoon maple flavoring

❖ ❖ ❖

Pastry for 1 9-inch 1-crust pie

❖ ❖ ❖

¾ cup chopped walnuts

❖ ❖ ❖

Whipped cream

The Pine Edge Inn

Mix together the eggs, sugar, corn syrup, milk, and maple flavoring. Pour into the pie crust. Sprinkle with the walnuts. Bake in a 350° oven for 45 minutes or until a knife inserted in the filling comes out clean. Cool.
  Serve topped with whipped cream. Serves 6.

The Lowell House

531 Wood Street
Old Frontenac, Minnesota 55026
(612) 345-2111

Frontenac? Like Shangri-La or Brigadoon, Old Frontenac is a place to stumble upon or be told the secret of by someone willing to share its magic. Situated about ten miles south of Red Wing, Minnesota, this mid-nineteenth century village of stately mansions graces the banks of the Mississippi River on the wide stretch called Lake Pepin.
  The Lowell House is an 1856 Greek Revival mansion with four large, bright guest rooms. One of these rooms has a private bath. Furnishings were not acquired quickly to open a

bed and breakfast but, rather, were gathered slowly over four generations. Art covers the high-ceilinged walls—the collection of the owners.

Cinnamon Rolls

1 ¼-ounce package active dry yeast
¼ cup warm water

❖   ❖   ❖

¾ cup water
⅓ cup nonfat dry milk
½ cup oil
½ cup sugar
1 teaspoon salt

❖   ❖   ❖

2 eggs, beaten
4½ to 5 cups unbleached flour

❖   ❖   ❖

2 tablespoons butter, softened
½ cup sugar
2 teaspoons cinnamon

❖   ❖   ❖

½ cup butter (1 stick), melted
½ cup brown sugar, firmly packed
½ cup pecan halves

In a small bowl dissolve the yeast in ¼ cup warm water. Set aside.

In a large mixing bowl combine the ¾ cup water, oil, ½ cup of sugar, and salt. Add the dissolved yeast and the eggs. Gradually stir in the flour to form a soft dough; beat vigorously. Cover and let rise in a warm place (80° to 85°) until double in bulk.

Turn the dough out on a lightly floured surface. Roll into a 9x18-inch rectangle. Spread the dough with 2 tablespoons of butter. Mix together ½ cup sugar and the cinnamon; sprinkle over the dough. Roll the dough lengthwise like a jelly roll. Cut into 1-inch thick slices.

Cover the bottom of a 13x9-inch pan with ½ cup melted butter. Sprinkle the brown sugar evenly over the butter, then evenly distribute the pecan halves over the sugar layer. Place the slices of dough evenly spaced over the mixture.

Place the pan in a cool oven and allow the rolls to rise until they touch and fill the pan. Bake in a 375° oven for 25 to 30 minutes.

Note: Rolls can be baked in 2 9-inch square pans. Increase by 2 tablespoons the amount of melted butter, brown sugar, and pecans used in the bottom of the pans.

Makes 18 rolls.

Eggnog

"This recipe is from my mother's annual New Year's Eve party, dating back to 1935. I have served leftover eggnog to my guests at breakfast and it was just as good January 1st after 8 A.M. as it was on December 31st. Now I make a practice of serving it when I am open winters for the first day of the year."

6 egg yolks
1 cup sugar
3½ cups whiskey

❖   ❖   ❖

6 egg whites

❖   ❖   ❖

3 cups whipping cream
3 cups light cream
1 tablespoon rum

❖   ❖   ❖

Nutmeg

Beat the egg yolks until lemon colored. Add the sugar; beat until very smooth. Slowly add the whiskey and beat in. Beat the egg whites until stiff peaks form; fold in. Whip the creams together until stiff and fold in. Slowly stir in the rum. Sprinkle the nutmeg over each serving. Serve chilled.

Serves 12.

Canterbury Inn

723 Second Street, Southwest
Rochester, Minnesota 55902
(507) 289-5553

Canterbury Inn, Rochester's first bed and breakfast, spoils its guests in the gracious surroundings of a restored Victorian home within three blocks of the Mayo Clinic and St. Mary's Hospital. The inn's informal, comfortable living room provides reading and writing materials, games and music, plus tea, and so forth each afternoon from 4:30 to 6:00. Full breakfasts feature a variety of specialties and the innkeepers conform to dietary needs or schedules. The inn offers central air conditioning, a cozy fireplace in the winter, and a shady porch in the summer. King, queen, and twin beds are available, and each of the four double rooms has a private bath with both shower and tub. Private, offstreet parking is provided. No pets are allowed.

Muffin Eggs

For each serving allow 2 eggs, 2 slices of cheese bread (or white bread and grated Parmesan cheese), and butter.

For each muffin cup prepare 1 slice of bread by removing a wedge from the bottom corners to the center.

Butter the bread generously on both sides, and push into greased muffin tins, forming bread cups. If you have used white bread, sprinkle with Parmesan cheese. Break an egg into each bread cup.

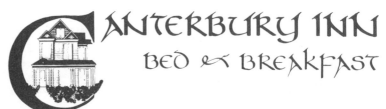

Bake in a 350° oven about 11 minutes, depending on the size of the egg. The eggs will continue to cook slightly even after removing them from the oven so take them out early unless they are to be served immediately.

Serves 2.

Minnesota Wild Rice Waffles

3 eggs, separated
1½ cups milk
1¾ cups sifted all-purpose flour
4 teaspoons baking powder
½ teaspoon salt
½ cup butter (1 stick), melted

❖   ❖   ❖

1 cup cooked wild rice

❖   ❖   ❖

Maple syrup

Beat the egg yolks with a fork or wire whisk; stir in the milk, flour, baking powder, salt and melted butter. Mix until smooth. Add the wild rice. In a separate bowl beat the egg whites until stiff and fold in. Bake in a hot waffle iron. Serve with maple syrup.

Serves 4.

Norwegian Fruit Soup

2 cups pitted prunes
1½ cups dried apricots
1 cup golden raisins
1 cup currants
1 cup dried tart cherries

❖   ❖   ❖

1 lemon, thinly sliced
4 sticks cinnamon

❖   ❖   ❖

½ cup pearl tapioca, soaked ½ hour

❖   ❖   ❖

1 cup fresh or frozen raspberries

Soak the fruits overnight in water to cover. Add the lemon and cinnamon; simmer gently about 45 minutes. Add the tapioca and simmer for 15 minutes more. Remove from the heat and add the raspberries.

Serves 4 to 6.

Driscoll's for Guests

1103 South Third Street
Stillwater, Minnesota 55082
(612) 439-7486

Driscoll's has had few structural changes since the Civil War. Period antiques adorn the rooms in this historically significant inn that is a half-mile walk from downtown Stillwater. Special packages for two or more nights are available, including dinner in one of Stillwater's finest restaurants, a riverboat cruise, riding, biking, canoeing, and cross country skiing. Special midweek rates are available for two or more nights. Guests awaken to the aroma of fresh homemade breads and hearty quiche. These plus an elaborate fruit plate are specially served by Mina, in one's room, on the sun-filled screened porch, or by a cozy fire.

Macadamia Nut Waffles

1¾ cups cake flour
2 teaspoons baking powder
1½ teaspoons salt

❖   ❖   ❖

3 egg yolks
1 cup milk

❖   ❖   ❖

1 teaspoon vanilla extract
5 tablespoons unsalted butter, melted

❖   ❖   ❖

3 egg whites
1 5-ounce can macadamia nuts, finely chopped

Combine the cake flour, baking powder and salt. Add the egg yolks and milk; beat with an electric mixer until smooth. Blend in the vanilla. Pour in the butter, mixing well. In a separate bowl, beat the egg whites until stiff and fold gently into the batter. Add the nuts. Bake in a hot waffle iron.

Makes 4 to 6 waffles.

Baked Cheese Fondues

6 eggs
1 cup milk
1½ cups grated mild Cheddar cheese
Salt and freshly ground pepper
12 drops hot sauce (or to taste)
1 teaspoon dried tarragon
2 tablespoons chopped fresh parsley

❖   ❖   ❖

Soft butter

Beat together the eggs and milk until blended well. Stir in the cheese, salt, pepper, hot sauce and herbs. Liberally butter 4 custard cups (1-cup size; earthenware works best) and divide the mixture among them, almost filling the cups. Bake in a preheated 350° oven for 30 minutes until puffy on top.

Serves 4.

Ginger Tea Cakes

1½ cups sifted cake flour
1½ teaspoons baking powder
¼ teaspoon baking soda
½ teaspoon salt
½ teaspoon cinnamon
¼ teaspoon ground cloves
1½ teaspoons ground ginger

❖   ❖   ❖

¼ cup butter (½ stick)
4 tablespoons brown sugar, firmly packed

❖   ❖   ❖

1 egg

❖   ❖   ❖

Boiling water
¼ cup butter (½ stick)
2 cups confectioners' sugar

3 tablespoons milk
1 teaspoon vanilla extract
Dash salt

Combine the flour, baking powder, soda, salt, and spices. Cream the butter well; add the sugar gradually and cream together until light and fluffy. Add the egg and beat well. Add the flour mixture alternately with the creamed mixture, beating after each addition. Add boiling water, mixing quickly to blend, until of muffin-batter consistency. Turn into small muffin pans, lined with paper cups, filling ½ full. Bake in a 375° oven for 20 minutes. Frost with Butter Frosting.

To prepare the frosting cream the butter, add the confectioners' sugar gradually, blending well after each addition. Continue adding the sugar, moistening with up to 3 tablespoons milk until spreadable. Add the vanilla and salt.

Makes 1½ dozen tea cakes.

The Lowell Inn

102 North Second Street
Stillwater, Minnesota 55082
(612) 439-1100

The Lowell Inn is an all-season, all-occasion inn. The founders, Arthur and Nelle Palmer, raised their family in the inn. Dining at the Lowell Inn is a culinary delight. The Garden Room has a bubbling spring that forms an indoor trout pool. The George Washington dining room is decorated in colonial style, and the Matterhorn Room evokes the feeling of camaraderie characteristic of Europe. Lovely French Provincial-style rooms and suites create an atmosphere of luxurious beauty.

Lowell Inn Crescent Rolls

1 2-ounce cake compressed yeast
Sugar
1 cup warm water (78° to 82°)

❖ ❖ ❖

¼ cup sugar
1 tablespoon salt
1 cup warm milk
7 to 8 cups all-purpose flour
3 eggs

❖ ❖ ❖

¼ cup butter (½ stick), melted

Sprinkle the yeast with sugar; soften in the warm water and set aside. Dissolve ¼ cup of sugar and the salt in the warm milk; add 2 to 3 cups of flour. Mix in the eggs and the yeast mixture; add the remaining flour until stiff but soft. Let rise until double in size and punch down; let rise again. Turn out on a floured board and let rest for 10 minutes.

Working with ⅓ of the dough at a time, roll into 9-inch circles and cut into 12 wedges. Brush the wedges with melted butter, roll into crescents and place on greased baking pans. Bake in a 400° oven for 10 to 15 minutes, until golden brown.

Makes 50 rolls.

Red Cabbage

1 medium head red cabbage, sliced
1 medium sweet onion, sliced
2 large apples, peeled and quartered
1 tablespoon bacon fat
1 teaspoon salt
½ cup sugar
1½ cups water
1 cup vinegar
1 bay leaf
2 whole allspice
2 whole cloves with heads removed
6 peppercorns

❖ ❖ ❖

Cornstarch to thicken

Combine all the ingredients except the cornstarch together in a large saucepan. Cover and simmer for 1½ hours.

Add a small amount of cornstarch to thicken. Serve.

Serves 18.

Old-Fashioned Maple Frango

¾ cup maple syrup
¼ cup Alaga syrup
4 egg yolks, warmed

❖ ❖ ❖

3 cups whipping cream

Warm the syrups slightly before adding to the egg yolks. Boil gently until thickened, then cool. Whip the cream and fold into the maple mixture. Pour into an 8x8x3-inch pan.

Makes 8 to 10 servings.

The Anderson House

333 Main Street
Wabasha, Minnesota 55981
(612) 565-4524

At the Anderson House hot bricks are delivered to the rooms at bedtime, guests may sign out one of the six cats for nighttime companionship, and shoes left outside the door are shined when returned the next morning. The feeling of moving backward in time is furthered by the black walnut and marble furniture that is typical of the mid-1800s, by primitive paintings and family portraits, and old-fashioned quilts on the beds. Guests may even believe great-grandmother is in the kitchen when they see the enormous breakfast rolls and bread tray with fifteen to twenty varieties of breads or smell the chicken and dumplings simmering on the stove. Grandma's famous sour cream raisin pie and strawberry rhubarb pie are served almost every day, as well as her fabulous cakes.

Rhubarb-Strawberry Coffee Cake

3 cups diced fresh rhubarb, cut in 1-inch pieces
1 16-ounce package frozen sliced sweetened strawberries, thawed
1 cup sugar
⅓ cup cornstarch

❖ ❖ ❖

3 cups all-purpose flour
1 cup sugar
1 teaspoon baking soda
1 teaspoon baking powder
1 teaspoon salt
⅛ teaspoon cinnamon
1 cup butter or margarine (2 sticks)

❖ ❖ ❖

1 cup buttermilk
2 eggs, slightly beaten
1 teaspoon almond extract

❖ ❖ ❖

¾ cup sugar
½ cup all-purpose flour
¼ cup butter or margarine (½ stick)
¼ cup flaked coconut

Combine the rhubarb and strawberries and cook about 5 minutes. Combine the sugar and cornstarch and add to the fruit. Cook until bubbly and thickened. Set aside and cool.

In a large mixing bowl combine 3 cups of flour, 1 cup sugar, soda, baking powder, salt, and cinnamon. Cut in 1 cup butter until the mixture resembles fine crumbs. In a separate bowl combine the buttermilk, eggs, and almond extract and beat; add to the dry ingredients, stirring just to moisten. Spread half of the batter in a greased 9x13x2-inch baking pan. Spread the cooled rhubarb filling over this and spoon the remaining batter in small mounds on top of the filling.

Make the topping by combining ¾ cup sugar and ½ cup flour, cut in ¼ cup butter until the mixture resembles fine crumbs. Add the flaked coconut. Sprinkle the topping over the batter. Bake in a 350° oven for 40 to 45 minutes.

Makes 12 servings.

Orange Rolls

"Probably our favorite roll. We serve them for fancy luncheons and other special events. Add McCaffrey perfected the recipe for our kitchens."

1 ³/₅-ounce cake compressed yeast
2 cups lukewarm milk

❖ ❖ ❖

½ cup orange juice
Grated rind of 2 oranges
1 teaspoon salt
⅓ cup sugar

❖ ❖ ❖

½ cup butter (1 stick), melted
1 egg, well-beaten
3½ cups flour

❖ ❖ ❖

½ teaspoon grated orange rind
1 tablespoon butter
½ cup brown sugar, firmly packed

❖ ❖ ❖

¼ cup orange juice
1 teaspoon lemon juice (pure)
¼ cup butter (½ stick), melted
Grated rind of 1 orange

❖ ❖ ❖

Confectioners' sugar

Dissolve the yeast with the milk. Set aside. In a separate bowl mix ½ cup of orange juice, grated orange rind, salt, and ⅓ cup of sugar. Add to the yeast mixture. Add ½ cup melted butter and the egg to the mixture. Thicken with 1½ cups flour, so it is thick enough to knead. Add the remaining flour and knead until soft. Let rise until double in bulk. Knead again and let rise until doubled in bulk. Punch down and roll quite thin. Cut rolls with round cutter and fold over as in Parker House rolls. Cook ½ teaspoon of orange rind with 1 tablespoon of butter and ½ cup of brown sugar. When heated, place under the flap of each roll. Close the flap tightly and let rise until very light. Bake in a 425° oven for 15 to 20 minutes.

Make the icing by combining ¼ cup orange juice, the lemon juice, melted butter, and orange rind. Gradually mix in enough confectioners' sugar to make the icing of spreading consistency. Spread the icing on the rolls when they are cool.

Makes 1½ dozen rolls.

Calico Muffins

3 tablespoons finely chopped green pepper
¼ cup finely chopped onion
1 2-ounce jar diced pimiento, drained
¾ cup shredded Cheddar cheese
2½ cups all-purpose flour
¼ cup cornmeal
2 tablespoons dried or fresh chives
2 tablespoons baking powder
1 teaspoon salt
¼ cup sugar

❖ ❖ ❖

2 eggs, beaten
1½ cups milk
¼ cup butter (½ stick), melted

Combine the green pepper, onion, pimiento, Cheddar cheese, flour, cornmeal, chives, baking powder, salt, and sugar.

Combine the eggs, milk and butter. Add to the dry ingredients and stir just until moistened. Do not beat.

Spoon into well-greased muffin cups. Fill ⅔ full and bake in a 400° oven for 20 to 25 minutes. Cool on wire racks.

Makes 1½ dozen.

Glazed Curried Chicken
with Rice

2 broiler-fryer chickens, quartered
Salt and pepper
3 tablespoons butter, melted

❖ ❖ ❖

1 cup chopped onions
5 slices bacon, finely diced
3 tablespoons all-purpose flour
1 tablespoon curry powder
2 cups chicken broth

¼ cup orange marmalade
2 tablespoons ketchup
2 tablespoons lemon juice

❖   ❖   ❖

6 cups hot cooked rice

Quarter the chickens, wash, and pat dry. Season with salt and pepper. Dip the chicken pieces into the butter, coating well on all sides. Place on a baking pan, skin side up. Bake uncovered in a 400° oven for 30 minutes.

While the chicken is baking make the sauce. Cook the onions and bacon over low heat until the onions are tender. Blend in the flour and curry powder. Stir in the broth and cook, stirring constantly, until thickened. Blend in the marmalade, ketchup and lemon juice. Spoon the sauce over the chicken and continue baking 30 minutes longer, or until the chicken is tender and richly glazed. Serve over beds of fluffy rice.

Serves 8.

Tennessee Chicken

6 chicken breast halves
6 tablespoons all-purpose flour
6 tablespoons shortening

❖   ❖   ❖

6 slices country ham
6 tablespoons ham fat
2 tablespoons butter or margarine
3 tablespoons all-purpose flour
2 cups milk
½ cup Sherry

❖   ❖   ❖

6 toast circles

❖   ❖   ❖

12 fresh mushrooms, broiled

Ask the butcher to cut the breasts, leaving the wing bone attached to the first joint. Carefully remove the skin and bones. Dredge in the flour, shake well to remove the loose bits. Brown the breasts in shortening in a heavy-bottomed frying pan, but do not cook until tender. In a separate pan, brown the country ham slices. Remove from the pan, trim off the fat and add the fat back to pan with the butter or margarine. Blend in the flour; add milk and

cook until thickened. Add the Sherry, stir well and season to taste. Place the chicken pieces in the sauce, cover the pan tightly and bake in a 325° oven until the chicken is tender.

To serve place a toast round on a plate and place on it a slice of ham which has been trimmed to fit. Over this put a chicken breast with the wing tip up. Decorate with 2 broiled mushroom caps. Ladle gravy over the top. Place in the oven until heated thoroughly. Serve immediately.

Makes 6 servings.

Grandma Senderauf's Wonderful Baked Beans

1 16-ounce package large dried
    lima beans

❖   ❖   ❖

3 large Bermuda onions
Salt
1 pound thick bacon
¾ cup light brown sugar,
    firmly packed

Cover the beans with water and soak overnight. Bring them to the boiling point the next morning in the same water in which they have been soaked. Simmer about 20 minutes. Drain and reserve 1 pint of the liquid in which they have been cooked.

Slice the onions into rings. Grease a 2-quart Pyrex baking dish. Place ⅓ of the beans in the baking dish. Cover the entire top with onion rings. Salt lightly. Cut the bacon crosswise into 4 sections. Add strips of the bacon until the entire area is covered. Dust lightly with ¼ cup of the brown sugar. Repeat the layers. If there is bacon left over, use it all on the top. Sprinkle with the last ¼ cup of brown sugar. Cover the casserole.

Bake in a 350° oven. After an hour, check to be sure there is liquid in the casserole. If it seems dry, add some of

the reserved bean liquid. The beans should be done in 2 to 3 hours, depending on the beans, your oven, and other factors.

Serves 6 to 8.

Corn and Onion Casserole

A five star recipe!

2 tablespoons margarine
1 large onion, sliced

❖   ❖   ❖

1 cup sour cream
¼ teaspoon salt
1 tablespoon finely chopped
    parsley
½ cup shredded Cheddar cheese

❖   ❖   ❖

1½ cups corn muffin mix
1 egg, well-beaten
⅓ cup milk
1 16-ounce can creamed corn
2 drops hot sauce

❖   ❖   ❖

¾ cup shredded Cheddar cheese

Melt the margarine in a skillet and sauté the onions until tender. In a bowl combine the sour cream, salt, parsley and ½ cup cheese. Combine and add to the onion mixture and set aside. Combine the muffin mix, egg, milk, corn, and hot sauce and mix well. Spread in a greased 9x9-inch pan. Cover with the sour cream mixture. Top with the remaining cheese. Bake in a 425° oven for 25 to 30 minutes. Wonderful served with Southern Fried Chicken.

Serves 8.

Carrots Anderson

1 cup ketchup
1 cup butter (2 sticks), melted
1 cup honey
1 20-ounce bag frozen carrots,
    whole miniature preferred

Blend the ketchup, butter, and honey in a blender. Cook the carrots as directed. Near the end of the cooking process, add the sauce. It sounds terrible, but everybody loves it. It makes an elegant dish.

Note: We suggest that you use carrot sticks in fresh vegetable season. Split each carrot down the middle, then in fourths. Makes 4 to 6 sticks from each carrot, depending on size.

Apple Folly

This is the Anderson House specialty.

    4 apples
    1 cup pecans
    1 29-ounce can peaches, drained
        (reserve liquid)
    24 almond macaroons, crumbled
    ¼ cup peach juice

Peel the apples and slice very thin. Butter a 1½-quart casserole dish, place a layer of apples in the bottom. Cover with successive layers of pecans, peaches, and macaroon crumbs until all the ingredients are used, ending with crumbs for the top layer. Pour peach juice over all. Set the casserole dish in a pan of hot water and bake in a 350° oven for 1 hour.

Serves 8. (This is a perfect accompaniment for fowl).

Belleweather Plantation Apple Pecan Pie

    2 cups all-purpose flour
    ¾ cup lard
    1 teaspoon salt
    6 to 7 tablespoons cold water
        ❖ ❖ ❖
    1 pound Granny Smith apples
    2 tablespoons lemon juice
    ½ teaspoon nutmeg
    ½ teaspoon cinnamon
    ¼ cup seedless raisins
    ½ cup sugar
        ❖ ❖ ❖
    1 cup brown sugar, firmly packed
    2 tablespoons all-purpose flour
    ½ cup butter (1 stick)
    ½ cup chopped pecans
    ¼ cup whole milk
        ❖ ❖ ❖
    2 tablespoons sugar
        ❖ ❖ ❖
    ½ cup butter (1 stick), softened
    1½ cups confectioners' sugar
    1 tablespoon boiling water
    1 tablespoon good brandy

To make the crust, work the flour, lard and salt together until crumbly. Add the cold water until the dough holds together. Divide the dough in ½ and roll into balls. Roll out one ball and line a 9-inch pie pan. Reserve the other ½ for the top pastry.

Wash, peel, core and slice the apples into the pie shell. Sprinkle with the lemon juice, nutmeg and cinnamon. Spread with raisins and ½ cup sugar.

In a small bowl mix the brown sugar, flour and butter, spread over the apple mixture. Sprinkle with pecans and most of the milk. Roll out the remaining dough, place over the filling, prick with a fork and brush with the remaining milk. Sprinkle 2 tablespoons of sugar over the top. Bake in a 450° oven for 10 minutes. Reduce to 350° and bake another 30 minutes.

To make brandied hard sauce, cream the butter until light. Beat in the confectioners' sugar, boiling water, and brandy.

Serve the hot pie with sauce spooned over the slices.

Serves 10 to 12.

Mississippi

Edgewood

412 Storm Avenue
Brookhaven, Mississippi 39601
(601) 833-2001

Edgewood, built in 1908, took four years to complete. With its many beautiful details, it is considered an architectural gem in the Greek Revival style. It has been completely restored over a thirty-year period by David Lovell, an architectural designer, who furnished it with fine antiques and beautiful chandeliers. Edgewood has recently been opened for tours, parties, and weddings. Eight rooms are available for overnight guests in the main house and the carriage house. Dinner is served by reservation.

Shrimp Mousse

**6 cups shrimps, peeled and
  deveined**

❖ ❖ ❖

**2 8-ounce packages cream cheese
1 cup mayonnaise
2 cups sour cream
½ cup finely minced green pepper
½ cup finely minced celery
½ cup finely minced green onion
¼ cup finely minced pimientos
½ cup chili sauce
⅛ teaspoon hot sauce
1 teaspoon salt
1 tablespoon Worcestershire sauce**

❖ ❖ ❖

**2 tablespoons unflavored gelatin
Juice of 2 lemons
¼ cup cold water**

❖ ❖ ❖

Watercress or parsley for garnish

Boil the shrimp in salted water, drain and finely chop. You must have 6 cups of shrimps. Cream together the cream cheese, mayonnaise and sour cream; add all vegetables and seasonings. Dissolve the gelatin in lemon juice and cold water. Heat over water in the top of a double boiler for 5 to 10 minutes. Gradually fold into the cheese-seasoning mixture. Add the shrimp and blend well. Pour into a 2-quart chilled ring mold; refrigerate overnight. Unmold; garnish with watercress or parsley. Serve as an hors d'oeuvre or as a main course.
Serves 8 to 16.

Crab Meat Edgewood

**3 10¾-ounce cans cream of
  mushroom soup
1½ soup cans milk
2 6-ounce cans lump crab meat
1 8½-ounce jar mushrooms
1½ cups cut parsley
1 cup butter (2 sticks), melted
Pepper to taste
1 to 1½ cups cracker crumbs**

Edgewood

204

Heat the soup and milk. In a buttered 9x13-inch casserole layer some of the crabmeat, mushrooms, and parsley. Pour in part of the soup. Drizzle with melted butter and sprinkle pepper over all. Repeat layers 2 or 3 times. Bake in a 350° oven until bubbly.

Serves 8 to 10.

Chicken Edgewood

**8 boned and skinned whole
    chicken breasts
Paprika
White pepper
Salt
1 cup butter (2 sticks)**

❖ ❖ ❖

**2 eggs, beaten
4 cups milk
2 cups bread crumbs**

❖ ❖ ❖

**2 tablespoons butter
½ cup chopped green onions
1 cup sliced fresh mushrooms
2 cups sour cream
1 10¾-ounce can cream of
    mushroom soup
1 10¾-ounce can cream of chicken
    soup
¼ cup chopped parsley**

Split the chicken breasts lengthwise. Sprinkle with paprika, pepper and salt. Place 1 tablespoon of butter in each breast and secure with a toothpick. Dip in beaten eggs and milk. Roll in bread crumbs. Brown in butter and place in a casserole dish. Make a sauce with 2 tablespoons of butter, the onions, and mushrooms. Add the sour cream and the soups. Heat well. Add the parsley and pour over the chicken breasts in the casserole. Cover and bake in a 325° oven for 45 minutes. Serve with rice pilaf.

Serves 8.

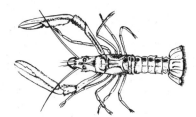

Green Bean Almondine
(Sweet and Sour Green Beans)

**3 slices bacon
½ cup sugar
½ cup vinegar
1 medium onion, thinly sliced
1 2-pound can green beans,
    drained
½ cup slivered almonds**

Fry the bacon until crisp and set aside. Into the skillet of bacon drippings add the sugar and vinegar. Separate the onion into rings and place in the skillet. Add the drained beans and almonds. Cover and simmer for 25 minutes. Sprinkle the crumbled bacon over the beans when ready to serve.

Serves 6 to 8.

Mississippi Mud Pie

**4 eggs, beaten
2 cups sugar
1½ cups all-purpose flour
1 teaspoon vanilla extract
1 cup butter (2 sticks)
⅓ cup cocoa
1½ cups chopped pecans**

❖ ❖ ❖

**1 6¼-ounce bag miniature
    marshmallows**

❖ ❖ ❖

**½ cup butter, melted
⅓ cup milk
3 tablespoons cocoa
1 1-pound box confectioners' sugar
1 teaspoon vanilla extract**

Combine the eggs, sugar, flour, and vanilla. In a saucepan melt the butter and add the cocoa. Add the egg mixture and beat well. Add the pecans. Bake in a greased 9x13-inch pan in a 350° oven for 25 to 30 minutes. As soon as the cake is removed from the oven, cover it with the marshmallows. Return the pan to the oven until the

marshmallows are slightly melted. To make the frosting, combine the butter, milk, and cocoa. Beat in the sugar and vanilla. Pour the frosting over the marshmallows and cool before cutting.

Serves 16.

Hamilton Place

105 East Mason
Holly Springs, Mississippi 38635
(601) 252-4368

Hamilton Place was built in 1838 by William F. Mason, Treasurer of the Illinois Central Railroad. The home is a typical Louisiana raised cottage; it is listed on the National Register of Historic Places and is filled with eighteenth and nineteenth century antiques. Guests may relax by the swimming pool or the year-round hot tub. Bikes are also available. The carriage house is now an antique shop. Holly Springs has an abundance of ante-bellum homes, an art gallery, museum, and a Green Line historical driving tour.

Strawberry Butter

**1 cup unsalted butter (2 sticks),
    softened
½ cup sifted confectioners' sugar
1 10-ounce carton frozen sliced
    strawberries, thawed and
    drained (reserve juice)**

Whip the butter until fluffy. Beat in the sugar, and add the strawberries. Gradually beat in the reserved strawberry juice. Store in the refrigerator. This butter freezes well. Serve on hot biscuits or rolls. Delicious!

Makes 1¾ cups.

Honey-Cream Dressing

2 eggs
¼ cup honey
¼ cup lemon juice
❖ ❖ ❖
1 cup whipping cream, whipped

Beat the eggs until soft and creamy. Add the honey and lemon juice. In a double boiler cook over hot water until thickened, stirring constantly. Cool. Fold in the whipped cream. Chill and serve with fruit.

Makes 1½ cups of dressing.

Cream Cheese Pound Cake

1 8-ounce package cream cheese, softened
1 cup unsalted butter (2 sticks)
½ cup unsalted margarine (1 stick)
3 cups sugar
6 eggs
3 cups all-purpose flour
1½ teaspoons vanilla extract

Cream together the cream cheese, butter, and margarine. Beat in the sugar. Alternately add 2 eggs and 1 cup of flour until all are added. Blend in the vanilla. Bake in a greased bundt pan. Place in a cold oven. Bake at 300° for 1½ hours. This cake has a wonderful, crispy top crust.

Serves 12.

Hamilton Hall

½ cup quick-cooking grits
¼ cup butter (½ stick)
Salt and pepper to taste
❖ ❖ ❖
¼ cup grated Parmesan cheese

In a saucepan bring the milk to a boil. Add the Gruyère and stir until melted. Add grits and stir until thick. Remove from heat; add the butter, salt, and pepper. Beat with a mixer for about 3 minutes. Pour into a greased casserole and sprinkle with Parmesan. Bake in a 350° oven for 30 minutes.

Serves 4.

ical section of Vicksburg. It is magnificently furnished with period antiques and gas-burning chandeliers. Overnight guests are accommodated in the original slave quarters, the turn-of-the-century guest cottage, or at the main house. Bedrooms are all furnished with period antiques and have private baths, color televisions, heating, and air conditioning. The price of the room includes a big southern breakfast, a tour of the house, and use of the swimming pool and jacuzzi hot tub.

Hamilton Hall

4432 State Boulevard
Meridian, Mississippi 39305

Gruyére Grits

2 cups milk (or half and half)
3 to 4 ounces Gruyère cheese

Anchuca

1010 First East
Vicksburg, Mississippi 39180
(601) 636-4931
1-800-262-4822 (Outside Mississippi)

Anchuca was built in 1830 in Greek Revival style in the center of the histor-

Broccoli-Cheese Casserole

1 cup boiling water
1 10-ounce box frozen chopped broccoli
❖ ❖ ❖
1 small onion, chopped
1 cup chopped celery
3 tablespoons butter
1 10¾-ounce can cream of chicken soup

1 soup can milk
1 8-ounce jar processed cheese
 spread
❖   ❖   ❖
2 cups cooked rice
Salt and pepper

Thaw the broccoli in water. Meanwhile, sauté the onion and celery in butter. Add the soup, milk and cheese. Heat briefly. Drain the broccoli. Add to the soup mixture. Add the rice and seasonings. Pour into a greased 9x13-inch casserole. Bake in a 350° oven for 30 to 40 minutes. Can be made ahead of time.
Serves 10 generously.

Cranberry-Apple Casserole

3 cups peeled chopped apples
2 cups fresh cranberries
2 tablespoons all-purpose flour
1 cup sugar
❖   ❖   ❖
3 1⁵/₈-ounce packages instant
 oatmeal with cinnamon and
 spices
¾ cup chopped pecans
½ cup all-purpose flour
½ cup brown sugar, firmly packed
½ cup butter or margarine (1 stick),
 melted
❖   ❖   ❖
Pecan halves
Fresh cranberries

Combine the apples, 2 cups cranberries, and 2 tablespoons flour, tossing to coat fruit; add 1 cup sugar, mixing well. Place in a greased 2-quart casserole. Combine the oatmeal, pecans, ½ cup flour, and brown sugar; add the butter and stir well. Spoon over the fruit mixture. Bake uncovered in a 350° oven for 45 minutes. Garnish with pecan halves and fresh cranberries.
Serves 6 to 8.

The Manor House

2011 Cherry Street
Vicksburg, Mississippi 39180
(601) 634-1861

The Manor House, an inn and club where members and guests may enjoy an overnight stay or a quiet lunch, provides an experience unparalleled anywhere else. The inn has three large bedroom suites and six bedchambers. The day begins with fresh fruit and croissants baked minutes earlier in the kitchen. Later on guests may enjoy the music of the grand piano in the foyer or unwind on the hardwood porches to the relaxing sounds of nature or listen to the calliope on the *Mississippi Queen* as she docks nearby. On Sundays a jazz band accompanies the tantalizing delights of a champagne brunch. The restaurant always offers delicious cuisine.

Mary's Seafood Gumbo

2 quarts boiling water
Salt and pepper to taste
Garlic to taste
2 pounds shelled shrimp
5 pounds skinless cod
1 pound crab meat
2 8-ounce jars oysters
2 tablespoons hot sauce
❖   ❖   ❖
2 cups lard
2 cups all-purpose flour
❖   ❖   ❖
Margarine
2 cups chopped onions
2 cups chopped green pepper
2 cups chopped celery
2 cups chopped okra
❖   ❖   ❖
4 cups stewed tomatoes
❖   ❖   ❖
Hot cooked rice

In a large soup kettle cook the shrimp, cod, and crab meat in seasoned boiling water. Add the oysters just before removing from heat. Add the hot sauce. Drain the fish (reserving liquid) and flake the cod. Prepare a roux with the melted lard and flour, stirring until golden brown. Add reserved liquid from fish and thin with water until of a soup consistency. Sauté the vegetables in margarine and combine with the shrimp, cod, crab meat, and oysters; add to the stock. Add the stewed tomatoes. Serve with rice.
Serves approximately 20.

Missouri

Borgman's Bed and Breakfast

Arrow Rock, Missouri 65320
(816) 837-3350

When guests arrive, they are shown to one of four spacious rooms where they can relax. They may prefer to enjoy the sitting room or porches, stop by the kitchen to visit with the cooks, wind up an old Victrola for a song, choose a game or puzzle, read a book, or just sit a spell and listen to the sounds of Arrow Rock. Grandma's Trunk may reveal a home-crafted item to purchase. In the morning, a family-style breakfast of freshly baked breads, juice or fruit, and coffee or tea begins the day.

Angel Biscuits

1 ¼-ounce package active dry yeast
½ cup warm water (115°)

❖ ❖ ❖

5 cups all-purpose flour
1 teaspoon baking soda
3 teaspoons baking powder
1 teaspoon salt
3 tablespoons sugar

❖ ❖ ❖

¾ cup shortening
2 cups buttermilk

Dissolve the yeast in the warm water. Mix together all dry ingredients; work in the shortening. Add the buttermilk, water, and yeast mixture; mix well. Place in a greased pan; chill. Use as desired.
Makes 2½ dozen biscuits.

Rhubarb Jam

5 cups rhubarb, finely cut
3 cups sugar
1 3-ounce package wild strawberry gelatin

Cover the rhubarb with sugar and let set until it draws juice. Cook over low heat until soft. Remove from heat; add the gelatin. Mix well until the powder is dissolved. Pour into pint jars and seal.
Makes 4 pints of jam.

Chunky Chicken Curry Soup

1 frying chicken, cut up
2 pieces celery
1 medium onion
4 cups water

❖ ❖ ❖

¼ cup butter (½ stick)
1 medium onion, diced
1 cup diced carrots
2 teaspoons curry powder
2 tablespoons cornstarch
¼ cup water
2 teaspoons salt
¼ teaspoon sugar
1 cup evaporated milk

Combine the chicken, celery, and onion with water and cook for 1 hour or until tender. Remove and cut the chicken into chunks; strain and reserve the stock. Sauté the diced onion and carrots in butter over low heat for 5 minutes. Add the curry powder and sauté 10 minutes more. Add the chicken stock. Mix the cornstarch with water; stir in the cornstarch mixture, salt, sugar, chicken, and milk. Cook until thick.
Serves 4 to 6.

Pinwheel Bread

2 ¼-ounce packages active dry yeast
2 cups warm water (110° to 115°)
2 cups milk
½ cup sugar
½ cup shortening
2 tablespoons salt
4 cups all-purpose flour

❖ ❖ ❖

4½ cups all-purpose flour

❖ ❖ ❖

¼ cup molasses
4½ cups whole wheat flour

Dissolve the yeast in the warm water. Add the milk, sugar, and shortening; beat in the salt and 4 cups of flour until smooth. Cover and let stand for 1 hour. Stir down and pour half of the batter (4 cups) into another bowl and add 4½ cups of all-purpose flour or enough to make a moderately stiff dough. Knead 6 to 8 minutes. To the other ½ of the batter add the molasses and whole wheat flour. Knead for 6 to 8 minutes;

cover and let rise for 45 to 60 minutes. Divide each portion into thirds and roll into rectangles. Place a rectangle of wheat dough on each rectangle of white dough and roll up tightly into loaves. Place in greased loaf pans. Cover and let rise for 45 to 60 minutes. Bake in a 350° oven for 45 minutes.

Makes 1 loaf.

Divinity Candy

4 egg whites, room temperature
½ teaspoon cream of tartar

❖   ❖   ❖

4 cups sugar
1 cup water
1 cup light corn syrup
2 teaspoons vanilla extract

Beat the egg whites. When foamy, add the cream of tartar. Beat until stiff.

Boil the sugar, water, and corn syrup to 250° on a candy thermometer. Beat the egg whites constantly while slowly pouring half the syrup mixture over them. Boil the rest of the syrup to 280°. Again beat the egg white mixture while slowly adding the rest of the syrup mixture. Add the vanilla. Let set until it cools. Drop with a spoon onto waxed paper. It will lose its glossy look.

Makes 80 pieces of candy.

The Victorian Guest House

3 Stillwell Place
Hannibal, Missouri 63401
(314) 221-3093

This gracious Victorian home, furnished with family heirlooms and hand-painted china, is just one-half mile from the historic Mark Twain Home area. The attractively furnished and air-conditioned guest rooms fea-

ture double or twin-sized beds. The warm hospitality of the Victorian Guest House is memorable.

French Puffs

⅓ cup margarine, melted
½ cup sugar
1 egg
1½ cups all-purpose flour
1½ teaspoons baking powder
½ teaspoon salt
¼ teaspoon nutmeg
½ cup milk

❖   ❖   ❖

⅓ cup margarine, melted
½ cup sugar
1 teaspoon cinnamon

Beat together all ingredients and bake in small greased muffin pans in a 350° oven for 15 to 20 minutes. While warm dip in the melted butter and roll in the sugar and cinnamon mixture.

Makes 12 puffs.

Boston Brown Bread

1 cup molasses
1 cup sour milk
1½ teaspoons baking soda
1 teaspoon salt
1 cup cornmeal
2 cups graham flour

Combine all ingredients and let stand for ½ hour before putting in well-greased and floured molds. (Boston bread molds always had lids. If one is not available use baking powder cans with metal lids.) This makes 3 baking powder cans-full. In a large pan or Dutch oven place cans on a trivet in 1 inch of cold water. Bring the water to a boil, cover, and steam for 3 hours. Add boiling water as necessary.

Serves 9.

Cherry Pecan Bread

¾ cup sugar
½ cup butter (1 stick), softened
2 eggs

❖   ❖   ❖

2 cups sifted all-purpose flour
1 teaspoon baking soda
½ teaspoon salt

❖   ❖   ❖

1 cup buttermilk
1 cup chopped pecans
1 10-ounce jar maraschino
    cherries, well-drained
1 teaspoon vanilla extract

Cream the sugar, butter and eggs until very fluffy. In a separate bowl, sift together the flour, baking soda and salt. Stir into the creamed mixture. Add the buttermilk and stir well; then add the pecans, cherries, and vanilla. Place in a well-greased 9x5-inch loaf pan. Bake in a 350° oven for 55 to 60 minutes. Remove from the pan and cool on a rack.

Makes 1 loaf, 12 servings.

Doanleigh Wallagh

217 East 37th Street
Kansas City, Missouri 64111
(816) 753-2667

Gracious, turn-of-the-century elegance is found at Doanleigh Wallagh, along with superb food and midwestern warmth. This handsomely restored eighty-year-old Georgian Colonial-style mansion has five bedrooms, each furnished with a private bath and antiques. Just five minutes from Kansas City's celebrated Country Club Plaza and Crown Center, Doanleigh Wallagh is in the Hyde Park area, with tennis courts and the lovely park just across the street.

Doanleigh Wallagh

Puff Pancakes

3 eggs
½ cup all-purpose flour
½ cup milk
3 tablespoons butter, melted
½ teaspoon salt

❖ ❖ ❖

Confectioners' sugar
Lemon wedges
Fruit-flavored syrup

Grease two 8-inch cake pans. In a small bowl, beat the eggs; stir in the flour and then the milk. Add the melted butter and salt. Pour the mixture into 2 greased 8-inch pans and bake in a 450° oven for 20 minutes. Serve with confectioners' sugar and lemon wedges or fruit flavored syrup.
Makes 2 pancakes.

Spicy Milk

½ cup water
¼ cup cinnamon red hots candy
¼ cup honey
1 tablespoon whole cloves

❖ ❖ ❖

4 cups milk

In a saucepan stir together the water, candy, honey and cloves. Bring to a boil and simmer for 5 minutes. Strain out the cloves. Slowly stir in the milk and heat.
Serves 6.

Down to Earth Lifestyles

Route 22
Parkville, Missouri 64152
(816) 891-1018

Down to Earth Lifestyles offers a quiet country setting near Parkville, between the Kansas City International Airport and downtown Kansas City. The private rooms are cozy, each with a private bath and telephone, and the living areas are spacious. This new, beautiful, earth-integrated home is surrounded by eighty-five acres of grounds that provide many opportunities for healthful exercise. The indoor heated swimming pool, the exercise room, and the jogging and walking trail (including exercise guidelines) are popular with guests. Breakfast is served as ordered, from country to continental.

Scrambled Eggs Supreme

6 eggs
½ cup grated Monterey Jack cheese
½ cup grated Cheddar cheese
½ cup cooked bacon (or ham), chopped
1 tablespoon water
2 tablespoons milk
1 teaspoon salt
½ teaspoon pepper
1 tablespoon onion soup mix
1 teaspoon Worcestershire sauce

Lightly beat the eggs with a whisk. Add the remaining ingredients and mix well. Scramble in a frying pan over medium heat until light and fluffy. If a pan other than non-stick is used, fry in 1 tablespoon of butter or oil.
Serves 6.

Bacon and Egg Bake

6 slices bacon
2 medium onions, sliced
1 10¾-ounce can cream of mushroom soup
1¼ cups milk
5 hard-boiled eggs, sliced
2 cups shredded Cheddar cheese
Salt and pepper to taste
English muffins, split and toasted

In a large skillet fry the bacon. Drain, leaving 2 tablespoons of grease in the skillet. Sauté the onions in the bacon grease. Stir in the soup, milk, eggs, cheese, and seasonings. Pour into a greased 10x6-inch pan and top with crumbled bacon. Bake in a 350° oven for 20 minutes. Serve over muffin halves.
Serves 6.

Egg-Ham-Cheese-Broccoli Strata

9 slices white bread
1 10-ounce package chopped broccoli, cooked and drained
12 ounces sliced sharp Cheddar cheese
2 cups cooked ham, diced
6 eggs, slightly beaten
3½ cups milk
2 teaspoons instant minced onions
½ teaspoon salt
¼ teaspoon dry mustard

Trim the crusts from the bread slices and reserve. Cut the slices diagonally to form 2 triangles. Arrange 9 triangles and crust trimmings on the bottom of a greased 9x13-inch pan. Alternate layers of broccoli, cheese and ham.

Arrange 9 remaining triangles on top. Combine the slightly beaten eggs, milk, onion, salt, and dry mustard. Pour over the bread.

Cover and refrigerate for 6 hours or overnight. Bake uncovered in a 325° oven for 55 minutes. Let set 10 minutes before cutting and serving.
Serves 12.

Montana

Lone Mountain Ranch

Box 145
Big Sky, Montana 59716

The Lone Mountain Ranch is known as one of the finest Nordic skiing centers in America, and the innkeepers pledge to make it better every year. Capacity is for about forty guests. The Old West atmosphere creates a warmth and ambience that adds greatly to the enjoyment of visiting the ranch.

An ideal destination for vacationing Nordic skiers, it has forty miles of double-tracked, machine-set trails in deep dry snow to make track skiing delightful. Available are a complete rental and retail shop, certified instruction, and guided all-day trips into the wilderness of Yellowstone and the Spanish Peaks. Snow coach trips to Old Faithful, guided overnight trips to the back country cabin, gourmet on-the-snow luncheons, horse-drawn sleigh rides, the cozy Horse Fly Saloon, evening entertainment, and the wood-fired hot tub are some of the reasons guests return year after year.

Café de Paris Butter

1 tablespoon tarragon
1 tablespoon sweet basil
1 tablespoon marjoram
1 tablespoon thyme
1 tablespoon sage
1 tablespoon rosemary
1 teaspoon fresh ground fennel
   seed
1 teaspoon fresh ground anise seed
1 tablespoon fresh cracked black
   pepper
2 fresh cloves garlic, chopped
2 bulbs shallots, chopped
1 pint Burgundy

❖   ❖   ❖

2 cups butter (4 sticks), softened
6 tablespoons chili sauce
1 tablespoon Worcestershire sauce

In a saucepan boil all the herbs in red wine until a paste forms.

In a mixing bowl beat the butter, chili sauce, and Worcestershire sauce until well-blended. Blend in the cooled herbs.

Serve with beef, shrimp, lobster, veal or lamb.

Makes 2 cups of butter.

Lentil Bean Soup

1 carrot, diced
2 stalks celery, diced
2 large onions, diced
¼ cup butter (½ stick)

❖   ❖   ❖

1 pound lentils
2 quarts water
8 ounces dried ham
Salt and pepper to taste
Worcestershire sauce to taste

❖   ❖   ❖

½ cup all-purpose flour
½ cup oil

In a soup kettle sauté the carrots, celery, and onion in the butter. Add the lentils, water, and dried ham, and add seasonings to taste. Boil for about 1½ hours.

In a small saucepan prepare a roux with the flour and oil. Stir until thickened and well-blended. Add the roux to the soup mixture until the soup is the desired consistency.

Serves 6 to 8.

Hot Bacon Dressing

8 ounces bacon, diced
2 large onions, diced

❖   ❖   ❖

6 egg yolks
1 teaspoon fresh cracked black
   pepper
½ teaspoon salt
2 tablespoons stone-ground
   mustard
2 tablespoons sugar
2 tablespoons vinegar
1 tablespoon Worcestershire sauce
2 tablespoons dill weed
½ cup salad oil

In a sauté pan, sauté the bacon until brown; add the onions and sauté until translucent. Drain and set aside.

In a mixer bowl combine the egg yolks, pepper, salt, ground mustard, sugar, vinegar, Worcestershire sauce, and dill weed on medium speed of the mixer. Slowly add the oil and blend well. Add the bacon and onions. If too thick, thin the dressing with vinegar.

Adjust the seasonings and serve within 30 minutes. Do not store.

Makes approximately 3 cups of dressing.

Oatmeal Bread

1½ cups water
2 tablespoons butter
1 tablespoon salt
1 cup quick-cooking oats

❖ ❖ ❖

1 ¼-ounce package active dry yeast
2 cups warm water (110° to 115°)
¾ cup molasses

❖ ❖ ❖

4 cups all-purpose flour
4 cups whole wheat or all-purpose flour

In a saucepan boil together the water, butter, salt and oats.

In a mixing bowl dissolve the yeast in the water; add the molasses. After the yeast activates, add 4 cups of flour; mix well. Add the remaining flour, mixing well. Knead until you have a soft dough. (You can add sunflower seeds, sesame seeds, or other grains). Let rise in a greased bowl until double in size; punch down. Shape into loaves or rolls, buns, etc. Let rise again. Bake in a 375° oven for 25 to 30 minutes.

Makes 2 loaves.

Pepper Kaka

1 cup butter (2 sticks)
1 cup sugar
½ cup molasses

❖ ❖ ❖

1½ tablespoons ginger
2 teaspoons cinnamon
2 teaspoons cloves
1 teaspoon baking soda
3½ cups all-purpose flour

❖ ❖ ❖

1 cup sliced almonds

Cream together the butter and sugar; add the molasses.

In a separate mixing bowl sift together the ginger, cinnamon, cloves, baking soda, and flour; add to the creamed mixture. Add the almonds to the dough. Roll into logs; chill and slice. Bake in a 325° oven until golden brown. Watch carefully to avoid burning.

Makes 24.

The Lehrkind Mansion: Bed and Breakfast

719 North Wallace
Bozeman, Montana 59715
(406) 586-1214

The Lehrkind Mansion is a bed and breakfast home with furnishings that resemble a museum. This home has been historically restored and furnished. Guests can sleep in Calamity Jane's brass bed and see Buffalo Bill Cody's gloves. Four double rooms and one single guest room are available. A master suite for two to eight people is complete with a private kitchen. This bed and breakfast can accommodate group events. A continental breakfast is provided each morning, and gourmet dinners are also served. The Lehrkind is near such activities as Yellowstone National Park and it is close to two major ski resorts. Blue ribbon fishing and hunting and professional guide services are available.

Banana Bread

"This recipe was great-great-grandmaw Herbert's, who homesteaded here in Montana. The bread could only be made at Christmastime. They went to town by wagon to a dry goods store that only stocked bananas at Christmas, and those were always over-ripe. Ripeness was the inspiration of the recipe!"

¼ cup shortening
¾ cup sugar
2 eggs
2 medium bananas, mashed
2¼ cups all-purpose flour
¼ cup sour milk
¾ teaspoon baking soda
¾ teaspoon baking powder
⅛ teaspoon salt
½ cup chopped nuts

In a large mixing bowl cream together the shortening and sugar; add the eggs and bananas. Add the remaining ingredients. Bake in a greased loaf pan in a 375° oven for about 50 minutes.

Makes 1 loaf.

The Voss Inn: Bed and Breakfast

319 South Willson
Bozeman, Montana 59715
(406) 587-0982

The Voss Inn is truly a "home away from home" for people who enjoy fine accommodations as well as personal service and hospitality. A lovingly restored 100-year-old mansion, it offers six guest rooms, each with large comfortable beds and a private bath. Guests can relax in comfortable surroundings and enjoy a style of gracious living reminiscent of an earlier time. Each guest room remains true to the old-fashioned charm of the inn. When breakfast is served each morning, guests may help themselves to fresh, homemade breakfast rolls from the unique, built-in warmer in the 1880s ornate radiator. For those who prefer, a full breakfast is served in the comfort of their room.

The Voss Inn

Place 6 rolls in each pan. Brush the tops with peanut oil. Refrigerate for 2 to 24 hours. Let set at room temperature for 20 minutes. Bake in a 375° oven for 20 minutes. Serve and enjoy piping hot.

Makes 24 rolls.

Sautéed Nectarines

Per serving:
1 nectarine (or peeled apple or
peach)
1 tablespoon butter, melted
1 teaspoon brown sugar, firmly
packed
Cinnamon and nutmeg to taste
Fresh cream

Slice the nectarine and sauté in butter over medium heat for 10 minutes. Add the sugar and spices. Sauté until tender. Serve warm topped with fresh cream.

Serves 1.

Eggs with Salsa

Per serving:
1 slice Canadian bacon
1 tablespoon salsa
1 large egg
2 tablespoons grated Cheddar
cheese

Grease one ramekin per serving. Stack the ingredients in each ramekin in the order listed. Bake in a 350° oven for 15 minutes. Wonderful and easy!

Serves 1.

Ruthmary's Sticky Buns

5½ to 6 cups all-purpose flour
½ cup sugar
1½ teaspoons salt
2 ¼-ounce packages active dry
yeast
❖ ❖ ❖
1 cup warm milk
⅔ cup water
¼ cup butter (½ stick), melted
2 eggs, room temperature
❖ ❖ ❖

¼ cup butter (½ stick), melted
¼ cup sugar
2 tablespoons cinnamon
½ cup brown sugar, firmly packed
❖ ❖ ❖
¼ cup butter (½ stick), melted
¼ cup brown sugar, firmly packed
4 tablespoons peanut oil

Stir together 5 cups of flour, ½ cup of sugar, salt, and yeast. In a separate bowl combine the warm milk, water, and ¼ cup of butter. Using a mixer with the dough hook, gradually add the liquid mixture to the dry mixture. Add the eggs. Gradually add ½ to 1 cup flour until the dough sticks to the hook. Knead for 10 minutes. Place the dough in a greased bowl and let it rise about 45 minutes. Punch down and roll out on a floured board into a long rectangle. Pour approximately ¼ cup of melted butter evenly over the dough. Sprinkle with ¼ cup of sugar, cinnamon, and ½ cup of brown sugar. Roll into a "log" shape. Cut 24 rolls. Using 4 9-inch round pans, divide ¼ cup melted butter equally between the pans. Sprinkle ¼ cup of brown sugar over the butter, again dividing equally.

Murphy's House Bed and Breakfast

2020 Fifth Avenue North
Great Falls, Montana 59401
(406) 452-3598

This lovely, white house with brown trim offers two rooms for guests, both with double beds. The rooms are attractively furnished with antiques and collectibles. Breakfast is served on the patio when the weather permits. The yard is landscaped with a profusion of flowers that evoke cheer and tranquility. Murphy's House is close to the Charles Russel Gallery and Home, the Great Falls of the Missouri River, and Giant Springs. It is on the way to Glacier Park and Yellowstone National Park.

Apple Coffee Cake

1 20-ounce can apple pie filling
2 teaspoons ground cinnamon

❖ ❖ ❖

3 cups all-purpose flour
1 cup sugar
1½ cups milk
½ cup butter or margarine (1 stick),
softened
3 teaspoons baking powder
1 teaspoon salt
3 eggs

❖ ❖ ❖

¼ cup brown sugar, firmly packed
¼ cup chopped nuts
2 tablespoons butter or margarine,
melted

Combine the pie filling and cinnamon; set aside. In a mixer bowl beat the flour, sugar, milk, butter, baking powder, salt, and eggs on low speed of the mixer for 30 seconds. Beat at medium speed for 2 minutes. Pour half of the batter (about 2 cups) into a greased 9x13-inch pan. Spoon half of the pie filling (about 1 cup) over the batter. Repeat with the remaining batter and pie filling. Sprinkle the brown sugar and nuts over the pie filling mix. Drizzle with melted butter. Bake in a 350° oven until a wooden toothpick inserted in the center comes out clean. Serve warm.
Serves 6 to 8.

Coffee Cake

¼ cup butter (½ stick)
1 cup sugar
2 egg yolks, well-beaten

❖ ❖ ❖

2 cups all-purpose flour
2 teaspoons baking powder
1 teaspoon salt
1 cup milk
2 egg whites, beaten

❖ ❖ ❖

1½ cups brown sugar, firmly
packed
2 tablespoons all-purpose flour
2 tablespoons melted butter
2 teaspoons cinnamon
1 cup nuts

In a medium mixing bowl cream ¼ cup of butter; add the sugar gradually. Add the egg yolks. In a separate bowl sift together 2 cups of flour, baking powder, and salt and add alternately with the milk to the butter mixture. Add the egg whites.
In a separate mixing bowl mix together the brown sugar, 2 tablespoons of flour, 2 tablespoons of butter, cinnamon, and nuts for the filling. Pour half the batter into a 9x13-inch baking pan. Add half of the filling, then the remaining batter and filling. Bake in a 350° oven until a cake tester inserted in the center comes out clean.
Serves 8.

Nebraska

The Rogers House

2145 B Street
Lincoln, Nebraska 68502
(402) 476-6961

To stay at The Rogers House is to experience the richness and warmth of a period when welcoming friends or strangers was a cultivated art. Within each bedroom the special touches of antique furnishings, a down comforter, and a private bath invite each guest to pause and refresh. Following the customary European tradition, each morning begins with a complimentary breakfast of a specially-prepared hot entree, fresh fruit, pastry, fresh-squeezed orange juice, and market-blend coffee.

Whether time is spent in solitude, perhaps with a Willa Cather book from the many volumes in the guest library, or in shared company before the fireplace or within one of the sunrooms, The Rogers House offers a very special place of lodging.

Pineapple Coffee Cake

½ cup margarine (1 stick), softened
1 cup brown sugar, firmly packed
2 eggs
1 teaspoon baking soda
1 cup sour cream
2 cups all-purpose flour
¼ teaspoon salt
1 teaspoon baking powder
1 teaspoon vanilla extract

❖ ❖ ❖

1 cup crushed pineapple, drained

❖ ❖ ❖

¼ cup sugar
⅓ cup brown sugar, firmly packed
½ cup chopped walnuts
¼ teaspoon cinnamon
¼ teaspoon nutmeg

Prepare the batter by creaming together the margarine and 1 cup brown sugar. Add the eggs and beat well. Combine the soda with the sour cream. Mix together the flour, salt, and baking powder, add alternately to the margarine mixture with the sour cream mixture. Add the vanilla; mix well.

Grease well a 9x13-inch pan. Pour in ½ of the batter. Spread the pineapple over this as a filling, and then add the remaining batter.

Make a topping by combining the sugar, ⅓ cup of brown sugar, walnuts, cinnamon, and nutmeg. Sprinkle the topping over the batter. Bake in a 350° oven for 25 to 30 minutes.

Serves 20.

Pecan Tarts

"These are especially nice at an afternoon tea or at a small reception."

2 8-ounce packages cream cheese, softened
1 cup butter (2 sticks), softened
3 cups all-purpose flour (approximately)
2 teaspoons baking powder

❖ ❖ ❖

6 egg yolks
1 cup plus 2 tablespoons brown sugar, firmly packed
2 pounds pecans, chopped
4 teaspoons vanilla extract

❖ ❖ ❖

Whipped cream (optional)

For tart pastry cup: Mix the cream cheese and butter until smooth. Add the flour and baking powder; continue adding flour until a nice ball forms. Form small balls and shape into small muffin pans.

Mix the egg yolks, brown sugar, pecans, and vanilla. Fill tarts with the nut mixture about ⅔ full. Bake in a 350° oven until golden brown, approximately 15 minutes. May be topped with whipped cream, if desired.

Serves 12.

❖ ❖ ❖ ❖ ❖ ❖

Nevada

Winters Creek Ranch

1201 Highway 395 North
Carson City, Nevada 89701
(702) 849-1020

Nestled among Ponderosa Pines with a spectacular view of the Sierra Nevada Mountains and Washoe Lake, this old horse ranch provides its guests an unusual experience. It is surrounded by the Toiyabe National Forest where wildlife abounds including deer, turkey, porcupine, and eagles. Guests often see such wildlife while riding horseback to the Cattlemen's Restaurant for a delicious dinner. The colonial-style ranch house has formally landscaped grounds and gardens. All guest rooms have private baths. The Colonial Suite, decorated in subdued colors, has a four-poster bed and a cozy fireplace. The Nevada Suite, with authentic Navajo rugs and western antiques, enjoys a magnificent view of Mt. Rose from its private deck. Oliver's Nook is a soft and cheerfully decorated room. The Gambrel Cottage, separate from the main house, overlooks the Washoe Valley. Complimentary hors d'oeuvres and wine are served at 4:30 P.M. in the living room, tastefully decorated in Victorian-style furnishings, complete with baby grand piano and fireplace.

Here guests are invited to read, play a game of darts, or tie their own fly for the next day's trout fishing.

Savory Eggs

2 cups grated sharp Cheddar
　　cheese
¼ cup butter (½ stick)
　　❖　　❖　　❖
1 cup light cream
½ teaspoon salt
¼ teaspoon freshly ground pepper
2 teaspoons Dijon mustard
　　❖　　❖　　❖
12 eggs, slightly beaten

Spread the cheese in a 13x9x2-inch baking dish. Dot with butter. Combine the cream, salt, pepper, and mustard. Pour ½ of this mixture over the cheese. Pour the eggs into the baking dish. Add the remaining cream mixture. Bake in a 325° oven for 40 minutes until set.
　　Serves 6 to 8.

Victoria's Monterey Eggs

1½ cups cubed ham
½ pound bacon, fried and crumbled
12 eggs
1 teaspoon seasoned salt
Dash pepper
1 4-ounce can diced green chilies
　　❖　　❖　　❖
1½ cups grated Monterey Jack
　　cheese
1 large avocado, thinly sliced
Tomato slices and mushrooms
　　(optional as garnish)

Spread the ham and bacon on the bottom of a greased 2½-quart quiche pan. Beat together the eggs, seasoned salt, pepper, and chilies. Pour the egg mixture on top of the ham and bacon. Bake in a 325° oven until set, about 30 minutes. Sprinkle the cheese on top of the set eggs, place avocado slices, also tomato slices and mushrooms if desired, on top of the cheese. Place under the broiler until the cheese is melted.

Spinach and Feta Scramble

½ cup frozen chopped spinach
　　❖　　❖　　❖
12 eggs
½ cup milk
Dash salt and pepper
2 tablespoons butter
　　❖　　❖　　❖
1 cup shredded Monterey Jack
　　cheese
½ cup crumbled Feta cheese
½ cup chopped mushrooms

Thaw the spinach and squeeze out the liquid. Set aside. Beat together the eggs, milk, salt, and pepper. Melt the butter in a large skillet, and scramble the eggs until partially set. Fold in the spinach, cheeses, and mushrooms. Stir slowly until cheeses melt. Serve hot.
　　Serves 4 to 6.

Orchard House

Post Office Box 77
Genoa, Nevada 89411
(702) 782-2640

Picturesque and historical Genoa is Nevada's oldest town. Set close to Lake Tahoe, Virginia City, Carson City, and Reno, it is an ideal location for those visiting this area of Nevada. Dating from the 1860s and surrounded by old fruit trees and extensive grounds, Orchard House has been in the same family for four generations. It offers an informal, relaxed atmosphere and comfortable accommodations.

Orange Rolls

2 10-ounce cans butter-flavored biscuits
½ cup butter (1 stick)
¾ cup sugar (scant)
2 tablespoons orange rind, grated (or cinnamon and nuts)
Glaze (optional)

Stand the biscuits on edge in a greased bundt pan. Heat the butter, sugar, and orange rind. Pour over biscuits. Bake in a 350° oven for 30 minutes. Turn out of the pan at once. Glaze, if you wish, with a confectioners' sugar and orange juice mixture. Cinnamon and nuts instead of the orange rind is a nice change.

Serves 8 to 10.

New Hampshire

The Steele Homestead Inn

Rural Route 1, Box 78
Antrim, New Hampshire 03440
(603) 588-6772

The Steele Homestead Inn has been renovated to conform to the time when it was built, 1810. Located in Antrim, which was named for its first inhabitant's native county in Ireland, the inn sits back from the main road on four acres of land. The expansive front lawn, flower-filled gardens, and small fruit orchard welcome guests, while the inn is bordered by a small forest of deciduous trees and evergreens. There are four large guest rooms, two with their own fireplaces and private baths. The price of lodging includes a hearty breakfast of favorite homemade specialties prepared by the innkeepers. A roomy, comfortable parlor, complete with fireplace, on the lower floor is available to guests for reading and relaxation.

Steele Eggs

¼ cup butter (½ stick)
¼ cup all-purpose flour
2 cups milk
1 cup sour cream
Worcestershire sauce to taste
Salt and pepper to taste

❖ ❖ ❖

12 hard-boiled eggs
1 cup grated sharp Cheddar cheese
1 teaspoon dry mustard
Sour cream to moisten

❖ ❖ ❖

Bread crumbs

Prepare white sauce with the butter, flour, and milk. Add sour cream, Worcestershire sauce, salt and pepper to taste. Pour the sauce into a shallow casserole (or individual ramekins, dividing equally). Slice the eggs in half, remove and mash yolks and mix with Cheddar cheese and dry mustard. Moisten the yolk mixture with the sour cream, just enough to be able to handle for stuffing into the whites. After stuffing the egg halves, place them in the white sauce. Sauce should not cover the eggs. Sprinkle with the bread crumbs and bake in a 325° oven for 30 to 45 minutes (or until bubbly and warm). Eggs may be prepared the night before and refrigerated. However, the innkeeper always prepares the sauce just before baking.
Serves 6.

Cinnamon Twists

1 cup sour cream
3 tablespoons sugar
⅛ teaspoon baking soda
1 teaspoon salt
1 ¼-ounce package active dry yeast

❖ ❖ ❖

1 egg
2 tablespoons shortening, softened
3 cups sifted all-purpose flour

❖ ❖ ❖

Butter, softened
⅓ cup brown sugar, firmly packed
2 teaspoons cinnamon

❖ ❖ ❖

Glaze

Heat the sour cream to lukewarm in a large saucepan. Remove from heat and stir in the sugar, soda, salt, and yeast. Stir until the yeast is dissolved, then stir in the egg, shortening, and flour. Mix well (use hand if necessary). Turn dough onto floured board, fold over several times until smooth, then roll into a 24x6-inch oblong. Spread with soft butter. Sprinkle bottom half of dough with a mixture of brown sugar and cinnamon. Fold other half over. Cut into 24 strips, 1 inch wide. Hold each strip at both ends and twist. Place on a greased baking sheet 2 inches apart. Press both ends of twists to baking sheet. Cover and let rise until light, approximately 1 hour. Bake in a 375° oven for 12 to 15 minutes until brown.

Freezes well after baking, but thaw before heating. The uncooked dough does not freeze well. Twists may be iced with confectioners' sugar and cream glaze.

Note from the innkeeper: We have used this same dough in several variations, including rolling into 2 rounds. Pat 1 round into a round cake pan, sprinkle with cinnamon and sugar, and attractively arrange thinly sliced apples in a circle, and top with a dough round. Dot with butter and sprinkle with some more cinnamon and sugar. Bake for 15 minutes with a foil cover. Uncover and bake another 15 minutes, or until a toothpick in-

218

serted in the center comes out clean. Very attractive and very popular. Makes 2 dozen.

Cheese Puffs

1 3-ounce package cream cheese
¼ pound sharp Cheddar cheese
½ cup butter (1 stick)
2 egg whites, stiffly beaten

❖ ❖ ❖

1 loaf firm white bread, unsliced

Melt the cheeses and butter in double boiler, stirring to a smooth and velvety consistency. Remove from the heat and fold in the egg whites. Trim crusts from the bread and cut into 1-inch cubes. Dip cubes into the cheese mixture until well coated. Place on an ungreased cookie sheet and refrigerate overnight (or freeze and bake when needed). Freezes very well. Bake in a 400° oven for 12 to 15 minutes until brown.
Makes 4 dozen.

The Bradford Inn

Main Street
Bradford, New Hampshire 03221
(603) 938-5309

Guests at the Bradford Inn enjoy a special brand of Yankee hospitality and informality. Built in the 1890s, it is furnished in a casual country manner geared for relaxation. Specialties of the dining room are roast duckling and veal. A full-service bar stocks fine wines.

Pâté Maison

¼ pound bacon
2 tablespoons brandy
1½ pounds beef liver, ground
1½ pounds calves liver, ground
½ pound pork liver, ground
2 eggs
¼ cup sour cream
Salt and pepper
Crushed garlic to taste
2 tablespoons brandy

❖ ❖ ❖

3 to 4 chicken livers
¼ pound bacon

❖ ❖ ❖

Lettuce
Green olives
Black olives
Pickle spear

Line a loaf pan with ¼ pound of bacon; sprinkle with 2 tablespoons brandy. Mix the ground liver with the eggs, sour cream, and seasonings. Mix well and pour on the remaining 2 tablespoons brandy, flambé. Mix well and fill the pan with ½ of the mixture. Place the chicken livers in a row down the center. Cover with the rest of the mixture and top with the remaining bacon. Cover with foil. Place the loaf pan in another pan of water and bake in a 300° oven for about 2 hours. Remove the foil; place the pan in cool water. Chill in the refrigerator for 24 hours. Turn out and arrange on a plate with a lettuce bed, cutting as many slices as needed. Garnish with green and black olives and a pickle spear.
Serves 6 to 8.

Polish Mushroom Soup

½ pound mushrooms (reserve 1 mushroom for garnish)
3 tablespoons butter
¼ teaspoon caraway seeds
½ teaspoon paprika
1 tablespoon all-purpose flour
4 cups chicken stock

❖ ❖ ❖

1 egg yolk
1 cup sour cream
2 tablespoons dillweed

Wash and dry the mushrooms, cut off stem ends. Sauté whole mushrooms in the butter with the caraway seeds and paprika until slighty tender. Sprinkle with flour and blend into the mushroom mixture. Add the chicken stock a little at a time, stirring constantly. Simmer covered for approximately 30 minutes. Whip the egg yolk in a bowl until creamy. Add the sour cream and dillweed; mix well. Add this mixture to the hot soup and whisk together. Garnish each serving with one small sliced mushroom.
Serves 8 to 10.

Salmon Imperial

2 to 3 pounds salmon steaks or fillets
2 tablespoons butter, melted
2 tablespoons lemon juice
1 teaspoon anchovy paste (per steak)
1 teaspoon dry mustard
1 clove garlic, crushed
½ teaspoon paprika

❖ ❖ ❖

Wild rice

Cut the salmon into 8-ounce portions and place on a greased broiler pan. Combine the butter, lemon juice, anchovy paste, mustard, garlic, and paprika. Baste salmon with the mixture. Broil approximately 5 inches from heat for 6 minutes; turn and baste again. Broil an additional 4 to 5 minutes or until the fish flakes easily with a fork. Serve on a bed of wild rice.
Serves 4 to 6.

Veal Oporto

12 medium veal scallops
Flour
6 tablespoons butter (¾ stick)
3 tablespoons olive oil
⅔ cup Port wine
Salt and pepper to taste

❖ ❖ ❖

½ cup heavy cream
Butter

❖ ❖ ❖

Buttered noodles
Toasted bread crumbs

Pound the scallops thin and flour lightly. Sauté in butter and olive oil turning to brown evenly. When brown and tender add wine and cook gently for 2 minutes. Season to taste. Remove the meat to a hot platter and add cream to the pan. Stir to scrape up all the brown bits and flavor with a little butter. Pour sauce over scallops. Serve on buttered noodles sprinkled with toasted bread crumbs.
Serves 12.

Peach Praline Pie

¾ cup sugar
3 tablespoons all-purpose flour
4 cups peeled and sliced fresh
    peaches
1½ teaspoons lemon juice

❖ ❖ ❖

⅓ cup brown sugar, firmly packed
¼ cup all-purpose flour
½ cup chopped pecans
3 tablespoons butter

❖ ❖ ❖

1 unbaked pie shell

In a large mixing bowl, combine the sugar and 3 tablespoons of flour, mix together. Add the peaches and lemon juice.

In a small bowl, combine the brown sugar, ¼ cup of flour, and the pecans, cut the butter in until the mixture becomes crumbly.

Sprinkle ⅓ of the nut mixture in an unbaked pie shell until it becomes a layer on the bottom, cover with the peach mixture and sprinkle the remaining nut mixture over the peaches. Bake in a 400° oven until the peaches are tender.

Note: If the pie browns too fast, lower the oven temperature.
Serves 6.

The Bernerhof

Box 381
Glen, New Hampshire 03838
(603) 383-4414

The Bernerhof is an Old World country inn set in the White Mountains of New Hampshire. Remaining true to its European tradition, it is small, personal in nature, with a focus on elegant dining; a friendly taproom; and simple, comfortable bed and breakfast accommodations. Each of the nine individually decorated inn rooms is light and airy, with flowers at the bedside. Both hall and private baths are available. To assure comfort, a second floor sitting room is provided for guests' exclusive use, letting them curl up and read, watch television, or socialize informally. A visit to the Finnish sauna will make guests' relaxation complete. During the summer, guests are invited to take a short stroll through the pines to the swimming pool; the more ambitious may follow the trail to the top of Mount Washington. Well-mannered children are welcome, and a playground is provided. Guests at The Bernerhof come not only to stay, but to dine; for it is widely known for its superb continental cuisine.

Delice de Gruyére

"This recipe has been a favorite of visitors of the Bernerhof since Claire Zumstein brought it here from Switzerland in the mid-fifties. Many food critics have commented upon it, and it was even featured in *Gourmet* magazine many years ago. This appetizer recipe takes the form of small cheese croquettes and is served as an appetizer, accompanied by a small serving of spiced tomato. (Recipe serves twenty persons, three each.)"

3 cups milk
½ cup butter (1 stick)
Salt and white pepper to taste
1¼ cups sifted all-purpose flour
½ pound Emmenthaler cheese,
    grated
½ pound Gruyère cheese, grated
6 egg yolks

❖ ❖ ❖

4 eggs, beaten
3 cups dried bread crumbs

❖ ❖ ❖

1 onion, finely chopped
2 28-ounce cans stewed tomatoes,
    drained
¼ cup finely chopped parsley
Fresh herbs (optional)

Bring the milk, butter, salt and pepper to a boil (be sure the butter is melted), take off the heat and add all of the flour, stirring thoroughly until achieving a mashed potato consistency. Immediately add all of the grated cheese, mixing thoroughly to a smooth texture or until the cheese has completely melted. Add the egg yolks, again mixing until a smooth yellow hue is achieved.

Chill for several hours in the refrigerator or until firm enough to mold. Molding into a shallow pan (approximately 6x10x2-inch) will allow for faster chilling. Once firm, cut into 8-ounce rectangles and roll into long (2 foot) ¾-inch in circumference strips on a well-floured board. Cut into 3-inch lengths, dip into the beaten eggs and coat in dried bread crumbs.

Sauté chopped onions lightly. Add the stewed tomatoes to the onions after squeezing most of the juice out and breaking up if whole. Add the chopped parsley. Fresh herbs may be added to season. Sauté breaded croquettes in butter in a heavy skillet until golden brown. Add the croquettes to the pan only after the butter begins to jump in the pan, otherwise they will soften before browning.

To serve, place three croquettes in a spoke arrangement on a small 8-inch plate with the heated spiced tomato in the center. Add a parsley sprig for color.
Serves 20.

The Stonebridge Inn

Route 9
Star Route 3, Box 82
Hillsborough, New Hampshire 03244
(603) 464-3155

The Stonebridge Inn

The Stonebridge Inn is a dream-come-true for the innkeepers, Nelson and Lynne Adame. A mid-1800s farmhouse, it has been restored and redecorated (much by their own hands) to create the kind of small country inn everyone has always hoped to find. The inn has four guestrooms, each with its own private bath. Whatever the season, there always is plenty to do at Stonebridge.

Mushroom Nut Strudel

Pastry stuffed with duxelles (mushroom paste) served as an appetizer or vegetarian entree.

1 cup minced onions
¼ cup butter (½ stick)
¾ pound mushrooms, minced
¼ cup Sherry
¼ teaspoon thyme
Salt and pepper to taste
½ cup ground toasted walnuts
2 8-ounce packages cream cheese, softened
1 pound phyllo dough
Melted butter

To prepare duxelles, sauté the onions in butter until soft. Add the mushrooms and sauté for 2 minutes. Add the Sherry and cook, stirring until the liquid evaporates. Add the thyme, salt, and pepper. Cool, and add the walnuts. Mix well. Beat the cream cheese until fluffy, add the mushroom mixture. Cut the phyllo dough in half (you will have 2 stacks approximately 2½x11 inches each). Cover the dough with a damp towel. Butter (using a brush and a light touch) 3 sheets of dough, putting about ¼ cup of the cream cheese mixture down the length of the right side, about an inch in from the edge. Fold the long top edge over about an inch. Do the same with the bottom and butter. Roll up the strudel starting at the right. Place on cookie sheet and brush with butter if ready to bake (or wrap in plastic wrap and freeze). Bake in a 375° oven for about 20 minutes or until golden. (The dough can also be cut into strips and folded up into strips or triangles for smaller appetizers.)

Makes about 14.

Harvest Bisque

1 2-pound butternut squash, peeled and cubed
4 cups chicken stock
2 Mac or Cortland apples, peeled and quartered
2 tablespoons lemon juice
Salt and pepper to taste
1 cup milk or cream

Cook the squash in chicken stock until tender, about 10 minutes. Add the apples, cook until soft. Purée squash and apples in processor. Reheat in stock, adding the lemon juice and seasonings to taste. Stir in milk or cream. Heat thoroughly, do not boil.

Note: The Mac apple or Macoun apple is a form of McIntosh.

Serves 6.

Raspberry Almond Pie

1 8-inch chocolate crumb crust
1 cup raspberry jam
½ cup butter or margarine (1 stick), softened
½ cup sugar
2 eggs
½ cup ground almonds

Spread jam in the pie crust. Cream the butter and sugar together. Add the eggs one at a time, beating after each addition. Stir in the almonds. Pour the batter over the jam. Bake in a 350° oven for 30 minutes or until delicately browned.

Serves 6 to 8.

The Inn on Golden Pond

Route 3
Post Office Box 126
Holderness, New Hampshire 03245
(603) 968-7269

Across the street from The Inn on Golden Pond is Squam Lake, the setting for the movie starring Katharine Hepburn and Henry Fonda. The inn itself is a gracious country home built in 1879 amid some of New England's most picturesque countryside. It sits on fifty-five acres of land, mostly wooded, with trails circling the property to provide an ideal setting for hikers, strollers, and cross country skiers. The grounds immediately surrounding the inn are spotted with meandering stone walls, old split rail fences, and a variety of flowers, shrubs, and shade trees. Each room is individually decorated; most have private baths, and all overlook the grounds. In cool weather one can curl up by a crackling fire in the sitting room and enjoy a good book or games and puzzles. In warmer weather the sixty-foot-long screened-in porch is the perfect spot to pass a few relaxed hours. Each morning guests are treated to a full breakfast featuring homemade breads and muffins.

Apple Harvest Pancake

¾ cup all-purpose flour
3 tablespoons sugar
¼ teaspoon salt
3 eggs
¾ cup light cream
2 tablespoons butter, melted

❖   ❖   ❖

2 large apples, thinly sliced

❖   ❖   ❖

2 tablespoons brown sugar, firmly packed
½ teaspoon cinnamon
2 tablespoons butter, melted

Mix the flour, sugar, salt, eggs, cream and 2 tablespoons of melted butter together in a 2-quart mixing bowl. Heat a 10-inch ovenproof skillet and brush with oil to prevent sticking. Pour in the batter all at once and cook until set over medium heat. Lay apples over the top, completely covering the surface. Combine brown sugar and cinnamon; sprinkle over the apples. Pour the remaining 2 tablespoons of butter over all. Bake in a 400° oven for 6 to 8 minutes. Serve warm.

Serves 3 to 4.

Oven Omelet

"This recipe can easily be prepared the night before. Cover and refrigerate overnight. Breakfast cooks with no effort in the morning!"

4 to 6 slices bread
1 pound bulk sausage
1 cup grated sharp Cheddar cheese

❖   ❖   ❖

6 eggs
2 cups milk
1 teaspoon salt
Dash pepper

Place the bread slices in a greased 13x9x2-inch baking dish. Brown the sausage in a skillet and drain off the excess fat. Spoon the sausage over the bread and sprinkle the mixture with cheese. In a medium mixing bowl beat the eggs, milk, salt and pepper. Pour over the bread and sausage mixture. Bake in a 350° oven for 35 minutes.

Serves 6.

The Forest Country Inn

Route 16A
Intervale, New Hampshire 03845
(603) 356-9772

The Forest Country Inn feels like a large turn-of-the century family home, with braided rugs on the floors, comfortable chairs everywhere, and antiques, crafts, and country collectibles, all designed to make guests feel at home. The inn has eleven rooms (most with private baths), and a beautiful little stone cottage has two more rooms, each with its own bath. The front room of the cottage, a favorite with honeymoon couples, has its own fireplace and screened porch.

The inn takes pride in its cooking. A hearty breakfast with homemade baked goods is served, and in some seasons dinner is also available. Guests may sit on the porches (one is glassed in and has a woodstove for cool days), others relax in the living room, sounding out a few tunes on the piano, while others stroll down the paths that wind through the twenty-five wooded acres. The swimming pool is warmed by solar heating. In winter guests have free use of the trails of the Intervale Nordic Learning Center, just across the street.

Cranberry Swirl Coffee Cake

¼ cup butter or margarine (½ stick), softened
1 cup sugar

2 eggs, well beaten
2 cups all-purpose flour
1 teaspoon baking soda
½ teaspoon salt
1 cup sour cream
1 teaspoon almond extract

❖ ❖ ❖

8 ounces whole cranberry sauce
½ cup chopped walnuts

Cream the butter and sugar together. Add the eggs, beat well. Mix together the dry ingredients and add alternately with sour cream. Add almond extract. Place ½ of the batter on the bottom of a greased tube pan. Swirl ½ of the cranberry sauce over batter. Sprinkle ½ of the walnuts over the sauce, then repeat layers. Bake in a 350° oven for 55 to 60 minutes.

Carlton's Cream of Cauliflower Soup

1 head cauliflower
3 cups water
2 onions, peeled and quartered
4 stalks celery, cut into 2-inch
   pieces

❖ ❖ ❖

3 tablespoons butter
3 tablespoons all-purpose flour
Salt to taste
¼ teaspoon mace
3 cups milk (or more to thin soup)
3 chicken bouillon cubes

❖ ❖ ❖

Parsley

Break the cauliflower into small pieces, and add with water, onions, and celery to a large pot. Simmer until tender. Remove vegetables and purée, reserving the cooking water.

In a large saucepan, melt the butter, adding the flour to make a roux. Cook for 1 minute or so to thicken, add salt and mace. Gradually add the cooking water, milk, and bouillon cubes. (If you have enough chicken stock, you can use it in place of the water, then just use a small amount of bouillon for flavoring.) Keep stirring until the mixture thickens and comes to a boil. Stir in the vegetable purée and heat thoroughly.

At this point, you can add more milk if you want to thin the soup a little. Garnish with parsley when serving.

Note from the innkeeper: Even people who do not like cauliflower have loved this one!

Serves 6.

Cranberry Relish Gelatin Mold

Great with roast turkey and other poultry dishes.

1 8-ounce can crushed pineapple

❖ ❖ ❖

1 3-ounce package cherry-flavored
   gelatin
½ cup sugar
1 cup hot water
1 tablespoon lemon juice

❖ ❖ ❖

1 cup ground cranberries
1 unpeeled orange, seeded and
   ground
¾ cup chopped celery
½ cup chopped walnuts

Drain the pineapple, reserving the syrup. Add water to the syrup to equal ½ cup. Dissolve the gelatin and sugar in hot water. Add the reserved syrup and the lemon juice. Chill until partially set. Add the fruits, celery, and walnuts. Chill overnight in a 5-cup ring mold.

Serves 8.

Autumn Apple Cake with Warm Galliano Sauce

1 cup vegetable oil
3 eggs, beaten
½ cup sugar
1 cup brown sugar, firmly packed
2 cups chopped apples
2½ cups all-purpose flour
1 tablespoon baking powder
1 teaspoon cinnamon
1 teaspoon nutmeg

½ teaspoon salt
1 teaspoon vanilla extract

❖ ❖ ❖

1¾ cups sugar
1 cup whipping cream
1 cup butter (2 sticks)
⅓ cup Galliano liqueur

Combine the oil and eggs, add the sugar, brown sugar, and apples, beat well. Beat in the flour, baking powder, cinnamon, nutmeg, and salt. Beat in the vanilla last. Pour into a greased 12-cup bundt pan or a 10-inch tube pan. Bake in a 350° oven for 45 minutes or until the cake tests done.

Make Galliano sauce by boiling together the sugar, whipping cream, and butter for about 4 minutes. Add the Galliano liqueur and simmer for 1 minute.

Cool the cake for 10 minutes, then cut and serve with warm Galliano sauce over the slices.

Makes 12 servings.

The Inn at Jackson

Main Street at Thorn Hill Road
Post Office Box H
Jackson, New Hampshire 03846
(603) 383-4321

Guests of The Inn at Jackson discover a six-room country mansion with a comfortable and relaxed atmosphere. Designed by Stanford White as a private home at the turn of the century, it now offers its guests beautiful views of the surrounding mountains. Varied activities such as cross country skiing and golf are popular. Many other family activities are available in the surrounding valley.

Patterson McMuffins

3 egg yolks, room temperature
3 tablespoons water
1 cup hot clarified butter
Lemon juice to taste
Salt to taste
Cayenne pepper to taste

❖ ❖ ❖

8 eggs
8 thin slices Canadian bacon
Butter
4 English muffins, halved and
**   toasted**

❖ ❖ ❖

Chopped parsley

Prepare a Hollandaise sauce by combining in a double boiler over simmering water the egg yolks and water and whip until frothy. Continue whipping until the egg mixture begins to thicken, then remove from the heat. Drizzle the hot butter into the egg mixture as you continue to whip. Add the lemon juice, salt, and pepper to taste.

Heat a skillet and prepare fried eggs and bacon in butter. Place toasted muffin halves on a plate, and layer each with a slice of Canadian bacon and a fried egg. Top with Hollandaise sauce and garnish with parsley.

Serves 4.

Cranberry-Blueberry Bread

4 cups all-purpose flour
1 cup sugar
2½ tablespoons baking powder
1 teaspoon salt

❖ ❖ ❖

1½ cups orange juice
6 tablespoons butter, melted
4 eggs, slightly beaten

❖ ❖ ❖

2 cups cranberries
1 cup blueberries
1 cup chopped walnuts
¼ cup grated orange rind

Sift the dry ingredients into a mixing bowl and make a well in the center.

The Inn at Jackson

Add the orange juice, butter, and eggs. Mix slightly, being careful not to overmix. Fold in the cranberries, blueberries, walnuts, and orange rind. Pour the batter into 2 greased loaf pans and bake in a 350° oven for 50 minutes or until done. Cool loaves on a rack.

Makes 2 loaves.

Chicken Hash
with Asparagus and Tomatoes and Bacon

1½ medium onions, diced
2 to 3 tablespoons bacon fat
3 cooked chicken breasts, diced
3 potatoes, parboiled and diced
6 to 8 strips fried bacon, crumbled
8 cooked asparagus stalks,
**   chopped**
4 tomatoes, diced
Salt, pepper, and garlic to taste

❖ ❖ ❖

Poached eggs (optional)

In a large fry pan cook the onions in bacon fat until translucent. Stir in the chicken and potatoes and continue cooking over medium-high heat. Stir the mixture constantly, making sure it does not burn, but brown well. Then add the bacon, asparagus, and tomatoes, and season to taste. Allow the mixture to heat thoroughly, and serve, topped with poached eggs if desired.

Serves 8 to 10.

Nestlenook Inn Bed and Breakfast

Box Q, Dinsmore Road
Jackson Village, New Hampshire 03846
(603 383-9443)

The Nestlenook Inn is a 150-year-old farmhouse. Its seventeen rooms nestle on sixty-five secluded acres on the banks of the sparkling Ellis River. Most of the ten bedrooms have private baths, and all are furnished in keeping with the historical character of the home. In addition to the inn, Nestlenook has three cottages, and the manger has been recently converted into five airy bedrooms with shared baths. Following a restful sleep, guests enjoy a full country breakfast each morning, prepared by the hosts. Morning fare includes homemade breads, fresh-cut fruits, cheese, juice, freshly brewed coffee, eggs, and bacon, or the specialty of the inn, French toast with walnuts, raisins, and cinnamon. The Nestlenook offers a variety of activities that include horseback riding, sleigh rides, and a ski touring center.

Nestlenook Inn's Beer Bread

3 cups all-purpose flour (or self-rising)
3 teaspoons baking powder (omit if self-rising flour is used)
1 cup sugar
1 teaspoon salt
1 12-ounce can beer (any brand, the cheaper the better!)

Combine all dry ingredients and add the beer. Stir until moist, adding a little water if necessary. Bake in a greased loaf pan in a 400° oven for 1 hour. Remove from pan and knock the bottom of the loaf—if it sounds hollow, it is done.

Serve hot or cold with pumpkin butter or fresh preserves (like Nestlenook's). Makes great toast or sandwiches.
Makes 1 loaf.

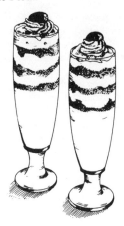

The Country Inn on Jefferson Hill

Route 2
Jefferson, New Hampshire 03583
(603) 586-7998

The Country Inn on Jefferson Hill is a charming Victorian home built in 1896. Sitting in the middle of the White Mountain National Forest, the inn is an ideal location for hikers and all those who appreciate the outdoors. Places to swim and skate are directly across the street, while golf is nearby. Mountain views abound, and there are acres of fields in which to relax. The name will soon be changed to The Jefferson Inn.

Baked Pancake

2 eggs, beaten
½ ounce nonfat dry milk
2 tablespoons water
2 tablespoons margarine, melted
1 tablespoon all-purpose flour
¼ teaspoon vanilla extract
1 tablespoon lemon juice (optional)

Mix the ingredients and beat until smooth. Pour into a preheated non-stick frying pan with an ovenproof handle. Bake in a 425° oven for 15 minutes. Sprinkle with lemon juice or jam.
Serves 1 to 2.

Pumpkin Bread

3½ cups all-purpose flour
3 cups sugar
2 teaspoons baking soda
1½ teaspoons salt
1 teaspoon nutmeg
2 teaspoons cinnamon
2 teaspoons allspice

1 cup oil
1 16-ounce can pumpkin
⅔ cup water
4 eggs
1 cup raisins

Mix together. Bake in greased loaf pans in a 350° oven for 1 hour.
Makes 2 loaves.

Cranberry Bread

1 cup sugar
2 tablespoons butter
1 egg
2 cups all-purpose flour
½ teaspoon baking soda
1 teaspoon baking powder
½ teaspoon salt
¾ cup orange juice
1 cup chopped cranberries
½ cup chopped nuts

Cream together the sugar, butter, and egg. Add the remaining ingredients, mix well and pour into a greased loaf pan. Bake in a 350° oven for 50 minutes.
Makes 1 loaf.

Anadama Bread

2 cups water
1 teaspoon salt
½ cup cornmeal
2 tablespoons shortening
½ cup warm water
2 ¼-ounce packages active yeast
1 teaspoon sugar
½ cup molasses
6 to 8 cups all-purpose flour

Combine the water, salt, cornmeal, and shortening and cook until thick; cool. Add the remaining ingredients and mix together; knead and let rise. Punch down and form into 2 loaves. Let rise again until doubled. Bake in a 375° oven for 40 to 50 minutes.
Makes 2 loaves.

Edencroft Manor

RFD No. 1, Route 135
Littleton, New Hampshire 03561
(603) 444-6776

Edencraft Manor

The Edencroft is a charming country inn with comfortable lodging, good food, and friendly hospitality. Six guest rooms, one with a fireplace, provide guests with firm beds and freedom from television. Most rooms have private baths. Beside the fireplace in the common room or in the full-service lounge overlooking the White Mountains one can meet other guests, browse through the selection of books and magazines, or play games. A soundproof children's corner is a plus. Trails for hiking, cross country skiing, or snowmobiling leave from the inn. Canoeing, swimming, or fishing are just two miles away at Moor Lake and major ski areas are fifteen minutes distant.

Kiwi Chicken

2 fryer chickens
Flour
Salt and white pepper to taste
Oil
White wine
4 garlic cloves
4 kiwi fruit
Chopped parsley

Quarter the chicken and dredge in flour, salt, and pepper to taste. Sauté the chicken in hot oil until golden brown, then layer in a Dutch oven. Pour enough wine over the chicken to cover. Crush the garlic cloves with the flat part of a knife and place around the chicken. Peel and slice kiwi and arrange around the chicken. Cover and bake in a 350° oven for 1 hour or until chicken is tender. Sprinkle with chopped parsley and serve from the Dutch oven, spooning the juice over the chicken.

Note: Do not be afraid of the garlic because the long cooking time removes the sharpness and gives the chicken a richer flavor. Also the cooking time and temperatures reflect cooking at a high altitude. Adjustments may be needed.

Serves 6 to 8.

Peanut Butter Torte

2¼ cups all-purpose flour
1¾ cups sugar
¾ cup butter (1½ sticks)
¾ cup milk
4 1-ounce packages unsweetened chocolate, melted
1½ teaspoons baking soda
1 teaspoon salt
¾ cup milk
3 eggs
1¼ teaspoons baking powder
1 teaspoon vanilla extract

❖   ❖   ❖

¾ cup peanut butter
2 cups whipped cream (or buttercream)

Sift the flour into a large bowl. Add the sugar and butter. Add ¾ cup milk, chocolate, soda, and salt. Beat with an electric mixer for 2 minutes. Add ¾ cup milk, eggs, baking powder, and vanilla. Beat for 2 more minutes. Pour into 3 greased 9-inch round cake pans.

Bake in a 350° oven for 30 minutes or until done. Allow to cool completely.

Beat the peanut butter until soft and creamy. Add the whipped cream (or buttercream), beating until stiff. Fill and frost cakes. Chill before serving. Serves 12.

The Lyme Inn

Lyme, New Hampshire 03768
(603) 795-2222
(603) 795-4404

At the Lyme Inn one finds such typical New England accouterments as poster beds, hooked rugs, hand-stitched quilts, wide pine floorboards, and a picket to close up the tavern. Stenciled wallpaper, wingback chairs, wicker furniture on the large screened porch, Currier & Ives samplers, and ten fireplaces add to the charm of this bed and breakfast establishment that was built in 1809. Leisurely meals are cooked to order; convenience foods are not to be found at the Lyme Inn. A complimentary breakfast is included in the room rates. The Tavern, small and intimate, features hot spirits in the winter and tall, cool libations in the summer.

The Lyme Inn

Indian Pudding

2 eggs, beaten
1 cup cornmeal
½ cup all-purpose flour
½ cup molasses
1 teaspoon salt
½ teaspoon ginger
½ teaspoon cinnamon

❖ ❖ ❖

2 quarts milk, scalded

On the top of the stove, combine all the ingredients but the milk in a saucepan and beat thoroughly. Slowly add the milk, stirring constantly until the mixture thickens. Pour into a well-greased baking dish and bake in a 350° oven for 30 minutes. Delicious served warm with ice cream or whipped cream. This also keeps well in the refrigerator and can easily be heated in a double boiler.

Serves 8.

Peep-Willow Farm

Noel Aderer
Bixby Street
Marlborough, New Hampshire 03455
(603) 876-3807

Peep-Willow Farm is a Thoroughbred horse farm that also caters to humans. Guests are invited to "help out" around the farm that contains twenty acres in the Marlborough hills, but riding is not permitted. Breakfast "New Hampshire" style is included.

Crab Bisque

1⅓ quarts light cream
1⅓ quarts half and half
¼ cup Sherry
¼ cup brandy
1 teaspoon white pepper
¼ pound lobster base

❖ ❖ ❖

1 small Spanish onion, finely chopped
¾ cup butter (1½ sticks)
2 stalks celery, finely chopped
1¾ cups all-purpose flour

❖ ❖ ❖

1¼ pounds crab meat
1 tablespoon butter
2 teaspoons white wine

Combine the light cream, half and half, Sherry, brandy, and white pepper in a large stock pot; heat. Once heated, add the lobster base, stirring very carefully.

Sauté the onions in a large skillet with the butter. Lightly brown the celery in the butter. Add the flour to make a stiff roux. (It should leave the sides of the pan when stirred.) Cook on top of the burner, stirring and lightly browning to cook out the flour taste.

Sauté the crab meat in a pan with 1 tablespoon of butter and the white wine, until very hot (180 degrees). Slowly thicken the soup with the roux, adding the crab meat when the soup is thick. Allow the soup to simmer 15 to 20 minutes after all the ingredients have been added, stirring constantly.

Serves 8 to 12.

Eclair Cake

Graham crackers (a little more than a 1-pound box)
2 3-ounce packages instant vanilla pudding
3½ cups milk
1 8- to 9-ounce container dairy whipped topping

❖ ❖ ❖

2 1-ounce squares unsweetened chocolate, melted
2 teaspoons light corn syrup
2 teaspoons vanilla extract
3 tablespoons butter or margarine, softened
1½ cups confectioners' sugar
3 tablespoons milk

Butter the bottom of a 9-inch pan and line with 2 layers of crackers. Prepare the pudding with the milk. Mix at medium speed for 2 minutes. Mix in the whipped topping. Pour ½ of the pudding mixture over the graham crackers. Cover with a single layer of crackers. Cover with the remaining pudding mixture, then another layer of crackers. Refrigerate for 2 hours, then frost with Eclair Icing.

Combine the remaining ingredients and beat until smooth. Spread on the cake and refrigerate for 24 hours.

Serves 6.

Coffee Butter Crunch Pie

½ package pie crust mix
1 1-ounce square unsweetened chocolate
¼ cup light brown sugar, firmly packed
¾ cup finely chopped walnuts
1 teaspoon vanilla extract
1 tablespoon water

❖ ❖ ❖

1 1-ounce square unsweetened chocolate
½ cup butter (1 stick)
¾ cup light brown sugar, firmly packed
2 teaspoons instant coffee powder
2 eggs

❖ ❖ ❖

2 cups heavy cream
2 tablespoons instant coffee powder
½ cup confectioners' sugar
Coarsely grated or shaved chocolate (optional)

Place the pie crust mix in a mixing bowl. Grind the chocolate in a nut grinder, or chop it coarsely and then grind it in a food processor or blender. Stir the ground chocolate into the pie crust mix. Stir in the sugar and walnuts. Mix in the vanilla and water; gradually drizzle the mixture over the pie crust mixture (do not pour it all in one place) while using a fork to stir and toss. The mixture will be lumpy and crumbly. Stir it very briefly, but do not try to make it smooth; it will hold together when pressed into place.

Adjust the rack to the center of the oven. Use a 9-inch ovenproof glass pie plate lined with aluminum foil. Bake the crust in a 375° oven for 15 minutes. Meanwhile, prepare the filling.

Melt the chocolate over hot water and set it aside to cool. In the small bowl of an electric mixer cream the butter. Add the sugar and beat at medium high speed for 2 to 3 minutes. Mix in the cooled melted chocolate and the instant coffee. Add the eggs one at a time, beating for 5 minutes after each addition, and scraping the bowl occasionally with a rubber spatula. Pour the filling into the cooled baked crust. Refrigerate for 5 or 6 hours, or overnight. The pie may be frozen now or it may be refrigerated for a day or two. If you freeze it, freeze until the filling is firm and then wrap airtight. To thaw the frozen pie, unwrap and let stand overnight in the refrigerator. Either just before serving or a few hours before, prepare the whipped cream topping.

In a chilled bowl with chilled beaters, whip the cream with the instant coffee and sugar until the cream holds a definite shape. Do not overbeat; it must be firm enough to hold its shape when the pie is served, but is more delicious if it is slightly creamy, rather than stiff. Spread the whipped cream smoothly over the filling, or apply it in fancy swirls, using a pastry bag fitted with a large star-shaped tube. Sprinkle the top with the grated or shaved chocolate if desired. Refrigerate until ready to serve.

Serves 6 to 8.

The Inn at Coit Mountain

HCR 63, Box 3
Newport, New Hampshire 03773
(603) 863-3583
1-800-367-2364

Nature's four seasons provide the backdrop to this gracious and historic Georgian home. Whether guests prefer the greening spring, languid summer afternoons, colorful autumn foliage, or winter-white mornings, they will delight in a stay at this inn. The library, with its oak paneling and massive granite fireplace, offers year-round charm and warmth, a good book, needlework, or a puzzle. Morning comes alive with the smell of freshly baked breads for the country breakfast before a corner fireplace. Dinners are available *by prior arrangements*. The bedrooms are spacious and comfortable, and some have fireplaces. A luxury suite with two rooms, bath, and king-sized bed is also available. The Lake Sunapee area provides a variety of recreation, including cross-country and alpine skiing in winter.

Sherried Creamed Eggs and Mushrooms on Toast

1½ pounds fresh mushrooms, sliced
2 tablespoons butter
Garlic salt to taste

❖ ❖ ❖

6 tablespoons butter
6 tablespoons all-purpose flour
2½ cups cream
½ teaspoon nutmeg
Dash hot sauce
Salt and pepper to taste
¾ cup Sherry

❖ ❖ ❖

8 hard-boiled eggs, sliced
Toast

Sauté the mushrooms in 2 tablespoons butter, add garlic salt and set aside.

In a medium saucepan melt 6 tablespoons butter, stir in the flour, then the cream, seasonings, and Sherry. Simmer until thickened, stirring occasionally to keep the sauce smooth.

Fold the eggs and mushrooms into the sauce and serve over the toast. Delightful!

Serves 8 to 10.

Lemon Pancakes
with Lemon Syrup

2 cups baking mix
2 cups milk
1 egg
Juice and grated rind of 2 lemons

❖   ❖   ❖

3 cups water
2 cups sugar
1 cup lemon juice
Grated rind of 1 lemon

Beat together the baking mix, milk, egg, and the juice and grated rinds of 2 lemons. Spoon by small amounts into a hot buttered skillet. (It is preferable to have the pancakes thin and small— silver dollar size.) The pancakes are ready to turn when the batter becomes bubbly and browns around the edges.

Make lemon syrup in a saucepan by combining the water, sugar, 1 cup of lemon juice, and grated rind of 1 lemon. Simmer for 5 to 10 minutes.

Serves 6.

Fresh Fruit with Brandied Cream

Fruit

❖   ❖   ❖

2 cups heavy cream
2 tablespoons confectioners' sugar
½ teaspoon vanilla extract

❖   ❖   ❖

5 tablespoons brandy

Wash and cut up any fresh fruit of the season. Whip heavy cream, confectioners' sugar and vanilla until thick but still runny, and add brandy. Pour over fruit.

Minted Fruit Bowl

Fresh fruits (melons, peaches, berries are best)

❖   ❖   ❖

1 tablespoon minced fresh or dried mint
¼ cup white crème de menthe

Cut up the fresh fruits and add mint and crème de menthe. Chill and serve.

The 1785 Inn

Post Office Box 9
North Conway, New Hampshire 03860
(603) 356-9025

At The 1785 Inn guests can dine, spend a relaxing evening, or enjoy a whole vacation. In this charming inn with a romantic colonial atmosphere, guests experience some of the best dining and one of the finest wine lists in America. For overnight guests there are fourteen individually decorated rooms, two guest living rooms with original fireplaces, a comfortable lounge furnished in Victorian antiques, and over four acres of beautiful property with several outdoor activities for all ages. Each room has its own unique character, and each is individually color-coordinated and furnished with its own comfortable country furniture. From The 1785 Inn guests can easily explore Mt. Washington Valley, relax in front of a fireplace, or enjoy the spectacular views.

Shrimp Capri with Avocados

1 hot pepper (preferably cayenne)
¼ cup clarified butter
Pinch garlic
5 jumbo shrimps
¼ cup white wine
2 tablespoons tamarind
2 tablespoons lemon juice

❖   ❖   ❖

3 black olives, sliced
5 cherry tomatoes, halved
½ avocado, sliced

Heat the pepper in clarified butter until the butter sizzles. Remove the pepper, and add the garlic and shrimps. Turn shrimps and add the wine, tamarind, and lemon juice. Cook until the shrimp reach the desired level of doneness. Add the olives, tomatoes, and avocado. Remove from the heat and serve.

Serves 1.

Blackberry Sorbet

2 pounds blackberries
1½ cups sugar
½ cup lemon juice
½ cup water
½ cup crème de cassis
5 eggs, well beaten

The 1785 Inn

Purée the berries and strain to remove seeds. Stir in the sugar, lemon juice, water, crème de cassis, and eggs. Place the mixture in the freezer. When it starts to freeze and has a 1-inch frozen ring around the edge, stir vigorously with a wooden spoon. Repeat stirring at the 1-inch phase at least 4 times. Cover and freeze until solid. Mix 1 last time, approximately 1 hour before serving.

Serves 14.

The Stonehurst Manor

Post Office Box 1900
North Conway, New Hampshire 03860
(603) 356-3271
1-800-525-9100 (New England except
 New Hampshire)

The Stonehurst Manor invites guests to experience the luxury of a vacation in a turn-of-the-century mansion. Set back from the highway on thirty-three acres of beautiful pine forest, it offers a country vacation that is truly magical. From the huge front door to the richness of old oak, stained glass, and deep carpeting in the library lounge, guests are surrounded by the grace and beauty of another era. Guests may savor gourmet cooking in the three dining rooms each evening. The large swimming pool, shuffleboard, tennis court, and color cable television are available to guests. The many attractions and activities of the Mt. Washington Valley area are nearby.

Corn Meal and Bacon Pancakes

2 strips bacon

❖ ❖ ❖

⅓ cup yellow corn meal
1 cup all-purpose flour
1 teaspoon salt
2 teaspoons baking powder

❖ ❖ ❖

1 egg
1¼ cups milk
1 tablespoon bacon fat

❖ ❖ ❖

Butter
Maple syrup

Fry bacon crisp and crumble, reserving 1 tablespoon of fat. Mix together the dry ingredients. In a small mixing bowl, combine the egg, milk, and bacon fat. Stir this mixture slowly into the dry ingredients, mixing well. The batter should be fairly thin (add more milk if necessary). Mix in the bacon. Cook the pancakes in a greased skillet or on a griddle, and serve with butter and maple syrup.

Serves 4.

Manor Pâté

This pâté is served with cornichons, which are tiny pickles shaped like the horns of an animal.

1½ pounds veal
1½ pounds pork
1 pound fresh unsalted pork fat,
** cubed**
¾ pound pork liver
4 eggs

3 tablespoons salt
1 tablespoon thyme
1 teaspoon black pepper
1½ teaspoons allspice
½ teaspoon powdered bay leaf
4 cloves garlic, minced
1 cup minced onions, sautéed in
** butter**
⅓ cup Madeira
½ cup Cognac
¼ cup unsalted, roasted, chopped
** pistachios**

❖ ❖ ❖

Additional pork fat for lining the
** mold**

❖ ❖ ❖

Cornichons

With a meat grinder, grind the veal, pork, and pork fat twice and place in a mixing bowl. Grind the pork liver twice and add to the pork and veal mixture. Add remaining ingredients (except additional pork fat). Beat until the mixture is well mixed (an electric mixer with a paddle is helpful).

Line a glass or earthenware terrine or loaf pan with thin slices of the fresh pork fat. Fill the mold with the pâté mixture and pack it into place, covering the top with additional slices of pork fat. Cover the mold with a lid or aluminum foil and place in a pan of hot water. Bake in a 350° oven for approximately 1½ hours or until the juices run clear when the pâté is punctured with a skewer.

Remove from the oven, but leave the

Stonehurst Manor

pâté in the water bath. Remove the top or foil and place a flat weight of approximately 3 pounds on the pâté. Let it cool to room temperature, then remove from the water bath and refrigerate overnight, with the weight still in place.

To serve, dip the chilled mold into a pan of hot water and unmold the pâté. Remove the excess fat from the outside and slice thinly. Serve with cornichons.

Serves 16.

Cream of Parsnip and Celery Knob Soup
with Smoked Gouda Cheese

Celery knob, also called celery root, tastes like celery and is related to the stalk celery family. It does, however, have a bit more flavor and a totally different texture. It is shaped like a turnip and should be peeled and washed before using.

¼ cup butter (½ stick)
1 medium onion, diced

❖   ❖   ❖

1 leek, white part only, thinly
   sliced
2 tablespoons all-purpose flour
1 pound parsnips, peeled and diced
1½ pounds celery knob, peeled and
   diced
5 cups chicken stock
1 teaspoon salt
½ teaspoon white pepper

❖   ❖   ❖

1½ cups heavy cream

❖   ❖   ❖

1 cup shredded smoked Gouda
   cheese

In a large saucepan, melt the butter and sauté the onions and leeks until they are soft but not brown. Stir in the flour and cook the mixture for 3 to 4 minutes. Add the parsnips, celery knob, chicken stock, salt, and pepper. Bring to a simmer and cook for 1 hour

or until the vegetables are very tender. Purée the soup in batches in a blender or food processor. Place the puréed soup in a clean pot, add the cream and return to a simmer. Correct the seasoning if needed. Ladle into bowls and top each portion with a mound of cheese.

Serves 10.

Trout with Pistachios

4 brook trout

❖   ❖   ❖

½ cup all-purpose flour
½ teaspoon salt
¼ teaspoon white pepper

❖   ❖   ❖

2 eggs
2 teaspoons water

❖   ❖   ❖

½ cup fresh bread crumbs

❖   ❖   ❖

1 tablespoon butter

❖   ❖   ❖

½ cup unsalted butter (1 stick)
½ cup chopped, unsalted, roasted
   pistachios

❖   ❖   ❖

2 tablespoons chopped parsley

To prepare the trout cut off the heads and butterfly them (slit open to the tail and remove the backbone and ribcage, which you can have done at the fish market if you like). Mix together the flour, salt, and pepper. In a separate bowl, beat the eggs with the water. Dip only the meat side of the trout into the flour mixture, then the eggs, and finally the bread crumbs. In a large frying pan heat enough oil to cover the bottom to a depth of ⅛ to ¼ inch. When hot, add the butter. As soon as the butter melts, place the trout in the pan, breaded side down (they may have to be cooked in two batches). When the breaded side is nicely browned, turn the fish and cook on the other side for 2 to 3 minutes or until a skewer can pass through the flesh with no resistance. Keep the cooked fish in a warm oven while you

cook the rest. Heat a smaller frying pan (approximately 8 inches). Add the ½ cup butter to the pan and when it foams, add the chopped pistachios. Sauté 1 minute. Arrange the trout on plates, spoon the pistachios over the fish, and sprinkle with the parsley.

Serves 8.

Veal Ribs
with Red Wine and Basil

4 14-ounce veal ribs with bone
Salt and pepper
½ cup all-purpose flour
6 tablespoons butter

❖   ❖   ❖

¾ cup red wine
1 cup rich brown veal stock
½ teaspoon dry mustard
Pinch salt and pepper

❖   ❖   ❖

½ cup unsalted butter, softened
5 tablespoons minced fresh basil
3 cloves garlic, minced

Trim the fat off the last 2 inches of the bone on the veal ribs, and push the remaining meat up toward the eye of the rib, resulting in 3 to 4 inches of exposed bone. Combine the salt and pepper with the flour; dredge the ribs. Clarify the 6 tablespoons of butter in a large heavy frying pan. Sauté the ribs over medium heat, browning on both sides. Then place the ribs in a baking dish, insert a meat thermometer in one of the ribs, and roast in a 375° oven until the thermometer reads 135°.

While the ribs are roasting make the sauce in the same frying pan used to brown the ribs. Pour out any remaining butter, then heat the pan and deglaze by adding the wine, allowing the wine to cook until reduced by half. Add the veal stock, mustard, salt and pepper; reduce until the sauce is thick and coats a spoon.

While the sauce is thickening, combine ½ cup of butter with the basil and garlic, mixing well. When the sauce has reached the desired thickness remove the pan from the heat and slowly add the basil-butter mixture in small amounts, beating well after each addition. When all of the butter mixture has been added, taste and adjust the seasonings if needed. If the sauce is very thick, then thin it slightly with warm water. Pour the sauce over the ribs and serve.

Serves 4.

Breast of Duck
With Pomegranate and Ginger

The pomegranate concentrate used in the recipe is available at Middle-Eastern and specialty food stores.

**4 10 to 12-ounce duck breasts,
    skinned and boned
¼ cup butter (½ stick)
Salt and pepper
2 teaspoons minced fresh ginger
    root
½ cup brandy
1 cup cream
3 tablespoons pomegranate
    concentrate
½ teaspoon dry mustard
Salt and pepper to taste**

❖ ❖ ❖

Watercress sprigs

Separate each duck breast into two pieces by removing the center strip of cartilage, just as you would a chicken breast. Heat the butter in a large sauté pan. Season the breast with salt and pepper. When the butter foams and then subsides, add the breasts to the pan. Cook for 3 to 4 minutes per side. They will still be quite pink inside. Carefully remove the breasts from the pan, reserving the butter. (Keep the breasts warm while the sauce is made.) Add the ginger to the butter, sauté briefly. Deglaze the pan with the brandy. Reduce the ginger and brandy mixture to about 2 tablespoons. Add the cream, pomegranate concentrate, and dry mustard. Reduce this mixture by ½, season to taste with salt and pepper.

To serve, slice the duck breasts across the grain at a 45° angle from the cutting board (in order to get a broader slice). Divide the sauce between four plates covering the surface evenly. Lay the duck breast slices on top of the sauce, overlapping them slightly to form two lines on each plate. Garnish with watercress sprigs.

Serves 4.

Brussels Sprouts
with Pear and Mustard Sauce

2 pints brussels sprouts

❖ ❖ ❖

**1 ripe Comice pear, peeled and
    sliced
½ cup unsalted butter (1 stick)
2 teaspoons Dijon mustard
Salt and freshly ground pepper**

Trim the brussels sprouts of outside leaves and stems. Cut an X in the stem end. Rinse in cold water, then cook in boiling salted water for 10 minutes or until just tender.

While the brussels sprouts are cooking, gently sauté the pear slices in 4 tablespoons of butter until heated through. Stir in the mustard and add the remaining 4 tablespoons of butter. When the brussels sprouts are cooked, toss them with the pear and mustard sauce. Season to taste with salt and pepper.

Serves 6.

Apple and Cheddar Cheese Crisp

**6 cups pared sliced apples
1 teaspoon cinnamon
1 tablespoon lemon juice
½ cup corn syrup
½ cup sugar
⅔ cup all-purpose flour
¼ teaspoon salt
⅓ cup butter
1 cup grated Cheddar cheese**

Arrange the apples in a greased 10x6x2-inch baking dish. Sprinkle them with cinnamon and pour the lemon juice and corn syrup over them. Combine the sugar, flour, and salt. Cut in butter until the mixture is the consistency of cornmeal. Gently mix in the cheese. Sprinkle this mixture over the apples. Bake in a 350° oven for 1 hour or until the apples are tender.

Serves 4 to 6.

Follansbee Inn

Post Office Box 92
North Sutton, New Hampshire 03260
(603) 927-4221

The Follansbee Inn is an authentic 19th century New England farmhouse with a porch, comfortable meeting room, and twenty-three quaint bedrooms. The inn is on the shore of peaceful Kazar Lake with a private pier for swimming, fishing, and boating, as well as cross country skiing right from the front door. Downhill skiing is only minutes away. A full country breakfast comes with the price of the room. Since this is a completely No Smoking inn, guests enjoy clean New Hampshire air inside and out.

Ethiopian Honey Bread
(Yemarina Yewotet Dabo)

**1 ¼-ounce package active dry yeast
¼ cup warm water (110° to 115°)**

❖ ❖ ❖

**1 egg
½ cup honey
1 tablespoon coriander
½ teaspoon cinnamon
¼ teaspoon cloves
1 teaspoon salt**

❖ ❖ ❖

**1 cup scalded milk
¼ cup melted butter
4 to 5 cups all-purpose flour**

Dissolve the yeast in the water. In a separate bowl combine the egg, honey, coriander, cinnamon, cloves, and salt; mix well. Add the yeast, milk, and butter. Beat in 1½ cups of flour, then gradually add the remaining flour. Let rise 1 hour or until doubled. Punch down; knead 1 or 2 minutes. Shape and place in a buttered loaf pan. Let rise for 1 hour. Bake in a 300° oven for 50 to 60 minutes.

Makes 1 large loaf.

Chicken Supreme

¾ cup honey
¾ cup dry Sherry
1½ cups chopped walnuts

❖ ❖ ❖

4 8-ounce boneless chicken breasts
Garlic powder
Leaf oregano
12 ounces extra sharp Cheddar cheese (cut into 8 thick slices)

❖ ❖ ❖

1 seedless orange (cut into twists)

Mix the honey and Sherry until well blended, add walnuts; set aside. Spread out the breasts and sprinkle with the garlic powder and oregano. Wrap each breast around 1½ ounces of thickly sliced cheddar and place each in a casserole dish unseasoned side up. Sprinkle again with garlic and oregano and top with 1½ ounces of cheese. Bake in a 350° oven for approximately 30 minutes until the breasts are cooked thoroughly. Remove from the oven and top each dish with 3 ounces of honey mixture. Return to the oven and heat for another 2 to 4 minutes. Top each with an orange twist.

Serves 4.

Bread Pudding

24 1-inch slices stale French bread
½ cup butter (1 stick), softened

❖ ❖ ❖

½ cup raisins

❖ ❖ ❖

6 eggs
1½ cups sugar
1 tablespoon vanilla extract
2 tablespoons cinnamon
1 teaspoon salt
4 cups milk, scalded

❖ ❖ ❖

½ cup dark brown sugar, firmly packed
¼ cup water
3 tablespoons dark rum, bourbon or liqueur
½ cup butter (1 stick), softened

Spread one side of each bread slice with softened butter. On a large baking sheet, place the bread slices in a single layer, buttered side up. Toast in the oven for 8 to 10 minutes or until brown; remove from the oven and place the bread slices in a shallow 2-quart baking dish. Scatter raisins over the top; set aside.

In a large bowl with a wire whisk, beat the eggs, sugar, vanilla, cinnamon and salt. Gradually add the scalded milk, whisking until thoroughly combined. Pour over the toasted bread. Press the bread slices down into the egg-milk mixture. Let stand for 2 hours, pressing bread slices into the egg-milk mixture occasionally. Place the casserole in a larger pan and place on the oven shelf. Pour boiling water into the larger pan, halfway up the sides of the casserole. Bake in a 350° oven for 1 hour or until the top of the pudding is golden brown. Remove the casserole from the water bath to a wire rack.

To prepare the sauce, in small saucepan combine the brown sugar, water and rum. Bring slowly to boiling. With a wire whisk, beat in ½ cup of butter until melted. Pour some sauce over the pudding. Serve the remaining sauce at the table. Serve warm.

Serves 8 to 10.

Chocolate Pecan Pie

"Tastes great with a dollop of freshly whipped cream."

1½ cups coarsely chopped pecans
1 6-ounce package semi-sweet chocolate chips
1 8-inch pie shell, partially baked

❖ ❖ ❖

½ cup light corn syrup
½ cup sugar
2 extra large eggs
¼ cup butter (½ stick), melted

Sprinkle the pecans and chocolate chips in the pie shell. In a medium mixing bowl blend together the corn syrup, sugar, and eggs. Mix in the melted butter. Pour the mixture slowly and evenly into the pie shell. Bake in a 325° oven for about 1 hour until firm.

Serves 6.

The Hilltop Inn

Main Street, Route 117
Sugar Hill, New Hampshire 03585
(603) 823-5695

The Hilltop Inn is an old Victorian home close to all the area attractions: alpine and nordic skiing, swimming, canoeing, fishing, biking, hiking, horseback riding, wind surfing, glider rides, Cannon Mountain, the Tram-Way, the Old Man of the Mountain, and the flume. After a day in Franconia Notch, guests can escape up to Sugar Hill, where they can enjoy New Hampshire's scenery and slow pace. The sunsets from the inn's kitchen window are spectacular. In the morning breakfast is cooked in the kitchen, which is the heart of the home. The Hilltop Inn is on Route 117 between Franconia and Lisbon.

German Apple Pancakes

10 eggs
1 cup all-purpose flour
2 tablespoons honey or sugar
1 teaspoon baking powder
1/8 teaspoon salt
2 cups milk
1/4 cup butter (1/2 stick), melted
2 teaspoons vanilla extract
1/4 teaspoon cinnamon
1/4 teaspoon grated nutmeg

❖ ❖ ❖

1 1/2 cups sugar
1 teaspoon cinnamon
1/2 cup unsalted butter (1 stick)
1/4 teaspoon grated nutmeg
2 to 3 Granny Smith apples, peeled and thinly sliced

Blend until smooth the eggs, flour, honey, baking powder, salt, and milk. Add the next 4 ingredients and blend well. Let the batter rest for at least 30 minutes at room temperature or overnight in the refrigerator.

Combine the sugar, cinnamon, and nutmeg. Use 2 ovenproof skillets. Divide the butter between them and melt, brushing the butter evenly over the bottom and sides of the pans. Remove from heat and sprinkle 1/2 cup of the sugar mixture over the butter in each pan. Layer the apple slices evenly in each and sprinkle with the remaining sugar mixture. Cook over medium heat until the mixture bubbles. Divide the batter and pour over the apples. Bake in a 425° oven for 15 minutes. Lower the heat to 350 degrees and bake 10 minutes more. Cut into wedges and serve alone or with heated maple syrup, or ice cream.
Serves 6.

Challah Bread
(French Toast with Sautéed Banana and Walnuts)

1 1/2 cups milk
1/2 cup sugar
3 teaspoons salt

The Hilltop Inn

1/3 cup butter
2 1/4-ounce packages active dry yeast
1/2 cup warm water
3 eggs, beaten
7 1/2 cups all-purpose flour
2 teaspoons poppy seeds (optional)

In a small saucepan combine the milk, sugar, salt, and butter. Heat slowly until the butter melts; cool to lukewarm. Sprinkle the yeast into warm water in a large bowl; stir until dissolved. Reserve 2 tablespoons of eggs. Add the milk mixture and the eggs. Gradually add the flour. Knead until smooth. Place in a greased bowl and let rise for 1 1/2 hours. Punch down and let rise for 1/2 hour. Punch down and divide into 2 parts. Divide each part into 3 pieces. Roll each piece and braid together. Let rise 1 hour. Brush the top with the remaining egg, sprinkle with poppy seeds and bake in a 350° oven for 30 minutes.

For French toast, slice thickly. Soak each slice on both sides in a mixture of beaten eggs, cream, and cinnamon. Sauté in unsalted butter until lightly brown on both sides. Serve with maple syrup and/or sliced bananas and walnuts which have been sautéed in a small amount of unsalted butter and cinnamon.
Makes 2 loaves.

Cheesy Broccoli-Sausage Delight

6 small baked pastry shells
1 pound brown sausage, crumbled
1 1/2 cups cooked chopped broccoli
6 eggs, scrambled
1/2 cup grated Cheddar cheese
1 cup prepared cheese soup
Parmesan cheese
Fresh chopped chives (optional)

Fill the pastry shells with a layer of each of sausage, broccoli, and eggs. Sprinkle the Cheddar cheese over each and bake in a 350° oven for 10 minutes. Prepare the cheese soup as directed on the can. Serve pastries with the cheese soup ladled over them and a garnish of Parmesan cheese. Chopped fresh chives add a nice touch of color and flavor sprinkled over the sauce.
Serves 6.

Apple-Raspberry Cheddar Crisp

2 cups unsalted butter (4 sticks), softened
2 tablespoons cinnamon
1 1/2 cups brown sugar, firmly packed
4 cups all-purpose flour
1 1/2 cups Cheddar cheese (optional)

❖ ❖ ❖

15 apples, peeled and quartered (or sliced)

3 cups raspberries (or strawberries
    or blueberries)
1 tablespoon cinnamon
2 tablespoons lemon juice

In a large mixing bowl mix together the butter, cinnamon, and sugar until well-blended. Gradually add the flour starting with 2 cups; add until the mixture is crumbly and dry to the touch. Add the Cheddar cheese if desired and mix well. Spread half of the crumbs in a large ungreased rectangular roasting pan. Combine the apples and raspberries; spread evenly over the bottom layer of crumbs. Sprinkle with cinnamon and lemon juice. Top with the remaining crumb mixture and bake in a 350° oven for 25 minutes.

Great served warm or cold, especially with fresh whipped cream or ice cream.

Serves 24.

The Birchwood Inn

Route 45
Temple, New Hampshire 03084
(603) 878-3285

While the Birchwood Inn was opened about 1775, the present brick structure was probably built circa 1800. The present barns were added in 1848, and the inn has remained in much the same form since that time. Two centuries have seen "the old hotel" entertain many overnight guests, Henry David Thoreau among them. In addition to the tavern, dining and guest room operations, the inn has housed the Temple Post Office, a small general store, the town meeting hall, and, most recently, an antique shop. One of the notable features of the inn is the dining room mural painted by the New England itinerant painter Rufus Porter. His works can also be found at Old Sturbridge Village in Massachusetts.

Fruited Bran Muffins

2 cups raisin and bran cereal
¾ cup milk
1 egg, beaten
¼ cup butter (½ stick), softened
1 apple, peeled and grated
1 orange, chopped
2 tablespoons grated orange peel
1 cup all-purpose flour
2½ teaspoons baking powder
½ teaspoon salt
1½ teaspoons cinnamon
6 tablespoons sugar

Combine in a large mixing bowl the cereal, milk, egg, and butter, mixing well. Add the fruits, peel, and dry ingredients. Mix evenly. Pour into greased muffin pans and bake in a 400° oven for 25 minutes. Enjoy for breakfast. These muffins are very popular at our inn.

Makes 12 muffins.

Cheddar Cheese Bread with Dill

2 cups all-purpose flour
2 teaspoons baking powder
1 tablespoon sugar
½ teaspoon salt
¼ cup margarine (½ stick)
1 cup grated Cheddar cheese
1½ teaspoons dillweed
1 egg
¾ cup milk

Sift into a large mixing bowl the flour, baking powder, sugar, and salt. Cut in the margarine until the mixture resembles coarse crumbs. Stir in the cheese and dillweed, mix well. Add the egg to the milk, pour into the dry ingredients, and stir quickly. Pour into a greased loaf pan and bake in a 350° oven for 40 minutes.

Note from the innkeeper: This is the most requested recipe of the non-sweet quick breads.

Makes 1 loaf.

Lemon Fried Chicken

2 chickens, cut up
1 cup flour
1½ tablespoons salt
Dash pepper
1 cup margarine (2 sticks)
    ❖ ❖ ❖
¾ pound fresh mushrooms, sliced
1 lemon, sliced paper thin
½ cup Sherry

Wash the pieces of chicken and pat dry. Combine the flour, salt, and pepper. Dredge the chicken in the mixture, coating well. Melt the margarine in a large fry pan. Brown the pieces of chicken on both sides; remove and place the pieces in a large casserole. To the remaining margarine in the fry pan add the mushrooms, lemon slices, and Sherry. Cook until thickened. Pour over the chicken and cover the casserole dish. Bake in a 325° oven for 1 hour.

Note from the innkeeper: This dish is served every Thursday night at our buffet and is a very popular dish indeed.

Serves 8.

Rum-Raisin Cheesecake Bars

⅓ cup butter or margarine,
    softened
⅓ cup brown sugar, firmly packed
1 cup all-purpose flour
½ cup chopped nuts
    ❖ ❖ ❖
1 8-ounce package cream cheese,
    softened
¼ cup sugar
1 egg
3 tablespoons rum
½ cup raisins

To make the crust cream together the butter and brown sugar, stir in the flour, and add the nuts. Press into an 8- or 9-inch square pan, reserving some of the crumbs to use as a topping. Bake in a 350° oven for 10 to 12 minutes. Cool.

With a mixer beat the cream cheese until fluffy. Add the sugar, egg, and rum, beat well. Then stir in the raisins. Spread the mixture over the cooked crust, then sprinkle with the remaining crumbs. Bake in a 350° oven for 20 to 25 minutes.

Makes 9 to 12 servings.

Blackberry Cream "Parfait"

20 large marshmallows
1½ cups juice of blackberries, cooked and strained
¼ cup crème de Cassis liqueur

❖ ❖ ❖

1 cup heavy cream, whipped

Place the marshmallows, juice, and liqueur into a double boiler and heat until marshmallows are melted. Remove from heat and cool completely. Chill whipped cream and fold gently into the chilled blackberry mixture. Serve in stem wine glasses or a "mousse" type glass.

Note: The innkeeper invented this light refreshing one!

Serves 7 to 8.

The Partridge Brook Inn

Hatt Road, Post Office Box 151
Westmoreland, New Hampshire 03467
(603) 399-4994

Once a tavern and then a station for the Underground Railroad, the Par-

tridge Brook Inn was built in 1790 by Captain Abiathar Shaw, a prosperous "nailmaker." The interior of the house bears many reminders of its past, from mortise-and-tenon doors and original fireplaces throughout to the unpainted wide boards in the dining room. Guests' rooms are spacious and comfortable (king, queen, and double-sized beds are available), and all have private baths. Those who take to the sporting life will find it right on the property. Trout fishing in Partridge Brook, nature walks, and blueberry picking are popular in spring and summer. In winter cross country skiing is just outside the door. Nearby Spofford Lake is ideal for swimming and boating and golf and tennis facilities are near.

Bran Date Muffins

1 cup boiling water
1 cup chopped dates
1 cup 100% bran cereal

❖ ❖ ❖

2 eggs, beaten
½ cup oil
1¼ cups sugar (or ¾ cup honey)
3 cups all-purpose flour
1½ tablespoons baking soda
Pinch salt
1 pint buttermilk
2 cups bran flake cereal (or raisin and bran cereal)
½ cup raisins (or chopped nuts)

Pour the boiling water over the dates and cereal. Set aside. In a large mixing bowl combine the eggs, oil, sugar, flour, soda, salt, and buttermilk. Add the date mixture, bran flake cereal, and raisins. Fill greased muffin cups ⅔ full. Bake in a 375° oven for 25 to 30 minutes.

Makes 2 dozen muffins.

Sunday Scramble

4 eggs
½ teaspoon salt
1 tablespoon mustard
8 cooked shrimps
½ piece matzo bread
1 teaspoon butter

Beat the eggs with a fork. Add the salt, mustard, and shrimps. Crumble the matzo and add to the mixture. Scramble in butter.

Serves 2.

Renee's French Toast Delight

1 8-ounce package cream cheese
½ cup chopped walnuts
1 teaspoon vanilla extract
12 slices firm white bread

❖ ❖ ❖

Partridge Brook Inn

4 eggs, beaten
¾ cup cream
1 teaspoon vanilla extract
Dash nutmeg
Butter

❖   ❖   ❖

1 12-ounce jar apricot jam
½ cup orange juice

❖   ❖   ❖

Sliced bananas

Combine the cream cheese, walnuts and vanilla. Spread on 6 slices of bread. Top with the remaining 6 slices of bread to form sandwiches.

Combine the eggs, cream, vanilla and nutmeg. Dip each sandwich into the mixture. Cook in butter in a skillet as for French toast.

Combine the jam and orange juice. Garnish the top of the diagonally cut toast with bananas. Serve apricot sauce over all.

Serves 4 to 6.

Hot Cider

6 cups apple cider
1 cinnamon stick

❖   ❖   ❖

¼ teaspoon nutmeg
¼ cup honey
3 tablespoons lemon juice
1 teaspoon grated lemon peel
1 18-ounce can unsweetened
    pineapple juice

In a large saucepan, heat the cider and cinnamon stick to boiling; reduce heat. Cover and simmer for 5 minutes. Uncover and add the remaining ingredients; simmer 5 minutes more.

Makes 16 servings of ½ cup each.

New England Shortbread Cookie

1 cup butter (2 sticks)
½ cup sugar
1 teaspoon vanilla extract
2 cups all-purpose flour
1 3½-ounce can coconut

½ cup slivered almonds (or finely
    chopped pecans)

❖   ❖   ❖

Confectioners' sugar

Combine in the order given. Form into rolls the size of half dollars. Wrap in waxed paper or foil and chill. Slice and bake in a 300° oven for 25 minutes until golden brown. Sprinkle with confectioners' sugar.

Makes 2 dozen cookies.

Stepping Stones

Bennington Battle Trail
Wilton Center, New Hampshire 03086
(603) 654-9048

This small bed and breakfast is in the picturebook village of Wilton Center, a quiet, rural retreat just sixty miles from downtown Boston. The gracious old house overlooks a sunny terrace and extensive gardens. Handwoven rugs and throws, down comforters, and fresh flowers brighten both bedrooms. The cozy living room offers good reading, stereo, and a warm fire; the solar breakfast room is bright with flowering plants and pottery. Throughout the house, handwoven fabrics contribute to the warm and friendly atmosphere. Included in the cost of the room is a home-cooked breakfast and afternoon tea. The cookie jar is always full of ginger cookies, a specialty; and a small refrigerator is available for guests' use.

Cinnamon Rolls

2 cups scalded milk
2 tablespoons sugar
¼ cup butter (½ stick)
1 teaspoon salt

❖   ❖   ❖

1 ¼-ounce package active dry yeast
2 eggs, beaten

5 to 5½ cups all-purpose flour

❖   ❖   ❖

Melted butter

❖   ❖   ❖

¾ cup brown sugar, firmly packed
1 tablespoon cinnamon
1 teaspoon nutmeg
Chopped nuts (optional)
Raisins (optional)

Combine the milk, sugar, butter, and salt. Cool until lukewarm. Add the yeast and eggs; beat well. Gradually add the flour and beat well. Place the dough in a bowl, cover with a damp cloth, and let rise until double. Turn out onto a floured board and roll into a thin rectangle. Brush with melted butter.

Combine the remaining ingredients and dust the dough. Roll up and slice into rolls. Place in 2 well-greased 9x13-inch pans. Bake in a 350° oven for 15 to 18 minutes.

Serves 16.

Chewy Ginger Cookies

2 cups sugar
1½ cups shortening (at least ½
    butter)
2 eggs
½ cup molasses

❖   ❖   ❖

1½ teaspoons ginger
2 teaspoons cinnamon
1½ teaspoons cloves
½ teaspoon nutmeg (preferably
    fresh grated)
½ teaspoon salt
3½ teaspoons baking soda
4½ to 5 cups unbleached flour

❖   ❖   ❖

Sugar

Cream together the sugar, shortening, eggs, and molasses until fluffy. Sift together dry ingredients and add to creamed mixture. Roll small (walnut-size) balls of dough in sugar, and bake on a cookie sheet in a 350° oven for approximately 10 minutes or until crinkled and brown.

Makes 3½ to 4 dozen cookies.

New Jersey

The Barnard-Good House

238 Perry Street
Cape May, New Jersey 08204
(609) 884-5381

Originally a fifteen-room summer cottage, this bed and breakfast was built in the French Second Empire architectural style with Mansard roof and a full veranda. The three-story home contains six guest rooms. An antique pump organ often serves as a catalyst for impromptu songfests. Complete gourmet breakfasts are served every morning.

Sweet Potato Pancakes

  1 9-ounce sweet potato, peeled
  1 small onion
      ❖ ❖ ❖
  2 eggs
  2 tablespoons all-purpose flour
  1/8 teaspoon cardamom
  Salt and freshly ground black
      pepper to taste
      ❖ ❖ ❖
  3 tablespoons oil

With a medium shredding disc in a food processor, shred the sweet potato and onion. Wrap in a towel and squeeze out the moisture. Transfer to a mixing bowl and stir to distribute the vegetables evenly. Insert a metal blade in the processor and process the eggs, flour, cardamom, salt, and pepper. Pulse about 3 times, scrape down and pulse again until smooth. Add to the sweet potato mixture and blend well. Heat the oil in a skillet over moderate heat and drop the batter mixture in by tablespoons. Cook the pancakes in oil about 1 minute on each side or until lightly browned.

Serves 6.

Plum Soup

  1¾ pounds plums, pitted and
      coarsely chopped
  1 cup dry white wine
  1 cup fresh orange juice
  ½ cup sugar
  1 to 1½ pieces cinnamon stick
  4 whole cloves
      ❖ ❖ ❖
  Sour cream

In a large non-aluminum saucepan combine the plums, wine, orange juice, sugar, cinnamon, and cloves. Bring to a boil over medium heat and skim off any foam that forms on the surface. Reduce the heat, partially cover and simmer, stirring occasionally until the plums are very tender, about 20 minutes. Discard the cinnamon sticks and cloves. Cool slightly and force through a food mill or use a food processor. Taste and add more sugar if necessary. Soup will taste less sweet when chilled. Cover and refrigerate at least 6 hours or overnight. Garnish with sour cream.

Serves 4 to 6.

Shellfish Crêpe Pie

  1 cup all-purpose flour
  1 cup water
  4 eggs
  ½ teaspoon salt
      ❖ ❖ ❖
  ¼ cup butter (½ stick)
  6 tablespoons unbleached flour
  2 cups milk
  Salt, freshly ground pepper to taste
  Marjoram to taste
  Dash Sherry (optional)
      ❖ ❖ ❖
  1 pound shellfish (shrimp, lobster,
      crab or combination)

Prepare the crêpes by combining 1 cup of flour, water, eggs, and salt, beating together until smooth. Refrigerate the batter for at least one hour. Cook in a crêpe pan. Makes 12 to 18 crêpes.

To make Bechamel sauce melt the butter in a heavy saucepan. Sprinkle in the flour and cook gently without browning. Meanwhile, in a separate saucepan, bring the milk to a boil. Remove both the pans from the heat. Pour the milk into the flour mixture, whisk vigorously. When the bubbling stops, return the pan to medium heat. Return to a boil, stirring constantly for 5 minutes. Season with salt, pepper, and marjoram. Thin with a little Sherry if desired.

Line a buttered pie plate with crêpes, overlapping them in a circle. Place the shellfish over the crêpes, then cover with ½ of the sauce. Make another layer of crêpes, top with the remaining sauce and then the cheese. Bake in a 350° oven for 15 to 20 minutes, until the top begins to brown and the cheese melts.

Note: This is a Barnard-Good original.

The Captain Mey's

202 Ocean Street
Cape May, New Jersey 08204
(609) 884-7793

The Dutch heritage at Captain Mey's Inn is truly evident in the Persian rugs on table tops, the Delft Blue collection, and the Dutch artifacts throughout. Guests are surrounded by rich, warm oak and Tiffany stained glass in this authentically restored inn. Rooms are spacious, with antiques, walnut bedsteads, marble-topped dressers, handmade quilts, and fresh flowers. The chestnut oak Eastlake paneling in the dining room, leaded glass window seat, and fireplace with its intricately carved mantel all contribute to the Victorian elegance of this inn. During the summer months guests can enjoy a leisurely breakfast or a refreshing glass of iced tea in the afternoon on the wrap-around veranda with wicker furniture. The full country breakfast consists of homemade breads, cakes, egg dishes, breakfast meats, cheese imported from Holland, fresh fruit, and jelly made from beach plums.

Built Circa 1890

The Captain Mey's

Dutch Cheese Bake

8 slices white bread, cubed
8 eggs
2 cups milk
8 ounces Gouda cheese, shredded
1 teaspoon dry mustard

❖ ❖ ❖

1 cup butter (2 sticks), melted

Place the bread cubes in a buttered 9x13-inch casserole. Mix the eggs, milk, cheese, and mustard in a blender, then pour the mixture over the bread. Refrigerate overnight.

Just before baking, pour the melted butter over the casserole. Bake in a 350° oven for 30 minutes.

Serves 8.

Quiche Mey

A crustless quiche.

6 eggs
2 cups heavy cream
½ cup fresh bread crumbs
½ teaspoon salt
¼ teaspoon nutmeg
3 tablespoons frozen orange juice concentrate
1 cup chopped spinach

Beat eggs and cream together. Stir in bread crumbs, salt, nutmeg, orange juice, and spinach. Pour into a buttered quiche dish. Bake in a 350° oven for 40 minutes (or 20 minutes in a microwave oven).

Serves 8.

The Chalfonte

301 Howard Street
Cape May, New Jersey 08204
(609) 884-8409

The Chalfonte, a 110-year-old Victorian hotel in the heart of the Historic District, is the oldest hotel in continual operation in Cape May. The rooms are simple, with no telephones, television, or air conditioning. Although the hotel is very basic (only eleven of the 108 rooms have a private bath), its guests return year after year. The dining room was originally built as a ballroom and seats 175 comfortably. Meals are served family-style at the long tables. Breakfast and dinner are included in the rates, but the dining room is open to the public as well. The long porches filled with rocking chairs and the quiet King Edward Room bar make relaxing a necessary part of the day.

Black-Eyed Peas and Ham Hocks

1 quart water
4 smoked ham hocks
1 pound black-eyed peas
3 onions, sliced
Pinch sugar
Pinch seasoning salt
1 teaspoon salt
1 teaspoon black pepper

Place the ham hocks in a medium saucepan, cover with water and bring to a boil. Cook for 1 hour. Add the peas, onions, sugar, salts, and pepper. Cook for 1 more hour or until peas are soft.
Serves 8.

Crab Meat Croquettes

3 tablespoons butter or margarine
4 tablespoons all-purpose flour
1 cup milk

❖ ❖ ❖

1½ pounds crab meat (backfin preferable)
¼ cup chopped parsley
¼ cup grated onion
¼ cup fresh lemon juice
2 eggs
1 tablespoon Worcestershire sauce
1 teaspoon pepper
2 dashes hot pepper sauce
¼ teaspoon dry mustard

❖ ❖ ❖

3 eggs
2 teaspoons salt

❖ ❖ ❖

Bread crumbs

❖ ❖ ❖

Fat for deep frying

Melt the butter in a small pan, add the flour, and cook over low heat. Add the milk and cook until the mixture thickens. Set aside.

Mix the crab meat with the parsley, onions, lemon juice, 2 eggs, Worcestershire sauce, pepper, hot pepper sauce, and dry mustard. Add the cooled cream sauce and shape into 2½- to 3-inch long croquettes. Beat 3 eggs and salt together in a small bowl. Dip each croquette in bread crumbs, then in beaten eggs, and then in bread crumbs again. Fry in deep fat at 375° until brown.
Makes 12 to 14 croquettes.

Eggplant Casserole

2 medium eggplants (about 2½ pounds), peeled and cubed
2 cups chopped onion

❖ ❖ ❖

1 28-ounce can tomatoes, drained and chopped (reserve juice)
1 teaspoon salt
½ teaspoon pepper
2 tablespoons Worcestershire sauce
¼ cup butter

❖ ❖ ❖

1½ tablespoons butter
2 tablespoons all-purpose flour

The Chalfonte

½ cup reserved tomato juice
(or milk)

❖ ❖ ❖

1 tablespoon butter
½ cup bread crumbs
Paprika

Simmer eggplant and onion in a large saucepan with water to barely cover. Cook until tender, about 5 to 7 minutes. Drain well. Add the tomatoes, salt, pepper, Worcestershire sauce, and ¼ cup of butter.

In a small pan melt 1½ tablespoons of butter, add the flour and cook over low heat until well blended. Add the tomato juice (or milk) and cook until thickened. Add to the eggplant mixture.

Melt 1 tablespoon of butter in a 2-quart baking dish. Sprinkle ½ of the bread crumbs into the melted butter. Add the eggplant mixture, then sprinkle the cheese, remaining bread crumbs, and paprika over the top. Bake in a 350° oven about 10 to 15 minutes, until heated through.

Serves 6.

Sweet Potato Pie

4 medium sweet potatoes

❖ ❖ ❖

2 eggs
1 cup sugar
1 teaspoon vanilla extract
Pinch salt
½ teaspoon ground nutmeg
½ cup butter (1 stick)
½ cup evaporated milk

❖ ❖ ❖

1 unbaked 9-inch pie shell

Boil the potatoes until soft, then peel and place them into a mixing bowl. Beat until there are no lumps left. Add the eggs, sugar, vanilla, salt, nutmeg, butter, and milk; beat until creamy. Pour into pie shell and bake in a 350° oven until crust is brown.

Serves 6.

The Duke of Windsor

817 Washington Street
Cape May, New Jersey 08204
(609) 884-1355

Wallis Warfield of Baltimore, later the Mrs. Simpson for whom Edward VIII renounced the British throne, had her "coming out" in Cape May. Therefore it is appropriate that this inn—grand in scale and Victorian in character—was named "The Duke of Windsor." It contains classic Queen Anne detailing, Tiffany stained glass, plaster ceiling medallions and moldings, as well as a dramatic forty-five foot tower. Two guest rooms fill the upper levels of the tower while it houses a first-floor conversation and game room. From the foyer a carved oak open stairway rises three floors. Some of the guest rooms have private baths. The Windsor is near fine restaurants and shops, tennis courts, and the beach. Bicycles are provided.

Banana Wheat Bread

1¼ cups unbleached flour
½ cup whole wheat flour

1 cup sugar
1 teaspoon baking soda
1 teaspoon salt
1½ cups thinly sliced bananas
¼ cup butter or margarine
(½ stick), softened
2 tablespoons orange juice
1 egg
¼ to ½ cup raisins

Blend all the ingredients in a large bowl. Beat 3 minutes at medium speed. Pour into a greased and floured loaf pan. Bake in a 325° oven for 60 to 70 minutes until a toothpick inserted in center comes out clean. Remove from pan to cool.

Makes 1 loaf.

Honey Twist Bread

1½ cups unbleached flour
¼ cup sugar
1 teaspoon salt
1 ¼-ounce package active dry yeast

❖ ❖ ❖

1 cup milk
3 tablespoons butter or margarine

❖ ❖ ❖

2 eggs (reserve 1 white)

❖ ❖ ❖

1½ to 1¾ cups unbleached flour

❖ ❖ ❖

¼ cup butter or margarine
(½ stick), softened
2 tablespoons honey
⅔ cup confectioners' sugar
Reserved egg white

In a large bowl, combine 1½ cups flour, sugar, salt, and yeast. In a small saucepan, heat the milk and 3 table-

THE *Duke of Windsor*

BED AND BREAKFAST INN

spoons of butter to 120° to 130° (butter does not need to melt). Add the warm liquid and 1 egg and 1 yolk to the flour mixture. Blend at low speed until moistened; beat 3 minutes at medium speed. Stir in the remaining 1½ to 1¾ cups flour to form a soft dough. Knead with a dough hook until smooth, about 1 minute. Cover; let rise in a warm place until light and doubled in size, 30 to 45 minutes. Grease a 12-cup fluted tube pan. Punch down dough. On floured surface, shape dough into long roll about 1 inch in diameter. Twist the roll into the prepared pan beginning at the inner edge and coiling out.

Combine ¼ cup butter, honey, and confectioners' sugar for a topping; blend until smooth. Brush dough with half of the topping. Let rise in a warm place until light and doubled in size, 30 to 45 minutes. Bake in a 350° oven for 25 to 30 minutes, until brown. Remove from pan, and brush warm bread with remaining topping.

Serves 12.

Banana-Pineapple Cake

3 cups all-purpose flour
1 teaspoon baking soda
1 teaspoon cinnamon
2 cups sugar
1 teaspoon salt

❖ ❖ ❖

1½ cups oil
1 8-ounce can crushed pineapple,
    with syrup
1½ teaspoons vanilla extract
3 eggs
2 cups diced bananas

In a large mixing bowl, sift together the dry ingredients, add the remaining ingredients and mix until blended. Do not beat. Pour into a greased round tube pan and bake in a 350° oven for 1 hour and 20 minutes. Cake will crack a little on top. Place the pan on a rack to cool.

Serves 12.

Cinnamon Swirl Cake

3 cups unbleached flour
1½ cups sugar
2 teaspoons baking powder
1 teaspoon baking soda
1 teaspoon salt
1 cup buttermilk
¾ cup butter or margarine
    (1½ sticks), softened
2 tablespoons orange juice
1 tablespoon grated orange peel
3 eggs

❖ ❖ ❖

¼ cup raisins

❖ ❖ ❖

½ cup brown sugar, firmly packed
⅓ cup all-purpose flour
2 teaspoons cinnamon
¼ cup butter or margarine
    (½ stick)

❖ ❖ ❖

1 cup confectioners' sugar
1 to 2 tablespoons orange juice

In a large mixing bowl, blend 3 cups of flour, 1½ cups sugar, baking powder, soda, salt, buttermilk, ¾ cup of butter, 2 tablespoons orange juice, and peel; beat 2 minutes at medium speed. Stir in the raisins. Pour ⅓ of batter (about 2 cups) into a greased and floured 12-cup fluted tube pan. In a small mixing bowl, blend the brown sugar, ⅓ cup flour, cinnamon, and ¼ cup butter until crumbly; sprinkle half of the mixture over the batter in pan. Pour another ⅓ of the batter into the pan. Sprinkle with the remaining filling mixture and top with the remaining batter. Bake in a 350° oven for 50 to 60 minutes or until a toothpick inserted in the center comes out clean. Cool upright in the pan 15 minutes; turn onto a serving plate. Cool completely. In a small bowl, blend the confectioners' sugar and 1 to 2 tablespoons of orange juice together for a glaze. Spoon over the cake.

Serves 12.

Perry Street Inn

20 Perry Street
Cape May, New Jersey 08204
(609) 884-4590 or
(201) 689-3940

Facing the Atlantic Ocean, the Perry Street Inn is not only near the beach but is also close to the mall and the historic district. Parking is provided. The rooms are nicely decorated with antiques, and rocking on the porch is a relaxing way to spend a few hours. A continental breakfast is served.

Sweet Potato Bread or Muffins

3 eggs
1½ cups sugar
1½ cups mashed sweet potatoes (or
    1 16-ounce can sweet potatoes,
    drained and mashed)
1 cup oil
2 teaspoons vanilla extract
2¼ cups all-purpose flour
1½ teaspoons baking powder
1½ teaspoons baking soda
1½ teaspoons cinnamon
1 teaspoon salt
¼ teaspoon ground cloves
¼ teaspoon ginger
¼ teaspoon nutmeg
Nuts or raisins (optional)

In a large mixing bowl, combine eggs, sugar, sweet potatoes, oil, and vanilla. Mix well with an electric mixer or by hand. Mix the dry ingredients and add to sweet potato mixture. Beat only enough to blend. Add the nuts or raisins last. Pour into 2 greased and floured 8-inch loaf pans or 48 tiny muffin cups. Bake in a 350° oven for 50 to 60 minutes for loaves, or 20 to 25 minutes for muffins. This freezes well.

Note from the innkeeper: This is our most requested recipe!

Makes 2 loaves or 48 tiny muffins.

Raspberry Torte

4 cups all-purpose flour
1 teaspoon salt
1½ cups butter or margarine
(3 sticks)
1 cup sugar
1 egg

❖ ❖ ❖

1 cup raspberry jam
¼ cup sliced almonds

Mix the flour, salt, butter, sugar, and egg together in a food processor or by hand. Press ⅔ of the dough onto a cookie sheet. Cover with raspberry jam. Use the remaining dough to roll into pencil strips and form a lattice top. Sprinkle with sliced almonds. Bake in a 350° oven for 30 to 35 minutes. Cool and cut into squares for pastries or into 1x2½-inch bar cookies. This keeps well in the refrigerator for up to a week.

Note from the innkeeper: This is an elegant, easy, and versatile cookie or pastry.

Makes 2½ to 3 dozen.

The Queen Victoria

102 Ocean Street
Cape May, New Jersey 08204
(609) 884-8702

Named in honor of the British monarch who loved the sea, the Queen Victoria was restored to its original elegance in celebration of the building's 1981 centennial. At the Queen Victoria guests can enjoy the personal service, comfort, and charm of a country inn and one of the innkeepers is

always on hand. It is furnished with authentic Victorian pieces of walnut, wicker, oak, and pine. Bedrooms have quilts on antique bedsteads and fresh flowers on the tables. In the morning a hearty country breakfast awaits guests in the dining room.

Mincemeat Brunch Cake

1 cup butter or margarine
(2 sticks), softened
1½ cups sugar
1½ teaspoons baking powder
1½ teaspoons vanilla extract
½ teaspoon grated orange peel
4 eggs
3 cups all-purpose flour

❖ ❖ ❖

2 cups mincemeat

❖ ❖ ❖

⅔ cup chopped walnuts

❖ ❖ ❖

1 cup confectioners' sugar
2 tablespoons orange juice

Cream together the butter and sugar. Beat in the baking powder, vanilla, and orange peel. Add the eggs, one at a time, beating well after each addition. Mix in the flour. Spread ⅔ of the batter into a 10x15-inch greased jelly roll pan. Spread mincemeat on top of batter. Drop remaining batter onto the mincemeat making 15 dollops. Sprinkle with chopped walnuts. Bake in a 350° oven for 35 to 40 minutes, or until a tester inserted in the center comes out clean. Stir together the confectioners' sugar and orange juice and drizzle over the cake while it is still warm. Cut in squares and serve warm.

Note from the innkeeper: This recipe is a Thanksgiving and Christ-

The Queen Victoria

mas morning breakfast tradition at the Queen Victoria.

Serves 12.

Aunt Ruth's Baked Eggs and Cheese

7 eggs
1 cup milk
2 teaspoons sugar
1 pound Monterey Jack or Muenster cheese, grated
4 ounces cream cheese, cubed
1 16-ounce container small curd cottage cheese
6 tablespoons margarine
½ cup all-purpose flour
1 teaspoon baking powder

Beat together the eggs, milk, and sugar. Add the cheeses and margarine. Mix well, then add the flour and baking powder. Pour into a greased 9x13-inch glass baking dish. Bake in a 325° oven for 45 minutes or until knife inserted in the center comes out clean. This may be made ahead of time and refrigerated. If the pan goes from refrigerator to oven, bake 60 minutes.

Note from the innkeeper: This recipe comes from a couple of their favorite guests, Jane Spangler and her mother-in-law, "Aunt Ruth."

Serves 12.

Sesame Cheddar Spread

1 8-ounce package cream cheese, softened
1 cup grated sharp Cheddar cheese
1 tablespoon soy sauce
2 tablespoons toasted sesame seeds

Blend or process cheeses together. Stir in the soy sauce and process until smooth. Stir in the sesame seeds. Serve with crackers.

Variations: Add 1 to 2 tablespoons of sour cream if a softer spread is desired. For a dip, substitute 1½ cups of sour cream for the cream cheese. For

cheese balls, combine all the ingredients except the sesame seeds. Form into small balls and roll in the sesame seeds, using more if necessary. (Adapted from Cooking for Compliments by the Knudsen Dairy, Los Angeles, CA.)

Makes about 1½ cups.

Curried or Spiced Fruit

1 16-ounce can sliced peaches
1 15¼-ounce can pineapple chunks
1 16-ounce can sliced pears
1 17-ounce can apricot halves
½ cup butter or margarine (1 stick), melted
¾ cup brown sugar, firmly packed
4 teaspoons curry powder (or 2 teaspoons cinnamon)
1 teaspoon cloves
1 teaspoon nutmeg

❖ ❖ ❖

2 bananas, sliced

Drain and combine the canned fruits. Melt the butter and add the sugar and flavorings; stir into the fruits. Cover and heat in a 350° oven for 30 minutes (or in a microwave oven for 5 minutes). Stir in the bananas just before serving.

A very versatile recipe. Use any combination of fresh and canned fruits you wish. Cherries, grapes, mandarin oranges, and even apple slices (simmered in juice to soften a bit) are good. Recipe can be doubled easily. Benefits from being combined ahead of time.

Note: This recipe was given to the Queen Victorian Inn by Cindy Janke, Washington, D.C.

Serves 8 to 12.

Rum Butter Frosted Brownies

1¼ cups margarine (2½ sticks)
¾ cup cocoa

❖ ❖ ❖

4 eggs
2 cups sugar
2 teaspoons vanilla extract
1 cup all-purpose flour
¼ teaspoon salt
1½ cups chopped walnuts

❖ ❖ ❖

½ cup margarine (1 stick), softened
1 1-pound box confectioners' sugar
4 tablespoons light rum

Melt 1¼ cups margarine in a saucepan; remove from the heat and beat in the cocoa until smooth. In a large mixing bowl beat the eggs until fluffy. Gradually beat in the sugar until the mixture is thick. Stir in the chocolate mixture and vanilla. Fold in the flour and stir, beat until well blended. Stir in the walnuts. Spread the batter evenly in a greased 10x15-inch pan and bake in a 350° oven for 30 minutes or until firm to the touch.

Blend ½ cup margarine with ½ of the sugar. Add the remaining sugar alternately with the rum until the frosting is of spreading consistency.

When the brownies are cooled, spread with the frosting and cut into bars.

Serves 8 to 12.

Chocolate Yogurt Cake

1 tablespoon all-purpose flour
1 teaspoon Dutch processed cocoa

❖ ❖ ❖

2 cups all-purpose flour
⅔ cup Dutch processed cocoa
1½ teaspoons baking soda

❖ ❖ ❖

½ cup butter or margarine (1 stick), softened
1½ cups sugar
2 eggs
1½ cups plain yogurt
1 teaspoon vanilla extract

Mix 1 tablespoon of flour with 1 teaspoon of cocoa and dust the inside of a greased 9-inch bundt or tube pan with this mixture, shaking out any excess. Sift 2 cups of flour and ⅔ cup of cocoa together with the baking soda; set aside. In a large mixing bowl cream the butter and sugar together. Beat in the eggs, one at a time. Add the flour mixture alternately with the yogurt, in three parts. Do not overmix. Stir in the vanilla. Pour the batter into the prepared pan and bake in a 350° oven for 45 to 55 minutes, until a tester inserted in the center comes out clean. Cool for 10 minutes before inverting onto a rack to cool completely.

Serves 16.

Windward House

24 Jackson Street
Cape May, New Jersey 08204
(609) 884-3368

Windward House, in the heart of Cape May's Historic District, was built during the Edwardian Period. It is an excellent example of the shingled-style cottage, a late Victorian architectural design developed about 1880 and used mostly in coastal resorts. It features upper and lower porches, a long central hall, large and airy rooms, and one of Cape May's finest collections of stained and beveled glass. Oak paneling and doors are complemented by a collection of antiques and family heirlooms. Windward House has private baths and small refrigerators in most rooms. It is close to the beach, the mall, and most of Cape May's restaurants and tour sites.

Crescent Date Honey Buns

½ cup butter or margarine (1 stick)
⅓ cup chopped pecans or walnuts
2 tablespoons brown sugar, firmly
    packed

2 tablespoons honey

❖ ❖ ❖

1 8-ounce can crescent dinner rolls

❖ ❖ ❖

12 pitted dates

Combine butter, pecans, brown sugar, and honey, and pour into an ungreased 8- or 9-inch square baking pan. Heat in the oven until the butter melts; stir and set aside. Separate crescent dough into 8 triangles. Cut dates in half and place 1½ dates inside each triangle and roll up. Place on top of the butter mixture, and bake in a 400° oven for 15 to 18 minutes; let cool for 3 minutes. Invert the pan and serve warm.

Makes 8 buns.

Party Tuna Mold

Tastes like crab or shrimp.

1 10¾-ounce can tomato soup,
    undiluted (or tomato bisque
    soup)
1 8-ounce package cream cheese,
    cubed

❖ ❖ ❖

1½ tablespoons unflavored gelatin
½ cup warm water

❖ ❖ ❖

1 pound white or light tuna,
    drained
6 tablespoons finely chopped onion
6 tablespoons finely chopped
    celery
4 tablespoons finely chopped green
    pepper
Salt and pepper to taste
⅓ cup mayonnaise (not salad
    dressing)

Place the tomato soup and cream cheese into a heavy saucepan. Heat gently, not to boiling, until a well-balanced sauce is achieved. (Stirring with a wire whisk is great!) Meanwhile, soak the gelatin in ½ cup warm water. Stir dissolved gelatin mixture into the sauce and remove from heat. Break tuna apart and stir into sauce, then add the vegetables and seasonings. Mix in the mayonnaise. Pour into a 1½-quart oiled mold or 2 smaller, oiled molds and refrigerate. After it is firm, remove from molds.

Broiled Crab Open Facers

1 6½-ounce can crab meat, drained
¼ cup mayonnaise
1 3-ounce package cream cheese,
    softened
1 egg yolk
1 teaspoon chopped onion
¼ teaspoon mustard
Dash of salt

❖ ❖ ❖

3 English muffins, split and toasted
Soft butter

Combine the crab meat, mayonnaise, cream cheese, egg yolk, onion, and seasonings. Spread the muffins with soft butter and top with the crab and cream cheese mixture. Broil 5 to 6 inches from heat for 2 to 3 minutes.

Serves 3.

Christmas Sugar Plums

1 egg white
¼ cup cold water
1 teaspoon cream of tartar
1 teaspoon vanilla extract

❖ ❖ ❖

6 cups sifted confectioners' sugar
¼ cup butter (½ stick), softened
½ cup unsweetened grated coconut
¼ cup chopped candied cherries
¼ cup chopped candied pineapple

❖ ❖ ❖

1½ pounds large pitted prunes

❖ ❖ ❖

Sugar

❖ ❖ ❖

Candied cherries

In a bowl beat egg white, cold water, cream of tartar, and vanilla until the mixture is frothy. Add confectioners' sugar, ¼ cup at a time, continuing to beat the mixture until it is thick and smooth. Add butter and combine the mixture well. Stir in coconut, cherries, and pineapple. Chill the filling, covered, for at least 48 hours.

Slit the prunes lengthwise, stuff each prune with 1½ teaspoons of the filling, then roll the prunes in granulated sugar. Garnish each sugar plum with a sliver of candied cherry and store in an airtight container.

Makes about 72 sugar plums.

Lemon Bars Deluxe

2 cups sifted all-purpose flour
½ cup sifted confectioners' sugar
1 cup butter or margarine (2 sticks)

❖   ❖   ❖

4 eggs, beaten
2 cups sugar
⅓ cup fresh lemon juice

❖   ❖   ❖

¼ cup all-purpose flour
2 teaspoons baking powder

Sift together the flour and confectioners' sugar. Cut in the butter until the mixture clings together. Press into a 13x9x2-inch baking pan and bake in a 350° oven for 20 to 25 minutes. Beat the eggs, sugar, and lemon juice together. Sift ¼ cup flour and baking powder together; stir into the egg mixture. Pour over the baked crust and return to the oven for an additional 20 to 25 minutes. Cool before cutting into bars.

Note from the innkeeper: This is the favorite breakfast sweet of my guests, and it is easy!

Makes 26 squares.

The Publick House

111 Main Street
Chester, New Jersey 07930
(201) 879-6878 or
(201) 879-4800

This authentic country inn and restaurant, built in 1810, combines fine

The Publick House

dining with charming accommodations. Each of its ten bedrooms is decorated in the style of the nineteenth century and is provided with a private bath and telephone. A complimentary breakfast is provided overnight guests. In addition, they may wish to avail themselves of the sumptuous Sunday brunch or dine in one of four indoor locations or on the veranda overlooking Main Street.

Golden Mushroom Soup

1 teaspoon butter
¾ cup diced celery
¾ cup diced onions
8½ cups water
4 ounces mushroom base
1 28-ounce can tomatoes, crushed
1½ pounds mushrooms, thickly sliced
2 tablespoons freshly chopped parsley
¼ teaspoon white pepper

Sauté butter, celery and onions for 10 to 15 minutes. Add the water, mushroom base, tomatoes, mushrooms, and parsley. Simmer for 2 hours and 30 minutes. Add the pepper and season to taste.

Makes 1 gallon.

Mustamaise Sauce

A dip for fried chicken, cheese fingers, and vegetables.

¼ cup dry mustard
1¼ cups honey
½ cup Dijon mustard
2 tablespoons Worcestershire sauce
2 quarts mayonnaise

In a mixing bowl combine the dry mustard, honey, Dijon mustard, and Worcestershire sauce. Mix well with a slotted spoon or wire whisk, making sure all the ingredients are blended smoothly. Add the mayonnaise, and mix well. Store in a sealed container for a maximum of 4 days until ready to use.

Makes 2½ quarts of sauce.

Chocolate Mousse Supreme

1 pint heavy cream
½ cup plus 1 tablespoon super fine sugar

❖   ❖   ❖

4 egg yolks
4 1-ounce squares semi-sweet chocolate

In a chilled bowl, whip the heavy cream with a fine wire whisk. Add the sugar while mixing. The cream will thicken and peak when complete. Refrigerate until needed.

Place the egg yolks in a bowl and beat well. Using a double boiler, melt the chocolate to a smooth consistency. Slowly add the melted chocolate to the egg yolks, stirring constantly. The temperature of the chocolate must not be over 115° or the yolks will scramble. Using a rubber scraper, fold in small amounts of the whipped cream at a time. When all whipped cream and chocolate have been mixed, refrigerate until stiff, approximately 30 to 40 minutes. Using a piping bag, pipe the mousse into decorative glasses.

Makes 10 to 12 servings.

Jerica Hill—A Bed and Breakfast Inn

96 Broad Street
Flemington, New Jersey 08822
(201) 782-8234

Built in 1901 by local businessman John B. Case as his family residence, Jerica Hill has recently been restored. In each of the five spacious, sunny guest rooms there are always fresh flowers and fruit. Jerica Hill is in the center of the historical area of Flemington, just two blocks off Main Street and within walking distance of many shops and restaurants. A continental breakfast of fresh fruits, homemade breads, and pastries is served guests in the dining room, and hot coffee and tea are always available. During good weather, the screened porch, filled with wicker furniture and plants, is a good place to enjoy a leisurely breakfast or to unwind in the afternoon. The large living room, with an open fireplace, well-stocked bookcases, daily *New York Times,* and television, is ideal for conversation or quiet reading.

Pear Bread for Jerica Hill

½ cup butter or margarine (1 stick), softened
1 cup sugar
2 eggs

❖   ❖   ❖

2 cups all-purpose flour
½ teaspoon salt
½ teaspoon baking soda
1 teaspoon baking powder
⅛ teaspoon nutmeg

❖   ❖   ❖

¼ cup plain yogurt or buttermilk
1 cup coarsely chopped pears (not peeled, must be fresh)
1 teaspoon vanilla extract

In a mixing bowl cream the butter; gradually beat in the sugar. Beat in the eggs, one at a time. Combine the dry ingredients, then add to the egg mixture, alternating with the yogurt. Stir in the pears and vanilla. Pour into a buttered 9x5x3-inch loaf pan. Bake in a 350° oven for 1 hour.

Ashling Cottage: A Victorian Seaside Inn

106 Sussex Avenue
Spring Lake, New Jersey 07762
(201) 449-3553

Sitting beneath sentinel sycamores, Ashling Cottage has served as a seaside haven for over 100 years. Its bedrooms are tastefully decorated and some have private porches or sunken bathrooms. Guests join the innkeepers in the solarium for a sumptuous buffet breakfast as they watch the sun rise over the ocean.

Ashling Cottage

Fruited Bran Bread

1½ cups sifted all-purpose flour
½ cup sugar
1 teaspoon baking powder
1 teaspoon baking soda
1 teaspoon salt

❖   ❖   ❖

1½ cups whole bran cereal
½ pound dried apricots, chopped (or 1½ cups golden raisins)
¼ cup butter (½ stick)
1½ cups hot water
1 egg
1 teaspoon vanilla extract

❖   ❖   ❖

¾ cup chopped nuts

Sift together the flour, sugar, baking powder, soda, and salt; set aside. In a mixing bowl, combine the cereal, apricots, butter, and hot water. Stir until the butter is melted. Beat in the egg and vanilla. Stir the dry ingredients and nuts into the cereal mixture only until combined. Spread evenly in a well-greased 9x5-inch loaf pan. Bake in a 350° oven for 60 to 75 minutes. Let cool for 15 to 20 minutes before removing from the pan. Cool completely before slicing.

Irish Yogurt Bread

4 cups all-purpose flour
¾ teaspoon baking soda
3 teaspoons baking powder
1 teaspoon salt

❖ ❖ ❖

1 cup currants
2 tablespoons caraway seeds

❖ ❖ ❖

2 eggs
1 cup plain low-fat yogurt mixed
  with water (mix in electric
  mixer)

Stir the dry ingredients together. Add the currants and caraway seeds; add eggs. Add yogurt and water mixture and stir until a sticky batter is formed. Knead on a well-floured surface for 1 minute, then shape into a ball and place in a well-greased round casserole. Mark a cross in the center with a sharp knife and bake in a 350° oven for 1 hour and 15 minutes. Wait 10 to 15 minutes before removing bread from casserole, then allow to cool on a wire rack. Slice thinly to serve. Freezes well and is best the day after baking.

Easter Pound Cake

1 cup butter (2 sticks)
2 cups sugar
4 eggs, beaten

❖ ❖ ❖

3 cups all-purpose flour
3 teaspoons baking powder
1 teaspoon baking soda
½ teaspoon salt

❖ ❖ ❖

1 16-ounce container sour cream
1 teaspoon vanilla extract

❖ ❖ ❖

¼ cup sugar
1 teaspoon cinnamon

Cream the butter and 2 cups of sugar together; add eggs. Combine dry ingredients together and add alternately with the sour cream to the batter, beginning and ending with dry ingredients. Mix just until the ingredients are blended together. Add the vanilla. Pour batter into 2 loaf pans. Mix ¼ cup of sugar with the cinnamon and sprinkle over the batter. Bake in a 350° oven for 50 to 60 minutes. Cool thoroughly. It is best served the next day.

Fruit Squares

1 cup butter (2 sticks)
1½ cups sugar
4 eggs, beaten
2 cups all-purpose flour
1 teaspoon vanilla extract
1 teaspoon lemon or orange extract

❖ ❖ ❖

1 21-ounce can pie filling (cherry,
  blueberry, peach, etc.)

❖ ❖ ❖

Confectioners' sugar

Cream the butter and sugar together. Add the eggs and flour, then add the flavorings, blending well. Spread in a well-greased 15x10x1-inch pan. Score the surface into 26 squares and spoon pie filling into center of each square. Bake in a 350° oven for 45 minutes. Cut into squares and sprinkle with confectioners' sugar. Cool and serve.

Makes 26 squares.

New Mexico

The Galisteo Inn

Box 4
Galisteo, New Mexico 87540
(505) 982-1506

The Galisteo Inn offers a unique environment designed with its guests' comfort and enjoyment in mind. The Main House is over 200 years old and sits on eight picturesque acres with a pond, pastures, and huge cottonwood trees spreading over green lawns. Guest accommodations are priced to fit a variety of budgets and tastes. The Galisteo Inn combines a homey atmosphere with the best in a modern facility. The cedar sauna, heated pool, and well-equipped exercise center provide pleasant relaxation. Therapeutic massage is available at additional cost. The restaurant serves fresh, innovative American cuisine; local produce and regional dishes are emphasized. Breakfast is included in the price of an overnight stay.

The recipes included here were provided by Marie O'Shea and Amy Toms.

Maple Piñon

1¼ cups unbleached flour
1 cup yellow or blue cornmeal
1 teaspoon cinnamon
4 teaspoons baking powder
½ teaspoon salt
1 cup coarsely ground piñon nuts,
    toasted lightly

❖ ❖ ❖

2 extra large eggs
½ cup unsalted butter (1 stick),
    melted
1¼ cups cream or half and half,
    warmed
1 teaspoon vanilla extract
1 cup pure maple syrup

Combine the dry ingredients and nuts; set aside. Beat the eggs well, then add the other wet ingredients (make sure the butter and cream are not too hot!). Combine the liquid and dry ingredients, stirring just enough to produce a batter. Fill greased or papered muffin pans ⅔ full. Bake in a 400° oven for 10 minutes, then rotate the pans and bake another 4 minutes or so until golden brown.

Makes 18 muffins.

Green Chili Lamb Blue Corn Enchiladas

1 pound lamb, cut into small pieces
2 cloves garlic, minced
1 small onion, diced
Olive oil
2 tomatoes, diced
2 green chilies, diced

❖ ❖ ❖

1 small onion, diced
2 cloves garlic, minced
¼ cup unsalted butter (½ stick)
3 tablespoons all-purpose flour
20 ounces green chilies
13 ounces green tomatillas
1 tablespoon cumin
2 teaspoons oregano
Salt and pepper to taste

❖ ❖ ❖

Oil
12 blue corn tortillas
1 pound Monterey Jack cheese,
    grated

❖ ❖ ❖

Sour cream

Sauté the lamb, 2 cloves of garlic, and the diced onion in olive oil until browned. Add the tomatoes and chilies, remove from heat and set aside. Sauté the remaining onion and garlic in butter. Sprinkle the flour over the mixture and heat until the mixture bubbles. Remove from heat. Purée the chilies and tomatillas together. Add the onion mixture and seasonings. Heat through and remove from heat immediately. Set aside.

In a medium sauté pan heat the oil until hot. Fry one tortilla until soft and pliable and remove it to a plate. Place a handful of cheese in the middle and top with some of the lamb mixture. Roll up and place in a greased roasting pan. Repeat until all the tortillas are used. Pour the sauce over the enchiladas and sprinkle with the remaining cheese. Bake in a 375° oven for 1 hour. Serve with sour cream and a salad.

Serves 6.

249

Galisteo Corn Meal Scones

2 cups unbleached white flour
1 cup blue or yellow corn meal
⅓ cup sugar
1 tablespoon baking powder
½ teaspoon baking soda
¾ teaspoon salt
1 teaspoon cinnamon

❖ ❖ ❖

¾ cup unsalted butter (1½ sticks),
    cut in small pieces
Currants, nuts, dried fruit, etc.
1 cup buttermilk

❖ ❖ ❖

½ cup corn meal

Combine the dry ingredients. Cut the butter into the flour mixture with a food processor or pastry cutter until it resembles small peas. Mix in the nuts and/or fruit. Mix in the buttermilk and turn onto a board sprinkled with about ½ cup of cornmeal. Knead lightly, then roll out to about ½- inch thick (try to keep the piece of dough as much in a square shape as possible—this will facilitate cutting it). With a knife or pizza cutter, cut the dough into triangles, squares, or rectangles (cookie cutters may also be used). Place the scones on an ungreased cookie sheet and bake in a 425° oven for 12 minutes, rotating the pan halfway through cooking time to insure even baking. Serve with jam.

Makes approximately 16 scones.

Llewellyn House Bed and Breakfast

618 South Alameda
Las Cruces, New Mexico 88005
(505) 526-3327 or
(505) 524-6978

Original serigraph prints by artist-in-residence Lynn Stenzel and other fine art from the adjoining Linda Lundeen Gallery are on display at the Llewellyn House. This adobe hacienda in the heart of Las Cruces evokes Mexican territorial days with its brick patios, balconies, and fireplaces. It has fourteen artistically decorated bedrooms, each named after a famous artist.

Mexican Eggs

16 to 18 corn tortillas
Oil

❖ ❖ ❖

½ cup diced tomatoes
⅓ cup chopped chilies

❖ ❖ ❖

3 tablespoons butter
1 small onion, minced
½ teaspoon ground cumin
1 tablespoon all-purpose flour
½ cup sour cream
1½ cups shredded Jack cheese
1½ cups shredded Cheddar cheese
6 eggs, lightly beaten

❖ ❖ ❖

Sour cream and/or guacamole

Cut the corn tortillas into ¼-inch strips and lightly fry in oil. Keep warm in the oven while preparing eggs.

Mix the tomatoes and chilies together in a small bowl as a salsa topping for the eggs. (Place them in the oven with the tortilla chips to warm slightly.)

For the eggs, melt the butter in a large frying pan. Add the onion and cumin; stir until the onion is limp. Mix in the flour; cook until bubbly. Remove from heat and blend in the sour cream. Stir over low heat until smooth and bubbly. Add the cheeses, stirring until melted. Stir in the beaten eggs and cook until the eggs look smooth and creamy, like soft scrambled eggs. (The texture becomes coarse with longer cooking.)

Place equal portions of tortilla strips on plates. Spoon eggs over the strips and garnish with tomato-chili mixture. Add a dollop of sour cream and/or guacamole on top and serve.

Serves 6.

Shrimp Soufflé

An appetizer.

2 4½-ounce cans medium deveined
    shrimp, drained
2 8-ounce packages cream cheese,
    softened
½ large onion, chopped
Juice of ½ lemon
Dash Worcestershire sauce
    (or to taste)

❖ ❖ ❖

Crackers

Mix all ingredients together and pour into a soufflé dish. Bake in a 350° oven for 30 minutes. Serve with crackers. Tastes best when it is mixed ahead of time, even a day ahead and baked shortly before serving.

Hot Ryes

1 cup finely grated Swiss cheese
¼ cup cooked crumbled bacon
1 4½-ounce can ripe olives,
    chopped
¼ cup minced green onions or
    chives
1 teaspoon Worcestershire sauce
¼ cup mayonnaise

❖ ❖ ❖

Party rye bread

Mix all ingredients together, spread on bread. Bake in a 375° oven for 10 to 15 minutes. May be frozen after baking.

Serves 36.

Frozen Margaritas

¼ cup Triple Sec
½ cup lime juice
¾ cup gold Tequila

Combine the ingredients in a blender. Fill the blender with ice and blend until smooth. Pour into salt-rimmed glasses.

Makes 4 generous servings or 6 moderate ones.

White Sangria

½ cup brandy
1 shot Triple Sec
1 lemon, sliced
Lemon juice to taste
1 cluster Thompson grapes
¼ cup sugar
White wine

Combine the brandy, Triple Sec, lemon slices, lemon juice, grapes, and sugar. Measure the amount of liquid and add white wine in a 3 to 1 ratio. Add ice; stir and serve.

Cheese Loaf

1 2-pound box Velveeta cheese, softened
1 8-ounce package cream cheese, softened
1 12-ounce can green chilies
1 8-ounce can black olives

❖ ❖ ❖

Mustard
Green olives

Place the softened Velveeta cheese between waxed paper and roll until it is an oblong shape. Remove the paper. Spread the softened cream cheese over the Velveeta with a spatula. Arrange the green chilies and black olives on top of the cream cheese. Place the cheese loaf on a platter and decorate with mustard and green olives.

Chili Con Queso

1 onion, finely chopped
2 tablespoons mayonnaise
1 2-pound box Velveeta cheese
1 8-ounce can evaporated milk
1 8-ounce can green chilies, diced

In a medium saucepan fry the onion in the mayonnaise. Add the cheese slowly until melted. Add the milk and then the chilies.

To reheat, place in a double boiler or heavy pan and heat slowly.

The Plum Tree

Box 1–A
Pilar, New Mexico 87571
(505) 758-4696

Pilar, a centuries-old village on the Rio Grande, is on Route 68 between Santa Fe and Taos. The Plum Tree has a cafe and a hostel. The Cafe features delicious wholesome food and the hostel, friendly comfortable lodging at low costs. Guests can hike, bike, birdwatch, rockhound, swim, cross-country ski, see petroglyphs, take a raft trip, go fishing, learn to kayak, study art, listen to live music, enjoy summer theater, and sunbathe. Near Pilar are downhill ski areas, Indian pueblos, and natural hot springs.

Scrambled Tofu

1 onion, diced
1 clove garlic
1 pound crumbled tofu
¼ cup green chilies
1 tablespoon Grey Poupon mustard
1 teaspoon cumin
¼ teaspoon oregano
1 teaspoon soy sauce

Sauté the onion and garlic. Add the tofu and continue to sauté. When thoroughly heated, add the chilies, mustard, cumin, oregano and soy sauce. Stir and serve.

Serves 2 generously.

Spanish Omelet

1 28-ounce can tomatoes, chopped
1 onion, chopped
1 tablespoon lemon juice
3 tablespoons chopped green chilies
1 teaspoon cumin
½ teaspoon oregano
1 teaspoon salt
1½ teaspoons Worcestershire sauce
1 teaspoon garlic powder

❖ ❖ ❖

3 eggs
Milk

❖ ❖ ❖

½ cup grated cheese

To make the salsa, combine the tomatoes, onion, lemon juice, chilies, cumin, oregano, salt, Worcestershire sauce, and garlic powder. Set aside. This improves after storing overnight.

In a small bowl whisk together the eggs and a little milk. In a large frying pan melt a pat of butter and pour in the egg mixture. Let the bottom cook; pull up the sides and let the top run under to continue cooking. Cook to taste. Place a generous amount of salsa over half the omelet and top with some of the cheese. With a spatula fold over the top half of the omelet. Leave in the pan for a moment to melt the cheese, and place on a serving plate.

Buckwheat Pancakes a la Mode

1 cup whole wheat pastry flour
1 cup rye flour
1 cup buckwheat flour
1 tablespoon cinnamon
1 tablespoon baking powder
3 cups milk
3 eggs
3 tablespoons oil

❖ ❖ ❖

Bananas
Vanilla yogurt
Maple syrup

Stir the flours, cinnamon and baking powder together. Add the milk, eggs, and oil and stir together until smooth. Heat the griddle or frying pan until water dropped on the surface dances across the top. Spoon batter onto a hot griddle and bake until bubbles begin to pop in the middle, then flip. They get golden brown.

Place three pancakes on a plate. Slice a banana on top, add a dollop of vanilla yogurt and maple syrup; indulge yourself.

Atole

2 cups water
¾ cup blue cornmeal
½ teaspoon cinnamon
1 teaspoon honey
Butter
Blueberries
Cream

Place water in a small saucepan and whisk in the blue cornmeal. Cook over medium heat until the mixture thickens. Stir in the cinnamon and honey. Spoon into bowls and top with generous pats of butter. Serve with blueberries and cream.
Serves 2.

Carob Pecan Cake

1 cup soy margarine (2 sticks)
1 cup honey
1 cup milk
4 eggs
1½ teaspoons vanilla extract

❖   ❖   ❖

1 cup unbleached flour
1 cup whole wheat pastry flour
1 tablespoon baking powder
1 teaspoon baking soda
1 cup sifted carob powder

❖   ❖   ❖

¼ cup soy margarine (½ stick)
¼ cup honey
1 cup milk
2 tablespoons cornstarch
½ cup freshly grated coconut
½ cup chopped pecans

In a large pan over low heat, gently melt 1 cup of margarine and 1 cup of honey. Remove from heat and add 1 cup of milk. Beat in the eggs and vanilla. Combine the dry ingredients and stir in until just blended. Pour the batter into a greased and floured 10-inch bundt pan and bake in a 350° oven for 50 minutes. Let cool for 10 minutes and place on serving platter.
   Prepare the topping by melting together ¼ cup of margarine and ¼ cup of honey; add 1 cup of milk and the cornstarch. Stir with a whisk over medium heat until thickened. Add the coconut and pecans. Pour the topping over the hot cake and enjoy.

The Grant Corner Inn

122 Grant Avenue
Santa Fe, New Mexico 87501
(505) 983-6678

Grant Corner Inn, a colonial manor home, is near the old plaza, among intriguing shops, restaurants, and galleries with ample guest parking on the premises. Built in the early 1900s as a private home, the recently renovated inn has nine charming guest rooms, each appointed with antiques and treasures from around the world. Antique quilts, brass and four-poster beds, armoires, and art work make each room special. Each room is modernized with private phones, cable television, and ceiling fans. Breakfast is served daily in front of a crackling fire in the dining room or on the front veranda in summer months. A varied menu includes such treats as banana waffles, eggs Florentine, and New Mexican soufflé. Complimentary wine is served in the evening.

Maple Spice Muffins

1¼ cups all-purpose flour
1½ cups whole wheat flour
½ cup quick oats
1 teaspoon baking soda
2 teaspoons baking powder
2 teaspoons cinnamon
½ teaspoon ground cloves

❖   ❖   ❖

2 eggs
1 cup plain yogurt
1 cup maple syrup
½ cup brown sugar, firmly packed
½ cup oil

❖   ❖   ❖

1 cup chopped walnuts
1 banana, mashed

❖   ❖   ❖

Maple syrup

Into a small mixing bowl, sift the flours, oats, soda, baking powder, and spices. Set aside. In a medium mixing bowl, combine the eggs, yogurt, maple syrup, brown sugar, and oil; beat thoroughly. Stir in the dry ingredients,

The Grant Corner Inn

nuts, and banana. Fill paper lined muffin tins ¾ full. Bake in a 400° oven for 20 minutes, or until the tops spring back when touched. Drizzle maple syrup over muffins and serve warm.

Makes 2 dozen muffins.

Savory Potato Pancakes

3 large potatoes, peeled
2 tablespoons finely grated onion
2 eggs
1 teaspoon salt
Pepper to taste
Freshly grated nutmeg to taste
⅓ cup all-purpose flour

❖ ❖ ❖

Oil and butter for frying

❖ ❖ ❖

Applesauce
Sour cream

Grate the potatoes by hand or in a food processor, pressing out excess moisture between 2 paper towels. Stir in the onion, eggs, salt, pepper, nutmeg, and flour. Heat a thin layer of oil and butter in large heavy skillet. Drop the potato mixture by heaping tablespoonfuls into the fat, flattening each mound with a spatula. Fry the pancakes for about 4 minutes on each side, until uniformly crisp and golden brown. Drain on paper towels. Serve hot with applesauce and sour cream.

Anne's Blue Corn Waffles

1 cup sifted cake flour
3 tablespoons sugar
1 tablespoon baking powder
½ teaspoon salt
¾ cup blue corn meal

❖ ❖ ❖

2 egg yolks
1¼ cups buttermilk
5 tablespoons butter, melted and cooled

❖ ❖ ❖

2 egg whites

❖ ❖ ❖

Honey-Orange Sauce (recipe follows)

Sift together the flour, sugar, baking powder, and salt; stir in blue corn meal and set aside.

Beat the egg yolks until thick and lemon colored. Beat in the buttermilk and butter. Add to dry ingredients and stir just until blended.

Beat the egg whites until stiff peaks form. Stir ⅓ of the whites into batter; gently fold in the rest.

Bake in a waffle iron and serve immediately with Orange-Honey Sauce.

Makes 6 to 8 waffles.

Orange-Honey Sauce

2 cups honey
4 teaspoons grated orange rind
½ cup freshly squeezed orange juice
4 teaspoons Grand Marnier or Triple Sec

Warm the honey in a saucepan; add the remaining ingredients and stir until combined.

Makes 2½ cups of sauce.

Vegetarian Brunch Torte

8 eggs
½ cup milk

❖ ❖ ❖

4 3-ounce packages cream cheese, softened
¼ cup roasted salted sunflower seeds
½ teaspoon finely chopped parsley
½ teaspoon chives
½ teaspoon oregano

❖ ❖ ❖

Cherry tomatoes

Grease 3 9-inch pie plates. Beat the eggs well; add the milk and blend. Divide the egg mixture equally among the pie plates. Bake in a 350° oven for 15 minutes, or until eggs have set. Cool

for 5 minutes. Beat the cream cheese with the sunflower seeds, parsley, chives, and oregano.

Unmold the 3 baked omelets. Place 1 on a warmed platter. Spread with ½ of the cream cheese mixture. Top with the second omelet, spreading with the remaining cream cheese mixture. Top with the third omelet. Cut the torte into wedges and serve immediately, garnishing with cherry tomatoes.

This torte is also well liked when filled with cream cheese and jam.

Serves 6.

Grant Corner Inn Orange Frappé

The fruit frappé has become very popular at Grant Corner Inn. Each morning the fruit blend changes. Any fresh fruit that is too ripe for the guest room fruit baskets finds its way to the blender for frappé. Preparation is simple, and infinite flavors are possible. The cook only needs to taste as he goes. The beauty in these drinks is that they need no sweetener other than the natural fruits. My one "hint" is that they be served very, very cold. During breakfast we keep prepared frappé and glasses in the freezer; then blend each frappé to order.

4 cups freshly squeezed orange juice
Juice of 1 lemon
1 large banana
6 strawberries, fresh or frozen
¼ cup whipping cream
6 ice cubes

❖ ❖ ❖

Fresh mint leaves

Blend all the ingredients except mint leaves, on high for 1 minute. Serve in frosted stemmed goblets, garnished with fresh mint leaves.

Serves 6.

Preston House Bed and Breakfast

106 Faithway Street
Santa Fe, New Mexico 87501
(505) 982-3465

Preston House is the elegant recreation of noted artist/designer Signe Bergman, who moved to Santa Fe in 1974 to pursue her painting career. When she was commissioned by the Santa Barbara Biltmore Hotel to paint its murals in 1978, Signe began to think about a hotel of her own. She is now able to bring her taste and sense of the good life to Preston House in Old Santa Fe. At Preston House a living memory stands gracefully between two centuries.

Champagne Jelly

2 cups champagne (flat is fine)
3 cups sugar
1 2¾-ounce package Certo liquid fruit pectin

Mix the champagne with the sugar in the top of a double boiler. Place over boiling water, stirring for 3 to 4 minutes until the sugar is dissolved. Remove the pan from heat and immediately stir in the Certo. Place in sterilized jars.
Makes 4 8-ounce jars.

Corn Bread with Red Pepper Jelly

1 cup all-purpose flour
¾ cup cornmeal
1 teaspoon baking powder
1 teaspoon baking soda

½ teaspoon salt

❖ ❖ ❖

3 tablespoons red pepper jelly
1 egg
2 tablespoons melted butter

Mix the dry ingredients together. In a separate bowl, mix the remaining ingredients together including the red pepper jelly. Combine and mix just until blended. Do not over mix. Turn into a greased 8-inch square pan and bake in a 425° oven for 20 minutes.
Serves 6 to 8.

Almond Shortbread

2 cups butter (4 sticks), room temperature
1 cup sugar
1 teaspoon almond extract
4 cups all-purpose flour
½ cup chopped roasted almonds

Cream the butter and sugar until light and fluffy. Add the almond extract and fold in the flour and nuts. Pat the dough or roll gently into a 7x10-inch rectangle, ³/₈-inch thick. Place on a baking sheet. Make cutting lines, refrigerate until cold. Cut and bake in a 275° oven for about 40 minutes, until lightly brown. Serve at tea time.
Makes 20 cookies.

Sunset House Bed and Breakfast

436 Sunset
Santa Fe, New Mexico 87501
(505) 983-3523

The Sunset House is a private residence with two rooms used for bed and breakfast guests. They share a bath between them. The house is located only four blocks from downtown Santa Fe, close to galleries, shops, and museums, and just fourteen miles from the Santa Fe ski area. Guests are invited to enjoy the living room fireplace in the winter and the outside decks in summer. The hearty continental breakfast consists of juice, coffee, homemade breads, coffee cakes, jams, and fruit or melon in season. Three fully equipped apartments are also available for nightly and weekly stays.

Cinnamon Rolls

These cinnamon rolls freeze well and do not dry out. One of our guests, Sandy Werner from Kansas, is a State Fair judge and gave us this one. It won first prize in the Texas State Fair and also the Kansas State Fair.

4 cups warm water
1½ cups sugar
2 ¼-ounce packages active dry yeast
1 tablespoon salt

❖ ❖ ❖

1 cup shortening
4 eggs

❖ ❖ ❖

Flour

❖ ❖ ❖

Cinnamon
Sugar

❖ ❖ ❖

Confectioners' sugar
Milk

Mix together the water, sugar, yeast, and salt. Let stand 20 to 30 minutes. Add shortening and eggs. Add enough flour for a stiff dough, let rise 1½ to 2 hours. Punch down and let rise 1 hour. Flatten the dough out on a greased counter and sprinkle with cinnamon and sugar. Make into cinnamon rolls and let rise till double in bulk. Bake in a 350° oven for 18 to 25 minutes depending on pan size and number of rolls. When taken out of the oven, cover with a hot towel (wet or very damp) and let the crust steam for about 10 to 20 minutes. Glaze with confectioners' sugar and milk glaze.
Makes 4 dozen.

The Mabel Dodge Luhan House

Post Office Box 3400
Taos, New Mexico 87571

The Mabel Dodge Luhan House is a private residence on six acres bordering the Taos Indian Reservation. The beautiful site was chosen by a wealthy patroness of the arts, Mabel Dodge Luhan, for the home that attracted to Taos a constant flow of her artistic and intellectual friends. D. H. Lawrence, Georgia O'Keefe, Thomas Wolfe, Aldous Huxley, Willa Cather, Robinson Jeffers, and numerous other painters, artists, and writers have been guests. The twenty-two room house is sequestered behind an adobe wall whose gates are ancient altar pieces. Huge cottonwood, beech, and elm trees shade the residence and the Flagstone Placita. In traditional Spanish colonial style, a long portal crosses the house, opening to the living room, bedrooms, and the log cabin studio. All main rooms have ceilings of viga and latia construction, arched pueblo-styled doorways, hand-carved doors, pueblo fireplaces, and dark hardwood floors. The home is registered as a New Mexico State Historical Site and is listed on the National Register of Historical Places.

Pastelitos Mexicanos

¾ cup water
6 tablespoons butter or margarine
¾ cup sifted all-purpose flour
3 eggs

❖ ❖ ❖

Grated Parmesan cheese

❖ ❖ ❖

1 teaspoon chicken base (or 1 chicken bouillon cube, crumbled)
½ cup finely chopped onion
1 8-ounce package cream cheese, softened
½ cup chopped ripe olives
1 tablespoon finely chopped green chilies (or to taste)

Heat the water and butter to boiling. Add the flour all at once and cook, stirring until the mixture forms a ball that follows a spoon around the pan. Remove from heat and add the eggs, one at a time, beating thoroughly after each addition. Drop the batter by small teaspoonfuls onto an ungreased baking sheet, and sprinkle with Parmesan cheese. Bake in a 400° oven about 30 minutes, until puffed and dry. Cool. The puffs freeze well before filling.

Mix together the chicken base, onion, and cream cheese. Stir in the olives and green chilies. Just before serving, split one side of each puff and stuff with a heaping tablespoon of the filling.

Makes about 3 dozen tiny puffs.

Pastelitos Picante

2½ cups grated Cheddar cheese
3 cups baking mix
1 pound hot sausage, ground
Dash cayenne pepper

Let the cheese soften to room temperature. Combine all ingredients and mix until very smooth. Form into small balls. Bake in a 400° oven for 30 minutes.

Makes about 100 balls, 1-inch in diameter.

Sopa De Chile Verde Con Queso

1 onion, minced
1 carrot, thinly sliced

3 medium potatoes, cubed
¾ cup lard or oil
3 cups chicken stock

❖ ❖ ❖

¼ cup all-purpose flour
1 cup water
1 cup nonfat dry milk

❖ ❖ ❖

6 green chili peppers, chopped
½ pound Cheddar or Monterey Jack cheese

Sauté the onion, carrot, and potatoes in lard or oil. Add the chicken stock; cook, covered, until tender. Combine the flour, water, and nonfat dry milk. When smooth, add to the vegetable mixture, stirring until well blended. Add the green chilies and cheese. Stir until the cheese is melted. Do not boil.

Serves 6 to 8.

Calavacitas

1 onion, chopped
4 teaspoons olive oil
4 medium summer squash or zucchini
½ cup chopped green chilies
1 16-ounce can whole kernel corn, drained (fresh corn is even better)
Salt and pepper
¼ cup milk
½ cup grated cheese

Sauté the onion in oil; add the squash and chilies. Mix and cook, covered, for 20 minutes. Add the corn and seasonings and cook 5 minutes longer. Add the milk and cheese, stirring constantly to prevent sticking until cheese melts.

Mabel's Grapefruit Cooler

Combine bourbon, grapefruit juice, and lightly crushed mint leaves. Shake with ice until frosty. (Use own taste for amount of bourbon to juice.)

Squash Soup

2 onions, diced
Butter

❖ ❖ ❖

5 potatoes, diced
2 cups well-seasoned chicken stock
　　(chicken boullion may be used)
5 medium yellow squash or
　　zucchini, unpeeled and
　　chopped
2 teaspoons curry powder
Salt and pepper to taste
1 cup milk, cream, or sour cream

❖ ❖ ❖

Fresh squash, chopped
Fresh dill, chopped
Parsley
Chives

Sauté onions in a small amount of butter. Next, cook the potatoes in the chicken stock until tender. Add the squash and sautéed onions; cook until tender. Add the seasonings and milk; cook until hot. Do not boil. Purée in a blender until very smooth. Serve in cups or small bowls with a garnish of chopped fresh squash and finely chopped fresh dill, parsley and chives.

Makes 3 cups.

Taos Valley Salad Dressing

2 tablespoons salt
2 teaspoons monosodium glutamate
2 teaspoons parsley flakes
1 teaspoon garlic powder
1 teaspoon pepper
½ teaspoon onion powder

❖ ❖ ❖

1 cup mayonnaise
1 cup buttermilk

In a small bowl combine the salt, monosodium glutamate, parsley flakes, garlic powder, pepper, and onion powder. Mix thoroughly. To 3¹/₈ teaspoons of this mixture add the mayonnaise and buttermilk. Store the dressing mixture and the dry ingredients in airtight containers in the refrigerator. The flavor of the dressing is best after 24 hours.

Variations: Creamy Herb Dressing. To the basic ingredients add 1 tablespoon chopped chives and ½ teaspoon dried crushed tarragon leaves. Stir and refrigerate.

Bleu Cheese. To the basic ingredients add ¼ to ½ cup crumbed bleu cheese.

Creamy Italian. To the basic ingredients add a dash of cayenne pepper and 1 teaspoon crushed, dried Italian seasoning.

Indian Fry Bread

2 cups unsifted all-purpose flour
½ cup nonfat dry milk
2 teaspoons baking powder
½ teaspoon salt
2 tablespoons lard, cut into ½-inch
　　bits
½ cup warm water

❖ ❖ ❖

Lard for frying

Combine the flour, nonfat dry milk, baking powder, and salt in a large bowl. Add the lard bits and rub the flour and fat together by hand until the mixture resembles flakes of coarse meal. Add water and toss the ingredients together until the dough can be gathered into a ball. Drape the bowl with a damp kitchen towel and let rest at room temperature about 2 hours. Divide the dough into 4 equal parts. Roll each into a circle about 7 to 8 inches in diameter and about ¹/₈-inch thick. In a heavy 10-inch skillet, melt the lard over moderate heat until it is very hot but not smoking. The melted fat should be about 1-inch deep. Fry the breads 1 at a time for about 2 minutes on each side, turning them once with tongs. The bread should puff and become crisp and brown.

Makes 4 loaves.

Chile Verde

3 pounds boneless pork shoulder,
　　cut in ½-inch cubes

2 tablespoons oil

❖ ❖ ❖

1 large clove garlic, minced or
　　mashed

❖ ❖ ❖

2 28-ounce cans (or quart jars,
　　1 pound 12 ounces each)
　　tomatoes
1 7-ounce can California green
　　chilies, seeded and chopped
½ teaspoon sugar
2 teaspoons ground cumin (or 1
　　tablespoon whole cumin seed,
　　crushed)

❖ ❖ ❖

Salt

Brown about ¼ of the pork at a time on all sides in heated oil; remove with a slotted spoon and set aside. Sauté the garlic in the pan drippings. In a large saucepan, combine the tomatoes and their liquid, the green chilies, and seasonings. Bring the tomato mixture to a boil, then reduce the heat to a simmer. Add the browned meat, the juices and the garlic. Cover and simmer for 2 hours, stirring occasionally. Remove the cover; simmer for about 45 minutes more until the sauce is reduced to the desired thickness and the meat is very tender. Add salt to taste.

Serves 6 to 8.

Spinach Enchiladas

1 cup sour cream
1 10¾-ounce can cream of chicken
　　soup
½ clove garlic
1 10-ounce package frozen spinach,
　　thawed and drained
1 3-ounce can jalapeno chilies (or
　　equivalent, frozen or fresh)

❖ ❖ ❖

1½ cups grated Monterey Jack
　　cheese
6 green onions, chopped
8 to 10 flour tortillas

❖ ❖ ❖

Finely chopped onion tops
Chives

To prepare the sauce, purée the sour cream, soup, garlic, spinach, and chilies in the blender. Roll the cheese and a little onion in each tortilla. Pour a little sauce on the bottom of a 9x12-inch cake pan, add the rolled tortillas, and cover with the remaining sauce. Bake in a 350° oven for 20 to 25 minutes or until the cheese melts. Serve garnished with finely chopped onion tops or chives.

Serves 8 to 10.

Crepas con Pollo
with Salsa de Chile Chipotle

2 tablespoons oil
1 medium onion, chopped
2 cloves garlic, mashed or pressed
1 16-ounce can tomato sauce
1 28-ounce can solid pack
    tomatoes, chopped
1 or more chile chipotle, chopped
Salt to taste

    ✦ ✦ ✦

2 cups chopped cooked chicken
2 tablespoons minced onion
Chile verde
2 tablespoons chopped raisins
2 tablespoons blanched chopped
    almonds

    ✦ ✦ ✦

5 eggs
1¼ cups milk
1½ cups sifted all-purpose flour
1 teaspoon salt
2 tablespoons melted butter

    ✦ ✦ ✦

1 pint sour cream
Grated cheese

To make Salsa de Chile Chipotle, in a saucepan heat the oil, add the onions and let them wilt. Then add the garlic, tomato sauce, tomatoes, chile chipotle, and salt. Simmer for 15 to 20 minutes. Set aside for later use.

To prepare the filling, combine the chicken, onion, chile verde, raisins, and almonds. Set aside, ready to be placed inside the crêpes as they are ready.

Prepare the crêpes in a mixing bowl, beating the eggs with a wire whisk until smooth. Add the milk, then the flour and salt. Stir in the butter; mix well. Pour about ¼ cup of batter into a 7-inch buttered Teflon pan. Lift the pan and tilt until the batter covers the bottom of the pan. When the crêpe has browned on the bottom, turn and brown lightly on the other side.

Take up each crêpe and keep warm; refill the pan with batter, continuing until all of the batter is used. While the cooked crêpes are warm, place 1 tablespoonful of the filling mixture in a strip through the center. Roll up the crêpe with the filling inside and place seam side down in a greased large shallow baking dish. When all the crêpes have been cooked, filled, and placed in the dish, cover them with the chipotle sauce, top with sour cream, and sprinkle with cheese. Bake in a 325° oven for 15 to 20 minutes.

Serves 6 to 8.

Pastel De Almendras

½ cup butter (1 stick)
1 cup all-purpose flour
2 tablespoons water

    ✦ ✦ ✦

1 cup water
½ cup butter (1 stick)
1 cup all-purpose flour
3 eggs
1 teaspoon almond extract

    ✦ ✦ ✦

1½ cups confectioners' sugar
½ cup chopped nuts
2 tablespoons butter
2 tablespoons water
1 teaspoon almond extract

To prepare the first layer, cut ½ cup of butter into 1 cup of flour with a pastry blender until the mixture resembles cornmeal. Sprinkle the mixture with 2 tablespoons of water. Stir with a fork until the mixture holds together. Divide the dough in half. Press onto a cookie sheet in 2 rectangles, 12x3 inches, leaving 3 inches between each.

To prepare the second layer, bring 1 cup of water and ½ cup of butter to a rolling boil. Add 1 cup of flour; blend. Stir and cook until the mixture leaves the sides of the pan, about 1 minute. Remove from the heat. Add the eggs, one at a time, beating briskly after each addition. Add 1 teaspoon of almond extract with the last egg. Spread the mixture evenly over each rectangle. Bake in a 350° oven for 1 hour or until the top is golden brown.

Prepare a glaze by combining the confectioners' sugar, nuts, 2 tablespoons butter, 2 tablespoons water, and 1 teaspoon almond extract. Spread the glaze over all.

Serves 6 to 8.

Biscochitos

1½ cups sugar
2 cups lard
2 eggs
6 cups all-purpose flour
3 tablespoons baking powder
1 teaspoon salt
2 tablespoons ground anise seed
2 tablespoons anise flavoring
1 tablespoon cinnamon
¼ cup brandy (optional)

Cream together the sugar and lard. Beat in the eggs until fluffy. Add the dry ingredients and flavoring. Add the brandy if desired. The dough can be rolled and cut to a fancy shape or formed into 2-inch diameter rolls. Wrap in waxed paper or plastic wrap and refrigerate until chilled. Slice into ¼ to ½-inch thick slices and bake in a 400° oven for 10 minutes or until lightly browned.

Makes about 3 dozen.

Cafe Las Palomas

Peel from 4 oranges
15 cloves
3 sticks cinnamon
½ cup confectioners' sugar
1 pint whiskey
8 cups strong coffee
1 quart Kahlua

    ✦ ✦ ✦

Vanilla ice cream

Combine the orange peel, spices, and sugar in a cast iron skillet. Heat, stirring constantly, until the sugar is melted. Add the whiskey and flambé for about 1 minute. Strain; pour into a larger pan with the coffee and Kahlua.

Heat just to boiling. Fill cups about ⅔ full; add ice cream to each cup and serve immediately.

Serves approximately 20.

Sagebrush Inn

Post Office Box 1566
Taos, New Mexico 87571
(505) 758-2254

The flavor of the old Southwest and of the artistic milieu of modern times are combined at the Sagebrush Inn. Spanish colonial architecture is reflected in the soft adobe walls, graceful portals, secluded patios, and piñon-burning fireplaces. Navajo rugs, carved santos, painted bultos, as well as pottery and paintings from the renowned art colony abound. Suites with fireplaces are for let, and some of the individual bedrooms also have fireplaces. The Sagebrush Inn features two restaurants: Los Vacqueros, and the Sagebrush Dining Room. Breakfast and dinner are served year-round.

Sagebrush Inn

Chicken-Chili Noodle Soup

1 large frying chicken, cut up
   (about 3½ pounds)
3 quarts water
2 bay leaves
2 teaspoons salt

❖ ❖ ❖

1 medium onion, chopped
1 cup diagonally sliced celery
1 medium tomato, chopped
2 ⁷/₈-ounce envelopes gravy mix
   for chicken
1 4-ounce can chopped green
   chilies
2 teaspoons Worcestershire sauce
2 teaspoons salt
¼ teaspoon pepper
⅛ teaspoon ground thyme

❖ ❖ ❖

2 cups extra wide egg noodles,
   uncooked

Combine the chicken, water, bay leaves, and 2 teaspoons salt in a large pot. Cover and simmer for 1 hour until tender. Discard the skin and bones; cut the chicken into 1-inch pieces. Skim the fat from the broth; remove the bay leaves. Return the cut-up chicken to the broth, and add the onion, celery, tomato, gravy mix, green chilies, Worcestershire sauce, 2 teaspoons salt, pepper, and thyme. Bring the soup to a boil; add the noodles. Cook for 8 to 10 minutes until the noodles are tender.

Serves 6 to 8.

Green Chili Huevos Rancheros

1 pound pork, diced
Pinch meat tenderizer

❖ ❖ ❖

1 cup chopped green chilies (mild,
   medium, or hot)
8 cups water
1 tablespoon garlic powder
1 tablespoon chicken base

❖ ❖ ❖

⅔ cup all-purpose flour
⅓ cup butter, melted
Maggi seasoning or salt
Dash Kitchen Bouquet (optional)
Butter
Corn tortillas
Eggs
Grated Cheddar cheese

In a large pot, sauté the pork with a pinch of meat tenderizer, and cook until brown. Add the green chilies and water, and bring to a boil. Add the garlic powder and chicken base. Make a roux using the flour and ⅓ cup of melted butter and add to the pork mixture. Let the roux boil for 3 to 4 minutes, stirring occasionally. Add Maggi seasoning or salt. Simmer, stirring occasionally. Add Kitchen Bouquet if desired. Melt butter in a pan and add corn tortillas, turning several times until soft. Cook the eggs as desired. To serve, place a tortilla on a plate and add a cooked egg. Top with the chili and grated Cheddar cheese. This chili is also excellent for burritos and enchiladas.

Makes 8 cups of chili.

New York

The Gregory House

Country Inn and Restaurant
Averill Park, New York 12018
(518) 674-3774

Built in 1830 as a private residence, The Gregory House is now an intimate country inn with twelve comfortably furnished guest rooms and a three star restaurant. Located near the Berkshire and Green mountains in upstate New York, the inn provides its visitors many natural, cultural, and historic attractions. For the less adventuresome, the solitude of lounging in front of the fire in the inn's common room or around the pool in the summer is enough reward.

Béarnaise Sauce

4 egg yolks
2 tablespoons lemon juice
2 tablespoons capers
2 teaspoons tarragon leaves
2 teaspoons tarragon vinegar

❖   ❖   ❖

1½ cups butter (3 sticks), melted

❖   ❖   ❖

2 tablespoons dried parsley flakes

Using a blender, blend at low speed the egg yolks, lemon juice, capers, tarragon leaves, and vinegar. When thor-oughly mixed, slowly add the melted butter, blending until thick and well mixed. Fold in the parsley flakes. Serve warmed.

Makes about 1 cup of sauce.

Chicken Cotelettes á L'Anglaise

1 whole chicken breast
Flour
Beaten egg
Bread crumbs, homemade

Split the breast in half and remove the bones. Cut each half-breast into 3 strips after pounding to tenderize. Dip strips into flour, then into beaten egg. Roll in bread crumbs (use a food processor to grind old rolls, breads, corn muffins, etc.). Sauté in hot oil for about 3 minutes. Turn and sauté for about 2 more minutes until golden brown and crisp. Serve with Bearnaise Sauce.

Serves 2.

Cranberry Apple Crisp

1½ cups fresh or frozen
    cranberries
5 cups (6 medium) apples, pared,
    cored, and sliced
⅓ cup sugar

❖   ❖   ❖

½ cup all-purpose flour
½ cup brown sugar, firmly packed
1 teaspoon cinnamon
¼ cup butter (½ stick)

Sort and rinse the cranberries. Layer cranberries and apples in a greased 9-inch square pan, sprinkling with ⅓ cup sugar as you layer.

In a bowl, mix together the flour, brown sugar, and cinnamon; cut in the butter. Sprinkle the mixture evenly over the apples and cranberries. Bake in a 375° oven for 45 minutes or until apples are tender.

Serves 9.

The Friends Lake Inn

Friends Lake Road
Chestertown, New York 12817
(518) 494-4751

Located in the Adirondacks over-looking Friends Lake, The Friends Lake Inn is conveniently situated just twenty minutes north of Lake George, one and one-half hours north of Al-bany, and one hour south of Lake Placid. Gore Mountain Ski Center is only fifteen minutes away. Formerly The Murphy's, it was built in the 1860s as a boarding house to accommodate the tanners who worked in the major industry of early Chestertown. The inn has been completely restored and re-furbished and now provides a pleasant, relaxed atmosphere for individuals, couples, or families. Downhill skiers, cross-country skiers, trail hikers, anglers, hunters, boaters, or "loafers" will appreciate the beauty of the Adirondacks and The Friends Lake Inn. Individually decorated with a warm country flair, each guest room is comfortable and relaxing. Many of the rooms have brass and iron beds and provide their occupants with magnificent lake views.

Veal Marsala

¼ cup unsalted butter (½ stick)
5 ounces veal medallions
Fresh ground pepper to taste
¼ teaspoon basil
¼ teaspoon oregano
¼ teaspoon finely chopped shallots
⅛ teaspoon minced garlic
2 black olives, chopped
2 strips prosciutto
1 teaspoon chopped green pepper
2 large mushrooms, sliced
Chopped parsley

❖ ❖ ❖

¼ cup Marsala wine

❖ ❖ ❖

Grated orange and lemon rind

Melt the butter in a heavy fry pan, quickly sauté the veal. Remove the veal from the pan, reserving the butter. Add to the butter the seasonings, shallots, garlic, olives, ham, green pepper, mushrooms, and parsley. Simmer for about 4 minutes. Return the veal to the pan, add the wine and simmer until the liquid is reduced by half. Serve garnished with orange and lemon rind.
Serves 1.

Alligator Dumplings

1 pound alligator meat
2 pounds veal scraps
Mint to taste
Salt and pepper to taste
8 egg whites
2 quarts heavy cream

❖ ❖ ❖

1 quart water
2 cups white wine
½ cup Brandy
5 peppercorns
1 bay leaf
2 sprigs parsley

Grind the meats to a paste; season to taste. Add the egg whites gradually. Put the mixture through a fine sieve. Place in a large bowl over ice. Stir in the cream until smooth. Keep the bowl over ice.

Make court bouillon by combining the water, wine, brandy, and seasonings in a shallow pan. Bring to a simmer. Shape the dumplings with a spoon; poach in the bouillon.

Note: Leftover bouillon should be strained and reserved for use later in Essence of Alligator Flambé soup.

Essence of Alligator Flambé

2 pounds alligator meat
2 pounds veal
4 pounds veal marrow bones
12 egg whites
3 carrots, diced
2 onions, diced
2 leeks, diced
½ cup diced celery
4 bay leaves
1 teaspoon thyme
1 teaspoon mint
20 peppercorns, crushed
3 cloves garlic
1 bunch parsley stems
1½ gallons strained chicken stock
1 gallon strained veal stock

❖ ❖ ❖

Strained court bouillon (reserved from Alligator Dumplings)

Grind together the alligator and veal meat. In a very large stock pot combine the ground meats, veal bones, egg whites, carrots, onions, leeks, celery, bay leaves, thyme, mint, peppercorns, garlic, and parsley stems. Add the chicken and veal stocks and bring just to a boil. Simmer for 2½ hours. Remove from the heat and strain through flannel or doubled cheese cloth. Return the clear broth to the stock pot.

Scrape the marrow from the boiled veal bones and add with the court bouillon to the soup; adjust the seasonings. Heat through.
Serves 8 to 10.

Dessert Soufflé

3 tablespoons cornstarch
¼ cup corn syrup
1½ cups orange juice
2½ tablespoons minced orange pulp
2 tablespoons grated orange rind
1½ teaspoons minced lemon pulp
½ teaspoon grated lemon rind

❖ ❖ ❖

4 egg whites
6 tablespoons sugar
12 orange segments, peeled and seeded
Pine nuts or pistachios

❖ ❖ ❖

Julienne of orange peel
Confectioners' sugar
6 orange segments, peeled and seeded

Combine in a saucepan the cornstarch, corn syrup, juice, orange pulp and rind, lemon pulp and rind. Simmer without boiling over moderate heat for 2 minutes, stirring constantly. Remove from the heat, set aside to cool.

Beat the egg whites in a mixing bowl until soft peaks form. Add the sugar a spoonful at a time, beating until stiff peaks form. When the orange and lemon mixture has cooled to room temperature fold in the beaten egg whites.

Butter 6 ramekin dishes, sprinkle lightly with sugar, and place 2 orange segments in each dish. Divide the soufflé mixture equally between the dishes. Top with nuts. Place the dishes on a baking sheet. Bake in a 375° oven for 7 to 10 minutes until golden.

Garnish each soufflé with julienne of orange peel, confectioners' sugar, and one orange segment. Serve immediately!

Note from the innkeeper: Contrary to the myth that soufflés are fragile, temperamental, and will disintegrate at a mere touch or by the gaze of an eye, the soufflé is one of the easiest of desserts. It should be baked at the last minute to insure perfection.

Serves 4.

Back of the Beyond

7233 Lower East Hill Road
Colden, New York 14033
(716) 652-0427

This charming country mini-estate is in the Boston Hills and ski area of western New York, about twenty-five miles from Buffalo and fifty miles from Niagara Falls. Accommodations are in a separate chalet with three available bedrooms, one bath, and a fully furnished kitchen. The dining/living room, piano, pool table, and fireplaces are available to guests. A rustic post/beam cabin in the woods will accommodate two more. A full country herbal breakfast is served daily, and the organic herb, flower, and vegetable gardens are for the delight of guests who want to stroll and relax on the grounds. A greenhouse and Herbtique Gift Shop is part of the complex, as are a large pond for swimming and lovely woods for hiking. Lawn games are provided for the summer and autumn visitors, and cross country skiing is free on the inn's own trails.

Swedish Caraway or Anise Rye Bread

½ cup honey
2 teaspoons herb salt (optional)
2 tablespoons vegetable oil
1½ cups milk, scalded
2 ¼-ounce packages active dry yeast
1 cup warm water (110° to 115°)
3 cups light rye flour
3½ cups unbleached flour
2 tablespoons caraway or anise seed

In a large mixing bowl combine the honey, salt, and oil with the scalded milk, cool to lukewarm. Dissolve the yeast in warm water and combine with the milk mixture. Add the rye flour gradually, then 2 cups of the unbleached flour, beating thoroughly. Add the remaining flour and seeds. Turn the dough onto a floured surface. It is important to let it rest for 10 minutes. Then knead until the dough is smooth and elastic. Place in a greased bowl, turning to grease the dough; cover and set in warm place to rise until doubled. Punch down once and let rise again (about 2 hours in all). Shape into round loaves and put into greased loaf pans. Cover and let rise again (about 40 minutes). Bake in a 375° oven for 45 to 50 minutes until loaves sound hollow when tapped. Place on a rack to cool and brush the tops with butter.

Makes 2 loaves.

Applesauce Mint Nut Bread

A quick bread that is great to make ahead, as it slices better and has more flavor after 2 or 3 days.

2 cups unbleached flour
¾ cup brown sugar, firmly packed
1 tablespoon baking powder
1 teaspoon herb salt (optional)
½ teaspoon baking soda
½ teaspoon cinnamon

½ teaspoon nutmeg
1 cup chopped nuts

❖   ❖   ❖

1 egg, beaten
1 cup applesauce
1 teaspoon dried mint or ¼ cup chopped fresh mint
¼ cup oil

Mix the dry ingredients and nuts together in a mixing bowl. Combine the egg, applesauce, mint, and oil; add to the dry ingredients and stir until just blended. Pour the batter into a greased loaf pan and bake in a 350° oven for about 50 minutes. Cool on a rack. When the bread is completely cool wrap in plastic or foil.

Makes 1 loaf.

Shash's Stash

Use grated Cheddar, Brie, Swiss, Parmesan, or any combination of cheeses you like best. Add enough mayonnaise to hold the grated cheese together. Season with a few drops of hot sauce and Worcestershire sauce. Flavor with chopped green scallions, shallot tops, or freshly grated shallot bulb. Green and/or red peppers may be added for color if desired. Add your favorite herbs for the final touch (dillweed, marjoram, lemon, thyme, etc.); blend well.

Spread on English muffin halves and broil until bubbly and lightly browned.

Sautéed Fruit Compote

Sauté sliced bananas in butter and lemon juice, until warmed. Before removing from pan, just before serving, add other fruits such as sliced kiwi, whole seedless grapes, strawberries, etc. Serve with a dollop of yogurt and honey on top. Garnish with fresh mint or lemon balm sprigs.

De Puy Canal House

Route 213
High Falls, New York 12440
(914) 687-7700
(914) 687-7777

The De Puy Canal House features a four-star restaurant operated since 1969 by John Novi in the tiny village of High Falls. A cabaret is located in the basement, along with an extensive wine cellar. The house has three guest rooms filled with art and artifacts.

De Puy Canal House

Mock Eggs Benedict with Scallops

An appetizer consisting of boufarette pastries topped with spinach, ham, scallops, and Hollandaise sauce.

4 cups all-purpose flour
**2 ¼-ounce packages active dry
    yeast**
Pinch salt
¼ cup oil
1¼ cups warm water (110° to 115°)
    ❖ ❖ ❖
4 cups coarsely chopped spinach
Splash white wine

**Splash fish sauce (available at
    oriental food stores)**
    ❖ ❖ ❖
**2 ¼-inch thick slices fresh baked
    ham**
**6 fresh large sea scallops,
    butterflied**
    ❖ ❖ ❖
¼ cup butter
2½ teaspoons lemon juice
3 egg yolks, well beaten
    ❖ ❖ ❖
½ cup butter (1 stick)
    ❖ ❖ ❖
**Salt and cayenne or white pepper
    to taste**

To make the boufarette dough combine in a large mixing bowl the 4 cups of flour, yeast, salt, and oil. Add the water a little at a time. Knead until the mixture forms a ball and is soft. Divide the dough into 4 equal parts; 2 portions for the boufarettes and the remainder can be made into bread rolls by forming and baking.

Stretch each of the 2 pieces of dough out until they form a circle approximately 6 inches wide. Drop each boufarette into hot (350°) oil; brown on one side, then on the other. Drain and place on a serving dish.

Steam the spinach in the wine and fish sauce until it is very limp, but do not overcook. With a slotted spoon, place ½ of the spinach on each boufarette.

Sauté the ham slices in a fry pan in a little butter for 30 seconds on each side, and place a slice on each spinach portion.

Splash each scallop with a little melted butter, then on each ham slice arrange 3 scallops in a circle with a hole in the center the approximate size of an egg yolk. Place the entire dish under a broiler until the scallops are half-cooked. To make Hollandaise sauce place ¼ cup of butter in the top part of a double boiler. Add the lemon juice and egg yolks; place over hot (not boiling) water. Cook slowly, beating constantly until the mixture begins to thicken. Add the remaining butter and cook until the sauce has the consistency of mayonnaise, beating con-

stantly. Remove from the hot water immediately and add the salt and pepper.

Remove the scallops from the broiler and spoon the Hollandaise sauce in the center of the scallops until the finished design resembles a sunny side egg. Place under the broiler again until the dish and the sauce are heated.

Shad Roe Salad

1½ pounds shad roe (or sole roe)
1 tablespoon chopped parsley
¼ large Spanish onion, minced
2 to 4 anchovies, mashed
3 tablespoons tahini sauce
1 tablespoon lemon juice
Mayonnaise to taste
Paprika to color
Boston lettuce

Cover the roe with water and poach for 3 minutes. Cool the roe and remove the skin. Mash the roe (or it may be put through a sieve or grinder). Add the parsley, onion, anchovies, tahini, and lemon juice. Slowly add the mayonnaise until the desired consistency is reached. Stir in enough paprika to color the salad a light pink. Chill and serve on a bed of Boston lettuce.

Serves 4.

Interlaken Lodge

15 Interlaken Avenue
Lake Placid, New York 12946
(518) 523-3180

The Interlaken Lodge, a quaint and romantic country inn, is in the breathtaking Adirondack Mountains between picturesque Mirror Lake and historic Lake Placid. It caters to those on a romantic holiday or on a family vacation. All of the twelve guest rooms have private baths and some have panoramic views and terraces. There is one two-bedroom suite. After a day of skiing, hiking, golf, tennis, shopping, sightseeing, or enjoying the fall foliage, guests will delight in returning to the Interlaken for a good dinner individually prepared by the chef. In the morning a continental breakfast featuring homemade pastries is delivered to guests' rooms. If preferred, guests with a hearty appetite may enjoy a full country breakfast in the dining room.

Interlaken Lodge

Pasta Interlaken

½ cup unsalted butter (1 stick)
1½ pounds mushrooms, sliced
3 leeks (white part only), sliced

❖ ❖ ❖

2 cups heavy cream
1 cup sliced sun-dried tomatoes (available in specialty food stores)
2 cloves garlic, crushed
1¼ cups grated fresh Parmesan cheese

❖ ❖ ❖

1 tablespoon unsalted butter
½ pound fresh shrimp, cleaned and deveined
½ pound scallops
1 cup fresh peas (or frozen petite peas)
Spinach and egg fettuccine (cooked)

Melt ½ cup of butter in a very large sauté pan over medium heat. Add the mushrooms and leeks; cover and cook for 5 minutes or until the vegetables have wilted. Add the cream and boil until the liquid is reduced by ½. Add the tomatoes, garlic, and cheese. Lower the heat and cook until the sauce is thickened, stirring constantly. Turn off the heat and set the sauce aside. Melt 1 tablespoon of butter in a small sauté pan; simmer the seafood until just cooked through. Add the peas; turn off the heat. Toss the cooked fettuccine with the sauce and seafood. Serve hot with more grated cheese on side.

Serves 6 to 8.

Quadruple Chocolate Suicide

1¾ cups half and half
2 tablespoons honey
6 egg yolks, room temperature
2 tablespoons sugar
1 teaspoon vanilla extract
Pinch salt
6 ounces bittersweet chocolate, chopped
3 tablespoons unsweetened cocoa
2 tablespoons dark rum

❖ ❖ ❖

2 cups whipping cream
¼ cup honey
12 egg yolks, room temperature
¼ cup sugar
1 teaspoon vanilla extract
Pinch salt
12 ounces bittersweet chocolate, chopped

❖ ❖ ❖

Whipped cream
Shaved chocolate mint bars

To make chocolate bittersweet ice cream scald the half and half in a heavy medium-sized saucepan. Stir in 2 tablespoons of honey. Combine 6 egg yolks, 2 tablespoons of sugar, 1 teaspoon vanilla, and a pinch of salt in a mixing bowl. Slowly whisk in the half and half mixture, return to the pan. Stir until the mixture is thick enough to coat the back of a spoon (180°), do not boil. Remove from the heat, add 6 ounces of chocolate, and stir until melted. Sift in the cocoa, whisking to blend. Add the rum. Strain into a container. Cool slightly. Cover and freeze at least 8 hours.

To make the chocolate mousse scald the cream in a heavy medium-sized saucepan. Add ¼ cup of honey and stir until dissolved. Combine 12 egg yolks, ¼ cup sugar, 1 teaspoon vanilla, and salt in a mixing bowl. Slowly whisk in the cream mixture. Return to the pan. Stir over medium-low heat until thick enough to coat the back of a spoon (180°), do not boil. Remove from the heat. Add the chocolate and stir until melted. Strain into a bowl; cool. Freeze until firm, at least 3 hours.

Place 2 scoops each of the ice cream and mousse side by side in either a dessert bowl or a molded chocolate bowl. Top with whipped cream and shaved chocolate.

Serves 6.

Three Village Inn

150 Main Street
Stony Brook
Long Island, New York 11790
(516) 751-0555

Three Village Inn, originally the Jonas Smith Homestead of 1785, offers modern comfort in an atmosphere of 1800. Thoroughly modernized as far as creature comforts are concerned, good food, good drink, and a good night's rest are assured. Outdoor activities, such as swimming, golf, fishing, and walking await the visitor.

Stony Brook is an old shipping and fishing village nestled in the hills of the north shore, with its own harbor and with Long Island Sound immediately adjacent. The restored Village Green and community shopping center add interest to Stony Brook's charm and take the visitor back in time to the early days of the Republic.

Cold Plum Soup

1 29-ounce can purple plums
1 cup water
⅔ cup sugar
1 cinnamon stick
¼ teaspoon white pepper
Pinch salt
½ cup heavy cream
½ cup dry red wine
1 tablespoon cornstarch
2 tablespoons lemon juice
1 teaspoon grated lemon rind

❖   ❖   ❖

1 cup sour cream
3 tablespoons Brandy

Drain the plums, reserving the syrup. Pit and chop the plums. In a medium saucepan, combine the plums with the reserved syrup, water, sugar, cinnamon stick, white pepper and salt. Bring the liquid to a boil over moderately high heat. Reduce to medium heat and cook the mixture 5 minutes, stirring occasionally. Stir in heavy cream. Combine the wine with the cornstarch, stir into the mixture. Cook, stirring constantly, until it is thickened. Stir in the lemon juice and rind. Remove the pan from the heat.

Measure out ½ cup of the soup mixture into a small bowl, whisk in the sour cream, then the Brandy. Stir the mixture into the soup, stirring until it is smooth. Let the soup cool. Chill, covered, for at least 4 hours.

Ladle the soup into cups and garnish each serving with a dollop of sour cream and a sprinkling of cinnamon.

Makes 6 to 8 servings.

Three Village Inn Apple Crisp

10 cups apples, sliced
1½ teaspoons cinnamon
2 teaspoons sugar, granulated

❖   ❖   ❖

1½ cups brown sugar, firmly
    packed
1 cup plus 2 tablespoons all-
    purpose flour
6 tablespoons butter (¾ stick)
6 tablespoons margarine (¾ stick)
½ teaspoon cinnamon
¼ teaspoon salt

Place the apple slices, 1½ teaspoons of cinnamon, and sugar in a bowl and mix thoroughly. Spread in a lightly buttered 9x13x2-inch baking dish. In a medium bowl combine the brown sugar, flour, butter, margarine, ½ teaspoon of cinnamon, and salt. Blend with a pastry blender until the mixture resembles coarse crumbs. Spread the crumbs evenly over the apple mixture and pat down. Bake in a 350° oven for 45 minutes or until the apples are thoroughly cooked. If the topping browns

too fast, place a sheet of brown paper over the pan. Serve slightly warm with whipped cream.

Makes about 10 servings.

Genesee Country Inn

948 George Street
Mumford, New York 14511
(716) 538-2500

The Genesee Country Inn and Conference Center is just twenty-five minutes from Rochester, New York, and less than a mile from the Genesee village and museum. Six acres of grounds include creeks, fully-stocked trout ponds, gardens, and a sixteen-foot waterfall. Guests awaken to the soothing sounds of Allens Creek, which flows beneath the inn foundation, and enjoy an ample breakfast in a splendid room overlooking the creek. Fall color tours, cross country skiing, antiquing, biking, and hiking are available and inn guests may enjoy year-round trout fishing.

Genesee Country Inn French Toast

12 1-inch slices French bread (slice
    on the diagonal)
1 8-ounce package cream cheese,
    whipped
2 eggs
2 to 3 tablespoons milk
½ teaspoon cinnamon
Butter
1 cup strawberry or apricot
    preserves

Slice bread. Coat each slice with whipped cream cheese on one side only. Put every two slices together to make a sandwich. Set aside.

Combine eggs, milk and cinnamon in a flat dish. Beat well.

Dip the sandwiches in egg mixture. Let stand a few minutes. Heat preserves in a saucepan until warmed. Heat a small amount of butter in a frying pan. Sauté sandwiches in the melted butter until golden. Serve with warmed preserves on top.

Serves 6.

circa 1833

Pleasant Valley Quince Jam

    4½ cups fully ripe quinces (about 3
        pounds)
    3 cups water
          ❖   ❖   ❖
    6½ cups sugar
          ❖   ❖   ❖
    1 box fruit pectin
    ½ cup lemon juice
    1 teaspoon ginger

Peel and core the quinces. Using a food processor, grind very fine. Place in a saucepan along with the water. Cook, covered, for about 15 minutes. (Fruit will darken and then lighten as it cooks.) Measure about 4½ cups of prepared fruit into a 6 to 8-quart saucepan. Measure the sugar and set aside. Add the pectin to the fruit, mix well. Add the lemon juice and ginger. Place over high heat and stir until the mixture comes to a full boil. Add the sugar all at once and again bring to a full rolling boil. Boil hard 1 to 2 minutes, stirring constantly. Remove from the heat. Skim off the foam. Fill 8 8-ounce heated jars (or equivalent) and seal, process in a hot water bath for 10 minutes.

Makes about 8 cups.

Easy Maple Syrup

This is an ideal recipe for maple syrup in an emergency and is just as good as the store variety.

    2 cups white sugar (or brown
        sugar, firmly packed)
    1 cup water
    ½ teaspoon maple flavoring
    ¼ cup butter (½ stick)

Heat the sugar in a saucepan. Add the water and bring to a full boil. Boil for 2 minutes. Remove from the heat and stir in the flavoring and butter. Store in the refrigerator.

Makes 1½ cups.

Wine Country Shrimp Appetizer

This recipe is easy but it has been a real hit with our conference guests. Genesee Country is on the fringes of wine country and we always use native New York State Sherry.

    1 cup soy sauce
    3 tablespoons Sherry
    1 pound large shrimps (16 to 20)
        cooked and shelled
          ❖   ❖   ❖
    ½ cup brown sugar
    1 pound bacon strips

Combine the soy sauce and sherry in a bowl, add the shrimps and marinate in the mixture for 30 minutes in the refrigerator.

Remove the shrimps from the marinade and sprinkle well with the brown sugar. Wrap each shrimp in a bacon strip and secure with a toothpick. Broil until the bacon is crispy and serve.

Serves 8 to 10.

The Garnet Hill Lodge

North River, New York 12856
(518) 251-2821

The Garnet Hill Lodge is a resort-inn and conference center in the Adirondacks, offering quiet beauty and comfort year round. The Log House has a restaurant, garnetstone fireplace, reading room, lounges, game room, and reception desk on the first floor. Upstairs are fourteen guest rooms, each with a private bath. Six rooms have balconies overlooking the lake and mountains. The Ski Haus is a two-level apartment adjoining the equipment center. This unit has a large bed/sitting room, private bath, sleeping loft, and a private entrance. The Big Shanty is a beautiful old manor house. The baronial main room is lined with shelves of books and is dominated by a garnetstone fireplace. Six bedrooms are upstairs, two with private baths. Dinner and breakfast is included with the daily and weekly room rates.

Tea Room Carrot Bread

    2 cups all-purpose flour
    1½ cups sugar
    2 teaspoons baking soda
    2 teaspoons cinnamon
    ½ teaspoon salt
    2 cups finely grated carrots
    ¼ cup chopped nuts (optional)
    ½ cup shredded coconut
    ½ cup raisins (optional)
    1 cup vegetable oil
    1 teaspoon vanilla
    3 eggs, slightly beaten

Sift the flour, sugar, soda, cinnamon, and salt together in a large bowl. Stir in the carrots. Add the nuts, coconut, and raisins. Stir in the oil, vanilla, and eggs. Pour into a greased 9x5x3-inch loaf pan. Bake in a 350° oven for 1 hour.

Serves 12 to 14.

New Orleans Veal Grillades

4 veal cutlets
Salt and pepper
Flour
3 tablespoons shortening or vegetable oil

❖ ❖ ❖

2 tablespoons all-purpose flour
1 onion, finely chopped
1 clove garlic, minced
3 sprigs parsley, finely chopped

❖ ❖ ❖

1 green pepper, finely chopped
3 to 4 stalks celery, finely chopped
1 cup water
½ teaspoon thyme
1 bay leaf, crushed
1 14½-ounce can tomatoes
Cayenne pepper to taste

Season the veal with salt and pepper, then dredge in flour. In a fry pan brown the veal in hot melted shortening; remove the veal, reserving the drippings.

Measure out 2 tablespoons of the drippings and place in a large saucepan or Dutch oven. Brown 2 tablespoons of flour over low heat, stirring often. Add the onion, garlic, and parsley.

In a small saucepan quickly parboil the green pepper and celery in the cup of water; add to the saucepan along with the veal, thyme, bay leaf, tomatoes, and cayenne pepper. Simmer for 2 hours or until the veal is tender.

Serves 6.

Broccoli Bake

2 10-ounce packages frozen chopped broccoli

❖ ❖ ❖

1 10¾-ounce can cream of mushroom soup
½ cup mayonnaise
1 egg, slightly beaten
1 small onion, grated
1 cup grated sharp cheese
4 ounces herb stuffing
¼ cup butter, melted

Cook the broccoli slightly; drain. Combine with the soup, mayonnaise, egg, onion, and cheese. Place in 2 1-quart casseroles. Toss the stuffing with melted butter; spoon over the broccoli mixture. Bake in a 350° oven for 30 to 35 minutes.

Serves 6 to 8.

Sautéed Leeks

2 pounds fresh leeks

❖ ❖ ❖

2 large onions, chopped
½ cup olive oil

❖ ❖ ❖

3 medium carrots, sliced
1 large tomato (or 1 14½-ounce can whole tomatoes)
1 teaspoon salt
¼ teaspoon white pepper

Remove the green tops and roots from the leeks; cut the white and light green parts into 2-inch pieces. Place in cold water and set aside to soak.

Using a medium saucepan, sauté the onion in olive oil. Drain the water from the leeks and add to the saucepan along with the carrots, tomato, salt, and pepper. Add enough boiling water to cover the vegetables. Cover the pan tightly and cook for 15 to 30 minutes, until tender.

Note from the innkeeper: May be served over hot rice. Excellent with broiled fish.

Serves 6.

Strawberry Castle Bed and Breakfast

1883 Penfield Road (Route 441)
Penfield, New York 14526
(716) 385-3266

A warm welcome awaits the guests of Strawberry Castle. They can wander the lawns and gardens, sit beneath the huge maple tree, and enjoy the birds singing. Strawberry Castle's rooms are large, comfortable, and pleasant, and are virtually unaltered from the original design. Sunning on the patio and swimming in the pool are among guests' most enjoyed experiences.

Strawberry Castle's Eggs Benedict

1 ham slice
1 cheese slice
1 croissant

❖ ❖ ❖

2 eggs
Béarnaise sauce
Parsley
Strawberries

Place the ham and cheese slices on the croissant; heat in a 375° oven for 10 minutes.

Poach the eggs. Place the croissant on a plate. Place one egg inside the croissant and the other egg on the plate next to the croissant. Lightly cover with Béarnaise sauce. Glaze under the broiler for 1 minute. Garnish with parsley and a ripe strawberry. Serve immediately. Enjoy.

Sage Cottage

Box 121
Trumansburg, New York 14886
(607) 387-6449

Sage Cottage, just north of Ithaca and minutes from Taughannock Falls, is located in a rejuvenated Gothic Revival home built about 1855. There are four guestrooms. Breakfast always includes fresh herb breads, biscuits, and jams made with herbs from the gardens.

Red Vinaigrette

2 tablespoons spicy mustard
2 tablespoons red wine vinegar
2 tablespoons tomato paste
3 tablespoons olive oil
2 tablespoons chives, minced
3 tablespoons water

Combine the mustard, vinegar and tomato paste in a blender; process. Add the olive oil; process to mix. Add the chives and water; process until dressing is creamy. Serve over salads.

Makes about 1 cup of dressing.

Orange Mint Cucumbers

2 tablespoons corn oil
2 tablespoons red wine vinegar
1 tablespoon orange juice, frozen
    undiluted
1 tablespoon chopped fresh
    spearmint (1 teaspoon dry)
2 large thin cucumbers

Combine the corn oil, red wine vinegar, orange juice and mint in the bowl of a blender; blend at low speed 15 seconds. Slice the unpeeled cucumbers very thinly. Pour the orange-mint mixture over the cucumbers; cover and chill in the refrigerator several hours. Serve in lettuce cups garnished with sprigs of mint or, in the winter, with orange slices.

Serves 4 to 6.

Caraway Crisps

Once upon a time caraway seeds were heated with sugar until it melted; they were called comfits. These little sweets were often used in cakes and other desserts. Caraway is reputed to give the gift of memory and cure fickleness. These tiny cookies are wonderful with lemon balm tea or fresh applesauce.

1 cup caraway seeds
❖ ❖ ❖
6 tablespoons butter
¾ cup dark brown sugar, firmly
    packed
1 egg
½ cup all-purpose flour
¼ teaspoon baking powder
1 teaspoon vanilla extract

Toast the seeds over low heat in a heavy skillet for 15 minutes, stirring frequently. Place the toasted seeds in a paper bag and crush with a rolling pin.

Cream the butter and sugar; beat until light; add the egg and blend. Combine the flour and baking powder; stir into the creamed mixture. Stir in the vanilla and crushed seeds. Drop by half teaspoonfuls on a greased cookie sheet at least 2 inches apart. (They spread a lot.) Bake in a 350° oven for 8 minutes. Let the cookies cool for one minute before removing from the pan. Let the cookie sheet cool before dropping on more cookies. Store in tightly covered container.

Makes 7 dozen cookies.

The Jeronimo

Walder Valley, New York 12588
(914) 433-1219

The Jeronimo is an informal resort on eighty rolling, wooded acres. Guests enjoy the indoor and outdoor pool and saunas, and tennis is available for those so inclined. Mental hiking, organized idling, and woolgathering are also encouraged. Three meals are served daily.

Linguine with Clam Sauce

1 pound linguine
❖ ❖ ❖
3 cloves garlic, minced
¼ cup peanut oil
1 6-ounce can minced clams
Oregano to taste
Minced parsley
Salt and pepper to taste

Cook the linguine according to the package directions.

While the pasta cooks prepare the sauce. In a saucepan fry the garlic in the oil. When the garlic browns, add the juice from the can of clams. Add the seasonings. Bring to a boil; simmer for 5 minutes. Add the clams a few seconds before serving (just enough time to heat them through and keep them tender).

When the linguine is done drain it well. Pour the sauce over pasta.

Serves 6.

Coq au Vin

1 broiler
½ cup peanut oil
1 cup chopped onion
2 cloves garlic, minced
¼ teaspoon oregano
½ teaspoon salt
3 tablespoons lemon juice

❖ ❖ ❖

1 cup Rhone red wine

Cut the broiler into 8 pieces. In a large skillet sauté the pieces of chicken in the oil. Remove the pieces when browned, place on a paper towel to drain. In the same oil sauté the onion and garlic. Add the oregano, salt, and lemon juice. Place the chicken pieces in a roasting pan; pour the sauce over the chicken. Cover; bake in a 350° oven for 45 minutes. Uncover; add the wine and bake an additional 10 minutes.
Serves 4.

Veal en Papillote

2 pounds veal, sliced thin (about 4x4-inches)
Oil
Paprika

❖ ❖ ❖

4 large onions
1 2¼-ounce jar capers
1 8-ounce can mushroom pieces
1 cup pimiento-stuffed olives, sliced across
1 clove garlic
1 teaspoon salt
½ teaspoon oregano
Pepper to taste

Marinate the veal in oil and paprika. Chop the vegetables finely. Add seasonings. Place each serving of veal in the center of a buttered 10-inch square of parchment paper. On each piece of veal, place 3 tablespoons of vegetable mixture. Double-fold the parchment paper to assure sealing (so no steam escapes and parchment puffs up). Place on a baking pan and bake in a 325° oven for 30 to 35 minutes. Serve immediately.
Serves 6.

Sweet and Sour Peppers

6 large green peppers (cut into 2-inch squares)
¼ cup vegetable oil
2 cloves garlic
¼ cup cider vinegar
¼ cup sugar
Salt and pepper to taste

In a large heavy skillet, sauté the peppers in oil on high heat. When they begin to soften, lower the heat. Add the garlic, vinegar, sugar, salt, and pepper. Cook until tender. Chill overnight. Serve cold.

Yellow Rice

Note from the innkeeper: Bijol may be purchased at Spanish-American groceries. If you have difficulty purchasing it, write to the Jeronimo.

1½ large onions, minced
1 clove garlic
½ cup oil
¼ teaspoon oregano
1 tablespoon lemon juice
½ cup canned tomatoes
1½ cups chicken broth
1 package Bijol
¾ teaspoon salt
1½ cups rice

❖ ❖ ❖

Pimiento

In a heavy saucepan sauté the onions and garlic in oil. Add the oregano, juice, tomatoes, chicken broth, Bijol, and salt. Bring to a boil and add the rice. Cover and simmer 20 minutes or until done. Garnish with pieces of pimiento.

North Carolina

The Grove Park Inn and Country Club

290 Macon Avenue
Asheville, North Carolina 28804
(704) 252-2711

The Grove Park Inn is a grand hotel. In 1913 this meant the daily polishing of coins so that guests, such as Thomas Edison, never received a tarnished silver dollar. In 1984 it meant the construction of a premier conference center capable of handling meetings of up to 1000. Today it means both returning to the early years in such ways as a leisurely horse-and-carriage ride through the pines and the enjoyment of an indoor sports complex to serve the most active guest any time of the year. Full amenities, combined with championship golf; an incomparable collection of restaurants, lounges, and shops; classic service, and rare atmosphere, make the Grove Park Inn the most complete year-round resort hotel in the Carolinas. Sitting on the western slope of Sunset Mountain, the inn looks toward the glorious Blue Ridge Mountains.

❖ ❖ ❖ ❖ ❖ ❖

Chicken and Oyster Gumbo

18 pounds chicken, cut in eighths
Pepper
2 cups clarified butter
1½ cups all-purpose flour

❖ ❖ ❖

8 large onions, diced
2 bunches celery, chopped
5 green peppers, chopped
2 ounces garlic, crushed

❖ ❖ ❖

1½ gallons chicken stock
Filé powder
Salt
½ cup Worcestershire sauce
5 bay leaves, crumbled
2 tablespoons allspice
1 tablespoon cloves
3 tablespoons thyme
Hot pepper sauce

❖ ❖ ❖

1 gallon oysters
Chopped onion tops
Parsley

Season the chicken with pepper. Brown in the butter; remove and add the flour to the butter. Cook on low to make a dark roux, 20 to 30 minutes. Add the vegetables and the chicken to the roux; cook for 5 minutes. Stir in the stock and seasonings; bring to a boil. Simmer for 1 hour and 30 minutes. Add the oysters and heat through. Garnish with chopped onion tops and parsley.

Serves 16 or more.

Veal Scallops with Gorgonzola Sauce

6 3½-ounce veal scallops
Flour for dredging
3 tablespoons olive oil

❖ ❖ ❖

½ cup Brandy
½ cup unsalted butter, cut into bits
¼ pound Gorgonzola, crumbled
½ cup heavy cream
Pepper

Dredge the veal scallops in the flour, shaking off the excess. In a large stainless steel or enameled skillet sauté the veal in oil over moderately high heat for 30 seconds on each side. As they are cooked transfer them with tongs to a platter; keep warm.

Add the Brandy to the skillet and deglaze the skillet, scraping up the brown bits clinging to the bottom and sides. Reduce the mixture by half over moderate heat. Reduce the heat to moderately low; whisk in the butter. Cook the mixture, whisking until the butter melts. Stir in the Gorgonzola and the cream. Cook the sauce, whisking until the cheese is melted. Season with pepper. Top the veal with the sauce.

Serves 6.

Flambéed Cherries

1½ pounds sweet dark cherries,
pitted
1 pint red wine

The Grove Park Inn

¼ **cup sugar**
Pinch of cinnamon
1 teaspoon cornstarch
2 tablespoons red currant jelly

❖ ❖ ❖

2 tablespoons Kirsch

Poach the cherries in the red wine with the sugar and the cinnamon. Drain the cherries and reduce the red wine to ¼ of its volume. Thicken with the cornstarch dispersed in a little water. Add the red currant jelly. Cook for 5 to 7 minutes. Place the cherries in a pan and stir in the sauce. Pour 2 tablespoons of warmed Kirsch over the cherries and ignite when ready to serve.

Serve with one scoop of vanilla ice cream and the cherries poured atop.

Serves 6.

Black Forest Cake

5 eggs
¼ **cup butter**
⅔ **cup all-purpose flour**
¼ **cup cocoa**
⅔ **cup sugar**

½ **cup cornstarch**
½ **cup sugar syrup**
2 teaspoons Kirsch
1 pint whipping cream, whipped
**9 1-ounce squares chocolate,
 shaved**

In a mixing bowl, mix the eggs and butter at medium speed for 2 to 3 minutes. Reduce speed and add the flour and cocoa. Add the sugar and cornstarch and mix. Bake in a greased 1¼-inch deep cake pan in a 350° oven for 20 to 25 minutes.

When cool, cut the cake into 3 layers. Combine the sugar syrup and Kirsch. Moisten the bottom layer with the Kirsch-sugar syrup. Spread whipped cream over the bottom layer of the cake to a thickness of ¼ inch. Place the second layer on top and spread it with the whipped cream. Place the remaining layer on top. Spread whipped cream over the top and sides of the entire cake. Sprinkle with shaved chocolate.

Note: Pitted and marinated red cherries may be placed between the individual layers.

Serves 12 to 16.

Balsam Lodge

Box 279
Balsam, North Carolina 28707
(704) 456-6528

Balsam Lodge consists of two lodgings, and guests may choose between the Main House and the Depot. The former is a home that was built in 1904. The latter, the original railroad station for the town, is made up of efficiency units fully equipped for housekeeping. It has an excellent view of one of the most picturesque spots in the Great Smoky Mountains.

Day begins with a continental breakfast served country-style in the Main House (served out on the porch, weather permitting). Day ends in the Main House with visiting in the parlor, playing cards or dominoes, and sampling some more of Marie's "treats" with a fresh cup of coffee or tea and a newfound friend.

Biscuits

2 cups all-purpose flour
1 tablespoon sugar
4 teaspoons baking powder
½ teaspoon salt
½ cup shortening
1 egg, beaten
⅔ cup milk

Mix together the dry ingredients; cut in the shortening. Mix the egg in the milk; then add to the mixture and blend well. Turn out on a floured surface and knead 8 to 10 times. Roll to ½-inch thickness and cut. Bake on an ungreased cookie sheet in a 425° oven for about 12 minutes. Serve immediately.

Makes 1½ to 2 dozen biscuits.

Applesauce Oatmeal Muffins

½ cup butter (1 stick)
¾ cup brown sugar, firmly packed
1 egg
1 cup all-purpose flour
½ teaspoon cinnamon
1 teaspoon baking powder
¼ teaspoon baking soda
¼ teaspoon salt
¾ cup applesauce
½ cup golden raisins
1 cup quick rolled oats
½ cup chopped nuts

Cream the butter; gradually add the brown sugar; cream until light and fluffy. Add the egg and beat well. Mix the dry ingredients and add alternately with the applesauce to the creamed mixture, stirring well. Add the remaining ingredients and mix well. Spoon into well-greased muffin cups. Bake in a 350° oven for 25 to 30 minutes or until done. Cool on a rack.

Makes 12 muffins.

Banana Muffins

½ cup shortening
1 cup sugar
1 teaspoon vanilla extract

2 eggs
3 large ripe bananas, mashed
1½ cups all-purpose flour
1 teaspoon baking soda
½ teaspoon salt

Cream together the shortening, sugar, and vanilla. Add the eggs and beat well. Blend in the mashed bananas. Add the flour, soda and salt. Bake in a 350° oven in greased and lightly floured muffin pans for about 15 minutes or until brown. Nuts may be added if desired.

Makes about 15 muffins.

Langdon House

135 Craven Street
Beaufort, North Carolina 28516
(919) 728-5499

Langdon House (circa 1732) represents building techniques and materials spanning 250 years, from the time of hand-forged nails and hand-wrought timbers to the twentieth century with central heating and cooling. The house has survived Indians, revolution, pirates, and the Civil War; and today it is in the heart of Beaufort's historic district. Restoration grounds, waterfront boardwalks, shops, restaurants, museums, churches, and the library are all just a block distant. Wild ponies on the banks across the creek, sailboats on the Intercoastal Waterway, blazing sunsets, and salt air breezes touch the senses. The first floor hall, parlor, and four bedrooms are reserved for visitors. Each guest room has a queen-size bed and a private bath. A full gourmet breakfast of fresh fruit, gourmet cheese, select breads and imported coffee and tea is served in guest rooms or in the parlor.

❖ ❖ ❖ ❖ ❖ ❖

Decadent Blueberry Waffles

½ cup blueberries, fresh or frozen

❖   ❖   ❖

1½ cups all-purpose flour
2 teaspoons baking powder
1 tablespoon sugar
½ teaspoon salt

❖   ❖   ❖

3 eggs, room temperature
1¼ cups half and half
½ cup butter (1 stick), melted

Wash, drain, and dry the fresh blueberries or defrost and separate the frozen berries. Sift all dry ingredients together; stir well with a whisk and then resift. Separate the eggs and set the whites aside; beat the yolks until lemon colored; add the half and half and butter and blend. Add the liquid ingredients to the dry and combine lightly. Beat the egg whites until stiff and fold into the batter. Lightly fold in the blueberries, creating blue streaks in the batter. Bake in a waffle iron in accordance with manufacturer's instructions.

Serves 5 to 6.

Wake 'Em Up Cinnamon and Raisin Waffles

¼ cup all-purpose flour
1 cup raisins
1¼ cups all-purpose flour
1 tablespoon baking powder
½ teaspoon salt
¼ teaspoon cinnamon
1 tablespoon sugar

❖   ❖   ❖

1¼ cups milk
2 eggs, separated
½ cup melted butter

Combine ¼ cup of flour with the raisins to make chopping easier. Chop the raisins into nice-sized bits. Set aside. Combine the remaining flour with the other dry ingredients; sift, stir well with a whisk and resift. Blend well the egg yolks, milk and butter. Lightly combine the dry and liquid ingredients until there are no lumps. Stir in the raisin bits. Beat the egg whites until they peak; gently fold them into the batter. Bake in a greased waffle iron until golden brown.

Serves 5.

Chocolate Chip - Whole Wheat Waffles

1 cup all-purpose flour
1 cup whole wheat flour
1½ tablespoons sugar
2 teaspoons baking powder
1 teaspoon baking soda
½ teaspoon salt

❖ ❖ ❖

2 cups buttermilk
3 eggs, separated
½ cup melted butter
¼ to ½ cup chocolate mini-chips

Sift together the dry ingredients; blend well with a whisk and resift. Separate the eggs and blend the yolks well with the buttermilk and melted butter. Lightly blend the dry ingredients with the liquid ingredients until there are no lumps. Beat the egg whites until

they peak and fold them along with the chocolate chips into the batter. Bake in a greased waffle iron until golden brown.

Serves 6.

Ragged Garden Bed and Breakfast

Sunset Drive
Post Office Box 1927
Blowing Rock, North Carolina 28605
(704) 295-9703

A touch of the past has come alive in this grandiose old home. Named Ragged Garden when it was built at the turn of the century, it sits on an attractive one-acre setting, surrounded by roses, rhododendrons, and majestic trees. It is close to the shops, art galleries, boutiques, parks, and attractions of Blowing Rock, just one block off Main Street. It has three different dining areas, including one for private dining, and it rents eight bedrooms for overnight lodging in its upstairs quarters.

Swiss Cheese Dressing

1 pound Swiss cheese, finely grated
1 gallon mayonnaise
1 medium onion, finely chopped
¼ cup Dijon mustard
¼ cup red wine vinegar
1 dash Worcestershire sauce
Salt and pepper

Blend together the cheese, mayonnaise, onion, mustard, and vinegar. Add the Worcestershire sauce, salt, and pepper to taste. Refrigerate. Keeps well for at least 3 months.

Makes 1 gallon.

Saltimbocca alla Romana

8 thin slices veal
Salt and pepper
½ cups all-purpose flour
Butter
8 thin slices prosciutto
8 thin slices Mozzarella cheese

Pound the veal. Sprinkle salt and pepper on each slice. Dredge the veal in flour and pat to remove excess flour. Melt the butter in a sauté pan over high heat. When the butter foams, place the veal in the pan. Do not crowd. Sauté for 1 minute on each side. Place the veal in an ovenproof serving dish. Place the prosciutto on each slice of veal. Place the cheese on top to cover. Place the dish within 4 inches of the broiler until the cheese melts. Serve immediately, preferably with buttered spinach linguine.

Serves 8.

Folkestone Lodge

Route 1, Box 310
West Deep Creek Road
Bryson City, North Carolina 28713
(704) 488-2730

The traveler who enjoys a peaceful, rural setting and a home-cooked breakfast should delight in Folkestone Lodge. Nearby activities include river rafting on the Nantahala River; the Cherokee Indian Reservation with its

museum, craft shops, and renowned outdoor drama "Unto These Hills"; the Biltmore House in nearby Asheville; the scenic drive through Maggie Valley, a pioneer farmstead and museum; and within walking distance of the lodge, tubing down Deep Creek, horseback riding, and hiking in the Great Smoky Mountains National Park. All rooms have private baths; each has one double bed. One room also has a three-quarter antique hide-a-bed.

Grandma's Old-Fashioned Oatmeal

2½ cups water
⅛ teaspoon salt
2 cups dry oatmeal
2 tablespoons sugar
½ teaspoon cinnamon
1 5-ounce can evaporated milk
3 tablespoons butter
2 tablespoons brown sugar, or more

Bring the water to a boil, add the salt. Stirring constantly, add the dry oatmeal gradually. Continue stirring. Add the sugar and cinnamon; cook 1 minute. Add the evaporated milk and reheat to boiling. Pour into a serving dish; top with butter and brown sugar.
Serves 6.

Fruit Cobbler

3 cups prepared fruit (strawberries, blackberries, blueberries, peaches or rhubarb)
1 cup sugar
½ teaspoon lemon juice
⅛ teaspoon salt
3 tablespoons cornstarch
¼ cup water
1 tablespoon butter
Biscuit dough top

Combine the fruit and sugar over low heat. Add lemon juice, salt and cornstarch dissolved in water. Stir con-stantly over medium heat until thickened. Pour into a greased cobbler dish; dot with butter. Cover with biscuit dough. Bake in a 450° oven until golden brown, approximately 15 to 20 minutes.
Serves 8 to 12.

The Fryemont Inn

Post Office Box 459
Bryson City, North Carolina 28713
(704) 488-2159

Near the Great Smoky Mountains National Park, the Fryemont thus is close to one of the world's finest wildlife sanctuaries. The park has more than 800 miles of streams, mountain peaks over 6000 feet high, endless biking trails, and abundant flora and fauna. Other attractions near the inn include whitewater rafting, horseback riding, the Blue Ridge Parkway, Fontana Dam and Reservoir, Cherokee Indian Reservation, the Biltmore House and Gardens, the Thomas Wolfe home, and Gatlinburg, Tennessee. The dining room is open for breakfast and dinner seven days a week. Dress is casual and comfortable. A modified American plan is available.

Cheese Soup

2 stalks celery, finely chopped
2 carrots, peeled and finely chopped
1 small onion, finely chopped
1 cup chopped fresh cauliflower
1 cup finely chopped broccoli
1 small clove garlic, crushed and minced
½ cup butter (1 stick)
½ cup all-purpose flour
3 cups strong chicken broth
Salt to taste
½ teaspoon pepper
2½ cups milk
2 cups grated Cheddar cheese
1 tablespoon Worcestershire sauce
¼ cup sliced almonds

Cook the celery, carrots, onion, cauliflower, broccoli, and garlic in butter

The Fryemont Inn

over medium heat for 6 minutes, stirring constantly. Stir in the flour. Cook, stirring constantly, for 3 minutes. Slowly add the broth, salt and pepper. Simmer covered over very low heat for 20 minutes. Add the milk, cheese and Worcestershire sauce. Cook over low heat for 10 minutes. Garnish with almonds. Can be made ahead, refrigerated and reheated in a double boiler. This actually enhances the flavor.

Serves 6.

Mushroom Business

8 slices bread, cut into sixths
¼ cup mayonnaise
½ teaspoon salt
¼ teaspoon pepper
1 pound mushrooms, sliced and sautéed in butter
½ cup finely chopped onion
½ cup finely chopped celery
½ cup finely chopped green pepper
2 eggs, beaten
1¾ cups milk
1 10-ounce can cream of mushroom soup
1 cup shredded Swiss cheese

Butter an 8-inch square baking pan or a 1-quart casserole dish. Place half of the bread slices in the bottom. Combine the mayonnaise with the salt and pepper, sautéed mushrooms and the finely chopped vegetables. Spread over the bread. Cover with another layer of bread squares. Combine the eggs and milk; pour over all. Cover and refrigerate overnight or all day. One hour before serving, pour the soup on top and spread around. Add another layer of lightly buttered bread squares. Sprinkle the cheese over the top. Bake in a 350° oven for 45 minutes to 1 hour or until puffed and brown.

Serves 8 to 10.

Carrot Soufflé

1 pound carrots, sliced, cooked, and drained
½ cup melted butter
⅓ cup brown sugar, firmly packed
¼ cup all-purpose flour

1 teaspoon baking powder
1 teaspoon vanilla extract
2 tablespoons dark rum
3 eggs

Combine the cooked carrots with the butter and purée. Add the remaining ingredients and mix very well. Pour into a greased and floured 1-quart casserole and bake in a 325° oven for 45 minutes to 1 hour or until the center is set and the top is lightly browned and puffed. Serve at once.

Serves 6.

Fudge Cake

1 cup butter (2 sticks)
1 cup water
6 tablespoons cocoa
2 cups sugar
2 cups well-sifted self-rising flour
2 eggs
½ cup sour cream
❖   ❖   ❖
½ cup butter, melted
¼ cup cocoa
6 tablespoons milk
1 1-pound box sifted confectioners' sugar
1 teaspoon vanilla extract

In a saucepan melt the butter and combine with the water. Add the cocoa and bring to a boil. Stir well and remove from heat. Add the sugar; mix well. Add the flour, stirring until smooth. Blend the eggs and sour cream into the mixture. Spread into a well-greased 13x9-inch baking pan. Bake in a 375° oven for 40 minutes or until done.

For the frosting, combine the remaining ingredients and pour over the cake as soon as it comes out of the oven. It will make a very fudgy cake. Pecans sprinkled over the top are good, too.

Serves 12 to 16.

Nu-Wray Inn, Inc.

Post Office Box 156
Burnsville, North Carolina 28714
(704) 682-2329

Nestled in the shadow of Mount Mitchell, the highest mountain east of the Mississippi, the Nu-Wray Inn is reached via the scenic Blue Ridge Parkway. Escapees from the summer's heat should bring sweaters because of the mountain breezes at this elevation (3,000 feet). Although daytime temperatures are pleasant for outdoor activities, guests usually sleep under blankets at night.

Christmas Morning Eggnog

6 eggs, separated
2 tablespoons sugar
1 pint milk
¼ cup Brandy or whiskey
Nutmeg

Beat the yolks well; then gradually add the sugar until the mixture is creamy. Pour in the milk slowly, beating constantly. Add the Brandy. Beat the egg whites until stiff; add to the mixture. Fill glasses; grate a little nutmeg on top and serve at once.

If richer eggnog is desired, add a cup of cream to 1 cup of milk. More or less Brandy may be used according to taste. A fork or wire whisk should be used instead of an egg beater.

Serves 6.

Syllabub

A holiday drink.

1 quart cream (24 hours old)
1 cup milk
1 cup sugar
1 teaspoon vanilla extract
1 to 2 cups grape juice
1 to 4 cups orange juice
1 to 4 cups Sherry

Have all ingredients cold, and place in large bowl. Beat with an egg beater until frothy; serve immediately.

Leroy's Holiday Salad

1 cup ground raw cranberries (measure after putting through food chopper)
1 cup sugar
1 3-ounce package lemon-flavored gelatin
1 to 2 cups boiling water
1 cup orange juice
2 teaspoons grated orange rind
1 8-ounce can crushed pineapple
1 to 2 cups broken pecans
1 cup celery, chopped

❖ ❖ ❖

Lettuce
Mayonnaise

Mix together the sugar and cranberries; let stand several hours. Add the gelatin to the boiling water and stir until dissolved. Add the orange juice and stir; add the remaining ingredients including the cranberry mixture and pour into a mold. Serve on crisp lettuce and garnish with mayonnaise.

Serves 6 to 8.

Pear Relish

1 gallon coarsely chopped pears
1 to 2 gallons coarsely chopped onions
14 green peppers, seeded and chopped
2 cups pickling salt

❖ ❖ ❖

2 quarts vinegar
4 cups sugar
2 tablespoons turmeric
2 tablespoons mustard seed

Combine the pears, onions, peppers, and salt; let stand overnight.

In the morning drain and rinse with 4 changes of water. Prepare a syrup with the vinegar, sugar, and spices. Cook 5 minutes; add the chopped mixture and simmer for 5 minutes. Pour into hot sterilized jars and seal.

Fills 8 8-ounce jars.

Carolina Relish

2 large cabbages, cored
6 onions, peeled

6 green peppers, seeded
6 apples, cored
6 cucumbers
6 tablespoons pickling salt

❖ ❖ ❖

1 bunch celery, chopped
6 cups vinegar
10 cups brown sugar, firmly packed
1 tablespoon pickling spices
1 tablespoon turmeric

In a food chopper coarsely grind all vegetables except the celery. Add salt, put in a cloth sack and let drip all night.

The next morning grind the vegetables again. Add the chopped celery. Mix together the vinegar, sugar, pickling spices and turmeric; add to the vegetables. Pack in sterile jars and seal. Keep in a cool place.

Makes about 5 quarts.

Mis' Sallie's Candied Yams

4 or 5 large yellow sweet potatoes
3 to 4 cups water
1 cup sugar
1 to 2 teaspoons salt
1 to 2 teaspoons nutmeg
1 to 2 cups butter

Wash and peel the yams. Cut lengthways in ¼-inch slices. Cover with water and boil until tender but not soft. Place in a baking pan and sprinkle the slices with sugar, salt, and nutmeg. Dot with butter and bake in a 350° oven until a syrup is formed, about 15 or 20 minutes.

Serves 4.

Sour Cream Pie

1 cup sour cream
³/₄ cups sugar
2 eggs, slightly beaten
1 teaspoon cinnamon
½ teaspoons nutmeg
½ teaspoons cloves
½ cup pecans

Nu-Wray Inn

Mix together the sour cream and sugar; add the slightly beaten eggs. Add the remaining ingredients. Pour into an unbaked 9-inch pie shell and bake in a 425° oven for 20 minutes. Reduce the heat to 325° and bake for 20 minutes more.

One cup undiluted evaporated milk plus one tablespoon of vinegar may be used in place of sour cream. Sweetened whipped cream and pecans may be placed on top to serve.

Serves 6.

Bully Pudding

2 eggs
1 cup milk
1 cup sugar
1 cup dates, chopped
½ cup butter (1 stick)
1 heaping tablespoon all-purpose flour
1 teaspoon baking powder
½ cups pecans, chopped

❖ ❖ ❖

Whipped cream

Combine the ingredients except whipped cream; pour into greased bread pans. Bake in a 325° oven for 1 hour. Spoon out of the pan and top with whipped cream.

Serves 6 to 8.

Butter Pie

1 egg
2 heaping tablespoons butter
¾ cup sugar
1 teaspoon all-purpose flour
½ teaspoon vanilla extract
Hot water
Pastry for 1 9-inch pie

Break the egg into a 2 cup measure; beat. Add the butter, sugar, flour, and vanilla. Pour in enough hot water to fill cup to the top and stir until well-blended. Pour into the pie shell and bake in a 350° oven.

Serves 6.

Tom Jones House

Post Office Box 458
Carthage, North Carolina 28327
(919) 947-3044

The house built in 1880 by Tom Jones, Vice-President of the Tyson-Jones Buggy Manufacturing Company, offers visitors an opportunity to relax in one of Carthage's most elegant historical homes and partake of an ample, delicious breakfast. The inn is well-situated; no golfer or hunter needs to be told about Pinehurst and Southern Pines, only minutes away. The house features a wrap-around front porch and a screened back porch for the warmer months. The back yard also has a large heated pool and jacuzzi, with a deck for sunning, and a gazebo and patio for sitting and sipping. In their rooms guests will find fruit-filled baskets, fresh flowers by their beds, plush terrycloth robes, imported soaps for soaking in a hot tub, and an array of reading materials. Handcarved wainscoting, nine fireplaces, a broad, curved staircase with fretwork, leaded glass windows, and twelve-foot ceilings are some of the features of the house that make a stay memorable.

Cinnamon Grapefruit

½ grapefruit
Sugar
Cinnamon
Maraschino cherry

Sprinkle the grapefruit with sugar and cinnamon. Microwave 1 minute. Top with a maraschino cherry.

Serves 1.

Pork, Cheese, Onion, and Potato Casserole

3 cups sliced boiled potatoes
1 large onion, chopped
3 cups cooked pork shoulder, cut into bite-sized pieces
1 pound sharp Cheddar cheese

Layer the potatoes, onion, pork, and cheese on top. Salt and pepper to taste. Bake in a buttered 3-quart casserole in a 375° oven for 30 minutes.

Serves 8 to 10.

High Hampton Inn and Country Club

Cashiers, North Carolina 28717
(704) 743-2411

High in the Blue Ridge Mountains, High Hampton Inn is a rustic but comfortable retreat. A huge stone chimney with four fireplaces is the focal point of the lobby. Bedrooms have walls of sawmill-finished pine and sturdy mountain-crafted furniture. Country ham, homemade breads, and vegetables from the kitchen garden grace the table while dahlias in the flower garden lift the soul. While all seasons are beautiful in Cashiers Valley with its caves, streams and surrounding craggy peaks, spring and fall are spectacular when the rhododendrons and dogwoods blossom and the leaves turn fiery colors. (Lower rates are in effect, too.)

High Hampton Sunday Fried Chicken

Have the chickens cut into quarters. Dip the quarters in evaporated milk. Season a pan of flour with salt and dip the chicken in this flour; roll the pieces around a bit. Fry in vegetable oil until nicely browned. Place in pans with drip pans under them and place in a 275° oven for 1 hour or so.

Serve with stewed corn, green beans, candied yams or rice.

One chicken serves 4 to 6.

Sauce

½ **pint cream, very stiffly whipped**
2 **egg yolks**
1 **cup sugar**
½ **teaspoon rum**

Beat the yolks; add the sugar and rum. Beat and add the cream just before serving.

Makes about 2 cups of sauce.

Plum Duff

½ **cup butter (1 stick)**
1 **cup brown sugar, firmly packed**
2 **cups prunes, cooked, pitted and**
    finely chopped
2 **eggs**
1 **cup all-purpose flour**
¹/₈ **teaspoon salt**
1 **teaspoon baking soda**
1 **tablespoon milk**

Melt the butter and add the sugar. Add the prunes and eggs; stir in the flour and salt. Dissolve the soda in milk and add to the prune mixture. Steam in a greased coffee can with a lid or a loaf pan with a lid on high temperature for 1 hour and 30 minutes in a covered kettle of water. Reduce the heat to low and steam for 30 minutes. Serve with sauce if desired.

Serves 2 to 4.

The Inn at Bingham School

Post Office Box 267
Chapel Hill, North Carolina 27515
(919) 563-5583

Built around 1835, the Bingham School was a preparatory school for young men seeking entrance to the University of North Carolina in nearby Chapel Hill. Although the school building itself no longer stands, the Headmaster's home, listed in the National Historic Registry, has been meticulously restored, and guests of the Inn at Bingham School enjoy these interesting accommodations. There are six spacious guest rooms with private baths. Guests are invited to gather in the living room and formal dining room or to roam the surrounding ten acres of farm and woodland. A full English breakfast is served either in the dining room or the airy sun room.

Baked Cheese Grits

Even Yankees like these.

1 **cup grits (do not use instant)**
2 **cups water**
1 **cup milk**
1 **teaspoon salt**
1 **cup New York sharp Cheddar**
    cheese
¼ **cup butter (½ stick)**
Several drops Tabasco sauce
2 **eggs, beaten**

Cook the grits in water, milk, and salt. When thick remove from the heat. Add the cheese, butter, and Tabasco. Beat the eggs and gradually add the hot grits. Pour in a 1½-quart greased casserole dish. Bake in a 350° oven for 30 minutes or until the top is brown.

Can be fixed 24 hours ahead and brought to room temperature before baking.

Serves 4 to 6.

Corn Fritters

1 **egg**
1 **cup all-purpose flour**
1 **teaspoon baking soda**
1½ **cups buttermilk**
1 **tablespoon butter, melted**
1 **cup grated fresh corn**

Mix the ingredients together and fry on a hot greased griddle like pancakes. Serve with butter and crisp bacon.

Serves 4.

The Homeplace

5901 Sardis Road
Charlotte, North Carolina 28226
(704) 365-1936

At the Homeplace the warm, friendly atmosphere hasn't changed since 1902. Situated on two and one-half wooded acres in southeast Charlotte, the Homeplace is conveniently located near shopping malls and downtown. The completely restored home has the original hand-crafted staircase, ten-foot beaded ceilings, heart-of-pine floors, and a formal parlor. During their stay at the Homeplace, guests can sleep in an 1890 oak high-back bed in the downstairs Victorian-style bedroom and enjoy the convenience of their own bath and private entrance to the wrap-around porch. Or they can sleep in one of two upstairs country bedrooms with twin beds, both sharing a large semi-private bath. Mornings are welcomed with a complete breakfast of eggs, homemade breads, pastries, jellies, and fresh fruit, coffee and tea served in the main dining area or on the screened porch when weather permits. Evenings can be enjoyed by gathering in the parlor for appetizers or desserts and southern hospitality.

Broiled Grapefruit

2 medium grapefruit
2 teaspoons sugar
½ teaspoon cinnamon
½ teaspoon nutmeg

Cut the grapefruit in half crosswise; remove the seeds, cut out the center core and loosen the sections. Place the cut side up in a broiler pan. Mix together the sugar and spices and sprinkle on each grapefruit. Broil until the sugar is bubbly, about 2 to 4 minutes.
Serves 4.

Breakfast Casserole

6 slices bacon
¼ cup green pepper, finely chopped
¼ cup onion, finely chopped
1 tablespoon butter

4 to 5 eggs
2 tablespoons milk
¼ teaspoon celery salt
Dash pepper
2 tablespoons chopped pimiento
½ cup shredded Cheddar cheese

Microwave the bacon until brown; crumble. In a glass pie plate combine the pepper, onion, and butter in the microwave. Cook on high for 1 minute. Combine the eggs, milk, celery salt, and pepper; stir in the pimiento and bacon. Pour into a pie plate with the pepper and onion; microwave on high for 1 minute and 30 seconds. Stir and cook on high 1 to 2 minutes more until set. Sprinkle the cheese on top; microwave for 30 to 45 seconds or until the cheese melts.
Serves 4 to 6.

Orange Cream Sauce

¾ cup whipping cream
2 tablespoons frozen orange juice, partially thawed
1 tablespoon sugar

Combine the ingredients until well blended. Cover and chill about 30 minutes, until slightly thickened.
Makes about 1 cup of sauce.

Honey Cream Sauce

¼ cup honey
½ cup half and half
2 tablespoons butter

Combine the ingredients and bring to a boil. Reduce heat and simmer for 10 minutes or until slightly thickened, stirring occasionally. Use as a sauce for prepared fresh fruit.
Makes about 1 cup of sauce.

Baked Apples

1 tart apple, cored (Rome apples are good)
2 tablespoons brown sugar
⅛ teaspoon cinnamon
1 teaspoon butter
2 tablespoons water

Slit the apple in several places to prevent bursting. Mix together the brown sugar, cinnamon, and butter; fill the apple. Place in a casserole and add the water. Microwave on high for 2 to 4 minutes.

To make more than 1 serving, add an additional 2 tablespoons of water for each stuffed apple and microwave an additional 2 to 4 minutes for each apple.
Serves 1.

The Homeplace

The Gingerbread Inn

Post Office Box 187
Chimney Rock, North Carolina 28720
(704) 625-4038

Spicy, hot gingerbread to take the chill off cool mountain nights is served to guests at the Gingerbread Inn as they relax in rocking chairs on decks overlooking the Rocky Broad River. Later they retire to rooms furnished with country furniture, home-sewn quilts, and ruffled curtains. The warm atmosphere of wicker, chintz, and cross-stitch is enhanced by ceiling fans, grapevine wreaths, and authentic antique toys. Breakfast usually features homemade raisin bread and specially prepared jams.

Added attractions are nearby Chimney Rock Park, Hickory Nut Gorge, and beautiful Lake Lure. Within easy driving distance are the Biltmore mansion and Flat Rock Playhouse. Trout fishing, hiking, and wading in icy mountain streams are other popular activities.

Cinnamon Blintzes

2 loaves bread, thinly sliced
2 8-ounce packages cream cheese
2 egg yolks
½ cup sugar

❖ ❖ ❖

1 cup margarine (2 sticks), melted
1 cup brown sugar, firmly packed
2 to 3 teaspoons cinnamon

Trim the crusts from the bread. Combine the cream cheese, egg yolks, and sugar. Spread the mixture on the bread and roll up. Mix together the margarine, brown sugar, and cinnamon; roll the bread in the mixture. Bake on a greased baking sheet in a 350° oven for 15 to 20 minutes. This is really delicious!

Serves 12 to 16.

The Lords Proprietors' Inn

300 North Broad Street
Edenton, North Carolina 27932
(919) 482-3641

Edenton, once the colonial capital of North Carolina, has been called "the South's prettiest town" because of the reach of Albemarle Sound from the foot of Broad Street, the lovely waterfront parks, the tree-lined streets flanked by fine eighteenth and nineteenth century homes, and the magnificent 1767 Court House with its green running to the water. The Lords Proprietors' Inn is part of this charming and historical environment. Offering seventeen elegant guest rooms, each with private bath and cable television, The Proprietors' Inn is furnished by local cabinetmakers and antique dealers.

Our Daily Bread

We do all of the kneading in the same bowl. It is tidier.

3 ¼-ounce packages active dry yeast
6 cups warm water (110° to 115°)
2 cups nonfat dry milk
½ cup sugar
2 eggs
7 cups unbleached flour

❖ ❖ ❖

½ cup unsalted butter (1 stick), melted

½ cup oil
3 tablespoons salt
13 to 14 cups unbleached flour
Cinnamon sugar (optional)

In a very large bowl mix together the yeast, warm water, dry milk, sugar, eggs and 7 cups of flour. Cover with plastic wrap and leave in a draft-free place to rise for about 1 hour. Stir down the dough with a wooden spoon and add the butter, oil, salt and enough more flour to make the dough kneadable but not stiff (usually a total of 5 pounds of flour is used in the recipe). At this point, use whole wheat or rye flour if desired. (We use about 1½ to 2 cups of whole wheat, about 1 cup of medium rye flour and all the rest unbleached white.) Knead the bread for 8 to 10 minutes until satiny. Cover again with plastic wrap and let rise for 1 hour or until double in bulk.

Push the dough down with clean hands sprayed with oil. Let rise 1 hour. Form into 4 or 5 loaves. Sprinkle cinnamon sugar into the middle of the loaf if desired. Place in non-stick loaf pans. Bake in a 350° oven for 45 minutes.

Makes 4 or 5 loaves.

Angel Bread

6 cups all-purpose flour
3 teaspoons baking powder
1 teaspoon baking soda
⅓ cup sugar
2 teaspoons salt

❖ ❖ ❖

2 ¼-ounce packages active dry yeast
½ cup warm water (110° to 115°)
1 cup oil
2 cups buttermilk

In a large mixing bowl mix together the flour, baking powder, soda, sugar, and salt. In a separate bowl dissolve the yeast in water; add the oil and buttermilk. Pour over the dry ingredients and mix thoroughly. Pull off pieces the size of a golf ball and place in greased muffin pans. Bake in a 400° oven for 15 minutes.

Makes 2 dozen muffins.

Skyline Apple Muffins

1½ cups brown sugar, firmly packed
⅔ cup oil
1 egg

❖   ❖   ❖

1 cup buttermilk
1 teaspoon salt
1 teaspoon baking soda
1 teaspoon vanilla extract
2 cups all-purpose flour
1½ cups chopped Granny Smith apples
½ cup chopped pecans

In a large mixing bowl mix together the brown sugar, oil, and egg. Combine the buttermilk, salt, soda, and vanilla. Add to the sugar mixture. Add the flour all at once; mix until there are no dry spots. Fold in the apples and pecans. Bake in greased muffin pans in a 350° oven for 30 minutes. Fill the muffin tins almost full for really big muffins.

Makes 1 to 1½ dozen muffins.

Banana-Nut Muffins

This is an old Edenton recipe for bread, but we make muffins instead. They are delicious and freeze well.

½ cup oil
1 cup sugar
2 eggs, beaten
3 bananas, mashed

❖   ❖   ❖

2 cups all-purpose flour
1 teaspoon baking soda
½ teaspoon baking powder
½ teaspoon salt
3 tablespoons buttermilk
1 teaspoon vanilla extract
½ cup chopped nuts

Beat together the oil and sugar. Add the eggs and bananas; beat well. Sift together the flour, soda, baking powder, and salt; add to the banana mixture with the buttermilk and vanilla. Beat well. Stir in the nuts. Bake in

greased muffin pans in a 350° oven for about 30 minutes.

Makes 12 to 15 muffins.

Country Lane

Post Office Box 627
Elkin, North Carolina 28621
(919) 366-2915

This unique "country place" awaits guests in the foothills of the Blue Ridge Mountains, thirty minutes from the Blue Ridge Parkway. Complete with tin roof, calico, braided rugs and mountain crafts, Country Lane has fifteen acres of tranquility overlooking the lovely Elkin Valley. The one bedroom has two single beds, a sitting room with queen-size sofa bed, and a private bath. A full Southern breakfast is served by the fireplace in the dining room or on the front porch in the summer. Golf privileges are available at the nearby Country Club. The Country Lane is forty-five minutes from Historic Old Salem in Winston-Salem, North Carolina. Hiking, canoeing, or rocking on the porch are part of the country charm of Country Lane.

Cheese Strata

8 slices white bread
6 eggs
2 cups milk
Salt and pepper to taste
2 tablespoons minced onion, instant or fresh
¼ cup butter (½ stick), melted
¾ pound Cheddar cheese, grated

Trim the crusts and cut the bread in cubes. Beat the eggs. Add the milk, seasonings, onion, and butter. Alternate layers of bread and cheese in an unbuttered casserole dish. Pour the liquid over all. Refrigerate overnight. Bake in a 350° oven for one hour.

Serves 8.

The Buttonwood Inn

190 Georgia Road
Franklin, North Carolina 28734
(704) 369-8985

The Buttonwood is a small country inn with four guest rooms that adjoins the Franklin golf course. The inn is furnished with many handcrafted pieces, some of which are for sale to inn guests. The Smoky Mountains, the Blue Ridge Parkway, and the Appalachian Trail are only a short distance from the inn. The area has excellent fishing, and wildlife is abundant in the Nantahala National Forest. Completely surrounded by tall pines, The Buttonwood is small and cozy and will appeal to those who prefer simplicity and natural rustic beauty. For those wishing to make their stay longer there is an apartment available by the week or month.

Strawberry Butter

½ cup unsalted butter (1 stick)
½ cup strawberry jam
1 tablespoon lemon juice

Whip the butter. Add the strawberry jam and lemon juice. Beat until smooth. Store in the refrigerator. Use for omelets, toast, and muffins.

Makes about 1 cup of butter.

Strawberry Omelet

3 eggs, separated
1 tablespoon sugar
1 tablespoon rum
Salt
2½ tablespoons sugar

2 tablespoons Strawberry Butter
2 tablespoons sour cream
2 large strawberries

Butter a 10-inch iron skillet or omelet pan. Beat the egg yolks with 1 tablespoon of sugar and the rum. Add the salt to the egg whites and beat until peaks form. Gradually add the remaining sugar. Fold into the egg yolks; pour into the skillet. Bake in a 325° oven for 20 minutes, until golden brown. Put Strawberry Butter on one side and fold over. Place on a warm plate. Top with the sour cream and strawberries.
Serves 3.

Crunchy Baked Bananas

2 large or 3 medium bananas
2 tablespoons brown sugar
½ cup miniature marshmallows
1 cup cornflakes
1 tablespoon butter, melted

Peel the bananas and cut lengthwise; arrange in a buttered dish. Sprinkle on the brown sugar and then marshmallows. Mix together the cornflakes and melted butter. Sprinkle on top. Bake in a 375° oven for 12 to 15 minutes.
Serves 4.

Lemon Cheese

½ cup butter or margarine (1 stick)
4 eggs
Pinch salt
Juice and grated rind of 3 lemons
2 cups sugar

Melt the butter in the top of a double boiler over hot water. Beat the eggs in a bowl with salt. Beat in the sugar, then lemon juice and rind. Beat for several minutes. Stir into the melted butter. Stir and cook until thickened, about 15 minutes. Pour into glass jars and store in the refrigerator. Will keep for several weeks.
Use on gingerbread muffins or in tart shells.

Gingerbread

2 eggs
¾ cup sugar
¾ cup molasses
¾ cup butter (1½ sticks), melted
½ teaspoon baking powder
2½ cups all-purpose flour
2 teaspoons baking soda
2 teaspoons ginger
1½ teaspoons cinnamon
½ teaspoon cloves
½ teaspoon nutmeg
1 cup boiling water

Beat the eggs slightly. Add the sugar, molasses, and melted butter to the eggs. Sift the dry ingredients and add to the sugar mixture. Slowly add boiling water. Bake in a buttered 13x9-inch dish in a 350° oven for about 30 to 40 minutes.
Serves 10 to 12.

Leftwich House

215 East Harden Street
Graham, North Carolina 27253
(919) 226-5978

The Leftwich House combines Southern hospitality with the European tradition of bed and breakfast. Built in the early 1920s, the Leftwich House has high ceilings and chandeliers, with one bedroom featuring a cherry four-poster bed and a 100-year-old cherry rocking chair. Another bedroom is decorated with quilts in navy and white.

Breakfast Casserole

1 10-ounce can crescent dinner
   rolls
1 pound sausage
6 eggs
2 tablespoons milk
Salt and pepper to taste
½ cup grated Swiss cheese

Line an 8- or 9-inch dish with the crescent roll dough. Brown the sausage and place over the rolls. Beat the eggs with the milk, salt, and pepper. Pour over the sausage. Sprinkle with Swiss cheese. Bake in a 350° oven for 30 minutes. It is better if made a day ahead of time.
Serves 4 to 6.

Chicken Pie

4 chicken breasts
1 onion

Leftwich House

1 carrot
1 teaspoon of salt
Pepper
1 sprig parsley

❖ ❖ ❖

6 tablespoons butter
1 small onion, chopped
5 tablespoons all-purpose flour
3½ to 4 cups chicken broth
½ cup milk or cream
Butter
½ cup peas (optional)
Crust for 1 9-inch pie shell

Cook the chicken breasts in water with the onion, carrot, seasonings, and parsley. When the chicken is done, dice and place the chicken in a buttered 9-inch baking pan.

In a large frying pan melt 6 tablespoons of butter. Sauté the onion, add the flour slowly. Add the chicken broth and bring to a boil, stirring constantly. Add the milk or cream. Pour over the diced chicken in the baking dish; dot with butter or margarine. Add the peas if desired. Cover with pie crust. Bake in a 350° oven for 30 to 40 minutes.
Serves 6.

Havenshire Inn

Route 13, Box 366
Cummings Road
Hendersonville, North Carolina 28739
(704) 692-4097

Havenshire Inn was built in 1882 by George Holmes, who led a group of English settlers to this area. The large redwood and cedar manor is perched atop Bowman's Bluff in the beautiful Blue Ridge Mountains, overlooking the rolling French Broad River, alpine pastures, and still forests. Guests of the Havenshire Inn enjoy a relaxing visit in some of the best summer climate in the nation. Golfing is only minutes away.

North Carolina Applesauce Muffins

½ cup butter (1 stick), softened
1 cup sugar
1 egg
1 cup unsweetened applesauce
1½ teaspoons cinnamon
½ teaspoon cloves
1 teaspoon allspice
½ teaspoon salt
1 teaspoon baking soda
2 cups all-purpose flour
½ cup nuts, chopped

Cream the butter and sugar. Add the egg. Stir in the applesauce and spices. Sift together the salt, soda, and flour. Add to the applesauce mixture and beat well. Stir in the nuts. Fill greased muffin tins ⅔ full and bake for 8 to 10 minutes. The batter keeps well in a refrigerator, and baked muffins freeze well (reheat before serving).
Makes 24 muffins.

The Hickory Bed and Breakfast

464 7th Street Southwest
Hickory, North Carolina 28603
(704) 324-0548

The Hickory Bed and Breakfast is a welcome and charming respite for weary travelers. Tastefully furnished guest rooms, complete with fresh-cut flowers, greet every visitor. Rooms include double or twin beds with furnishings ranging from contemporary to traditional styles. Downstairs, two sitting rooms offer comfortable sitting chairs for reading and relaxation. Outdoors, a built-in swimming pool is open from May 1 to October 1. In every service The Hickory offers friendly and gracious hospitality.

Whole Wheat Buttermilk Pancakes

1 cup buttermilk
2 tablespoons oil
1 egg

❖ ❖ ❖

½ cup whole wheat flour
½ cup unbleached flour
1 teaspoon baking powder
½ teaspoon baking soda
½ teaspoon salt

Combine the buttermilk, oil, and egg. Add the dry ingredients and mix just until moistened. Fry in a hot lightly greased skillet.
Serves 3.

Apple-Molasses Muffins

2 cups all-purpose flour
⅓ cup molasses
¼ cup brown sugar, firmly packed
¼ cup milk
¼ cup butter (½ stick)
1 egg
1 teaspoon baking soda
1 teaspoon cinnamon
½ teaspoon allspice
½ teaspoon salt
½ cup chopped nuts
2 apples, diced

Grease and flour 1 pan to yield 12 medium-sized muffins. In a large mixing bowl, combine all ingredients except the apples and nuts. Beat well, scraping sides of the bowl. Stir in the apples and nuts. Spoon into pan. Bake in a 375° oven for 20 minutes. Leave in the pan 5 minutes before moving to racks.
Makes 12 muffins.

Blueberry Cornbread

This bread freezes well.

½ cup butter (1 stick)
¾ cup sugar
2 eggs
1 cup yellow corn meal
1½ cups all-purpose flour
2 teaspoons baking powder
½ teaspoon salt
1½ cups milk
½ cup blueberries
Flour

With an electric mixer, cream the butter with the sugar. Add the eggs and cornmeal. Sift together the flour, baking powder and salt. Add ⅓ of the flour mixture to the cornmeal mixture, then ½ cup of milk. Beat. Repeat twice until 1½ cups of milk have been used. Carefully stir in ½ cup of blueberries dredged with flour. Turn into a greased 9-inch square pan. Bake in a 375° oven for 40 minutes or until a tester comes out clean. Serve steaming hot.
Serves 8.

Colonial Pines Inn

Box 2309
Hickory Street
Highlands, North Carolina 28741
(704) 526-2060

A quiet country guest house, Colonial Pines Inn is on a secluded hillside, half a mile from Main Street. Surrounded by the spruce, hemlock, pine and rhododendron of Nantahala Forest, it has wide porches and a lovely mountain view. Rooms in the main house include private baths, breakfast, and the use of a comfortable living room with antique furnishings, fireplace, television and grand piano. A separate cottage is also available.

Colonial Pines Inn

Bailey's Corn-Oat Muffins

1 cup all-purpose flour
1 teaspoon baking powder
½ teaspoon baking soda
½ teaspoon salt

❖ ❖ ❖

½ cup cornmeal
½ cup old-fashioned oats
1 cup buttermilk
1 egg
⅓ cup brown sugar, firmly packed
6 tablespoons butter
¾ cup coconut
½ cup nuts

Mix together the flour, baking powder, soda, and salt; set aside. In a separate bowl mix together the cornmeal, oats, and buttermilk. Add the egg, sugar, and butter. Add the flour mixture and stir until blended. Add the coconut and nuts. Spoon into 12 2½-inch muffin cups. Bake in a 400° oven for 20 to 25 minutes.
Makes 12 muffins.

Crustless Sausage Quiche

2 cups milk or half and half
6 eggs, lightly beaten
1 teaspoon dry mustard
1 pound bulk sausage, browned and drained

½ pound Cheddar cheese, grated
6 slices whole wheat bread, cubed, with crusts removed

Combine the milk, eggs, mustard, sausage, and cheese. Pour over the bread cubes in a greased casserole. Refrigerate for 24 hours. Bake in a 325° oven for 1 hour.
Serves 6.

Applesauce Molasses Bread
with Currants

1 cup margarine (2 sticks)
2 cups sugar
6 eggs
2 cups applesauce
½ cup molasses

❖ ❖ ❖

4 cups flour
2 teaspoons baking powder
1 teaspoon salt
1 teaspoon cinnamon
½ teaspoon nutmeg
2 cups currants
1 cup nuts, chopped

Cream the margarine and sugar. Add the eggs, applesauce, and molasses. In a separate bowl combine the remaining ingredients. Stir together the mixtures just until blended. Pour into 3 small greased bread pans. Bake in a 350° oven for 1 hour.
Makes 3 loaves.

Cataloochee Ranch

Route 1, Box 500
Maggie Valley, North Carolina 28751
(704) 926-0285 (winter)
(704) 926-1401

Cataloochee Ranch spreads across a thousand acres in the Great Smoky Mountains and has catered to its guests for over fifty years. Refreshing mountain breezes from the peaks share the sunshine, while warm fires welcome the cool nights. At Cataloochee guests can stay in their own cabin with an open fireplace and a private bath, or in the stone and hewn-log main ranch house. In both cases they will be surrounded with the rustic beauty and charm of hand-made quilts, antiques, and furniture carved from native cherry and walnut. The ranch's varied, bountiful meals feature seasonal garden vegetables and homemade jams.

Cataloochee Puffed Toast

1 loaf white bread, unsliced
2 cups all-purpose flour
4 teaspoons baking powder
½ cup sugar
½ teaspoon salt
½ teaspoon cinnamon
½ teaspoon nutmeg
1 egg
1 teaspoon vanilla extract
1½ cups milk
2 teaspoons oil

❖ ❖ ❖

Confectioners' sugar
Honey and maple syrup

Cut thick diagonal slices from a loaf of unsliced white bread. Spread the slices out to dry overnight. Make a thick batter with the next 10 ingredients. Coat the slices with batter and fry quickly in 2 inches of hot oil. Fry until golden and crisp on both sides. Drain on paper towels. Sprinkle with confectioners' sugar. Serve with honey and maple syrup.
Serves 8.

Cataloochee Escalloped Onions

When these escalloped onions come out of the oven, they keep diners guessing about how they were made. Vidalia onions are good, but any onions will be sweet and mild cooked by this method. Our ranch-goers have requested this recipe time and time again over the years.

5 medium onions
¾ cup grated Cheddar cheese
1 5⅓-ounce can evaporated milk
Salt and pepper
Parmesan cheese

Slice the onions in ½-inch slices and cook in salted water until just tender. Drain and place in a greased 1-quart casserole. Add the cheese and seasonings; pour the evaporated milk over all. Bake in a 375° oven until the milk and cheese have blended into a sauce. For a stronger cheese flavor, sprinkle the top with Parmesan cheese.
Serves 4 to 6.

Pine Ridge Inn

2893 West Pine Street
Mount Airy, North Carolina 27030
(919) 789-5034

At Pine Ridge Inn, surrounded by the Blue Ridge Mountains, guests are treated to the luxury of the past. Built in 1948, Pine Ridge Inn has private bedroom suites, a swimming pool with sun deck, a large indoor hot tub, an exercise room, and many amenities of a grand hotel. A continental breakfast is served each morning. Pine Ridge offers bed and breakfast for the traveling executive, the executive spouse, the visiting relative accustomed to traveling first class, or to a couple looking for a truly luxurious weekend away from home. Golf privileges at Cross Creek Country Club are available to guests.

The following recipes make up a Thanksgiving menu for twenty-four guests.

Dill Dip in Rye Bread Boat

2 tablespoons seasoned salt
4 tablespoons dill weed
4 tablespoons parsley
4 cups sour cream
4 cups real mayonnaise
4 tablespoons chopped green onion
4 2-pound loaves rye bread
(unsliced)

Mix together all the ingredients except the rye bread; chill. Cut a rectangular hole in 2 of the loaves of bread. Scoop out the interior and cut into bite-sized cubes. Cut the other loaves into bite-sized cubes. Store the cubes and bread in an airtight container. Just before serving pour the dill dip into the hollowed loaves of bread and serve with the cubes. When all "dippers" are gone, cut the hollowed loaves and eat.
Serves 32 to 40.

Mushroom Soup

Polish and Shiitake mushrooms are available in specialty shops.

4 to 6 large dried Polish
mushrooms
12 large dried Shiitake mushrooms
3 quarts homemade or canned beef
broth
5 medium carrots, peeled, trimmed,
and finely diced
2 large onions, peeled and finely
chopped

5 stalks celery with leafy tops, trimmed and finely diced
2 tablespoons finely chopped fresh parsley
1 pound fresh domestic mushrooms, wiped, trimmed, and sliced
3 tablespoons chopped fresh dill (or 2 tablespoons dried dill)
1 tablespoon coarse (kosher) salt (omit if using canned beef broth)
½ teaspoon freshly ground pepper
½ cup very small dried macaroni (bows, squares, alphabet)

❖ ❖ ❖

2 tablespoons butter
2 tablespoons flour
1 cup sour cream

Soak the dried mushrooms for four hours in 2 cups cold water. In a large pot, bring the broth to a simmer. Add the carrots, onions, celery, and parsley to the broth. Cook, uncovered over low heat for 20 minutes, stirring occasionally. Drain the mushrooms that have been soaking; strain and reserve the liquid. Cut the mushrooms into pieces slightly larger than the diced vegetables. Add the mushrooms and liquid to the soup. Simmer for 15 minutes. Add the sliced fresh mushrooms, dill, salt (if using homemade beef broth) and pepper to the soup. Simmer for 15 minutes. Bring the soup to full boil, stirring constantly. Add the macaroni. Reduce the heat to a gentle boil and stir occasionally with a slotted spoon to prevent the macaroni from sticking. Cook the soup another 4 to 7 minutes, or until the macaroni is done to taste.

Melt butter in saucepan and blend in the flour, stirring until the mixture is smooth. Add 2 tablespoons of the sour cream and stir until it is well blended. Combine this mixture with the rest of the sour cream. When the macaroni tests done, add the thickened sour cream to the soup, and stir constantly. Simmer gently for about 3 minutes. Serve very hot.

Serves 8 to 12.

Fruit and Nut Stuffing
for a 20 Pound Turkey

18 whole pitted prunes
½ cup dried currants
1 cup dark raisins
24 dried apricot halves
¼ cup Bourbon

❖ ❖ ❖

⅔ cup whole cashews
1 cup unsalted walnut pieces

❖ ❖ ❖

3 tart cooking apples, unpeeled, cored and chopped
3 large onions, peeled and diced
2 celery stalks, diced
¼ cup butter (½ stick), melted
2 cups whole raw cranberries
1 teaspoon ground cloves
¼ teaspoon cayenne pepper
1 teaspoon ground ginger
1 teaspoon dried chervil leaves
1 teaspoon finely minced fresh parsley leaves
2 teaspoons salt
½ teaspoon freshly ground black pepper
2 eggs, slightly beaten
1 teaspoon ground cinnamon
Giblet broth

Combine the prunes, currants, raisins, and apricot halves in a bowl and pour the Bourbon over the fruit. Cover and soak overnight. In a skillet heat 2 teaspoons of vegetable oil and add the cashews and walnuts. Toast, stirring until golden.

In a large skillet combine the apples, onions and celery with the butter. Cook the mixture over moderate heat, stirring occasionally, until the onions are soft and the celery is tender, about 10 minutes. Transfer the onion mixture to a large mixing bowl. Add the fruit and all remaining ingredients, adding enough giblet broth to moisten the dressing well. Gently mix the stuffing with 2 large spoons until evenly blended. Set the stuffing aside while preparing the turkey for roasting.

Makes approximately 9 cups.

Roast Turkey
with Fruit and Nut Stuffing

1 18- to 20-pound turkey
Salt
Fruit and Nut Stuffing
¼ cup butter (½ stick), softened
2 tablespoons snipped fresh rosemary leaves (or 2 teaspoons dried rosemary)
2 tablespoons snipped fresh thyme leaves (or 2 teaspoons dried thyme)
1 cup dry Vermouth
Rosemary and thyme sprigs

Rinse the turkey inside and out with cold water, and pat dry with paper towels. Sprinkle the cavity with salt. Turn the turkey breast-side down and loosely stuff the neck cavity with about 2 cups of stuffing. Pull the neck skin over the cavity and fasten it to the back of the turkey with skewers. Turn the turkey breast-side up and fold the wing tips underneath the turkey so that the tips are almost touching. Lightly stuff the main cavity with about 6 to 7 cups of stuffing. Place a double layer of aluminum foil over the exposed stuffing to prevent its charring as the bird roasts. Tie the drumsticks together with twine. Rub softened butter over the skin. Place the turkey breast-side up on a rack in a roasting pan and roast in the lower half of a 325° oven for 2½ hours. Add the herbs and vermouth to the pan drippings. Roast the turkey until done, from 1 hour to 1 hour and 30 minutes longer. Remove the rack containing the turkey and allow to rest 20 minutes before carving. Transfer the turkey to a heated platter and garnish with sprigs of rosemary and thyme.

Onions Stuffed with Spinach

24 medium yellow onions, each about 2½ inches in diameter
2 tablespoons unsalted butter
¼ teaspoon ground black pepper

1 cup homemade or canned
chicken broth

❖ ❖ ❖

2 pounds fresh spinach
2 tablespoons olive oil
2 large cloves garlic, peeled and
finely chopped
2 tablespoons finely chopped fresh
parsley leaves
⅓ teaspoon nutmeg
2 teaspoons salt
¼ cup unsalted butter
¾ teaspoon black pepper

Partially fill a large saucepan with water and bring to a boil. Add the unpeeled onions and boil uncovered for
10 minutes. Drain the onions and cool
them by running cold water over
them. Trim off the root ends and peel
off the outer layer. Cut off the top third
of each onion and hollow out the centers, reserving the removed portions.
The onion shells should be about ⅓-
inch thick. Place the onion shells in a
large, shallow baking dish. Dot with 2
tablespoons of butter, sprinkle with ¼
teaspoon of pepper, and add the
chicken broth to the dish. Cover the
dish and braise the onions in a 350°
oven for 30 minutes, basting occasionally.

Trim and discard the stems of the
spinach. Wash well. Place in a pot,
cover and steam over low heat for 3 to
5 minutes. Drain well and squeeze to
remove excess moisture. Heat the
olive oil in a skillet. Add the garlic and
sauté briefly over low heat. Chop the
reserved onion portions and add along
with the spinach, parsley, nutmeg, salt
and the remaining ¼ cup of butter and
¾ teaspoon of pepper. Cook over low
heat, stirring constantly, for about 5
minutes. Remove from heat and purée
in a blender or food processor. Remove the onions from the oven when
done and fill with the hot purée. Serve
with the braising juices.

Serves 24.

Squash and Apple Bake

8 pounds squash (butter or
butternut)
2 cups brown sugar, firmly packed
1 cup butter or margarine
(2 sticks), melted
¼ cup all-purpose flour
4 teaspoons salt
2 teaspoons mace
8 baking apples, cored and cut into
½-inch slices

Halve each squash; remove the seeds
and fibers. Pare the squash. Cut into ½-
inch slices. Mix together the brown
sugar, butter, flour, salt, and mace. Arrange the squash in ungreased, oblong
baking dishes, 12x7x2-inches; top
with apple slices. Sprinkle the sugar
mixture over the top. Cover and bake
in a 350° oven until the squash is tender, 50 to 60 minutes.

Serves 24.

Caramelized Pumpkin Pie

2½ cups pumpkin
¼ cup milk
2 eggs, slightly beaten
1 cup sugar
1 tablespoon all-purpose flour
¼ teaspoon salt
½ teaspoon lemon extract
½ teaspoon vanilla extract
½ tablespoon butter, melted
1 unbaked pastry shell

❖ ❖ ❖

1 cup pecans
¼ cup melted butter
1 cup brown sugar, firmly packed

Mix the pumpkin, milk, eggs, sugar,
flour, salt, extracts, and butter and
pour into the pastry shell. Bake in a
425° oven for about 10 minutes. Reduce the heat to 350° and bake 40 minutes until done. Mix the pecans,
melted butter and brown sugar. Sprinkle over the top of the pie. Place pie
under the broiler until the topping is
caramelized.

Serves 6 to 8.

Winborne House

Bed and Breakfast in Historic
Murfreesboro
333 Jay Trail
Murfreesboro, North Carolina 27855
(919) 398-5224

Guests spend the night with a warm
and friendly couple in the restored
Winborne House. They may relax on
the front porch, take a walk in a quiet
place, and enjoy a continental breakfast. Town tours are available.

Sticky Buns

Chopped nuts
Frozen bread rolls (18 or 24 in
package)
1 package butterscotch or vanilla
pudding (not instant)
½ cup margarine (1 stick)
½ cup brown sugar, firmly packed

Cover the bottom of a greased bundt
pan with nuts. Place the frozen rolls
over the nuts in the pan. Sprinkle the
pudding over the rolls. Bring the butter
and sugar to a rolling boil and pour
over the rolls. Cover with plastic wrap
and let stand overnight. If refrigerated,
leave at room temperature about 1
hour before baking. Bake in a 350°
oven for 20 to 30 minutes.

Makes 18 to 24 buns.

Easy Croissants

1 package active dry yeast
1 cup warm water (110° to 115°)
¾ cup evaporated milk
⅓ cup sugar
1½ teaspoons salt
1 egg
1½ cups all-purpose flour
¼ cup oil
4 cups all-purpose flour
1 cup cold butter (2 sticks)

In a medium bowl, let the yeast dissolve in 1 cup warm water. Add evaporated milk, sugar, salt, egg, and 1½ cups flour. Beat to a smooth batter. Add the oil and set aside. In a large bowl cut the butter or margarine into the remaining 4 cups flour, until the butter particles are the size of kidney beans. Pour the yeast batter over and carefully fold in until all the flour is moistened. Cover with plastic wrap and refrigerate for 2 hours to 4 days.

Remove the dough to a floured board; press and knead about 6 times to release the air bubbles. Divide into 4 parts. Roll each part of the dough into a 16-inch circle. Cut with a sharp knife into 8 equal pie-shaped wedges. Loosely roll each wedge toward its point; curve into a crescent, point side down. Place on an ungreased baking sheet, allowing space around each croissant. Let rise in a draft-free place (do not speed rising by placing in warm spot), from 2 to 4 hours. Bake in a 325° oven for 18 minutes. For coffees, spread jam on the wedges before rolling; frost with plain confectioners' frosting when baked.

Serves 8.

The Oakwood Inn

411 North Bloodworth Street
Raleigh, North Carolina 27604
(919) 832-9712

Guests of The Oakwood Inn stay in a beautiful Victorian neighborhood. Built as a home in 1871, it is listed on the National Register of Historic Properties. It has recently been restored to reflect the elegance and charm of its time. The individual character of each room has been enhanced by a variety of period antique furnishings, draperies, and accessories. Many original details remain, including names scratched on the windowpane in 1875.

Nine fireplaces and Victorian furnishings make Oakwood Inn a special place to stay.

French Toast

6 eggs
½ cup baking mix
2 tablespoons sugar
½ teaspoon cinnamon
1½ cups milk
1 loaf day-old French bread

Beat the eggs. Blend in the baking mix, sugar, cinnamon and milk. Mix until smooth. Cut the bread in 1-inch slices. Soak in batter on both sides until saturated. Fry in a wide frying pan over medium heat in ¼-inch oil.

Serves 6.

Popovers

4 eggs
1 cup milk
1 cup unbleached flour
½ teaspoon salt
¼ cup butter (½ stick), melted

Beat together the eggs and milk; add the flour and salt. Beat with a fork until the mixture is uniform.

Preheat a muffin pan in a 375° oven for 5 minutes. Brush the cups and top of the surface generously with melted butter. Fill the muffin cups ⅔ full with batter. Work quickly so that the pan stays hot. Bake in a 375° oven 35 minutes. Do not open the oven while baking. If necessary, prick a hole in the top with fork immediately after baking to let steam escape so they will hold their shape.

Makes 1 dozen popovers.

Dill Bread

⅓ cup Parmesan cheese, grated
½ cup butter (1 stick), melted
½ teaspoon dill weed
2 tablespoons parsley, chopped
1 teaspoon lemon juice
2 10-ounce cans refrigerated
  biscuits

Mix together the first 5 ingredients and pour into a bundt pan. Line the biscuits on the edge around the pan. Bake in a 425° oven for 20 to 25 minutes.

Serves 12.

Melrose Inn

211 Melrose Avenue
Tryon, North Carolina 28782
(704) 859-9419

Melrose Inn has eighteen private rooms and full dining facilities. New owners have renovated it to return its old charm. A full breakfast is included with each room, and lunch and dinner are served to the public each day. Reservations are appreciated.

Potato Balls Melrose

1½ pound potatoes
2 egg yolks
½ cup grated Parmesan cheese
¼ cup grated Romano cheese
2 tablespoons butter
1 tablespoon finely chopped onion
1 tablespoon fresh minced garlic
¼ cup chopped parsley
1 teaspoon oregano
Salt and pepper
2 eggs, beaten
Flour
Bread crumbs
Oil

Peel and boil the potatoes in salted water. In a large mixing bowl combine the egg yolks and both cheeses. Mash the cooked potatoes and add to the cheese-egg mixture. Melt the butter in skillet. Add onion and garlic and sauté until golden brown. Add to the potato mixture. Add the parsley, oregano, salt, and pepper to taste. Mix until the mixture is smooth. Form into small balls the size of large pecans. Beat the eggs until well-blended. Roll the po-

Melrose Inn

4 teaspoons baking soda
4 teaspoons cinnamon
4 cups coarsely chopped pecans
8 eggs, beaten
8 cups applesauce
1 cup butter (2 sticks), melted
4 cups raisins

Sift together dry ingredients. Add the chopped pecans. Mix together the eggs, applesauce, and butter. Add to the dry ingredients. Add the raisins. Stir until blended. Pour into 8 greased loaf pans. Bake in a 350° oven for 45 to 50 minutes.

Makes 8 loaves.

tato balls in flour, then in the beaten eggs. Coat with bread crumbs and chill for at least 1 hour. Heat the oil to frying temperature (350° to 375°). Fry a few balls at a time until golden brown.

Makes 30 potato balls.

Edna Mae's Pudding

3 medium yams
2½ cups milk
3 eggs
2 cups sugar
2 teaspoons cinnamon
½ cup slivered almonds
½ cup butter (1 stick)
½ cup Bourbon or Canadian
   whiskey

Peel and grate the yams. Place in a 2-quart casserole and add the milk to prevent the potatoes from turning dark. Beat the eggs well; add the sugar and cinnamon and mix well. Slowly add the almonds. Add to the potato mixture. Cover the potatoes with dots of butter, using the entire amount. Bake in a 300° oven for 2 hours. Just prior to serving, pour whiskey over the pudding. Serve hot, as a vegetable.

Serves 8 to 10.

Mill Farm Inn

Post Office Box 1251
Tryon, North Carolina 28782
(704) 859-6992

Guests at Mill Farm Inn enjoy a true home-like atmosphere in this inn. Attractive bedrooms with private baths primarily with king-sized beds; the spacious living room has a glowing fireplace; and the Pacolet River flows past the rear boundary of the large yard in which the inn sits. Bird-watching is a favorite pastime here. A complimentary continental breakfast of specialty breads that vary daily, English muffins, cereal, juice, preserves and jelly, coffee, tea and milk is served each morning.

Applesauce-Nut Bread

16 cups all-purpose flour
6 cups sugar
½ cup baking powder
8 teaspoons salt

Stone Hedge Inn

Post Office Box 366
Tryon, North Carolina 28782
(704) 859-9114

A weary traveler seeking a good meal and the comforts of home or a couple enjoying a cozy getaway weekend will find what they are looking for at the Stone Hedge Inn. Excellent, well-prepared food and fine hospitality are fundamental. The serendipity is the spectacular setting at the base of Tryon Mountain. Guest rooms range from a cottage with fireplace that sits next to the pool to three rooms in the Main Inn. Two rooms in the inn offer double beds, and another with twin beds is a two-room suite with fireplace. A full breakfast is served every morning.

Veal Lafayette

1 5-ounce veal leg or loin
Flour, seasoned
Ripe avocado, seeded and peeled
Ripe tomato
Salt, pepper, sweet basil
Swiss cheese, sliced

Pound the veal and slice into 3 pieces. Dredge with flour and sauté in butter until done. Place on a platter alternately with avocado and tomato; sprinkle with salt, pepper, and basil. Cover with the Swiss cheese and place under the broiler until the cheese is melted.

Serves 3.

Cajun Shrimp Diane

6 large shrimps
¼ teaspoon thyme
¼ teaspoon basil
¼ teaspoon oregano
1/8 teaspoon white pepper
1/8 teaspoon pepper
½ teaspoon cayenne pepper
½ teaspoon salt
1/8 teaspoon curry powder
4 mushrooms, sliced
¼ teaspoon chopped garlic
½ green onion, chopped
1 tablespoon butter, melted
1½ teaspoons raw butter
2 tablespoons shrimp stock (stock from shells)
Parsley
Hot cooked noodles

In a saucepan sauté the shrimp, spices, mushrooms, garlic, and onion in the melted butter until almost done. Add the raw butter and stock. Shake the pan until the butter is melted. Add the parsley. Serve over noodles.

Serves 2.

Hallcrest Inn, Inc.

299 Halltop Road
Waynesville, North Carolina 28786
(704) 456-6457

Overlooking the Waynesville Valley in beautiful western North Carolina sits a 110-year-old farmhouse now known as Hallcrest Inn. This small country inn features home-style cooking served around the large lazy-susan tables. The charm of the old house is enhanced by the many family treasures and keepsakes throughout. Its warm hospitality bespeaks the genuine pleasure its owners, Russell and Margaret Burson, take in catering to their guests.

Chicken Pie

1 fryer chicken
2 cups chicken stock
1 10¾-ounce can cream of celery soup

❖ ❖ ❖

1 cup self-rising flour
1 cup buttermilk
½ cup butter (1 stick), melted

Cook the chicken in boiling water to cover until tender. Remove the skin and bones. Cut into bite-sized pieces; place the chicken in the bottom of a greased casserole. Combine the chicken stock with the cream of celery soup and pour over the chicken.

Combine the flour, buttermilk, and butter and spoon over the top of the casserole. The crust rises to the top as it bakes. Bake in a 350° oven for 40 to 50 minutes. Let stand for 10 minutes before serving.

Serves 6.

Barbecued Meatballs

1 pound ground chuck
½ cup bread crumbs
1 teaspoon salt
½ cup evaporated milk

❖ ❖ ❖

1 cup ketchup
1 green pepper, chopped
1 onion, chopped
3 tablespoons sugar
¼ cup vinegar
1 tablespoon Worcestershire sauce

In a medium bowl combine the ground chuck, bread crumbs, salt, and evapo-

rated milk. Shape into balls and arrange in a baking pan.

Combine the remaining ingredients and spoon over the meatballs. Bake in a 375° oven for 45 minutes.

Serves 4 to 6.

Copper Pennies

½ cup vinegar
¾ cup oil
¾ cup sugar
1 tablespoon mustard
1 green pepper, chopped
1 onion, chopped

❖ ❖ ❖

4 16-ounce cans sliced carrots, drained

In a blender combine the vinegar, oil, sugar, mustard, green pepper, and onion. Blend and pour over the carrots. Let stand for 24 hours. This keeps well in the refrigerator.

Serves 6.

Brown Rice

2 cups water
1 envelope onion soup mix
¼ cup butter (½ stick)
1 cup rice
1 tablespoon Kitchen Bouquet

Bring the water, soup mix, and margarine to a boil. Add the rice and Kitchen Bouquet. Stir, cover and simmer for 20 minutes.

Serves 3 to 4.

Chess Pie

1 cup brown sugar, firmly packed
1/3 cup sugar
3 eggs
¼ cup all-purpose flour
2 tablespoons milk
½ cup butter (1 stick), melted
1 teaspoon vanilla extract

Combine all the ingredients and pour into an unbaked 9-inch pie shell. Bake in a 300° oven for 45 minutes.

Serves 8.

The Colonel Ludlow House

Summit and West Fifth
Winston-Salem, North Carolina 27101
(919) 777-1887

This charming Victorian house built by Jacob Lott Ludlow in 1887 has been restored and converted into a luxurious bed and breakfast inn. The formal parlor, dining room, and unique guest rooms (each with a private bath and some with a two-person whirlpool tub) are furnished with beautiful period antiques. In the historic west end community of Winston-Salem, it is within walking distance of restaurants, cafés, shops, and parks. Only slightly farther away, but also within walking distance, is the downtown business district.

Tropical Chicken Salad

1 lemon
1 orange
1 Golden Delicious apple
1 cup pineapple
3 cups cooked and cubed chicken
½ cup celery, thinly sliced
1 cup mayonnaise
½ teaspoon basil, freshly chopped
2 ounces Grand Marnier
3 ounces slivered almonds, toasted

Wash and remove the peel from the lemon and orange, being careful not to include the pith. Finely chop the peel. Cut the orange into sections; squeeze and reserve the juice. Squeeze the lemon and combine the lemon juice and orange juice. Core and dice the apples and pineapple. In a large glass or stainless steel bowl, combine the chicken, celery, apples, pineapple and fruit peel. Stir in the juice mixture. Refrigerate at least 1 hour. Mix together

the mayonnaise, basil, and Grand Marnier; fold into the chicken mixture. Sprinkle individual servings with toasted almonds.

Makes 4 main dish servings.

Nut Bread with Ginger Spread

2½ cups all-purpose flour
1 cup sugar
1 teaspoon salt
2 teaspoons baking powder
2 cups walnuts, chopped
2 eggs
1 cup milk

❖   ❖   ❖

⅔ cup cream cheese
⅓ cup butter
¼ cup crystallized ginger, finely chopped
½ teaspoon salt

Sift together the flour, sugar, salt, and baking powder. Beat the eggs vigorously until thick. Blend in the milk.

Fold in the flour mixture and nuts. Pour into a greased and floured 1-quart pan. Bake in a 350° oven for 1 hour. Turn out the bread onto a cake rack to cool.

Cream together the cream cheese and butter until light and fluffy. Mix in the ginger and salt. Store covered in the refrigerator. Serve with bread.

Makes 1 loaf.

Colonel Ludlow Fresh Fruit Cup

3 to 4 kinds of fresh fruit, cut in bite-sized pieces
1 tablespoon vanilla yogurt
¼ cup granola
Shredded coconut, almond slivers, or fresh mint

In a sherbet glass combine the fresh fruit. Top with yogurt and granola. Garnish with coconut, almond slivers or mint. Delicious and very filling.

Serves 1.

The Colonel Ludlow House

North Dakota

Kaler Bed and Breakfast

Route 2, Box 151
Lidgerwood, North Dakota 58053

The Kaler home, in rural Lidgerwood, is a six-bedroom country home owned by innkeepers Mark and Dorothy Kaler. Guests live with them in their home, and the delicious country breakfast each morning is part of the fare.

Triticale Egg Bread

Triticale is a grain grown on the farm. It can be found at specialty shops and natural food stores.

½ cup nonfat dry milk
½ cup butter or margarine (1 stick)
2 teaspoons salt
½ cup sugar
2 cups boiling water
2 ¼-ounce packages active dry yeast
2 eggs, beaten
4 cups triticale flour
4½ cups unbleached flour

In a large mixing bowl, combine the milk, butter, salt, and sugar. Pour in the boiling water. Cool to lukewarm (110° to 115°). Add the yeast and eggs. Add the flour, 1 cup at a time, starting with the triticale first. Turn the dough onto a floured board and knead until smooth and elastic. Place the dough in a greased bowl, cover, and let rise until doubled in bulk (about 1½ hours). Punch down, and let rise until doubled again. Place in greased loaf pans and bake in a 375° oven for 30 minutes.
Makes 2 loaves.

Fruit Pizza

For this recipe almost any combination of fresh fruits may be used, such as strawberries, blueberries, pineapple, kiwi, grapes, bananas, etc.

1½ cups all-purpose flour
¾ cup confectioners' sugar
½ cup butter (1 stick), melted
❖ ❖ ❖
1 8-ounce package cream cheese
½ cup sour cream
½ cup sugar
½ teaspoon vanilla extract
Fresh fruits
❖ ❖ ❖
½ cup sugar
2 tablespoons cornstarch
½ cup orange juice (or pineapple juice)
½ cup water
1 teaspoon lemon juice

Combine the flour, confectioners' sugar, and butter. Press the mixture onto the bottom of a 12-inch buttered pizza pan. Bake in a 325° oven for 15 minutes.
While the crust bakes mix together the cream cheese, sour cream, sugar, and vanilla. Spread evenly over the baked, partially cooled pizza crust. Top with assorted fresh fruits.

Make a glaze by mixing the sugar and cornstarch well. Gradually add the liquids. Cook in a saucepan until the mixture thickens. Drizzle over the pizza and chill.
Serves 4 to 6.

Buns

This dough can also be used for kuchen.

1 quart milk
❖ ❖ ❖
2 ¼-ounce packages active dry yeast
¼ cup water
1 teaspoon sugar
❖ ❖ ❖
3 eggs, beaten
1 cup sugar
4 teaspoons salt
1 cup corn oil
11 cups all-purpose flour (approximately)

Boil the milk. Cool to lukewarm. In a cup dissolve yeast in warm (110° to 115°) water, add 1 teaspoon of sugar and let rise to fill the cup. Place the milk in a large bowl. Add the eggs, 1 cup sugar, salt, corn oil and yeast mixture. Add the flour to make a soft dough; knead for 10 minutes. Let rise for 1 hour. Punch the dough down. Let rise for 45 minutes to 1 hour. Form into buns and let rise for 2 hours. Bake in a 375° oven for 12 to 15 minutes.
Makes 4½ dozen buns.

291

Eva's Bed and Breakfast

Star Route, Box 10
Wing, North Dakota 58494

Eva's Bed and Breakfast is in the rolling hills three miles west of Wing on Highway 36, two miles north, and one-fourth mile west. The home is a ranch style, built in 1983. It has two bedrooms, an office, kitchen, dining room, living room, and a utility room on the main floor, and two bedrooms, bath, and large family room with fireplace, hot tub, and television in the basement. The innkeepers are semi-retired and help with their son's 3,500-acre ranch and farm. Pony rides are available and a tour of the farm/ranch operation can be arranged. Area interests include Michel Lake for good fishing, picnics, and boating. Other attractions are the zoo, Heritage Center, museums, and libraries.

Pan-Fried Chicken

½ to ¾ cup oil
1 3 to 4-pound chicken, cut up
1 cup all-purpose flour
Salt and pepper
Garlic salt
Paprika

Put the oil in a large fry pan and heat over medium high heat. While it heats, place the chicken and flour in a paper sack and shake until all the pieces are well-floured. When the oil is hot put the chicken in the pan, sprinkle it generously with salt, pepper, garlic salt, and paprika. When the chicken is brown, turn and sprinkle the other side with the seasonings. Fry until brown; place in small roaster and bake in a 350° oven for 30 minutes.
Serves 4 to 6.

Swedish Meatballs

1 pound ground beef
¾ cup bread crumbs
1 onion, diced
1 egg
1 tablespoon parsley flakes
1 teaspoon salt
1 teaspoon pepper

❖ ❖ ❖

1 10¾-ounce can cream of celery
   soup
1 soup can milk

Combine in a mixing bowl the ground beef, bread crumbs, onion, eggs, and seasonings. Add ¼ cup of the soup to the mixture; form into meatballs and brown in a large skillet.
In a medium saucepan combine the remaining soup and milk to make a sauce. Add the meatballs and heat for about 15 minutes.
Serves 6.

Fresh Strawberry Pie

¾ cup sugar
2 tablespoons cornstarch
1½ cups water
1 3-ounce package strawberry
   gelatin
4 cups fresh strawberries
1 baked 9-inch pie shell
Whipped cream or ice cream

Mix the sugar and cornstarch together; blend in the water. Cook until boiling, stirring constantly; reduce heat. Cook until thick and clear, stirring occasionally. Add the gelatin, stirring to dissolve. Place the strawberries in the pie shell; pour the gelatin mixture over them. Chill until firm. Top with whipped cream.
Serves 6.

Rhubarb Pie

Pastry for 1 9-inch 2-crust pie
1½ cups sugar
3 tablespoons all-purpose flour
½ teaspoon nutmeg
1 tablespoon butter
2 eggs, well beaten
3 cups chopped rhubarb

Line a 9-inch pie pan with ½ of the pastry. Blend together the sugar, flour, nutmeg, and butter. Add the eggs; beat until smooth. Place the rhubarb in the pie shell and cover with the mixture. Top with the remaining pastry cut into fancy shapes. Bake in a 450° oven for 10 minutes, then lower the temperature to 350° and bake 30 minutes longer.
Serves 6.

Ohio

The Frederick Fitting House

A Bed and Breakfast Country Inn
72 Fitting Avenue
Bellville, Ohio 44813
(419) 886-4283

Frederick Fitting was a prominent Bellville citizen who built this home in 1863. A contractor, farmer, and financier, he brought the railroad to Bellville. His home reflects the grand midwestern tradition of rural hospitality in a village setting. It has three rooms for guests: The Colonial Room, The Shaker Room, and The Victorian Room. Each is decorated as its name suggests. The semi-private bath is newly remodeled with hand-painted Italian tile and matching wallpaper. The Village of Bellville offers visitors a highly regarded smorgasbord restaurant named "The San-Dar," a fine golf course, hard surface tennis courts, an abundance of Victorian homes with intricate nineteenth-century gingerbread trim, pleasant walks, jogging trails in all directions, and a collection of little shops along main street. Canoeing and skiing (both downhill and cross-country) are available within a few minutes' drive.

Dutch Babies with Fresh Strawberries

2 tablespoons butter
2 eggs
½ cup milk
½ cup all-purpose flour
Dash salt
¼ teaspoon nutmeg

❖　❖　❖

2 cups sliced strawberries or other fresh berries
Confectioners' sugar
Vanilla yogurt
Nutmeg

Melt the butter in a pie plate in a 425° oven. In mixing bowl, beat the eggs and milk together. Add the flour, salt, and nutmeg; mix well, leaving mixture a bit lumpy. Remove the pie plate from the oven and pour the mixture into it. Bake 12 to 15 minutes. Will rise dramatically on the sides. Remove from oven, slice in half, putting ½ on each of 2 serving plates. Top with sliced strawberries; sprinkle with confectioners' sugar. Place a dollop of vanilla yogurt in the middle; sprinkle yogurt with nutmeg.
Serves 2.

Ham and Cheese Crêpes

2 tablespoons butter
2 tablespoons all-purpose flour
1 cup milk, heated
Salt and cayenne pepper

2 cups shredded Swiss or Cheddar cheese
1 cup finely chopped cooked ham
1 tablespoon minced chives

❖　❖　❖

12 crêpes

❖　❖　❖

White grapes

Melt the butter. Stir in the flour and cook, stirring constantly, until paste bubbles a bit, about 2 minutes. Add the hot milk, continuing to stir as the sauce thickens. Bring to a boil. Add salt and pepper to taste, lower heat and cook, stirring, for 2 to 3 minutes more. Stir in the cheese until melted. Add ham and chives. Place approximately 4 tablespoons of the ham and cheese sauce in each crêpe, roll up and heat in a 250° oven for 20 minutes, just enough to warm them through. Serve with white grapes to balance the spiciness of the cayenne pepper.
Makes 12 crêpes.

Shaker Pumpkin Loaves

2 cups sugar
1 cup butter (2 sticks), melted
3 eggs
2 cups pumpkin

❖　❖　❖

2 cups all-purpose flour
½ teaspoon salt
½ teaspoon baking powder
1 teaspoon baking soda
1 teaspoon cloves
1 teaspoon cinnamon
1 teaspoon nutmeg

In a mixing bowl beat the sugar and butter to blend. Beat in eggs, one at a time, and continue beating until light and fluffy. Then beat in the pumpkin.

In a separate bowl, sift together the flour, salt, baking powder, soda, and spices. Beat this mixture into the pumpkin mixture. Divide batter between 3 greased loaf pans (7½x3½x2¼ inches). Bake in a 325° oven for 60 minutes.

Makes 3 loaves.

Hot Gingered Cider

2 quarts apple cider
1 cup dried apricot halves
1 cup golden raisins
1 cup dried apple slices
¾ cup ginger-flavored brandy
2 cloves
½ teaspoon ginger
¼ teaspoon cinnamon

❖   ❖   ❖

1 cup Bourbon
Cinnamon sticks

Combine all the ingredients except the Bourbon and cinnamon sticks in a large stainless steel or enamel saucepan. Let stand covered at room temperature for at least 1 hour. Then heat the cider mixture over medium heat until hot; remove from the heat. Remove and discard the cloves. Stir in the Bourbon. Adjust the seasonings to taste. Garnish with cinnamon sticks. Serve hot.

Serves 16.

Grandma Sowash's Hazelnut Cookies

8 egg whites
1 pound confectioners' sugar
¾ pound ground almonds
1 pound hazelnuts, very finely
  ground
1 teaspoon vanilla extract

Beat the egg whites until very stiff. Slowly add confectioners' sugar. Beat for 15 minutes. Add the almonds, ha-

The Frederick Fitting House

zelnuts and vanilla. Drop by teaspoonfuls on waxed paper on a cookie sheet. Bake in a 350° oven for about 12 minutes.

Note: 2 pounds of hazelnuts in the shell make 1 pound shelled; 1¾ pounds of almonds in the shell make ¾ pound shelled.

Makes 2 dozen cookies.

The Beach House

213 Kiwanis Avenue
Chaska Beach
Huron, Ohio 44839
(419) 433-5839

This spacious private home on the shore of beautiful Lake Erie is in the heart of vacation activities such as boating, biking, island hopping, golfing and summer theater. Ten minutes away is Cedar Point Amusement Park and Historic Milan, with its many lovely homes, antique shops and museums. The three guest rooms share a bath and are located in one wing of the house, with a private entrance. The rooms are tastefully decorated. A continental breakfast included in the price of the room consists of home-baked goodies, fresh-squeezed juices, and fruit in season. Weather permitting, breakfast is served on the screened-in summer porch overlooking the lake and greenhouse.

Brunch Egg Casserole

¼ cup butter (½ stick)
¼ cup all-purpose flour
1 cup milk
1 cup cream (or half and half)
¼ teaspoon thyme
¼ teaspoon marjoram
¼ teaspoon basil
1 pound sharp Cheddar cheese,
  shredded
18 to 24 hard cooked eggs, thinly
  sliced
1 pound bacon, cooked and
  crumbled
¼ cup chopped parsley
Buttered bread crumbs

In a medium saucepan melt the butter. Add the flour, milk, and cream, stirring until the sauce thickens. Stir in the herbs and Cheddar cheese. Mix well until all of the cheese has melted. Place some of the eggs in a casserole, sprinkle half of the bacon and parsley over the eggs. Add the cheese sauce. Repeat. Sprinkle the bread crumbs on top. Refrigerate. Bake in a 350° oven for 30 minutes. Can be prepared a day or 2 in advance and refrigerated.

Serves 8 to 10.

Hot Pineapple Butter

    3 tablespoons butter
    1 9-ounce can crushed pineapple
        with syrup
    2 tablespoons brown sugar
    Dash nutmeg

In a saucepan melt the butter. Stir in the remaining ingredients and heat until slightly reduced. Serve warm with French toast.

Sticky Butterscotch Pecan Rolls

    1 1-pound loaf frozen bread dough
    ½ cup coarsely chopped pecans
    ½ cup butter (1 stick)
    ⅔ cup brown sugar, firmly packed
    1 3¾-ounce package instant
        butterscotch pudding mix

Thaw the bread in a plastic bag in the refrigerator overnight and keep refrigerated until about 3 hours before baking. Sprinkle about ½ of the pecans in the bottom of a 9- or 10-inch bundt or tube pan without a removable bottom. Melt and cool the butter. Cut the bread dough in quarters lengthwise to make 4 strips; cut each strip into 8 pieces. Roll each piece in melted butter, brown sugar, and then in the pudding mix and place in the pan. Place the remaining pecans in the pan. If any butter, sugar or pudding mix is left, sprinkle over the rolls. Let stand in a warm place for 2½ hours or until double in bulk. Bake in a 350° oven for about 30 minutes. Invert the pan onto a plate and leave for 5 minutes so the butter will drip down. Serve warm and let guests pull off rolls.

Serves about 8.

Green Coffee Cake

    1 18¼-ounce package golden butter
        cake mix
    1 3½-ounce package instant
        pistachio pudding mix
    4 eggs
    ½ pint sour cream
    ½ cup oil
    ½ teaspoon almond extract
    Green food color
            ❖   ❖   ❖
    ½ cup chopped nuts
    1 tablespoon sugar
    1 teaspoon cinnamon

Mix together the cake mix, pudding mix, eggs, sour cream, oil, almond extract, and food color. In a separate bowl combine the nuts, sugar, and cinnamon. Pour ½ of the batter into an Angel food or bundt pan, then add ½ of the topping. Repeat. Do not preheat the oven. Bake in a 350° oven for 1 hour. Allow to cool in the pan for 1 to 2 hours. Good with cream cheese.

Serves 16.

Spinach Quiche

    1 12-ounce package Stouffers
        spinach soufflé
    1 deep-dish pie crust
    ¾ pound sausage
    2 teaspoons chopped onion
    ½ cup chopped mushrooms
    2 tablespoons butter, melted
    2 eggs, beaten
    3 tablespoons milk
    ¾ cup cheese

Prepare the spinach soufflé according to the directions on the package. Prick the pie crust all over and bake in a 400° oven for 7 to 10 minutes. Brown the sausage and pour off the fat. Sauté the onion and mushrooms in butter; combine with the beaten eggs and milk. Mix with the soufflé and pour into the crust. Arrange the cheese and sausage decoratively on top. Bake in a 400° oven for 25 to 30 minutes. Let stand 5 minutes before slicing.

Note: Use pork sausage with Cheddar cheese. Use Italian sausage with Mozzarella cheese.

Serves 6.

The Inn on Kelleys Island

Box 11
Kelleys Island, Ohio 43438
(419) 746-2258

Guests of the Inn on Kelleys Island may relax on the Victorian porch overlooking Lake Erie, chat with other guests in front of a crackling fire in the marble fireplace, or cast a line off the private beach. Built in 1876, the home became an inn about 1905. It is the former home of Captain Frank Hamilton, a marine historian of the Great Lakes and Kelleys Island. In the National Historic District of Kelleys Island, the inn is conveniently near the ferry dock and only minutes from the island's restaurants. Its beautiful surroundings, relaxing atmosphere, and old-fashioned charm make this a delightful place to visit.

The Inn's Victorian Lawn Party Wine Coolers

    ⅓ portion wine
    ⅓ portion lemon/lime soft drink
    ⅓ portion juice (orange juice,
        lemonade, limeade all work
        well)

Mix, serve with lemon or lime slices for garnish.

The Inn's Twist Salad

For a speedy salad, cook the pasta the night before serving.

1 pound cooked Rotini (twist)
  vegetable pasta
1 cup Italian dressing
½ head broccoli, cut into flowerets
1 15-ounce can garbanzo beans
⅔ cup cubed cheese
½ cup black olives, sliced

Combine all the ingredients in a salad bowl. Serve chilled.
Serves 16.

The Old Stone House Bed and Breakfast Inn

133 Clemons Street
Marblehead, Ohio 43440
(419) 798-5922

This rambling, four-story house is on the shore of Lake Erie facing Kelley's Island. The Captain's Tower, room 12, is the original "widow's walk" on the roof that affords a commanding view of the lake. The guest rooms on the second and third floors are decorated in white and Williamsburg blue, are carpeted, and have deep-silled windows that also look out on the lake. The five guest rooms and two large bathrooms on the second floor are air conditioned. On the third floor are six more guest rooms and three bathrooms. The original poplar wood floors in these rooms are covered only

The Old Stone House

by a few braided and hooked rugs, and the windows on the third floor have small panes of glass that open to catch the cool lake breezes. Guests can read or watch television in the sitting room on the third floor. An English breakfast is included with the room.

Sausage Croissants

8 sausage links
1 can crescent dinner rolls

Cook the sausage completely; cool. Wrap each link in a dinner roll and bake in a 350° oven until the rolls are golden brown, serve warm.
Makes 8.

The Oberlin College Inn

Oberlin, Ohio 44074

Located on the historic campus of one of America's most respected colleges, The Oberlin College Inn has been known for its gracious hospitality since 1833. Today the inn serves a wide variety of functions, from providing a room for the night, to an elegant dinner for two, to a wedding reception for 200 guests. For years, the inn's quiet, relaxed atmosphere and excellent facilities have made it a favorite setting for meetings, seminars, conferences, receptions, and banquets. Oberlin College has an active cultural life of more than 1000 events annually to which visitors at the inn are welcomed.

Salade d'Epinards (Spinach Salad)

1 pound fresh spinach
2 eggs
2 teaspoons Dijon mustard
3 tablespoons white vinegar
2 tablespoons lemon juice
Salt and pepper to taste
¾ cup walnut oil
6 ounces fresh green beans
3 tablespoons chopped onion
¼ cup plus 2 tablespoons chopped
  walnuts

Pluck the stems from the spinach and wash the leaves in cold water. Dry with paper towels. Beat the eggs with the mustard, vinegar, lemon juice, salt and pepper. Slowly beat in the oil. Wash and trim the green beans; combine with the spinach, onion, and walnuts in a large bowl. Add the dressing and toss. Serve on chilled plates.
Serves 4.

Mousseline de St. Jacques Au Coulis de Homard

¾ pound fresh scallops
1¼ teaspoons salt
¼ teaspoon pepper
1 egg
1 egg white

❖   ❖   ❖

1 pound cooked lobster meat
¼ teaspoon tarragon
1 teaspoon salt
3 tablespoons white wine
2 cups heavy cream

Place the scallops, salt, and pepper in a blender and process until smooth. Add the egg and the egg white, blending well. With the blender running, gradually add the cream. Refrigerate for 30 minutes. Butter 6 ramekins or muffin cups and fill with the mousse. Set in a pan of water and cover with buttered waxed paper. Bake in a 350° oven for 20 minutes.

Chop the lobster meat very fine. Place in a saucepan over moderate heat. Add the remaining ingredients and reduce until thickened, about 10 minutes, stirring frequently. Turn the mousses out onto individual plates, ladle Lobster Sauce over each and serve.

Serves 6.

Tournedos Echalote

6 shallots, chopped
1¼ cups white wine
½ cups plus 1 tablespoon white
    vinegar
1½ cups unsalted butter (3 sticks)
Salt and white pepper

❖ ❖ ❖

1 3-pound beef tenderloin, trimmed
Butter
Flour
Salt and pepper
12 slices French sourdough bread,
    toasted

For the Beurre Blanc, combine the shallots, wine, and vinegar in a saucepan. Bring to a boil and reduce to about 6 tablespoons of liquid. Remove from heat and beat in the butter, bit by bit. Season with salt and white pepper.

Slice the tenderloin into ¼ pound tournedos (small steaks). Melt 1 to 2 tablespoons of butter in a large sauté pan over high heat. Dredge the tournedos in flour and sauté about 3 minutes on each side. Remove from heat. Season to taste with salt and pepper. Trim the crusts from the toast and set 2 pieces on each plate. Place the tournedos over the toast and cover with Beurre Blanc.

Serves 6.

Courgettes Farcies (Stuffed Zucchini)

6 small zucchini
2 tablespoons olive oil
1 teaspoon chopped garlic
1 tablespoon chopped shallots
6 mushrooms, diced
1 tablespoon tomato paste
¼ cup grated Gruyère cheese

Split the zucchini in half lengthwise. Scoop out the pulp, taking care not to break through the skin. Chop the pulp. Heat the oil in a sauté pan over high heat. Add the garlic, shallots, zucchini pulp, and mushrooms. Sauté for 1 minute. Add the tomato paste and cheese; stir until well-blended and remove from the heat. Fill the zucchini shells with the mixture. Bake in a 350° oven for about 20 minutes.

Serves 6.

Pumpkin Cheesecake

1 cup graham cracker crumbs
4 tablespoons butter, melted
2 tablespoons grated orange rind

❖ ❖ ❖

¾ cup canned pumpkin
1 cup sugar
3 egg yolks
1 tablespoon cinnamon
1¼ teaspoons ground ginger
½ teaspoon salt
½ teaspoon mace
2 tablespoons heavy cream
1½ teaspoons grated orange rind

❖ ❖ ❖

¾ cup sugar
3 8-ounce packages cream cheese
2 egg yolks
2 eggs
1 tablespoon all-purpose flour
½ teaspoon vanilla extract
½ teaspoon rum extract

Mix the crumbs with the butter and orange rind until pliable. Press into the bottom and sides of a 9-inch springform pan. Bake in a 375° oven until lightly browned, about 10 minutes. Cool before filling.

In a medium mixing bowl combine the pumpkin, 1 cup sugar, 3 egg yolks, the cinnamon, ginger, salt, mace, cream, and orange rind. Set aside.

Mix the remaining ¾ cup sugar into the cream cheese until fluffy. Add the remaining egg yolks and the whole eggs, one at a time, mixing well. Blend in the flour, vanilla, and rum extract. Fold the pumpkin mixture into the cream cheese mixture. Pour gently

into the crust and bake in a 325° oven for 1 hour and 30 minutes or until a cake tester inserted in the center comes out clean. Allow to cool and refrigerate before serving.

Serves 12 to 16.

Zane Trace Bed and Breakfast

Box 115, Main Street
Old Washington, Ohio 43768
(614) 489-5970
(614) 489-5734

Built in 1859, this Italianate Victorian home on the Old National Trail and in Zane Grey territory has historical charm aplenty. A feeling of spaciousness abounds in this nineteenth century home with its three guest rooms. Two rooms are spacious with queen size beds and fireplaces, one of the two has an adjoining single bedroom-sitting room available. An elegant parlor for conversations is furnished as parlors of yesteryear were. A card and reading room is available for entertainment, along with a large, screened porch overlooking the heated swimming pool. Many historical sites and museums as well as three major lakes for boating and recreation, are nearby. The Zane Grey Museum, depicting the great Western novelist, is in nearby Zanesville. Continental breakfast is provided.

Cheese Ball

2 8-ounce packages cream cheese,
    softened
1 8-ounce can crushed pineapple,
    drained
1 cup chopped pecans
¼ cup chopped green pepper
2 tablespoons finely chopped onion
1 teaspoon seasoned salt

❖ ❖ ❖

1 cup chopped pecans

In a mixing bowl combine the cream cheese, pineapple, 1 cup of pecans, green pepper, onion, and salt. Roll into a ball and refrigerate until the ball is firm enough to hold its shape. Roll in the remaining nuts and refrigerate until ready to be served.

Serve with fancy crackers or bits of dark rye bread. Absolutely delicious! A good crowd pleaser.

Vermont Nut Bread

½ cup brown sugar, firmly packed
¾ cup cold water
½ cup molasses
¾ cup milk

❖ ❖ ❖

2 cups graham flour
1 cup bread flour
1⅓ teaspoons salt
2½ teaspoons baking powder
1 teaspoon baking soda

❖ ❖ ❖

¾ cup nuts (walnuts, etc.)

Mix together the brown sugar and cold water. When the lumps are dissolved, add the molasses and milk. In a separate bowl, sift together the graham and bread flours, salt, baking powder, and salt. Add the liquids to the dry ingredients. Add the nuts. Pour into a greased loaf pan. Bake in a 300° oven for 1½ to 2 hours.

Makes 1 loaf.

Ginger Cookies

The combination of ginger and molasses is considered by many cooks as a very effective digestion aid.

2 cups molasses
1 tablespoon ginger
1 tablespoon vinegar
1 tablespoon baking soda
Pinch salt
1 cup sugar
2 eggs, beaten
6 cups all-purpose flour
    (approximately)

In a large saucepan, bring the molasses just to a boil; remove from heat.

Add the ginger, vinegar, soda (carefully, for it will fizz up), salt, sugar, and eggs. Stir in enough flour that the dough will roll; cut with a cookie cutter while dough is warm. Place on a greased cookie sheet. Bake in a 350° oven for 10 to 12 minutes.

Makes 3½ to 4 dozen.

The Cider Mill

Post Office Box 441, Second Street
Zoar, Ohio 44697
(216) 874-3133

Zoar Village, founded in 1817 by a group of Germans seeking freedom from religious persecution, was a successful commune when the pioneers built their steam-operated mill in 1863. To increase efficiency, they used the building as a cabinet shop during the off season. Now renovated, it is a bed and breakfast called the "Cider Mill." Somehow the serenity of these early settlers lingers in the atmosphere to provide a tranquil stay for modern travelers. A delicious breakfast is served from the country kitchen each morning.

Hot Spiced Cider

2 3-inch sticks cinnamon
2 teaspoons whole cloves
2 teaspoons whole allspice
1 gallon apple cider
⅔ cup sugar
2 whole oranges, washed

Tie spices in a cheese cloth or place in a tea ball. Add to cider along with the sugar and whole oranges. Heat to boiling; cover and simmer 20 minutes. Serve hot.

Serves 16.

Sausage and Egg Soufflé

6 eggs
2 cups milk
1 teaspoon salt
1 teaspoon dry mustard
6 slices bread, cubed
1 pound mild sausage, cooked and
    drained
1 cup grated cheese

Beat the eggs; add the milk, salt, and mustard. Combine this mixture with the cubed bread, sausage and cheese. Pour into a greased 8x12-inch baking dish and refrigerate overnight. Bake in a 350° oven for 45 minutes. Let stand at least 5 minutes before serving.

Serves 4.

Zoar Brezl (Zoar Pretzels)

1 2-ounce cake compressed yeast
2 cups milk, scalded and cooled
1 cup water
6 to 8 cups sifted all-purpose flour
6 tablespoons lard or shortening
2 tablespoons sugar
1 teaspoon salt

❖ ❖ ❖

1 tablespoon lye
2 quarts water
Salt

Combine the ingredients as for rolls. After mixing a medium dough, let it rise in a warm place for 20 minutes. Cut off pieces of dough the size of an egg. Roll and shape into pretzels. Place on a cloth on a warm baking board. Let rise. Dip each one in hot lye water. (1 tablespoon lye to 2 quarts water.) Place on greased cookie sheets. Sprinkle with salt and bake in a 400° oven until brown. These will be about 3 inches across with a crisp crust and soft inside.

Makes approximately 3 dozen.

Oklahoma

Clayton Country Inn

Route 1, Box 8
Clayton, Oklahoma 74536
(918) 569-4165

Clayton Country Inn is in the heart of Oklahoma's beautiful Kiamichi Mountain Country, easily accessible from Tulsa, Oklahoma City, and Dallas. The inn has six large, comfortable guest rooms and the nearby cottage has two complete apartments, each with living room, bedroom, equipped kitchenette, and fireplace. The great room in the inn is for guests' use; its high, log-beamed ceiling, natural rock fireplace, easy chairs and big sofas, television, and wide windows with a view of the mountains and river create a restful setting for games, reading, or loafing. The knotty pine and fireplace theme is carried from the great room into the dining room where guests enjoy excellent food prepared with the utmost care.

Bran Muffins

5 cups sifted all-purpose flour
3 cups sugar
5 teaspoons baking soda
2 teaspoons salt
1 teaspoon cinnamon
½ teaspoon allspice
1 12-ounce package bran and raisin cereal

❖ ❖ ❖

4 eggs, beaten
1 quart buttermilk
1 cup oil
1 15-ounce can crushed pineapple

Mix the dry ingredients together. Add eggs, buttermilk, oil, and pineapple. Pour batter into muffin cups or greased muffin tins and bake in a 400° oven for 15 to 20 minutes.
Makes 2 dozen.

Squash Casserole

2 cups cooked mashed squash
¼ cup sugar
½ cup mayonnaise
½ cup grated Cheddar cheese
½ cup cracker crumbs
½ cup chopped onion
1 egg, beaten

❖ ❖ ❖

½ cup cracker crumbs
¼ cup butter (½ stick), melted
½ cup chopped pecans

Combine the squash, sugar, mayonnaise, cheese, ½ cup of cracker crumbs, onion, and egg. Place into a 1½-quart casserole dish and top with cracker crumbs, melted butter, and pecans. Bake in a 350° oven for 40 minutes.
Serves 4 to 6.

Ham Loaf

1½ pounds ground ham
½ pound ground pork
2 eggs
1 cup bread crumbs
1 cup milk

❖ ❖ ❖

1 cup brown sugar, firmly packed
½ cup water
1 teaspoon mustard
½ cup pineapple juice

Combine the ham, pork, eggs, bread crumbs, and milk. Shape into a loaf and place in a pan. Combine the brown sugar, water, mustard, and pineapple juice; pour over the loaf. Bake in a 350° oven for 1½ hours.
Serves 6.

Redbud Reservations

Post Office Box 23954
Oklahoma City, Oklahoma 73123
(405) 720-0212

Whether travelers want down home hospitality or a touch of elegance, this Oklahoma reservation service has inns available. All of their accommodations have been inspected for comfort and cleanliness, and guests will find the hosts friendly and knowledgeable about restaurants, sight-seeing, and shopping. A continental breakfast is included as part of the bed and breakfast plan. Redbud Reservations offers fine accommodations in almost every area of Oklahoma.

Cheesy Eggs and Bacon

¼ cup finely chopped onion
½ cup butter or margarine (1 stick)
½ cup all-purpose flour
½ teaspoon salt
⅛ teaspoon pepper
4 cups milk
1½ cups shredded Swiss cheese (6 ounces)
1 cup diced Canadian bacon
1 2-ounce jar chopped pimiento
16 hard-boiled eggs, quartered

❖ ❖ ❖

1½ cups soft bread crumbs
3 tablespoons butter or margarine, melted

❖ ❖ ❖

Toast points

In a saucepan cook the onion in ½ cup of butter until tender. Blend in the flour, salt, and pepper. Add the milk; cook and stir until bubbly. Add the cheese, bacon, and pimiento; stir until the cheese melts.

Place ½ of the eggs in the bottom of a 3-quart casserole. Spoon ½ the sauce over the eggs. Repeat layers. Cover, and chill up to 24 hours. Toss the bread crumbs with 3 tablespoons of melted butter. Wrap and refrigerate until ready to bake.

Bake the casserole in a 375° oven for 45 minutes. Sprinkle with the buttered crumbs, and bake about 15 minutes longer. Serve over toast points.

Serves 14 to 16.

Barbecued Meatballs

1 cup bread crumbs
½ cup milk
1 pound lean ground beef

❖ ❖ ❖

1½ tablespoons Worcestershire sauce
3 tablespoons sugar
¼ cup vinegar
½ cup ketchup
½ cup water
½ cup chopped onion
½ cup chopped bell pepper
½ teaspoon celery seeds

Combine the bread crumbs, milk, and ground beef together and form into meatballs. Mix the remaining ingredients for the sauce and pour over the meatballs in a casserole dish. Bake in a 350° oven for 1 hour. Great with garlic bread and salad.

Serves 4.

Fruit Medleys

For each serving cut into bite-sized pieces any of the following fruits: seedless red and green grapes, strawberries, bananas, peaches, pears, pineapple, mandarin oranges, or sweet cherries.

¼ cup yogurt or sour cream
¼ cup whipped cream
1 tablespoon sugar
¼ teaspoon cinnamon
Dash nutmeg
Dash cloves

Make a sauce for the fruits with the yogurt, whipped cream, sugar, and spices, and pour over the fruit. Serve chilled.

Serves one.

Grandmother's Butterscotch Pie

1 cup all-purpose flour
1 teaspoon salt
⅓ cup oil
3 tablespoons milk

❖ ❖ ❖

1 cup brown sugar, firmly packed
¼ teaspoon salt
¼ cup all-purpose flour or cornstarch (or combine 3 tablespoons cornstarch and 2 tablespoons flour)

2 cups milk
3 to 4 egg yolks
1 tablespoon butter
1 teaspoon vanilla extract

❖ ❖ ❖

3 to 4 egg whites
½ teaspoon cream of tartar
6 tablespoons sugar
½ teaspoon vanilla extract

To prepare the pie shell combine 1 cup of flour, 1 teaspoon of salt, oil, and 3 tablespoons of milk. Mix together well and roll out slightly larger than the pie pan. Place in the pie pan, prick several times, and decorate the edge as desired. Bake in a 425° oven for 8 to 10 minutes.

For the filling mix together well in a medium saucepan the brown sugar, ¼ teaspoon salt, and the remaining flour and/or cornstarch. To avoid having lumps form in the mixture stir the milk in slowly. Cook over medium heat until the mixture is thick, stirring constantly. Remove from the heat when thickened.

Beat the egg yolks in a small bowl, add in the butter; then slowly add a small quantity of the hot mixture, stirring constantly so as not to overcook the yolks. Then stir the warmed yolk mixture into the saucepan.

Return the saucepan to the heat; cook 1 to 2 minutes longer. Remove from the heat and add 1 teaspoon of vanilla. Pour into the baked pie shell.

Make the meringue by beating the egg whites and cream of tartar until frothy. Gradually beat in the sugar a tablespoonful at a time. Add ½ teaspoon of vanilla; continue beating until stiff and glossy. Spread the meringue over the pie filling, sealing around the edge, and swirling into peaks. Bake in a 400° oven for 8 to 10 minutes. Cool away from drafts; then chill. Serve when cold.

Serves 6.

Oregon

Chanticleer Bed and Breakfast Inn

120 Gresham Street
Ashland, Oregon 97520
(503) 482-1919

In Chaucer's *Canterbury Tales* "Chanticleer and the Fox" is a barnyard fable whose origin comes from the heart of Europe. Chanticleer Bed and Breakfast Inn reflects this same European country feeling. This snug and cozy six-room guest house is situated in a quiet residential neighborhood, a short walk from the Oregon Shakespearean Festival, Lithia Park, and the shops and restaurants of Ashland's Plaza. The Rogue River's white water rafting and Mount Ashland's ski slopes are in close driving distance. Some of the inn's rooms overlook the Bear Creek Valley and Cascade Foothills; others open onto a peaceful brick patio. Guest rooms are furnished with antiques, fluffy comforters, and fresh flowers, and each room has a private bath and is air-conditioned. The spacious living room offers books and magazines to curl up with while warming one's toes by the open hearth fireplace. A full breakfast is served in the sunny dining room; by request, guests may have breakfast in bed.

Cheese Baked Eggs

Here's a recipe everyone asks for at the Chanticleer. It is simple yet deliciously rich. It is served with croissants and fresh fruit for a wonderful breakfast.

> 1 teaspoon butter, melted
> 1 tablespoon cream
> 1 egg
> Salt and pepper
> Grated Havarti cheese

Butter a 3½-ounce ramekin or custard dish; add the cream. Gently crack a large egg into the ramekin. Season with salt and pepper. Sprinkle Havarti cheese on top. Bake in preheated 425° oven for 8 to 10 minutes, or until the white is firm and the center is still soft.
Serves 1.

Hersey House

451 North Main Street
Ashland, Oregon 97520
(503) 482-4563

A spacious front porch beckons guests into this turn-of-the-century Victorian home, now fully restored. Inside, the L-shaped staircase leads to the four guest rooms, one of which has a private balcony overlooking the Cascade foothills and the Rogue Valley. Another has a pleasing view of Mount Ashland. Each room has a private bath. Breakfast is set each morning overlooking the colorful English country garden. House specialties include gingerbread pancakes, Eggs Hersey, sourdough pancakes, and avocado omelets. In the late afternoon a social hour in the main parlor gives guests a chance to exchange news of the day's pleasures. Ashland's Plaza, Lithia Park and the Oregon Shakespearean Festival theaters are all a short walk from the inn.

Hersey House

Eggs Hersey

8 hard-cooked eggs

❖ ❖ ❖

⅓ cup butter, melted
1½ teaspoons Worcestershire sauce
Mustard to taste
4 slices boiled ham, ground
Several sprigs of fresh parsley, chopped
4 to 5 green onions with tops, chopped

3 cups rich white sauce

❖ ❖ ❖

**1 to 1½ cups grated Parmesan or
mild Cheddar cheese**

Cut the eggs lengthwise, lift out the yolks. Mash the yolks, add melted butter, Worcestershire sauce, and mustard. Add the ground ham, parsley, and onions. Stuff the mixture into whites. Place in a greased baking dish or individual ramekins. Top with white sauce. May be made ahead and refrigerated at this point. Bake in a 350° oven for 15 to 20 minutes. Top with grated cheese halfway through baking.

Serves 8.

Kate's Avocado Omelet Filling

This recipe makes enough filling for 2 omelets, which can be prepared according to your preference.

1 medium-sized ripe avocado
1½ tablespoons mayonnaise
1 tablespoon fresh lemon juice
**1 tablespoon finely chopped red
   onion**
Salt and pepper

Halve the avocado, remove the pit, peel, and trim away any brown spots. Finely chop or mash the avocado; combine in a bowl with the mayonnaise, lemon juice, and onion. Mix thoroughly and season with salt and pepper.

Place the filling in the omelets and serve with mild red salsa, hot green salsa, and sour cream.

Serves 2.

Hersey Bacon

½ pound thick sliced bacon
Brown sugar, enough to coat bacon

Roll the bacon in brown sugar to coat. Place on a greased broiler rack. Bake in a 300° oven for 30 to 40 minutes until browned to taste.

Serves 8.

Gail's Brown Sugar Syrup

1 cup brown sugar, firmly packed
¼ cup water

Bring to a boil in a saucepan. Boil only until sugar melts into a syrup. Serve on sourdough pancakes.

Makes 1 cup.

Oregon Caves Chateau

Post Office Box 128
Cave Junction, Oregon 97523
(503) 592-3400

The Oregon Caves Chateau is nestled in the mountains east of Cave Junction, in the Oregon Cave National Forest.

The chateau operates from about mid-June to early September each year. Built in 1834, the chateau stands six stories high and provides rustic accommodations, although some of the rooms have modern facilities. Some pleasures to be enjoyed here are invigorating mountain air, the sound of rushing water (from the nearby waterfalls), a better than average dining room, no television, no telephones (except at the front desk), and the national park at the doorstep. Available activities include visiting the Oregon Caves National Monument, exploring the caves, and hiking the trails to enjoy the splendid waterfalls.

Shrimp Newberg

1 tablespoon minced shallots
1 tablespoon butter

❖ ❖ ❖

½ cup butter (1 stick), melted
All-purpose flour

❖ ❖ ❖

1 quart half and half
1 quart whipping cream

❖ ❖ ❖

Oregon Caves Chateau

2 tablespoons butter
2 tablespoons minced celery
1 tablespoon minced shallots
2 to 3 ounces Marsala wine
Salt to taste
1/8 teaspoon paprika
Pinch cayenne pepper
Pinch nutmeg

   ❖ ❖ ❖

2 pounds frozen large shrimp,
    thawed, shelled, and deveined

   ❖ ❖ ❖

Croutons

In a medium saucepan sauté 1 tablespoon of shallots in 1 tablespoon of butter until soft. Prepare a roux with ½ cup of butter, adding flour and cooking until almost hard. Mix with a wooden spoon. Add some lumps of the roux to the shallots. Add the half and half and whipping cream. Bring to a boil, continually adding roux and blending with a wire whisk until all the roux is blended into the cream and the mixture is thick. Pour through a strainer.

In a small sauté pan melt 2 tablespoons butter; sauté the celery and 1 tablespoon shallots until soft. Then add the wine and flambé. Add this mixture to the cream sauce, blending with a whisk. Add the seasonings and blend.

Place the shrimp in a large casserole dish and cover with the sauce. Bake in a 350° oven until done, about 8 minutes. Garnish with croutons.

Serves 8.

Madison Inn Bed and Breakfast

660 Madison Avenue
Corvallis, Oregon 97333
(503) 757-1274

The Madison Inn is a well-maintained historical home facing Central Park on a quiet street in downtown Corvallis. Oregon State University is within walking distance, a feature especially convenient for visiting professors from throughout the world. The five-story home offers comfortable guest rooms and varied breakfasts that may include fruit-studded scones and individual puffed pancakes, served with fresh fruit or juice and custom-blended coffee or tea. For quiet comfort, pleasant surroundings and conversation, the Madison Inn is a good choice.

The Madison Inn Buttermilk Scones

3 cups all-purpose flour
1/3 cup sugar
2½ teaspoons baking powder
½ teaspoon baking soda
¾ teaspoon salt
¾ cup firm butter or margarine
    (1½ sticks), cut in small pieces
¾ cup chopped pitted dates,
    currants, or raisins
1 teaspoon grated orange peel
1 cup buttermilk

   ❖ ❖ ❖

1 tablespoon cream or milk
    (approximately)
¼ teaspoon cinnamon
2 tablespoons sugar

In a large bowl, stir together the flour, sugar, baking powder, soda, and salt until thoroughly blended. Using a pastry blender or 2 knives, cut the butter into the flour mixture until it resembles coarse cornmeal. Stir in the fruit and orange peel. Make a well in the center of the butter-flour mixture; add the buttermilk all at once. Stir the mixture with a fork until the dough pulls away from the sides of the bowl. With your hands, gather the dough into a ball; turn out onto a lightly floured board. Roll or pat into a ½-inch thick circle. Using a 2½-inch heart (or other shaped) cutter, cut into individual scones. Place 1½ inches apart on lightly greased baking sheets. Brush tops of scones with cream; sprinkle lightly with a mixture of the cinnamon and sugar. Bake in a 425° oven for 12 minutes or until the tops are lightly browned. Serve warm.

Makes about 18 scones.

Marjon Bed and Breakfast Inn

44975 Leaburg Dam Road
Leaburg, Oregon 97489
(503) 896-3145

This elegant bed and breakfast offers luxury along the McKenzie River. A garden containing 2,000 azaleas and 700 rhododendrons, and a natural fern bed that slopes to the river contribute to the charming atmosphere of the Marjon Bed and Breakfast Inn. Breakfast is served on a covered terrace, weather permitting. Accommodations for two couples are available at this beautiful inn with an oriental atmosphere.

Marjon Upside Down Sunrise Surprise

4 ½-inch thick slices fresh tomato
5 fresh mushroom caps
Fresh broccoli flowerets
Salt and pepper to taste
¼ cup olive oil (or bacon fat or
    cooking oil)
⅔ cup hickory smoked barbecue
    sauce

   ❖ ❖ ❖

½ teaspoon cream of tartar
8 eggs, separated
Salt and pepper to taste

Prepare in a thoroughly greased 10-inch skillet or teflon skillet the following: arrange in an attractive design the fresh tomato slices in the center of the skillet, fresh mushroom caps, tops down, one in the center and the other 4 between each tomato slice. Place the fresh broccoli flowerets around the center arrangement of the tomatoes and mushrooms so it looks like a wreath. Use small pieces of broccoli flowerets (no stems) and place side by side with flower heads down. Sprinkle with salt and pepper. Drizzle with oil and then with barbecue sauce.

In a mixing bowl combine the cream of tartar with the egg whites and beat until stiff. In a separate bowl beat the egg yolks until thick and lemon-colored, add salt and pepper. Fold the egg whites and yolks together and spoon over the arrangement in the skillet. Lightly smooth over with a spatula to cover the arrangement and evenly distribute the mixture. Cook slowly on top of stove on low heat about 15 minutes. Bubbles will still appear through uncooked puffy top and mixture will look moist. Place skillet in a preheated 425° oven for 5 minutes. Reduce heat to 350° and bake until light brown on top and no imprint remains when touched lightly, about 30 minutes. Remove from the oven. Place a serving plate on top of the skillet; carefully turn skillet upside down onto the serving plate. Mixture will look beautiful with the arrangement on top.

Serve immediately.

Makes 4 pie-shaped servings.

The Pringle House

114 Northeast 7th Street
Post Office Box 578
Oakland, Oregon 97462
(503) 459-5038

Standing on a rise overlooking downtown Oakland, The Pringle House of-fers satisfying bed and breakfast accommodations to travelers at a moderate price. Constructed in 1893 by Z. L. Dimmick and returned to most of its original Victorian design by Jim and DeMay Pringle, it is one of many homes and businesses on the National Historic Register in this city of 850 people. Arriving guests find ample space for relaxing in their rooms, in the comfort of the parlor, or perhaps in the winged-backed chairs in front of the living room fireplace. In the dining room, where coffee and tea are available at the self-service corner, guests gather each morning for breakfast of fresh juice, coffee or tea, fruits and melons in season, cheeses, hot breads, jams and jellies, and perhaps a "house specialty." Activities in Oakland include a historic walking tour, a visit to the city museum, antique shops, and the carriage works, where fine horse-drawn carriages are made.

The Pringle House

Mini Quiches

1 cup margarine (2 sticks), softened
2 3-ounce packages cream cheese, softened
2 cups all-purpose flour

❖ ❖ ❖

2 2¼-ounce cans deviled ham
1 medium onion, chopped
2 teaspoons margarine
½ cup grated American or Swiss cheese
2 eggs, slightly beaten
½ cup milk
1⅛ teaspoons nutmeg
Dash pepper

Beat together the margarine and cream cheese until fluffy. Gradually add the flour, mixing to a smooth dough. Chill thoroughly. Shape the dough into 1-inch balls, then press evenly into 24 1⅞-inch muffin cups to make crust. Spoon deviled ham into each cup. Sauté onion in 2 teaspoons of margarine until soft, not brown. Mix with ¼ cup of the cheese. Scatter over the ham. Combine the remaining cheese, eggs, milk, nutmeg, and pepper. Spoon evenly into the cups. Bake in a preheated 450° oven for 10 minutes. Reduce the heat to 350° for 15 minutes until the custard is set and quiches are golden brown. Serve warm. To freeze, allow them to cool, then wrap and freeze. Reheat in a 350° oven for 15 minutes before serving.

Makes 24 individual quiches.

Berry Butter

This is a sweet butter made with frozen sliced strawberries (or fresh). Delicious on croissants, waffles or pancakes, coffee cakes and breads.

1 cup unsalted butter (2 sticks), softened
1 tablespoon honey
½ cup frozen sliced strawberries in syrup, thawed

With an electric mixer, whip the butter with the honey until soft and light. On high speed gradually beat in the berries. Store covered in the refrigerator. Keeps up to 4 weeks. It's pretty!

Makes ¾ cup.

Crème Caramel

¼ cup sugar

❖ ❖ ❖

4 eggs
¼ cup sugar
2 cups milk
1 teaspoon vanilla extract
¼ teaspoon salt

❖ ❖ ❖

Lemon peel twists

Grease 6 custard cups. Put ¼ cup of sugar in a small pan; heat over medium heat until melted and a light caramel color, stirring constantly. Pour immediately into the greased cups.

Using a whisk or a fork, beat the eggs and ¼ cup of sugar in a large mixing bowl until well-blended. Add in the milk, vanilla, and salt; blend well. Divide the mixture between the custard cups.

Put the cups into a 13x9-inch baking pan. Fill the pan with hot water to come halfway up the sides of the cups. Bake in a 325° oven for 50 to 55 minutes, until a knife inserted in the center of the custard comes out clean. Remove the cups from the pan and allow to cool. Cover and refrigerate until chilled, about 1½ hours.

To serve unmold each custard onto a chilled dessert plate, allowing the caramel topping to drip from the cup onto the custard. Garnish with lemon peel twists.

Serves 16.

❖ ❖ ❖ ❖ ❖ ❖

Wolf Creek Tavern

An Original Stagecoach Stop
Post Office Box 97
Wolf Creek, Oregon 97497
(503) 866-2474

Wolf Creek Tavern authentically portrays the evolutionary changes and adaptations it has undergone since 1870 as a roadside inn. Therefore the restoration reflects the tavern's various historical periods, rather than one in particular. As it has in the past, it functions today by providing food and beverages, as well as meeting and overnight accommodations for the local and traveling public. On the ground floor are the central stair and hallway, ladies' parlor, and men's sitting room. On the second floor, the original ballroom-dormitory space and the two small sleeping rooms have been reconstructed to the pre-1905 era and have

been adapted for use as banquet and meeting rooms. The building has modern amenities, including bathrooms for each of the eight guest chambers. To every extent possible, the building reflects its character and evolution as a wayside inn from the 1870s to the present.

Poppyseed Dressing

1½ cups sugar
2 teaspoons dry mustard
2 teaspoons salt
⅔ cup vinegar
3 tablespoons onion juice (optional)

❖ ❖ ❖

2 cups oil
3 tablespoons poppyseeds

Mix together all ingredients except oil and poppyseeds. Allow sugar to completely dissolve. Add the oil very slowly while beating in a blender or food processor, then add the seeds and beat 1 minute longer.

Store in a cool place or refrigerate.
Makes 3 cups.

Pennsylvania

Springs Valley Inn

Church Road
R.D. 1, Box 532
Avondale, Pennsylvania 19311
(215) 268-2597

The Springs Valley Inn was built originally as a barn. It has been drastically remodeled and developed into a beautiful country inn in a rural setting. The dining room provides a balcony for secluded dining, and the lower dining room, called the Thomas Eakins Room after the artist whose work is featured in high quality reproductions, is available for private parties and banquets. A gourmet chef presides over the new, modern kitchen, and delicious meals are served daily. A sixteen-unit motel has recently been added to the facilities.

Cream of Mushroom Soup

½ cup butter (1 stick), clarified
¼ pound onions, chopped fine
½ pound mushrooms, washed and
    chopped fine
¾ cup all-purpose flour
1½ quarts chicken stock, hot
1 pint milk, hot
½ pint light cream
Salt and pepper to taste

Sauté the onions and mushrooms in butter until soft. Do not brown. Add the flour; stir until smooth. Cook for five minutes. Gradually add the hot chicken stock, stirring until smooth. Simmer for 7 or 8 minutes until thick and smooth. Whip as necessary. Add the hot milk and cream; season to taste.
    Serves 12.

The Mountain House

Mountain Road
Delaware Water Gap, Pennsylvania 18327
(717) 424-2254

In the beautiful Pocono Mountains of Pennsylvania, the Mountain House Inn has been in continuous operation as an inn since 1870. Directly on the Appalachian Trail and within walking distance of the Delaware River, it is an ideal vacation spot for the outdoors enthusiast. In addition, it has an outdoor pool and is close to many of the famous Pocono Mountains attractions. Guests get a homey feeling as they enter the door into the century-old parlor and are greeted by the inn's dog, Peanut. The warmth is carried through to the guest rooms. The antique-filled dining room serves good old-fashioned fare, and all baking is done on the premises, including the honey wheat bread served with each meal. The inn is open year round.

Smoked Egg Dip

2 dozen hard-boiled eggs
½ teaspoon Tabasco sauce
1 tablespoon liquid smoke
1 tablespoon Worcestershire sauce
½ tablespoon dry mustard
2 cups mayonnaise
Salt and pepper to taste

Peel and clean the eggs; do not separate. In a mixing bowl crush the eggs with a fork or grind in a food processor if one is available. Add the Tabasco, liquid smoke, Worcestershire sauce and mustard to the eggs. Add the mayonnaise a little at a time, stirring to blend all the ingredients completely. Add salt and pepper. Top with a few dashes of paprika. Serve with fresh breads or crackers.
    Makes approximately 4 cups.

Broiled Haddock a la Casino

1 pound fresh haddock fillet (or
    other light white fish)
¼ cup butter (½ stick)
Juice of one fresh lemon
½ green pepper
1 whole pimiento
2 ounces chopped onion
¾ cup fresh bread crumbs
Paprika
Lemon wedges

Place the haddock in a shallow broiling pan. In a sauté pan melt the butter and add the remaining ingredients except the bread crumbs. Sauté until well-blended, and the peppers and onions are soft. Add the bread crumbs to the mixture. Spoon an adequate amount of mixture on top of the haddock. Place in the broiler, cooking until the fish is fork tender. The mixture may burn if placed too close to the broiler coils. Serve topped with a sprinkle of paprika and a fresh lemon wedge garnish.

Serves 2.

The Inn at Fordhook Farm

105 New Britain Road
Doylestown, Pennsylvania 18901
(215) 345-1766

Friendly, comfortable, and quietly elegant, The Inn at Fordhook Farm, still the Burpee (seed company) family home, offers the tranquility and beauty of a 200-year-old house and sixty acres of meadows, woodlands, gardens, and historic buildings. Guests will enjoy the large bedrooms furnished with family antiques and mementos, the full traditional breakfast in the beamed dining room, and afternoon tea by the fire or on the terrace under the shade of giant old linden trees. The inn is near Valley Forge, New Hope, and Philadelphia.

Old-Fashioned Oatmeal Pancakes

2 cups rolled oats
2 cups buttermilk
❖ ❖ ❖
2 eggs, lightly beaten
¼ cup butter (½ stick), melted and cooled
½ cup raisins (optional)
❖ ❖ ❖
½ cup all-purpose flour
2 tablespoons sugar
1 teaspoon baking powder
1 teaspoon baking soda
½ teaspoon ground cinnamon
¼ teaspoon salt

In a bowl, combine the oats and buttermilk; stir to blend well. Cover and refrigerate until the next day.

Just before cooking, add the eggs, butter and raisins (if desired); stir just to blend. In another bowl, stir together the flour, sugar, baking powder, soda, cinnamon and salt; add to the oat mixture and stir just until moistened. If the batter seems too thick, add more buttermilk (up to 3 tablespoons). The batter will be thicker than normal pancakes. Preheat a griddle or large frying pan over medium heat; grease lightly. Spoon the batter, about ¼ cup for each cake, onto the griddle; spread the batter out to make 4-inch circles. Cook until the tops are bubbly and appear dry; turn and cook the other side until browned.

Serve with butter, syrup or jam.

Makes about 1½ dozen pancakes.

Blueberry Gingerbread

½ cup butter (1 stick)
1 cup sugar
1 egg
2 cups all-purpose flour
1 teaspoon cinnamon
½ teaspoon ginger
½ teaspoon salt
1 teaspoon baking soda
1 cup sour milk

3 tablespoons molasses
1 cup blueberries
3 tablespoons sugar

Cream together the butter and sugar. Mix in the egg. Sift together the flour, cinnamon, ginger, and salt. Dissolve the soda in the sour milk; mix alternately with the dry ingredients to the creamed mixture. Add the molasses; fold in the blueberries. Pour the batter into a greased and floured 9x9-inch pan. Sprinkle sugar on top of the batter. Bake in a 350° oven for 50 minutes.

Serve warm with whipped cream or vanilla ice cream, or make into muffins for a delightful breakfast treat.

Serves 12.

Shady Lane Lodge—A Bed and Breakfast Inn

Allegheny Avenue
Eagles Mere, Pennsylvania 17731
(717) 525-3394

The Shady Lane Lodge is a quiet bed and breakfast inn in the picturesque mountain-top village of Eagles Mere, known as "The Town Time Forgot." It provides visitors a lovely step into the past.

The lodge has seven guest rooms, all with private baths; it also has two sitting rooms and a dining room. Guests enjoy a quiet wooded setting within walking distance of the lake; gift and antique shops are nearby, too. Winter sports include cross country skiing, tobogganing, and ice skating.

Apple Muffins

1 egg
½ cup milk
¼ cup oil
1 cup grated apples

❖ ❖ ❖

1½ cups all-purpose flour
½ cup sugar
½ teaspoon cinnamon
2 teaspoons baking powder
½ teaspoon salt

❖ ❖ ❖

¼ cup brown sugar, firmly packed
¼ cup broken nuts
½ teaspoon cinnamon

In a mixing bowl beat the egg, stir in the milk, oil, and grated apples. In a separate bowl mix the flour, sugar, cinnamon, baking powder, and salt; combine with the apple mixture. The batter should be lumpy. Pour into a greased 12-cup muffin pan; fill the muffin cups ⅔ full. Mix together the brown sugar, nuts, and cinnamon; sprinkle over the batter. Bake in a 400° oven for 25 to 30 minutes. Serve warm.

Makes 12 muffins.

The Guesthouse at Doneckers

The Guesthouse at Doneckers

322–324 North State Street
Ephrata, Pennsylvania 17522
(717) 733-8696

Pampering guests is the aim of the innkeepers of the Guesthouse at Doneckers. Refreshing coolers or pots of hot tea on request, chocolates on the pillow at night, a balcony deck for sunning, a cozy parlor for relaxing at night, good food in the restaurant—all these and more add up to a feeling of elegance and well being. The Guesthouse has twelve rooms, each individually decorated with cherry wood vanities, folk art, designer linens, and fine crystal. The restaurant specializes in French cuisine.

Crème Crecy Soup

1½ to 2 gallons chicken stock
1 large onion
Butter
8 pounds grated carrots
½ stalk celery
2 pounds chef's or regular
    potatoes, peeled and chopped
Pinch nutmeg
1 tablespoon curry powder
1 to 1½ quarts heavy cream
1½ cups butter (3 sticks)
Pinch salt and pepper
Chopped fresh chervil (optional)
Chopped parsley (optional)

In a stock pot bring the chicken stock to a boil. Set the pot aside; keep the stock hot.

In a separate large pot, sauté the chopped onion in butter until it becomes translucent. Add the grated carrots. Cover the pot and steam; do not allow the bottom of the pot to scorch. Stir occasionally. The carrots should turn a bright orange. Add the hot chicken stock to the carrot mixture. Add the potatoes. Bring to a boil and boil for 10 minutes.

Purée the soup. Add the heavy cream gradually. The consistency should be that of any cream soup. Season the soup with the curry powder, nutmeg, salt, and pepper. Add the chopped chervil and parsley for color and texture if desired.

Serves 10 to 12.

Paupiette de Veau

1 clove garlic
¼ pound grated carrots
¼ pound grated celery
⅛ pound grated mushrooms
2 tablespoons butter
1 tablespoon all-purpose flour
1 teaspoon thyme

❖ ❖ ❖

4 veal scallops
Salt and pepper to taste
1 tablespoon butter
Oil

❖ ❖ ❖

½ cup white wine
2 cups veal stock
1 tablespoon butter

❖ ❖ ❖

1 stalk parsley

In a saucepan cook the garlic and vegetables with 2 tablespoons of butter until tender. Stir in the flour and cook until smooth; add the thyme. Remove from heat and set aside.

Pound the veal into uniform rectangles and season with salt and pepper. Spread the vegetable mixture evenly on each veal scallop; roll as for a jelly roll and secure with skewers. In a sauté pan heat 1 tablespoon of butter and a drop of oil. Sauté the veal rolls until brown on all sides. Transfer the veal to a serving platter, cover with foil and keep warm in a low oven.

Pour the white wine into the sauté pan used for the veal and reduce by half. Add the veal stock, simmer for a few minutes, and slowly stir in 1 tablespoon of butter. Taste and season if necessary. Pour the sauce on the bottom of 4 serving plates and arrange the sliced veal rolls on top. Garnish with parsley.

Serves 4.

Salmon Ardennes-Style in Foil Cases

1 10-ounce salmon fillet
2 tablespoons dry white wine
Lemon slice
Freshly ground pepper
2 slices bacon
Salt
1 teaspoon finely chopped parsley
Pinches chopped garlic
Thyme and bay leaf to taste

❖ ❖ ❖

2 teaspoons finely chopped shallots
Pepper
1 tablespoon heavy cream
2 tablespoons butter
Salt
1 teaspoon lemon juice

Cut the salmon into 2-inch slices and place in a small bowl with the wine, lemon slice and a grind or so of pepper. Marinate for 1 hour.

Drain the salmon, reserving the marinade for later. Wrap the salmon slices in the bacon and if desired salt lightly. Oil a square of aluminum foil large enough to hold the salmon pieces comfortably. Place the salmon on one half of the foil and sprinkle with the parsley, garlic, thyme and bay leaf. Fold over the other half of the foil and seal it tightly. Bake in a 400° oven for 12 to 15 minutes.

While the salmon is cooking, make the butter sauce. Strain the marinade and pour it into a small saucepan with the shallots and a grind or 2 of pepper. Add a little water so that the shallots will cook. Reduce the liquid to about half, add the cream and reduce again by half. Stir in the softened butter, salt, and lemon juice. The sauce should be quite thick and creamy. Transfer the salmon to a serving plate, open the foil case and serve the butter sauce separately. Garnish with lemon if desired.

Serves 1.

Ratatouille Nicoise

3 medium eggplants
3 sweet red peppers
3 zucchini
1 medium onion
3 cloves garlic
2 tablespoons olive oil
½ teaspoon thyme
1 bay leaf
½ cup olive oil
8 tomatoes
Salt and pepper to taste

Peel the eggplants and cut in 1-inch cubes. Remove the seeds from the peppers and cut into thin strips. Slice the zucchini in ¼-inch thick rounds. Chop the onion and garlic. Heat 2 tablespoons of oil in a flame proof casserole. Add the onion and garlic, thyme and bay leaf. Cook without browning for 6 to 7 minutes. Sauté each of the vegetables separately in skillet in the remaining oil. Add each to the onion as

it is done (2 or 3 minutes for the eggplant and zucchini, 10 minutes for the peppers). Peel the tomatoes and squeeze out the seeds; chop coarsely and add to the other vegetables. Add salt and pepper. Simmer the ratatouille for 45 minutes.

Serves 6.

Gateau Marjolaine

"This cake is Fernard Point's masterpiece of pastry. Marjolaine means 'sweet marjoram,' though neither flower nor herb have anything to do with it. For decoration the chef stencils the famous pyramid on the sugared top of the cake. It is served every day at the Pyramid. I, for one, would never tire of it," says Chef de Cuisine, Jean Maurice Juge.

1½ cups blanched almonds
1 cup hazelnuts (skinned)
1½ cups sugar
8 egg whites
Salt
¼ teaspoon cream of tartar

❖ ❖ ❖

1 cup sugar
⅓ cup water
⅛ teaspoon cream of tartar
8 egg yolks
1½ cups butter (3 sticks), cubed
1 teaspoon vanilla
¼ cup praline powder
3 1-ounce pieces semi-sweet
    chocolate
1 tablespoon water

❖ ❖ ❖

6 1-ounce pieces of semi-sweet
    chocolate

In separate pie plates spread the blanched almonds and the skinned hazelnuts. Bake in a 450° oven for 20 minutes or until brown, shaking the pans occasionally. Remove and let cool. Grind 1 cup at a time in an electric blender on high speed for about 5 seconds and empty into a bowl. Mix the ground nuts with 1½ cups of sugar.

In a separate bowl beat the egg whites, a pinch of salt, and ¼ teaspoon of cream of tartar until stiff. Gradually fold in the sugar-nut mixture.

Line a baking sheet with waxed paper and butter lightly. On the paper mark 4 bands about 12 inches long and 4 inches wide. Spread these bands quickly with the meringue-nut mixture. Bake in a 250° oven for about 30 minutes or until crusty on top, but still pliable. Invert onto waxed paper, and carefully remove the waxed paper from the bottoms of the bands. Cool.

In a saucepan combine 1 cup of sugar, ⅓ cup of water, and ⅛ teaspoon of cream of tartar. Bring to a boil and boil rapidly to 240° on a candy thermometer, or until the syrup spins a long thread. Gradually beat the hot syrup into the egg yolks and continue to beat until the mixture is cool and thick. Beat in the butter one cube at a time. This makes 1 quart of butter cream.

Measure 1 cup of the butter cream and flavor it with 1 teaspoon of vanilla.

Measure a second cup of butter cream and flavor it with ¼ cup of praline powder.

Melt 3 ounces of semi-sweet chocolate with 1 tablespoon of water and stir into the remaining butter cream.

Chill all of the butter cream until firm enough to spread.

Melt 6 ounces of semi-sweet chocolate in a double boiler over hot water. Cut circles 2½ inches in diameter from waxed paper and spread these rounds with a thin coating of the melted chocolate. Place the rounds on a cookie sheet and chill in the refrigerator.

On a serving plate place a meringue band and spread with the vanilla cream. Top with a second meringue band and spread with the praline cream. Top with another meringue band and spread with part of the chocolate cream. Top with the fourth meringue band. Frost the sides with the remaining chocolate cream and sprinkle the top heavily with confectioners' sugar. Carefully peel the waxed paper from the bottom of the chocolate wafers and decorate the sides of the cake by overlapping the wafers all the way around.

Serves 12 to 16.

Academy Street Bed and Breakfast

528 Academy Street
Hawley, Pennsylvania 18428
(717) 226-3430

This large Italianate-style Victorian home was built in 1865 by Civil War hero Joseph Atkinson, on a hill near the Lackawaxen River. It miraculously survived the "Great Flood" when most other houses nearer the river were washed away. Restored within the last decade by commercial artist Dennis Corrigan, it has oversized windows and high ceilings and is bright and airy. Seven bedrooms are available for guests.

Baked Broccoli-Egg Custard

1 10-ounce package frozen chopped broccoli
Butter
6 eggs, beaten
1¼ cups milk
Bacon or ham, chopped (optional)
1 tomato, peeled and chopped

In a large skillet sauté the broccoli in butter. Combine the eggs and milk; add the broccoli. Chopped bacon or ham may be added to the egg mixture if desired. Pour into a greased 9x13-inch dish. Place the dish in a pan of hot water. Sauté the chopped tomato in butter and layer over the egg mixture. Bake in a 350° oven for 1 hour and 15 minutes until set.

Serves 6 to 8.

Academy Street

Corn Pudding

1 10-ounce box frozen corn, thawed
1 cup milk
½ cup bread crumbs
2 eggs, beaten
1 cup shredded Cheddar cheese
1 teaspoon mustard
1 teaspoon salt
1 tablespoon finely chopped onion
1 tablespoon finely chopped green pepper

Mix together all of the ingredients and pour into a greased 1½-quart baking dish. Place the dish in a pan of hot water. Bake in a 350° oven for 1 hour.

Serves 4.

Settler's Inn

4 Main Avenue
Hawley, Pennsylvania 18428
(717) 226-2993
(717) 226-2448

This Tudor-style home, built in 1927, was purchased in 1980 by the present innkeepers, who have restored and reopened it as a place of elegant entertainment and comfort. Each of the sixteen guest rooms is different although they all are alike in that they have been furnished with period furnishings. Games, reading materials, and television are provided in a central living room.

Lunch and dinner are available in the dining room, which enjoys a fine reputation in the area. The decor of hand-made quilts, early American memorabilia, hanging plants, and soft lighting lends to relaxation. Dress is casual and families are welcome. The complimentary cheese bar is always inviting.

Cinnamon Raisin or Nut Swirl Bread

**2 cups very hot water
2 cups oats
¼ cup butter (½ stick)
1 tablespoon salt
6 tablespoons honey**

❖   ❖   ❖

**2 ¼-ounce packages active dry
  yeast
½ cup warm water (110° to 115°)
4 to 5 cups all-purpose flour
½ cup sugar
2 teaspoons cinnamon
1 cup nuts or raisins**

Mix the hot water, oats, butter, salt, and honey. Cool slightly until just warm. Dissolve the yeast in the warm water. Add to the oat mixture. Mix in 4 to 5 cups of flour (enough so that the dough is not sticky). Knead for 10 minutes. Place in a greased bowl and let rise for 1 hour. Punch down and roll to a square approximately 1-inch thick. Sprinkle with sugar, cinnamon, and nuts or raisins. Roll up and cut in half. Place in 2 greased loaf pans and let rise for 45 minutes. Bake in a 375 ° oven for 45 minutes.

Makes 2 loaves.

Cinnamon Nut Bread

**5 cups all-purpose flour
1 cup sugar
1 cup brown sugar, firmly packed
2 tablespoons plus 1 teaspoon
  baking powder
2 teaspoons salt
2 teaspoons cinnamon
6 tablespoons oil
2½ cups milk
2 eggs
1 cup nuts**

Mix together the dry ingredients. Add the remaining ingredients and mix gently. Pour into 2 greased loaf pans. Bake in a 350° oven for 1 hour.

Makes 2 loaves.

Rum Raisin Bread

**5 cups all-purpose flour
1 cup sugar
1 cup brown sugar, firmly packed
2 tablespoons plus 1 teaspoon
  baking powder
2 teaspoons salt
6 tablespoons oil
2½ cups milk
2 eggs
1½ teaspoons rum extract
1 cup raisins**

Mix together the dry ingredients. Add the remaining ingredients and mix gently. Pour into 2 greased loaf pans. Bake in a 350° oven for 1 hour.

Makes 2 loaves.

Whole Wheat Bread

**3 to 4 cups all-purpose flour
3 cups whole wheat flour
1 cup rolled oats
3 ¼-ounce packages active dry
  yeast
1 tablespoon salt
3 cups milk
¼ cup honey
¼ cup butter or margarine
  (½ stick)**

Combine 2½ cups of flour, whole wheat flour, oats, yeast, and salt. Heat the milk, honey, and butter until quite warm and the butter is melted. Add to the dry ingredients. Beat 100 strokes or with a mixer at medium speed for 2 minutes. Add the remaining flour and knead. Add more flour if the dough is sticky. Knead for 10 minutes. Place in a greased bowl. Cover and let rise until doubled in size, about 1 hour. Punch down and divide into 3 parts. Shape into round loaves. Place on greased cookie sheet and let rise for 45 minutes. Bake in a 400° oven for 30 minutes.

Makes 3 loaves.

Peach Bread

**5 cups all-purpose flour
1 cup sugar
1 cup brown sugar, firmly packed
2 tablespoons plus 1 teaspoon
  baking powder
2 teaspoons salt
6 tablespoons oil
2½ cups milk
2 eggs
2 cups chopped fresh or canned
  peaches
2 teaspoons vanilla extract**

Mix together the dry ingredients. Add the remaining ingredients and mix gently; pour into 2 greased loaf pans. Bake in a 350° oven for 1 hour.

Makes 2 loaves.

Almond Bread

**5 cups all-purpose flour
1 cup sugar
1 cup brown sugar, firmly packed
2 tablespoons plus 1 teaspoon
  baking powder
2 teaspoons salt
6 tablespoons oil
2½ cups milk
2 eggs
1½ teaspoons almond extract
1 cup slivered almonds**

Mix together the dry ingredients. Add the remaining ingredients and mix gently; pour into 2 greased loaf pans. Bake in a 350° oven for 1 hour.

Makes 2 loaves.

Ash Mill Farm

Route 202
Post Office Box 202
Holicong, Pennsylvania 18928
(215) 794-5373

Ash Mill Farm is a country bed and breakfast centrally located on ten acres of wooded farmland in the rolling hills of historic Bucks County. The eighteenth century plaster-over-stone house, with its high ceilings, light-filled rooms, and broad central stair, bespeaks a more gracious heritage than the traditional Pennsylvania fieldstone farm house.

Decorated in keeping with its past and present, Ash Mill Farm has four guest bedrooms, two with private bath and two with semi-private bath, that are comfortably furnished and accented with handcrafted quilts and family antiques. Mornings at Ash Mill Farm begin with a continental-plus breakfast served in front of an open fire in winter and on the stone porch in spring and summer. The guest living room is a place for quiet relaxation and afternoon tea.

Ash Mill Farm Quiche

½ pound broiled bacon, chopped
Pastry for 1 9-inch 1-crust pie
1½ cups shredded Swiss cheese
3 eggs
1½ cups light cream
Dash nutmeg
Dash pepper
Dash cayenne pepper

Spread the bacon evenly over the pie shell. Cover the bacon with Swiss cheese and set aside. Beat the eggs, light cream, and seasonings. Pour into the pie shell. Bake in a 350° oven for 35 to 40 minutes or until the center appears firm when shaken gently. Let cool 10 minutes before serving.

Serves 6.

Raisin Bran Muffins

1 15-ounce box raisin and bran cereal
3 cups sugar
5 cups all-purpose flour
5 teaspoons baking soda
2 teaspoons salt
1 cup oil
4 eggs, beaten
1 quart buttermilk

Mix together the dry ingredients; add the oil, eggs, and buttermilk. Store in a closed container in the refrigerator for up to 6 weeks. When ready to bake, fill greased muffin pans. Put the remaining batter back in the refrigerator until needed. Bake in a 425° oven for 18 minutes.

Makes 5 to 6 dozen.

Kane Manor Country Inn

Kane, Pennsylvania 16735
(814) 837-6522

The Kane Manor was the home of the family of General Thomas L. Kane. The mansion, built in 1896, is situated in a private wildlife sanctuary atop a mountain in the Allegheny National Forest. The inn has ten guest rooms, dining room, Rathskellar, and gift shop. Activities include fishing, hiking, swimming, boating and cross-country skiing. Each guest room has special touches that include apple baskets and jars of candy kisses. The slogan is "Come Home" to the Kane Manor Country Inn.

Fettucine Alfredo

An appetizer.

Noodles
⅓ cup grated Parmesan cheese
⅓ cup whipping cream
Bacon bits

Cook the noodles in salted boiling water; drain. In a saucepan combine the noodles, Parmesan, and cream. Mix over medium heat, stirring constantly, for 3 minutes. Place in a shallow crock and sprinkle with bacon bits.

Serves 1.

Passion: A Cocktail Beverage

1 ounce rum
2 teaspoons grenadine
6 ounces pineapple juice
Orange slice for garnish
Cherry for garnish

Fill a shaker with ice. Add the rum, grenadine, and pineapple juice. Shake; pour into a brandy snifter. Top with an orange slice and a cherry.

Serves 1.

Kane Manor

Scallops Tarragon

3 mushrooms, sliced
2 green onions, sliced
¼ cup parsley butter
¼ teaspoon tarragon
10 scallops
1½ cups white wine
Parmesan cheese

Sauté the mushrooms and onions in the parsley butter for 2 minutes. Add the tarragon, scallops, and wine. Cook until tender. Place in a shallow crock and sprinkle with Parmesan cheese.
Serves 2.

Peanut Butter Cream Pie

1 cup peanut butter
½ cup sugar
6 tablespoons milk
1 cup heavy whipping cream
1 8-inch graham cracker pie crust, baked

Cream together the peanut butter, sugar, and milk. Whip the cream in a separate bowl until stiff. Fold the peanut butter mixture into the cream. Mix well until very smooth. Pour into the baked graham cracker crust and keep refrigerated.
Serves 6.

Longwood Inn

815 East Baltimore Pike
Kennett Square, Pennsylvania 19348
(215) 444-3515

Longwood Inn is a small inn found just outside Kennett Square, the Mushroom Capital of the World. All the rooms have telephones and color television. The inn is located in the midst of several well known attractions, such as beautiful Longwood Gardens, The Franklin Mint, Winterthun Museum, and the Brandywine Museum, which features Andrew Wyeth paintings.

In the restaurant adjacent to the inn, guests may enjoy a full country breakfast while relaxing in a booth overlooking the flower garden. Fresh flowers adorn the tables during luncheon, and diners may choose between the candlelit Colonial Dining Room or the more intimate Victorian room. Breakfast, luncheon, and dinner are served daily. A small cocktail lounge is adjacent.

Longwood Cream of Crab

10 to 12 hard-shell crabs
1 gallon water
5 stalks celery, chopped
1 onion, chopped
2 tablespoons Old Bay Seasoning

❖ ❖ ❖

5 ounces butter
2 ounces finely chopped celery
Grated rind of 1 lime
1 ounce finely chopped onion
3 ounces chopped ginger root
1 clove garlic, chopped
1 pound hard-shell crab meat
½ pound snow crab meat
6 cups warm milk
5 tablespoons all-purpose flour
½ cup cornstarch
2 cups half and half
Dash Tabasco sauce
Dash pepper
Dash salt
Pinch Old Bay Seasoning

To make the crab stock steam the crabs and remove from the pan when done. Allow the crabs to cool; pick the meat from the shells and place the shells back in the pan and add the water, celery, onion, and Old Bay Seasoning. Simmer for 1 hour. Strain through cheesecloth.

In a saucepan melt the butter and sauté the celery, lime rind, onion, gingerroot, and garlic. Do not brown. Add the crab meat and snow crab; cook for 2 minutes. Add the strained crab stock and pour in the heated milk. Mix together the flour, cornstarch, and half and half; add to the crab mixture and stir until creamy. Add more cornstarch if needed. Add the seasonings. Serve hot.
Makes 1 gallon.

Fresh Stuffed Rainbow Trout
with Mussel Sauce

1 egg
1 teaspoon Pommery mustard
Dash Tabasco sauce
Salt to taste

Pepper to taste
Dash Worcestershire sauce
1 teaspoon chives
½ cup mayonnaise
1 slice white bread, diced
1 pound lump crab meat
½ pound Canadian snow crab meat
1 teaspoon diced red pepper

❖ ❖ ❖

2 dozen fresh mussels
2 teaspoons finely chopped shallots
1 teaspoon butter
1½ cups heavy cream
½ cup Port wine

❖ ❖ ❖

1 fresh 12-inch Rainbow trout

To make the Crab Imperial Stuffing whisk the eggs, and add the mustard, Tabasco sauce, salt, pepper, Worcestershire sauce, chives, and mayonnaise. Add the bread cubes. Mix well and let the mixture sit for 5 minutes. Add all of the crab meat and red pepper. Mix well, being careful not to break the lumps of crab meat. Refrigerate for 2 hours.

To make the mussel sauce, steam the mussels until tender and remove the shells. In a heavy saucepan, sauté the shallots in butter for about 1 minute over medium heat. Add the cream, Port wine, and mussels. Cook for 3 minutes, but do not boil or the sauce will separate.

Split and bone the trout. Stuff with about 4 ounces of Crab Imperial Stuffing. Bake in a 350° oven for 10 to 15 minutes or until done. Cover with the mussel sauce and serve immediately.

Serves 4.

Mushroom à la Grecque

2 to 3 dozen mushrooms
1 pound lean bacon, finely chopped
½ pound ham, finely chopped
1 quart ground seasoned croutons
1 pound grated Feta cheese
¼ pound Romano cheese
¾ pound tomatoes

Steam the mushrooms just until tender, approximately a minute and a half. Be careful not to overcook.

In a mixing bowl combine the bacon, ham, croutons, Feta and Romano cheese. To prepare the tomatoes, scald in boiling water, remove the skins and finely chop. Add the tomatoes to the mixture and mix thoroughly. Stuff each mushroom with 2 ounces of filling. Cook in a 350° oven for approximately 10 to 12 minutes. Serve immediately.

Makes 2 to 3 dozen stuffed mushrooms.

The Stranahan House

117 East Market Street
Mercer, Pennsylvania 16137
(412) 662-4516

A 150-year-old building, The Stranahan House provides a peaceful night's rest and a delicious breakfast amidst antique furnishings rich in the area's heritage. This classic red brick home is near the center of town just a few steps from stately Mercer County Courthouse, and conveniently close to an array of historical and recreational sites. The two guest rooms are on the second floor. One is furnished with Victorian furniture that was made in Philadelphia; it has a double bed, ceiling paddle fan, mauve carpeting, and blue and mauve floral stripe wallpaper. The other room has two double beds in cherry—1830 spool rope beds that are roped, but supported, to give guests a firm, comfortable night's rest. It has a working fireplace, and its walls are stenciled in an old-fashioned border.

Spinach Sausage Quiche

1 9-inch pie shell
½ pound bulk sausage
¼ cup chopped green onion
1 clove garlic, minced
1 10-ounce package frozen chopped spinach, cooked and drained
½ cup herb stuffing mix
1½ cups shredded Monterey Jack cheese
3 eggs, mixed
1½ cups half and half cream
2 tablespoons Parmesan cheese
Paprika

In a skillet cook the sausage, green onion, and garlic; drain. Add the spinach and the stuffing mix. Sprinkle the Monterey Jack cheese, then the sausage mixture, into the shell. In a bowl, combine the eggs and half and half; pour over the sausage. Bake in a 375° oven for 30 minutes. Sprinkle with Parmesan and paprika. Bake 15 minutes longer or until a knife inserted in the center comes out clean. Let stand 10 minutes before cutting and serving.

Serves 6.

French Breakfast Puffs

3 cups all-purpose flour
1 tablespoon baking powder
1 teaspoon salt
½ teaspoon nutmeg

❖ ❖ ❖

1 cup sugar
⅔ cup shortening
2 eggs
1 cup milk

❖ ❖ ❖

¾ cup butter (1½ sticks), melted
2 teaspoons cinnamon
1 cup sugar

Stir together the flour, baking powder, salt, and nutmeg; set aside. In a mixer bowl cream together 1 cup of sugar, shortening, and eggs. Add the flour mixture to the creamed mixture alternately with the milk, beating well after each addition. Fill greased muffin cups

⅔ full. Bake in a 350° oven for 20 to 25 minutes. Dip in the melted butter, then in the cinnamon-sugar mixture.

Makes 24 puffs.

Teri's Rhubarb Walnut Sticky Muffins

1 cup finely chopped rhubarb
¼ cup butter (½ stick)
¾ cup brown sugar, firmly packed
⅓ cup chopped walnuts

❖ ❖ ❖

⅓ cup butter
⅓ cup sugar
1 egg
1¾ cups all-purpose flour
2 teaspoons baking powder
½ teaspoon salt
½ teaspoon nutmeg
½ cup plus 2 tablespoons milk

Combine the rhubarb, ¼ cup of butter, brown sugar and walnuts; mix until blended. Divide this mixture into the bottom of 12 well-greased muffin cups. Beat together ⅓ cup of butter, the sugar and egg until fluffy. Mix together the flour, baking powder, salt, and nutmeg. Add the dry ingredients to the butter mixture alternately with the milk. Blend and spoon on top of the rhubarb. Bake in a 350° oven for 25 to 30 minutes. Invert onto a cooling rack and let stand for a few minutes before removing from the pan and serving.

Makes 12 muffins.

Jackson Center Stromboli

This recipe can be adapted to anyone's taste. Try it with broccoli and cheese, or spinach and sausage. A favorite with the family! Easy to make!

1 loaf freshly made bread dough
(or frozen dough)
Egg and milk wash

4 slices Provolone cheese
Pepperoni
Grated Mozzarella cheese
Sautéed onions, mushrooms, green
peppers (optional)
Italian tomato sauce (optional)
Sprinkle of parsley
Parmesan cheese
Oregano

Punch out the air bubbles in the dough. Roll into a large rectangle on a lightly floured surface. Brush with the egg and milk wash. Place the remaining ingredients of your choice down the middle ⅓ of rectangle. Fold up the outer thirds (sides) of the rectangle over the center. Brush the top with egg and milk wash. Sprinkle with Parmesan cheese and oregano. Bake in a 350° oven on a greased baking sheet for 20 minutes or until lightly browned.

Serves 4 to 6.

Peanut Butter Pie

1 8-ounce package cream cheese,
softened
1 cup crunchy peanut butter
1 16-ounce container frozen
whipped topping, thawed
1½ cups sifted confectioners' sugar
1 9-inch graham cracker crust (or
chocolate wafer crust)

❖ ❖ ❖

1½ 1-ounce squares unsweetened
chocolate
1 14-ounce can sweetened
condensed milk
½ cup butter (1 stick)
1 teaspoon vanilla extract

In a large mixing bowl combine the cream cheese and peanut butter. Beat at medium speed with an electric mixer until light and fluffy. Gradually add the whipped topping and confectioners' sugar. Continue beating until smooth. Spoon the filling into the pie crust. Freeze for 8 hours or overnight.

To prepare the Fudge Sauce, melt the chocolate and milk in a double boiler. When thoroughly blended and thick, remove from heat and add the butter and vanilla. Serve warm over each slice of pie.

Serves 6.

Blair Creek Inn and Lodging

Mertztown, Pennsylvania 19539
(215) 682-6700
(215) 682-4201

The Blair Creek Inn is a renovated country barn that has two mini-suites, the "loft" and the "stable." Both are fully air-conditioned, with private baths and working fireplaces, and both overlook the lush gardens that supply the fresh flowers for the inn. Service includes a complimentary continental breakfast, with fresh juices, pastries, coffees, and fresh fruit that will always include fresh strawberries, a signature of the inn.

Blair's Spinach Balls

2 10-ounce packages frozen
spinach, thawed
3 cups dry bread crumbs with herb
seasonings
1 large onion, finely chopped
6 eggs, well beaten
¾ cup grated sharp cheese
½ teaspoon pepper
½ teaspoon thyme
2 teaspoons Worcestershire sauce

In a mixing bowl combine all of the ingredients. Measure approximately a teaspoonful of the mixture and shape into balls. Place on cookie sheets and freeze. Store in the freezer in plastic bags. Remove from the freezer as needed and thaw slightly before baking. Bake in a 350° oven for about 20 minutes.

Makes approximately 50 spinach balls.

Chicken Salad Empress

2 hard boiled eggs, finely diced
9 pieces bacon, chopped and lightly fried
4 pounds cooked boned chicken, diced
1 teaspoon chopped fresh chives
1 teaspoon Worcestershire sauce
1 medium onion, chopped
4 ounces fresh pineapple
Few sprigs parsley, finely chopped
3 stalks celery, chopped
⅓ teaspoon lemon juice
Salt and pepper to taste
Sugar to taste
Mayonnaise

Blend together all of the ingredients with homemade mayonnaise to taste. It is best to refrigerate the salad for 4 hours before using. Place on a plate with Romaine lettuce. Garnish with tomatoes, baby corn, artichokes, and white asparagus.
Serves 6 to 8.

Blair Creek Inn

Sour Cream Quiche Lorraine

Pastry for 1 9-inch 1-crust pie

❖ ❖ ❖

6 slices bacon, chopped and sautéed
¼ cup chopped onions, sautéed and seasoned to taste
¼ cup shrimp or crab meat
¼ cup shredded Swiss cheese
1 teaspoon Parmesan cheese

❖ ❖ ❖

¼ teaspoon baking powder
1 teaspoon all-purpose flour
1¾ cups sour cream
4 eggs

Bake the pie shell in a 400° oven for 20 minutes. In the baked pie shell place in layers the bacon, onions, shrimp, and cheeses. In a mixing bowl combine the baking powder, flour, sour cream, and eggs. Beat the mixture well and pour over the layers in the pie shell. Bake in a 400° oven for 40 minutes. Garnish and serve.
Serves 6.

Basic Beef Stock Recipe

6 pounds marrow bones, split
2 gallons water
1 teaspoon salt
½ teaspoon pepper
4 bay leaves
¼ teaspoon rosemary
4 carrots, peeled and halved
1 medium head white cabbage, chopped in quarters
3 large onions, peeled
2 celery tops (cut about 5 inches from the top, with greens)
1 bunch parsley, tied with string

This soup must simmer for 8 straight hours (it cannot be done in a 2-day period). Combine all of the ingredients in a large soup pot. After 6 hours of simmering, add 1 quart of water and continue to simmer. When it begins to cool, skim off the fat. Skim the fat off twice before the next step. Pour the skimmed broth through a colander lined with cheesecloth. This will produce a clear broth.
Makes 1 gallon of stock.

Liver Dumpling Soup

1 quart Beef Stock
4 stale Kaiser rolls
½ cup lukewarm milk
9 ounces beef liver
1 onion
1 bunch parsley
2 tablespoons butter
2 eggs
Marjoram to taste
Salt and pepper to taste
Chives for garnish

In a large pot cook the beef stock over low heat. Cut the rolls into thin slices and place in a deep bowl. Add the milk. Grind the liver. Finely chop the onion and parsley, sauté in butter. Combine all of the ingredients except spices with the rolls and work into a dough. Add the spices to taste. Shape the dough into 4 large dumplings and place in the beef stock. Cover and cook for 20 minutes. Garnish with fresh chopped chives.
Serves 4.

Frangelica Cheese Pie à la Blair Creek Inn

1⅓ cups honey graham cracker
    crumbs
1½ tablespoons sugar
¼ cup unsalted butter (½ stick)

    ❖ ❖ ❖

2 8-ounce packages cream cheese,
    softened
½ cup sugar
1 tablespoon all-purpose flour
2 eggs
2 tablespoons Frangelica liqueur
⅔ cup toasted skinned hazelnuts

Combine the crumbs, sugar, and butter. Press the mixture evenly onto the bottom and sides of an ovenproof 9-inch ceramic or glass pie plate.

In a large bowl cream together the cream cheese, sugar, and flour. Beat in the eggs, one at a time, beating well after each addition. Beat the mixture until smooth. Stir in the Frangelica and ⅓ cup of the hazelnuts. Pour the filling into the shell and bake in a 350° oven for 30 to 35 minutes or until the filling is set. The filling may crack while baking. Let the pie cool on a rack. Finely chop the remaining hazelnuts and garnish the pie. Chill for 2 hours before serving.

Serves 6.

Tulpehocken Manor Inn and Plantation

650 West Lincoln Avenue
Myerstown, Pennsylvania 17067
(717) 866-4926
(717) 392-2311

Tulpehocken Manor Plantation is a 150-acre working farm on which grain

crops are raised and Black Angus beef cattle are bred. Tours are offered daily at a nominal donation.

Within the complex the Michael Ley Manor offers individual rooms with shared hall baths, for occupancy on a daily basis.

The Christopher Ley House has group facilities for up to twelve people, with five bedrooms, one and one-half baths, kitchen, and dining-living room. This guest house is rented on a daily basis.

The attic apartment in the Michael Spangler House is a large one-room efficiency guest apartment with kitchen and bath for up to six people.

Each of the five guest apartments in the George Spangler House has its own kitchen and private bath. These apartments accommodate from two to five people and may be rented on a daily basis during the summer season, and weekly or monthly during off season.

White Coconut Custard Pie

2 cups all-purpose flour
¼ cup water
½ to ⅔ cup oil

    ❖ ❖ ❖

1 cup sugar
2 tablespoons cornstarch
3 cups milk
2 cups coconut
3 egg whites, stiffly beaten

In a mixing bowl mix the flour, water, and oil with a fork. Form into a ball; divide the ball into 2 parts. Roll between sheets of waxed paper. Place in 2 9-inch pie pans. Bake in a 450° oven for 12 to 15 minutes.

Mix the sugar with the cornstarch; gradually add the milk. Cook in a double boiler or a saucepan over low heat until thick. Remove from heat and stir in the coconut. Fold in the beaten egg whites; pour into the 2 pie shells. Cool before serving.

Makes 2 9-inch pies.

Backstreet Inn

144 Old York Road
New Hope, Pennsylvania 18938
(215) 862-9571

Tucked away on a quiet street, this small inn was built in 1750 and is on a three-acre plot containing a rippling stream. Nevertheless it is within walking distance of the center of town. The Backstreet Inn is surrounded by towering shade trees and flowering plants and has an old wishing well and secluded pool. Croquet wickets are set up on the sprawling lawn. All rooms are comfortably furnished and mornings at Backstreet welcome guests to a home-cooked gourmet breakfast in the garden breakfast room; afternoon tea and maid service are included.

Scrambled Eggs à la Rolf

2 eggs
2 tablespoons cream cheese,
    crumbled

    ❖ ❖ ❖

Mozzarella cheese
Mashed potatoes
1 egg, beaten
Flour
Olive oil

In a small frypan scramble the eggs with cream cheese. Set aside and keep warm.

Surround a small stick of Mozzarella cheese with mashed potatoes, dip in egg, dredge in flour, and fry in olive oil.

Serve the fried potato mixture surrounded by scrambled eggs. Sausage, country ham, or bacon may be served on the side if desired.

Serves 1.

Raspberry Grand Marnier Toast

28 slices Viennese bread
Butter

❖   ❖   ❖

1½ cups orange juice
1 cup Melba sauce
1 cup raspberries (fresh or frozen)
½ cup Grand Marnier

Fry the bread in butter until golden brown. Place 2 slices per serving on warmed plates.

In a saucepan combine the orange juice, Melba sauce, and raspberries. Bring to a boil. Add the Grand Marnier. Serve over the toast.

Serves 14.

Vegetable Quiche

1 cup shredded Swiss cheese
⅓ cup minced onions
1 cup each cooked carrots,
**   broccoli, cauliflower**
Pastry for 1 2-crust deep dish pie
4 eggs
2 cups half and half
¾ teaspoon sugar
⅛ teaspoon pepper
⅛ teaspoon salt

Put the Swiss cheese, onions, and vegetables in a pie shell. Mix the eggs, half and half, sugar, pepper and salt. Cover the pie filling. Bake in a 350° oven for 1 hour.

Makes 1 quiche.

Logan Inn

10 West Ferry Street
New Hope, Pennsylvania 18938
(215) 862-5134

The Logan Inn was built in 1722 in the 250-year-old town of New Hope as part of the Ferry Tavern. Carl Lutz, co-owner and gourmet cook, provides many magnificent dishes for his guests. New dishes constantly appear on the menu. The public areas of the Logan Inn are filled with contrasts. The bright and open spaces in the dining room are contrasted by small and dark intimate areas such as the adjoining bar. Decor is Early American, with ten guest rooms available with private and shared baths.

Chicken Logan au Peche

4 large half-breasts of chicken,
**   boned and skinned**
Salt
White pepper
2 tablespoons butter
1 tablespoon brown sugar
¼ teaspoon grated fresh ginger
**   root (or ½ teaspoon minced**
**   candied root)**
1 ripe peach, peeled and sliced
1 tablespoon Major Grey's Chutney
**   (optional)**
Flour
1 egg, beaten
¾ cup dry white bread crumbs

Flatten the chicken breasts between sheets of waxed paper as thin as possible without tearing. Salt and pepper to taste. In a small saucepan melt the butter. Add the sugar and ginger root; stir until the sugar is dissolved. Add the peach slices and simmer for 1 minute. Cool. Place the peach slices in each flattened breast. Fold envelope-style (long bottom side of breast up and over peach, fold sides in next, fold top flap over all). Chill for at least 1 hour.

Dust with flour, dip in the beaten egg, roll in the bread crumbs. Chill. Heat the oil to 350° and fry for about 10 minutes. Drain and serve.

Serves 4.

Supreme of Chicken Tarragon

3 chicken breasts, skinned, boned
**   and halved**
Salt and pepper to taste
1½ teaspoons chopped fresh
**   tarragon (or ¾ teaspoon dried**
**   tarragon)**
Flour
6 tablespoons clarified butter
18 medium mushroom caps
⅓ cup white wine (or vermouth)

Season the breasts with salt and pepper. Sprinkle the chopped tarragon on both sides; press in. Dredge lightly with flour. In a large skillet (or 2 medium pans) over medium heat, sauté the breasts in butter until just firm, ap-

Logan Inn

proximately 18 to 20 minutes. Remove and keep warm.

Sauté the mushrooms in the same pan until warmed through. Do not overcook. Deglaze the pan with the wine and reduce slightly. Arrange the mushrooms on the breasts and spoon the pan juices over.

Note: Delicious served on fried croutons with asparagus tips. For croutons use crustless French bread that has been fried in butter until crisp and colored.

Serves 3.

Shrimp Logan

¼ cup butter (½ stick)
1 medium onion, chopped

❖ ❖ ❖

1 cup raw long grain rice
1 cup beef stock (canned consommé)
Salt and pepper

❖ ❖ ❖

½ cup butter (1 stick)
1 tablespoon chopped fresh dill (or ½ tablespoon dry dill)
½ cup white wine (or vermouth)
32 medium-sized raw shrimp (16 to 20 per pound), peeled, with tails on

❖ ❖ ❖

Watercress or parsley for garnish

In a pot with a tight cover, melt ¼ cup of butter and add the onion. Sauté until tender. Add the rice and stir for 2 to 3 minutes. Add boiling stock and seasonings. Cover; place over low heat and cook until all moisture is absorbed. Fluff with a fork.

In a large pan melt the butter over medium heat. Add the dill, then the wine. When bubbly, add the shrimp. Cook briefly until the shrimp are just firm. Do not overcook.

Press the rice pilaf into 4 custard cups and invert onto individual serving dishes. Surround the sides of each rice mound with 8 shrimp, all curved in one direction, with tails up. Carefully pour the pan juices equally around the rice. Garnish with watercress or parsley on top of the rice mound.

Serves 4.

Sole Veronique

6 fillets of sole
Salt and white pepper to taste
2 teaspoons lemon juice (or ½ cup vermouth)

❖ ❖ ❖

½ cup milk
1 cup cream
¼ cup butter (½ stick)
¼ cup all-purpose flour
1 cup seedless grapes
1 cup blanched slivered almonds

Season the sole fillets with salt and pepper. Poach in one layer in simmering water to barely cover the fillets with lemon juice (or vermouth) added, until the fish flakes easily with a fork. Do not overcook. Remove the sole carefully with spatulas. Drain and place in a single layer in a heatproof buttered oven dish or platter. Reduce the poaching liquid to ½ cup. Add the milk and cream and bring to a boil.

In a saucepan melt the butter and add the flour; when well-blended, cook gently for a minute. Add the boiling cream mixture to the roux and stir vigorously with a whisk until thick and smooth. Place grapes around and on the sole. Cover with the sauce and sprinkle with almonds. Place under a broiler until the sauce bubbles and the almonds are toasted.

Serves 6.

Apple Cake
with Hot Buttered Rum Sauce

2 cups sugar
½ cup butter (1 stick), softened
2 eggs
2 cups all-purpose flour
1 teaspoon baking powder
¾ teaspoon baking soda
½ teaspoon salt
½ teaspoon nutmeg
½ teaspoon cinnamon
1½ cups chopped walnuts

3 to 4 peeled diced apples (3 cups)

❖ ❖ ❖

1 cup sugar
½ cup light cream or half and half
2 tablespoons butter
¼ cup dark rum (or to taste)

In a mixing bowl add the sugar slowly to the softened butter and beat well until creamy. Add the eggs one at a time. Combine the dry ingredients and add gradually to the creamed mixture. Add the nuts and apples. Bake in a greased tube pan in a 350° oven for 60 minutes or until a tester inserted in the center comes out clean. After 15 minutes invert onto a rack to cool.

Heat the sugar and cream over low heat until well-dissolved. Add the butter and rum. Serve hot over the cake.

Serves 12.

Pineapple Hill

R.D.3
Box 34C
New Hope, Pennsylvania 18938
(215) 862-9608

Pineapple Hill is a spacious Bucks County farmhouse built about 1780. Nestled on five acres overlooking a bend along scenic River Road beside the Delaware River, the inn beckons invitingly to guests. Inside, the central hall leads to a parlor displaying country and primitive furniture, old quilts, folk art, and Persian carpets. On the other side of the hallway is a second sitting room with a big bay window. The guest rooms upstairs are furnished similarly and have either brass, spindle, or rope beds; blanket chests; and chests of drawers.

Guests can enjoy the many attractions of New Hope and the surrounding area, including many fine restaurants, important historical sites, parks, rafting or tubing on the Delaware, antiquing, arts and craft galleries, and beautiful scenery. They also may enjoy the parlor fireplace with a

Pineapple Hill

good book or play a game of backgammon. In the summer they can lounge beside the pool located within the stone ruins of the farm's original barn. Breakfast includes a fresh fruit salad and croissants with homemade jams and jellies. Afternoon refreshments are also included in the rates, as are complimentary after-dinner beverages.

Sun Tea
with Fresh Mint

In a ½-gallon clear glass jar place 4 tea bags. Pick about 5 healthy sprigs of peppermint or spearmint (sprigs approximately six inches in length). Wash and then crush well. Add the mint to the jar, fill the jar with water and put on the lid. Place the jar in the sun for about 3 hours (more doesn't seem to hurt the flavor). Remove the tea bags and mint and store the tea in the refrigerator. The mint gives such a nice flavor to the tea that even a sweet-toothed non-tea drinker loves it with no sugar added. Guests find it to be the perfect refresher on a hot summer day, and fresh mint from your own garden makes it special.
Serves 8.

Fresh Fruit Sundae

1 honeydew melon (and/or other melons in season)
1 cantaloupe
1 pineapple
2 peaches
1 Granny Smith apple
Juice of 2 oranges
½ pint strawberries
½ pint red or green seedless grapes
½ pint blueberries and raspberries (or blackberries)
Mint sprigs

❖　❖　❖

Plain yogurt
Granola
Coconut
Raw unsalted sunflower seeds
Honey

Choose the fruit according to what is in season and most tasty at the moment; cut fruit into bite-sized pieces. Pour the juice on the peaches and apples to prevent browning. Stir well, pushing apples and peaches below the surface, avoiding too much air contact and therefore further reducing the risk of browning. On top, sprinkle the strawberries, red or green seedless grapes, blueberries and raspberries (or blackberries). Garnish with healthy sprigs of fresh mint.

After helping themselves to fruit, guests then choose from any (or all) of the toppings; the yogurt, granola, coconut, sunflower seeds, and honey. This makes a perfect breakfast served with a large fresh croissant, homemade jams, coffee, teas, juices and milk.

The Wedgwood Inn

111 West Bridge Street
New Hope, Pennsylvania 18938
(215) 862-2570

This gracious two-and-a-half story structure with a gabled hip roof has been offering lodging since 1950 and is eligible for the National Register of Historic Places. Surrounded by manicured landscaping, the building features a large veranda with scrolled wood brackets and turned posts, a porte-cochere, and a gazebo. Hardwood floors, lofty windows, and antique furnishings create a comfortable nineteenth century feeling in each of the eight bedrooms. In addition, the innkeepers have filled their inn with Wedgwood pottery, original art, handmade quilts, and fresh flowers. Guests can relax with a good book or can have a friendly conversation in the parlor. Days begin with breakfast, which is served every morning in the sun-porch, the gazebo, or in one's private bedroom. The continental-plus breakfast includes freshly squeezed orange juice, homemade baked goods, hot croissants, fresh fruit salad, and coffee and tea. Days end with a tot of almond liqueur at bedside and mints waiting on the pillows of turned-down beds. The Wedgewood is also a place where innkeepers-to-be are trained.

Wassail

"We serve wassail as people check in on Fridays which enhances a warm welcome."

- 1 gallon apple cider
- 2 quarts cranberry juice
- 1 tablespoon aromatic bitters
- 4 cinnamon sticks
- 1 tablespoon white allspice
- 2 oranges, studded with cloves
- 2 cups rum (optional)

Combine the ingredients and heat gently. Serve warm. This drink also sends wonderful aromas throughout the house.

Serves 30.

Hot Buttered Wedgwood

"This is a favorite of Carl's—he makes his own almond liqueur (excellent, too!) which is served to guests at their bedside as part of the evening turn-down service."

- 2 ounces almond liqueur
- 1 cup hot tea, cider or apple juice
- 1 tablespoon whipped unsalted butter
- Twist of orange peel
- 1 cinnamon stick

Pour the almond liqueur into a mug. Fill with the hot drink; add the butter and orange peel. Garnish with a cinnamon stick.

Serves 1.

Dave's Banana Blueberry Muffins

- 3 large very ripe bananas
- ¾ cup sugar
- 1 egg
- ⅓ cup melted butter
- 1 cup fresh or frozen blueberries
- 1 teaspoon baking soda
- 1 teaspoon baking powder
- ½ teaspoon salt
- 1½ cups all-purpose flour

Mash the bananas. Add the sugar and slightly beaten egg. Add the melted butter and the blueberries. Combine the dry ingredients and stir very gently, add to the banana mixture. Bake in a 375° oven for 20 minutes.

Makes 12 muffins.

Rich Delicious Orange Tea Muffins

- 1½ cups all-purpose flour
- ½ cup sugar
- 2 teaspoons baking powder
- ½ teaspoon salt
- ½ cup butter, melted
- ½ cup fresh orange juice
- 2 eggs
- Grated rind of 1 orange
- 1 cup fresh or frozen raspberries (optional)
- ½ cup coconut (optional)

Combine the flour, sugar, baking powder, and salt; blend well. Melt the butter. Remove from heat and stir in the orange juice, eggs, and orange rind; beat. Add the raspberries and coconut if desired. Stir the liquid into the dry mixture and blend until just moistened. Spoon into well-greased muffin cups. Bake in a 375° oven for 15 to 20 minutes.

Makes 1 dozen muffins.

Applesauce Bran Muffins

- 1 cup All Bran cereal
- ¼ cup milk
- 1 cup applesauce
- ⅓ cup oil
- 1 egg
- 1½ cups all-purpose flour
- 3 teaspoons baking powder
- ½ teaspoon baking soda
- ½ teaspoon salt
- 1 teaspoon cinnamon
- ⅓ cup brown sugar, firmly packed

Stir the bran, milk, applesauce, oil, and egg together. Stir together the dry ingredients. Add the bran mixture to the dry ingredients, stirring just to moisten. Bake in a 375° oven for 15 to 20 minutes. Raisins or nuts are optional.

Makes 24 muffins.

Ricotta Pineapple Muffins

- 1 egg
- Oil
- 1½ cups Ricotta cheese
- 1 cup crushed well-drained pineapple
- 2 cups all-purpose flour
- ½ cup sugar
- 1 tablespoon baking powder
- ½ teaspoon baking soda
- ½ teaspoon salt

In a measuring cup place the egg and add enough oil to make ½ cup. Add the egg and oil mixture to the Ricotta cheese and mix until smooth. Add the crushed pineapple. In a separate bowl combine the dry ingredients, add to the wet ingredients and blend gently. Fill greased muffin cups ⅔ full. Bake in a 400° oven for 25 minutes.

Makes 1 dozen muffins.

Lemon Yogurt Bread

- 3 cups all-purpose flour
- 1 teaspoon salt
- 1 teaspoon baking soda
- ½ teaspoon baking powder
- 1 cup sesame seeds (or 1 cup poppy seeds)
- 3 eggs
- 1 cup oil
- 1 cup sugar
- 2 cups lemon yogurt
- 2 tablespoons fresh squeezed lemon juice

Sift together the flour, salt, soda, and baking powder; stir in seeds. Beat the eggs in a large bowl. Add the oil and sugar; cream well. Add the yogurt and lemon juice. Spoon into 2 greased loaf pans or 1 large bundt pan. Bake in a 325° oven for 1 hour.

Makes 2 loaves.

Chocolate Chip Mousse

1 18-ounce package chocolate chip cookies, crumbled
Chocolate syrup
1 quart fresh cream, whipped
Chocolate shavings

In a large glass bowl layer the crumbled cookies, chocolate syrup, and whipped cream. Chill in the refrigerator for at least 4 hours or overnight. Top with chocolate shavings before serving.

Serves 20.

Lemon Poppy Seed Coffee Cake

½ cup poppy seeds
½ cup milk

❖ ❖ ❖

1½ cups butter (3 sticks)
1¼ cups sugar
2 tablespoons grated lemon rind
1 tablespoon grated orange rind
8 egg yolks
2 cups cake flour
¾ teaspoon salt

❖ ❖ ❖

¾ teaspoon cream of tartar
⅛ teaspoon salt
8 egg whites
¼ cup sugar

Soak the poppy seeds in milk for 4 hours.

In a mixing bowl cream the butter and 1¼ cups of sugar. Add the lemon and orange rinds and the egg yolks. Add the flour and salt. Beat for 5 minutes. Add the poppy seeds and milk.

In a separate mixing bowl beat the cream of tartar and ⅛ teaspoon of salt with the egg whites. Beat until stiff,

gradually adding ¼ cup of sugar. Fold into the poppy seed mixture and pour the batter into 2 greased and floured 8x8-inch baking pans. Bake in a 350° oven for 40 to 60 minutes.

Serves 16.

Pleasant Grove Farm

R.D. 1, Box 132
Peach Bottom, Pennsylvania 17563
(717) 548-3100

Located in beautiful, historic Lancaster County, this 160-acre dairy farm has been a family-run operation for 102 years, earning it the title of "Century Farm" by the Pennsylvania Department of Agriculture. As a working farm, it provides guests the opportunity to experience daily life in a rural setting. Four rooms and a shared bath, plus one loft for children, are available, as well as a motor home that is equipped for four persons. Tenting in the yard, an above-ground swimming pool, sand for children to play in, a pond for fishing, and hiking in the meadow are among the facilities and activities on the farm. Pleasant Grove is also an excellent starting point for day trips to such attractions as Longwood Gardens, the Gettysburg Battlefield, Hershey Park, Dutch Wonderland, and the birthplace of Robert Fulton.

Sausage Egg Brunch Casserole

This is mixed the night before and stored in the refrigerator to be baked the next morning.

1½ pounds pork sausage
8 slices bread, cut in pieces
¾ pound grated Cheddar cheese
4 eggs
Dash of salt
2½ cups milk
¾ tablespoon mustard (optional)

Brown the crumbled sausage and drain. Spread the bread cubes over the bottom of a 9x13-inch baking dish. Cover bread cubes with sausage, then cover with the Cheddar cheese. Beat the eggs; add a dash of salt, the milk, and mustard if desired. Pour the egg mixture over the bread, sausage, and cheese in the pan. Refrigerate overnight. The next morning bake in a 375° oven for 30 to 40 minutes.

Serves 4 to 6.

Ham and Cheese Strata

12 slices bread
½ cup ground cooked ham
4 ounces American or Cheddar cheese, grated
5 eggs
3 cups milk
½ teaspoon dry mustard

Trim the crusts from the bread; place 6 slices on the bottom of a buttered 9x13-inch baking dish. Layer on top ½ of the ham and cheese. Cover with the remaining 6 slices of bread and repeat the ham and cheese layer. Combine the eggs, milk, and mustard. Pour over the layers in the casserole. Cover and refrigerate overnight. Bake in a 350° oven for 1 hour. Slice in squares and serve.

Serves 4.

Gelatin Apple Dessert

6 3-ounce packages strawberry gelatin
5 cups boiling water
3 cups diced apples

2 bananas, diced
1 cup crushed pineapple with juice

❖ ❖ ❖

½ cup sour cream
1 8-ounce package cream cheese
½ cup sugar
½ cup chopped nuts

Dissolve the gelatin in water. Let it gel until slightly thickened. Add the apples, bananas, and pineapple; stir until well-blended. Pour into a 9x13-inch pan and chill until firm.

To make the topping, whip the sour cream, cream cheese, and sugar until fluffy. Add the nuts and spread the mixture over the gelatin.

Serves about 15.

Rhubarb Dessert

3 cups rhubarb, cut in 1-inch pieces
½ 3-ounce package strawberry
    gelatin
1 cup sugar (or to taste)
1 cup crushed pineapple

Simmer the rhubarb just until tender. Add the gelatin and sugar; stir until dissolved. Add the pineapple. Chill.

Serves 4.

Funnel Cakes

3 eggs
2 cups milk
¼ cup sugar
2 cups all-purpose flour
1 cup whole wheat flour
1 cup cornmeal
⅛ teaspoon baking soda
½ teaspoon salt
2 teaspoons baking powder

❖ ❖ ❖

Confectioners' sugar
Cinnamon and sugar

In a large mixing bowl beat the eggs. Add the milk and dry ingredients; beat until smooth. Pour about ¼ cup of batter at a time through a funnel into deep fat and fry until golden brown, turning once. Remove from the fat and serve warm. Sprinkle with confectioners' sugar or cinnamon and sugar if desired.

Makes 6 to 8 large cakes.

Society Hill Hotel/ Philadelphia

301 Chestnut Street
Philadelphia, Pennsylvania 19106
(215) 925-1919

Built in 1832, this twelve-room "urban inn" delights its guests with small,

Society Hill Hotel/Philadelphia

cozy rooms that echo its rich past. The hotel's brass beds, fresh flowers, and European breakfast served to guest rooms have proven a successful combination. The hotel's restaurant boasts a European atmosphere where each night jazz piano appeals to guests and professionals who live and work nearby. Light fare, large windows overlooking Independence National Park, and an outdoor cafe lend to its congenial atmosphere.

Whole Wheat Crêpes

1½ cups milk
2 tablespoons oil
3 eggs
1¼ cups whole wheat flour
Dash salt

❖ ❖ ❖

2½ pounds blanched vegetables
10 ounces grated Jarlsburg cheese
½ pound Brie

❖ ❖ ❖

Sour cream
Applesauce

In a blender combine the milk, oil, eggs, flour, and salt; blend until smooth. Pour a small amount of batter at a time into a preheated oiled crêpe pan or an 8-inch sauté pan.

Fill each crêpe with 3 ounces of vegetables (a combination of thinly sliced carrots, zucchini, cauliflower, and broccoli flowerets is good), and ½ ounce of Jarlsburg and Brie. Roll up the crêpes. Place in a baking pan and top with 2 ounces of grated Jarlsburg. Bake in a 325° oven for 20 minutes. Serve with a dollop of both sour cream and applesauce.

Serves 8.

Tattersall

Cafferty and River Road
Post Office Box 569
Point Pleasant, Pennsylvania 18950
(215) 297-8233

A romantic getaway in a village setting, this lilac-and-cream mansion of the early nineteenth century is now a delightful bed and breakfast inn. The historical Bucks County inn, eight miles north of New Hope along River Road, has seven spacious, air-conditioned guest rooms with private baths. It boasts an antique phonograph collection, including a 1903 Edison cylinder phonograph. Breakfast is served in the dining room, in the bedroom, or on the veranda. Cider and cheese are offered in the common room each afternoon.

Quick Raisin Bread Muffins

1 tablespoon active dry yeast
½ cup warm water (110° to 115°)
³/₈ cup oil (6 tablespoons)
¼ cup honey
½ cup warm water
1 teaspoon salt
1 egg
2 cups all-purpose flour
1 cup whole wheat flour
¼ cup wheat germ
½ cup raisins
Corn oil margarine

Dissolve the yeast in warm water and set aside for 10 minutes. Mix the oil, honey, and warm water. Add the salt, egg, and yeast mixture. Blend in both flours and the wheat germ. Add the raisins. This batter is sticky, but needs no kneading. Spoon the batter into 18 greased 2½-inch muffin cups. Cover and let rise in a warm place for ½ hour. Bake in a 375° oven for 15 minutes. Brush the tops with corn oil margarine before serving.

Makes 18 muffins.

Timberline Lodges

44 Summit Hill Drive
Strasburg, Pennsylvania 17579
(717) 687-7472

Timberline Lodges is nestled in the heart of Amish farmland in the quiet country surroundings of Lancaster County. Through the windows of the Hearthroom Restaurant, guests can gaze down over the beautiful landscape. Timberline features tableside cooking and fireside dining. There is no charge for the spectacular sunsets.

Piña Colada Bread

½ cup butter (1 stick), softened
1 cup sugar
3 eggs

Tattersall

1 teaspoon vanilla extract
¼ cup rum (dark preferred)
½ cup cream of coconut
3 cups crushed pineapple

❖   ❖   ❖

2¼ cups all-purpose flour
1 tablespoon baking powder
1 teaspoon baking soda
1 teaspoon salt
1 cup coconut (medium flake)

Cream the butter and sugar. Add the eggs, vanilla, rum, cream of coconut, and pineapple.

Mix the dry ingredients. Add to the wet mixture. Pour into a well-greased loaf pan. Bake in a 350° oven for 1 hour, or until it tests done.

Makes 1 loaf.

Filet Mignons with Shrimp Sauce

12 shrimp with shells (16 to 20 per
    pound)
2 stalks celery
1 small onion
1 clove garlic
1 bay leaf
Pinch thyme
Pinch cayenne pepper
1½ cups water
½ cup dry white wine
1 cup heavy cream
2 tablespoons cold butter

❖   ❖   ❖

2 teaspoons sour cream
1½ teaspoons prepared
    horseradish
⅛ teaspoon dry vermouth
Pinch cayenne pepper
12 ounces jumbo lump crab meat

❖   ❖   ❖

4 8-ounce filet mignons
Puff pastry

Remove the shells from the shrimp. Set the shrimp aside. In a stock pot combine the shells, celery, onion, garlic, seasonings, water and wine. Bring to a boil. Reduce to ½ cup of liquid. Strain through a double layer of cheesecloth into a sauce pot. Reduce the stock again to 2 tablespoons of liquid. Add cream. Simmer, *do not boil,* until the sauce thickens. Add the shrimp to cook. Just before serving, remove the

shrimp; set aside and keep warm. Remove the pan from heat. Whisk in the butter in small chunks. (For a nice presentation, split the shrimp lengthwise leaving the shrimp connected at the small end.)

Meanwhile, thoroughly mix the sour cream, horseradish, vermouth, and pepper. Blend in the crab meat, leaving lumps of meat as large as possible.

Broil the filets to the desired doneness, allowing for the fact that they will be heated in the oven (leave rare for medium rare; medium rare for medium). Butterfly each filet. Warm the crab meat mixture. Put ¼ of the mixture in each filet and wrap with puff pastry. Bake in a 500° oven until the pastry is browned. Top with 3 shrimp on each filet and the desired amount of sauce.

Serves 4.

Shrimp and Scallops Moutarde

12 shrimp (under 10 per pound)
12 large sea scallops

❖   ❖   ❖

Asparagus spears

❖   ❖   ❖

1 cup heavy cream
¼ cup reduced shrimp stock
1 teaspoon Sherry
2 tablespoons Moutarde de Meaux
    Pommery
1½ teaspoons Dijon mustard

Curl each shrimp around a scallop. Place a skewer in each shrimp and scallop to hold the shape. Broil over mesquite charcoal.

Arrange the shrimp and scallops over green asparagus spears. Combine the cream, stock, Sherry, Moutarde de Meaux Pommery, and Dijon mustard. Pour over the shrimp and asparagus.

Serves 2.

❖ ❖ ❖ ❖ ❖ ❖

Bittersweet Frangelica

1½ cups butter (3 sticks)
2 cups sugar
8 eggs
2¾ cups all-purpose flour
½ teaspoon baking powder
½ teaspoon salt
1 teaspoon vanilla extract

❖   ❖   ❖

½ cup sugar
1 cup water
½ cup Frangelica liqueur

❖   ❖   ❖

⅔ cup sugar
¼ cup water
1 large egg
3 egg yolks
1 teaspoon vanilla extract
½ pound unsalted butter (2 sticks)

❖   ❖   ❖

16 ounces semi-sweet chocolate
¼ cup Crisco

❖   ❖   ❖

1½ cups finely ground hazelnuts
Whipped cream

Cream butter. Gradually add sugar and beat until fluffy. Add eggs one at a time. Beat after each addition. Add the next 3 ingredients. Add the vanilla. Beat the mixture until light and fluffy; pour into a greased tube pan. Bake in a 350° oven for 1 hour. Cool on a cake rack.

To make the imbibing syrup, dissolve the sugar in water over medium heat. Cool. Add the Frangelica liqueur and set aside.

To make the butter cream filling, mix the sugar and water in a saucepan. Simmer to 238° or the soft-ball stage. Beat the egg and yolks with the vanilla. Pour the sugar syrup into the eggs in a thin stream. Add the butter, a lump at a time, into the sugar and eggs. Beat until smooth. Reserve ½ cup.

Melt the chocolate and Crisco together in the top of a double boiler; set aside.

Cut the tube cake into 3 equal layers. Sprinkle the imbibing syrup on all 6 surfaces of the cake until it is absorbed. Spread ½ of the butter cream filling on the bottom layer. Sprinkle with ¾ cup of ground hazelnuts. Repeat with the next layer. Add the top layer of cake. Spread ½ cup of reserved butter cream thinly over the outside of the cake to prevent crumbling.

Ice the cake with the melted chocolate. Garnish each slice with a dollop of whipped cream topped with a sprinkle of hazelnuts. Serve thin slices. This is a very rich cake.

Serves 16.

Pace One Restaurant and Country Inn

Thornton Road
Thornton, Pennsylvania 19373
(215) 459-3702

Pace One has that breath of fresh air for which city people search and Ted Pace's famous country cooking is served with an extra helping of friendly service in an eighteenth-century restored stone barn. The country inn, with rooms for overnight accommodations, is newly opened. Its rooms all have private baths or showers. A continental breakfast is available every morning, consisting of coffee, juice, Danish and fresh fruit. Lunch, dinner and Sunday brunch are available in the restaurant. Meeting and banquet facilities for up to eighty people are available.

Pace One Restaurant's Squash-Apple Bisque

**2 apples, peeled and cored
1 small butternut squash, peeled
    and seeded
6 cups chicken stock
1 small onion, diced
½ teaspoon dried rosemary
½ cup butter (1 stick)
½ cup all-purpose flour
Milk to taste (optional)**

Grate the apples and squash on a medium grater. Place the chicken stock in a large pot and add the apples, squash, onion, and rosemary. Bring to a boil, then lower the heat and simmer for 30 minutes. Meanwhile, in a small saucepan, melt the margarine. Allow to cool without solidifying. Whisk in the flour and return the saucepan to low heat. Cook, stirring constantly, for about 7 minutes, until the mixture changes to a lighter color. Pour into the stock in a fine stream, stirring with a whisk until smoothly blended. Simmer the soup for 15 minutes. Milk may be added to adjust the consistency.

Serves 6 to 8.

Pace One Restaurant's New England Pudding

**3 16-ounce cans chunk pineapple,
    drained
4 apples, cored and cut into chunks
1½ cups walnuts, coarsely chopped
1 cup brown sugar, firmly packed
4 eggs
2 cups sugar
2 cups all-purpose flour
1½ cups butter (3 sticks), melted
Vanilla ice cream**

Mix the pineapple and apples. Place in a 12x7-inch pan. Mix the walnuts and brown sugar and spread on top of the fruits. Whip the eggs, add the sugar,

and blend. Add the flour and butter to the egg mixture and blend well. Spread the batter over the fruit, concentrating it in the center of the pan. Bake in a 325° oven until golden brown, about 25 minutes. Spoon into bowls and serve with vanilla ice cream.

Serves 12.

Willaman Jersey Farm

R.D. 2
Transfer, Pennsylvania 16154
(412) 962-2556

A country experience awaits guests of the Willaman Jersey Farm. The twelve-room farmhouse has two double bedrooms (one with crib) for guests, and the two full bathrooms are shared with the family. Here is the opportunity to observe a farm family at work, to meet livestock and cuddle kittens, and to walk in quiet woods and open pastures. Breakfast and supper are served daily, and the "bottomless" cookie jar is always there for the hungry. No smoking is permitted in the buildings, and the hosts request no alcohol or pets. Shenango Reservoir, a nine-hole golf course, and community tennis courts offer off-the-farm fun at less than ten minutes distance.

Broccoli Salad

**1 bunch broccoli, cut in small
    pieces
½ pound bacon, cooked and
    crumbled
½ cup diced sharp cheese
1 red onion, diced**

    ❖ ❖ ❖

**½ cup salad dressing
¼ cup sugar
1 teaspoon vinegar**

Combine the broccoli, bacon, cheese and onion. Mix together the salad dressing, sugar, and vinegar; toss with the salad.

Serves 4.

French Bread

1 tablespoon shortening
1 tablespoon salt
1 tablespoon sugar
1 cup boiling water
1 cup cold water
1 ¼-ounce package active dry yeast
5½ to 6 cups all-purpose flour
1 egg white, slightly beaten

Place the shortening, salt, and sugar in a large bowl. Add the cup of boiling water, stirring until the shortening is melted. Add the cold water to the shortening mixture. Add the yeast. When it bubbles, stir the flour in gradually. Knead for 5 minutes (by the clock—it must feel springy or the bread will be heavy). Place the dough in a greased bowl to rise until doubled in bulk. Punch down and shape into 2 long loaves. Place on a greased cookie sheet to rise again. When light, brush with the slightly beaten egg white and slash 3 times diagonally. Bake in a 375° oven for 35 to 45 minutes. For a soft crust brush with oil or shortening when the bread comes from the oven.

Makes 2 loaves.

Lemon Sponge Pie

¼ cup melted butter
1 cup sugar
3 tablespoons all-purpose flour
3 egg yolks, slightly beaten
Juice and grated peel of 1 lemon
1 cup milk
3 egg whites, stiffly beaten
Pastry for 1 9-inch 1-crust pie crust

Blend the butter with the sugar and flour. Add the egg yolks, lemon juice and peel. Stir in the milk and fold in the egg whites. Pour into the pastry lined pie pan. Bake in a 450° oven for 8 minutes; reduce the oven to 325° for 25 minutes.

Serves 6.

Upper Black Eddy Inn

River Road, Route 32
Upper Black Eddy, Pennsylvania 18972
(215) 982-5554

The Upper Black Eddy Inn, in upper Bucks County, is a historic building on both the Delaware Canal and Delaware River. Built in 1830 as an inn, it served the needs of canal travelers and the men who worked the barges in the middle of the last century. Today its six bedrooms (sharing two baths) offer overnight accommodations, and its two dining rooms (one with a bar) offer a menu emphasizing French cuisine. Breakfast is included for house guests only. Lunch, dinner, and Sunday brunch are served. The inn is conveniently located for all the historic, cultural, and natural attractions in Bucks County and western New Jersey.

Il Diplomatico

5 tablespoons rum
5 teaspoons sugar
1¼ cups strong espresso coffee (do not substitute American coffee)

1 16-ounce pound cake (homemade, mix or frozen)

❖ ❖ ❖

4 eggs, separated
1 teaspoon sugar
6 ounces semisweet chocolate (bits or grated)

❖ ❖ ❖

1½ cups heavy cream
2 teaspoons sugar
1 teaspoon vanilla extract, rum flavoring, or both
Chocolate curls, candied fruit, or walnuts

Line a rectangular bread pan with greased waxed paper, extending it up the sides above the rim. Combine the rum, sugar, and coffee. Cut the pound cake into ¼-inch thick slices. Dip each briefly on both sides in the coffee-rum mixture. Place on the sides and bottom of the pan to completely line it with soaked pound cake.

Beat the egg yolks with 1 teaspoon of sugar until pale yellow. Melt the chocolate and mix into the beaten yolks. Beat the egg whites until they form stiff peaks. Combine a small portion of whites with the chocolate-yolk mixture to lighten it; then add the remaining whites, folding gently with a whisk until just combined. Spoon the chocolate mixture into the cake-lined pan. Cover top with more rum-soaked slices of cake. The cake may be pieced if necessary. It will be covered at serving.

Refrigerate overnight or up to 1 week. Loosen the paper from the pan and turn the dessert out onto a serving platter, waxed paper protruding out. Lift the pan off and carefully peel off the waxed paper.

Whip the chilled cream in a chilled bowl with 2 teaspoons of sugar and flavoring until stiff. Cover all exposed surfaces of the cake with whipped cream. Decorate as desired with chocolate curls, candied fruit, or walnuts. Refrigerate until serving time.

Serves 16.

Rhode Island

Hotel Manisses

Spring Street
Block Island, Rhode Island 02807
(401) 466-2421

As a long-established summer hotel, the Manisses has been renovated but still retains the atmosphere of the 1870s. Even the staff dresses in fashions of that time. In the parlors are stained glass windows that reflect old-fashioned flower gardens, an outdoor fountain, and Victorian garden furniture. Nevertheless, the eighteen guest rooms all have private baths, and some have Jacuzzis and refrigerators. A complete restaurant serves excellent food. The owners also operate the 1661 Inn, which has twenty-five rooms and serves breakfast, as well as the 1661 Inn Guest House.

Cold Cucumber Sauce

2 cups minced cucumbers, seeds removed
2 teaspoons salt

❖ ❖ ❖

2 cups sour cream
1 cup mayonnaise
1 tablespoon lemon juice
¼ cup minced onion
¼ cup chopped fresh dill

1 teaspoon sugar
¼ cup chopped fresh parsley
Salt and white pepper

Place the cucumbers in a large bowl, add the salt and blend well; place in a sieve to drain for 20 minutes. Then press the cucumbers against the sieve to squeeze out the excess moisture.

Place the sour cream into a mixing bowl; stir in the mayonnaise; then the lemon juice. Add the remaining ingredients and mix well. Stir in the cucumbers. Adjust the seasonings to taste (add more lemon juice if desired).

Serve with fish, smoked meats, or vegetables.
Serves 4.

Halibut
with Green Peppercorn Cream Sauce

2 7-ounce halibut fillets or steaks

❖ ❖ ❖

Butter
1 tablespoon green peppercorns
2 tablespoons Brandy
1 tablespoon dry vermouth
1 cup heavy cream
Salt and pepper to taste

Bake halibut in a 350° oven for 15 to 20 minutes or until just starting to become flaky to the touch.

In a saucepan heat a small amount of butter and sauté green peppercorns for 1 minute; add Brandy and vermouth. Reduce by half, add cream and reduce by half. Season with salt and pepper. Serve over fish.
Serves 2.

Monkfish Grenoblaise

2 8-ounce monkfish fillets, peeled
Salt and pepper to taste
Flour
2 tablespoons clarified butter

❖ ❖ ❖

2 tablespoons butter
1 tablespoon capers
1 tablespoon lemon juice

Season the monkfish with salt and pepper, then dredge in flour. Sauté the fillets in clarified butter, cooking about 5 minutes on each side. Remove the fillets to a serving dish. Drain the pan.

Using the same pan brown 2 tablespoons of butter, add the capers and lemon juice. Stir and pour over the fillets. Garnish with freshly chopped parsley.
Serves 2.

Oysters Chelsea

12 oysters on the halfshell, loosened
1 cup butter, softened (2 sticks)
3 cloves garlic, minced
1 large shallot, minced
1 tablespoon chopped fresh parsley
½ teaspoon prepared mustard
¼ teaspoon white pepper
1 tablespoon lemon juice

❖ ❖ ❖

¼ cup blanched almonds, sliced

Arrange the oysters in a baking pan. Mix all the ingredients except almonds together and blend until smooth. Place a heaping teaspoon of the butter mixture on each oyster. Sprinkle with about 5 slices of almonds. Bake in a 400° oven for 10 minutes or until the almonds begin to brown.

Serves 4.

Fairfield-by-the-Sea

527 Green Hill Beach Road
Green Hill, Rhode Island 02879
(401) 789-4717

Fairfield-by-the-Sea is an artist's contemporary house in a country setting. It is south of U.S. Route 1 between Westerly and Wakefield. This comfortable, airy house with its eclectic collection of art and interesting library offers its guests beauty and seclusion. Continental breakfasts are included in the rates. Homemade hot breads and elegant fruit are served, and farm fresh eggs often are included. Beautiful Green Hill Beach on Block Island Sound is a walk or bike ride away, and Theatre-by-the-Sea is just down the road in Matunuck. Golfing, bird watching, tennis, sailing, nature trails, fine shops, museums, historical sights, antique shops, craft shops featuring local craftsmen, high quality restaurants, and horseback riding are among the most popular activities. Fishing, both fresh and saltwater, is excellent.

Sportsman's Breakfast

1 English muffin
3 slices Swiss cheese
1 slice ham or Canadian bacon
1 anchovy (optional)
1 slice tomato
2 slices canned or fresh pineapple

Split the English muffin. On one muffin half layer 1 slice of cheese, ham, anchovy, tomato, and another slice of cheese. On the other muffin half layer the remaining cheese slice and 2 pineapple slices. Place on a baking sheet; bake in a 450° oven until the cheese is melted and the sandwich is hot. Serve and enjoy immediately!

Serves 1 with a hearty appetite.

Aunt Grace's Easy Beef Stew

To this basic recipe you may add your favorite vegetables. Layer them in the casserole over the meat, onions, and green pepper.

2 pounds stewing beef
2 medium onions, sliced
1 chopped green pepper

❖ ❖ ❖

¾ cup chili sauce
¾ cup water
1½ teaspoons salt
⅛ teaspoon pepper

❖ ❖ ❖

1 10-ounce package frozen baby lima beans
Sour cream

Place the beef in a large casserole dish. Arrange the onion and green pepper, and other vegetables if desired.

Combine in a bowl the chili sauce, water, and seasonings. Pour over the meat and vegetables. Cover and bake in a 350° oven for 2 hours. Break apart and add the lima beans. Cover and bake 45 minutes more. This may be cooked in a crock pot instead; adjust cooking times accordingly.

Garnish with a dollop of sour cream and serve with a green salad and crisp French bread.

Serves 6.

Duckling à l'Orange

1 5-pound duckling
1 teaspoon salt
¼ teaspoon black pepper
1 teaspoon ginger
1 orange (including rind), sliced
1 onion, sliced

❖ ❖ ❖

1 cup freshly squeezed orange juice
¼ cup honey

❖ ❖ ❖

Rinds of 2 oranges, slivered
1 tablespoon flour
Orange slices and parsley for garnish

Season the neck and body cavities of the duckling with a mixture of salt, pepper, and ginger. Mix the orange and onion slices together and stuff the body cavity. Place the duckling on a rack in a roasting pan and roast in a 450° oven for 20 minutes. Reduce the heat to 350° and roast 1½ hours longer. Pour off and reserve the fat as it accumulates.

Combine the orange juice and honey to make a basting sauce; baste the duckling every 20 minutes while it is roasting.

Place the slivers of rind in a saucepan; cover with water. Boil for 10 minutes, then drain well and pat dry. Return the rind to the pan. Combine 2 tablespoons of the reserved fat with the peel. Add the flour and cook for a few minutes, stirring constantly. Set aside.

Remove the duckling to a platter and cover it with foil to keep it hot. Skim the fat from the roasting pan. Add water to the drippings from the pan to measure 1½ cups; then heat and stir in the roasting pan until all the brown bits come free in the water. Add this liquid to the rind and flour mixture in the saucepan. Cook and stir until the sauce is thick.

Garnish the duckling with orange slices and parsley. Serve the sauce as gravy.

Serves 4.

Beef Stroganoff

An old family recipe.

1 pound beef strips, cut into 2x2½-
    inch strips (or ground beef)
2 tablespoons oil
½ cup sliced onion
1 clove garlic, minced
1 6-ounce can mushrooms,
    undrained (or 1 pint fresh
    mushrooms)
2 drops Tabasco sauce
1 tablespoon Worcestershire sauce
¼ teaspoon pepper
¼ teaspoon paprika
Dash nutmeg
1 10¾-ounce can tomato soup

❖ ❖ ❖

1 cup sour cream

Using a skillet or kettle, brown the
beef in oil. Add the onion and garlic;
when browned add the mushrooms,
seasonings and soup. Simmer until the
beef is tender.

About 5 minutes before serving add
the sour cream. Heat but do not allow
to boil.

Serve with noodles or rice, a green
salad, and a crisp bread.

Serves 4 to 6.

Mrs. Lewis's Rhode Island Baked Clams

These may be used as a main course or
as an appetizer. Fresh clams may be
used instead of canned ones. They
should be steamed first and then finely
chopped.

1 clove garlic, minced
1 medium onion, finely chopped
2 tablespoons butter
8 to 10 mushrooms, finely chopped
    (optional)

❖ ❖ ❖

1 10½-ounce can minced clams
1/8 teaspoon pepper
1 tablespoon dried parsley

❖ ❖ ❖

2 tablespoons cornstarch
¼ cup cold water

❖ ❖ ❖

½ cup butter (1 stick)
1½ cups bread crumbs

❖ ❖ ❖

Lemon wedges

In a small skillet sauté the garlic and
onions in 2 tablespoons butter. Add the
mushrooms, sauté over medium heat
until translucent and soft, stirring often.

Drain the clams and set aside, adding the juice to the skillet. Also add
pepper and parsley.

In a cup mix the cornstarch and cold
water until smooth; stir into the skillet.
Bring the mixture to a boil, stirring
constantly until thick. Remove from
the heat and add the clams. Fill 12 to
15 shells with the mixture.

Melt ½ cup of butter in the same skillet; remove from the heat and add the
bread crumbs. Mix thoroughly and
spread on top of the clam mixture.
(This dish may be frozen at this point
and baked later if desired.) Bake in a
450° oven for 10 to 15 minutes on the
highest rack.

Serve with a wedge of lemon.

Rusty's Braised Fish—Chinese Style

10 pieces fish (or 10 whole fresh
    porgies)
Flour
Oil

❖ ❖ ❖

2 tablespoons oil
2 cloves garlic, minced
1 medium onion, finely chopped
2 tablespoons soy sauce
1 tablespoon honey (or sugar)
½ teaspoon ginger
1 cup chicken stock (or fish stock)

❖ ❖ ❖

Hot cooked rice

Dredge the fish with flour. Heat some
oil in a large skillet; brown the fish 1
minute on each side; then sauté for 2
minutes on each side. Drain the oil and
pile the fish carefully in the skillet. Set
aside and keep warm while preparing
the sauce.

Place 2 tablespoons oil in a sauté
pan. Sauté garlic and onion; add soy
sauce, honey, and ginger. Pour this
sauce over the fish. Add the stock,
cover, and poach over low heat for 20
minutes. Serve with rice.

Serves 8 to 10.

Pat's Plum Tart

¾ cup ice cold butter (1½ sticks)
2 cups plus 2 tablespoons all-
    purpose flour
¼ cup sugar
1 teaspoon baking powder
1/8 teaspoon salt
1 teaspoon lemon rind
1 egg

❖ ❖ ❖

2 pounds purple plums
¼ cup sugar
2 tablespoons all-purpose flour
1 teaspoon cinnamon

Dice the butter and keep chilled. In a
large bowl combine the flour, sugar,
baking powder, salt, and rind. Add the
butter and cut into flour mixture with a
pastry blender. In a small bowl or cup
beat the egg. Add the egg to the flour
mixture; mix until the mixture holds
together, it may be crumbly. Pat the
pastry into the bottom of a 9-inch
springform pan and up the sides.

Wash and slice the plums. Place the
plums, skin side up, over the pastry.
Mix together and sprinkle over the
plums the sugar, flour and cinnamon.
Bake in a 400° oven for 30 to 40 minutes. Cool 20 minutes and then remove
the sides of the pan. Serve warm with
whipped cream or ice cream, if desired. Best if eaten the same day.

Serves 16.

Bed and Breakfast at the Richards'

104 Robinson Street
Narragansett, Rhode Island 02882
(401) 789-7746

Guests of this ten-room home first encounter a stone walkway, a weathered fence, and a tree-filled yard. The living room fireplace invites guests to make themselves at home, and the wicker, antiques, and chintz that fill the house lend it a country air. The three guest bedrooms include two with double beds and one with a kingsize bed or two twins. One of the rooms has a private bath and private entrance; the other two share a bath. Nearby attractions include the Matunuck Theatre-by-the-Sea, summer concerns on the Village Green, shopping, good restaurants, tennis, fishing, great beaches, and Newport. Breakfast each morning includes such delights as Johnnycakes, cheese blintzes, blueberry muffins, and freshly-ground coffee and tea.

Steven's Johnnycakes

1 cup corn meal
1 teaspoon salt
1 teaspoon sugar
½ cup milk
1 cup boiling water

Mix the corn meal, salt, and sugar. Add milk and boiling water; mix well. Batter will be thin. Drop by tablespoonfuls onto a medium hot well-greased griddle. Cook for 6 minutes, turn and cook for about 2 minutes more. Serve with maple syrup.
Serves 4.

Broiled Tomatoes

5 fresh tomatoes
½ cup bread crumbs
½ cup grated Parmesan cheese
2 tablespoons snipped chives
¼ cup minced parsley
¼ cup butter (½ stick), melted

Slice the tomatoes ½-inch thick; discard the ends. Place on a broiler pan. Mix the remaining ingredients and place an equal portion of the mixture on the top of each tomato. Broil 5 minutes until hot; serve immediately. A nice accompaniment to egg dishes.
Serves 4.

Narragansett Strudel

This strudel is named for our town. This is very easy because you use fresh seafood salad from your local market, but be sure it is not too runny. Salad should consist of lobster, fish, celery, shrimp, and peppers.

12 sheets phyllo pastry
1 cup butter (2 sticks), melted
1 cup fine dry bread crumbs
1 pound seafood salad

Lightly dampen a tea towel. Lay a sheet of phyllo on the towel. Brush with melted butter and sprinkle lightly with bread crumbs. Repeat four times, ending with the 6th sheet of phyllo. Place ½ of the seafood salad on the narrow edge of phyllo, leaving a 2-inch border on each side. Fold in the sides and roll up the pastry. Place the roll on a buttered baking sheet. Brush with the melted butter. Repeat using the remaining filling and phyllo. Bake in a 400° oven for 20 minutes.
Serves 8 to 10.

Blueberry Slump

3 cups blueberries
¼ cup water

¼ cup sugar
Cinnamon to taste

❖ ❖ ❖

1 cup all-purpose flour
2 teaspoons baking powder
2 tablespoons sugar
3 tablespoons butter
½ cup milk

Butter a 1-quart dish. Place the blueberries in a dish with the water. Sprinkle with ¼ cup sugar and cinnamon.

In a separate bowl sift the flour, baking powder and 2 tablespoons of sugar. Work the butter in with your fingertips. Moisten with the milk. Drop by tablespoonfuls on the blueberries. Bake in a 400° oven about 20 minutes. Serve hot with whipped cream.
Serves 4.

The Melville House

39 Clarke Street
Newport, Rhode Island 02840
(401) 847-0640

Staying at The Melville House is like taking a step into the past. Built about 1750, it is in the heart of the old hill section of Newport, one block up the hill from Thames Street with its brick market and wharves, and around the corner from Touro Synagogue and Trinity Church. Off-street parking is provided in the backyard so guests may leave their cars and walk to restaurants, shops, and points of interest. Seven rooms furnished in traditional colonial style are available with both private and shared baths. A continental breakfast featuring homemade granola and muffins is served in the breakfast room each morning. The living room has an interesting collection of old appliances.

Chocolate Chip Pumpkin Muffins

May be made 1 or 2 days before servings.

½ cup unblanched almonds, sliced

❖ ❖ ❖

1⅔ cups all-purpose flour
¾ cup sugar
1 tablespoon pumpkin pie spice
1 teaspoon baking soda
¼ teaspoon baking powder
¼ teaspoon salt

❖ ❖ ❖

2 eggs, beaten
1 cup pumpkin (half of a 1-pound can)
½ cup butter (1 stick), melted
1 cup chocolate chips

Spread the almonds on a baking sheet and bake for 5 minutes, just until lightly browned. Set aside to cool.

In a large bowl thoroughly mix the flour, sugar, pie spice, soda, baking powder, and salt.

In a separate bowl combine the eggs, pumpkin and butter; whisk until blended. Stir in the chocolate chips and almonds. Pour over the dry ingre-dients and fold in with a spatula until the dry ingredients are moistened. Spoon the batter into greased muffin cups. Bake in a 350° oven 20 to 25 minutes or until puffed and springy to the touch. Turn out onto a rack to cool. Wrap in a plastic bag and keep for 1 or 2 days. Reheat before serving.

Makes about 14 muffins.

Sweet Currant Muffins

⅓ cup butter
½ cup sugar
1 egg
½ cup sour cream
1½ cups all-purpose flour
1½ teaspoons baking powder
½ teaspoon salt
⅔ cup currants

❖ ❖ ❖

¼ cup butter (½ stick), melted
½ cup sugar
1 teaspoon cinnamon

Cream ⅓ cup of butter with ½ cup of sugar; add the egg. Blend in the sour cream and dry ingredients just until mixed. Stir in the currants. Grease muffin cups and fill ⅔ full. Bake in a 375° oven for 20 minutes.

Melt ¼ cup of butter. In a small bowl mix ½ cup of sugar with the cinnamon. While the muffins are warm, dip the tops in melted butter and then dip in the cinnamon-sugar mixture.

Makes about 10 muffins. This recipe can be doubled.

The Wallett House: A Bed and Breakfast Inn

91 Second Street
Newport, Rhode Island 02840
(401) 849-5177

The Wallett House, built in 1930, is in Newport's historical Point section overlooking the harbor. Interior decorating, with many mirrors and glass accents, is in Art Deco style with shades of purple predominating. It has a reception hall for weddings and other social events, with catering services provided. Open the entire year, the Wallett House is within walking distance of other mansions, synagogues, churches, boutiques, fine restaurants, sandy beaches, the marina, and lots of shopping opportunities.

Greek Doughnuts (Svingi)

4 cups water (or 3 cups water and 1 cup milk)
1 tablespoon butter
2 cups farina
⅛ teaspoon salt

❖ ❖ ❖

The Melville House

**8 eggs
Olive oil**

❖ ❖ ❖

**Confectioners' sugar (optional)
Cinnamon (optional)
Honey (optional)**

Boil the water, add the butter, farina and salt; stir until the mixture thickens. Remove from the heat and let stand. When cool, add the eggs, one at a time and mix well. Dough should be of a soft consistency. Working with greased hands, form the dough into medium-sized balls, making a hole in the center.

Fry in a heavy pan in ample hot olive oil until golden on both sides, frying no more than three doughnuts at a time, as they puff up. Serve sprinkled with confectioners' sugar and cinnamon or with honey, whichever is preferred.

Makes 12 doughnuts.

Loukoumathes

Drop doughnuts.

**2 ¼-ounce packages active dry
  yeast
½ cup warm water (110° to 115°)**

❖ ❖ ❖

**¾ cup scalded milk
¼ cup sugar
1 teaspoon salt
⅓ cup soft shortening
2 eggs
3½ cups sifted all-purpose flour**

❖ ❖ ❖

Oil

❖ ❖ ❖

**Honey
Cinnamon**

Add the yeast to water in a cup and set aside. Pour the scalded milk into a mixing bowl; add the sugar and salt. Blend together and cool to lukewarm. Stir the yeast mixture well and add to the milk mixture. Mix in the shortening, eggs, and flour. Beat vigorously until the batter is smooth. Cover and let rise about 30 minutes or until doubled. Stir down and let rest.

Pour oil about 2 inches deep in a heavy frypan; heat to 350°. Drop the batter from a teaspoon into the hot oil, frying until golden brown. Drain on absorbent paper. Dilute the honey with a little warm water and drizzle over the loukoumathes while they are still warm. Sprinkle with cinnamon.

Makes approximately 2 dozen.

Pastry Squares
(Pasta Flora)

**2 eggs
½ cup butter (1 stick)
1 cup sugar
2 heaping teaspoons baking
  powder
1 teaspoon vanilla extract
3 cups all-purpose flour**

❖ ❖ ❖

1 16-ounce jar pineapple preserves

❖ ❖ ❖

**1 egg, beaten
Maraschino cherries**

Blend the eggs, butter, sugar, and baking powder until smooth. Add the vanilla, then gradually work in the flour, blending thoroughly. Divide the dough, reserving about ¼ of it for a lattice topping. With the remaining portion line the bottom of a greased 10x14-inch oblong pan. Spread the pineapple preserves evenly over this.

Roll out the reserved dough into strips and form a lattice topping over the pineapple preserves. Brush the lattice strips with beaten egg and bake in a 350° oven until the pastry is golden brown. When the pastry has cooled, cut it into squares and garnish each square with a maraschino cherry.

Serves 12.

Pineapple Surprise
(Pasta Pari)

**1 cup butter (2 sticks)
½ cup sugar
1 ounce Cognac
1 teaspoon baking powder**

**1 egg
2 cups all-purpose flour**

❖ ❖ ❖

1 12-ounce jar pineapple preserves

❖ ❖ ❖

**12 eggs, separated
1 1-pound box confectioners' sugar
1 teaspoon baking powder
1 ounce Cognac
Almond extract, or rind of one
  lemon
1½ pounds almonds, blanched and
  finely ground**

Cream the butter and sugar together until well-blended. Add 1 ounce of Cognac, baking powder and 1 egg; mix thoroughly. Now gradually add the flour and work together to form a soft dough. Line the bottom of a 10x14-inch oblong pan with the dough.

Spread the pineapple preserves evenly over the dough.

Beat together the 12 egg yolks, confectioners' sugar, baking powder, remaining Cognac, and almond extract. Add the almonds and blend thoroughly. In a separate bowl beat the egg whites until stiff but not dry. Fold the egg mixture into the beaten egg whites. Carefully spread this over the pineapple preserves. Bake in a 350° oven for about 40 minutes.

Serves 12 to 16.

Apple Rice Pudding

3 cups cooked rice

❖ ❖ ❖

**2 eggs
½ cup sugar
¼ teaspoon salt
½ cup sour cream
1 cup grated Cheddar cheese
1 cup milk
1 tart cooking apple, chopped
⅓ cup raisins**

❖ ❖ ❖

**1 tablespoon butter or margarine,
  melted
¼ cup brown sugar, firmly packed
1 tablespoon all-purpose flour
½ teaspoon ground cinnamon**

Measure the rice into a large mixing bowl. In a small mixing bowl beat the eggs with the sugar and salt. Add the sour cream, cheese, and milk; mix thoroughly and pour over the rice. Add the apple and raisins; stir well. Pour into a buttered shallow 2-quart baking dish.

Combine the butter, brown sugar, flour, and cinnamon. Sprinkle over the rice mixture. Bake in a 375° oven for 30 to 35 minutes or until a knife inserted in the center comes out clean.

Serves 6.

Bed and Breakfast at Highland Farm

4145 Tower Hill Road
Wakefield, Rhode Island 02879
(401) 783-2408

In this old New England farmhouse built in the early 1800s, three bedrooms with double beds are available. Highland Farm covers twenty-eight acres and is ten minutes from the ocean. Nearby points of interest include shopping, the famous Narragansett Pier, Galilee Fishing Village, charter boats, the Village of Kingston, the University of Rhode Island, Newport (30 minutes away). In addition to the full cookie can, guests enjoy eggs, pancakes, cereal, juice, coffee, tea, hot muffins, fruit, and wonderful conversation.

Elephant Stew:
(Copious Collations)

    1 elephant
    Brown gravy
    Salt and pepper
    2 rabbits (optional)

Cut the elephant into bite-sized pieces; should take about 2 months. Add enough brown gravy to cover. Salt and pepper to taste. Cook over a kerosene fire for about 4 weeks at 460°. This will serve about 3800 people. If more are expected, two rabbits may be added. But do not add the rabbits unless necessary, as most people do not like to find a hare in their stew.

Serves approximately 3,800.

Rye Cakes

    1 cup sour milk (1 cup milk and 1
      tablespoon vinegar)
    1 egg
    2 tablespoons sugar
    1 cup all-purpose flour
    1 cup rye or whole wheat flour
    ½ teaspoon baking soda

In a mixing bowl combine all the ingredients. Heat some oil in a heavy fry pan. Drop in the batter by spoonfuls. Drain on a paper towel.

Makes 1½ dozen rye cakes.

Molasses Cookies

A recipe from Mrs. Sumner's grandmother.

    ½ cup sugar
    ½ cup molasses
    ½ cup oil
    ½ cup hot water
    2 teaspoons baking soda
    2 teaspoons ginger
    3¼ cups all-purpose flour

In a mixing bowl combine all the ingredients and let stand for 10 minutes. Roll out the dough the size of a 10½x15½-inch cookie sheet, grease the sheet, and place the dough on it. Bake in a 350° oven for 12 minutes or until done. Immediately cut into squares.

Makes 1½ dozen cookies.

❖ ❖ ❖ ❖ ❖ ❖

Pineapple Cookies

    1½ cups sugar
    ⅓ cup shortening
    ½ cup crushed pineapple, drained
    2 eggs
    3 cups all-purpose flour
    1 teaspoon vanilla extract
    1 teaspoon baking soda

In a mixing bowl combine all the ingredients, drop by spoonfuls onto a greased baking sheet. Bake in a 350° oven until brown.

Makes 2½ dozen cookies.

J. Livingston's Guest House by the Sea

39 Weekapaug Road
Weekapaug, Rhode Island 02891
(401) 322-0249

J. Livingston's Guest House by the Sea is directly across the street from the Breachway, a waterway that invites fishing at almost any hour, and is bordered in back by a natural wildlife preserve. It is also less than one-half mile from one of Rhode Island's most beautiful beaches.

Furnishings include many original artworks of the owner and other artisans, such as knotted lampshades, wallhangings, needleworks, paintings, and prints in the stenciled rooms. Fare includes a continental buffet breakfast consisting of juice, fruit, cereal, a variety of homemade breads, bagels, hot muffins, or the pastry of the day. The Guest House is open during the off-season, making it a quiet retreat from October to May.

Spicy Peach Muffins

4½ cups all-purpose flour
1 teaspoon salt
4½ teaspoons baking powder
¾ cup sugar
¾ cup brown sugar, firmly packed
½ teaspoon nutmeg
1 teaspoon cinnamon
2 eggs
¾ cup vegetable oil
1¼ cups milk
2 peaches, peeled and diced

Combine the flour, salt, baking powder, sugar, brown sugar, and spices. Slowly add the eggs, oil, and milk. Stir in the diced peaches. Fill greased muffin pans ⅞ full. Bake in a 400° oven for 25 to 30 minutes.

Makes 1½ to 2 dozen muffins.

Apple-Nut Coffee Cake

½ cup shortening
1 cup sugar
2 eggs
1 teaspoon vanilla extract

❖ ❖ ❖

2 cups all-purpose flour
1 teaspoon baking powder
1 teaspoon baking soda
¼ teaspoon salt

❖ ❖ ❖

1 cup sour cream
2 cups finely chopped apple

❖ ❖ ❖

½ cup chopped nuts
½ cup brown sugar, firmly packed
1 teaspoon cinnamon
2 tablespoons all-purpose flour

In a mixing bowl cream together the shortening and sugar. Add the eggs and vanilla; beat well. Sift together 2 cups of flour, baking powder, soda, and salt; add to the creamed mixture alternately with the sour cream. Fold in the chopped apple and spread the batter into a greased 13x9-inch pan.

In a separate bowl combine the nuts, brown sugar, cinnamon, and 2 tablespoons flour. Mix well and sprinkle over the batter. Bake in a 350° oven for 35 to 40 minutes.

Serves 16.

South Carolina

The Willcox Inn

Colleton Avenue and Whiskey Road
Aiken, South Carolina 29801
(803) 649-1377

The Willcox Inn is one of the few remaining aristocratic southern inns. The roster of its guests has included President Franklin D. Roosevelt, Winston Churchill, and the Duke of Windsor. Though closed from the 1950s until 1983, it is now restored and is presided over by an Argentine hostess, The Contessa Bianca Lovatelli. All three meals are served in the dining room. A special package is offered for honeymooners. The inn has retained its European flair.

The Willcox's Own Sweet Roll

1 8-ounce carton sour cream
½ cup sugar
½ cup butter (1 stick), melted
1 teaspoon salt
2 ¼-ounce packages active dry yeast
½ cup warm water (105 to 115°)
2 eggs, beaten
4 cups bread flour

❖ ❖ ❖

2 8-ounce packages cream cheese, softened
¾ cup sugar
1 egg, beaten
⅛ teaspoon salt
2 teaspoons vanilla extract

❖ ❖ ❖

2 cups confectioners' sugar
¼ cup milk
2 teaspoons vanilla extract

In a heavy saucepan scald the sour cream. Remove from the heat; add ½ cup of sugar, butter, and 1 teaspoon of salt. In a large mixing bowl dissolve the yeast in warm water; stir in the sour cream mixture and 2 eggs. Gradually stir in the flour to make a soft dough. Cover tightly and chill overnight.

With a mixer or food processor make the filling by combining the cream cheese, ¾ cup of sugar, 1 egg, ⅛ teaspoon of salt, and 2 teaspoons of vanilla; blend well and set aside.

Divide the dough into 4 equal portions. Working with 1 portion at a time, place on a heavily floured board, knead 4 or 5 times, and roll into a 12x8-inch rectangle. Over each rectangle spread ¼ of the filling, leaving a ½-inch margin around the edges. Beginning at the long side, roll up jelly-roll style, pinching edges and end to seal. Place the rolls, seam side down, on greased baking sheets. Make 6 equally spaced cross-shaped cuts across the top of each loaf. Cover and let rise in a warm place for 1 hour or until doubled in bulk. Bake in a 375° oven for 15 to 20 minutes.

Make a glaze by combining the confectioners' sugar, milk, and 2 teaspoons of vanilla. Spread the loaves with the glaze while they are still warm.

Makes 4 12-inch loaves.

Marinated Carrots

1 pound carrots, peeled and sliced
½-inch thick
1 onion, sliced in rings
1 bell pepper, sliced

❖ ❖ ❖

1 cup sugar
1 tablespoon dry mustard
1 tablespoon Worcestershire sauce
½ cup oil
1 teaspoon salt
¾ cup vinegar

Cook the carrots just until tender; drain and cool. Combine in a 2-quart refrigerator dish with the onion and bell pepper. In a medium-sized saucepan combine the remaining ingredients. Bring to a boil; remove from the heat and cool. Add to the vegetables. Stir or toss. Cover and refrigerate for 24 hours.

Serves 4.

The Cedars Bed and Breakfast

1325 Williston Road
Post Office Box 117
Beech Island, South Carolina 29841
(803) 827-0248

The moment guests enter the drive, they know this is a special place. Tucked away on twelve park-like acres, The Cedars is a step back in time to a more genteel way of life. The completely renovated house is furnished in the traditional manner and accented with antiques. The guest bedrooms feature queen-size poster beds, ceiling fans, fireplaces, and modern private or semi-private baths. Guests are welcome to fully enjoy the house and its amenities, to read and relax in the upstairs parlor, sip lemonade on the wide veranda, have afternoon tea or sherry, and stroll the grounds. Dogwood, wisteria, redbud, and crape myrtle bloom in profusion, while mockingbirds sing their greetings. A continental breakfast is served each morning by the fireplace in the country kitchen or in the formal dining room. Within easy access is Aiken and its famed thoroughbred country and Augusta, home of the Masters Golf Tournament, many fine restaurants, antique shops, and restored historic "Old Towne."

Pear Marmalade

4 pounds firm ripe pears
1 orange
1 lemon
3 pounds sugar

Wash the pears; remove the seeds and cores. Cut into quarters, then into eighths crosswise. Wash the orange and lemon. Cut off the ends and remove the seeds. Cut into eight chunks. Chop all the fruit in a food processor, being careful to keep it chunky. Pour the fruit and sugar in a large saucepan and bring to a boil. Reduce the heat and continue cooking, stirring frequently, until clear and shiny. Pour into sterilized jars and seal.
Makes 3 to 4 pints.

Chicken Breasts with Mustard Tarragon Sauce

3 whole chicken breasts
3 tablespoons butter
Salt and pepper

❖ ❖ ❖

1 clove garlic, minced
2 tablespoons flour
1 tablespoon fresh tarragon
2 tablespoons Dijon mustard
1 cup heavy cream

Prepare the breasts by removing skin and bones, split in half, and pound slightly to an even thickness. Sauté the breasts in butter, salt and pepper to taste, and remove to a heated platter.

Add the garlic to the pan drippings and cook until softened. Stir in the flour, cooking until golden; then mix in the mustard, tarragon, and cream. Simmer, stirring until the sauce is slightly thickened. Pour over chicken breasts.
Serves 6.

Orange Curried Rice

½ cup chopped onion
¼ cup butter (½ stick)
2 teaspoons curry powder
1 cup uncooked rice
1 cup orange juice
1 cup chicken broth
1 teaspoon salt
½ cup seedless raisins
1 bay leaf

In a heavy saucepan sauté the onions in butter until soft. Stir in the curry powder and rice; cook and stir two minutes. Add the remaining ingredients and stir with a fork. Bring to a boil, lower the heat, cover, and simmer 20 minutes. Remove bay leaf.
Serves 6.

The Cedars

Pear Mincemeat

5 pounds firm pears
1 pound seedless raisins
1 orange
4 cups sugar
¾ cup cider vinegar
1 tablespoon cinnamon
1 tablespoon nutmeg
1 tablespoon allspice
2 teaspoons cloves

Core the pears and cut into eight chunks. Cut the orange into large chunks and remove the seeds. In a food processor coarsely chop the pears and orange. Combine all the ingredients in a large pot and bring to a boil. Reduce the heat and simmer uncovered for about two hours or until thick, stirring occasionally. Use to make two pies, or seal in sterilized jars.

Makes about 2 quarts.

Indigo Inn

One Maiden Lane
Charleston, South Carolina 29401
1-800-922-1340 (in South Carolina)
1-800-845-7639 (Toll Free)

Eighteenth century charm abounds at the Indigo Inn, from the elegant lobby with its Sheraton sideboard (circa 1700) and oriental motif to the beautifully appointed rooms decorated with eighteenth century antiques and reproductions. Down pillows and comforters complete the luxury, and most rooms contain two comfortable queen-size beds. The famous hunt breakfast, consisting of homemade breads, ham biscuits, fruits of the season, and coffee is served each morning on the sideboard. Guests may choose to partake of this delicious breakfast in the lobby, their rooms, or the lush courtyard. The Indigo Inn is in the heart of the Historic District of Charleston and is within

easy walking distance to the open air market, churches, mansions, and fine restaurants of Old Charleston.

Blueberry Bread

1 cup butter (2 sticks)
2½ cups sugar
6 eggs
4 cups all-purpose flour
1 teaspoon salt
2 teaspoons baking powder
2 teaspoons baking soda
2 cups sour cream
2 teaspoons vanilla extract
3 16½-ounce cans blueberries, drained

In a mixing bowl combine the butter, sugar, and eggs. In a separate bowl combine the flour, salt, baking powder, and soda; add to the butter mixture. Add the sour cream and vanilla. Gently fold in the blueberries. Pour into 2 large or 3 small greased loaf pans. Bake in a 350° oven for 50 minutes.

Makes 2 to 3 loaves.

Prune Bread

4 eggs
3 cups sugar
1 cup oil
3 cups self-rising flour
1½ teaspoons nutmeg
1½ teaspoons cinnamon
2 4½-ounce jars prune baby food
1 cup chopped nuts (optional)

Mix the eggs, sugar, and oil together in a mixing bowl. Add the flour and spices; then add the prunes and nuts. Pour into 2 greased loaf pans. Bake in a 350° oven for 50 to 60 minutes.

Makes 2 loaves.

The Lodge Alley Inn

195 East Bay Street
Charleston, South Carolina 29401
(803) 722-1611

The Lodge Alley Inn takes its name from the Marine Lodge of Freemasons established in the alley in 1773, where Charleston defied the British-imposed tax by holding her own tea party in 1774. It is in Charleston's historic district, offering thirty-four inn rooms, each with a fireplace, thirty-seven one- and two-bedroom suites, each with a kitchen, and a two-bedroom penthouse. The inn also has facilities for private meetings and functions, dining in the French Quarter Restaurant, and relaxation in the Charleston Tea Party Lounge, eighteenth century parlor, courtyard, and gardens. Lodge Alley Inn is within easy strolling distance of historic homes, fine restaurants, and shops.

Lobster Soufflé with Américaine Sauce

1 cup water
½ cup butter (1 stick)
1 cup all-purpose flour
3 medium eggs
❖ ❖ ❖
4 ounces lobster meat, puréed
2 ounces Sherry
1 teaspoon salt
Dash cayenne pepper
❖ ❖ ❖
4 tablespoons butter, melted
½ cup fine bread crumbs
❖ ❖ ❖
4 egg whites
Pinch cream of tartar
❖ ❖ ❖

**Shells of one lobster, finely
   chopped
5 tablespoons butter
½ cup minced carrots
1 cup minced leeks
1 cup minced celery
1 cup minced onion
½ teaspoon minced garlic**

✦ ✦ ✦

**6 tablespoons flour
1 cup brandy
2 cups white wine
3 tablespoons tomato paste
1 quart fish stock
1 teaspoon thyme
1 bay leaf
½ tablespoon tarragon**

✦ ✦ ✦

Salt and pepper to taste

Make a puff paste in a small saucepan by bringing the water and ½ cup of butter to a boil; sprinkle in the flour and mix well with a wooden spoon. Cook over low heat, stirring constantly until smooth; allow to cool for five minutes. Add the eggs one at a time, allowing one minute between each, stirring constantly; continue to stir for 5 more minutes.

Combine with the puff paste the lobster purée, Sherry, salt, and cayenne pepper. Mix together until smooth.

Prepare 4 8-ounce soufflé cups by coating well the bottoms and sides with 4 tablespoons of melted butter and then with the bread crumbs.

In a mixing bowl beat the egg whites with cream of tartar until they hold soft peaks. Fold in the lobster mixture; combine well but do not beat. Pour into the soufflé cups and bake in a 450° oven for 10 to 15 minutes. Serve with Américaine sauce.

To prepare the Américaine sauce, sauté the shells in 5 tablespoons of butter in a medium saucepan until the butter turns a reddish brown. Add the carrots, leeks, celery, and onion, sauté until soft. Add the garlic and sauté one more minute. Stir in the flour. Add in the brandy, wine, tomato paste, stock, thyme, bay leaf, and tarragon. Simmer for 1 hour. Strain through a fine sieve and season with salt and pepper.

Serves 4.

Veal with Morels

½ cup morels

✦ ✦ ✦

**8 2-ounce veal slices
Salt and pepper
Flour
¼ cup butter (½ stick)**

✦ ✦ ✦

**1 cup Madeira
2 cups heavy cream
Salt and white pepper to taste**

Place the morels in a small bowl; cover with water, and set aside.

Pound the veal slices until they are very thin, season with salt and pepper, and coat lightly with flour. In a medium frypan sauté the veal in the butter, then place on a serving platter.

Add the Madeira to the pan and reduce to ½. Add the cream and the water from the morels; cook until the sauce is thick. Add the morels and season to taste. Pour the sauce over the veal slices.

Serves 4.

Marinated Vegetables

**½ cup virgin olive oil
½ teaspoon minced garlic
2 tablespoons dill, chopped
1 teaspoon salt
⅛ teaspoon white pepper
12 medium mushrooms
2 cucumbers
3 tomatoes
1 pound asparagus**

Mix together the olive oil, garlic, dill, salt, and pepper in a large bowl. Cut the stems from the mushrooms. Peel, seed, and slice the cucumbers. Peel and quarter the tomatoes. Briefly steam and cool the asparagus. Place all the vegetables in the bowl, cover, and refrigerate 24 hours. Drain the oil and arrange on chilled platters.

Serves 6.

The Shaw House

8 Cyprus Court
Georgetown, South Carolina 29440
(803) 546-9663

The Shaw House is a spacious home with antique-filled rooms. Guests can enjoy a beautiful view of the Willowbank Marsh. The hostess has intimate knowledge of the area, including historical sites, gift shops, and restaurants. A complimentary southern home-cooked breakfast is included, with fresh hot bread and individual pots of coffee. The Shaw House is near Myrtle Beach, Pawley Island, and Charleston.

Angel Biscuits

**1 ¼-ounce package active dry yeast
¼ cup warm water (110 to 115°)
2½ cups all-purpose flour
½ teaspoon baking soda
1 teaspoon baking powder
1 teaspoon salt
2 tablespoons sugar
½ cup shortening
1 cup buttermilk**

Dissolve the yeast in warm water; set aside. Mix the dry ingredients in the order given; then cut in the shortening. Stir in the buttermilk and the yeast mixture; blend thoroughly. The dough is ready to refrigerate or roll. Turn the dough out onto a floured board and knead lightly. Roll out and cut with a biscuit cutter and place on a greased baking sheet. Let the dough rise slightly before baking in a 400° oven for 12 minutes. The dough will keep up to 2 weeks in the refrigerator.

Makes 24 biscuits.

Baked Grits

2 cups grits
1 cup milk
4 eggs, beaten
1 cup grated cheese
1 8½-ounce box of corn bread mix

Combine all the ingredients; mix well. Place in a 2-quart glass baking dish. Bake in a 350° oven for 45 minutes. Serves 6.

Windsong—A Bed and Breakfast

Route 1, Box 300
Mayesville, South Carolina 29104

Windsong is a large, spacious house in an excellent location for people wanting a rural setting for their vacation or needing a place to stop on their travels north and south. Its comfortable guest rooms have a separate entrance, and the house's balconies and porches provide ample opportunity for relaxation and conversation. The miles of private, isolated country trails surrounding Windsong invite long, quiet walks.

Tomato Juice

20 pounds medium tomatoes (about 40)
2 tablespoons lemon juice
2 tablespoons prepared horseradish
1 tablespoon plus 1 teaspoon seasoned salt
1½ teaspoons Worcestershire sauce
1 teaspoon hot sauce

Core and quarter the tomatoes. Place in two large Dutch ovens; cover and cook over medium heat 45 minutes, stirring occasionally, until the tomatoes are soft. Remove from the heat; press through a food sieve, reserving the tomato juice. Return the juice to a Dutch oven and stir in the remaining ingredients; simmer until thoroughly heated. Quickly pour into 9 hot sterile pint jars, leaving ½-inch of head space; cover at once with metal lids and screw on bands. Process in a boiling water bath 15 minutes.
Makes 9 pints.

Kosher Dill Pickles

12 pounds cucumbers
1 ½-ounce jar dillweed
10 cloves of garlic
2 quarts water
1 quart apple cider vinegar
¾ cup pickling salt

Slice or quarter the cucumbers and pack into 10 sterile quart jars. Add one clove of garlic and one teaspoon of dillweed to each jar. Combine the water, vinegar, and salt; bring to a boil. Pour over the cucumbers in the jars until all are covered; seal immediately. Age for about two weeks before using.
Makes approximately 10 quarts.

Windsong

Orange Sugared Nuts

1½ cups pecan halves
½ cup sugar
¼ cup water
1 teaspoon grated orange rind

Place all the ingredients in a large heavy skillet; cook over medium heat until the water evaporates and the nuts have a sugary look. Pour the nuts onto a greased baking sheet, separating them quickly with a fork. Cool and store in a covered container in refrigerator.

Serendipity, An Inn

407 71st Avenue North
Myrtle Beach, South Carolina 29577
(803) 449-5268

Serendipity is a small complex in Spanish Mission style, surrounded by lush tropical vegetation. The setting is a quiet side street less than 300 yards from the Atlantic Ocean, away from noise and traffic. It offers active days, memorable evenings, and relaxed sleeping at night. The "Garden Room" is the place for the complimentary Continental breakfast and socializing. Also, a heated pool, spa, and brick patio with fountain provide opportunity for conversation and relaxation. All bedrooms are spacious and air-conditioned and have color televisions and private baths. Also available are efficiency units and family-sized apartments.

Garlic Grits

1 cup instant grits
¼ cup butter (½ stick)
¼ cup milk
1 16-ounce roll garlic cheese, shredded
1 egg, beaten
Dash Tabasco sauce

Cook the grits according to the package instructions. Remove from the heat and mix in the butter, milk, cheese, egg, and Tabasco. Place in a 1-quart baking dish and bake in a 375° oven for 30 minutes. Serve with eggs or sausage.
Serves 4.

Dump Cake

1 16-ounce can crushed pineapple
1 21-ounce can cherry pie filling
1 18¼-ounce package deluxe yellow cake mix
1 cup pecans, chopped
2 tablespoons butter, thinly sliced

Dump the undrained pineapple into a buttered 13x9-inch baking pan and spread evenly over the bottom of the pan. Dump the cherry pie filling and spread. Dump the dry cake mix onto the cherry layer; spread evenly. Sprinkle pecans over the top and dot with butter slices. Bake in a 350° oven for 45 to 50 minutes.
Serves 12.

Pineapple Pudding

5 slices white bread
2 eggs, beaten
½ cup butter (1 stick), melted
❖ ❖ ❖
½ cup sugar
1 tablespoon all-purpose flour
1 16-ounce can crushed pineapple

Tear the bread into small pieces and stick to the bottom and sides of a buttered 1-quart casserole. In a mixing bowl combine the eggs and butter, mixing well. In a separate bowl mix the sugar and flour; then add to the egg mixture. Stir in the pineapple, mixing well. Pour over the bread and bake in a 375° oven for 30 minutes.
Variations: Canned apples, cherries, or pumpkin pie mixture may be substituted for the pineapple.
Serves 4.

Bed and Breakfast at Summerville

304 South Hampton Street
Summerville, South Carolina 29483
(803) 871-5275

The primary unit offered for bed and breakfast is the restored servants' quarters dating from 1865. A large room with beamed ceilings, it has a fireplace in the sitting area and a double bed in the sleeping area. A bath with a shower, fully equipped kitchen, heat and air conditioning, two worn bikes and a grill are part of the facilities. Accommodations are also available in the main house (listed on the National Register of Historic Places) in a large upstairs room furnished with antiques, including a canopy bed. The bath is private but not connected. The

room opens to the upstairs porch, where a light breakfast can be served; breakfast is also served by the pool or in the greenhouse as weather permits. Complimentary wine and soft drinks, fruit, and flowers are provided for guests. The pool, open late-May to mid-September, is available to guests at most hours.

Gingerbread Muffins

1 cup shortening
1 cup sugar
1 cup molasses
4 eggs
❖ ❖ ❖
2 teaspoons baking soda
1 cup buttermilk
❖ ❖ ❖
4 cups all-purpose flour
2 teaspoons ginger
½ teaspoon cinnamon
½ teaspoon cloves
½ cup pecans, chopped
1 cup raisins

In a mixing bowl cream the shortening and sugar until light and fluffy. Stir in the molasses; then add the eggs one at a time beating well after each.

Dissolve the soda in a cup with the buttermilk. In a separate bowl combine the flour with the spices and add to the creamed mixture alternately with the buttermilk. Stir in the pecans and raisins. Store the batter in an airtight container in the refrigerator. When ready to bake fill greased muffin cups ⅔ full. Bake in a 350° oven for about 20 minutes or until done. To bake unchilled, reduce baking time to 15 minutes. Batter may be stored for several weeks in the refrigerator.

Makes about 6 dozen muffins.

Bacon Biscuit Bars

2 cups biscuit mix
6 cooked bacon slices, crumbled
½ cup shredded sharp Cheddar
** cheese**
½ cup cold water

In a mixing bowl combine the biscuit mix, bacon, and cheese. Add water; stirring until the dough clings together. Knead gently 5 times on a lightly floured board. Roll into a 10x6-inch rectangle; cut lengthwise with a floured knife into 1-inch strips; then crosswise into thirds. Bake on an ungreased baking sheet in a 450° oven for 10 minutes. Serve hot.

Makes 18 bars.

Gingered Fruit Compote

1 apple, sliced
1 orange, sectioned
1 banana, sliced
¼ cup orange juice
2 teaspoon ginger, freshly grated
Mint sprigs

In a serving dish combine and mix the first 5 ingredients. Cover and chill at least 2 hours. Garnish with mint.

Serves 2.

South Dakota

Bed and Breakfast at Skoglund Farm

Route #1, Box 45
Canova, South Dakota 57321
(605) 247-3445

The Skoglund Farm is a farmhouse that brings back memories of Grandpa's home. Decorated in country-style, with antiques and collectibles, it expresses the personality of the innkeepers. It has four rooms for guest use and provides guests with a continental breakfast served country-style every morning. Nearby attractions are the Corn Palace, the Doll Palace, and the "Little House on the Prairie."

Orange Jello Salad

1 16-ounce can mandarin oranges
1 16-ounce can crushed pineapple
1 6-ounce package orange gelatin

❖   ❖   ❖

1 8-ounce carton whipped topping
1 8-ounce carton cottage cheese

Drain the juices from the oranges and pineapple into a saucepan; heat to the boiling point; remove from the heat. Mix in the gelatin, stirring until dissolved.

When the gelatin has cooled, stir in the fruits, whipped topping, and cottage cheese. Refrigerate overnight before serving.
Serves 9.

Buttermilk Salad

1 cup buttermilk
1 8-ounce carton frozen whipped topping, thawed
1 3-ounce package vanilla instant pudding mix
1 16-ounce can mandarin oranges, drained
1 16-ounce can crushed pineapple, drained

❖   ❖   ❖

Chocolate stripe cookies, crumbled

In a mixing bowl combine the buttermilk, whipped topping, and pudding mix. Stir in the oranges and pineapple. Cover and refrigerate until ready to serve.

Just before serving, add the cookie crumbs.
Serves 4.

Quick Rolls

2 ¼-ounce packages active dry yeast
2½ cups warm water (110° to 115°)
1 18¼-ounce package yellow cake mix
4½ cups all-purpose flour

❖   ❖   ❖

½ cup butter (1 stick), melted
½ cup brown sugar
Cinnamon
½ cup chopped nuts

Dissolve the yeast in warm water. Add the cake mix and flour. Knead the dough; then let it rise until double. Roll out on a lightly floured surface. Spread with melted butter; sprinkle with brown sugar, cinnamon, and nuts. Roll up jelly-roll fashion; then slice into ½-inch thick sections. Place on 2 baking sheets. Bake in a 350° oven for 20 minutes.
Makes 2 dozen rolls.

Party Cake

1 18¼-ounce package white pudding-cake mix

❖   ❖   ❖

1 20-ounce can crushed pineapple, undrained
1 3-ounce package vanilla instant pudding mix

❖   ❖   ❖

1 8-ounce carton whipped topping

Prepare the cake mix according to the package directions. Bake in a 9x13-inch pan.

When the cake is baked, poke holes in the top with a meat fork. Pour the crushed pineapple over the top, allowing it to soak into the holes. Prepare the pudding according to the package directions; spread in a layer over the pineapple. Refrigerate until ready to serve. Serve with whipped topping.
Serves 16.

343

Fitch Farm

Box 728
Milesville, South Dakota 57567-0728
(605) 859-2040

This bed and breakfast is a ranch farm about a two-hour drive from the Black Hills. At the Fitch Farm the inn-keeper makes quilts and weaves, and her wares can be purchased. Guests can observe a wheat farm in opera-tion, and they can enjoy the prairie west as people there experience it.

Old-Fashioned Pioneer Prairie Cracked Wheat Cereal

Cracked wheat can be obtained by sorting the chaff from the wheat and then by grinding the seed into meal. This recipe is especially good if sugar is sprinkled on top.

1 cup cracked wheat
3 cups water
❖ ❖ ❖
1 cup dates (or dried prunes)
1 cup light cream
½ cup chopped nuts
¼ cup honey
1 teaspoon cinnamon
¼ teaspoon lemon juice
⅛ teaspoon salt

Combine the cracked wheat and water in a saucepan, cover, and bring to a boil. Reduce the heat and cook until the water is absorbed, about 25 to 30 minutes. Remove from the heat and stir in dates, cream, nuts, honey, cinna-mon, lemon juice, and salt. Serve hot as a cereal or cold as a pudding; with additional milk or cream as desired.
Serves 4.

Lake Side Farm

Rural Route 2, Box 52
Webster, South Dakota 57274
(605) 486-4430

This farm home in the northeast lake region of South Dakota is part of a modern dairy farm. The farm raises oats, corn, barley, and alfalfa hay for the cattle, the few sheep, and two horses that live there. Fishing, boat-ing, and water recreation is nearby. Guests are welcome to tour the farm and watch the dairy operation in action. Children are welcome, but smoking, drinking, and pets are not.

Fruit Soup

¼ cup pearl tapioca
❖ ❖ ❖
2 cups dried mixed fruit
½ cup raisins
½ cup prunes
1 stick cinnamon
¾ cup apple juice
1 tablespoon lemon juice
4 thin slices lemon
1 quart water
❖ ❖ ❖
Heavy cream

Soak the tapioca overnight in cold wa-ter according to package directions.
Combine in a saucepan the dried mixed fruit, raisins, prunes, cinnamon, juices, lemon, and water. Cook until the fruit is tender. Add the tapioca and cook until it is transparent. Remove the cinnamon stick. Serve warm or cold, with cream.
Serves 10 to 12.

Rhubarb Jam

5 cups chopped rhubarb (fresh or frozen)
4½ cups sugar
❖ ❖ ❖
1 3-ounce package raspberry gelatin (or strawberry, cherry, or orange)

Place the rhubarb and sugar in a heavy saucepan with a tiny bit of water. Sim-mer over low heat until tender. Stir in the gelatin until dissolved. Pour into hot jars and seal.
Fills 4 8-ounce jars.

Caramel Pudding

This pudding is inverted to be served and the brown sugar is on top, making it so delicious. It is also unusual be-cause it is cooked in a double boiler without being stirred.

1 cup brown sugar, firmly packed
4 slices bread
❖ ❖ ❖
2 eggs
2 cups milk
½ teaspoon vanilla extract
½ teaspoon salt

Use a double boiler over medium heat and have the water in the bottom por-tion simmering. Place the brown sugar in the top portion. Generously butter and then dice the bread. Add to the brown sugar, but do not stir.
In a mixing bowl beat the eggs with a fork, then add the milk, vanilla, and salt. Pour this mixture into the double boiler with the sugar and bread. Again, do not stir.
Cover and simmer for 1 hour. To re-move the pudding, run a knife around the edge and then turn it out onto a serving dish. Serve the pudding plain, or with cream, whipped cream, or ice cream.
Serves 4.

Hachland Vineyard

Hachland Hill Dining Inn and Catering
   Service
1601 Madison Street
Clarksville, Tennessee 37040
(615) 255-1727—Hachland Vineyard (in
   Joelton)
(615) 647-4084—Hachland Hill Dining Inn

Hachland Vineyard, in the Nashville area, offers fine fare in a restored cedar log house built around 1805. Those who love old things will revel in the wide pine board floors and hand-rubbed logs that only time-mellowed wood can have. The Vineyard, with its private guests rooms, is the ideal spot for corporate retreats, business meetings, seminars, as well as private family gatherings. The Vineyard sleeps twenty-five.

Hachland Hill Inn in Clarksville is 45 minutes northwest of downtown Nashville. The grand ballroom can seat 300 people for a private dinner. The adjoining terrace and garden rooms overlook wild flower gardens and a bird sanctuary. Roaring fires burn throughout the mansion from late September until May. Three of Clarksville's oldest log houses have been reconstructed in the garden area where old-fashioned barbecue suppers with square dances are held. Hachland Hill sleeps fifteen.

At both settings, Hachland Properties provide unlimited menu selection from such international cuisine as chateaubriand to "down-on-the-farm" country suppers of southern fried chicken, Tennessee country ham, and biscuits.

Hachland Hill Inn

Filet Mignon
with French Marinade and Brandy Glaze

½ cup oil
1 tablespoon lemon juice
3 teaspoons sugar
1 cup red wine
½ teaspoon salt
½ teaspoon cracked pepper
¼ teaspoon dried marjoram
¼ teaspoon dried thyme

❖ ❖ ❖

6 filet mignons

❖ ❖ ❖

¼ cup Brandy
¼ cup water
2 tablespoons Worcestershire sauce

Combine the oil, lemon juice, sugar, wine, and seasonings. Marinate the filets for at least 1 hour.

Grill the filets in ½ butter and ½ oil to the desired doneness.

Combine the Brandy, water, and Worcestershire to make the glaze. Sprinkle onto the filets, coating both sides. Heat quickly on each side on a hot grill. Serve immediately.

Serves 6.

Southern Barbecued Rabbit

1 tablespoon vinegar
1 tablespoon sugar
1 tablespoon dry mustard
3 tablespoons Worcestershire sauce
6 ounces chili sauce or relish
1 teaspoon salt
1 teaspoon black pepper
1 10¾-ounce can bouillon
1 medium onion, minced
2 cloves garlic, minced
½ cup butter (1 stick), melted
2 drops Liquid Smoke (if desired)

❖ ❖ ❖

1 dressed rabbit

Combine all the ingredients (except the rabbit) to make the barbecue sauce. Place the rabbit in a buttered baking dish and pour the sauce over it. Bake in a 350° oven for 1½ hours, or until tender.

Serves 2 to 4, depending on the size of the rabbit.

Southern Baked Stuffed Idaho Potatoes

6 Idaho baking potatoes
½ cup butter (1 stick)
1 cup sour cream
1 tablespoon minced onion
Celery salt to taste
Salt and pepper to taste
½ cup crumbled crisp-cooked bacon

Bake the potatoes. When they are done, split them lengthwise and scoop the potatoes out of the shells. While they are still hot, whip the potatoes with the butter, sour cream, salts, and pepper. Add more sour cream if necessary. Spoon the mixture back into the shells. Sprinkle the tops with bacon crumbs. Serve hot.
Serves 6.

Southern Butterscotch Sauce

⅓ cup butter
1 cup brown sugar, firmly packed
2 tablespoons light corn syrup
⅓ cup heavy cream

Bring all the ingredients to a boil, stir, and cool.
Makes 1⅔ cups of sauce.

Southern Tutti-Fruiti

1 29-ounce can Elberta peaches
1 20-ounce can pineapple chunks
1 20-ounce can crushed pineapple
3 cups sugar

❖ ❖ ❖

½ cup sliced maraschino cherries
1 cup Bourbon or rum

Drain the juice from the cans of peaches, chunked, and crushed pineapple into a saucepan. Add the sugar and boil for 5 minutes. Remove from the heat.
Chop the peaches; then add them to the syrup along with the pineapple and the cherries. Place in the refrigerator to chill. When the mixture has completely cooled, stir in the Bourbon or rum. Store in the refrigerator.
Serves 8.

Southern Butter Pound Cake

2 cups butter (4 sticks)
6 egg yolks
1 pound sugar
1 pound flour
Vanilla extract to taste (or almond extract)
6 egg whites
1 heaping teaspoon baking powder

❖ ❖ ❖

1 cup confectioners' sugar
1 teaspoon vanilla extract
2 tablespoons warm water

In a large mixing bowl cream the butter and egg yolks until fluffy. Add the sugar, flour, and vanilla to taste. Beat the egg whites until stiff peaks form; fold into the batter. Add the baking powder last, being very careful to mix thoroughly. Pour into a greased 10-inch tube cake pan and bake in a 325° oven for 1 hour.
Prepare the glaze by combining the confectioners' sugar, 1 teaspoon of vanilla, and 2 tablespoons of warm water, or enough to make a smooth paste. Glaze the cake while it is still hot.
Serves 16.

Buckhorn Inn

Tudor Mountain Road
Gatlinburg, Tennessee 37738
(615) 436-4668

The Buckhorn Inn sits on thirty acres atop a peaceful hilltop less than one mile from the entrance to the Great Smoky Mountain National Park. Built in 1938, the inn, with its guest cottages and main lodge, provides all the comforts desired in a mountain retreat. The guest rooms are spacious and have private baths. The dining room invites guests to the evening meal served in country surroundings.

Zucchini Soup

8 small zucchini, sliced
1 cup water
1 small onion, minced
2 tablespoons chicken bouillon granules
2 teaspoons Season-All salt
1 teaspoon fresh parsley

❖ ❖ ❖

¼ cup cornstarch
3 cups milk
3 tablespoons butter
2 tablespoons chicken bouillon granules

In a medium saucepan cook the zucchini in water with onion, 2 tablespoons chicken bouillon, Season-All, and parsley until tender.
Place the cornstarch in a small bowl. Gradually stir in a small amount of the milk, mixing until all of the cornstarch is dissolved. Combine in a saucepan the cornstarch mixture, the remaining milk, butter, and 2 tablespoons chicken bouillon granules. Simmer over medium heat, stirring occasionally, until the mixture is thickened.
Purée the zucchini mixture in a blender; then add it to the thickened mixture in the saucepan. Serve hot.
Makes 8 cups of soup.

Amala's Chocolate Sauce

4 ounces German's chocolate
1½ cups sugar
½ cup butter (1 stick)
1 cup whipping cream
1 tablespoon Amaretto

Melt the chocolate, sugar, and butter in the top of a double boiler over hot water. Add the cream and stir until thickened. Remove from the heat and add Amaretto.

Makes 2½ cups of sauce.

Sweet Corn Bread

½ cup butter (1 stick)
1 cup sugar
2 eggs
1 cup yellow cornmeal
1½ cups all-purpose flour
2 teaspoons baking powder
½ teaspoon salt
1½ cups milk

In a mixing bowl cream the butter and sugar together. Add the eggs, beat well; then add corn meal. Sift the flour with baking powder and salt. Stir in alternately with the milk. Pour into a greased 8-inch square pan and bake in a 375° oven for 30 to 35 minutes, or until done. If muffins are desired, bake in a greased muffin pan 15 to 20 minutes.

Serves 12.

Big Spring Inn

315 North Main Street
Greeneville, Tennessee 37743
(615) 638-2917

Big Spring Inn is a three-story brick Victorian home with leaded and stained glass windows, spacious porches, and a rolled dormer. The house is decorated in a charming mix of antiques and reproductions with the accent on comfort and privacy. Upon arrival, the tired traveler is treated to a cozy chair in the guest parlor, a refreshing beverage, and the afternoon paper. Each of the five guest rooms is different, and all have the thoughtful touch of fresh flowers, a small snack, and thick terrycloth robes. Also available for guests is a quiet upstairs library and a tree-filled yard large enough for an afternoon stroll. Breakfast, included in the room rate, consists of homemade bread or muffins, along with a variety of egg dishes. Early or late risers will find hot coffee, homemade muffins, and assorted cold cereals.

Orange Oatmeal Muffins

2 tablespoons brown sugar
2 teaspoons all-purpose flour
1 teaspoon butter, melted
¼ teaspoon cinnamon

❖ ❖ ❖

1 cup all-purpose flour
1 cup quick-cooking oats, uncooked
½ cup pecans, chopped
¼ cup sugar
2 teaspoons grated orange rind
2 teaspoons baking powder
½ teaspoon salt

❖ ❖ ❖

½ cup orange juice
¼ cup milk
3 tablespoons oil
1 egg, beaten

Combine the brown sugar, 2 teaspoons of flour, butter, and cinnamon, mixing until crumbly; set aside. In a mixing bowl combine 1 cup of flour, oats, pecans, sugar, orange rind, baking powder, and salt, stirring well. Make a well in the center. In a separate bowl combine the orange juice, milk, oil, and egg. Add to the dry ingredients; stir just until moistened. Spoon the mixture into greased muffin pans, filling ¾ full. Sprinkle with the cinnamon mixture and bake in a 425° oven for 15 minutes.

Serves 12.

Rye Muffins

1 cup rye flour
½ cup all-purpose flour
1 teaspoon salt
1 tablespoon baking powder

❖ ❖ ❖

2 tablespoons butter
1 egg, well-beaten
1 cup milk
2 tablespoons molasses
1 tablespoon grated orange peel
1 tablespoon caraway seeds

Sift together the dry ingredients into a mixing bowl. In a separate bowl cream together the butter and egg, then add the milk and molasses. Add the liquid mixture in the dry ingredients; then add the orange peel and caraway seeds. Stir just until moistened. Pour into a well-greased muffin pan and bake in a 400° oven for 12 to 15 minutes.

Makes 9 muffins.

Special Scrambled Eggs

3 eggs
1 tablespoon buttermilk
1½ teaspoons mayonnaise
Salt and pepper to taste
1 tablespoon butter
1 slice bacon, cooked and crumbled

In a mixing bowl beat the eggs, buttermilk, mayonnaise, salt, and pepper with a fork until well-blended. Melt the butter in a small skillet; add the egg mixture. Cook over low heat until the eggs are partially set, lifting the edges gently to allow uncooked portions to flow underneath. Cook until the eggs are set but still moist. Sprinkle with bacon and serve immediately.

Serves 1 to 2.

Viennese Orange Coffee

2 teaspoons grated orange rind
Ground coffee to brew 4 to 5 cups
¼ teaspoon cinnamon
½ teaspoon Brandy extract
Water to make 4 to 5 cups

Place the orange rind in a paper filter or filter basket; top with ground coffee, and sprinkle with cinnamon. Pour Brandy extract over the coffee mixture. Add water to the coffee maker and brew. Serve immediately with cream and sugar to taste.
Serves 4.

German Lentil Soup

12 cups beef stock
½ pound dried lentils
❖   ❖   ❖
5 celery stalks, diced
3 carrots, diced
1 large onion, diced
❖   ❖   ❖
½ cup butter (1 stick)
¾ cups all-purpose flour
❖   ❖   ❖
1 small tomato, diced
½ pound knockwurst, diced
3 tablespoons dry red wine
¼ teaspoon white pepper
❖   ❖   ❖
2 pounds potatoes, peeled and
**   diced**
❖   ❖   ❖
¼ cup red wine vinegar

Place the stock in a large saucepan, bring to a boil. Add the lentils and boil until tender, about 1½ hours.
Add the celery, carrots, and onion to the soup and boil until tender, about 15 minutes. While it cooks, prepare the roux. Melt the butter in a small saucepan, whisk in the flour and stir the mixture for 3 minutes.
Reduce the cooking temperature of the soup to low. Add the tomato, then whisk in the roux. Add the knockwurst, red wine, and white pepper; cook 30 minutes more.
Increase the cooking temperature to high; add the potatoes and boil until tender, stirring frequently. Stir in the vinegar and serve.
Serves 8.

Walnut Toaster Bread

1½ cups all-purpose flour
3 teaspoons baking powder
1¼ teaspoons salt
1 teaspoon baking soda
1½ cups whole wheat flour
❖   ❖   ❖
1¼ cups buttermilk
1 cup walnuts, chopped
½ cup honey
¼ cup oil
2 teaspoons lemon rind, grated
1 large egg

Sift the flour, baking powder, salt and soda. Stir in the whole wheat flour.
Combine the buttermilk, walnuts, honey, oil, lemon rind, and egg; mix well. Add to the dry ingredients, stir until just moistened. Pour into a greased 9x5-inch loaf pan. Place the pan on the lower oven rack and bake at 350° for about 55 minutes, or until the bread tests done. Let stand in the pan 10 minutes; turn out onto a rack to cool. Serve toasted or plain.

Variation: Add 1 cup of chopped prunes into the batter with the walnuts.

Mountain Breeze Bed and Breakfast

501 Mountain Breeze Lane
Knoxville, Tennessee 37922
(615) 966-3917

This two-story Cape Cod home is on a quiet cul-de-sac in a wooded country setting just two and a half miles from Interstate 40/75. It is warmly furnished with antiques. Freshly baked cookies await each guest in the comfortably furnished bedrooms. On warm days the guests can enjoy a lovely wooded view while having breakfast outside on the deck. Coffee is ready and waiting for early risers. Area interests include historic sites, restored mansions, numerous lakes, University of Tennessee activities, American Museum of Science and Energy, Museum of Appalachia, Smoky Mountain National Park, Dolly-

Mountain Breeze

wood, Gatlinburg, and the Cherokee National Forest.

Mountain Breeze Fresh Apple Cake

4 cups peeled, diced apples
2 cups sugar
1 cup chopped nuts

❖ ❖ ❖

½ teaspoon nutmeg
1 teaspoon cinnamon
2 teaspoons baking soda
3 cups all-purpose flour
½ teaspoon salt

❖ ❖ ❖

1 cup cooking oil
1 teaspoon vanilla extract
2 eggs, well-beaten

Mix together the apples, sugar, and nuts in a mixing bowl; let stand for 1 hour, stirring often.

Add the dry ingredients to the apples, mixing well. Then add the oil, vanilla, and eggs; mix well. Pour the batter into a greased and floured tube pan and bake in a 350° oven for 1 hour.

This cake may be served as the dessert after a full breakfast or as part of a continental breakfast.

The Peabody

149 Union Avenue
Memphis, Tennessee 38103
(901) 529-4000

The Peabody, a hallmark of Southern hospitality since 1869, was officially reopened on September 1, 1981, after undergoing a $25 million renovation. Named to the National Register of Historic Places, the fourteen-story hotel is an excellent example of Italian renaissance revival architecture. The lobby of the Peabody is a world of stately elegance, with white marble floors beneath handpainted beamed ceilings, skylights of handpainted etched glass, and decorated wrought iron chandeliers. In the center of the spacious lobby stands the Peabody fountain, where since the early 1930s the famous Peabody ducks have marched in single file to and from their rooftop penthouse. The original guest rooms have been elegantly remodeled, with each of the 454 rooms now more luxurious and spacious than ever. All rooms are tastefully and elegantly furnished. The exhibit hall, ballroom and meeting rooms make this hotel an ideal place for business meetings, too. Within walking distance are Beale Street, where the "blues" were born, riverboat cruises on the Mississippi, ballet, and marvelous restaurants. Elvis Presley's Graceland mansion is only a few minutes' drive away.

Smoked Salmon Mousse

6 ounces smoked salmon
3 egg whites
Pinch nutmeg
Salt and cayenne pepper to taste
4 ounces cream

Cut the salmon into ½-inch pieces; place in a food processor along with the egg whites, nutmeg, and a little salt and pepper. Allow the food processor to run continuously for 1½ minutes until you have an evenly consistent purée. Then add the cream and continue to process until you have a smooth creamy consistency. Poach a sample and check for seasoning. Place the mousse in 4 greased cups. At this point you may add a blanched julienne of vegetables for garnish. Place the cups in a pan half-way submerged in hot water. The pan should be covered. Bake in a 350° oven until a paring knife may be inserted and removed clean.

Chef Ralph Bouton.
Serves 4.

Rack of Lamb with Goat Cheese Pesto

2-3 pound racks of lamb, bones cracked and backbones removed
Salt and pepper

❖ ❖ ❖

¼ pound goat cheese (such as Saint Maure, Montrachet or Pyramide)
¼ cup pine nuts
¼ cup minced fresh parsley
3 medium cloves garlic
¼ cup walnut oil
2 tablespoons fresh lemon juice
¾ cup fresh breadcrumbs

"French" the lamb racks by cutting and scraping off the meat and fat between the rib bones. Remove the flat, gristly bone on the larger end of meat by inserting a sharp boning knife between the fat and bone and cutting around the bone. Trim off the fell (papery membrane covering meat). Cut off most of the fat, leaving a thin layer around the meat. Sprinkle the lamb with salt and a generous amount of pepper.

To prepare the pesto blend the cheese, pine nuts, parsley, and garlic in a processor using on/off turns. With the machine running, gradually add the walnut oil and lemon juice through the feed tube and mix until thick. Spread the pesto generously over the meat. Press the breadcrumbs into the pesto to coat completely. Set the lamb meat side up in a roasting pan. Bake in a 400° oven until a meat thermometer inserted in the thicker portion of the meat (without touching bone) registers 130° (for rare), 25 to 30 minutes. Let stand while preparing the sauce.

Serve with Leek Sauce.
Chef Ralph Bouton.
Serves 4.

Leek Sauce

1 cup fish stock
¼ to ½ potato, peeled and grated
1 leek, chopped
Salt and pepper to taste
¼ cup cream

Bring the fish stock to a boil. Add the potato; cook for 10 to 15 minutes. The potato will thicken the stock. With the stock at a rapid boil, add the chopped leek. Cook for only 5 minutes, enough to soften the leek but not long enough to spoil the brilliant green color. At this time remove the pot from the heat and allow the liquid to cool slightly. Then place the liquid in a blender or food processor and purée totally so that there are no strings. Remove from the blender and season. Just before serving, add the cream and check the seasonings again.

Makes 2 cups.

Vegetable Terrine

8 ounces green beans
2 small zucchini, trimmed
3 medium carrots, peeled and trimmed
8 ounced asparagus, trimmed
8 ounces fresh mushrooms, stems cut off
4 cups tightly packed spinach, washed and stems removed
1 small onion, peeled and quartered
1½ pounds boneless, skinless chicken breasts, trimmed of fat and cut into 1 inch pieces
1¼ teaspoons salt
¼ teaspoon freshly ground pepper
2 egg whites
1½ cups heavy cream

Cut the zucchini and carrots into strips, or process with the french fry disc on a food processor. Steam the green beans for 18 minutes; drain and reserve. Steam the zucchini about 7 minutes, the carrots 10 minutes, and the mushrooms for 2 minutes. Steam the spinach for 5 minutes and squeeze the excess water out when cooled. To make a chicken mousse, drop the onion through the feed tube of a food processor with the metal blade in place and the motor running. Process until finely chopped, about 10 seconds. Add chicken pieces and process for 3½ minutes or until smooth. Add the salt, pepper, egg whites and spinach and process for 30 seconds. With the motor running, slowly pour the heavy cream through the feed tube until it is absorbed. Scrape down the work bowl and process 15 seconds more. (You may make the mousse one day in advance and store it covered with plastic wrap in refrigerator.) When ready to assemble the terrine, preheat the oven to 350°. Butter a 8½x4½x2½-inch loaf pan. Spoon about 1 cup of the mousse into the pan and spread evenly with a spatula. Use about half the carrot strips to make a single layer, placing the strips about ¼ inch in from the sides of the pan. Cover the carrot layer with about 3 tablespoons of the chicken mousse. Make a layer of mushrooms, cover with 3 tablespoons of mousse. Make layer of asparagus, again covering with mousse. Make another layer of carrots and cover with the remaining mousse. Cover the terrine with foil, place in a shallow baking dish, pour boiling water halfway up the side of the pan, and bake in the center of the oven for 35 minutes or until a knife inserted in center comes out clean. Remove to a wire rack and cool for 15 minutes. Pour off the juices, invert onto a cutting surface, and cut into ½-inch slices with a serrated knife.

Chef Ralph Bouton.
Serves 8.

Red Tomato Chutney

4 pounds ripe tomatoes, peeled and chopped
1 pound dessert apples, peeled, cored and chopped
1 pound onions, minced
12 ounces golden raisins
12 ounces dark raisins
1 teaspoon dry mustard
2 teaspoons allspice
1 tablespoon salt
1 tablespoon cayenne pepper
3 cups brown sugar, firmly packed
3¾ cups vinegar

Place all of the ingredients in a large heavy saucepan and bring to a boil. Reduce the heat and simmer, stirring frequently, until the chutney is thick. Seal in sterile jars and label.

Chef Ralph Bouton.

Makes approximately 12 cups.

White Chocolate Mousse in an Almond Cookie Shell

3 egg whites
2 tablespoons sugar
2 tablespoons flour
½ cup almonds, sliced and toasted

❖　❖　❖

1 cup sugar
½ cup water

❖　❖　❖

8 egg whites

❖　❖　❖

6 egg yolks
1 tablespoon white rum
1 pound white chocolate, melted

❖　❖　❖

Raspberry purée
Fresh raspberries

To make the almond cookie shell put 3 egg whites in a bowl and beat briefly. Add 2 tablespoons of sugar and flour, then whisk. Stir the almonds into the mixture. Butter a sheet pan and spoon tablespoons of the mixture onto the pan. Spread slightly with the back of a spoon to form circles about 2 inches apart. Bake in a 350° oven for 5 to 7 minutes. Remove from the oven and while still hot mold into small cups by placing over a rolling pin. Set aside to dry or form into funnel shape by molding around cream horn forms.

To make the mousse heat 1 cup of sugar and the water in a saucepan until it reaches the soft ball stage. In the bowl of a mixer place 8 egg whites and beat until medium stiff, beating first on medium speed and then on high. Add the sugar-water mixture to the egg whites and continue to beat briefly until a stiff meringue is formed. Place the egg yolks into a metal bowl and beat over heat with a whisk. Add rum to the egg yolks, still beating over heat. Fold the yolks into the whites; then fold in the melted chocolate. Refrigerate 3 to 4 hours. To serve place one scoop of mousse in each almond cookie shell. Garnish with raspberry purée and fresh berries.

Chef Ralph Bouton.
Serves 12.

Miss Anne's Bed and Breakfast

3033 Windemere Circle
Nashville, Tennessee 37214
(615) 885-1899

Miss Anne's Bed and Breakfast is a cozy little place that is furnished with many interesting collectibles. Four guest rooms are available, with a full breakfast included in the price. The home is within easy access of all Nashville attractions and shopping.

Cheese Grits Casserole

1 cup quick-cooking grits
4 cups water
1 teaspoon salt

❖ ❖ ❖

½ cup butter (1 stick)
1 cup grated Cheddar cheese
¼ teaspoon garlic powder
2 eggs, beaten

Place the grits, water, and salt in a medium saucepan, cook according to package directions. Add the butter and cheese; stir until melted. Add the garlic powder and eggs. Pour into a buttered 1½-quart casserole. Bake in a 350° oven for 30 minutes.

Serves 8.

Low Calorie Broiled Grapefruit

2 tablespoons diet margarine, melted
1 teaspoon brown sugar substitute
¼ teaspoon rum flavoring
6 grapefruit halves

❖ ❖ ❖

Maraschino cherries (optional)

In a small bowl combine the butter, brown sugar substitute, and rum flavoring. Drizzle one teaspoon of mixture evenly over each grapefruit half. Broil until golden brown. Place a maraschino cherry in center if desired.

Serves 6.

Sweet Potato Bread

1 cup water
1 cup oil
2 cups cooked mashed sweet potatoes
3 cups sugar
3 eggs
1 cup chopped nuts

❖ ❖ ❖

3½ cups self-rising flour
1 teaspoon salt
1 teaspoon ginger
1 teaspoon nutmeg
½ teaspoon cloves
½ teaspoon baking powder
2 teaspoons cinnamon
2 teaspoons baking soda

In a large mixing bowl combine the water, oil, sweet potatoes, sugar, eggs, and nuts. Sift together the remaining dry ingredients. Mix together well with the sweet potato mixture. Pour into 2 large greased loaf pans. Bake in a 325° oven for 1½ hours.

Makes 2 loaves.

Parish Patch Farm and Inn

Normandy, Tennesse 37360
(615) 857-3441

On the banks of the famous Duck River, the Parish Patch Farm and Inn has become well known as the perfect retreat. This 750-acre, working farm is also convenient to Opryland USA, the Jack Daniels and George Dickel distilleries, Tennessee Walking Horse farms, and picturesque towns with names like Bugscuffle, Wartrace and Bell Buckle. There are ample opportunities for outdoor activities such as hiking, fishing, canoeing, biking, or experiencing the day-to-day operations of the farm. Comfortable rooms have handsome walnut and cherry paneling and are centrally heated and air-conditioned. Most have plush down pillows, private baths, and color television. Fireplaces and a swimming pool add to the appeal of the inn. Guests awaken to the aroma of hot biscuits baking, and they can enjoy classic country dinners with an elegant flair, from southern fried chicken to chicken Cordon Bleu.

Mexican Dip

1 1¼-ounce package taco seasoning
2 pounds lean ground beef, browned
2 16-ounce cans refried beans
1 16-ounce carton sour cream
8 ounces grated Mozzarella cheese
Black olives, sliced

Combine the taco seasoning with the ground beef. In a 13x9-inch casserole dish place in layers the beans, ground beef, sour cream, cheese, and olives. Heat in a 300° oven until hot, about 30 minutes. Serve with tortilla chips.

Makes 4 cups of dip.

Whole Baked Beef Tenderloin

**1 4-pound beef tenderloin roast
Salt and pepper to taste
Garlic to taste**

❖   ❖   ❖

**2 onions, quartered
1 pound fresh mushrooms, sliced
4 to 6 ribs celery, sliced diagonally
1 lemon, sliced thin, quartered**

❖   ❖   ❖

**1 24-ounce bottle catsup
¼ cup water
Worcestershire sauce to taste
Juice of 1 lemon**

Season the roast with salt, pepper, and garlic. Place in a roasting pan. Surround the roast with onions, mushrooms, celery, and lemon.

Make a sauce by combining the catsup, water, Worcestershire sauce, and lemon juice; pour over the roast.

Bake in a 350° oven for 45 minutes. It is perfect cooked medium rare.

Serves 12.

Parish Patch Potatoes

**3 pounds cooked whipped potatoes
½ cup butter (1 stick)
6 ounces cream cheese
1 green pepper, chopped
1 bunch scallions, sliced (part of tops)
1 2-ounce jar chopped pimiento
½ cup grated Cheddar cheese
½ cup grated Parmesan cheese
Salt to taste
¼ teaspoon saffron (for color if desired)
Sour cream (for extra moistness if needed)**

Combine all the ingredients. The mixture should be fairly moist; if not, add some sour cream. Place in a 2-quart ovenproof serving dish. Bake in a 350° oven for 30 minutes.

Serves 6.

Fudge Pie

**2 squares unsweetened chocolate
½ cup butter (1 stick)
1 cup sugar
2 eggs
2 tablespoons all-purpose flour
1 teaspoon vanilla extract
½ cup pecans**

Melt the chocolate and butter. Add the sugar, eggs, flour, vanilla, and nuts. Bake in a greased 9-inch pie pan in a 350° oven for 20 to 25 minutes.

Note: Delicious served with peppermint ice cream or Cool Whip mixed with 2 tablespoons Crème de Menthe and a strawberry on the side. This recipe is always a big hit!

Serves 6.

Homestead House Inn

Post Office Box 79
Pickwick Dam, Tennessee 38365
(901) 689-5500
(601) 667-3556 (Off Season)

Built in 1843, Red Sulphur Springs Hotel has at one time included a health spa, a general store, dining room, tavern, livery stable, post office, and several thousand acres of land on which annual fox hunts were the social highlights of the season. The three sulphur springs were popular attractions, and people came to bask in the red, chalybeate, and clear water sulphur springs bath houses.

During the 1870s, Jesse and Frank James hid out here between raids. At its peak Red Sulphur Springs had thirty-two rooms, and its guests entertained themselves by bowling, playing tennis, hunting, and horse racing. During the Civil War, it was occupied by both Union and Confederate armies, and after the Battle of Shiloh, it was converted into a hospital and used by both sides.

Following World War I, the owners closed the hotel, and it was used as a home and/or a boarding house for the next twenty-five years. In the 1960s it was converted to a restaurant. Its current owners purchased the building and the remaining fourteen acres of land in 1984, renovating and changing it to a bed and breakfast inn. The facilities now consist of five bedrooms and three baths available to guests, but use of the entire house is encouraged. A continental breakfast is served to guests in the dining room with white linens and china. The inn has many antiques. The area is noted for boating, fishing, and golfing.

Strawberry Bread

This recipe was requested by the "White House." Strawberry bread is always a part of the complimentary continental breakfast that is served at the Homestead House Inn.

**3 cups all-purpose flour
2 cups sugar
1 tablespoon cinnamon
1 teaspoon baking soda
1 teaspoon salt
3 eggs, well-beaten
1¼ cups corn oil**

❖   ❖   ❖

2 10-ounce packages frozen sliced strawberries, thawed

Line the bottom of 2 loaf pans with aluminum foil; lightly grease the pans. In a large mixing bowl, combine the flour, sugar, cinnamon, baking soda, and salt. Make a well in the center of this mixture. Pour the eggs and oil in the well. Stir until the dry ingredients just become moist.

Pour the thawed strawberries and juice into a container. With a slotted spoon, dip out the strawberries and gently stir into the above mixture. Then add the juice gradually, stirring until the batter is of the proper consistency. The amount of juice varies in

Homestead House

strawberries when thawed, and you do not want the batter to be too thin. Pour into the prepared loaf pans. Bake in a 350° oven for 1 hour or until the loaves test done. Let cool in the pans for 15 minutes. With a knife loosen sides of loaves from pans; turn out. Let loaves cool completely before slicing.

Makes 2 loaves.

Newbury House

Historic Rugby
Post Office Box 8
Rugby, Tennessee 37733
(615) 628-2441
(615) 628-2269

Newbury House was Rugby's first boarding house, in use in 1880. Sash and pulley cords on the windows reveal an 1879 patent date. In 1882 board and lodging was advertised at $4.50 to $6.50 per week, with a single meal for 25¢. Late in the nineteenth century, the Nelson Kellogg family

bought Newbury, lived there for several decades, and continued to take in occasional boarders; but by the 1950s Newbury stood empty. Historic Rugby completed restoration of Newbury House and again opened it to overnight guests in the spring of 1985. Five upstairs bedrooms are furnished in the Victorian period, as is the guests' parlor downstairs.

Harrow Road Café Spoon Rolls

1 ¼-ounce package active dry yeast
2 cups lukewarm water (110° to 115°)
¾ cup butter (1½ sticks)
¼ cup sugar
1 egg, well beaten
4 cups self-rising flour
¼ cup cornmeal

Combine the yeast and the water and stir to mix. Melt the butter; add to the sugar in a large bowl. Add the beaten egg and dissolved yeast mixture. Add the flour and cornmeal; stir until well-mixed. Bake in greased muffin tins in a 400° oven for 15 to 20 minutes.

This dough may be kept in the refrigerator in a covered container. It gets better as it ages.

Makes about 24 rolls.

Harrow Road Café Shepherd's Pie

½ cup chopped onion
1 cup thinly sliced carrots
½ cup butter (1 stick)

❖ ❖ ❖

2 cups chopped roast beef
1 cup gravy made from roast beef drippings
1 bouillon cube
4 teaspoons chopped parsley
2 bay leaves
Dash sage
Salt and pepper to taste

❖ ❖ ❖

4 cups mashed potatoes
½ cup grated sharp Cheddar cheese
Fresh parsley

In a medium saucepan sauté the onion and carrots in butter just until tender. Add into the saucepan the roast beef, gravy, bouillon, parsley, spices, and seasonings; simmer for 10 minutes for flavors to combine. If the consistency is thin or soupy add a little flour to thicken. Remove the bay leaves. Divide the mixture between 4 individual casserole dishes. Spread a layer of mashed potatoes smoothly over the top of each casserole. Mark the top of the potatoes with the tines of a fork; then sprinkle with cheese. Bake in a 375° oven until hot and cheese is golden and bubbly. Garnish with fresh parsley.

Serves 4.

Pioneer Cottage

Historic Rugby
Post Office Box 8
Rugby, Tennessee 37733
(615) 628-2441
(615) 628-2269

This charming cottage, where Rugby's founder, Thomas Hughes, stayed during his first visit there, was the first frame house to be erected on the townsite in 1880. Appropriately dubbed "The Asylum," the cottage quickly became a temporary home for many incoming settlers. The dwelling was renamed Pioneer Cottage in 1883. Travelers and settlers continued to find haven there, except for brief periods when the structure was used as a temporary drugstore and later as headquarters for the Rugby Musical and Dramatic Club.

Pioneer Cottage was completely restored by Historic Rugby in 1982. Today's lodgers will find the exterior of the cottage looking much as it did 100 years ago, with the interior carefully balanced between authentic restoration and comfort. The cottage contains one bedroom on the first floor and two on the second, a large parlor, a screened back porch, fully equipped kitchen, and modern bath-and-a-half. Kitchen, bathroom, and bedroom linens are furnished. Meals can be enjoyed at the nearby Harrow Road Café, which features Cumberland Plateau home cooking and serves breakfast and lunch.

Harrow Road Café Chocolate Pound Cake

3 cups all-purpose flour
3 cups sugar
1 cup cocoa
3 teaspoons baking powder
⅛ teaspoon salt

❖ ❖ ❖

1 cup butter (2 sticks), melted
1½ cups milk
3 teaspoons vanilla extract
3 eggs
¼ cup light cream

Sift all the dry ingredients together. Make a well in center and add the butter, milk and vanilla, beat five minutes. Add the eggs, one at a time, alternating the cream, beating well after each addition. Pour the batter into a greased and floured 10-inch tube pan. Bake in a 325° oven for 1¼ hours. Cool on a rack and then remove from the pan.

Serves 16.

The Simpson Place, Inc.

Route 2, Box 165
Seymour, Tennessee 37865
(615) 453-8762

The Simpson Place offers an escape at reasonable rates for those who enjoy a quiet farmhouse away from the tourist-oriented hustle and bustle of Pigeon Forge and Gatlinburg. Four rooms, each with a private bath, are available. The Blue Ridge Mountains and the wooded countryside surround it, yet the Simpson Place is within sixty miles of all points of interest in the Great Smoky Mountain region.

Muscadine Jelly

Muscadine is a hard variety of grapes grown in the south. Cook the fruit until it is soft. Extract the juice by putting the mixture through a jelly bag. (May use 2 layers of cheesecloth.) Do not squeeze the bag so the jelly will be clear. When juice stops dripping, measure the quantity. For each cup of juice add ¾ cup of sugar. Use a deep kettle to allow for rapid boiling without stirring until it is ready to remove from the heat. As it thickens 2 large drops will form as the spoon is tilted. Time will be about 15 to 20 minutes. Pour into sterilized jars; fill within ¼-inch of the top. Seal with paraffin.

Three Fruit Marmalade

Wash 1 orange, 1 grapefruit, and 1 lemon. Cut the fruit into pieces, remove the seeds, and purée in a food processor. Measure the fruit purée, then place in a bowl. For each cup of purée add 3 cups of water. Let the mixture stand overnight.

The next day place the mixture in a saucepan and bring to a boil. Let the mixture stand again overnight.

The third day measure the mixture again. For each cup of the mixture add 1 cup of sugar. Mix well and boil over medium heat until the mixture jells. Add a few grains of salt if desired. Pour into sterile jars and seal.

Fills 4 to 5 8-ounce jars.

Pumpkin Butter

Peel a pumpkin, remove the seeds, and cut into pieces. Cook the pumpkin until tender. Drain off the liquid; mash or purée in a blender. Add equal amounts of sugar and pumpkin. Boil to desired consistency. Add pumpkin pie spices to taste; stir well. Pour into sterile jars and seal. Very good!

Corn Bread

1 cup all-purpose flour
¾ cup cornmeal
3 teaspoons baking powder
1 teaspoon salt
2 tablespoons sugar
2 eggs, beaten
1 cup milk
¼ cup oil (or melted shortening)

Mix all the ingredients and bake in well-oiled 8-inch iron skillet in a 400° oven for 20 to 25 minutes.
Serves 6 to 8.

The Flow Blue Inn: Bed and Breakfast

Box 495
Sweetwater, Tennessee 37874-0495
(615) 442-2964

A collection of Flow Blue China gives this bed and breakfast home its name. Near the Cherokee National Forest and Hiwassee College, the Flow Blue Inn displays the works of local artists for purchase. Decorated in eclectic style, it contains materials from an antebellum plantation and Victorian stained glass. Visitors sleep in brass beds and enjoy the serenity of this secluded mountain setting. Breakfast is served at guests' convenience. Pets may be accommodated on the grounds; smoking and social drinking are accepted. Complimentary wine is included.

Dr. Pedigo's Nothin' Muffins

You may substitute other fruit in season.

1 package bran muffin mix
1 egg, beaten
½ cup milk
2 tablespoons honey
1 tablespoon cinnamon
1 tablespoon ginger
1 banana, mashed

Combine all the ingredients in a mixing bowl, blend well. Pour the mixture into a well-greased muffin pan. Bake in a 450° oven for 10 to 15 minutes. Delicious!
Makes 12 muffins.

Old English Wassail

1 gallon apple cider
6 2-inch cinnamon sticks
1 tablespoon whole cloves
1 tablespoon ground allspice (or whole allspice)
2 pieces mace
1 pod red pepper
1 to 2 cups brown sugar (if you prefer it very sweet)
2 cups Bourbon or Rum (optional)

Combine all the ingredients except the Bourbon in a large saucepan. Bring to a boil and allow to simmer 30 minutes. You may add Bourbon or Rum just before serving if desired. This is great cooked in a pot over a wood stove.
Serves 30.

Ledford Mill and Museum

Route 2, Box 152
Wartrace, Tennessee 37183
(615) 298-5674

Ledford Mill was built by Sanford Ledford at the headwaters of Shippmans Creek in Moore County, Tennessee in the early 1880s and continued to be operated by his family until 1942. The forty-two-inch grindstones, powered by a water turbine, ground wheat and corn for the local population and several whiskey stills in the area.

The first renovation was completed in the early 1970s by a local businessman, and further restoration is being done by its present owners. The building is on the National and Tennessee Historic Registers. A small apartment suitable for a couple or a family of four is available for bed and breakfast accommodations.

Honey Butter

½ cup butter (1 stick), softened
⅓ cup mild flavored honey

Blend the butter and honey until smooth. Refrigerate and use as desired.
Variations: For Orange or Lemon Honey Butter: add 2 tablespoons fresh orange or lemon juice and 1 teaspoon of grated peel.
For Prune Honey Butter add ½ cup uncooked prunes, pitted and chopped.
For Cinnamon Honey Butter add 1 teaspoon cinnamon.
Makes ¾ cup of butter.

Honey Punch

1 quart cranberry juice
1 46-ounce can pineapple-
   grapefruit juice
½ cup honey

❖ ❖ ❖

1 liter ginger ale

Mix the juices and honey together and chill. Add the ginger ale just before serving. Pour over ice.
Serves 12 to 16.

Honey French Dressing

⅓ cup honey
⅓ cup oil
⅓ cup vinegar
⅓ cup catsup
½ teaspoon salt
½ teaspoon pepper
½ teaspoon celery seed
½ teaspoon paprika

Combine all the ingredients in a blender until well-blended. Serve over mixed greens or fruit.
Makes 1⅓ cups dressing.

Cranberry Corn Bread

½ cup butter (1 stick), softened
1 cup sugar
2 eggs, beaten
1 cup sour milk (or buttermilk)

❖ ❖ ❖

2 cups all-purpose flour
1 cup yellow cornmeal
4 teaspoons baking powder
½ teaspoon salt

❖ ❖ ❖

2 cups fresh cranberries, chopped

In a mixing bowl cream together the butter and sugar; add in the eggs and sour milk, mix well. Sift the dry ingredients together and add gradually to the liquid mix. Fold in the cranberries. Pour into a greased 9-inch square pan.

Bake in a 400° oven for 25 minutes or until the center springs back when pressed gently.
Serves 9 to 12.

Molasses Corn Cake

¾ cup cornmeal
1 cup all-purpose flour
3 teaspoons baking powder
¾ teaspoon salt

❖ ❖ ❖

¾ cup milk
¼ cup molasses
1 egg, well beaten
2 tablespoons melted shortening
½ to 1 cup chopped ripe peaches

Sift the dry ingredients into a mixing bowl. Add the milk, molasses, egg, shortening, and peaches; mix well. Place in a shallow buttered 8-inch square pan and bake in a 425° oven for 20 minutes.
Makes 9.

Forrest Hall Corn Sticks

¾ cup cornmeal
1 cup all-purpose flour
3 teaspoons baking powder
¾ teaspoon salt

❖ ❖ ❖

1 cup milk
1 egg, well beaten
¼ cup shortening, melted
½ cup boiling hot hominy

Sift the dry ingredients into a mixing bowl. Add the milk, egg, shortening, and hominy, mix well. Turn into buttered cornstick pans. Bake in a 350° oven for 20 minutes.
Makes 6 cornsticks.

Hush Puppies

6 cups cornmeal
4 cups all-purpose flour
3 tablespoons baking powder
3 tablespoons salt
6 tablespoons sugar
8 eggs, lightly beaten
½ cup oil
1 cup buttermilk
5 tablespoons chopped parsley
1 cup dry onion flakes

Combine all the ingredients in a large bowl. Shape into small balls and deep fry until golden brown and crusty on the outside.
Makes 35 to 50 hush puppies.

Herb Corn Bread

1⅔ cups all-purpose flour
1 tablespoon baking powder
¼ teaspoon onion salt
½ teaspoon salt
2 tablespoons sugar
¾ cup yellow cornmeal
½ teaspoon celery salt
¼ teaspoon oregano
¼ teaspoon thyme

❖ ❖ ❖

1 egg, slightly beaten
1½ cups milk
¼ cup butter (½ stick), melted

Sift the flour with baking powder, onion salt, salt, and sugar into a mixing bowl. Stir in the cornmeal, celery salt, and herbs.
Combine the egg, milk, and melted butter; add all at once to the dry ingredients. Stir until the dry ingredients are well-moistened but still lumpy. Pour into a well-greased 8-inch square baking pan, muffin pan or cornstick pan. Bake in a 425° oven for 25 to 35 minutes until the top is golden brown. Serve hot.
Serves 8.

Bobota Village Corn Bread

This is a Greek recipe.

1 cup white cornmeal
1 cup all-purpose flour
1 teaspoon baking powder
¼ teaspoon baking soda
½ teaspoon salt
¼ cup sugar

❖ ❖ ❖

3 tablespoons honey
⅓ cup orange juice
¾ cup warm water
3 tablespoons oil, heated
1 teaspoon grated orange rind
½ cup currants (or raisins)

❖ ❖ ❖

½ cup confectioners' sugar

Sift all the dry ingredients together into a large bowl. Combine the honey, orange juice, water and warm oil. Stir into the dry mixture, beating until smooth. Fold in the orange rind and currants. Pour the batter into a well-greased 7-inch square pan. Bake in a 375° oven for 35 minutes. Leave in pan to cool; sprinkle with confectioners' sugar and serve immediately.
Serves 9.

Old-Fashioned Scrapple

1 pound boneless pork, cooked and
    chopped
1 cup cornmeal
1 14½-ounce can chicken broth
¼ teaspoon thyme
¼ teaspoon salt

❖ ❖ ❖

¼ teaspoon pepper
½ cup all-purpose flour
3 tablespoons oil

In a large saucepan combine the pork, cornmeal, chicken broth, thyme, and salt. Bring to a boil, stirring often. Reduce the heat and simmer about 2 minutes or until the mixture is very thick, stirring constantly. Line an 8-inch square baking pan with waxed paper, letting the paper extend 3 to 4 inches above the top of pan. Spoon the pork mixture into the pan. Cover and chill in the refrigerator 4 hours or overnight.

Just before serving, remove the pan from the refrigerator, unmold; cut the scrapple into 12 squares. Combine the flour and pepper; dust the squares with the flour mix. In a large skillet brown the scrapple on both sides in hot oil (adding more oil if necessary).
Serves 12.

Turkey with Rice

Great for leftover turkey.

¾ cup honey
6 tablespoons prepared mustard
Salt
1½ teaspoons curry powder
6 tablespoons turkey drippings
6 cups diced cooked turkey

❖ ❖ ❖

3 cups cooked rice

In a saucepan mix the honey, mustard, salt, curry powder, and drippings thoroughly. Combine lightly with diced turkey and heat, stirring lightly. Serve over hot cooked rice.
Serves 8.

Ham Hocks and Black-Eyed Peas

3 cups dried black-eyed peas
12 cups water
3 pounds smoked ham hocks
1¼ cups chopped onion
1 cup chopped celery
1 teaspoon salt
⅛ teaspoon cayenne pepper
1 bay leaf
1 10-ounce package frozen cut okra

Rinse the peas. In a 6-quart Dutch oven, combine the water and peas. Bring to a boil and simmer 2 minutes. Remove from the heat; cover and let stand for 1 hour. (Or combine the water and peas and soak overnight.)

Return the Dutch oven to the heat; do not drain. Stir in the hocks, onion, celery, salt, cayenne pepper, and bay leaf. Bring to a boil. Cover, simmer until the hocks are tender and the beans are done, about 1½ hours. Stir in the okra; cook until tender, from 10 to 15 minutes. Discard the bay leaf. Season to taste. Serve with onions and cornbread.
Serves 6.

Hopping John

1 cup black-eyed peas
8 cups water

❖ ❖ ❖

6 slices bacon
¾ cup chopped onion
1 clove garlic, minced

❖ ❖ ❖

1 cup rice
2 teaspoons salt
¼ teaspoon pepper

Rinse the black-eyed peas. In a large saucepan combine the peas and water; bring to a boil, then boil for 2 minutes. Remove from the heat and let stand for 1 hour. Drain, reserving 6 cups of the cooking liquid.

In a heavy 3-quart saucepan, cook the bacon, onion, and garlic until the bacon is crisp and the onion is tender but not brown. Remove the bacon; drain on paper towels; crumble and set aside.

Stir the black-eyed peas, rice, salt, pepper, and the reserved cooking liquid into the mixture in the saucepan. Bring to a boil; cover and reduce the heat. Simmer 1 hour, stirring occasionally. Stir in crumbled bacon. Turn into a serving bowl. Serve immediately. Serve with onions and cornbread.
Serves 8.

Carrots in Honey Sauce

½ teaspoon salt
1 cup water
12 medium carrots, sliced

❖ ❖ ❖

⅓ cup honey
1 teaspoon lemon juice
2 tablespoons oil

Combine the salt and water in a saucepan; heat to boiling. Add the carrots; continue to boil for 5 minutes, then reduce the heat. Cover and cook until tender, 12 to 15 minutes; then drain. Cook and stir the remaining ingredients in a skillet until bubbly; add the carrots. Cook 2 to 3 minutes uncovered over low heat, stirring occasionally, until the carrots are glazed.

Serves 6.

Corn Meal Cookies

1 cup butter (2 sticks), softened
1 cup sugar
2 egg yolks
1 teaspoon grated lemon peel
1½ cups all-purpose flour
1 cup yellow corn meal

❖ ❖ ❖

Sugar for topping

Place the butter and 1 cup of sugar in a medium-sized mixing bowl and beat with an electric mixer until lighter in color and well blended. Add the egg yolks and mix well. Stir in the lemon peel, flour and corn meal; mix well. Wrap the dough in a plastic bag and chill 3 to 4 hours until firm.

Roll out the dough on a very lightly-floured surface or between sheets of waxed paper to ¼-inch thickness. Cut into heart shapes, using 2½-inch cutter. Place on an ungreased baking sheet and sprinkle with additional sugar. Bake in center of a 350° oven about 8 to 10 minutes until edges are browned. (Or the dough may be rolled into a 2-inch cylinder before chilling and cut into rounds about ¼-inch thick before baking.)

Makes 2½ dozen cookies.

Healthy Oatmeal Cookies

2 cups rolled oats
½ cup nonfat dry milk
½ cup wheat germ (optional)
½ teaspoon salt
¼ teaspoon cloves
1 teaspoon cinnamon
½ cup dried fruit
½ cup unsweetened coconut
½ cup nuts, chopped

❖ ❖ ❖

2 eggs
½ cup oil
½ cup honey

In a mixing bowl combine the dry ingredients, fruit, and nuts; stir to mix. In a separate bowl beat the eggs; add oil and honey, mix well. Add to the dry ingredients, stir until thoroughly blended. Drop by teaspoonfuls onto a greased cookie sheet. Bake in a 300° oven for about 20 minutes.

Makes 1½ dozen cookies.

Gingerbread

2¾ cups all-purpose flour
1 teaspoon baking soda
1 teaspoon salt
2 teaspoons baking powder
1 teaspoon ginger
1 teaspoon cinnamon

❖ ❖ ❖

1 egg, beaten
1 cup oil
¾ cup honey
¾ cup molasses
1 cup buttermilk
1 cup raisins

Sift flour, soda, salt, baking powder, and spices together, set aside. In a mixing bowl cream the egg and oil together. Add the honey in a fine stream, beating constantly. Add molasses, beating constantly. Add the dry ingredients alternately with buttermilk, beating until smooth after each addition. Add the raisins. Pour into 2 well-greased loaf pans or one 13x9-inch pan. Bake in a 325° oven for 30 to 50 minutes or until the cake tests done. Cool for 5 minutes, then turn onto wire racks and cool. Serve with whipped cream.

Makes 2 loaves.

Texas

The Hotel Jefferson Historic Inn

124 West Austin
Jefferson, Texas 75657
(214) 665-2631

The Hotel Jefferson is in the heart of Jefferson's riverfront district, which is within walking distance of many of Jefferson's fine antique shops, restaurants, museums, and gift shops. The building was erected in 1851 for use as a cotton warehouse when Jefferson was a large inland port and the building was on the riverfront. Since then the building has been used as a livery stable, skating rink, concert hall, saloon, and hotel with a restaurant. The Hotel Jefferson offers fine, old-world accommodations with private baths and antiques, combined with modern conveniences.

A Preacher's Julep

2 cups green mint, slashed or chopped
2 cups sugar
2 lemons
1 quart water

Place the chopped mint in a large stew pan. Peel the lemons and shred the rind; sprinkle over the mint. Place the sugar and water in stew pan; add the juice of both lemons and bring to a boil. Remove from the heat and pour over the mint and lemon rinds. Cover the mint and let stand until cool. When cool, use a potato masher to press more mint into the juice. Strain off the juice. There should be 1 quart. Place in the refrigerator and add to tea in equal parts as needed. Serve with a cherry and a sprig of mint.

Makes 1 quart.

Tanya's Mayonnaise Rolls

1 cup self-rising flour
½ cup milk or buttermilk
1 heaping tablespoon mayonnaise
Dash salt

Mix the flour, milk, mayonnaise and salt. Pour into greased muffin cups and bake in a 400° oven for 15 to 20 minutes or until brown.

Make 6 rolls.

The Black Swan House Dressing

These recipes are from the Black Swan Restaurant, down the street from the Hotel Jefferson. The Black Swan specializes in Cajun cuisine, and dining is a treat.

2 cloves garlic, crushed
2 tablespoons sugar
½ teaspoon dry mustard
1½ teaspoons salt
4 tablespoons sour cream
5 tablespoons red wine vinegar
1 cup oil
2 tablespoons chopped parsley
Coarsely ground pepper to taste

In a food processor place the garlic, sugar, mustard, salt and sour cream. Add the vinegar. Blend on continuous speed. In a thin stream, slowly add oil. When blended, fold in the parsley and pepper.

Makes 2½ cups of dressing.

Cajun Shrimp Scampi

1½ cups margarine (3 sticks)
1 teaspoon minced garlic
1 teaspoon salt
1 teaspoon cayenne pepper
½ teaspoon white pepper
1 teaspoon black pepper
½ teaspoon thyme
1 teaspoon basil
¾ cup white wine
1 cup chopped green onions
½ pound crabmeat, picked over
1 pound shrimp, peeled and deveined

In a medium saucepan melt the margarine and add the garlic and all of the spices. Cook until the margarine starts bubbling. Add the wine, green onions, crabmeat and shrimp. Cook until the shrimp turns pink. Do not overcook.

Serves 4 to 6.

New Orleans-Style Bread Pudding

6 eggs
2½ cups sugar
1 tablespoon cinnamon
1 tablespoon nutmeg
1 tablespoon vanilla extract
½ cup melted margarine
1 quart milk
6 cups bread crumbs (preferably French bread)
1 cup chopped pecans
1 cup raisins

❖ ❖ ❖

2 cups confectioners' sugar
2 tablespoons evaporated milk (or whole milk)
2 tablespoons rum

Whip the eggs until frothy. Add the sugar, spices, vanilla, and margarine; mix well. Add the milk and bread crumbs. Mix and let soak for 15 minutes. Add the pecans and raisins. Pour into a greased pan. Bake in a 350° oven for 45 minutes or until set.

Mix together the confectioners' sugar, 2 tablespoons of milk, and the rum. Serve over hot bread pudding.
Serves 6 to 8.

Sam's Sawdust Pie

"This is Sam Litzenberg's recipe. Sam has a restaurant in Marshall, Texas, called The Hungry Potter. The restaurant is next door to the Marshall Pottery."

1½ cups sugar
1½ cups graham cracker crumbs
1½ cups coconut
1½ cups chopped nuts (pecans are best)
½ cup chocolate chips
7 egg whites

❖ ❖ ❖

Pastry for 1 9-inch 1-crust pie

Mix all ingredients and turn into the unbaked pie shell. Bake in a 350° oven for 35 minutes or until the center is firm. Don't cut until cool.
Serves 6.

Wise Manor

312 Houston Street
Jefferson, Texas 75657

Wise Manor is a quiet retreat in a Victorian home that houses family antiques of three generations. Rates are reasonable. Breakfast is continental (at a modest extra charge), or reservations can be made at the second oldest hotel in Texas, the Excelsior House, for a sumptuous plantation breakfast.

Apricot-Nut Bread

1½ cups dried apricots
½ cup butter (1 stick)
1 cup sugar
2 eggs
¾ cup orange juice
2 cups sifted all-purpose flour
3 teaspoons baking powder
¼ teaspoon baking soda
¾ teaspoon salt
1 teaspoon grated orange rind
1 cup chopped nuts

Soak the apricots in water for 30 minutes; drain and chop. Cream the butter and sugar. Beat the eggs and add alternately with the orange juice. Add the dry ingredients, apricots, orange rind, and nuts. Pour into a lined 9x5-inch loaf pan. Bake in a 350° oven for 1½ hours. This is delicious toasted, buttered, and served with coffee.
Serves 10 to 12.

La Borde House

601 East Main Street
Rio Grande City, Texas 78582
(512) 487-5101

The La Borde House Hotel was built 1877–98 by Francois La Borde. Com-

pletely renovated and brought up-to-date in recent years, the hotel has retained the original balconies, trim, and color. Its nine rooms are furnished with original Victorian furniture, as is the large parlor. The rear building contains thirteen efficiency apartments. The decor of the restaurant is in keeping with the Victorian atmosphere.

Guacamole with Shrimp

1 pound shrimp (about 24 per pound)
Juice of 1 lemon
2 teaspoons salt
Pinch thyme
4 ripe avocados
¾ cup lime juice
1 clove garlic, crushed
Pinch cayenne pepper
4 small peppers, peeled, seeded and diced
Corn or tostado chips

Shell and devein the shrimp; leave the tails intact. Bring 2 quarts of water to a boil, add the lemon juice, salt and thyme. Add the shrimp and simmer for 5 minutes. Remove from heat and let cool in cooking liquid. Drain and refrigerate. Halve the avocados lengthwise and remove the pits. Scoop out the pulp, being careful to reserve the shell halves intact. Mash the avocados coarsely with the lime juice. Stir in the remaining ingredients except the corn chips. Pile the mixture into the reserved shells and embed the shrimp, tails out, in guacamole. Serve on 1 plate on a lettuce bed and surround with corn chips. Can be made ahead, covered with plastic wrap, refrigerated.
Serves 8.

Gazpacho
(Cold Spanish Soup)

3 cups tomato juice
3 tablespoons wine vinegar

½ cup olive oil
3 garlic cloves, crushed
1 tablespoon salt
3 medium onions, peeled and
    chopped
3 large cucumbers, peeled and
    chopped
3 peppers, seeded and quartered
3 teaspoons minced fresh cilantro
Pepper to taste

❖   ❖   ❖

Sour cream

Place the tomato juice, wine vinegar, olive oil, garlic, salt, and onion in a blender or food processor and mix for a few seconds. Add the remaining ingredients except sour cream and blend until a smooth texture is obtained, do not overblend. Season with fresh ground pepper. Chill before serving. Serve in a goblet with a dollop of sour cream.
Serves 24.

Chicken Cilantro

12 chicken breasts, boned and
    skinned
1 cup butter or margarine (2 sticks)
½ cup oil
6 large cloves garlic, minced
3 medium onions, chopped
1 cup chopped cilantro
½ cup lemon juice
Salt and pepper to taste
Hot cooked rice

Cut the chicken into ¼-inch pieces. In a large frying pan melt the butter; add the onions, garlic, cilantro, lemon juice and sauté until the onion is tender. Add cut up chicken, salt, and pepper; cook for about 5 minutes or until the chicken is done. Pour over about 6 cups of steamed rice.
Serves 12.

Mexican Stuffed Chicken Breasts

7 boneless chicken breasts, halved
1 27-ounce can green chile strips
16 ounces Monterey Jack cheese,
    shredded

2 eggs, beaten
Bread crumbs
Chopped tomatoes

Pound the chicken breasts very thin with a mallet. Place 1 ounce of chile strips on each breast. Sprinkle Monterey Jack cheese over the chile strips. Fold ⅓ of the breast over the chile and cheese, then fold the other ⅓ over. Double-bread the chicken breasts, dipping in the beaten egg and bread crumbs. Let sit for 10 minutes.

Deep fry the chicken breasts for 5 minutes, turning to insure even browning. Place on serving plates and sprinkle with Monterey Jack cheese and chopped tomatoes. Serve with rice and a vegetable.
Serves 14.

Flan Carmelisado
(Custard with Caramel Topping)

1 cup sugar
12 eggs
2 cups sugar
7 cups milk
2 cinnamon sticks
2 teaspoons vanilla extract

In a large skillet caramelize 1 cup of sugar over medium heat, stirring constantly until the sugar is melted and browned. Pour immediately into the bottoms of 12 buttered custard cups. Beat the eggs until foamy; gradually add the remaining sugar, beating well after each addition. Heat the milk with the cinnamon sticks over medium high heat to just below boiling. Add the milk to the egg mixture, stirring until the sugar is dissolved. Strain the egg mixture; add the vanilla. Pour into the caramel-lined cups. Set the cups in a pan of hot water. Bake in a 350° oven for 1 hour and 10 minutes or until a knife inserted comes out clean. Serve warm. Butterscotch or caramel topping can be substituted.
Serves 12.

Menger Hotel

204 Alamo Plaza
Post Office Box 1399
San Antonio, Texas 78295
(512) 223-4361

San Antonio's historic Menger Hotel has been in continuous operation across Crockett Street from the Alamo since 1859, just twenty-three years after the battle that turned a mission into the shrine of Texas liberty. The original structure has been restored, and in recent years modern additions and facilities have been added while preserving the traditional atmosphere. Among the rooms and suites of the original wing of the Menger are authentically restored nineteenth century accommodations furnished with priceless antiques. The new, attached Motor Inn features oversized guest rooms with double-double beds, color television, and free in-room movies. Some rooms have private balconies overlooking the tropical pool and patio area; others overlook the Alamo. Room service dining is a Menger tradition. The Patio Room overlooks the swimming pool area; it is open for lunch and dinner in an atmosphere of casual elegance. Easy listening music for dancing accompanies evening cocktails and dining.

Art Abbott's Cheese Soup

1 cup finely diced celery
1 cup finely diced carrots
½ cup diced onions
3 tablespoons butter
3 tablespoons all-purpose flour
½ tablespoon salt
1 teaspoon All-N-One seasoning
1 quart chicken broth
2 cups milk
1 cup diced American cheese

In a saucepan sauté the celery, carrots, onions, and butter over low heat until the vegetables are soft. Be very careful not to scorch. Add the flour, salt, and seasoning; stir well. Blend in the broth, milk, and cheese. Stir until the cheese is melted. If the soup is too thick, add more milk or broth. This soup is very good reheated.

Serves 6 to 8.

Menger Hotel Spinach Pudding

3 cups cooked spinach
½ small onion
½ green pepper
1½ cloves garlic
4 eggs
1 teaspoon salt
¼ teaspoon pepper
Dash nutmeg
2 cups finely ground bread crumbs (no crusts)
½ cup softened butter (1 stick)

Put the spinach, onion, green pepper, and garlic through a grinder, using a fine blade. Add the eggs and seasonings; mix well. Mix in 1½ cups of the crumbs. Spread the butter onto a clean dish towel, forming a 9- to 10-inch square. Sprinkle with the remaining bread crumbs. Drop the spinach mixture into the center and form into a roll about 1½ inches thick. Wrap the cloth loosely around the roll. Tie ends and middle securely with string. Steam for 20 minutes.

Serves 10 to 12.

Weimar Country Inn

101 Jackson
Post Office Box 782
Weimar, Texas 78962
(409) 725-8888

For over 100 years, Weimar Country Inn has provided comfortable lodging and country cooking for travelers. Located midway between Houston and San Antonio, it is ideal for honeymoons, historic excursions, corporate meetings, or relaxing. Nine rooms with authentic Texas decor welcome the inn's guests. The rooms boast Texas names, Victorian antiques, and handmade quilts. Guests awaken to a complementary continental breakfast of coffee, juice, and home-baked kolaches served in the upstairs parlor.

Poppy Seed Dressing

1½ cups sugar
2 teaspoons dry mustard
2 teaspoons salt
⅔ cup vinegar
3 tablespoons onion juice or minced onion
2 cups oil
3 tablespoons poppy seeds
¼ teaspoon garlic powder

Mix the sugar, mustard, salt, and vinegar. Add the onion juice and stir it in well; add the oil, stirring constantly, and continue to beat until thick. Add the poppy seeds and beat for a few minutes. Store in the refrigerator. If the dressing is too thick, add more oil and vinegar.

Note: Add grenadine to prepared mixture to make it a beautiful rose color to top off a fruit salad, chicken salad, or a lettuce salad.

Makes 3½ cups dressing.

Teriyaki Chicken Sauce

½ cup soy sauce
¼ cup oil
1 tablespoon brown sugar
1 tablespoon Sherry (optional)
1 teaspoon garlic powder
½ teaspoon ginger

Mix thoroughly. Dip chicken in mixture and cook on a grill. Do not soak the chicken in the sauce. Use the remainder of the sauce on top of the cooked chicken. Best when served with white rice.

Serves 4.

Weimar Country Inn

Utah

The Center Street Bed and Breakfast Inn

169 East Center
Logan, Utah 84321
(801) 752-3443

The Center Street Bed and Breakfast in the heart of Cache Valley is a 107-year-old Victorian inn with ten guest rooms. Four are in the main house and six are in the old carriage house. Those in the main house are elegant suites used for special occasions or for a night away from home. All of these rooms have private baths, televisions, and VCRs; and breakfast is served in the room by the staff wearing nineteenth century dress. The Blue Room is furnished with 100-year-old antiques. The Garden Suite provides flowers, ruffles, and a heart-shaped Jacuzzi. The Jungle Bungalow is complete with a waterfall, environmental sounds, and Jacuzzi. And The Desert Oasis has a sultan's tent over a king-size bed, a ceramic camel, and a clear panel for gazing at the stars. Area interests include water and snow skiing, fishing, and beautiful scenery. A continental-plus breakfast is served daily.

Ann's Homemade Bread

⅔ cup milk
¼ cup butter (½ stick)
❖ ❖ ❖
2 cups warm water
¼ cup sugar
1 ¼-ounce package active dry yeast
1 tablespoon salt
4 cups all-purpose flour
2 cups wheat flour

Warm the milk and butter together. In a large bowl combine the water, sugar, yeast, salt, and milk mixture. Add the flours. Knead until smooth and elastic, adding as little additional flour as possible. Let rise until doubled; punch down. Let rise until doubled again. Form into 2 loaves and place in greased loaf pans. Bake in a 350° oven for 50 minutes.

Makes 2 loaves.

Peterson's Bed and Breakfast

95 North 300 West
Monroe, Utah 84754
(801) 527-4830

Situated in rural south-central Utah, Peterson's Bed and Breakfast is near five national parks and four national forests. It is also near the new Fremont Indian Museum and Park. It has a suite of two rooms with a private bath, and a third room with a private bath.

Danish Peach Fritters

This is a very old Danish recipe.

1 cup all-purpose flour
1½ teaspoons baking powder
¼ teaspoon salt
2 tablespoons sugar
❖ ❖ ❖
1 egg
⅓ cup milk
1 tablespoon shortening, melted
8 canned peach halves
Sugar

Sift the flour; add the baking powder, salt, and sugar. Beat the egg and milk together. Add the dry ingredients and mix well. Add the shortening and mix well. Dip the peach halves into the batter and brown in oil in a shallow pan. Sprinkle with sugar and serve warm.

Makes 8 fritters.

The Old Miners' Lodge

615 Woodside Avenue
Post Office Box 2639
Park City, Utah 84060-2639
(801) 645-8068

The Old Miners' Lodge is a restored 1893 building in the National Historic District of the colorful resort town of Park City. It was built as housing for local miners seeking their fortunes from the surrounding ore-rich hills. Now its rooms have been named after some of these colorful personalities and restored to the furnishings of their time. Guests begin each morning with a hearty country-style breakfast. In the evening the large living room becomes a gathering place for guests, and complimentary refreshments are served. A revitalizing outdoor hot tub welcomes everyone back after a satisfying day outdoors. The area provides year-round recreation to its visitors, such as skiing, snowmobiling, hot air ballooning, golf, tennis, hiking, and horseback riding.

The Old Miner's Lodge

Mary's German Pancake

3 eggs
¾ cup milk
¾ cup all-purpose flour
Pinch salt

❖ ❖ ❖

2 tablespoons butter, melted
Lemon juice (real or reconstituted)
Filling (applesauce or any fresh berries, mashed)
Cinnamon sugar

Place approximately ¹/₈-inch of oil (enough to just cover the bottom of pan) in an 8-inch cast-iron frying pan. Place the pan in the oven to get hot. In a blender combine the eggs and milk; mix. Add the flour and salt; mix. Remove the pan from the oven and gently pour the mixture into the hot pan. Bake for about 20 minutes, until the pancake rises and browns.

When the pancake is done, remove from the pan and place on a plate. Allow the pancake to fall. Pour a small amount of lemon juice and butter over the top. Cover with filling. Sprinkle with cinnamon sugar. Roll the pancake up. Butter the top and sprinkle with cinnamon sugar. Slice into pieces.

Note: The pancake rises best if the milk and eggs are at room temperature.

Serves 2 to 4.

The Washington School Inn

543 Park Avenue
Park City, Utah 84060
(800) 824-1672
(800) 824-4761 (In Utah)

Open year round, the Washington School Inn was built in 1889 and is on the National Register of Historic Places. It has twelve guest rooms, all with private baths, and three suites. On the first level are a whirlpool spa, dry sauna, and ski lockers and changing rooms. A large living room with fireplace and an elegant dining room are attractive to guests year round.

Kona Banana Bread or Muffins

½ cup margarine (1 stick)
1 cup sugar
2 eggs
¾ cup mashed very ripe bananas

❖ ❖ ❖

1¼ cups all-purpose flour
¾ teaspoon baking soda
½ teaspoon salt

Cream the margarine and sugar until light. Add the eggs, one at a time, beating well after each addition. Stir in the banana. Sift together the dry ingredients and add to the banana mixture. Mix until well-blended. Pour into a greased loaf pan. Bake in a 350° oven for 30 to 35 minutes.

For muffins, pour into a greased muffin pan and bake in a 375° oven for 20 to 25 minutes.

Makes 1 loaf or 12 muffins.

Chez Fontaine

45 North 300 East
Provo, Utah 84601
(801) 375-8484

Provo's Chez Fontaine Bed and Breakfast is in the heart of Mormon Country. Just blocks from Brigham Young University, the inn offers home accommodations to visitors. Guests are invited to relax on the porch or enjoy lawn games near the fish pool and fountain, from which the inn takes its name. Guests can also enjoy games in the parlor or retire to spacious rooms filled with Mormon pioneer furniture. Refreshments are placed in guest rooms each evening; they might include fresh fruit and cheese, homemade cookies, or fruit breads, along with hot or iced beverage.

Dorothy's Chocolate Zucchini Cake

½ cup margarine (1 stick)
½ cup oil
1¾ cups sugar
2 eggs
1 teaspoon vanilla extract
½ cup sour milk

❖ ❖ ❖

½ teaspoon cinnamon
½ teaspoon cloves
2½ cups all-purpose flour
¼ cup cocoa
½ teaspoon baking powder
1 teaspoon baking soda

❖ ❖ ❖

2 cups finely diced zucchini
¼ cup chocolate chips

Cream the butter, oil, and sugar. Beat in the eggs. Add the vanilla and sour milk. In a separate bowl mix the dry ingredients; add to the wet ingredients in small amounts. Lightly mix in the zucchini and chocolate chips. Pour into a 9-inch square pan. Bake in a 325° oven for 40 to 50 minutes.

Serves 12 to 16.

Dorothy's Blitz Torte

½ cup sugar
½ cup margarine (1 stick)
1 tablespoon milk or water
1 tablespoon vanilla extract
4 egg yolks
1 cup all-purpose flour
1 teaspoon baking powder

❖ ❖ ❖

4 egg whites
1 cup sugar
1 teaspoon vanilla extract
Chopped nuts

❖ ❖ ❖

⅔ cup sugar
Juice and grated rind of 1 lemon
1 large or 2 small eggs, slightly beaten
½ pint whipping cream, whipped

Cream ½ cup of sugar and the margarine together, adding the sugar in small quantities. Add the milk, 1 tablespoon of vanilla, and the egg yolks. Add the flour and baking powder and pour into 2 greased 9-inch cake pans that have tabs to loosen the bottoms, or are lined with waxed paper.

Beat the egg whites until stiff. Add 1 cup of sugar and 1 teaspoon of vanilla. Pour over the batter. Sprinkle a few chopped nuts on the batter. Bake in a 300° oven for 30 minutes.

In a double boiler mix ⅔ cup of sugar, the lemon juice, rind, and eggs. Cook until the mixture thickens somewhat. Cool. Fold in the whipped cream. Spread this filling between layers of cake. Refrigerate. May be made 1 day in advance and refrigerated.

Serves 12 to 16.

Seven Wives Inn

217 North 100 West
Saint George, Utah 84770
(801) 628-3737

Along the walking tour of St. George, just across from the Brigham Young home and two blocks from the historic Washington County Court House, lies Seven Wives Inn, southern Utah's first bed and breakfast inn. The inn offers traditional hospitality in delightful surroundings. Each bedroom is named after one of the seven wives of the late B. F. Johnson, who spent considerable time in the St. George area. A gourmet breakfast is served each morning in the elegant dining room. A swimming pool is on the premises.

Sausage en Croute

3 or 4 green onions, chopped
5 or 6 large mushrooms, sliced
1 pound regular sausage

❖ ❖ ❖

¾ cup cottage cheese
½ cup butter (1 stick), room temperature
1 cup flour

❖ ❖ ❖

3 ounces grated Monterey Jack cheese

Sauté the onions and mushrooms in a little butter. In a separate skillet fry the sausage until no longer pink. Drain. Refrigerate in separate containers until morning.

In a food processor whip the cottage cheese until fluffy. Add the butter and pulse until only small chunks are visible. Add the flour and blend until a dough forms. Turn out onto plastic wrap, forming a ball. Refrigerate until firm, preferably overnight.

In the morning roll out the dough into about a 12x18-inch rectangle. Add the sausage down the center; top with the onion-mushroom mixture, then the grated cheese. Slash the protruding crust about 6 times each side and lap over the filling by sections, one side and then the other. Place on a cookie sheet. Bake in a 350° oven for 30 minutes or until browned. May be made ahead and frozen. Allow longer baking time from frozen state.

Serves 6 to 8.

Whipped Cream Pecan Cinnamon Rolls

This recipe belonged to the innkeeper's grandmother.

    1 cup whipping cream
    1½ cups all-purpose flour
    4 teaspoons baking powder
    ¾ teaspoon salt
    2 tablespoons butter, melted
    Cinnamon and sugar

         ❖ ❖ ❖

    ½ cup light brown sugar, firmly
        packed
    ½ cup pecans, chopped
    2 tablespoons whipping cream (or
        evaporated milk)

In a medium mixing bowl whip the cream. Add the flour, baking powder and salt. Blend with a fork until a dough forms. Knead slightly. Roll out on a floured board into a ¼-inch thick rectangle. With a pastry brush, spread melted butter over the entire surface. Sprinkle sugar and cinnamon over the dough. Roll up like a jelly roll; cut into ¾-inch segments. Bake in a 425° oven until very lightly browned.

In a small bowl mix the brown sugar, pecans, and 2 tablespoons whipping cream until well-blended. Remove the rolls from the oven. Spread the topping on each roll. Return to the oven and bake until the topping starts to bubble.

Makes 12 to 15 rolls.

Surprise Soufflé

    6 eggs, separated
    1 cup heavy cream
    1 cup grated Swiss cheese
    2 cups cooked rice
    ½ teaspoon salt
    ⅛ teaspoon white pepper
    4 slices bacon, cooked and
        crumbled
    4 green onions with greens,
        chopped and sautéed

Beat the egg whites until stiff; set aside. Beat the egg yolks slightly; add the cream, Swiss cheese, rice, salt, pepper, bacon, and onions. Fold in the beaten egg whites. Pour into a greased soufflé dish. Bake in a 350° oven for about 45 minutes or until set.

Serves 6 to 8.

Fudge

    1 12-ounce package semi-sweet
        chocolate chips
    1 can sweetened condensed milk
    3 tablespoons butter
    ½ teaspoon vanilla extract
    1 cup walnuts

In the top of a double boiler melt the chocolate chips with the sweetened condensed milk. Stir to blend smooth when melted. Turn off the heat. Add the butter. When melted, blend in together with the vanilla and walnuts. Cool slightly. Turn out into an 8x8-inch pan, which has been lined with waxed paper. Refrigerate. When cool, cut in squares. Store in the refrigerator or wrap the fudge if setting out for any length of time.

Makes 24 squares.

The Eller Bed and Breakfast

164 South 900 East
Salt Lake City, Utah 84102
(801) 533-8184

The Eller Bed and Breakfast became known locally as the "Fortunato Anselmo Home" when it was the residence of Italy's vice consul for Utah and Wyoming from 1920 until 1950. Built in 1903, it is close to downtown Salt Lake City, historic Temple Square, the genealogy library, and the University of Utah. Newly refurbished, it serves breakfast family-style on a large oak table in the dining room.

Seven Wives Inn

Anselmo Inn Cinnamon Bread

1½ cups milk
6 tablespoons sugar
1¾ teaspoons salt
3 cups all-purpose flour
2 eggs
1 2-ounce cake compressed yeast
1½ cups warm water (85°)
3 cups all-purpose flour
Cinnamon and sugar
Nuts

Scald the milk, sugar, and salt. Cool. Add 3 cups of flour and the eggs. Dissolve the yeast in the warm water and add to the milk mixture. Let rise for 30 minutes. Add 3 cups of flour and let rise again. Roll into balls and dip in melted butter. Roll in the cinnamon and sugar mixture, and roll in crushed nuts. Fill an angel food cake pan ⅔ full. Bake in a 350° oven for 1 hour.
Serves 12.

Guest Pleasin' Abelskivers

3 eggs, separated
2 cups buttermilk
2 cups all-purpose flour
3 tablespoons sugar
1 teaspoon baking soda
½ teaspoon salt
1 teaspoon baking powder
Shortening

Beat the egg yolks and add the buttermilk. Add the dry ingredients gradually, beating well. Beat the egg whites until stiff and fold them into the other mixture. Melt ¼ teaspoon shortening in each cup of an abelskiver pan and fill each with batter. Cook until bubbly, then turn with a sharp instrument (we use an ice pick). Keep rotating it until the toothpick test shows they are fully cooked. Serve with preserves, syrup or honey butter. You may also cook with pieces of apple, whole-kernel corn or other fillings in the middle. Simply add the filling before you turn it for the first time.
Makes 2 dozen abelskivers.

Salt Lake City Taffy

This is a family activity in which guests are invited to participate.

4 cups sugar
1 cup white cider vinegar
3 cups water
2 teaspoons vanilla extract

In a heavy saucepan stir the sugar, vinegar and water together well.

Cook over high heat, stirring only once or twice until it starts boiling. Cook to 256°. Take off the stove. Add the vanilla, but do not stir. Pour on a cold greased cookie sheet. Let it cool, but stretch it as soon as possible (grease your fingers well). Lay strips of well-stretched taffy on a cabinet covered with waxed paper. Mark and cut, using cold knives. Wrap in small pieces of waxed paper.
Makes 3 to 4 dozen pieces of taffy.

Divinity-Peanut Roll

A nightstand treat.

2½ cups sugar
½ cup light corn syrup
½ cup cold water
¼ teaspoon salt
2 egg whites, beaten stiff
1 teaspoon vanilla extract

❖ ❖ ❖

1 cup or more peanut butter
1 cup chopped walnuts

Cook the sugar, corn syrup, water, and salt until a small amount dropped in cold water forms a soft ball or the syrup is at 242° on a candy thermometer. Pour the hot syrup slowly into the beaten egg whites. Continue beating until it begins to lose its gloss and holds soft peaks. Stir in the vanilla. Spoon onto 2 greased strips of 20-inch wide waxed paper. Butter hands or spoon; flatten the divinity to 16x8-inches each. Melt the peanut butter. Spread on the divinity. Roll up as with a jelly roll. Roll in walnuts. Cut in ½-inch slices. This is easier to make if two people work together on it.
Makes 5 dozen slices.

Sundance

Post Office Box A-1
Sundance, Utah 84604
(801) 225-4107

Sundance, the home of Robert Redford's Sundance Institute and Institute for Resource Management, is a town where one can hike the nature trail, browse through the general store, and spend an evening at the summer theater. Inns throughout the canyon are available, and there are two good restaurants in town, the Tree Room and the Grill Room.

Honey Pecan Chicken

2 cups butter (4 sticks)
2 cups honey
½ cup lemon juice (preferably fresh)
1 cup chopped pecans (set aside a few halves for garnish)
Chicken breasts

Combine the butter, honey, lemon juice, and pecans in a saucepan. Simmer over medium heat for 35 to 45 minutes or until the sauce is thickened like a caramel sauce. Charbroil boneless, skinned chicken breasts. Pour enough sauce over the chicken to cover. Garnish with pecan halves.
Makes 1 quart.

Roasted Breast of Pheasant

2 fresh pheasants
Salt and pepper
½ cup coarsely chopped onion
½ cup coarsely chopped celery
½ cup coarsely chopped carrot
¼ cup minced shallot
1 cup champagne vinegar
2 cups Chardonnay wine
4 cups pheasant stock (or other poultry stock)
½ cup heavy cream
Olive oil
Roasted pine nuts
Spiced Cranberry Apple Chutney

Bone the breast and thigh meat of pheasants. Set aside bones, the breast and thigh meat. Place the bones and excess fat in roasting pan; sprinkle with salt and pepper. Mix in the chopped onion, celery, carrots. Roast in a 350° oven for 1 hour or until nicely browned.

Place the bones in a stock pot, cover with water. Simmer for 3 hours; strain and set aside. There should be 4 cups of pheasant stock (can be made a day or two ahead). In a heavy saucepan place the shallots, champagne vinegar, and Chardonnay. Over medium heat reduce until almost all is evaporated; do not scorch. Add the pheasant stock and cook until reduced by ½. Add the heavy cream and reduce until the sauce is thick and creamy, about 20 minutes.

To cook the pheasant pieces, lightly rub each piece with olive oil. Charbroil skin side down and turn to finish browning until done. Slice the meat on an angle.

Spoon some sauce on each serving plate and arrange the slices on the sauce. Sprinkle with roasted pine nuts. Serve with Spiced Cranberry Apple Chutney.

Serves 4 to 6.

Spiced Cranberry Apple Chutney

1 pound fresh cranberries
1 cup water
1 cup sugar

❖   ❖   ❖

2 green apples
¼ cup Cabernet wine vinegar
2 tablespoons lemon juice
⅓ cup sugar
1 tablespoon cinnamon
½ teaspoon cloves
1 tablespoon freshly grated ginger
½ cup chopped walnuts

In a saucepan combine the cranberries with the water and 1 cup of sugar. Bring to a boil; simmer for 10 minutes. Peel, core, and cube the apples. Place in another saucepan with the wine vinegar, lemon juice, ⅓ cup of sugar, cinnamon, cloves, ginger, and walnuts; lightly cook until the apples are soft. Add to the cranberry mixture. Cool and refrigerate.

Makes 4 cups of chutney.

Hill Farm Inn

R.R. 2, Box 2015
Arlington, Vermont 05250
(802) 375-2269

Hill Farm Inn is a country inn in the true sense of the word. Surrounded by neighboring farms, it is set on two and one-half acres of lawns and gardens. Spectacular views in every direction make the setting unsurpassed for artists and photographers, as well as for those just seeking a tranquil, scenic vacation spot. The main inn has six guest rooms on the second floor, and the 1790 guest house next door has five guest rooms. Five of the eleven rooms have private baths. All rooms are spacious and comfortable, and many have beautiful views of the mountains. Dur-

ing the summer and fall months, several cabins are available, each with full bath. The common rooms are used by guests, whether visiting with new friends around the living room fireplace, doing puzzles and playing table games in the dining room, or dining in front of its antique fireplace.

Spaghetti Squash Primavera

1 medium spaghetti squash

❖ ❖ ❖

6 to 8 large tomatoes, cut up
1 large onion, coarsely chopped
2 teaspoons marjoram
2 teaspoons basil
2 cloves garlic, crushed

❖ ❖ ❖

Fresh vegetables
Parmesan cheese (optional)

Split the spaghetti squash in half; scoop out seeds and place cut side down on a greased baking sheet. Bake in a 350° oven for 35 to 45 minutes. Scoop out with a fork; it will come out in strands like spaghetti. Drain if needed. Set aside.

In a large saucepan simmer tomatoes, onion, marjoram, basil, and garlic over low heat for 2 to 3 hours, until much of the liquid from the tomatoes has evaporated.

Cut into pieces whatever is available fresh from the garden (flowerets of broccoli or cauliflower, zucchini slices, green pepper strips, corn, etc.) Add to the tomato mixture, simmer about 15 to 20 minutes, until crisp-tender. To serve, spoon the tomato/vegetable mixture over the spaghetti squash. Sprinkle with Parmesan cheese if desired.

Serves 6 to 8.

Hill Farm Inn

London Broil

This is particularly good cooked on the grill but can be cooked in the broiler.

½ cup Worcestershire sauce
½ cup soy sauce
¼ cup lemon juice
¼ cup dry Sherry
1 clove garlic, crushed
Ginger to taste
Tarragon to taste
1 cup oil

❖ ❖ ❖

3 to 4 pounds top round, about
    1½-inches thick

Combine all the marinade ingredients, mix well. Pour over the top round and marinate for at least six hours, turning once. Grill or broil 7 to 10 minutes per side. Slice thin. Serve medium rare.

Serves 12 to 16.

Eastwood House Bed and Breakfast

River Street
Bethel, Vermont 05032
(802) 234-9686

Eastwood House is in the middle of the White River valley of central Vermont where many sporting activities are available. Breakfast at this bed and breakfast begins with juice, tea or coffee, Vermont cheese, and fresh fruit, followed by a homemade bread, pumpkin pancakes with Vermont syrup, or abelskivers (Danish pancakes). Formerly a stagecoach stop and tavern, it has been restored to its original character. The Federal-style brick house, built in 1817, contains five fireplaces, four of which are in the bed chambers. Each guest room is decorated individually.

Abelskivers (Danish Pancakes)

This finger food is a favorite with children.

2 cups all-purpose flour
2 teaspoons salt
2 teaspoons baking soda
4 egg yolks
Peel of 1 lemon, grated (optional)
2 cups buttermilk

1 tablespoon Sherry (optional)
4 egg whites

❖   ❖   ❖

Melted butter

In a large mixing bowl combine the dry ingredients; add egg yolks, lemon peel, buttermilk, and Sherry; mix well. Beat egg whites until stiff; fold into the flour mixture. Heat abelskivers pan (cast iron pan with half-spheres) until a drop of water will sizzle in it. Put ½ teaspoon melted butter in each cup. Add mixture until level in cup. Turn each as soon as shell forms. Turn ¼ turns. Turn again to form ball. Cook until center is done. Serve with sugar, syrup, or preserves.

Makes 6 to 8.

Artichoke Spread

This is a favorite with skiers after a day on the slopes.

2 14-ounce cans artichoke hearts
   (chopped)
1 cup mayonnaise
1 cup grated Parmesan cheese
3 cloves minced garlic

❖   ❖   ❖

Paprika

Mix together the artichoke hearts, mayonnaise, cheese, and garlic. Place in a 1½-quart casserole; sprinkle with paprika. Bake in a 350° oven for 20 to 30 minutes or until brown and bubbly. Serve hot with crackers.

Makes 3½ to 4 cups.

Poplar Manor

R.R. 2
Bethel, Vermont 05032
(802) 234-5426

Built about 1810 by the son of Ebenezer Putnam, one of Bethel's earliest settlers and a general in the Revolutionary War, Poplar Manor is set back from the road at the end of a long driveway. This white clapboard house is surrounded by meadows and cornfields, and its wide floorboards and exposed beams are furnished with antiques, collectibles, art, and many plants. The inn has five upstairs guest rooms; they all share baths. A generous breakfast is served each morning, including juice, cereals, a variety of homebaked breads or muffins, and coffee. The Poplar Manor is within easy driving distance of restaurants and shops, as well as sports activities, scenic drives and walks, and antique shops.

Wassail Bowl in a Pot

1 gallon Vermont apple cider
3 tablespoons Vermont maple syrup
   (grade A)
Juice of 3 lemons
6 cinnamon sticks
Apple slices and/or orange slices

Combine the ingredients and heat over medium heat to the boiling point (but do not boil) and serve. You may start with half the recipe and then add as necessary.

Serves 16.

J. W. Hibbard, Carriagemaker (1852-1910)

Zucchini Bread

The secret ingredient in this recipe is nutmeg. At the Poplar Manor whole nutmeg is ground for this bread.

> 2 cups sugar
> 3 eggs, beaten
> 1 cup oil
> 2 cups grated zucchini (shred some unpeeled to give bread more color and texture)
> 3 cups all-purpose flour
> 1 teaspoon salt
> 1 teaspoon baking soda
> 1 teaspoon baking powder
> 3 teaspoons cinnamon
> ¾ teaspoon nutmeg
> 1 teaspoon vanilla extract
> 1 cup raisins, coated with flour

Mix ingredients in order. Place in 2 greased loaf pans. Bake in a 350° oven for 1 hour. Cool for 20 minutes before removing from pan. These freeze well.
Makes 2 loaves.

The Churchill House Inn

Route 73
Brandon, Vermont 05733
(802) 247-3300

From the beginning, this century-old farmhouse has offered hospitality to the traveler. Built by the Churchill family in 1871, it was a halfway house for patrons of the adjoining mill and store. That spirit of hospitality remains, and a blend of original furnishings, antique pieces, and modern bedding provide a homelike atmosphere. The inn has nine guest rooms and seven and one-half baths. Recent additions include a pool, sauna, and screened-in porch. The inn is known for its intimate atmosphere and its good food, especially its homemade breads, soups, and desserts. The inn's location in the Green Mountain National Forest offers ideal surroundings for the active person. Excellent hiking, biking, fishing, or cross-country skiing await the guest at the door.

Tomato Curry Soup

> ½ cup onion, chopped fine
> ¼ cup butter (½ stick)
> 2 teaspoons curry powder (more if desired)
> 1 28-ounce can crushed tomatoes (or use fresh in season)
> 2 14½-ounce cans chicken stock
> ¼ cup sour cream
> Chopped chives for garnish

Sauté onion in butter until transparent. Add in curry powder, stirring over low heat for a few minutes to blend flavors. Add the tomatoes and chicken stock. Bring to a boil, then reduce heat and simmer about 15 to 20 minutes. Just before serving, stir in sour cream. Garnish with chopped chives.
Serves 6.

Spinach Spoon Bread

This family favorite makes a nice accompaniment for fish.

> 1 10-ounce package frozen chopped spinach
> ❖ ❖ ❖
> 1 medium onion, chopped
> 1 tablespoon butter
> 1 tablespoon all-purpose flour
> ½ teaspoon salt
> ½ cup milk
> 2 eggs, slightly beaten
> 1 cup sour cream
> ½ cup butter (1 stick), melted
> ¼ teaspoon salt
> 1 8½-ounce package corn muffin mix
> ❖ ❖ ❖
> ½ cup shredded Cheddar cheese

Cook spinach according to package directions; drain well. Sauté onion in 1 tablespoon butter. Blend in 1 tablespoon flour and ½ teaspoon salt. Blend in milk and stir until smooth. Combine with spinach, eggs, sour cream, butter and salt. Stir in corn muffin mix. Pour the mixture into a greased 1½-quart casserole. Bake in a 350° oven for 30 to 35 minutes or until a wooden pick inserted in center comes out clean. Sprinkle the top with shredded cheese; bake about 2 minutes more to melt cheese. Serve warm.
Serves 8.

Almond Puff

> ½ cup butter (1 stick)
> 1 cup all-purpose flour
> 2 tablespoons water
> ❖ ❖ ❖
> ½ cup butter (1 stick)
> 1 cup water
> 1 teaspoon almond extract
> 1 cup all-purpose flour
> 3 eggs
> ❖ ❖ ❖
> 1½ cups confectioners' sugar
> 2 tablespoons butter, softened
> 1½ teaspoons almond extract
> 1 to 2 tablespoons warm water
> ❖ ❖ ❖
> Chopped nuts

Cut ½ cup of butter into 1 cup of flour. Sprinkle 2 tablespoons of water over the mixture. Mix well with a fork; form into a ball. Divide in half. On an ungreased baking sheet pat each half into a strip 12x3 inches. Strips should be about 3 inches apart.

In a medium saucepan bring ½ cup butter and 1 cup water to a rolling boil; remove from heat and quickly stir in 1 teaspoon of almond extract and 1 cup of flour. Stir vigorously over low heat until the mixture forms a ball, about 1 minute. Remove from heat and beat in eggs, one at a time, until smooth. Divide in half; spread each half evenly over the strips, covering completely. Bake in a 350° oven about 60 minutes or until topping is crisp and brown. Make glaze by combining confectioners' sugar with 2 tablespoons of butter. Add 1½ teaspoons of almond extract. Beat, gradually adding 1 to 2 tablespoons of water, until smooth.

When the strips have cooled frost them with the glaze and sprinkle generously with nuts.

Serves 12.

Strawberry Glacé Pie

3 tablespoons cornstarch
⅔ cup water
1 cup crushed strawberries
1 cup sugar
Dash salt

❖ ❖ ❖

1 quart firm ripe strawberries
1 baked 9-inch pie shell
½ cup whipped cream

In a medium saucepan dissolve cornstarch in a little of the water; add the remaining water, crushed strawberries, sugar, and salt. Cook over medium heat until thick. Arrange the whole strawberries, stem side down, in the baked pie shell; cover with the cooked mixture. Chill until set. Garnish with whipped cream.

Serves 8.

Host Home with Eileen and Charles Roeder

Post Office Box 203
Brandon, Vermont 05733
(802) 247-6137

Stone Mill Farm, one mile east of Brandon Village, is nestled in the heart of foliage country. Guests may walk the logging trail through the cedars; enjoy the pool; help feed the ducks, chickens, geese, or pigs; gather eggs and berries in season; or enjoy a peaceful night's stayover. A continental breakfast is provided, served informally on the porch.

Corn Fritters

4 to 5 ears fresh corn
1 to 2 tablespoons all-purpose flour
2 tablespoons milk
½ teaspoon salt
1 teaspoon sugar
1 teaspoon baking powder
1 egg, separated

Cut the corn from the cobs and scrape the cobs. Add the flour, milk, salt, sugar, and baking powder; add the beaten egg yolk. Beat the egg white, and fold into the corn mixture. Fry in solid vegetable shortening, turning once.

Makes 6 fritters.

Clam Pie

"This is a great appetizer for a chilly evening. When we serve this appetizer, many of our guests tease us because clam pie is certainly not to be considered a regional dish."

1 6½-ounce can minced clams
1 teaspoon lemon juice
½ medium onion, grated
1 tablespoon parsley flakes
6 tablespoons butter, melted
½ teaspoon oregano
Dash pepper
³/₈ cup seasoned bread crumbs

❖ ❖ ❖

Muenster cheese, cut in strips
Parmesan cheese

Simmer the clams, clam juice, and lemon juice for 5 minutes. Add the onion, parsley, butter, oregano, pepper, and bread crumbs. Place in an 8-inch pie plate. Place strips of Muenster cheese on top. Sprinkle with grated Parmesan. Bake in a 350° oven for 20 minutes.

Serves 8.

Pot Pie Dumplings

These are particularly good with stewed chicken.

1 egg
3 tablespoons milk
2 cups all-purpose flour

❖ ❖ ❖

Broth

Beat the egg; add the milk, then enough flour to make a stiff dough. Roll thin and cut into 1x2-inch strips. Drop into the boiling broth, cover and simmer for 20 minutes.

Serves 4.

Shire Inn

Post Office Box 37
Chelsea, Vermont 05038
(802) 685-3031

The Shire Inn offers comfortable, elegant accommodations for guests traveling through central Vermont and the upper Connecticut River Valley. Built in 1832, by a successful Chelsea chair manufacturer, the inn has an ample village setting of seventeen acres. A variety of flowers and herbs grow and bloom in the large gardens during the spring and summer. Picnics and cross-country skiing make Shire an inn for all seasons. The inn's six rooms are distinctive. Some have fireplaces and full bath, and all are furnished with period antiques that complement the elegant brick architecture. A complete breakfast is included in the cost of lodging.

Sherry and the Devil

Easy to prepare, yet elegant enough for a special dinner. The mustard spices the chicken, which is then simmered in Sherry. This makes a great combination.

6 boneless split chicken breasts
Dijon mustard
Salt and freshly ground pepper
Parsley
2 cups bread crumbs
¼ cup olive oil
3 tablespoons butter

❖ ❖ ❖

¾ cup Sherry
2 tablespoons butter

Coat the chicken with the mustard, covering the chicken completely. Sprinkle with salt and pepper. Add the parsley to the bread crumbs and coat the chicken with this mixture. Fry in a 10-inch skillet in the oil and 3 tablespoons of butter for about 3 to 5 minutes on each side until brown. Drain most of the oil off; turn the heat down. Add the Sherry, pouring over the chicken. Remove the chicken to a serving platter and stir the butter and Sherry, scraping the pan drippings. Pour over the chicken.

Serves 6.

Shire's Scallops

A new twist on scampi, this delightful dish can be made with scallops or shrimp, or a mixture of the two. Caraway seeds liven this seafood treat, which can be served as an appetizer or main course.

6 tablespoons butter
3 cloves garlic, chopped
½ teaspoon caraway seeds
Salt and freshly ground pepper
Parsley
1½ pounds bay scallops, unwashed
Juice of 1 lemon
2 to 3 tablespoons fine dry bread
** crumbs**
Dash wine or Sherry (optional)

In a skillet, melt the butter. Add the garlic, caraway seeds, salt, pepper, and parsley. Cook and stir over medium heat for 2 to 3 minutes. Add the scallops and sauté for approximately 5 minutes. Sprinkle with lemon juice, bread crumbs, and wine. Stir to combine.

Serves 4 to 6 main-course servings or 8 to 10 appetizers.

Screwdriver Veal

Flour
Salt and pepper
Paprika
6 veal or chicken cutlets
¼ cup olive oil
3 tablespoons butter
2 cloves garlic
¾ cup orange juice
¾ cup vodka
Parsley
Dash cayenne pepper

In a plastic bag combine flour with salt, pepper, and enough paprika to slightly color the flour pink. Add the cutlets to the flour and toss to coat completely. Put oil, butter, and garlic in a 10-inch skillet or fry pan and heat until hot. Add the cutlets and cook until browned on both sides, approximately 3 to 5 minutes on both sides. Remove the cutlets to a platter and drain oil.

Reduce the heat and add orange juice, vodka, parsley, and cayenne pepper to pan and stir to scrape up the pan drippings. You may sprinkle some flour in the pan and stir to thicken the gravy. Immediately add the cutlets, return the heat to high and cook for 1 more minute.

Serves 6.

Brandied Chocolate Cake

1 18-ounce package chocolate cake
** mix**
1 3⁵/₈-ounce package instant
** chocolate pudding mix**
½ teaspoon nutmeg
4 eggs
¾ cup Brandy
¾ cup oil

❖ ❖ ❖

1 6-ounce package instant
** chocolate pudding mix**
3 cups cold whipping cream
¼ cup Brandy

In a large bowl combine the cake mix, the 3⁵/₈-ounce package of chocolate pudding mix, the nutmeg, eggs, brandy and oil. With an electric mixer at low speed mix for 1 minute, then at medium speed mix for 3 minutes. Pour into 3 greased and floured 8-inch cake pans. Bake in a 350° oven for 25 minutes, or until a knife inserted in the center comes out clean. Cool completely on a wire rack.

Shire Inn

Prepare the 6-ounce package of pudding according to package directions, using the whipping cream instead of milk; add the brandy.

Place ⅓ of the filling on 1 layer of cake and spread evenly. Place the second layer on top and cover with filling. Top with the third layer and cover with filling. Garnish with chocolate or orange shavings.

Serves 10.

The Inn at Long Last

Box 589
Chester, Vermont 05143
(802) 875-2444

On the village green in Chester, The Inn at Long Last has thirty guest rooms, each with its own decorative theme. All rooms have private baths; a few are suites. The chef offers a menu of six to seven entrees each night, always including seafood and featuring local produce when possible. Guests are welcomed each morning with a muffin and a full breakfast. The inn also features a library where, in front of the fireplace and against a backdrop of good books and soft light, guests enjoy cocktails and a good-night Sherry. The innkeeper, Jack Coleman, is the author of *Blue Collar Journal,* which later was made into a television movie. His book is in the library, too! The inn also has a tennis court, a swimming pool, and a fishing stream.

Chester's village green, long and narrow, is a constant lure for photographers and art lovers. The antique shops provide hours of shopping opportunities. The village's buildings are a rarity in New England; thirty of its Pre-Civil War buildings are faced in rough, but gleaming, mica schist. Ski slopes are nearby, and a steam train carries visitors through some of the region's most dazzling fall foliage.

Peach Soup with Amaretto

8 fresh ripe peaches with skins
2 cups apple juice
⅛ cup sugar
¼ cup Amaretto Di Saronna
Juice of ½ lemon
½ teaspoon vanilla extract
1 cup plain yogurt

Place peaches, sugar, apple juice, Amaretto, lemon juice and vanilla in a blender. Purée until smooth. Lightly whip yogurt and add to the soup. Chill.
Chef Michael Brown.
Serves 8.

Toasted Almond Soup

2 tablespoons finely chopped
**   shallots**
1 tablespoon finely chopped garlic
2 tablespoons butter
¼ cup white wine
2 quarts chicken broth
2 tablespoons almond paste
½ cup blanched sliced almonds,
**   finely chopped**

❖ ❖ ❖

¼ cup butter (½ stick)
4 tablespoons all-purpose flour

❖ ❖ ❖

1 pint heavy cream
Salt and white pepper to taste
¼ cup blanched sliced almonds,
**   lightly toasted**

In a heavy soup pot over low heat, sauté the shallots and garlic in 2 tablespoons of butter. Just as they begin to brown, add the white wine. Simmer until reduced by half. Add the chicken broth; whisk in the almond paste and finely chopped almonds. Bring to a boil, then simmer for 30 minutes.

In a separate pan melt the remaining butter and whisk in the flour. Cook the roux for 5 minutes or until it smells nutty. Reserve.

After simmering the soup for 30 minutes, add the heavy cream, then whisk in the roux and stir vigorously until well-blended. Simmer for 10 minutes, then purée through a food mill, or process in a blender and strain. Adjust the seasonings. Serve in warmed bowls with a few toasted slivers of almonds.

Chef Michael Brown.
Serves 12.

Sun-Dried Tomato Basil Mayonnaise

1 5-ounce jar sun-dried tomatoes in
**   oil**
½ cup olive oil
2 eggs yolks
½ teaspoon salt
¼ teaspoon fresh ground pepper
1½ teaspoons chopped fresh basil
1½ teaspoons red wine vinegar

Process the jar of sun-dried tomatoes until smooth. Add the olive oil. Whip the yolks until fluffy and add the seasonings. Gradually add the tomato and oil mixture, making sure it is totally blended before adding more. Add the vinegar intermittently.
Serves 8.

Crab Meat Timbale

1 tablespoon gelatin
3 tablespoons lemon juice

❖ ❖ ❖

½ small onion, finely chopped
1 rib celery, finely chopped
2 teaspoons chopped fresh basil
1 teaspoon chopped fresh parsley
1 teaspoon salt
½ teaspoon fresh ground pepper
1 cup mayonnaise

❖ ❖ ❖

1 pound crab meat

❖ ❖ ❖

Sun-Dried Tomato-Basil Mayonnaise

Place the gelatin in the lemon juice and warm on low heat to dissolve. Mix together the onion, celery, basil, parsley, salt, pepper, and mayonnaise. Add the gelatin and lemon juice and blend together with a wire whisk. Add this mixture to the crabmeat. Place into eight chilled 6-ounce ceramic ramekins or molds and chill 4 hours until set.

To unmold the Crabmeat Timbale, run a knife around the edge and set upside down in a plate presentation of lettuce and the Sun-Dried Tomato-Basil Mayonnaise. Pull the mold up, leaving the crabmeat in place.

Chef Michael Brown.

Serves 8.

Grilled Vermont Lamb Loin Chops
with a Garlic-Spearmint Demi-Glacé

Vermont-raised lamb is slightly gamey and very flavorful.

12 loin chops
Salt and pepper to taste
1 tablespoon butter, clarified if possible
2 tablespoons finely chopped shallots
4 tablespoons finely chopped garlic
2 tablespoons Crème de Menthe
2 tablespoons red wine
1 quart rich beef stock, unsalted
1 teaspoon molasses
3 tablespoons chopped fresh spearmint

Grill the lamb chops on a hot fire and season with salt and pepper on both sides.

To make the sauce, in a medium gauge pan heat the butter and add the garlic and shallots. Sauté until brown. Deglaze the pan with Crème de Menthe and red wine. Add the beef stock and molasses, season with salt and pepper, and bring to a boil. Lower the heat to simmer and reduce until a sauce consistency. Skim the foam from the top as it gathers and stir every 5 minutes to prevent scorching. Strain and add the spearmint. Place sauce in each of 6 serving plates and place 2 lamb chops on the sauce on each plate.

Chef Michael Brown.

Serves 6.

Rum Raisin Cheesecake

½ cup raisins
¼ cup dark rum

❖ ❖ ❖

5 8-ounce packages cream cheese
1¼ cups sugar
2½ ounces arrowroot
5 eggs
2 egg yolks
½ cup heavy cream

Soak the raisins in the rum for 15 minutes. Whip the cream cheese and sugar until lightly fluffy. Blend in the arrowroot. Add the eggs and yolks gradually and mix until smooth. Fold in the heavy cream and then gently stir in the raisins and the rum in which they have soaked. Pour into a greased 10-inch springform pan and set in a hot water bath that comes halfway up the sides. Bake in a 325° oven for 60 to 75 minutes or until done. Remove to cool before unmolding. Serve bottomside up and decorate with whipped cream.

Chef Michael Brown.

Serves 12.

Mountain Top Inn

Mountain Top Road
Chittenden, Vermont 05737
(802) 483-2311 (In Vermont and Canada)
1-800-445-2100 (Toll free)

The altitude of Mountain Top Inn is 2000 feet, so it commands a spectacular view of the Green Mountains, which also are reflected in the lake. The inn's post-and-beam construction, combined with many fireplaces and polished furniture, creates a warm retreat. The maple sugar house on the premises produces the fine maple syrup served in the dining room. There are thirty-five guest rooms in addition to fifteen cottage and chalet units. Other amenities include a cocktail lounge; a room outfitted with exercise equipment, whirlpool, and sauna; childcare programs; indoor tennis and racquetball courts; heated outdoor pool; and a lighted outdoor skating rink. Depending on the season, guests have recreational choices of horse-drawn sleigh rides or hay rides, skiing, tobogganing, and sledding; lake-oriented sports such as boating, wind surfing, fishing, and swimming; pitch 'n putt golfing; and hiking or horseback riding throughout the 1000-acre grounds or adjacent national forest.

Mountain Top Inn

Butternut Squash Soup

**2 pounds butternut squash,
   trimmed and cleaned
1 quart water
1 tablespoon salt**

✦ ✦ ✦

**½ cup diced celery
½ cup diced onion
½ cup diced bell pepper
¼ cup butter (½ stick), melted
¼ cup white wine
1 teaspoon tarragon leaves
½ teaspoon cinnamon
½ teaspoon nutmeg
¼ teaspoon cloves
4 cups chicken stock**

✦ ✦ ✦

**¼ cup all-purpose flour
¼ cup butter (½ stick), melted
½ cup Vermont maple syrup
¼ cup dry Sherry**

Trim and seed the squash. Cover with water and salt; cook until soft, approximately 40 minutes. Strain out the squash, reserving 2 cups of liquid.

Sauté the diced vegetables in ¼ cup of butter and wine for 5 minutes. Add the herbs and spices. Add the chicken stock and 1 cup of reserved liquid. Bring to a boil; then thicken with a roux made by mixing the flour with ¼ cup of melted butter. Add the cooked squash which has been puréed in a blender or food processor with the remaining 1 cup of reserved liquid. Cook, stirring often, on low heat for 5 minutes. Add the syrup and Sherry. Mix well. Serve.

Serves 12 to 16.

Lime Sesame Dressing

**8 limes
1 medium white onion
¾ cup red wine vinegar
2 cups olive oil
½ cup honey
Salt and white pepper to taste
2 tablespoons sesame seeds**

Peel the limes and purée in a food processor or blender. Dice the onions and add to the blender; purée. Add the remaining ingredients and blend well.

Makes 3½ cups.

Apple Brulee

**6 apples, cored and sliced
½ cup raisins
¼ cup walnuts
¼ cup all-purpose flour
½ teaspoon cinnamon
½ teaspoon nutmeg
¼ teaspoon cloves
½ teaspoon ginger
½ cup brown sugar, firmly packed**

✦ ✦ ✦

**4 egg yolks
1 14-ounce can sweetened
   condensed milk
½ cup heavy cream**

Combine the apples, raisins, and walnuts. Sift the flour, spices and brown sugar over the fruit. In a separate bowl mix the egg yolks, sweetened condensed milk, and cream. Pour over the apple mixture; stir well and pour into a covered casserole dish. Bake in a 350° oven for 30 to 45 minutes, until the apples are cooked through. Serve in bowls with a dollop of heavy cream.

Serves 6.

Mountain Top Chocolate Cake

**1 cup sugar
2 cups all-purpose flour
1 teaspoon baking soda
Pinch salt
⅔ cup cocoa**

✦ ✦ ✦

**1 cup lukewarm water
1 cup mayonnaise
½ cup sour cream
½ teaspoon vanilla extract**

✦ ✦ ✦

**4 1-ounce squares unsweetened
   chocolate
¾ cup sugar
½ to ¾ cup heavy cream
Flavoring (sugar, vanilla, Kahlua,
   Amaretto or rum)**

Sift the dry ingredients together. In a separate bowl combine the water, mayonnaise, sour cream, and vanilla. Mix thoroughly. Add the dry ingredients and mix completely. Pour into 2 greased and floured 9x13-inch cake pans. Bake in a 350° oven for about 30 to 35 minutes or until a toothpick inserted in the center comes out clean. Cool to room temperature before frosting.

Heat and mix the chocolate and ¾ cup of sugar until smooth and well-blended. Cool to room temperature, then blend in the whipped cream (whipped with sugar, vanilla, and/or Kahlua, Amaretto, rum, etc.). Refrigerate until the right frosting consistency is reached. Frost the cake.

Serves 12 to 16.

Tulip Tree Inn

Chittenden Dam Road
Chittenden, Vermont 05737
(802) 483-6213

The Tulip Tree Inn is a gracious, rambling country house furnished with a variety of personally-collected antiques. Visitors in its ten guest rooms enjoy hearty breakfasts and delicious candlelit dinners in the picturesque dining room. The paneled den with its stone fireplace provides the ideal spot for total relaxation; this is the room for chess, backgammon, or relaxing. After a day outdoors, guests can soak in the hot tub and, in summer, enjoy lounging by the swimming pool. Cocktails are served in the library/tap room; a wine list is available.

Ice Cream Pie

**2 teaspoons butter, softened
2 tablespoons graham cracker
   crumbs**

✦ ✦ ✦

1 6-ounce package semi-sweet
  chocolate chips
4 egg whites
Pinch salt
2 tablespoons sugar

❖ ❖ ❖

4 egg yolks
2 tablespoons sugar
½ teaspoon vanilla extract

❖ ❖ ❖

1 pint ice cream
Nuts for garnish

Grease a 9-inch pie plate with butter. Coat sides and bottom of plate with crumbs. Melt chocolate bits in top of a double boiler over hot, not boiling, water. Beat egg whites with salt until foamy. Gradually beat in 2 tablespoons of sugar and continue beating until stiff. In another large bowl, beat the egg yolks with the remaining 2 tablespoons of sugar until thick and lemon-colored. Stir in the vanilla. Gently stir in chocolate. Fold in the egg whites. Fill pie plate. Bake in a 350° oven for 15 minutes. Cool to room temperature for 2 hours. Fill shell with ice cream. Garnish with nuts.

Serves 8.

Cheesecake

4 8-ounce packages cream cheese
4 eggs
1¾ cups sugar
1 teaspoon vanilla extract
½ cup sour cream

Butter an 8-inch soufflé dish. Blend all the ingredients until smooth. Pour into the prepared pan and place the pan inside a slightly larger pan containing hot water to a depth of ½-inch. Bake in a 325° oven for 1½ hours, then turn off the oven and let the cake sit 20 minutes. Lift cake pan out of water and cool for 3 hours. Unmold.

Serves 10.

Chocolate Cheesecake

1 cup mini chocolate chips

❖ ❖ ❖

2 8-ounce packages cream cheese
¾ cup sugar
½ cup sour cream
4 eggs

❖ ❖ ❖

2 tablespoons mini chocolate chips

Prepare an 8 or 9-inch springform pan by wrapping it in aluminum foil. Butter the inside of the pan.

In the top of a double boiler melt 1 cup of chips. Set aside to cool.

Blend until smooth the cream cheese, sugar, sour cream, and eggs. Add in melted chocolate, mix well. Pour into the prepared pan. Sprinkle 2 tablespoons of chips on top. Place the pan in a larger pan which contains water 1-inch deep. Bake in a 325° oven for 1 hour. Chill.

Serves 12.

Pumpkin Cheesecake

4 8-ounce packages cream cheese
1½ cups dark brown sugar, firmly
  packed
5 eggs
¼ cup all-purpose flour
1 teaspoon cinnamon
1 teaspoon allspice
¼ teaspoon ginger
¼ teaspoon salt
1 16-ounce can (2 cups) pumpkin
  purée
Maple syrup and walnuts for
  garnish

Butter a 9 or 10-inch springform pan. Beat cream cheese and sugar until fluffy. Add the remaining ingredients except maple syrup and walnuts. Pour into prepared pan. Bake in a 325° oven for 1½ to 1¾ hours. Serve garnished with maple syrup and walnuts.

Serves 12.

The Craftsbury Inn

Craftsbury, Vermont 05826
(802) 586-2848

This warm, attractive Vermont inn offers gracious accommodations and superb food. Its ten guest bedrooms and family suite are decorated with heirloom and custom-made quilts, antique wicker furniture, popular books, and works by local artists. The vegetable-herb garden provides the Craftsbury Inn with fresh produce. All food is made in the kitchen, including baguettes, ice creams, pastries, and sorbets.

Many recreational activities are available. In summer and fall, canoeing nearby rivers, swimming in one of four nearby lakes, fishing, sailing, tennis, or golfing on Vermont's oldest golf course are available. In winter the area offers the finest and most consistent cross country skiing in the East. The nearby Craftsbury Nordic Ski Center has 100 kilometers of wilderness trail.

Carrot and Orange Soup

4 large onions, sliced
3 pounds carrots, peeled and
  chopped
8 cups chicken stock (preferably
  homemade)
2½ cups orange juice
Salt and white pepper
Tabasco sauce
Chopped parsley (optional)
Grated orange rind (optional)

In a large pot sauté the onions in butter until golden and softened. Add the carrots and chicken stock. Bring to a boil, reduce the heat to a simmer, and simmer for 50 minutes. Purée in batches

The Craftsbury Inn

Spread the garlic mayonnaise on the fish. Place the fish in individual oven-proof dishes and pour white wine half-way up the side of the fish. Bake in a preheated 425° oven for 10 minutes per inch of fish.

Makes 1 cup.

Gary-Meadow Dairy Farm

R.R. 1, Box 11
Craftsbury, Vermont 05826
(802) 586-2536

The Gary-Meadow Dairy Farm offers one room off the main section of this 1884 restored Cape Cod farmhouse. The room can accommodate two to four people. The reasonable rates include a tour of the 750-acre Holstein dairy farm and a full country breakfast. The hosts have four children, and a sandbox, swings, toys, and babysitting are available. Antique hunting, concerts, drama, biking, swimming, hiking, canoeing and the wonderful fall foliage are among the most popular area recreational activities.

in a food processor until quite smooth. Add the orange juice, salt, and white pepper to taste, and add a few dashes of Tabasco. Garnish with chopped parsley or grated orange rind.

Serves 12 to 15.

Eggplant Soup with Curry

4 to 5 large eggplants, peeled and chopped
2 large onions, chopped
2 cups chopped celery
2 large cloves of garlic, minced
½ cup butter (1 stick)
8 cups chicken stock (homemade)
1 teaspoon thyme
1 teaspoon basil
1 teaspoon salt
1 cup heavy cream
1 tablespoon curry powder

In a large kettle cook the vegetables in the butter over moderate heat for 15 minutes, stirring often. Add the chicken stock, thyme, basil, and salt. Simmer for 40 minutes. Blend the mixture in batches in a processor with steel blade until smooth. Transfer to another container and add the heavy cream and curry powder.

Serves 12 to 15.

Poached Fish
with Garlic Mayonnaise

10 cloves garlic
1 egg
1½ tablespoons lemon juice
½ cup olive oil
½ cup oil
Salt
Cayenne pepper

❖ ❖ ❖

Fish of choice (halibut steaks, bluefish fillets, or swordfish steaks
White wine

In a small saucepan of boiling water boil the unpeeled garlic cloves for 15 minutes. Drain and peel them. In a food processor using the steel blade, blend the garlic with the egg and lemon juice. With the motor still running, add olive oil and oil in a stream. Add additional lemon juice, salt, and cayenne pepper to taste.

Double Treat Cookies

3 cups all-purpose flour
2 teaspoons baking soda
½ teaspoon salt
1 cup melted margarine
1 cup peanut butter
1 cup M&Ms
1 cup sugar
1 cup brown sugar, firmly packed
2 eggs
1 teaspoon vanilla extract

Mix the ingredients and drop by spoonfuls onto an ungreased cookie sheet. Bake in a 350° oven for 10 minutes.

Variations: Substitute chocolate chips, peanuts, raisins, or whatever is available for the M&Ms.

Makes 2½ to 3 dozen cookies.

Apricot-Oatmeal Bars

1½ cups all-purpose flour
1 teaspoon baking powder
½ teaspoon salt
1½ cups rolled oats
1 cup light brown sugar, firmly
    packed
¾ cup butter (1½ sticks), melted
1 12-ounce jar apricot preserves

Combine the flour, baking powder, salt, oats, brown sugar, and butter to form a crumb mixture. Press half of the crumb mixture into a greased 9-inch pan. Spread the apricot preserves over the crust. Sprinkle the remaining crumbs over the preserves. Bake in a 350° oven for 40 minutes.

Serves 9 to 12.

Raisin-Filled Cookies

2 eggs
1 cup sugar
½ teaspoon salt
1 teaspoon nutmeg
1 teaspoon lemon extract
3 teaspoons baking powder
½ cup melted butter
½ cup milk
3 cups all-purpose flour

❖   ❖   ❖

1 9-ounce box raisins
1 cup sugar
2 tablespoons all-purpose flour
1 cup water

Mix together the eggs, 1 cup of sugar, salt, nutmeg, lemon extract, baking powder, butter, milk, and 3 cups of flour to form the dough.

In a saucepan combine the raisins, 1 cup of sugar, 2 tablespoons of flour, and water. Cook over medium heat until thick. Stir to prevent burning.

Roll the dough on a floured board. Cut rounds of pastry; place 1 to 2 teaspoons of raisin filling on ½ of the rounds, cover with the remaining rounds and tap the edges closed. Bake in a 400° oven for 12 to 15 minutes.

Makes 3 dozen cookies.

Marble West Inn

Post Office Box 22
Dorset, Vermont 05251
(802) 867-4155

The Marble West Inn is a Greek-revival home with a formal entrance hallway, fir floors, and marble pilasters. From the front porches one has an admirable view of the nearby mountains. Ponds on the grounds are home for trout. It's just a short trip by car or on foot, to Dorset's village green. During the winter, guests can begin cross country skiing from the front door.

Vermont Maple Wheat Bread

1 ¼-ounce package active dry yeast
1 cup warm water (110° to 115°)
2 cups sour cream
⅔ cup maple syrup
2 egg yolks
2 teaspoons salt
½ teaspoon baking powder
2 cups whole wheat flour
4½ to 5 cups unbleached flour

Mix the yeast and water. Let sit for 5 to 10 minutes. Add all ingredients except the unbleached flour and beat vigorously. Gradually add the unbleached flour. Knead for at least 10 minutes. Be careful, for it is fragile. Let rise until doubled in bulk. Punch down and put in 2 greased loaf pans. Let rise and

Marble West Inn

bake in a 375 ° oven for 45 minutes. Brush tops with butter.

Makes 2 loaves.

Marble West Chicken Soufflé

2 boneless chicken breasts, split
Butter
Thyme

❖   ❖   ❖

⅔ cup Hellman's mayonnaise
⅓ cup sour cream
⅓ cup fresh ground Parmesan
    cheese

Sauté the chicken in butter for 5 minutes on each side or until slightly brown. Sprinkle ground thyme over each breast arranged in shallow baking dishes.

Combine the mayonnaise, sour cream, and Parmesan in a bowl. Place some of the mayonnaise mixture on each chicken breast. Bake in a 350° oven about 40 minutes until golden brown.

Serves 4.

Vermont Rhubarb Cake

2 cups chopped fresh rhubarb
½ cup sugar
¼ cup all-purpose flour

❖ ❖ ❖

½ cup butter (1 stick)
1½ cups sugar
1 egg, beaten
2½ cups all-purpose flour
1 teaspoon baking soda
½ teaspoon salt
1 cup milk
1 teaspoon vanilla extract

❖ ❖ ❖

½ cup sugar
1 teaspoon cinnamon
½ cup coconut

❖ ❖ ❖

Fresh whipped cream (8-ounce carton)

Sprinkle the rhubarb with ½ cup of sugar and ¼ cup of flour; set aside. Cream the butter and 1½ cups sugar. Stir in the egg and beat well. Sift twice 2½ cups of flour, baking soda, and salt. Add this to the butter mixture. Add the milk and vanilla; mix well. Stir in rhubarb mixture. Pour batter into a greased and floured 9x13-inch cake pan and sprinkle with mixture of ½ cup of sugar, cinnamon, and coconut. Bake in a 350° oven for about 50 minutes; test for doneness. Cool and serve with the fresh whipped cream.

Serves 12 to 14.

❖ ❖ ❖ ❖ ❖ ❖

Doveberry Inn

Route 100
Dover, Vermont 05356
(802) 464-5652

A country inn with eight individually decorated guest rooms, each with a private bath, the Doveberry Inn's accommodations range from modest double-bed rooms to a luxurious suite with private sun deck. Guests can relax with a good book or quiet game beside the fireplace in the common room. The innkeeper's home-cooked meals are served in two candlelit dining rooms. A good selection of modestly priced wines and beers are available, and crusty homemade Canadian oat bread and desserts are favorites. Afternoon tea and a full country breakfast are included at no extra charge. Dinners are among the best values in the region. Nearby are ski areas, cross country skiing, championship golf, tennis, antique and craft shops, five restaurants, hiking, and water sports.

Savory Roasted Lamb

Leg of lamb

❖ ❖ ❖

2 cups bread crumbs
2 eggs
¼ cup oil
2 tablespoons Parmesan cheese

1½ teaspoons each chopped dried tarragon, parsley, chives, and chervil
Salt and pepper to taste

❖ ❖ ❖

1 carrot
2 ribs celery
1 medium onion

❖ ❖ ❖

½ cup Dijon mustard
2 tablespoons soy sauce
1 teaspoon crushed garlic
¾ teaspoon each chopped dried tarragon, parsley, chives, and chervil
3 tablespoons olive oil

❖ ❖ ❖

½ cup all-purpose flour
1 cup chicken broth
Salt and pepper to taste
¼ cup red wine (optional)

Bone a leg of fresh American lamb or have a butcher do it. Cut off heavy pieces of fat and tendon. Prepare stuffing by mixing bread crumbs, eggs, oil, cheese, 1½ teaspoons each of herbs, the salt, and pepper. Press stuffing into the inside of lamb. Roll into the original shape and tie securely at 2-inch intervals to enclose stuffing.

Coarsely chop carrot, celery, and onion; place in the bottom of a roasting pan. Place the lamb on a rack over the chopped vegetables. Combine the mustard, soy sauce, garlic, and ¾ teaspoon each of the herbs. Add the olive oil a few drops at a time after the other ingredients have been well-blended. Coat the lamb with this mixture. If time permits, coat an hour or two before roasting. Cover with clear plastic wrap and refrigerate. Remove the plastic wrap and roast lamb approximately 2½ hours in a 325° oven or until juices run very faintly pink when the meat is stuck with a thin paring knife.

If a gravy is desired, remove roasted lamb and rack from pan, keeping meat on a warm platter. Strain fat and pan juices into a small bowl. Discard vegetables and pour 3 tablespoons of the melted fat back into roasting pan. Discard the rest of the melted fat, reserving the pan juices. Heat fat in pan over medium heat and stir in flour to form a thick roux. Stir roux over low heat until browned, being careful not to burn. Add pan juices from the small bowl and chicken broth. Taste and add salt and pepper if necessary. (Optional: stir in wine and cook for 5 minutes over low heat.) Strain gravy.

Serves 16.

Blueberry Cheesecake

Butter
½ cup ground walnuts (or pecans)
½ cup ground vanilla wafers

❖ ❖ ❖

2 8-ounce packages cream cheese, softened
1 8-ounce carton cottage cheese
1 cup sugar
1 tablespoon vanilla extract
4 eggs
3½ cups sour cream

❖ ❖ ❖

2 tablespoons cornstarch
½ cup cold water
1 pint fresh blueberries (or frozen)
¾ cup sugar

Generously butter bottom and sides of a 10-inch springform pan and dust with a mixture of walnuts (or pecans) and ground vanilla wafers. Shake out the loose crumbs.

In a large mixing bowl beat together with a large whisk the cream cheese, cottage cheese, 1 cup sugar, and vanilla. Beat in eggs one at a time; then sour cream, beating just long enough to blend ingredients. Do not overbeat. Pour into the pan and bake in a 350° oven for about 1½ hours, or until a toothpick comes out almost dry. Cool on a rack for two hours; then refrigerate overnight.

Combine cornstarch with cold water in a saucepan, stirring well. Bring to a boil. Add fresh (or frozen) blueberries and ¾ cup sugar; simmer until thick. Cool to room temperature and spread over the top of the refrigerated cake. Remove the sides of the pan.

Serves 14.

Inwood Manor

East Barnet, Vermont 05821
(802) 633-4047

Once the main lodging for the world's largest croquet factory, Inwood Manor is now a charming guest house near the quaint little village of East Barnet. The twenty acres surrounding the manor assure privacy in an idyllic setting. The manor offers tastefully restored guestrooms, home cooked meals freshly prepared by the hosts, and the congeniality of New England in a pleasant, relaxed atmosphere. Guests may walk to the waterfalls, explore the beautiful countryside, or visit the White Mountains of New Hampshire only minutes away. Complimentary Continental breakfast is included with the room, and a full breakfast is available for house guests.

Best Guacamole in Town

2 ripe avocadoes, peeled
½ small red onion, chopped
2 tomatoes, coarsely chopped

1 cup grated Monterey Jack cheese
Coriander
Cumin
Oregano
½ teaspoon sea salt
1 clove garlic, minced
Juice of 1 lime

Place ingredients in a food processor and use pulse button to coarsely blend. If you like a creamier dip, run longer.

Note: For a sodium reduced dip, substitute any non-salt, herbal, or other spiced seasoning.

Makes 2 cups.

Cheese Balls

A cheese lover's delight.

6 egg whites

❖ ❖ ❖

3 cups grated Cheddar cheese
2 tablespoons all-purpose flour
Dash cayenne pepper

❖ ❖ ❖

Cheese crackers

In a mixing bowl beat egg whites until stiff. Fold in the cheese, flour, and pepper. Shape the mixture into small balls.

Crumble the cheese crackers until fine; roll the balls in the crumbs and then deep fry until golden. Delicious!

Inwood Manor

Bastoncini di Carate Marinate

Clean carrots thoroughly but do not peel to maintain sweetness. Serve as an appetizer or as a delicious side dish for meat or fowl. Best prepared a day ahead.

1 pound carrots
Salt to taste

❖ ❖ ❖

½ cup olive oil
⅓ cup red wine vinegar (or to taste)
Oregano
2 cloves garlic, minced

Cut carrots into 2-inch strips. Steam or boil until crisp-tender. Place in a 1½-quart casserole dish and salt to taste.

Combine the oil, vinegar, a sprinkle of oregano, and garlic. Mix well; then pour over the carrots. Cover and refrigerate, preferably overnight. Serve cold.

Serves 4.

Sweet Carrots with Dill or Basil

1 pound carrots

❖ ❖ ❖

3 tablespoons butter
1 to 2 tablespoons Vermont maple syrup
Salt and pepper to taste
2 teaspoons dill seed or sweet basil

Cut carrots into diagonal slices; steam or boil for 10 minutes in a large saucepan; drain water. To the carrots add butter, syrup, salt, pepper, and your choice of dill seed or basil. Simmer 10 to 15 minutes more, until the carrots are tender. Delicious!

Serves 4.

Torta di Chocolata

Be advised that this dessert can cause the addiction of chocolate lovers and headaches for the chocolate non-lovers!

1 pound unsweetened butter (4 sticks)
1 12-ounce package semi-sweet chocolate chips
4 1-ounce squares unsweetened chocolate
1 cup sugar
1 cup demitasse (or espresso or strong coffee)

❖ ❖ ❖

8 to 10 eggs

❖ ❖ ❖

Strawberries and orange slices for garnish
Confectioners' sugar

In a large saucepan melt the butter with the chocolate chips and squares. Add the sugar and coffee, blend well.

In a large mixing bowl whisk the eggs; then gradually whisk in the chocolate mixture. Pour into 2 well-greased 9-inch pans. Bake in a 350° oven for 1 hour or until a thin crust forms on top. Remove from the oven, allow to cool for 5 minutes, shake pan to loosen and remove to serving platter.

Serve on dessert plates (with doilies if desired) with a strawberry and an orange slice. Sprinkle with confectioners' sugar.

Serves 16.

Burke Green

R.R. 1, Box 81
East Burke, Vermont 05832
(802) 467-3472

Burke Green, a country guest house in Vermont's Northeast Kingdom, provides a quiet country setting in a spacious farmhouse. Built about 1840 but remodeled with modern conveniences, the inn retains the original

wooden beams and delightful old-fashioned fixtures. The view of Burke Mountain is spectacular.

Guests find a friendly, relaxing atmosphere in the British tradition of bed and breakfast. Each comfortable room has one double or two single beds; guests may choose to have a private or shared bath (perfect for families). Rates are modest, and breakfast is available. Burke Green is located 2.7 miles from the village of East Burke in the midst of ample summer and winter activities for entertainment.

Heavenly Jam

This old Yankee recipe has a delicious flavor.

2 oranges
1 lemon

❖ ❖ ❖

4 cups finely cut peaches
1 16-ounce can crushed pineapple
1 6-ounce jar maraschino cherries
7 cups sugar

Cut the oranges and lemon into small sections, leaving the rind on. Remove the seeds, then chop fine in a blender. Place into a large saucepan with the remaining ingredients. Simmer uncovered until the fruit is translucent and the liquid has thickened. Seal in sterile jars or refrigerate.

Makes 4 to 6 8-ounce jars.

Coconut Tarts

This recipe came from the northeast section of England near Newcastle-on-Tyne where the innkeeper visited in 1965.

6 tablespoons butter
⅓ cup sugar
1 egg
Milk
1 cup shredded coconut
6 drops almond extract

❖ ❖ ❖

Pastry (any kind)
Jam

In a mixing bowl cream butter and sugar until light. In a cup beat the egg with a bit of milk, add to creamed mixture along with coconut and almond extract.

Line tart cups with pastry. Place ½ teaspoon of jam in the center of each cup. Spread the coconut mixture to cover the jam. Bake in a 350° oven for 15 to 20 minutes, until golden brown.

Makes 24 tarts.

Dropped Scones

This recipe came from a bed and breakfast inn in Scotland. Nice for breakfast or tea time.

¾ cup self-rising flour
¼ teaspoon salt
1 tablespoon butter
⅓ cup sugar

❖ ❖ ❖

1 egg
3 tablespoons milk
6 drops lemon flavoring

In a mixing bowl combine flour and salt. Cut in the butter, then add sugar. Beat together egg and milk, add with lemon flavoring to the flour mixture; mix well. Drop 1 tablespoonful at a time onto a greased griddle heated to 350°. Brown and turn. Cool on a wire rack. These are traditionally served fresh at room temperature, spread with butter.

Makes 2 dozen scones.

Cooper Hill Lodge

Cooper Hill Road
Post Office Box 146
East Dover, Vermont 05341
(802) 348-6333

A thirteen-room country inn, Cooper Hill Lodge is in the Green Mountains of southern Vermont. On a quiet country road at an elevation of 2,400 feet, the inn commands a 100-mile view of Vermont, New Hampshire, and Massachusetts. The lodge's atmosphere is homey and relaxed. Home-cooked meals with freshly baked breads and desserts are a treat for inn guests. A variety of fruits and vegetables are grown on the inn's property. Children are welcome.

Cranberry Nut Coffee Cake

1½ cups sifted all-purpose flour
¼ teaspoon salt
2 teaspoons baking powder

❖ ❖ ❖

¼ cup butter (½ stick)
½ cup sugar
1 egg
⅔ cup milk
½ teaspoon vanilla extract

❖ ❖ ❖

¼ cup brown sugar
½ cup chopped nuts
¼ teaspoon cinnamon

❖ ❖ ❖

⅔ cup cranberry pulp

❖ ❖ ❖

1 cup confectioners' sugar
½ teaspoon vanilla
1 tablespoon water

Combine the flour, salt, and baking powder. In a large mixing bowl cream the butter and sugar until light and fluffy. Beat in the egg, milk, and ½ teaspoon vanilla. Add the flour mixture and beat well. Pour into a greased 9-inch square pan.

Combine the brown sugar, nuts, and cinnamon in a small bowl; sprinkle over the batter. Then spoon the cranberry pulp over the top. Bake at 400° for 20 to 25 minutes.

To make icing combine confectioners' sugar, ½ teaspoon of vanilla, and water. Spread over cake while it is still warm.

Serves 6.

Stuffed Pork Chops

6 pork chops, 1¼ to 1½ inches thick (3½ to 4 pounds)
Salt and pepper
1½ cups toasted bread cubes
½ cup apple, chopped, unpared
½ cup shredded sharp Cheddar cheese
2 tablespoons golden raisins
2 tablespoons butter, melted
2 tablespoons orange juice
¼ teaspoon salt
⅛ teaspoon cinnamon

Have a pocket cut in each chop along the fat side. Salt and pepper inside of pockets. Toss together bread cubes, apple, cheese, and raisins. Combine melted butter, orange juice, salt, and cinnamon. Pour over bread mixture and mix gently. Stuff into pork chops lightly. Place in a shallow baking pan. Bake in a 350° oven for 1¼ hours. Cover lightly with foil. Bake 15 minutes more.

Serves 6.

Rhubarb Crumble

½ teaspoon salt
1½ cups all-purpose flour
¼ teaspoon cinnamon
½ cup sugar
⅓ cup butter

❖ ❖ ❖

4 cups rhubarb, chopped
1 cup sugar
⅛ teaspoon salt
1 tablespoon lemon juice

Mix salt, flour, cinnamon, and ½ cup sugar. Cut in butter with a pastry blender until crumbly. Place half of this mixture in a 9-inch square pan.

Mix rhubarb, 1 cup sugar, salt, and lemon juice. Layer over the crumbs in pan. Cover with remaining crumb mixture. Bake in a 375° oven for 45 to 50 minutes. Good served warm with whipped cream or a scoop of ice cream.

Berkson Farms

Enosburg Falls, Vermont 05450
(802) 933-2522

Situated on 600 acres in the Missisquoi River valley, Berkson Farms is a century-old farmhouse with eight newly renovated rooms offering a beautiful Vermont view. Guests enjoy a spacious living room and library, as well as a comfortable family and game room. The Berkson can easily accommodate twelve to fourteen guests. The innkeepers serve a Vermont-style breakfast of farm fresh eggs, milk from the dairy, fresh creamery butter, and maple syrup made on the farm. In the evening, a country-style dinner is served in the dining room around the old wooden dining table. Berkson Farms offers four seasons of country living.

Old-Fashioned Pancakes

1 cup all-purpose flour
1 cup milk
1 egg
1 teaspoon baking powder
1/8 teaspoon baking soda
Margarine
Maple syrup

Combine the flour, milk, egg, baking powder, and soda. Melt 1 teaspoon margarine in a hot skillet. Pour enough batter into the skillet to make a small pancake, and cook until bubbles appear on the pancake. Turn and cook a few seconds more. Serve with maple syrup.

Serves 2 to 4.

Homemade Muffin Mix

Use as a starter mix for wonderful variations of muffins.

10 cups all-purpose flour
1½ cups sugar
⅓ cup baking powder
1 tablespoon salt
2¾ cups shortening

Stir together the flour, sugar, baking powder and salt. With a pastry blender, cut in the shortening until the mixture resembles coarse crumbs. Stores up to 6 weeks at room temperature in a well-sealed container.

Makes about 14 cups of mix.

Lemon-Blueberry Muffins

2 tablespoons sugar
2½ cups Homemade Muffin Mix
½ teaspoon finely shredded lemon peel
1 egg, beaten
⅔ cup milk
1 cup blueberries, drained

Stir together the sugar, muffin mix and lemon peel; add the egg and milk. The batter will be lumpy. Fold in the blueberries. Fill greased muffin cups ⅔ full. Bake in a 400° oven for about 20 minutes.

Makes 12 muffins.

Gelatin Fruit Salad

2 3-ounce packages strawberry gelatin
2 cups boiling water
1 13½-ounce can crushed pineapple, undrained
2 10-ounce packages frozen strawberries
2 large bananas, sliced
1 cup chopped pecans (optional)
2 tablespoon lemon juice

Mix the gelatin with the boiling water; stir until dissolved. Add the pineapple, berries, bananas, pecans, and lemon juice. Stir. Pour into a 2-quart dish and refrigerate overnight. Unmold before serving.

Serves 8 to 10.

Barbecued Spare Ribs

3 pounds country-style spare ribs
Celery salt
Garlic salt
Meat tenderizer
Oregano

❖ ❖ ❖

6 ounces regular barbecue sauce
¼ teaspoon curry powder
Dash Worcestershire sauce
1 tablespoon A-1 sauce
1 tablespoon soy sauce
Oregano
Onion flakes or salt

Trim the ribs of excess fat; separate the ribs. Parboil in water for 15 minutes with a little celery salt, garlic salt, meat tenderizer, and oregano.

In a bowl combine the barbecue sauce and the remaining ingredients. Soak the ribs in the sauce mixture. Barbecue over high heat, turning regularly. As the ribs are done, put back in the extra barbecue sauce. When all of the ribs are done, cover with aluminum foil. Bake in a 350° oven for 10 minutes.

Serves 4.

Hamburger Side Dish

1 pound ground beef
1 16-ounce can corn or fresh corn
1 16-ounce can kidney beans
Salt and pepper
Soy sauce

In a saucepan cook the ground beef; drain off the extra fat. Add the corn and kidney beans. Add salt and pepper and soy sauce to taste. Heat until bubbly and lower the heat to simmer for about 5 minutes.

Serves 4.

Sister-in-Law's Doughnuts

3 eggs
1¼ cups sugar
1 teaspoon nutmeg
¼ teaspoon ginger
Pinch salt
¼ cup melted shortening
2 cups milk
6 or more cups all-purpose flour
2 teaspoons baking soda
1 teaspoon baking powder

Beat the eggs and sugar together; add the nutmeg, ginger, salt, and melted shortening, mix well. Stir in half of the milk and half of the flour, the soda, and baking powder. Add the remaining milk and enough flour so the dough handles easily. Turn the dough onto a floured board and roll out to ³/₈-inch thick. Cut with a doughnut cutter and slide the doughnuts into hot oil with a wide spatula. Turn the doughnuts as they rise to the surface. Fry until golden brown, 1 to 1½ minutes. Remove from oil and drain on paper towels.

Makes 2½ dozen doughnuts.

Dutch Babies

5 tablespoons butter
6 eggs
1½ cups milk
1½ cups all-purpose flour

In a 13x9-inch pan, melt the butter in a 400° oven. In a bowl with a wire whisk or egg beater, beat the eggs, milk and flour. Tilt the melted butter around the sides of a pan, pour in the batter and bake for 20 minutes (it will puff up). Serve with maple syrup.

Serves 6.

Fair Meadows Dairy Farm Bed and Breakfast

Box 430
Franklin, Vermont 05457
(802) 285-2132

Nestled in the northwest corner of Vermont, this American Bed and Breakfast offers peace, quiet, and comfort. The farm, which guests have enjoyed visiting for years, is a traditional Vermont dairy farm. The century-old farmhouse, surrounded by green meadows and quiet woods, is filled with an assortment of plants and antiques. The four large, airy bedrooms have double beds, with cribs also available. Guests are welcome to read books from the family library, enjoy a game of cards, or watch television in a spacious living room. Bicycling, hiking, cross-country skiing, and swimming are just a few of the activities accessible nearby. Major ski areas in Vermont and Quebec are 45 minutes to one hour distant. Breakfast is served in a pine-paneled room overlooking lawns and flowers.

Maple Cream Cheese Pie

1 8-ounce package cream cheese
1 14-ounce can sweetened
**   condensed milk**
⅓ cup lemon juice
2 tablespoons Vermont maple syrup
1 9-inch graham cracker pie crust

❖   ❖   ❖

1 cup Vermont maple syrup
½ cup water

1½ tablespoons cornstarch
¼ cup water
1 egg, beaten

Beat the cream cheese until fluffy and then add the condensed milk, lemon juice, and 2 tablespoons of maple syrup. Beat well. Pour the mixture into pie shell and chill.

In a saucepan bring to a boil 1 cup of maple syrup and ½ cup of water. Dissolve the cornstarch in ¼ cup of water. Add to the syrup, stirring constantly.

Return to a boil and then remove from heat. Add a small amount of syrup mixture to the beaten egg. Return to the pan, stirring until thick. Spread on top of the pie and garnish with chopped walnuts.

Serves 6.

Vermont Maple Cake

4 eggs
¾ cup maple syrup
½ teaspoon vanilla extract
¼ teaspoon salt
1 cup all-purpose flour
½ teaspoon baking powder

❖   ❖   ❖

1 cup Vermont maple syrup
2 egg whites, stiffly beaten

Separate the eggs; beat separately. Heat ¾ cup syrup to a boiling point. Slowly pour in yolks, beating constantly. Fold in beaten whites, vanilla, salt, flour, and baking powder. Bake in greased tube pan in a 325° oven for 50 minutes.

To make maple frosting boil 1 cup of syrup until it spins a thread (firm but not hard ball when tested in cold water). Add slowly to stiffly beaten egg whites, beating constantly. Beat until stiff enough to spread on cake.

Cobble House Inn

Post Office Box 49
Gaysville, Vermont 05746

The Cobble House Inn, an 1864 Federal-style mansion, has six bedrooms, each with a private bath. Now totally renovated, the inn features carved fireplaces, inlaid cherry and bird's-eye maple floors, and a collection of antiques that fills the rooms. Each bedroom has an interesting bed that is the center of attraction.

Set in the Green Mountains, the inn offers a panoramic view for several miles. It also has a 400-foot lawn on the White River, an excellent fishing and swimming spot. The innkeeper, Beau Benson, attended L'Academie de Cuisine in Bethesda, Maryland, and worked for three years as a chef in Washington, D.C. before opening this inn. It has a twenty-seat dining room.

Sautéed Pork Tenderloin
in Crabapple Sauce

½ cup butter (1 stick)
1 8-ounce jar crabapple jelly
4 7-ounce portions pork tenderloin
All-purpose flour
Salt and pepper to taste
½ cup dry white wine

In a sauté pan melt the butter. Melt the jelly in a microwave until loose and liquid-like. Slice the pork tenderloin into ½-inch slices and dip the slices in flour. Sauté in the melted butter until brown; do not burn the butter. When the slices are browned, add salt, pepper, and wine. Reduce the wine by ½. When the wine has reduced, pour the jelly liquid over the pork, shaking the pan until the mixture is bubbly. Serve at once.
Serves 4 to 6.

Veal Florentine

This is a sautéed dish, so the cooking is quick and preparation is a must. Have all of the ingredients at your fingertips.

4 6-ounce portions fresh veal
    scallopini
1 cup frozen chopped spinach,
    thawed and well-drained
¼ cup heavy cream
Dash fresh nutmeg
6 ounces Brie cheese
All-purpose flour
½ cup butter (1 stick)
½ cup dry white wine
3 tablespoons minced shallots
1 clove garlic, minced
1¾ cups heavy cream

Place the veal between waxed paper and pound it flat. In a blender or food processor purée the spinach with ¼ cup of heavy cream and the nutmeg. Cut the skin off the Brie and slice into 8 strips. Lightly flour the veal.

Melt the butter in a large sauté pan or 2 medium pans. When the butter is sizzling, quickly brown the veal and remove to a warm covered plate. The veal will be rare at this stage. Lower the heat and add to the sauté pan the wine, shallots, and garlic. Reduce. Add 1¾ cups of cream and reduce by ½.

While the sauce is reducing, arrange the veal into 4 6-ounce piles. Cover each portion with ¼ of the spinach mix and top with 2 strips of Brie. Place in a microwave oven or under a broiler until cheese is melted, about 1 or 2 minutes. Cover each portion with sauce and serve.

Note: It is very important not to overcook the sauce or it will separate. The veal will be tender only if you don't overcook. It will finish cooking when you melt the cheese. The entire cooking process is only 10 minutes, so preparation is a must! A very elegant entree.
Serves 4.

Raspberry Cloud

This can be made 2 hours ahead and kept in the refrigerator.

1 pint heavy cream
Confectioners'' sugar to taste
1 10-ounce package frozen
    raspberries
½ cup blackberry liqueur

Whip the cream with the sugar. Purée the thawed and drained raspberries and add the blackberry liqueur. Fold the puréed mixture into the whipped cream and pipe into stemmed glasses. Top with a fresh raspberry if available.
Serves 6 to 8.

Guildhall Inn

Box 129
Guildhall, Vermont 05905
(802) 676-3720

Guildhall Inn was built in the early 1800s in Guildhall, the oldest town in the Northeast Kingdom of Vermont. Beautifully restored, the inn offers a quiet escape to the country in an attractive, comfortable manner. Guests can enjoy hiking, canoeing, biking, and cross-country skiing and many nearby tourist attractions. In keeping with its tradition of hospitality, Guildhall Inn serves delicious home-cooked New England meals for its guests and the public.

Old-Fashioned Oatmeal

1 cup water
¼ cup old-fashioned oatmeal
2 tablespoons chopped apple
1 tablespoon raisins
1 teaspoon sunflower seeds
    (optional)

Combine water and oatmeal in a small saucepan. Add apple, raisins, and sunflower seeds. Cook over medium heat for approximately 7 minutes. Top it off with a dab of butter; sprinkle on some brown sugar.

Serves 1.

Herb Vinaigrette Dressing

4 medium cloves garlic, crushed
½ cup plus 2 tablespoons red wine
**   vinegar**
½ cup plus 2 tablespoons oil
½ teaspoon salt
½ teaspoon pepper
Pinch celery seed
½ teaspoon each dry mustard, dill
**   weed, oregano, basil**
2 small scallions, minced
1 tablespoon lemon juice

Combine all ingredients, mixing well. Makes 1½ cups.

Cottage Pudding Cake

⅓ cup butter, softened
1¼ cups sugar
1 egg
1¾ cups all-purpose flour
3 teaspoons baking powder
1 teaspoon salt
1 cup milk

❖   ❖   ❖

½ cup butter (1 stick)
¾ cup sugar
¼ cup light brown sugar, firmly
**   packed**
½ cup light cream
1½ teaspoons vanilla extract
1 teaspoon freshly grated nutmeg
3 tablespoons rum

In a large mixing bowl cream butter and 1¼ cups of sugar. Add egg and beat well. Sift together the flour, baking powder, and salt; add alternately with milk to creamed mixture. Blend well and pour into a greased 8-inch pan. Bake in a 375° oven for 25 minutes.

Make nutmeg sauce by placing butter, ¾ cup of sugar, brown sugar, and cream into a saucepan. Cook slowly for 15 minutes, stirring occasionally. Add vanilla, nutmeg, and rum. Serve warm over cottage pudding cake.

Serves 6.

Saxon Inn

Post Office Box 337
Jericho, Vermont 05465
(802) 899-3015

The Saxon Inn is a small inn with five guest rooms, each with a private bath. All rooms have large windows to enhance the spectacular views. Breakfast is served either in the combination living-dining room with a wood burning stove or beside the fireplace in another room. The seven and one-half-acre front lawn and the heavily wooded nature trails invite strolling.

Hot Cheddar Dip

Great with any unsalted cracker, and wonderful on hamburgers.

1 cup grated sharp Cheddar cheese
½ cup mayonnaise
1 small onion, finely minced

Combine the ingredients and place in a small casserole dish. Bake in a 400° oven for 20 minutes.

Serves 2 to 4.

The Vermont Inn

Route 4
Killington, Vermont 05751
(802) 773-9847

Nestled in the beautiful Green Mountains and surrounded by spectacular mountain views, the Vermont Inn has a country sophistication of its own. This area of the Green Mountains offers the East's best skiing, as well as year-round activities and outdoor sports. The rooms have the look of warm country charm; some of the rooms have private baths and others share facilities. Built as a farmhouse in the nineteenth century, the Vermont Inn is well-known for its fine dining and lodging. The original wood beams are exposed in the living and game rooms, where guests may enjoy congenial company by the warmth of the wood-burning stove, around the piano, or watching television. The lounge provides a rustic setting where guests may gather.

Cream of Tomato Soup

8 cloves garlic, minced
4 cups finely chopped onion
½ cup oil
2 cups finely chopped celery tops
4 cups finely chopped green
**   peppers**
16 cups tomato purée
1 tablespoon sugar
3 tablespoons salt
4 cups water
8 bay leaves
32 whole black peppercorns
16 whole cloves
2 cups heavy cream
3 10¾-ounce cans condensed
**   tomato soup**

In a heavy saucepan sauté the garlic and onion with the oil. Add the celery tops, peppers, tomato purée, sugar, salt, water, bay leaves, peppercorns, and cloves. Bring to a boil; reduce the heat to simmer and simmer uncovered for 1 hour. Press the mixture through a coarse sieve. Stir in the cream and the tomato soup. Heat.

Serves 25.

French Mushroom Soup

2 pounds fresh mushrooms, sliced
½ cup butter (1 stick)
½ cup all-purpose flour
2 quarts milk
1 tablespoon basil
1 teaspoon rosemary
1 10¾-ounce can beef consommé
    (or 1 bouillon cube plus 1 cup
    water)
Worcestershire sauce to taste
Sherry to taste
Salt and pepper to taste
Sour cream

Sauté the mushrooms in the butter; add the flour and blend well. Add the milk and bring to a boil. Add the basil, rosemary, consommé, Worcestershire sauce, and Sherry. Season with salt and pepper. Serve with a dollop of sour cream.

Serves 8.

Fresh Boston Scrod a la Maison

1 cup mayonnaise
1 cup buttermilk
1 cup lemon juice
1 teaspoon minced garlic
Salt and pepper to taste

❖ ❖ ❖

8 6-ounce fillets fresh Boston scrod
2 cups bread crumbs
Lemon garnish

Mix the mayonnaise, buttermilk, lemon juice, garlic, and seasonings until they form a batter; coat the fish fil-lets with the batter and then the bread crumbs. Bake in a 450° oven for 12 to 15 minutes on a greased baking sheet. Serve with a lemon garnish.

Serves 8.

Cheesecake

1 16-ounce carton cottage cheese
4 8-ounce packages cream cheese
4 eggs, slightly beaten
1½ cups sugar
1½ tablespoons lemon juice
1 teaspoon vanilla extract
¼ cup all-purpose flour
¼ cup cornstarch

❖ ❖ ❖

1 pint sour cream
½ cup butter (1 stick), melted

In a food processor cream together the cottage cheese, cream cheese, eggs, sugar, lemon juice, vanilla, flour, and cornstarch and pour into a large bowl. Add the sour cream and melted butter and mix thoroughly. Pour into a but-tered springform pan. Bake in a 350° oven for 1 hour. Reduce the heat to 275° and bake 45 minutes longer.

Serves 12 to 16.

Frozen Cranberry Pie

1 8-ounce package cream cheese
8 ounces whole cranberry sauce
½ pint heavy whipping cream
½ cup sugar
1 9-inch baked and cooled pie shell

❖ ❖ ❖

Whipped cream or cranberry sauce
    and Kirsch garnish

Mix the cream cheese and cranberry sauce together with an electric mixer at high speed until blended; slowly add the heavy cream and sugar and whip until thickened. Pour into the pie shell; cover with plastic wrap and place in the freezer. Remove a few minutes before serving. Garnish with whipped cream or top with hot whole cran-berry sauce flavored with Kirsch.

Serves 8.

The Highland House: A Country Inn

Route 100
Londonderry, Vermont 05148
(802) 824-3019

The Highland House is an 1842 white colonial inn, with swimming pool and tennis court, set on thirty-two acres. It has seventeen rooms, fifteen with pri-vate baths and four with private sitting rooms. Rates include a full breakfast. Special features include the expansive maple-shaded lawn, the fisherman's net hammock, croquet, and horse-shoes. The Highland House is open to the public for dinner Wednesday through Sunday by reservation. It pro-vides classic dining with homemade soups, breads, and desserts.

Cream of Zucchini Soup

2 to 2½ pounds zucchini
1 medium onion, chopped
Chicken stock
1½ tablespoons dillweed
1 cup heavy cream

Slice unpeeled zucchini; place in a large saucepan with onion. Add enough stock to cover the mixture. Add the dillweed; cover and cook for 30 minutes or until vegetables are soft. Remove from heat and purée in the blender, one cup at a time. Add cream. Heat thoroughly without boiling.

Serves 4.

Cheddar Cheese Bread

2 cups all-purpose flour
1 ¼-ounce package active dry yeast
2½ cups shredded sharp Cheddar
  cheese
1¾ cups milk
3 tablespoons oil
2 tablespoons sugar
2 tablespoons oregano
1 teaspoon salt

❖   ❖   ❖

3 to 3¼ cups all-purpose flour

In a large mixing bowl stir together 2 cups of flour and the yeast. In a saucepan heat Cheddar cheese, milk, oil, sugar, oregano, and salt just to lukewarm (115 to 120°). Add to the flour mixture. Beat at low speed of mixer for ½ minute, scraping sides of the bowl constantly. Beat 3 minutes at high speed. Stir in as much of the remaining flour as you can mix with spoon.

Turn the dough out on a lightly floured surface. Knead in enough of the remaining flour to make a moderately stiff dough. Continue kneading 8 to 10 minutes more or until the dough is smooth and elastic. Shape into a ball. Place in a lightly greased bowl, turning once to grease. Cover. Let rise in warm place for about 1¼ hours. Punch down. Divide dough in ½. Shape into 2 loaves. Place in 2 greased loaf pans. Cover and let rise until doubled. Bake in a 350° oven for 40 to 45 minutes.

Makes 2 loaves.

Marinara Sauce

¼ cup olive oil
2 cups coarsely chopped onions
½ cup sliced carrots
2 to 3 cloves garlic

❖   ❖   ❖

1 28-ounce can tomatoes
1 8-ounce can tomato sauce
Salt and pepper to taste

❖   ❖   ❖

1 teaspoon oregano
1 teaspoon basil
¼ cup butter (½ stick)

Heat oil in a large frypan. Add onions, carrots, and garlic. Cook and stir until soft and brown. In the meantime, put the tomatoes through a foodmill. Add tomatoes and tomato sauce to the carrot-onion mixture. Add salt and pepper. Partially cover and simmer for 30 minutes. Remove from heat and put the mixture through foodmill. Return to the pan and add herbs and butter. Cook (partially covered) slowly for 30 minutes.

Makes 6½ to 7 cups.

Apple Crisp

6 cups sliced apples
1 cup pine nuts (or walnuts)
¾ teaspoon cinnamon
¾ teaspoon nutmeg

❖   ❖   ❖

⅓ cup butter
1 cup brown sugar, firmly packed
1 cup oats

Place apple slices in a greased 10-inch square pan; add pine nuts and spices. Using a pastry blender, cut the butter into the brown sugar and oats. Sprinkle over the top and bake in a 375° oven for 30 to 40 minutes.

Serves 6.

Kentucky Derby Pie

½ cup butter (1 stick), melted
¾ cup sugar
½ cup all-purpose flour
2 eggs, lightly beaten
1 tablespoon Bourbon

❖   ❖   ❖

¾ cup semi-sweet chocolate chips
1 cup chopped nuts

❖   ❖   ❖

1 unbaked 8-inch pie shell

In a mixing bowl cream butter and sugar. Stir in the flour, then the eggs and Bourbon. Spread the chocolate chips and nuts in the bottom of the pie shell. Pour in the filling. Bake in a 350° oven for 30 to 40 minutes. Serve warm with ice cream.

Serves 6.

Echo Lake Inn

Post Office Box 142
Ludlow, Vermont 05149
(802) 228-8602

An authentic historic inn, Echo Lake Inn has hosted President Coolidge and President McKinley along with Henry Ford, Thomas Edison and Andrew Carnegie. Attractions include tennis, swimming, boating, fishing, hiking, and cycling, and the inn is minutes to golf, horseback riding, and downhill skiing. The cuisine, featuring unique sauces, homemade pasta, and desserts, has won culinary awards. Depending on the season, cocktails and dinner are served on the porch or in the Basket Case Lounge. The inn is open year round.

Award Winning Citrus Pasta Appetizer

Juice of 3 lemons
Juice of 3 oranges
Juice of 1 lime
⅓ cup Triple Sec
1½ cups all-purpose flour
½ teaspoon salt
2 eggs

❖   ❖   ❖

2 cups Sauterne
¼ cup Triple Sec
1 shallot, minced
3 cups chicken stock (or canned
  chicken broth)
¼ cup butter (½ stick)
½ cup all-purpose flour
2 cups heavy cream

❖   ❖   ❖

Echo Lake Inn

Duck and Mushroom Soup

1 duckling

❖ ❖ ❖

1 onion, chopped
2 ribs celery
1 carrot, chopped
Sprigs parsley
Thyme
Marjoram
1 bay leaf

❖ ❖ ❖

1 onion, cut in 1-inch cubes
1 clove garlic, minced
2½ pounds mushrooms
1 cup Port wine
1 teaspoon thyme
1 bay leaf
1 quart duck stock
¼ cup melted butter
½ cup all-purpose flour
1 pint heavy cream
Salt and pepper

1 apple
1 pear
3 bell peppers (1 red, 1 yellow, 1
    green)

❖ ❖ ❖

1 teaspoon salt
1 tablespoon oil
2 tablespoons butter

In a saucepan combine the lemon, orange, and lime juices. Add the Triple Sec. Bring to a boil, lower the heat, and reduce to the consistency of a very thick syrup. Place the flour on a board and make a well in the center. Combine the egg and salt and place in the center of the flour. Add 3 tablespoons of the syrup. With a fork or by hand fold the flour into the egg and syrup until well-blended. Knead until a smooth ball of dough is formed. Knead the dough for about 10 minutes. Let the dough stand for 1 hour. Roll out and stretch the dough, sprinkling with flour to keep the dough from sticking. Roll about 10 times until the dough is paper thin and translucent. Let it dry about 30 minutes. Before it becomes brittle, roll the dough into a scroll and cut diagonally into strips any width desired.

Combine the wine, Triple Sec, and shallots in a saucepan. Bring to a boil and reduce by ¼. Add the chicken stock, return to a boil and reduce by ⅓.

Melt the butter and mix in the flour until a smooth paste is formed. Cook for 10 minutes over low heat, stirring occasionally. When the wine and broth mixture has reduced, add to the flour and butter in a saucepan. Simmer for 10 minutes. Blend in the heavy cream and simmer for 15 minutes, stirring occasionally. Strain the sauce through a fine strainer and reserve.

Core the apple and pear. Cut in half and slice. Leave the skins on, as this adds to the color of the dish. Seed the peppers; cut in half, lengthwise. Cut in ½-inch wide julienne strips. Reserve.

Bring a large saucepan filled with water to a boil. Add 1 teaspoon of salt and 1 tablespoon of oil. Add the pasta. Cook until al dente.

Meanwhile, in a large sauté pan melt 2 tablespoons of butter. Over medium heat, sauté the peppers for about 3 to 4 minutes. Add the fruit and cook for 1 minute. Add the cream sauce and then lower heat to a slow simmer.

When the pasta is ready, drain well and turn out onto a serving dish. Cover with the sauce mixture and serve.

Serves 16.

Roast the duck on wire racks until done, about 2 to 2½ hours. Let cool. Remove all meat from the breast and legs and cut into fine julienne strips. Reserve the meat. Reserve the bones and scraps; discard the skin and fat.

To prepare the duck stock, place all of the scraps and bones from the roasted duck in a large saucepan. Add the chopped onion, celery, carrot, a few sprigs of fresh parsley and the herbs. Fill with water and bring to a full boil. Lower the heat to a simmer. Simmer for 3 to 5 hours. Remove from heat and strain through a fine strainer. Discard the scraps.

In a large soup pot, sauté the diced onion and garlic until translucent. Add the mushrooms. Cook until the mushrooms are slightly browned. Add Port wine, thyme, and bay leaf. Bring to a boil and simmer a few minutes. Add the duck stock. Bring to a full boil and lower the heat to a simmer. Simmer for 1 hour.

While the soup is simmering, melt the butter over low heat. Add flour gradually until it forms a thick paste. Cook over low heat for 5 minutes and reserve. Remove the soup from the heat. Strain through a colander and return the stock to the heat. Place the strained mushroom mixture in a food processor or sieve and process to a purée.

When the stock returns to a boil, add the butter and flour paste gradually until it becomes thickened. Simmer for about 10 minutes, stirring occasionally. Remove and strain through fine strainer to remove any lumps. Combine the thickened stock and mushroom purée; mix well. Add the heavy cream, salt, and pepper to taste. Serve piping hot with julienned duck meat sprinkled on the top.

Serves 6 to 8.

Hazelnut Pork
in Port Wine Sauce

2 eggs
½ cup milk
Hazelnuts, finely ground
1 cup all-purpose flour
8 boneless pork loin medallions,
    about ½-inch thick

❖ ❖ ❖

1 cup Port wine
1 shallot, minced
¼ cup wine vinegar
1 cup heavy cream
1 cup butter (2 sticks)

In a medium-sized bowl blend the eggs and milk. Place the ground nuts in a separate bowl and the flour in a third bowl. Dredge the pork in flour, then dip into the egg mixture. Bread the meat in the nuts, pressing them onto the meat firmly. In a large sauté pan melt a little butter. Place the pork in the pan and brown one side. Turn the pork over and put the pan in a 375° oven for 5 to 10 minutes.

To make the Port wine sauce, in a small saucepan place the Port wine, shallot, and wine vinegar. Bring to a boil and reduce by ¾. Add the heavy cream. Return to a boil and reduce by ¾ again. Cut 1 cup of butter into small chips. Reduce the heat to the lowest possible flame. Slowly add the butter chips, blending with a whip as they melt. Be careful to start slowly with

only 1 or 2 chips and gradually build up until all of the butter has been blended into the sauce, to protect against separation. Remove from heat and serve with the pork.

Serves 8.

Lamb Chops
with Pasta and Garlic Hollandaise

¼ pound spinach linguine
¼ pound tomato linguine
2 to 3 cloves peeled garlic
1 cup Hollandaise sauce
Loin lamb chops
Fresh parsley, chopped

Cook the pasta al dente and then rinse under cold water to remove the starch. In a small oven-proof dish, place the garlic cloves sprinkled with a little oil. Bake in a 350° oven until light golden brown. Remove from the oven and crush into a paste. Reserve.

Prepare a normal Hollandaise sauce according to your favorite recipe. Blend in the garlic paste and let stand. Charbroil the lamb chops until medium-rare to medium. Just before they are ready to serve, rinse the pasta under very hot water to reheat it. Divide the pasta onto serving plates; place the chops on top of the pasta and spoon the sauce over each chop. Sprinkle with chopped parsley and serve.

Serves 8.

Chocolate Decadence
with Raspberry Sauce

1 pound dark sweet chocolate,
    broken into pieces
½ cup plus 2 tablespoons butter

❖ ❖ ❖

4 eggs
1 tablespoon sugar
1 tablespoon all-purpose flour

❖ ❖ ❖

2 cups heavy cream
1 tablespoon confectioners' sugar
1 teaspoon vanilla extract

❖ ❖ ❖

Chocolate shavings
1 10-ounce package frozen
    raspberries, thawed (or ½ cup
    fresh raspberries)
1 tablespoon Kirsch
2 tablespoons sugar

Butter an 8-inch springform pan. Place an 8-inch round of waxed paper on the bottom. Butter the waxed paper and flour the pan. Melt chocolate and butter together in a heavy saucepan over low heat. Mix to blend. Cool.

Place the eggs and sugar in the bowl of an electric mixer and place the bowl over hot water, stirring until the sugar is dissolved and eggs are warm. Remove and beat at high speed until the whipped eggs are cool and tripled in volume. Fold in the flour. Fold half of the whipped egg mixture into the melted chocolate and butter. Carefully fold in the remaining egg mixture. Pour the batter into the prepared pan and bake in a 425° oven for 15 minutes. Remove from the oven and cool in the pan. Place the cake, still in the pan, in the refrigerator until very firm.

Whip the cream with the sugar and vanilla until stiff. Remove the cake from the refrigerator. Carefully remove it from the pan, invert onto a serving platter, and peel off the waxed paper. Working quickly, frost the top and sides of the cake with ⅔ of the whipped cream and place the rest in a pastry bag fitted with a star tube; make decorative rosettes around the perimeter. Decorate the center of the cake with chocolate shavings and return to the refrigerator. Chill until firm.

To make the raspberry sauce, place the raspberries and juices in a food processor fitted with the steel blade. Process until puréed. Strain into a bowl. Add the Kirsh and sugar. Stir to blend. Serve each slice of cake with several spoonfuls of raspberry sauce on the side.

Serves 16.

The Governor's Inn

86 Main Street
Ludlow, Vermont 05149
(802) 228-8830

The Governor's Inn

Built originally by Vermont Governor William Wallace Stickney as his private dwelling, The Governor's Inn stands as a classic example of the fine craftsmanship of the late Victorian period (circa 1890). As a stylish, romantic, intimate village inn, it now has become a haven for enjoying life's pleasures and a base for exploring Vermont. The Governor's Inn is less than one mile from Okemo Mountain, popular for its skiing facilities. At this inn guests find excellent food, a cozy room, friendliness, and warm, generous hospitality.

Apple Butter

2 cups unsweetened applesauce
½ cup sugar
1 teaspoon cinnamon
¼ teaspoon allspice
Pinch ginger
Pinch cloves

In a saucepan combine the ingredients and bring to a boil. Reduce the heat and simmer for 1 hour. Cool. Serve on pear bread.
Makes 2½ cups.

Rum Raisin French Toast

¾ cup rum raisin ice cream, melted
3 eggs, beaten
1 tablespoon dark rum
¼ teaspoon cinnamon
5 tablespoons finely ground walnuts
6 tablespoons butter
6 (or more) slices raisin bread

Scoops of rum raisin ice cream
Vermont maple syrup

Combine the melted ice cream, eggs, rum, cinnamon, and walnuts in a bowl. Beat with a wire whisk until well-mixed. Dip the raisin bread into the egg mixture, coating well on both sides. Sauté in butter over medium-low heat until toasted. Serve with a scoop of rum raisin ice cream with Vermont maple syrup poured over all.
Serves 3 to 4.

Eggs Ville Ludlow

4 trout fillets, halved
1 cup milk
1½ cups all-purpose flour
½ teaspoon salt
¼ teaspoon freshly ground pepper
Vegetable oil or bacon fat
16 poached eggs
Hollandaise sauce
Watercress

Dip the trout in milk and set aside for 5 minutes. Roll in flour seasoned with salt and pepper. Shallow fry in hot oil until crisp and nicely browned, about 5 minutes. Remove with tongs and drain. Place a piece of trout on each of 8 heated breakfast plates. Top fish with 2 poached eggs and some Hollandaise sauce, and garnish with crisp watercress.
Serves 8.

The First Lady's Cheese Spread

½ cup dry white wine
Juice of 2 lemons
¼ cup freshly snipped chives
1 tablespoon white pepper
3 cloves garlic, minced
2 tablespoons sweet basil
2 teaspoons marjoram
4 8-ounce packages cream cheese

Simmer the wine, lemon juice, and seasonings in a small saucepan for 15 minutes. Place in a food processor with the cream cheese. Mix well. Chill for several days to ripen. Serve at room temperature with crackers.
Makes about 2½ cups.

The Governor's Grog

½ cup fresh lemon juice
¼ cup sugar
1 cup cranberry juice
1 cup orange juice
1 cup strong tea
12 cloves
Dark rum
Orange slices
Cinnamon sticks
Maraschino cherries

Heat the lemon juice, sugar, cranberry juice, orange juice, strong tea, and cloves together, but do not boil. Pour into glass coffee mugs and add 2 ounces of dark rum to each mug. Garnish with a fresh orange slice, a cinnamon stick, and a maraschino cherry.

Makes about 4 cups.

Iced Victorian Tea

1 cup water
2 tablespoons sugar
3 whole cloves
1 cinnamon stick
2 tea bags
2 cups apricot nectar
2 tablespoons frozen orange juice
    concentrate

❖ ❖ ❖

Club soda
Dark rum
Grand Marnier

❖ ❖ ❖

Orange slices
Strawberries

In a saucepan combine the water, sugar, cloves, cinnamon, and tea bags. Simmer for 5 minutes, then allow to stand for 15 minutes. Strain into a glass container. Add the apricot nectar and orange juice concentrate. Stir. Allow to cool and then refrigerate. When ready to serve, pour over ice in a Brandy snifter and add club soda to each glass. Add 1 ounce of light rum and a splash of Grand Marnier to each. Garnish with a fresh orange slice and a plump, ripe strawberry, stem and all.

Also wonderful without the rum and Grand Marnier.

Makes about a quart and will serve 8 with a little sip for the cook.

Okemo Snowberry

Try this lovely warm cheer after a brisk walk in the clear, cool Vermont air. Double the recipe to share with a friend!

1 ounce vodka
1½ ounces strawberry liqueur
½ ounce simple syrup
1 ounce lemon juice
5 ounces water
½ ounce Kirschwasser
Fresh strawberry and thin slice
    lemon for garnish

In a small saucepan, heat the vodka, strawberry liqueur, syrup, lemon juice, and water, being careful not to boil. Pour this mixture into a large glass mug. Float the strawberry, lemon slice, and Kirschwasser on top of the drink.

Serves 1.

Game Hens Grand Marnier
with Orange Pecan Stuffing

½ cup chicken broth
1 cup mandarin orange segments
1 cup chopped scallions
2 cups sliced celery
2 tablespoons butter
3 cups cooked white rice
½ cup chopped pecans
Salt and pepper to taste

❖ ❖ ❖

4 game hens
½ cup butter (1 stick)
Salt and white pepper

❖ ❖ ❖

¼ cup Grand Marnier
1 cup chicken stock
2 tablespoons roux
1 11-ounce can Mandarin orange
    segments, drained

Make the orange pecan stuffing by combining the broth and oranges. Sauté the scallions and celery in butter until just tender but still crisp. Add the rice, pecans, salt, and pepper. Add the combined broth and orange slices and mix well. One teaspoon of poultry seasoning may be added, if you wish a more seasoned stuffing.

Prepare the game hens and stuff with orange pecan stuffing. Spread butter on the hens; salt and pepper them, and arrange in a shallow baking pan. Roast in a 350° oven for 1 hour. Remove the hens to a warming platter.

To make the Grand Marnier Sauce, pour off the excess grease in the roasting pan. Add the Grand Marnier and ignite. When the flames burn out, stir in the chicken stock and deglaze the pan. Stir in the roux and continue to cook until slightly thickened. Add the drained mandarin orange slices. Place the hens on heated serving dishes and pour the hot sauce over them, coating the entire hen.

Serves 4.

The Governor's Braised Quail

9 quail
Fonds de braise (1 carrot and 2
    onions, sliced)
Butter
Chicken stock

❖ ❖ ❖

12 ounces ginger preserves
Watercress
Cherry tomatoes

Truss the quail and sear in a 450° oven for 10 minutes, until lightly browned. Sauté the fonds de braise in butter and place the birds on the sautéed vegetables. Add the chicken stock to cover the quail halfway. Bring the stock to a light boil; cover the braising pot tightly and braise in a 325° oven for 40 minutes. Remove the quail from the braising liquid when done. Cool to room temperature. When cool, cover lightly with clear wrap and refrigerate.

When ready to serve, heat the chilled quail with the strained preserves to glaze them. Arrange on a plate with watercress and cherry tomatoes. This recipe allows for three quail per person. Prepare a day or two in advance of your picnic.

Serves 3.

Meatballs for a Santa Watch

"We know this recipe is magic because Santa has arrived every year."

3 pounds ground beef
1½ cups cracker crumbs
3 eggs
½ cup minced onion
2 tablespoons chopped parsley
1 cup milk, scalded
Salt and pepper to taste

❖ ❖ ❖

¾ cup ketchup
½ cup water
¼ cup cider vinegar
¼ teaspoon pepper
2 tablespoons brown sugar
1 tablespoon chopped onion
2 tablespoons Worcestershire sauce
1½ teaspoons salt
1 teaspoon dry mustard
6 to 10 drops hot sauce

Mix the beef, cracker crumbs, eggs, onion, parsley, milk, salt, and pepper well and form into small, firm balls. Bake on cookie sheets in a 350° oven for 15 minutes. Drain well.

To make the sauce heat the ketchup, water, vinegar, pepper, brown sugar, onion, Worcestershire sauce, salt, mustard, and hot sauce. Add the meatballs. Transfer to a chafing dish and serve.

Makes 150 meatballs.

Steak with Horseradish Cream

1 pound flank steak
⅓ cup soy sauce
⅓ cup white wine
2 tablespoons oil

❖ ❖ ❖

1 large clove garlic
1 1½-ounce piece fresh horseradish, peeled and cut in half
1 cup heavy whipping cream
1 tablespoon red wine vinegar
1 teaspoon Worcestershire sauce
½ teaspoon salt
3 drops hot sauce

Slice the steak into 5-inch strips. Combine the soy sauce and white wine in a shallow, glass baking dish. Add the steak and marinate in the refrigerator for 24 hours. Brush the steak with oil and broil on a rack 6 inches from the heat for 1 minute on each side, and then 5 minutes on each side. Allow to cool. Brush with the marinade juices. When cold, cut into very thin, diagonal slices. Serve with toothpicks for dipping into horseradish cream.

To make the horseradish cream drop garlic into food processor with steel blade and with motor running, through the feed tube and mince finely. Add the horseradish and continue to mince. With the machine still running, pour the cream through the feed tube in a slow stream, and process until the mixture is thick and fluffy. Add the vinegar, Worcestershire sauce, salt, and hot sauce. Blend for 5 seconds. Serve immediately with steak slices and crackers.

Serves about 10.

The Governor's Inn Mushroom Strudel

6 cups minced mushrooms, tops and stems
1 teaspoon salt
¼ teaspoon curry powder
6 tablespoons Sherry
¼ cup chopped shallots
¼ cup butter (½ stick)
1 cup sour cream
3 tablespoons dry bread crumbs

❖ ❖ ❖

1 16-ounce package frozen phyllo dough, thawed
½ cup butter (1 stick), melted
1 cup dry bread crumbs
Sour cream
Chopped parsley

Sauté the mushrooms with the seasonings, Sherry, and shallots in butter until the mushrooms are wilted and the liquid is gone. This will take about 20 minutes over medium-low heat. Allow to cool. Add the sour cream and dry bread crumbs. Refrigerate overnight.

Unwrap the phyllo dough carefully. Place a sheet of dough on a large breadboard. Brush with melted butter and sprinkle with bread crumbs. Repeat until you have 4 layers. Spoon half of the mushroom mixture onto the narrow end of the dough. Turn the long sides of dough in about 1 inch to seal the filling; then roll the dough up like a jelly roll. Brush the completed roll with butter and sprinkle with a few more crumbs. Place on a lightly greased cookie sheet. Mark with a sharp knife into eight equal slices. Repeat the above process using the remaining mushroom filling. Bake in a 375° oven for 40 minutes. Garnish with a small dollop of sour cream and chopped parsley. Serve hot.

Makes 16 slices.

Lamb Gourmet

1 750 ml bottle dry red wine
2 teaspoons fresh rosemary
6 tablespoons chopped shallots
2 ribs celery, chopped
2 carrots, grated
½ teaspoon freshly ground pepper
4 cloves garlic, crushed
½ bunch parsley, chopped

❖ ❖ ❖

1 cup veal stock
½ cup butter (1 stick)
Loin lamb chops, about 3 or 4 ounces each
Clarified butter
Olive oil

Combine the wine, rosemary, shallots, celery, carrots, pepper, and garlic in a pot. Bring to a boil, reduce heat, and simmer 20 minutes. Cool. Place the lamb chops in a flat, shallow, glass baking dish, and pour cooled marinade over them. Cover and refrigerate for three days, turning the chops over once during the marinating period.

After three days remove the lamb, strain the liquid, and boil it down to 1 cup. Add the veal stock and continue to boil until the liquids are reduced to 3 tablespoons. Remove from the heat and slowly whisk in the butter, 1 tablespoon at a time, until a well-blended emulsion forms. Pan fry the lamb in clarified butter and olive oil, turning frequently. Place the chops in a pool of sauce on a heated dinner plate.

The marinade is sufficient for 16 lamb chops.

Vitello Tonnato

Olive oil
Fonds de braise (1 carrot, sliced, and 2 onions, sliced)
1 4-pound veal shoulder roast
1 quart veal stock
Bouquet garni

❖   ❖   ❖

1 6½-ounce can tuna fish, packed in oil
3 egg yolks
2 tablespoons lemon juice
1 teaspoon Dijon mustard
1½ cups olive oil
6 anchovy fillets
1 tablespoon capers
Braising liquid
Light cream
Pepper

❖   ❖   ❖

3 hard-boiled eggs, quartered
Lemons
Black brine-cured olives
Parsley
Capers

In a heavy-bottomed braising pot heat the olive oil. Sauté the fonds de braise briefly; remove from the pot and add a little more olive oil. Brown the veal roast on all sides. Return the fonds de braise and add the bouquet garni to the pot. Add the veal stock until it comes halfway up the roast and heat to a boil. Place a lid on the braising pot and place it in a 325° oven to braise for 20 minutes. Turn the meat over and continue braising until a meat thermometer reads 150° (about 3 hours). Remove the meat from the pot and cool. Strain the braising liquid and cool.

To make the sauce drain the tuna fish and reserve the oil. Make a mayonnaise out of the egg yolks, lemon juice, mustard, and tuna oil (measure the tuna oil and add enough olive oil to equal 1½ cups). Do not salt the mayonnaise. In a blender purée the tuna fish, anchovy fillets, and capers. Add just enough braising liquid to make this mixture smooth. Add this purée to the mayonnaise and blend. Thin this sauce to a spreading consistency by adding more braising liquid and light cream. Correct the seasoning with pepper and lemon juice, if necessary.

When the veal is cool, slice it into medium-thin slices and arrange them on a platter. Spread sauce on each of the slices and refrigerate. The sauce will gel slightly due to the stock. When the sauce has set, garnish the platter with hard-boiled eggs, lemon wedges, black olives, and little bouquets of parsley. Sprinkle with capers.

Serves 10 to 12.

Bluefish Flambé

4 ½ pound bluefish fillets
2 tablespoons butter, melted
3 tablespoons minced onion
½ teaspoon salt
¼ teaspoon freshly ground pepper
7 tablespoons gin
2 tablespoons butter, melted

Grease a broiler pan that is just large enough to accommodate the fish and place them in it side by side. Pour 2 tablespoons of melted butter over the fillets and sprinkle with the onion, salt, and pepper. Place 3 inches below the broiler and let the fish start to brown.

Meanwhile, mix gin with 2 tablespoons butter. When fish is done, remove to heated dinner plates. Pour gin over fish and flambé.

Serves 4 with drama.

Country-Style Shrimp Remoulade

1 cup finely minced celery
1 cup finely minced green onions
1 cup finely minced parsley
½ cup cornichons, finely minced
2 tablespoons crushed garlic
2 cups good quality coarsely ground mustard
¼ cup horseradish
1½ cups oil
½ cup red wine vinegar
1 teaspoon salt or to taste
2 tablespoons Worcestershire sauce

❖   ❖   ❖

Romaine lettuce
2 pounds boiled shrimp, peeled, deveined and chilled

Combine all of the ingredients except the lettuce and shrimp. Mix with a wire whisk until well-blended.

Place a portion of lettuce on chilled salad plates and top with equal portions of shrimp. Spoon ¼ to ½ cup of sauce into little dishes and place on the edge of the salad plates.

Serves 8 or 10, depending on the size of the shrimp.

Salmon au Champagne

4 slices fresh salmon
1 bay leaf
1 sprig fresh thyme
Salt and pepper
Court bouillon

❖   ❖   ❖

1 onion, finely chopped
2 shallots, chopped
1 tablespoon butter
½ cup dry Champagne
¼ cup heavy cream
Sliced mushrooms for garnish

Place the slices of salmon in cold court bouillon and bring slowly to a boil. As soon as the liquid starts to simmer, remove the cooking pan to the edge of the heat and poach the fish very gently for 5 minutes. Remove, drain, and place the fish on warmed serving dishes.

To make the Sauce au Champagne cook the onion and shallots gently in the butter. Do not allow to brown. When the vegetables are soft, add the Champagne. Allow the liquid to reduce slowly by half. Add the cream and, stirring all the time, reduce the sauce until thickened. Strain the sauce and pour it over the poached salmon. Place a few sliced mushrooms on top as garnish. This is good served with fresh green peas and steamed small red potatoes.

Serves 4.

Oysters Benedict

This is served as a hot appetizer. It could, however, be served as an entree for dinner or at brunch.

48 medium-sized oysters
Clarified butter
Salt and white pepper
24 toast rounds
24 slices Canadian bacon
Hollandaise sauce
Fresh parsley

Sauté the drained oysters in clarified butter over a low flame until the edges of the oysters begin to curl. Carefully salt and pepper to taste. Place 2 rounds of toast on 12 individual serving dishes and top the toast with Canadian bacon. Place 2 oysters on top of the bacon and spoon on Hollandaise sauce. Garnish with a crisp sprig of parsley. Serve at once.

Serves 12.

Poached Pears in Kir

4 firm pears (almost, but not quite ripe)
Juice of 1 lemon
2½ cups dry white wine
½ cup Crème de Cassis
½ cup sugar

Drop the pears into a bowl of cold water which contains the juice of 1 lemon. In an enameled saucepan combine the wine, Crème de Cassis, and the sugar. Bring to a boil and stir until the sugar is dissolved. Simmer this syrup for 5 minutes. Drain the pears and place them in the syrup. Cover. Poach the pears in the syrup for about 10 to 20 minutes, or until they look slightly transparent. Transfer the pears with a slotted spoon to a bowl. Bring the syrup to a boil and reduce to about 2 cups. Pour this reduced syrup over the pears and allow to stand until cooled to room temperature. Serve in stemmed dessert dishes and pour a little syrup over each serving.

Serves 6.

Baked Indian Chowder

½ cup butter (1 stick)
5 chopped leeks
¼ cup all-purpose flour
Corn cut from 12 ears
2 cups cooked pumpkin
1 quart light cream
2½ cups Chablis
1 cup dry Sherry
½ cup chicken stock
Dash white pepper
Dash allspice

❖ ❖ ❖

½ pound lean bacon
Vermont Cheddar cheese

In a good-sized chowder pot melt the butter. Add the chopped leeks, flour, corn, cooked pumpkin, light cream, chablis, dry Sherry, chicken stock, white pepper, and allspice. Simmer for about 15 minutes.

Meanwhile, fry the bacon. Drain the bacon, chop it into smallish pieces, and set aside. Whip one blender full of chowder into a smooth purée. Return the purée to the bacon pan and simmer for 5 minutes to pick up flavor. Combine with the mixture in the chowder pot. Add the reserved bacon and simmer for 30 minutes.

Ladle chowder into oven-proof bowls or individual baking dishes. Top each dish with a slice of Vermont Cheddar cheese. Bake in a 400° oven for 30 minutes. Serve bubbling hot.

Serves 6 for a complete meal, or 8 as an appetizer.

Bourbon Squash Soufflé

2 teaspoons soft butter
2½ pounds butternut squash, peeled, seeded and cubed
6 tablespoons Bourbon
½ teaspoon salt
Pepper to taste
¼ teaspoon nutmeg
¼ cup butter (½ stick)
2 tablespoons Vermont maple syrup
1 egg yolk
3 egg whites, room temperature
Pinch cream of tartar

Place a collar of foil around a soufflé dish and grease with 2 teaspoons of soft butter. Cook the squash until tender, drain well, and purée it in a food processor. Flavor it with Bourbon, salt, pepper, nutmeg, butter, and maple syrup. Cool this purée to room temperature. Beat the egg yolk until thick and whisk into the purée; set aside. Beat the egg whites until foamy. Sprinkle in the cream of tartar and continue to beat until stiff. Fold the whites rapidly into the purée. Spoon the soufflé mixture into the prepared soufflé dish.

Bake in a 325° oven for 50 minutes.

Serves 8.

Marble Asparagus

2 bunches fresh asparagus
2 cups water

❖ ❖ ❖

2 pounds lump crabmeat
¼ cup butter (½ stick), melted
½ cup dry Sherry
2 tablespoons all-purpose flour
2 cups light cream
Whipped cream
4 to 6 tablespoons grated Parmesan cheese

Rinse the asparagus and cut off the hard end of the stems. With a sharp paring knife, peel the remaining stem, being very careful not to cut the tender tips. Steam over boiling water until just crisp-tender. Remove and divide among 4 to 6 buttered ramekins.

Sauté the crabmeat in melted butter over low heat in a heavy skillet. Add the dry Sherry and simmer until reduced by half. Add the flour and light cream. Cook until thickened. Spoon the crab meat mixture over the asparagus. Top each ramekin with whipped cream and sprinkle each with 1 tablespoon of Parmesan cheese. Place in a 400° oven to brown the cream.

Serves 4 to 6.

Rice Salad Village Inn

2 cups uncooked long grain white rice
Salt
½ cup butter (½ stick)
Salt and pepper to taste
½ cup toasted, slivered almonds
1 14-ounce jar marinated artichoke hearts, drained and quartered
½ cup cooked fresh peas (do not use canned)
¼ cup chopped pimiento
1 bunch scallions, thinly sliced
½ pound marinated sliced mushrooms
½ cup sliced black olives
½ pound salami, diced
½ cup chopped fresh parsley

❖   ❖   ❖

1½ teaspoons dried basil
1½ teaspoons dried tarragon
1 teaspoon Dijon mustard
¼ cup red wine vinegar
¼ cup oil
Salt and pepper to taste
Watercress
Cherry tomatoes

In a large pot add the rice and salt to boiling water. Cook over low heat for 18 minutes. Drain and rinse with warm water. Add the butter, salt, and pepper. Dry in a 250° oven for 30 minutes, stirring occasionally with a fork. Transfer to a large bowl. Add the almonds, artichoke hearts, peas, pimiento, scallions, mushrooms, black olives, salami, and parsley.

To make the vinaigrette dressing mix the basil, tarragon, mustard, vinegar, oil, salt, and pepper. Add this to the rice mixture; mix well. Pack tightly into an oiled ring mold or bundt pan. Refrigerate overnight. Unmold and garnish with watercress and cherry tomatoes. This recipe can be doubled. Serves 12.

Beehives

Double recipe pie crust
8 perfect, extra-large peaches
¼ cup butter (½ stick)
1 egg
2 cups confectioners' sugar
1 teaspoon vanilla extract
1 tablespoon Brandy
Nutmeg

Roll the pastry into an oblong and cut strips 1-inch wide. Wash and dry the peaches. They must be perfect. Wrap the strips of pie crust around them, starting from the bottom, until the peach is entirely covered. Pat and patch the crust as you go along so there are no holes. Seal the edges. Place the beehives on a cookie sheet. Bake in a 400° oven for 40 minutes. Serve hot with hard sauce.

To make the sauce cream butter and add the egg; mix well. Gradually work in 2 cups or more of confectioners' sugar. The definite amount of sugar to add will depend upon whether a tight or not so tight hard sauce is desired. Flavor with vanilla and brandy.

To eat, break the beehive in half, remove the stone, and spoon a heaping tablespoon of hard sauce into the cavity. Sprinkle with nutmeg. The peach skin has disappeared! What an absolutely divine dessert!

Serves 8.

Chocolate Rum Roll

5 egg yolks at room temperature
½ cup sugar
6 ounces chocolate bits
3 tablespoons dark rum

❖   ❖   ❖

5 egg whites

❖   ❖   ❖

1 cup heavy whipping cream, whipped
3 tablespoons confectioners' sugar
2 tablespoons Amaretto liqueur
Sliced almonds

Beat the egg yolks until thick and lemon-colored; add the sugar and beat until a ribbon forms. Melt the chocolate bits with rum in a double boiler over hot water; add to the sugared yolks. Beat the egg whites until stiff, and fold quickly into the chocolate-egg mixture. Pour the batter over greased waxed paper in a jelly roll pan. Bake in a 350° oven for 10 minutes. Reduce the oven temperature to 325° and continue to bake for 5 minutes. Remove the cake from the oven and cover with a damp tea towel; refrigerate for 1 hour. Flip the cake out of the pan. Remove the waxed paper and spread cake with whipped cream flavored with confectioners' sugar and Amaretto. Roll up the cake; cover with clear wrap, and refrigerate. To serve, slice with a serrated knife. Serve with the cut side up garnished with a few sliced almonds.

Makes about 10 slices.

Peach Ice
with Raspberry Melba Sauce

1 29-ounce can peaches

❖   ❖   ❖

1 cup sugar
½ cup light corn syrup
1 cup peach juice from canned peaches

❖   ❖   ❖

1 cup peach-flavored Brandy
¼ cup lemon juice

❖   ❖   ❖

1 10-ounce container frozen raspberries at room temperature
Raspberry liqueur
⅓ cup red currant jelly
2 tablespoons cornstarch

Combine the sugar, corn syrup, and 1 cup of reserved peach juice in a small saucepan. Bring the mixture to a boil, stirring constantly until the sugar dissolves; reduce heat and simmer for three minutes. Cool.

Place the peaches in a food processor and with a metal blade process until smooth. Add the peach-flavored Brandy and process until combined. Combine the sugar mixture, peach mixture, and lemon juice. Stir well and pour into an 8-inch square metal pan. Freeze.

When ready to serve, scoop the peach ice into Champagne glasses and top with Raspberry Melba Sauce.

To make the Raspberry Melba Sauce drain berries, reserving juice. Add the raspberry liqueur to the reserved juice, making ⅔ cup. Combine the juice, jelly, and cornstarch in a saucepan. Cook until clear and thick. Do not boil. Stir in the raspberries and cool.

Serves 10.

The Wildflower Inn

Star Route
Lyndonville, Vermont 05851
(802) 626-8310

Located in Vermont's secluded Northeast Kingdom, the Wildflower Inn is part of a 500-acre farm that includes a working dairy operation. The inn has sixteen bedrooms with a scenic view from every window. The groomed cross-country ski trails that run throughout the property are connected to the inn. Downhill skiing at Burke Mountain is just four miles away. Whether in the dining room or on the dining porch, full country breakfasts are hearty and delicious, with fresh eggs, homemade breads, and fresh fruits. A specialty of the house is the pancakes; made from a mixture of several grains, they are surprisingly light and fluffy.

Wildflower Inn Pancake Mix

3 cups unbleached flour
2½ cups whole wheat flour
½ cup oatmeal
1 cup raw wheat germ
1 cup cornmeal
5 tablespoons baking powder
1 tablespoon salt

Combine the ingredients and mix well. Store in a tightly covered container in the refrigerator.

Wildflower Inn Pancakes

3 cups Wildflower Inn Pancake Mix
2 cups milk
½ cup oil
2 eggs

Beat all of the ingredients until just mixed. Bake on a 400° griddle.

Variation: To the 3 cups of dry pancake mix add 2 tablespoons of ginger, 1 teaspoon of cloves, and 1 teaspoon of cinnamon. Add the milk, oil, and eggs and bake on a 400° griddle. Serve with warm homemade applesauce and whipped cream.

Serves 6 to 8.

The Wildflower Inn

The Inn at Manchester

Box 41
Manchester, Vermont 05254
(802) 362-1793

Four beautiful acres surround the Inn at Manchester. Enhanced by a grove of birch trees, a brook (home of two resident trout), and mountains in the background, this restored Victorian mansion has nineteen bedrooms, thirteen with private baths. The three sitting areas for guests include a television and game room. In winter guests sip their wine and munch on crackers and cheese by the fireplaces. A full country breakfast is served, including cottage cakes, omelets, apple or blueberry pancakes, homemade breads and granola, fresh juice or fruit, and Vermont maple syrup.

Potato-Leek Soup

4 leeks
1 medium onion
1 bunch scallions
3 tablespoons butter
1 quart chicken broth
5 potatoes, peeled and thinly sliced
1 cup cream
Fresh chives

Chop the leeks, onion, and scallions; sauté in butter until slightly brown. Add the broth and potatoes and cook until soft. Purée in a blender, adding the cream. Reheat. Serve with chopped fresh chives as a garnish.

Serves 6 to 8.

Sue's Endive Salad

2 Granny Smith apples
Lemon juice
1 head Romaine lettuce, cut up

2 endives, chopped
½ cup walnuts

❖ ❖ ❖

½ cup oil
3 tablespoons raspberry vinegar
2 tablespoons heavy cream
Dash garlic powder

Cut the apples into small chunks. Sprinkle with lemon juice and place in a big bowl. Add the lettuce, endive, and the walnuts.

Mix the oil, vinegar, cream, and garlic powder well. Add at last minute before serving.

Serves 4.

Manchester Highlands Inn: The Victorian Inn

Highland Avenue
Manchester Center, Vermont 05255
(802) 362-4565

The Manchester Highlands Inn is a graceful Victorian mansion and carriage house. Its peaked roofs, three-story turret, handsome oak and maple woodwork, and tin ceilings take guests back to another era. They enjoy the nostalgia of bygone days while relaxing by the stone fireplace in a cozy room, enjoying the wafting aromas of homemade breads and pies, or while dreaming and rocking on the front porch. Fresh coffee and a delicious snack always await guests in the dining room. A country breakfast of waffles, pancakes, and muffins begins the day. Each evening a different entree is served, along with homemade soups, breads, salad bar, vegetables, and desserts. The Manchester Highlands Inn is on a quiet side street in scenic Manchester Center, just minutes from a variety of recreational and cultural activities, and it is open for all seasons.

Orange Whole Wheat Pancakes

2 eggs
¼ cup oil
2 cups whole wheat flour
½ teaspoon baking soda
½ teaspoon salt
1½ to 2 cups orange juice

Beat the eggs and oil together. Sift together the dry ingredients and add to the eggs. Gradually add the orange juice until you have a batter of the consistency you like. Fry the pancakes on a medium hot griddle and serve immediately.

Serves 3 to 4.

Maple Nut Muffins

¼ cup butter (½ stick), melted
½ cup sour cream
⅔ cup maple syrup
2 eggs
½ cup applesauce

❖ ❖ ❖

1 cup quick-cooking oats
1¼ cups whole wheat flour
¾ cup chopped walnuts
½ tablespoon baking powder
¼ teaspoon salt

Blend the butter, sour cream, maple syrup, eggs, and applesauce. Add dry ingredients all at once and stir until

Manchester Highlands Inn

just blended. Fill greased muffin cups ⅔ full. Bake in a 375° oven for ½ hour or until done. These are unbelievably good.

Makes 12 to 15 muffins.

Easy Mushroom Quiche

**Pastry for 1 9-inch 1-crust deep dish pie
2 cups shredded Cheddar cheese
1 3-ounce can sliced mushrooms, drained
1 1⁵/₈-ounce can fried onion rings
4 eggs**

Sprinkle the shredded cheese on the pie crust. Layer the mushrooms over the cheese, then the onion rings. Beat the eggs and pour over the layers in the pie crust. The onion rings will rise to the top. Bake in a 350° oven for 50 minutes.

Serves 6.

French Onion Soup

This soup is very filling, a meal itself when served with a salad.

**3 tablespoons butter
6 medium onions
4 cups beef broth
½ cup tomato juice
Salt and pepper
Croutons
Grated and shredded cheese
(Vermont Cheddar)**

Melt the butter in a large pot. Sauté the onions. Add the broth and tomato juice; season with salt and pepper. Cook for a few minutes until heated through. Pour into crocks. Top with croutons, then cheese. Brown the top in the oven.

Serves 4.

Italian Meatball Soup

**1 pound lean ground chuck
¼ cup bread crumbs
1 tablespoon parsley
Minced onion
Oregano
Salt
Pepper**

❖   ❖   ❖

**1 quart chicken broth
1 pound fresh-cut or frozen spinach
1 cup tortellini**

Combine the first 6 ingredients. Shape into small meatballs. Brown in the oven. Drain the meatballs and add to the chicken broth along with the spinach. Simmer for 10 minutes. Cook and drain the tortellini. Add to the soup just before serving.

Serves 8 to 10.

House Dressing

**2 tablespoons plain yogurt
2 tablespoons mayonnaise
½ teaspoon powdered garlic
½ teaspoon parsley
1 teaspoon Parmesan cheese
Salt and pepper**

Blend all of the ingredients together. This is best if it sets a day or so (refrigerated) before using.

Makes ¼ cup.

Broiled Scallops (Baltimore Style)

Arrange scallops in individual shells or baking dishes. Sprinkle with garlic salt, paprika, and freshly ground pepper. Melt butter and lemon juice; sprinkle over the scallops. Broil 4 minutes turning often, sprinkle with bread crumbs, then broil 1 additional minute.

Variations: Fillet of sole and flounder may be broiled using the same method.

1 pound of scallops makes 3 servings.

Family Chili

**1 cup chopped onion
1 cup diced green pepper
2 pounds ground chuck
½ cup butter (1 stick)
2 cloves garlic, minced
1½ teaspoons salt
3 tablespoons chili powder
1½ teaspoons paprika
¼ teaspoon cayenne pepper
6 whole cloves
4 cups cooked tomatoes
2 15-ounce cans kidney beans**

Brown the onion, green pepper, and ground chuck in the butter. Add the minced garlic, seasonings, and tomatoes. Cover and cook over low heat about 1 hour. Add the kidney beans during the last 15 minutes of cooking time.

Serves 8 to 12.

Biscotti Facile

This is an Italian recipe that is served at Christmas in the afternoon with coffee and tea.

**6 cups all-purpose flour
2 cups confectioners' sugar
1¾ tablespoons baking powder
1½ cups shortening
5 eggs (reserve one white)
1 teaspoon almond extract or anise**

Sift the flour; measure and resift with the sugar and baking powder. Cut the shortening in by hand until the mixture resembles cornmeal. Make a well in the center of the flour. Add the eggs (5 yolks and 4 whites) and flavoring. Knead for 5 minutes. Pinch off pieces of dough the size of an apricot and roll between palms into strips the size and thickness of a finger. Beat reserved egg white with a fork and brush onto cookies. Place 1 inch apart on greased cookie sheet. Bake in 350° oven for 10 minutes.

Variations: To the dough add chopped nuts or roll strips of dough in sesame seeds.

Makes 6 dozen.

Orange Pound Cake

1 cup butter (2 sticks)
2 cups sugar
4 eggs
Pinch salt
Grated orange rind
1½ teaspoons vanilla extract
1 cup milk
3 cups all-purpose flour
2 teaspoons baking powder

❖ ❖ ❖

1 cup sugar
¼ cup butter (½ stick)
⅓ cup orange juice

Cream 1 cup of butter with 2 cups of sugar. Add the eggs, salt, orange rind, and vanilla. Add the milk, flour, and baking powder. Pour into a greased 10-inch bundt pan or 2 9x5-inch loaf pans. Bake in a 350° oven for 1 hour or until done. Leave in the pan. As soon as the cake is done, dissolve 1 cup of sugar, and ¼ cup of butter, in the orange juice, and cook about 2 minutes. Pour over the hot cake and let it set until the cake is cool.

Variation: You may substitute lemon rind and lemon juice for a lemon cake.

Serves 12 to 16.

River Meadow Farm

Post Office Box 822
Manchester Center, Vermont 05255
(802) 362-3700

The River Meadow Farm is a remodeled farmhouse that the town of Manchester Center operated as a "poor farm," from 1829 to 1945. Purchased in 1949 by its present owner, it has been remodeled and run as a bed and breakfast since the early 1950s. River Meadow accommodates ten people in the five bedrooms, and offers such comforts as the large country kitchen with a fireplace, a dining room, a den with a television, and a living room with fireplace and baby grand piano. Its more than eighty acres of meadow and woods are perfect for hiking, cross-country skiing, and fishing at the famous trout stream, called Battenkill River, that borders the farm. River Meadow Farm is within easy driving distance of Manchester Center for shopping, fine restaurants, an art center, and skiing at Stratton, Big Bromley, and Magic Mountain.

Zucchini Bread

2 cups sugar
1 cup oil
3 eggs

❖ ❖ ❖

1 cup whole wheat flour
2 cups all-purpose flour
1 teaspoon baking powder
1 teaspoon baking soda
1 teaspoon salt
3 teaspoons cinnamon
½ cup walnuts
2 cups grated zucchini
½ cup raisins

Beat sugar, oil, and eggs until light. Add dry ingredients, nuts, and zuc-

chini. Pour into greased 4½x8½-inch pans. Bake in a 350° oven for 55 minutes.

Makes 6 small loaves or 1 loaf.

Swift House

25 Stewart Lane
Middlebury, Vermont 05753
(802) 388-2766

The Swift House is a village inn in a Federal-style home with eight elaborately carved fireplaces, all working, and some of them in the guest rooms. Furnished with Queen Anne and Chippendale antiques, it also has four-poster beds and oriental rugs. Dinner by candlelight is served in front of the fireplace on white linen tablecloths, with real silver. Spacious lawns and formal gardens form the view from the terraces. Recreational opportunities include miles of hiking trails, trout fishing in Otter Creek, and swimming and sailing at nearby lakes. Golf and skiing are nearby. Guests enjoy a dinner menu that changes nightly, offering the finest selections.

Swift House Inn Shrimp, Chicken and Smoked Sausage Louisiana

1 pound Kielbasa, sliced thinly
2 tablespoons olive oil

❖ ❖ ❖

1 large onion, chopped
1 large green pepper, chopped
5 ribs celery, chopped
2 tablespoons oil

❖ ❖ ❖

2 cloves garlic, minced
1 hot jalapeno pepper, seeded and
  minced
1 tablespoon oregano
1 tablespoon chili powder
1 tablespoon cumin
Salt

❖   ❖   ❖

1 28-ounce can whole peeled
  tomatoes, drained (reserve
  liquid)

❖   ❖   ❖

16 large shrimp (1 pound), cleaned
  and shelled
4 boneless chicken breasts, cubed
2 tablespoons olive oil
4 cups cooked brown natural rice

Sauté Kielbasa in 2 tablespoons oil until brown; set aside. Sauté onion, green pepper, and celery in 2 tablespoons oil for 5 minutes or until soft. Add garlic, hot pepper, oregano, chili powder, cumin, and salt; sauté another minute. Add tomatoes and reserved Kielbasa. Stir, adding some of the reserved tomato liquid if needed. Set aside until ready to serve. (Can be made ahead to this point early in the day and reheated just before sautéing shrimp and chicken.)

Sauté shrimp and chicken in 2 tablespoons olive oil until just cooked, about 5 minutes, and stir into the hot Kielbasa mixture. Serve over steamed brown rice.

Serves 8.

syrup to chocolate mixture and stir until smooth; cool. Beat egg whites until stiff; fold into chocolate mixture. Beat 2¼ cups heavy cream until stiff and fold into chocolate mixture. Spoon into large wine glasses and chill two hours.

Serves 8.

The Hortonville Inn

R.D. #1, Box 14
Mount Holly, Vermont 05758
(802) 259-2587

The Hortonville Inn, a short distance from the Okemo Mountain Ski Area, enjoys its picturesque setting and boasts thirteen landscaped and wooded acres for its guests. Trails abound for cross country skiing. The rooms in the 150-year-old home are large, airy, and homey. Each has a radio, television and VCR, and the inn has an entertainment area with a video machine and a library of over 200 movies, games, and many books. The fireplace is an ideal place to warm oneself with a cup of hot chocolate or tea and a few chocolate chip cookies. A continental breakfast, consisting of freshly made juice and homemade pastries from the inn's kitchen, is included with the room.

Grammy's Carrot Timbales

2 cups grated raw carrots
½ cup Italian-style bread crumbs

❖   ❖   ❖

2 eggs
1 teaspoon salt
2 tablespoons shortening, melted
½ cup milk

Mix the grated carrots with the bread crumbs. Beat the eggs and add to them the salt, shortening, and milk. Add this mixture to the carrot and crumb mixture. Fill a greased muffin pan with equal amounts of mix; set in a pan of hot water and bake in a 300° oven until firm.

Serves 6.

Swift House Inn Grand Marnier Chocolate Mousse

¼ cup sugar
¼ cup Grand Marnier
4 ounces sweet chocolate
3 tablespoons heavy cream
2 egg whites
2¼ cups heavy cream

Cook the sugar and Grand Marnier over low heat until the sugar is dissolved but not colored. Set aside. Melt the chocolate in a double boiler. Stir in 3 tablespoons heavy cream. Add sugar

The Hortonville Inn

Bobbi's Cream Puffs

2 cups water
1 cup butter (2 sticks)
½ teaspoon salt
2 cups all-purpose flour
8 eggs

❖ ❖ ❖

2 3-ounce boxes instant French
vanilla pudding
2⅔ cups milk
1 pint heavy cream
2 teaspoons confectioners' sugar
½ teaspoon vanilla extract

In a saucepan combine the water, butter, and salt; bring to a boil over medium heat. Remove from heat and mix in the flour. Return to heat over low flame and stir until a ball forms. Remove from heat and stir in eggs one at a time. Beat with a hand mixer until shiny, 1 minute. Drop by teaspoonfuls 2-inches apart on an ungreased cookie sheet. Bake in a 400° oven for 20 to 35 minutes or until golden brown.

Mix the pudding with the milk and blend until well-mixed. Chill in the refrigerator. Whip the heavy cream with confectioner's sugar and vanilla; chill. Fold the cream mixture into the pudding mixture and chill again. Fill puffs that have been cut in half. Place the top half on puff and sprinkle with confectioners' sugar. Enjoy!

Makes 3 dozen puffs.

Walnut Pie

1 cup white corn syrup
1 cup dark brown sugar, firmly
packed
⅓ teaspoon salt
⅓ cup butter, melted
1 teaspoon vanilla extract
3 eggs, slightly beaten
1 cup walnuts

Mix the syrup, sugar, salt, butter, and vanilla. Add the slightly beaten eggs. Pour into a 9-inch unbaked pie shell. Sprinkle walnuts over the filling. Bake in a 350° oven for approximately 45 minutes.

Serves 6.

The Inn at Norwich

225 Main Street
Norwich, Vermont 05055
(802) 649-1143

The Inn at Norwich was built in 1797 as a stagecoach stop by Jasper Murdock, who established a base for hospitality that has passed down through the years. The inn's present keepers, Barbara and Gene Bellows, are carrying forward this tradition. The atmosphere at the inn is comfortable, with a fire glowing in the living room fireplace during the winter months. Many of the newly decorated guest rooms feature four-poster or brass beds. Each room has a private bath and telephone. While guests may want to take advantage of the area's attractions and beauty, many are tempted to curl up with a good book and relax. The town of Norwich is a "picture postcard" town composed of well-kept homes, an authentic general store, and a delightful cross-section of people. An evening in one of the candlelit dining rooms provides a romantic setting for leisurely dining.

Chicken Elizabeth

8 ounces cream cheese, softened
½ cup butter (1 stick)
1 teaspoon pepper
1 teaspoon basil
1 teaspoon minced garlic
1 teaspoon oregano
1 teaspoon thyme
1 teaspoon tarragon
1 teaspoon parsley

❖ ❖ ❖

4 boneless chicken breasts
12 cherry tomatoes, halved
4 ounces prosciutto ham, paper
thin
White wine

To make Boursin cheese mix cream cheese, butter, and herbs. Blend thoroughly.

The Inn at Norwich

Pound chicken breasts to uniform thickness. Line each breast with 1 ounce of ham, 3 halved tomatoes and ¼ cup of the Boursin cheese mixture. Roll up the chicken and place seam side down in a baking pan. Top with a dollop of remaining cheese and sprinkle with white wine generously. Bake in a 375° oven for 30 minutes.

Melissa D. Munday, Executive Chef
Serves 4.

Scallop Pesto

1 pound salt pork
1 bunch fresh basil
1 bunch fresh parsley

❖ ❖ ❖

3 tablespoons chopped garlic
1 cup Parmesan cheese

❖ ❖ ❖

½ cup white wine
1½ pounds bay scallops
12 ounces cooked pasta (rotini)

To make pesto grind salt pork after trimming off rind. You may have the butcher do this for you. Chop basil and parsley. Combine in food processor with salt pork. Add garlic and cheese. Pulsate machine. Pesto can be made ahead and refrigerated or frozen.

Heat a large saucepan to sizzling; add wine and scallops. Stir for 2 minutes. Add pesto and reduce heat until melted. Stir in cooked pasta.

Melissa D. Munday, Executive Chef
Serves 4.

Sweetbread and Kidney Casserole

1 sheet frozen puff pastry, thawed

❖ ❖ ❖

8 ounces veal sweetbreads
1 quart water
1 tablespoon lemon juice
1 teaspoon salt

❖ ❖ ❖

8 ounces veal kidney
1 red apple, sliced
1 green apple, sliced

2 tablespoons mustard
Chopped shallots
½ cup Calvados (or Applejack)
½ cup heavy cream
4 slices crisp bacon, crumbled

Place a 3-inch square of pastry in each of 4 muffin cups. Push down and weight centers with small ramekins or foil. Bake in a 375° oven until golden brown.

Prepare sweetbreads by placing in a saucepan with water, lemon juice, and salt. Heat to boiling, simmer for 20 minutes, then drain. Rinse in cold running water, pat dry with paper towels. Remove the membrane, cut out veins and connective tissue.

Slice sweetbreads and kidney. Flour only the kidney slices, sauté in hot buttered pan for 3 minutes. Add sweetbreads, apples, mustard, and shallots. Cook two more minutes. Add Calvados and flame. Reduce heat; add cream and bacon, cooked until thickened and reduced slightly. Serve in pastry cups.

Melissa D. Munday, Executive Chef
Serves 2.

White Chocolate Strawberry Mousse

This is a simple but elegant dessert deserving of your finest glassware. Garnish with fresh strawberries, chocolate leaves, and whipped cream flavored with strawberry juice.

20 ounces fine white chocolate

❖ ❖ ❖

1 quart fresh strawberries
½ cup strawberry preserves
2 cups heavy cream, whipped stiff
8 egg whites, stiffly beaten

Melt the chocolate in the top of a double boiler. Set aside. Purée the strawberries; strain and reserve liquid. Place the berries in a saucepan, add preserves and cook over low heat until the combination thickens. Remove from the heat; cool slightly. Fold into

melted chocolate. Fold in whipped cream. Fold in egg whites.

Melissa D. Munday, Executive Chef.
Serves 8 to 10.

Yankees' Northview Bed and Breakfast

R.D. #2, Box 1000
Plainfield, Vermont 05667
(802) 454-7191

Northview is a nine-room colonial home set on a hill and surrounded by stone walls and white fences. The location assures guests of enough quiet to enjoy the sounds of the seasons, while being close to Montpelier, the state capital, and to Barre, the home of the world's largest granite quarry. Excellent sports and recreational opportunities, as well as many unique points of interest (including historical Kent Corner and Museum) are within easy reach. The rooms, many with hand-stenciled walls, are furnished with antiques and reproductions. Three guest rooms share a full bath. One double-bedded corner room has a canopied rope bed; another boasts a hand-crocheted bedspread and quilts. The third room with twin beds has a large hooked rug done in dusty roses. Guests are greeted with fresh flowers and begin each morning with a hearty breakfast complete with homemade pastries, muffins, and jams. Often breakfast is served outside on the garden patio overlooking the meadows and mountains; in cooler weather it is served close to the pot-belly stove in the large kitchen or in the stencilled dining room.

No-Knead Rich Sweet Dough

¾ cup milk
½ cup sugar
2 teaspoons salt
½ cup margarine
½ cup warm water
2 ¼-ounce packages active dry yeast
1 egg
4 cups all-purpose flour

❖ ❖ ❖

2 to 3 teaspoons ground cardamom seeds (optional)
1 cup raisins (optional)

Scald milk; stir in sugar, salt and margarine; cool to lukewarm. Measure water into large warm bowl. Sprinkle in yeast and stir until dissolved. Stir in lukewarm milk mixture, egg and half the flour; beat until smooth. Add cardamom and raisins if desired. Stir in remaining flour to make a stiff batter. Cover tightly and refrigerate at least 2 hours. Dough may be kept in refrigerator for 3 days. To use, simply cut off amount needed and shape as desired.

If cardamom seed is used, make 2 or 3 braids out of the dough; brush tops with milk and sprinkle generously with sugar. Let rise and bake at 350 degrees for 20–30 minutes.

If no cardamom is used, shape into 2 or 3 9x12-inch rectangles. Sprinkle with cinnamon and sugar, raisins and/or diced apples. Roll up as jelly rolls, place in 9-inch pie plates in a ring shape. Let rise and bake. Frost with a confectioners' sugar frosting (lemon flavored is great!) and top with chopped nuts. Serve piping hot or warm. These can be baked and frozen, wrapped in foil (without frosting) and then reheated to piping hot. Serve frosted.

Serves 12 to 16.

The Quechee Inn at Marshland Farm

Clubhouse Road
Quechee, Vermont 05059
(802) 295-3133

Originally the eighteenth century farmstead of Vermont's first Lieutenant Governor, the Quechee Inn at Marshland Farm has twenty-two beautifully appointed guest rooms with private baths and color cable television. Complimentary buffet-style Continental breakfasts are provided for all inn guests. Bike and canoe rental, fly fishing instruction, and a cross-country skiing learning center with groomed trails are available at the inn. Guests enjoy privileges at the nearby private Quechee Club for golf, tennis, indoor and outdoor swimming, squash, and downhill skiing. Guests dine in an atmosphere of country elegance and browse in the Quechee Inn Keepsakes giftshop.

Harvest Chowder

1 large potato, peeled and cubed
2 pints chicken stock
Roux
1 large onion, minced
2 ribs celery, minced
1 large carrot, finely chopped
Butter
½ cup broccoli flowerets
½ cup cauliflower flowerets
2 strips bacon, cooked and crumbled
1 pint light cream
Salt and pepper to taste

Place the potatoes in cold, salted water and bring to a boil. Cool and reserve.

Bring the chicken stock to a boil and thicken with a flour and butter roux; bring back to boiling, then simmer. Sauté the onions, celery, and carrots in butter for 10 minutes, stirring continually. Add the broccoli and cauliflower for the last 5 minutes of cooking. Strain the chicken stock into this mixture and add the bacon and potatoes. Bring to a boil and simmer until the vegetables are just done. Add light cream and gently return to just boiling. Serve.

Serves 8.

Pork Normandy

3 1½-ounce pork tenderloins
Flour for dredging
Salt and pepper
¼ cup butter (½ stick)
1 teaspoon minced shallots
3 large mushrooms, sliced
1 ounce Brandy
3 ounces apple cider
¼ cup heavy cream
⅓ apple, julienned

Dredge the pork in flour seasoned with salt and pepper and sauté in butter over high heat. Add the shallots and mushrooms. Add Brandy away from the heat. Return to heat and flambé. Remove the pork and reserve. Add the apple cider. Reduce by ½. Add the heavy cream and reduce by ½. Add the julienned apple and reserved pork. Return to heat before serving.

Serves 1.

Sole Almondine

1 6- to 8-ounce fillet of sole
Flour for dredging
¼ cup butter (½ stick)
Salt and pepper
¼ cup white wine
Juice of ¼ lemon
Roasted blanched almonds, sliced
Parsley, chopped

Dredge the sole in flour and sauté in ¼ cup of butter. Sauté the side from which the skin has been removed first and the fish will hold together better.

Season with salt and pepper. Turn the fish and deglaze the pan with white wine and lemon juice. Add the almonds and parsley. Remove the fish to a plate, keeping it warm. Reduce the cooking liquor by half. Add 2 tablespoons of butter and remove from heat. Swirl to incorporate into the sauce. Pour over the fish and serve.

Serves 1.

Seafood Rissole

1 large onion, finely minced
¼ cup butter (½ stick)
1 3½-ounce package langostinos
1 cup dry white wine
Salt and pepper
Roux
Puff pastry dough (10x10 sheet)
1 egg, beaten
Sesame seeds
Hollandaise sauce (optional)

Sauté onions in butter until transparent. Add langostinos, white wine, and salt and pepper to taste. Bring to a boil and simmer for 15 minutes. Thicken with roux to a moderate stiffness. Adjust seasonings and cool.

Roll the puff pastry dough to ⅛-inch thickness. Cut dough into 12 squares. Egg wash the edges and divide the stuffing evenly between the pieces of dough. Fold the squares into triangles and press the edges together with a fork. Egg wash the surfaces and sprinkle with sesame seeds. Bake in a 350° oven for 12 to 18 minutes, until golden brown. Serve plain or with Hollandaise sauce on the side.

Makes 12 squares.

French Silk Pie

This dessert is famous at the Quechee Inn. It is sure to satisfy anyone's craving for sweets and chocolate.

2 egg whites
¼ teaspoon cream of tartar
½ cup sugar
2 to 3 tablespoons nuts, chopped
❖ ❖ ❖

½ cup unsalted butter (1 stick)
¾ cup sugar
1½ ounces unsweetened chocolate
1 teaspoon vanilla extract
2 eggs
❖ ❖ ❖
1 cup heavy cream
1 tablespoon Crème de Cacao
Shaved chocolate

Prepare a 9-inch meringue shell by combining the egg whites and cream of tartar in a large mixing bowl and beating until they hold soft peaks. Add the sugar gradually, beating until peaks are formed and the sugar is dissolved. Spread in a well-buttered 9-inch pie pan. Build up the sides using a round soup spoon. Sprinkle the bottom of the shell with chopped nuts. Bake in a 275° oven for 1 hour. The shell will color slightly. Cool.

Beat the softened butter with an electric mixer until fluffy. Add sugar gradually and beat until smooth. Melt the unsweetened chocolate in a double boiler and add with the vanilla to the creamed mixture. Beat in 2 eggs, 1 at a time, beating at least 2 to 3 minutes after each. The mixture should be fluffy and pale chocolate-colored, with the sugar dissolved. Pour this mixture into the meringue shell.

In chilled bowl, beat the cream and Crème de Cacao until it holds its shape. Spread over the mixture in the pie shell. Garnish with shaved chocolate. Chill. This pie will keep overnight. However, it will keep longer if not topped with the whipped cream until ready to serve.

Note: Try melting chocolate in the microwave. It saves a lot of time, mess, and bother.

Serves 6 to 8.

Placidia Farm Bed and Breakfast

R.R. 1, Box 275
Randolph, Vermont 05060
(802) 728-9883

This hand-hewn log house was used as a weekend retreat by the hosts before they decided to open it to travelers. Its large bedrooms have double beds and private baths; rollaway cots and room fans are available as requested. The living room, with its television, stereo, and radio, provides a place for socializing. Breakfast is served on the sunporch, with the hosts joining guests for coffee and conversation once the meal is served. Local activities include hiking and cross country skiing on the property. Pets are not welcome; nonsmokers are preferred.

Hot Crab Meat Cocktail Dip

3 8-ounce packages cream cheese
½ cup mayonnaise
⅔ cup dry white wine
Garlic salt
2 teaspoons prepared mustard
2 teaspoons confectioners' sugar
1 teaspoon onion juice
Dash seasoned salt
3 10¾-ounce cans crab meat

Mix the cream cheese, mayonnaise, and wine; add all of the seasonings. Pick over the crab meat. Fold into the mayonnaise mixture gently. Heat in a double boiler and serve hot in a chafing dish with crackers and rounds of toasted party rye.

If this recipe is to be halved, use 2 cups crab. This dip can be frozen.

Makes 3 pints; serves 30.

Hot Bean Casserole

1 large onion, chopped
1 clove garlic, minced
3 tablespoons bacon drippings
2 10-ounce packages frozen lima beans, cooked
1 16-ounce can beans in tomato sauce
1 16-ounce can kidney beans
½ cup ketchup
¼ cup water
3 tablespoons vinegar
1 tablespoon brown sugar
1 teaspoon dry mustard
1 teaspoon salt
¼ teaspoon pepper
Bacon strips

Sauté the onion and garlic in bacon drippings. Add to the beans. Add the remaining ingredients. Place in a greased 2-quart casserole with the bacon on top. Bake in a 300° oven for 30 minutes. Great with steak.

Serves 4 to 6.

Fruit Kuchen

1½ cups all-purpose flour
¾ cup butter (1½ sticks)
½ teaspoon salt
1 egg
2 tablespoons milk
3 cups fruit (apples, rhubarb, peaches)

❖ ❖ ❖

3 eggs, beaten
1 cup sugar
2 tablespoons all-purpose flour
¾ cup milk

❖ ❖ ❖

½ cup all-purpose flour
½ cup sugar
2 tablespoons butter
Cinnamon

Mix 1½ cups of flour, ¾ cup of butter, and salt as for a pie crust. Add 1 egg. Add 2 tablespoons of milk; beat. When the liquid is absorbed, pat the dough into a 9x13-inch pan. Do not roll out. Place the fruit on the dough.

Mix 3 eggs, 1 cup of sugar, 2 tablespoons of flour, and the milk; pour over the fruit.

Mix ½ cup of flour, ½ cup of sugar, and 2 tablespoons of butter until crumbly. Spread over the top of the fruit. Sprinkle with cinnamon to taste. Bake in a 350° oven for 40 to 50 minutes.

Serves 6 to 8.

Never-Fail Brownies

½ cup butter (1 stick)
1 cup sugar
4 eggs
1 teaspoon vanilla extract
1 cup all-purpose flour
1 16-ounce can chocolate syrup
½ cup chopped nuts

❖ ❖ ❖

1 cup sugar
6 tablespoons milk
6 tablespoons butter
½ cup chocolate chips

Cream the butter and sugar. Add the eggs, one at a time, beating after each. Add the vanilla, flour, chocolate syrup, and nuts. Pour into a jelly roll pan. Bake in a 350° oven for about 25 minutes.

For the frosting, combine 1 cup of sugar, milk, and 6 tablespoons of butter in a saucepan. Bring to a boil and boil for 3 minutes. Add the chocolate chips; beat well. Spread on the brownies.

Serves 8.

Prune Streusel Cake

2 cups all-purpose flour
1½ cups sugar
1 teaspoon salt
1¼ teaspoon baking soda
1 teaspoon cinnamon
1 teaspoon cloves
1 cup soft prunes, cut up
⅔ cup prune juice
½ cup oil
3 eggs
1 cup chopped nuts

❖ ❖ ❖

½ cup sugar
2 tablespoons soft butter
2 tablespoons all-purpose flour

Sift together 2 cups of flour, 1½ cups sugar, salt, soda, cinnamon, and cloves. Add the prunes and juice. Add the oil, eggs, and nuts. Blend thoroughly with an electric mixer at low speed for 1 minute. Pour into a greased and floured 9x13-inch pan.

Combine ½ cup of sugar, butter, and 2 tablespoons of flour. Sprinkle over the batter. Bake in a 350° oven for 35 to 40 minutes.

Serves 8 to 10.

Liberty Hill Farm

Rochester, Vermont 05767
(802) 767-3926

Liberty Hill is a 100-acre farm nestled between the White River and the Green Mountains. The house is 150 years old and contains five guest bedrooms and three shared baths. It has three living room areas, so there is plenty of space for guests to read, work jigsaw puzzles, compete in board games, or relax and watch the fire in the fireplace stove. Breakfast is served between 8:00 and 9:00 A.M. and consists of fruit, juice, coffee, tea, bacon, eggs, pancakes, sausage, and homemade coffee cakes. Dinner is served family style at 6:00 P.M. and usually consists of a roast, 3 vegetables, salad, homemade breads, and homemade desserts.

This is a beautiful area providing plentiful diversion for the outdoor enthusiast, with many museums and cultural events that take place through the year. Sleigh rides are fun in the winter, and in the summer guests enjoy lighting bonfires on the beach. The White River is known for trout fishing, and the Green Mountain National Forest, stretching for miles behind the farm has many old logging roads and country roads for hiking and cross-country skiing. Five major downhill ski areas are within thirty minutes of the farm.

Cranapple Coffee Braid

1 3-ounce package cream cheese
¼ cup butter (½ stick)
2 cups baking mix
⅓ cup milk

❖ ❖ ❖

½ can (16-ounce) whole cranberry sauce
1 apple, peeled and chopped
1 teaspoon sugar
½ teaspoon cinnamon

❖ ❖ ❖

1 cup confectioners' sugar
1 teaspoon butter
1 tablespoon milk
1 tablespoon cranberry juice

Cut the cream cheese and ¼ cup of butter into the baking mix until crumbly; blend in the milk. Turn onto a floured surface and knead for 1 minute. On waxed paper roll the dough to a 12x8-inch rectangle. Turn onto a well-greased cookie sheet; remove the waxed paper.

Mix the cranberry sauce, apple, sugar, and cinnamon; spread down the center of the dough. Make 2-inch cuts at 1-inch intervals on the long sides. Fold the strips over the filling alternately. Bake in a 425° oven for 12 to 15 minutes.

To make the glaze combine the confectioners' sugar, 1 teaspoon butter, milk, and cranberry juice until of the right consistency for glaze. Drizzle over the warm braid.

Serves 8 to 12.

Icelandic Baked Haddock

3 tablespoons butter
¼ cup all-purpose flour
Salt and pepper to taste
¼ teaspoon nutmeg
1½ cups milk
¾ cup grated Cheddar cheese
2½ pounds haddock, skinned and boned
¼ cup Sherry (optional)
Paprika to taste

To make the white sauce, melt the butter in a pan and stir in the flour and spices until smooth. Gradually stir in the milk. Cook until smooth and thick. Add the cheese; stir until melted. Place the haddock in a greased baking dish. Sprinkle with salt and pepper. Pour the sauce over the haddock. Add the sherry and sprinkle liberally with paprika. Bake in a 325° oven for 45 minutes.

Serves 4.

Almond Butter Cake

1 cup butter (2 sticks), softened
1 cup sugar
Dash salt
1 egg
2 cups all-purpose flour

❖ ❖ ❖

1 cup almond paste
½ cup sugar
1 egg
Sliced almonds

Combine the butter, 1 cup of sugar, salt, 1 egg, and the flour. Knead together by hand. Pat ½ of the dough into a 9-inch round pan.

Combine the almond paste, ½ cup of sugar, and 1 egg. Add water if too stiff. Place in the pastry shell. Pat the remaining dough on top. Brush with beaten egg and milk; sprinkle with sliced almonds. Bake in a 350° oven for 1 hour. Cool for at least 30 minutes.

Serves 8.

Frost on the Pumpkin Pie

1¼ cups graham cracker crumbs
3 tablespoons sugar
½ teaspoon cinnamon
¼ teaspoon nutmeg
⅛ teaspoon cloves
⅓ cup butter, melted

❖ ❖ ❖

1 can vanilla or sour cream vanilla frosting
1 cup sour cream
1 cup canned pumpkin
1 teaspoon cinnamon
½ teaspoon ginger
¼ teaspoon cloves
1 8-ounce container whipped topping, thawed

In a small bowl combine the graham cracker crumbs, sugar, ½ teaspoon of cinnamon, nutmeg, ⅛ teaspoon of cloves, and butter; stir until blended. Reserve 2 tablespoons for topping; press the remaining crumbs over the bottom and sides of a 9- to 10-inch pie pan. Bake in a 350° oven for 6 minutes.

In a large bowl combine the frosting, sour cream, pumpkin, 1 teaspoon of cinnamon, ginger and ¼ teaspoon of cloves. Beat with an electric mixer at medium speed for 2 minutes. Fold in 1 cup of whipped topping; pour into the cooled crust. Spread the remaining topping over the filling; sprinkle with the reserved crumbs. Refrigerate at least 4 hours or until served.

Store in the refrigerator. Regular whipped cream can be used, it just requires longer refrigeration before being served. The pie is quite rich, a nice change of pace from the traditional pumpkin pie.

Serves 6.

The Londonderry Inn

Route 100
South Londonderry, Vermont 05155
(802) 824-5226

The Londonderry Inn's twenty-five comfortable guest rooms are part of what was the Melendy Dairy Farm 150 years ago. A former woodshed is now the dining room, enhanced by Audubon prints and soft candlelight. The breakfast buffet is hearty enough for the big eater, yet tempting to those who rarely partake of this meal. The dinner menu changes nightly and includes traditional American fare, continental specialties, and some creative surprises. Southern Vermont's vast recreational opportunities are easily accessible to guests of the Londonderry.

Duckling Paté

6 duckling livers
Meat and skin from one cooked
    duckling
1 pound of veal

❖   ❖   ❖

Salt and pepper to taste
¼ teaspoon nutmeg
1/8 teaspoon cloves
Dash cayenne
6 green peppercorns
¼ cup chopped shallots
Oil
½ cup butter (1 stick)
1 ounce Cognac (or Brandy)
1 cup bread crumbs

Grind the meats very fine. Sauté meats in a large frypan with salt, pepper, nutmeg, cloves, cayenne, peppercorns, and shallots in oil and butter. Cook until done. Adjust seasonings. Add Cognac (or Brandy) and bread crumbs. Mix and press into a buttered mold.

Chill for at least 4 hours. Remove from mold and slice.
    Makes 3 to 3½ cups.

Honey Mint Salad Dressing

2 cups oil
¼ cup dried mint leaves (or ½
    bunch fresh mint leaves)
½ cup tarragon vinegar
½ cup honey
1 teaspoon basil
½ cup lime juice
1 teaspoon salt
½ cup white Crème de Menthe

Combine all the ingredients. Mix well. Especially good on fruit or as a lamb marinade. Makes 4½ cups.

Kedron Valley Inn

Route 106
South Woodstock, Vermont 05071
(802) 457-1858

Kedron Valley is one of the oldest inns in Vermont, operating since the early 1800s. Today all rooms have private baths. The food is mouthwatering "nouvelle Vermont," prepared by a professional chef who is also a lifetime Vermonter, and featuring unique combinations of local products. Golf, indoor and outdoor tennis, and athletic facilities including swimming pool, squash and aerobics are only five minutes up the road. Activities available in the area include skiing, horse-drawn sleigh rides, swimming in the spring-fed pond, or trail rides at the nearby stables.

Gingered Parsnip Soup

2 medium white onions
Clarified butter
8 medium parsnips, peeled and
    sliced
2 tablespoons grated fresh ginger
    (or 1 tablespoon powdered
    ginger)
Salt and pepper to taste
4 cups chicken stock
Parsley, chopped

Peel and roughly chop the onions. Sauté the onions in a heavy pan with clarified butter until translucent. Add the parsnips to the onion and sauté. Add the ginger, salt, and pepper. Stir for about 1 minute. Add the chicken stock and simmer until the parsnips become soft. Drain the parsnips and reserve the liquid; place the parsnips in a food processor and purée. Return the purée to the liquid and simmer for 10 minutes. Adjust the seasonings and serve. Garnish with chopped parsley.
    Serves 6.

Salmon Admiral
with Caper Sauce

1 fresh whole salmon (Norwegian is
    best)
2 pounds sole fillets
2 egg whites
Juice of 1 lemon
Salt and white pepper
Fish stock

❖   ❖   ❖

2 shallots
1 tablespoon fresh tarragon
¼ cup capers
½ cup white wine
1 cup butter (2 sticks)

Fillet the salmon and remove the bones and skin. Butterfly, slicing each fillet open by making a horizontal cut almost through the entire fillet. Then unfold to open. Place the fillets on sheets of plastic wrap. Place the sole in a food processor with a metal blade and purée. Add the egg whites and lemon juice. Purée to a mousse consistency and season to taste. Spread ½ of the mousse onto each salmon fillet evenly. Roll each fillet with mousse tightly to resemble a jelly roll. Wrap tightly and place in the freezer to set for about 1½ hours. Remove the rolled fillets from the freezer and unwrap. Slice into serving sized slices. Poach the slices in fish stock until the salmon is almost completely pink. Do not boil or overcook.

To make the caper sauce, chop the shallots and tarragon. Place in a saucepan with the capers and white wine. Simmer until most of the liquid has evaporated (leave about 2 tablespoons of liquid). Slice the butter into small chunks. Remove the saucepan from heat and swirl the butter into the liquid, slice by slice, until the sauce is thickened (may require more butter). Hold at room temperature. Spoon over the poached salmon slices just before serving.

Serves approximately 15.

Golden Kitz Lodge and Motel

R.D. #1, Box 2980
Mountain Road (Route 108)
Stowe, Vermont 05672
(802) 253-4217

In this quaint old Vermont farmhouse guests experience the charm and old world elegance of a bygone era. Each of the ten rooms has a different name that tells its own story, such as the "Dutch daffodil room," the "Charleston pink mums room," or "Granny's patchwork room." The six motel rooms behind the lodge have two double beds and a single. Breakfast in the cozy "international 1747 room" offers

a choice of omelets, English muffins with honey, walnut pancakes with pure Vermont maple syrup, or sesame seed Belgian waffles. Area attractions include antique hunting, beautiful scenery, skiing, and ice skating. This is an area that can be enjoyed in all seasons.

The Golden Kitz Lodge Motel Kitchen Helpers

There is a motto here of using "helpers" and not being a slave in the kitchen. Favorite helpers include:

Chicken or beef base
Dried minced onions
Parsley flakes
Celery salt
Onion and garlic powder
Frozen mixed vegetables
Canned condensed soup

Sassy Sausage Dip

Combine cottage cheese, plain yogurt, bacon bits, sausage chunks, helper seasonings, and sweet pickle relish. Add a dollop of mustard for a tangy touch.

Winning Wine and Walnut Cheese Dip

To cheddar cheese in a crock add helper seasonings, Burgundy or Port wine, and walnuts. A winning combination!

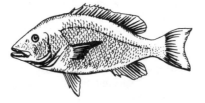

Bountiful Beautiful Bean Tweed Soup

Pick up a dozen or so different varieties of dried beans at your local health food store. Throw a handful of each kind (except lentils and split peas) into a big bowl of water and soak overnight. Cover lightly so that gases can escape. Boil a ham bone for a couple of hours (next day). Then throw in all the beans including the smaller unsoaked lentils and split peas. Simmer for about an hour. Dump in some chopped celery. Fifteen minutes later add all of the helpers including the mixed vegetables. You can also add any kind of small pasta, like elbow macaroni, shells, or vegetable swirls that have been partly cooked. Now, you can add chopped ham, or crisp crumbly bacon, or bite size pieces of hot dog—or add all! This soup takes more time, but it's a bountiful meal, and worth it!

Celestial Celery Soup

To 1 10¾-ounce can cream of celery soup add milk, butter, chicken base, and all the other helpers except mixed vegetables. Then add celery seed and chopped walnuts. This delicious soup tastes like you have been cooking for hours.

Marvelous Mushroom and Spinach Soup

To 1 10¾-ounce can of cream of mushroom soup add milk, frozen chopped spinach, chicken base, and all of the other helpers except the mixed vegetables. Then add chopped hard-boiled eggs. Simply marvelous!

Indecently Corrupting Indian Corn Chowder

To 1 10¾-ounce can of corn chowder add more crushed and whole corn, milk, butter, chicken base, and all of the other helpers but the vegetables, and a drizzle of molasses. Then sprinkle crispy bacon bits on top. You'll go back for more . . . and more. Be careful, it's addicting.

Yummy Yogurt and Avocado Soup

Combine the avocado pulp, plain yogurt, milk, all of the helpers but the vegetables and meat base. Add a drizzle of Italian salad dressing to give it more zip. So easy . . . and irresistible! Serve hot or cold.

Without the milk, it makes a great dip, or, with more Italian dressing, put it on your salad.

Fabulous Fudge Sauce

In the top of a double boiler combine unsweetened baking chocolate, butter, salt, milk, vanilla extract, and molasses. (Use all ingredients to your own discretion and taste.) This is a wicked after dinner treat.

The Green Mountain Inn

Aurora Enterprises, Ltd.
Box 1309
Stowe, Vermont 05672
(802) 253-7100

The Green Mountain Inn has 63 units, all warmly decorated with antiques. Rooms range in size from small rooms with twin beds to medium-sized rooms with canopy beds. A hotel section at the rear of the inn provides suites as well. Two restaurants, a cocktail bar, a gift shop, and an athletic club provide activities for varied interests.

Trastevere Salad Dressing

This dressing is served on a salad of fresh endive or arugula and radicchio.

16 tomatoes, peeled, seeded, and diced
2 yellow onions, sliced
6 cloves garlic, minced

❖ ❖ ❖

4 cups olive oil
Freshly ground pepper
¼ cup lemon juice
2 teaspoons sugar
Salt to taste

Place tomatoes, onions, and garlic in a large saucepan. Simmer lightly over medium heat; remove. Blend in oil, pepper, lemon juice, sugar, and salt. Serve at no less than room temperature.

Keith Martin, Chef.
Makes 5½ cups.

Chicken Quenelles

1 tablespoon butter
1 tablespoon all-purpose flour
½ cup chicken stock

❖ ❖ ❖

1 pound boneless, skinless, fatless white chicken meat

❖ ❖ ❖

5 egg whites
1 cup heavy cream
Salt and pepper to taste
Pinch cayenne and nutmeg

❖ ❖ ❖

1 quart chicken stock

In a small saucepan melt the butter, stir in the flour until well-mixed. Add stock and cook until thickened. Set aside.

Process raw chicken in a food processor. Add thickened stock; process until smooth. Remove to a metal mixing bowl set on ice. Blend in 1 egg white at a time; then work in cream. Mix well; add seasonings. Cover and refrigerate overnight.

Boil chicken stock; reduce to a simmer. Drop in spoonfuls of quenelles mixture and poach approximately 3 minutes. Serve on a bed of fresh spinach which has been steamed with sesame seeds. Garnish with a tomato rose in the center and light cream sauce or Hollandaise over each quenelle.

Keith Martin, Chef.
Serves 6 to 8.

Filet Mignon with Raspberry Sauce

2 8-ounce filets mignons
Butter

❖ ❖ ❖

1 shallot, diced fine
1 small tomato, peeled, seeded, and diced
2 to 3 tablespoons raspberry vinegar
½ cup beef stock
1 tablespoon demi-glace
8 fresh raspberries
1 teaspoon chopped fresh parsley
Salt and pepper to taste

In a sauté pan brown the filets mignons in butter over high heat. Place pan with filets in a 350° oven to cook until the desired internal temperature is reached, approximately 8 to 10 minutes for rare. Remove the filets to a heated platter.

Place the pan with drippings over medium heat on the stove top; add shallots, tomato, and vinegar. Reduce to a syrup. Add stock and demi-glaze; bring to a boil. Add raspberries, parsley, salt, and pepper. Spoon over filets.
Serves 2.

Blueberry-Apple Crumb Pie

2½ tablespoons butter
2½ tablespoons shortening
1 cup all-purpose flour
Ice Water
Minute tapioca

❖ ❖ ❖

3 cups fresh blueberries (or frozen wild Maine blueberries)
3 to 4 Granny Smith or MacIntosh apples, sliced
²/₃ cup sugar
1½ tablespoons all-purpose flour
1½ tablespoons cornstarch
½ teaspoon cinnamon
Dash nutmeg

❖ ❖ ❖

1 cup sugar
¾ cup all-purpose flour
⅓ cup ground walnuts
6 tablespoons butter

Prepare pie crust in a mixing bowl. Cut 2½ tablespoons of butter and the shortening into 1 cup of flour. Mix with just enough ice water to hold dough together. Wrap in plastic and refrigerate 1 hour. Roll out crust, place in a 9-inch pie pan. Flute the edges. Sprinkle the bottom lightly with minute tapioca.

Prepare the filling by mixing together blueberries, apples, 1½ tablespoons flour, cornstarch, lemon juice, cinnamon, and nutmeg. Place the mixture in the pie shell.

Prepare a topping by mixing together ⅓ cup of sugar, ⅓ cup flour, walnuts, and 2 tablespoons of butter.

Sprinkle the mixture over the pie. Bake in a 350° oven for 45 to 60 minutes, until blueberries bubble.
Serves 6 to 8.

Grey Fox Inn

Route 108
Mountain Road
Stowe, Vermont 05672
(802) 253-8921

The Grey Fox Inn offers a variety of accommodations, all with private bath and/or shower. The scenery and year-round activities make this one of the top resorts in the northeast in all seasons. It is within walking distance of the cinema and Stowe's famous nightspots, and one and one-half miles from the scenic village.

Sunshine Salad

1 head Romaine or iceberg lettuce, torn in pieces
1 bunch green onions, sliced
1 8-ounce can mandarin oranges, drained
¼ cup chopped pecans
1 avocado, peeled and diced
Bottled Italian dressing (not creamy)
Croutons

Toss the salad ingredients with the dressing and serve topped with croutons.
Serves 4.

Ginger Chicken
with Lime

2 whole chicken breasts
¼ cup olive oil
½ teaspoon salt and pepper
2 large garlic cloves, minced
1 tablespoon fresh minced ginger
Parsley
Lime wedges

Roll the chicken in oil and spices. Bake in a 425° oven for 15 minutes or until done. Garnish with parsley and sprinkle with lime at table.
Serves 4.

Grey Fox Inn

Roast Pork
with Deviled Sauce

2 tablespoons butter
1 thin slice onion
2 tablespoons all-purpose flour
1 cup beef broth
¼ teaspoon salt
⅛ teaspoon pepper
2 tablespoons chopped sautéed onion
1 tablespoon snipped parsley
1 tablespoon vinegar
¼ teaspoon tarragon leaves
¼ teaspoon thyme leaves
1 pork roast or 8 pork chops, cooked
Snipped parsley

Heat the butter in a skillet over low heat until golden brown. Add the onion slice; cook and stir until the onion is tender. Blend in the flour. Cook over low heat, stirring until the flour is deep brown. Remove from heat. Stir in the broth. Heat to boiling, stirring constantly. Boil and stir for 1 minute. Stir in the salt, pepper, sautéed onion, parsley, vinegar, tarragon leaves, and thyme leaves; simmer for 1 minute. Serve over the pork roast and sprinkle with extra snipped parsley.
Serves 8.

Chocolate Eclair Cake

2 3¾-ounce packages instant pudding (vanilla or banana)
3 cups milk
1 9-ounce carton non-dairy whipped topping

❖ ❖ ❖

¼ cup milk
¼ cup cocoa
1 cup sugar
½ teaspoon salt
2 tablespoons butter
1 teaspoon vanilla extract

❖ ❖ ❖

Graham crackers

Combine the pudding and milk. Fold in the whipped topping. Beat with an electric mixer at medium speed for 2 minutes.

Combine the milk, cocoa, sugar, and salt. Boil for 1 minute. Remove and add the butter and vanilla. Mix well. Cool.

In a 1-quart glass dish layer alternately the graham crackers and pudding, beginning and ending with the crackers. Add the cocoa topping and chill overnight.

Serves 8.

Ski Inn

Stowe, Vermont 05672
(802) 253-4050

Set back from the highway amid the evergreens, the Ski Inn is a traditional old New England inn made comfortably modern. This quiet, restful place provides a flat hiking road, trout stream, and cookout facilities on the twenty-eight acres of woodlands adjacent to the Mount Mansfield ski area. Daily room rates include the breakfast and dinner meals.

Apple Crunch

1 cup oats
½ cup all-purpose flour
1 cup brown sugar, firmly packed
½ cup butter (1 stick)

❖ ❖ ❖

3 cups apples, chopped
1 tablespoon all-purpose flour
1 teaspoon cinnamon
Pinch salt
1 tablespoon water
½ cup sugar

Mix the oats, flour, and brown sugar; cut in the butter until crumbly. Place ½ of the mixture in the bottom of a baking pan.

Combine the apples, flour, cinnamon, salt, water, and sugar; place in the pan over the oat mixture. Cover with the remainder of the mixture. Bake in a 350° oven for 45 minutes.

Serves 6.

Knoll Farm Country Inn

Bragg Hill Road
Waitsfield, Vermont 05673
(802) 496-3939

From the front porch of Knoll Farm, one can view the Lincoln Mountain Range with its three ski areas, Mad River Glen, Sugarbush, and Sugarbush North. The emphasis continues to be on simple country living, as it was fifty years ago when this was a flourishing hill farm. The farmhouse is converted for vacationing, with modern conveniences, light and airy rooms, firm beds, three baths, and plenty of hot water. Farm-grown, home-cooked meals are served family style. Breakfasts are hearty; fresh milk, butter, eggs, vegetables, and meats, are prepared in traditional Vermont ways. The innkeepers gladly prepare vege-tarian meals or meet other special dietary needs on request. Nature trails for hiking are nearby. The farm has many animals including a small herd of shaggy-haired Scottish highland cattle, cows, calves, chickens, a friendly pig, ponies, colts, horses, cats, kittens, and several amiable dogs.

Knoll Farm Vegetable Chowder

"Or Cream of Leftover Vegetable Soup. We serve this soup every day, with endless variations. It is a good meal for vegetarians."

1 cup butter (2 sticks)
1 medium onion, chopped
3 or 4 ribs celery, diced
1 teaspoon basil
1 teaspoon dill weed
1 teaspoon celery salt
2 carrots, peeled and thinly shaved
1 cup mushrooms, freshly sliced
1 small zucchini, diced
1 package onion soup mix (optional)
1 cup all-purpose flour
3 quarts milk, whole or skim
Leftover vegetables (broccoli, peas, corn, cabbage, etc.)
Cooked potatoes, cut up (or rice)

Melt the butter in a large pot. Add the onion and celery. As these vegetables cook over medium heat add the basil, dill weed, and celery salt, stirring constantly. Add the carrots, mushrooms, and zucchini. Add the soup mix if desired, stirring constantly to keep the vegetables from sticking. Slowly stir in the flour until all of the vegetables are coated and the butter is absorbed. Slowly add part of the milk until there is enough liquid to make a cream sauce. Add the rest of the milk, leftover vegetables, and the potatoes or rice. Simmer over low heat until thick, but do not boil. This chowder is best if made ahead and reheated. It can also be added to a new batch of soup with more leftovers.

Serves 16 to 20.

Chicken with Rosemary

1 broiler-fryer, cut up
Salt and pepper

❖ ❖ ❖

1½ tablespoons parsley
1 onion, chopped
1 clove garlic, chopped
2 tablespoons oil

❖ ❖ ❖

3 tablespoons oil
2 tablespoons butter
¼ teaspoon rosemary
¼ cup cider vinegar

❖ ❖ ❖

3 cups hot cooked rice
6 tablespoons grated Romano
    cheese
⅛ teaspoon pepper
3 tablespoons butter, melted

Season the chicken with salt and pepper; set aside.

In a large skillet, sauté the parsley, onion, and garlic in 2 tablespoons of oil. Remove the vegetables; set aside. Add 3 tablespoons of oil to the pan and fry the chicken until golden brown. Add the butter and sprinkle the rosemary over the chicken. Add the cider vinegar and the reserved vegetables to the pan. Cover and braise until the chicken is tender. Add more liquid if needed. Remove the chicken. Thicken the pan juices with a little flour and water blended until smooth.

Toss the hot rice with the Romano cheese, pepper, and melted butter. Serve the chicken with the rice mixture and the gravy.

Serves 8 to 10.

Meat Loaf

2 extra large eggs, beaten
¾ cup vegetable juice
1 medium onion, chopped
Several fresh mushrooms, chopped
1 cup old-fashioned rolled oats
1 teaspoon basil
1 teaspoon dill
1 teaspoon seasoned salt
1 tablespoon Worcestershire sauce
1 pound ground beef
¼ pound ground sausage,
    unseasoned

Mix the eggs with the vegetable juice. Add the onion and mushrooms. Add the oats, basil, dill, seasoned salt, and Worcestershire sauce and stir well. Mix in the ground beef and sausage. Mix well with a wooden spoon. Put into a large loaf pan and bake in a 375° oven for 1 hour.

Serves 6 to 8.

Zucchini Relish

This relish is a good way to use up the over-abundant zucchini you have in your garden. Our guests enjoy it with meats, especially meat loaf.

⅓ cup pickling salt
12 cups coarsely ground zucchini
2 green peppers, coarsely ground
2 sweet red peppers, chopped
4 cups coarsely ground onions
1 teaspoon turmeric
1 teaspoon curry powder
1 teaspoon celery seed
1 tablespoon cornstarch
½ teaspoon pepper
3 cups vinegar
4½ cups sugar

In a large enamel pan, mix the pickling salt into the vegetables. Let stand overnight. Drain, rinse with cold water, and return to the pan. Mix together the remaining ingredients and add to the vegetables. Boil for 20 minutes. Pour into sterilized jars and seal.

Makes about 12 pints.

The Valley Inn

Box 8, Route 100
Waitsfield, Vermont 05673
(802) 496-3450
1-800-451-4590 (toll free)

This thirty-five-year-old inn with its Tyrolean flavor has been improved over the years to provide the best in comfort and convenience. In addition to family rooms accommodating four to six people, there are adjoining rooms for couples, private rooms with double and twin beds, and even separate accommodations for children. Most rooms have private baths, while a few have bathrooms "just across the hall." Bedrooms are fully carpeted, and each bed is topped with a warm quilt. Regularly scheduled wine and cheese parties produce a festive atmosphere, as do impromptu fondue parties and moonlight cross country outings.

Three Cheese Ball

1 8-ounce package cream cheese
1 cup shredded Cheddar cheese
1 cup shredded blue cheese
1 tablespoon minced onion
1 tablespoon Worcestershire sauce
½ cup chopped walnuts

Soften the cheeses at room temperature for about 2 hours. Place everything except the walnuts in a large bowl and whip until blended. Chill. Shape into a ball and roll in the walnuts. Wrap in waxed paper and refrigerate until completely chilled. Serve with crackers.

Makes 1 cheese ball.

Spinach Cheese Nuggets

This recipe is easy and fast when the ingredients are blended in a food processor.

2 10-ounce packages frozen
    chopped spinach
1 small onion, finely chopped
4 eggs, beaten
½ cup Parmesan cheese
½ teaspoon thyme
2 cups stuffing mix

Thaw and barely cook the spinach; drain thoroughly. Combine with the remaining ingredients and shape into small balls. Place on a cookie sheet and freeze. Place in plastic bags until ready to use. Bake in a 350° oven for 20 minutes.

Makes 60 nuggets.

Cream of Summer Squash Soup

4 cups water
1 pound crookneck squash, chopped
1 large onion
2 tablespoons instant chicken bouillon granules
2 tablespoons butter
2 tablespoons all-purpose flour
2 egg yolks, slightly beaten
1 cup light cream

In a saucepan combine the water, squash, onion, and bouillon granules. Simmer covered for about 15 minutes or until the squash and onion are tender. Place half the mixture in a blender or food processor. Cover and blend until smooth. Remove and place in a bowl. Repeat with the remaining mixture.

In a large saucepan, melt the butter; stir in the flour. Add the blended squash mixture and stir until thickened and bubbly. Stir about 1 cup of the hot mixture into the beaten egg yolks. Return to the pan; stir in the cream. Heat through, but do not boil.

Serves 6.

Salad Dressing

1 cup oil
½ cup sugar
1 teaspoon dry mustard
1 teaspoon salt
¼ cup minced onion
¼ cup white vinegar
1 tablespoon celery seed

Combine everything in a bowl and whip with vigor. This dressing gets jelly-like after chilling for about 1 hour.

Makes 1½ cups.

Applesauce Raisin Bread

2 eggs
2 cups applesauce
1 cup sugar
½ cup brown sugar, firmly packed
½ cup butter (1 stick), melted
4 cups all-purpose flour
4 teaspoons baking powder
1½ teaspoons salt
1 teaspoon baking soda
1 teaspoon cinnamon
2 teaspoons nutmeg
1 cup raisins and nuts

Mix the eggs, applesauce, sugars, and butter until smooth. Add the dry ingredients. Mix until smooth. Add the raisins and nuts. Pour into 2 greased loaf pans and bake in a 350° oven for 45 to 60 minutes. Cool on a rack for 1 hour. This is delicious toasted the next day.

Makes 2 loaves.

Mom's Pork Chops

8 ½-inch center-cut pork chops
1 1⅝-ounce envelope dry onion soup mix
1 32-ounce jar spaghetti sauce
Onion slices
Green pepper slices
Mushroom halves

In a large skillet lightly brown the pork chops. Season with salt and pepper. Add the soup mix and spaghetti sauce. Smother the top with onions, peppers, and mushrooms. Cover and cook over medium heat for 45 minutes or until the pork chops are tender.

Served with buttered noodles and fresh vegetables, this is a super dinner.

Variation: Summer squash and zucchini may be used in place of the onion, green pepper, and mushrooms.

Serves 4.

Jaeger Schnitzel

1 large green pepper
1 medium onion
2 carrots

Mushrooms, sliced
2 sausage links, cut up
3 to 4 tablespoons all-purpose flour

❖ ❖ ❖

½ cup red wine
½ cup water
1 10-ounce can beef gravy
1 tablespoon dry mustard
1 tablespoon dill weed

❖ ❖ ❖

8 ½-inch thick pork chops

❖ ❖ ❖

Cheese noodles

Chop the pepper, onion, and carrots into bite-sized pieces; combine with the mushrooms and sausage. In a large saucepan sauté the vegetables and sausage until partially cooked. Drain off the grease. Add the flour and mix well. Add the wine, water, gravy, mustard, and dill weed. Simmer for several hours until thickened.

When the sauce is ready, sauté the pork chops until golden brown. Pour the sauce over the pork chops and serve with hot cheese noodles.

Serves 4.

Veal Escalopes

Sliced fresh mushrooms
Black pepper to taste
Lemon juice
Tarragon leaves
3 thin slices veal
Cream Sherry

❖ ❖ ❖

Hot rice or buttered noodles

In a medium saucepan sauté the mushrooms in butter; remove from the pan. Pound the pepper, lemon juice, and tarragon leaves into the veal slices. Add butter to the pan and gently sauté the veal slices; remove from the pan and keep warm. Add about 1 ounce of cream sherry and reduce. Pour over the veal. Serve with hot rice or buttered noodles.

Serves 2.

Pineapple Soufflé

2 eggs
¼ cup sugar
2½ cups crushed pineapple,
    drained
2 tablespoons all-purpose flour
½ cup butter (1 stick)
4 slices bread
Cinnamon and sugar mixture

Beat the eggs and sugar in a 1-quart casserole. Mix the pineapple and flour. Add to the egg mixture; stir slightly. Melt the butter in a saucepan. Add the bread slices. When the bread has absorbed all of the butter, place on top of the casserole. Lightly sprinkle with sugar and cinnamon. Bake in a 350° oven for 45 minutes. Serve hot with ham or roast beef.

Serves 4.

Blush Hill House

Blush Hill Road
Waterbury, Vermont 05676
(802) 244-7529

Once used as a stagecoach stop between Waterbury and Stowe, the Blush Hill House is in the center of Stowe, Sugarbush, and Balton Valley ski areas. It is directly across the road from the Blush Hill Country Club, which offers a nine-hole golf course. Miles of marked trails make the area a mecca for hiking and cross-country skiing. It is also near a state-protected lake with boating, swimming, and fishing.

Blush Hill Corn Bread

1 cup yellow cornmeal
1 cup all-purpose flour
2 tablespoons sugar

4 teaspoons baking powder
½ teaspoon salt
1 cup milk
¼ cup shortening
1 egg

❖   ❖   ❖

12 slices cooked bacon
Vermont maple syrup
Confectioners' sugar

Blend the first 8 ingredients about 20 seconds. Beat vigorously 1 minute. Pour into a greased 8-inch square pan. Bake 20 to 25 minutes or until golden brown. Serve warm, topped with 2 slices of bacon and Vermont maple syrup. Sprinkle with confectioners' sugar.

Serves 6.

Orange Date Bread

Rind of 1 orange, grated
1 cup water
½ cup chopped dates
¾ cup sugar
2 tablespoons butter
1 egg, beaten
1 cup butter (2 sticks)
2 cups all-purpose flour
2 teaspoons baking powder
½ teaspoon salt

Mix together the rind, water, and dates in a saucepan and boil gently. Add sugar and butter; stir until dissolved and remove from heat. When cooled, stir in remaining ingredients. Place in a buttered 8x4-inch loaf pan. Bake in a 350° oven for about 45 minutes or until it tests done. Serve sliced with cream cheese, homemade preserves, smoked turkey or homemade apple jelly.

Makes 1 loaf.

The Inn at Thatcher Brook Falls

R.D. 2, Box 62
Waterbury, Vermont 05676
(802) 244-5911

Centrally located in Vermont's ski country, the Inn at Thatcher Brook Falls is a recently restored "country

The Inn at Thatcher Brook Falls

Victorian" mansion with thirteen guest rooms, all individually decorated and with private baths. Several guest rooms have fireplaces. The inn offers superb cuisine in the three dining rooms. The cozy fireplaced tavern is called "Bailey's" after the dog that almost always is asleep in front of the fireplace. During the summer months, canoe and bike tours and golf and tennis packages are available. The host is a former PGA golf pro and is available for private lessons upon arrangement. In the winter months cross-country skiing begins at the front door.

Fillet of Sole a la Thatcher

2 ounces crab meat
2 large shrimp, chopped
2 pinches fresh dill, finely chopped
Pinch pepper
Pinch white pepper
4 sheets phyllo pastry dough
6 to 8 ounces fresh fillet of sole

❖ ❖ ❖

½ cup cream Sherry
¾ quart heavy cream
1 teaspoon lobster base
1 teaspoon roux

In a mixing bowl, combine the crab meat, chopped shrimp, and seasonings. On a counter or work area, lay out the phyllo dough 1 sheet at a time, brushing with melted butter between sheets. After the fourth sheet, spread the stuffing on the middle of the pastry, then place the sole on top of the stuffing. Fold the phyllo dough around the sole, making sure the ends are wrapped neatly. Bake in a 350° oven for 10 to 15 minutes or until the phyllo dough turns a light shade of brown.

To make the Sherried shrimp sauce, in a very hot sauté pan pour ½ cup of cream Sherry. Flambé and let 95% of the alcohol burn off. Add the cream. Bring the mixture to a boil and then whip the lobster base into the mixture. Add the roux and bring to a boil; maintain until the liquid thickens to a heavy cream consistency.

Makes enough sauce for 10 to 12 servings.

The Colonial House

Route 100
Weston, Vermont 05161
(802) 824-6286

Colonial House is an inn in which guests can enjoy the hospitality of the innkeepers and partake of the many recreational activities in the area. Its large living room, complete with player piano and open fireplace, provides a place to visit, relax, or enjoy the view. Over 150 miles of hiking and cross country skiing trails are immediately accessible, and several alpine ski mountains are in the area. Guests awaken to the aroma of cinnamon-raisin bread fresh from the oven, mingled with the smell of fresh coffee. The leisurely country breakfasts include pancakes and farm fresh eggs. Nearby is the town of Weston, nestled in the Green Mountains, with its country stores, intriguing shops, small museums, craft center, town green, and beautiful churches. Weston Priory is just north of the town. Hiking, swimming, golf, tennis, and canoeing are available nearby.

Savory Soup

1¼ teaspoons Italian seasonings
1½ cups chopped onions
1½ cups chopped celery
1½ tablespoons butter
1½ grated unpeeled zucchini
1½ cups chicken/turkey stock
2 cups light cream
½ cup milk
¼ teaspoon white pepper
2 chicken bouillon cubes

Sauté the seasonings, onions, and celery in butter until transparent. Add the zucchini and stock. Simmer for 30 minutes. Just before serving, add the

The Colonial House

cream, milk, pepper, and bouillon. Heat to serving temperature, but do not boil.

Serves 8 as a first course.

Mandarin Orange Salad Dressing

A little care with the arrangement of the lettuce and orange slices pays off with an attractive presentation.

½ cup sugar
2 teaspoons dry mustard
⅔ cup apple cider vinegar
½ cup honey
1 teaspoon minced onion
1 tablespoon celery salt
2 cups oil

❖ ❖ ❖

Mandarin orange sections

Add all of the ingredients except the oil and oranges and beat well. Add the oil and beat until well-mixed and almost transparent. Very good over a mixture of lettuces and spinach leaves. Garnish with several mandarin orange sections before serving the salad.

Makes 3½ cups.

Burgundy Berry Pie Filling

A magnificent pie. The cranberries cut the sweetness often found in blueberry pie while enhancing the flavor.

1½ cups whole cranberries, fresh or frozen
2 cups non-sweetened blueberries, fresh or frozen
1 cup sugar
3 tablespoons cornstarch
Dash salt
Pastry for 1 8-inch 2-crust pie
1 tablespoon butter
Juice of ¼ lemon

❖ ❖ ❖

Vanilla ice cream

Combine the cranberries and blueberries. Combine the sugar, cornstarch, and salt. Stir in the mixed berries and

spread into an 8-inch pie pan lined with pastry. Top the filling with 1 tablespoon of butter and the lemon juice. Add the top crust and flute the edges. Bake in a 400° oven for 35 minutes; reduce the heat to 375° for about 20 minutes until golden brown and the juice is bubbly. Cool partially. Serve with a scoop of vanilla ice cream.

Serves 6.

Brownie Pie

3 egg whites
¼ teaspoon salt
¾ cup sugar
½ teaspoon vanilla extract
¾ cup chocolate wafer crumbs
½ cup chopped walnuts

❖ ❖ ❖

½ pint whipping cream, whipped
Chocolate jimmies for garnish

Beat the egg whites and salt until soft peaks form. Gradually add the sugar. Then add the vanilla and beat until very stiff peaks form. Fold in the wafer crumbs and walnuts. Spread evenly in a lightly buttered 9-inch pie plate. Bake in a 325° oven for 30 to 35 minutes. Cool thoroughly. Spread with sweetened whipped cream. Pipe on decorative whipped cream and sprinkle on chocolate jimmies for a final touch. Chill well for 3 to 4 hours before serving.

Serves 6.

The Inn at Weston

Route 100
Weston, Vermont 05161
(802) 824-5804

Built as a farmhouse in 1848, The Inn at Weston is now a pleasant rambling building with wood stoves, exposed beams, and warm pine plank floors.

Located in the picturesque village of Weston in the Green Mountains of southern Vermont, it has been featured in many national magazines and guides. Guests are invited to savor the friendly country atmosphere and the fresh and creative cuisine. The inn has been placed on the National Register of Historic places as part of the Weston Village Historic District.

Apple Cheddar Quiche

3 apples, diced
3 tablespoons butter
1 partially baked 10-inch pie shell
1½ cups grated sharp Cheddar cheese

❖ ❖ ❖

4 eggs
2 egg yolks
1 cup cottage cheese
1½ cups half and half

❖ ❖ ❖

1 teaspoon sugar
¼ teaspoon cinnamon
Dash salt

In a medium frypan sauté apples in butter for 5 minutes. Place in the pie shell; top with Cheddar cheese.

In a mixing bowl beat together the eggs, yolks, cottage cheese, and half and half. Pour over the apples and cheese. Combine the sugar, cinnamon, and salt; sprinkle over the top. Bake in a 375° oven for 30 to 45 minutes, until the custard is firm.

Serves 6.

Apple Butter

5 pounds apples
2 cups cider
1 cup sugar
3 teaspoons cinnamon
1½ teaspoons cloves
¼ teaspoon allspice
Dash nutmeg

Quarter apples; cook in a large saucepan with cider, sugar, and spices. Cook until the apples are soft but still retain their shape a bit. Cool and refrigerate.

Can be mixed with sour cream or mayonnaise for a fruit salad dressing.

Nonie's Apple Chutney

1 lemon, finely chopped
1 clove garlic, minced
5 cups diced apples
2¼ cups brown sugar, firmly
 packed
1 cup chopped, crystallized ginger
1 cup orange juice
1½ teaspoons salt
1¼ teaspoons cayenne
1 teaspoon each cloves, cinnamon,
 and allspice
1 medium onion, chopped
2 cups cider vinegar
1 15¼-ounce can pineapple chunks
1 8-ounce can sliced water
 chestnuts, diced
1 cup sliced almonds
1½ cups raisins
1 cup Sherry

Place all the ingredients in a large pot and cook about 1 hour. The fragrance is fantastic. Spoon into sterilized jars. Seal.

Fills 6 to 8 8-ounce jars.

Strawberry Jam

Include 1 pint unripe berries so you have enough pectin.

2 quarts fresh strawberries
2 cups sugar
2 tablespoons lemon juice

Wash and hull strawberries. Then purée them in blender or food processor. Add sugar and lemon juice and cook in a large saucepan over medium heat; stirring frequently until the mixture thickens to the desired consistency (it will thicken as much as you wish). Spoon into sterilized jars and seal.

Fills 8 8-ounce jars.

The Inn at Weston

Fresh Strawberry Daiquiri

1 cup ripe strawberries, washed
 and stemmed
1 tablespoon sugar (or more)
¾ ounce lime juice
1½ ounces rum
4 to 6 ice cubes
Fresh mint

Place strawberries, sugar, lime juice, rum, and ice cubes into a blender. Blend for 45 seconds. Pour into a Brandy snifter. Garnish with fresh mint.

Serves 1.

Carrot Soup

1 pound carrots, sliced
2 tablespoons butter
2 tablespoons oil
 ❖ ❖ ❖
2 cups chicken broth
¼ cup butter
¼ cup all-purpose flour
2 cups milk
1 teaspoon cardamom
Salt and pepper

In a medium saucepan sauté sliced carrots in 2 tablespoons butter and oil until tender. Reserve ½ cup of the carrots. Purée remaining carrots in a blender with broth. In a saucepan melt ¼ cup butter. Add flour and cook 2 to 3 minutes, stirring with a wire whisk. Add milk and cook over medium heat, stirring until the sauce thickens. Combine sauce, carrots, and carrot purée. Season with cardamom, salt, and pepper. Heat in a double boiler and serve.

Serves 4 to 6.

Champagne Melon Peach Soup

A refreshing summer cooler.

1 ripe cantaloupe
2½ pounds frozen peaches, lightly
 sweetened
¼ bottle Champagne
Fresh mint

Remove meat from the melon and purée in a blender with peaches. Chill this mixture well. At serving time, fill Champagne glasses ⅔ full with chilled fruit purée. Top with Champagne. Garnish with a sprig of fresh mint.

Serves 12 to 16.

Rosy Beet Soup

A lovely rose color and rich flavor.

3 to 4 medium fresh beets

❖ ❖ ❖

2 to 3 cups chicken broth
¼ to ½ cup sour cream
2 to 4 tablespoons lemon juice
Salt

Peel and slice beets. Place in a medium saucepan; cover with water and cook until tender enough to pierce with a fork. Combine in a blender with broth; blend thoroughly. Add sour cream. Season with lemon juice and salt. Blend again. Serve well-chilled in your prettiest bowls or stemmed glasses.
Serves 4 to 6.

Summer Soup

1 medium onion, diced
3 medium summer squash, thinly
    sliced
2 carrots, sliced
3 ribs celery, sliced
4 cups chicken stock
    (approximately)
Salt and pepper
Sour cream, cherry tomatoes, and
    chives for garnish

In a medium saucepan sauté onion in butter. Add vegetables. Pour in enough chicken stock to just cover vegetables. Simmer, covered, until vegetables are quite soft. Purée in a blender; season with salt and pepper. Serve chilled with a dollop of sour cream, diced cherry tomatoes, and chives. Also delicious hot.
Serves 4 to 6.

Vermont-Style Fish Soup

1 Spanish onion, chopped
3 tablespoons butter
1 teaspoon thyme
½ teaspoon saffron
4 cups water

1 cup dry white wine
2 pounds scrod fillets, chopped
½ cup Brandy
2 cups whipping cream
Salt and pepper

In a medium saucepan sauté onion in butter until soft. Add thyme and saffron. Cook until onion is golden. Pour in the water and wine; add scrod. Bring to a boil and immediately lower heat; simmer 15 minutes. Add Brandy; simmer 10 more minutes. Add cream. Season. Heat well (do not boil) and serve.
Serves 6.

White Gazpacho

3 medium cucumbers
5 ribs celery, chopped
1 clove garlic, minced
3 cups chicken broth
3 cups sour cream
1 tablespoons white vinegar
White pepper
Minced chives (or scallions)
Diced cherry tomatoes

Purée cucumbers, celery, garlic, and chicken broth in blender. Whip in sour cream and flavor with white vinegar and white pepper to taste. Serve chilled with chives and tomatoes.
Variations: For a vegetarian recipe, substitute celery juice for chicken broth or purée celery and extra cucumber for broth. Try adding lemon juice instead of vinegar. You may also add 1 to 2 avocados in place of 1 to 1½ cups sour cream.
Serves 6.

Chocolate Mint Sauce

8 ounces semi-sweet chocolate
¼ cup Peppermint Schnapps
½ cup whipping cream

Melt the chocolate in the top of double boiler. Mix in the Schnapps and whipping cream. Heat through. Delicious served on your favorite ice cream.
Makes 1½ cups.

Country Blanquette of Veal

Sprigs fresh parsley
¼ teaspoon thyme
5 peppercorns
1 bay leaf
2 celery tops
1 clove garlic, peeled and halved

❖ ❖ ❖

2 cups all-purpose flour
½ teaspoon salt
1 teaspoon paprika
2½ pounds diced veal
1 carrot, sliced
¼ pound diced ham
1 Spanish onion
4 cups veal stock (or chicken)

❖ ❖ ❖

3 tablespoons butter
3 tablespoons all-purpose flour
½ cup dry white wine
½ teaspoon marjoram

❖ ❖ ❖

1 cup heavy cream
2 egg yolks
Fresh peas
Chives

Place in a cheesecloth bag the parsley, thyme, peppercorns, bay leaf, celery tops, and garlic.
Combine 2 cups of flour, salt, and paprika. Dredge the veal in this mixture; sauté lightly in butter. Place in a Dutch oven with carrot, ham, onion, and cheesecloth bag. Add stock and bring to a boil. Reduce heat, cover, and simmer for 1½ hours. Discard cheesecloth bag and onion. Remove the veal, ham, and carrots from the pan and set aside. Reduce broth by boiling down to half.
Melt the butter in a small frypan; add 3 tablespoons of flour. Cook 5 minutes, stirring constantly. Add to the stock in the Dutch oven along with wine and marjoram. Cook until thickened.
Combine the cream and egg yolks. Reduce the heat under the Dutch oven to low. Gradually add the cream to the hot mixture, whisking constantly until smooth. Return the veal, ham, and carrots to the pan. Top with fresh peas and chives.
Serves 8.

Florentine de Mer

1 cup water
½ cup dry white wine
¼ onion, chopped
1 sprig parsley
1 celery top
1 bay leaf
Pinch thyme

❖ ❖ ❖

¾ pound scrod fillets
½ pound sea scallops
1½ cups chopped spinach
2 shallots, minced
¼ cup heavy cream
1 tablespoon lemon juice
Dash nutmeg
¼ teaspoon salt
¼ teaspoon pepper

❖ ❖ ❖

1 package phyllo pastry
Melted butter

❖ ❖ ❖

Hollandaise sauce

In a medium saucepan place the water, wine, onion, parsley, celery, bay leaf, and thyme; heat. Place scrod and scallops into the liquid, bring to a boil and simmer 3 minutes. Remove the scrod and scallops; cut into 1-inch pieces. Combine with the spinach, shallots, cream, lemon juice, nutmeg, salt, and pepper.

Lay out 2 sheets of phyllo and brush with melted butter. Top with 2 more sheets. Brush with melted butter. Cut in ½. Place ¼ of the filling on each half. Bring in sides and roll up the sheet to make a small packet. Place on a buttered baking sheet. Repeat the process with the remaining phyllo and filling. Bake in a 400° oven 10 to 15 minutes, until brown. Lower temperature to 325° and bake an additional 5 to 10 minutes. Top with Hollandaise sauce.

Serves 8 to 12.

Spicy Bourbon Pot Roast

1 3 to 4 pound top round roast
3 slices raw bacon, chopped
Flour
Oil

Oregano
Basil
Salt
Pepper
1 cup Bourbon

Make deep slits in the fatty portion of roast. Insert pieces of chopped bacon. Flour roast lightly and braise in oil. Place in a heavy oven-proof casserole. Season with a pinch of oregano, basil, salt, and pepper. Add 1 cup of Bourbon. Cover and bake in a 325° oven for 2 to 3 hours, until tender.

Serves 12 to 16.

Vermont Pork and Apple Pie

4 medium potatoes
½ cup milk
3 tablespoons butter
Salt and pepper

❖ ❖ ❖

2 pounds pork, cubed
Flour
Butter
1 small onion, diced
Salt and pepper
1 teaspoon sage

❖ ❖ ❖

½ cup applesauce

❖ ❖ ❖

3 apples, thickly sliced
3 to 4 tablespoons butter

❖ ❖ ❖

Paprika

Boil the potatoes until tender. Drain and mash with the milk, 3 tablespoons of butter, salt, and pepper. Set aside.

Dredge cubed pork in flour; sauté in a large frypan until golden with onion, salt, pepper, and sage. Divide the mixture between 4 au gratin dishes and top with applesauce.

Flour the apple slices lightly and sauté in 3 to 4 tablespoons of butter for 5 minutes. Layer over the pork mixture and top with the reserved mashed potatoes. Sprinkle with paprika. Bake in a 350° oven for 20 minutes.

Serves 4.

Broccoli Cheese Strudel

2 small heads broccoli, trimmed, diced, and steamed until tender
1½ cups grated Cheddar cheese
½ cup freshly grated Parmesan
1 cup cottage cheese (or pot cheese)
1 medium onion, diced
2 cloves garlic, minced
2 eggs
Salt and pepper to taste

❖ ❖ ❖

1 16-ounce package phyllo dough
Melted butter
Fine bread crumbs

Combine the broccoli, Cheddar, Parmesan, and cottage cheese, onion, garlic, eggs, salt, and pepper to make filling.

Lay out two layers of phyllo pastry and brush lightly with melted butter. Sprinkle fine breadcrumbs on each layer to absorb moisture during baking. Repeat with more layers until a total of eight sheets are prepared. Spread broccoli filling onto phyllo, leaving a border of 2 inches on each side. Bring in sides and roll up strudel. Place on a buttered baking sheet. Lightly butter top of strudel and cut through top of pastry to indicate size of servings and to facilitate cutting later. Place strudel in a preheated 400° oven for 10 to 20 minutes until browned. Lower heat to 350° and bake 15 to 20 minutes longer.

Serves 12 to 16.

Vermont Cheddar Cheesecake

⅓ cup fine bread crumbs
¼ cup grated Parmesan cheese

❖ ❖ ❖

4 8-ounce packages cream cheese
¼ cup all-purpose flour
5 eggs
3 egg yolks
⅓ cup heavy cream
2 to 3 cups grated sharp Cheddar cheese

1 medium onion, diced and sautéed
   in butter
2 small cloves garlic, minced
⅓ cup flat beer

Butter a 10-inch cheesecake pan. Combine bread crumbs and Parmesan; sprinkle over pan bottom. Beat together the cream cheese, flour, eggs, yolks, and cream. Fold in Cheddar, onion, and garlic. Add beer last. Pour the mixture into the prepared pan. Place pan into larger pan filled with 2 inches of boiling water. Bake in a 250° oven for 1 hour and 40 minutes. Turn off heat and leave in the oven for 1 hour. Cool 2 hours before unmolding.
Serves 12 to 20.

❖ ❖ ❖ ❖ ❖ ❖

Sour Cream Apple Pie

2 tablespoons all-purpose flour
¾ cup sugar
¾ teaspoon cinnamon
⅛ teaspoon salt
1 egg
1 teaspoon vanilla extract
1 cup sour cream
6 apples, sliced
   ❖   ❖   ❖
⅓ cup all-purpose flour
⅓ cup sugar
½ teaspoon cinnamon
Butter

Preheat oven to 400°. Sift together 2 tablespoons flour, ¾ cup sugar, ¾ teaspoon cinnamon, and salt. Stir in egg, vanilla, and sour cream. Fold in apples and spoon into a pie shell. Bake in a 400° oven for 15 minutes. Reduce to 350° and bake 30 minutes longer. Meanwhile, combine ⅓ cup flour, ⅓ cup sugar, and ½ teaspoon cinnamon. Blend in butter until crumbly. Sprinkle mixture over pie and bake in a 400° oven for 10 minutes more.
Serves 6.

Raspberry Cream

3 cups partially thawed
   unsweetened raspberries
1 to 1½ cups sugar
1 tablespoon lemon extract
2½ cups sour cream
Sprig of mint or whipped cream for
   garnish

Purée berries and sugar in a food processor for about 2 minutes. Then add lemon extract and ½ cup of the sour cream. Purée for 30 seconds. Pour this into a large bowl and fold in the rest of the sour cream. Portion out into 12 stemmed wine glasses and chill 2 to 3 hours. Serve with a sprig of mint and/or a spoonful of whipped cream.
Serves 12.

Windham Hill Inn

West Townshend, Vermont 05359
(802) 874-4080

Since its beginning as a nineteenth-century Vermont family farm, Windham Hill Inn has enjoyed a history of comfortable living. Each of the rooms in the restored farmhouse has a view of the mountains. They are filled with antiques, oriental rugs, handmade quilts, old photographs, and paintings that will attract those who love the feeling of stepping into the charm of the past but in the comfort of the present. Days at Windham Hill begin with a hearty country breakfast and end with the evening's candlelight dinner and relaxation in the common rooms. In between, the surrounding countryside beckons with a diversity of summer and winter sports activities, historic villages with antique shops, summer theatre and festivals, and brilliant fall foliage.

Refreshing Tomato Soup

A summer favorite. Chill well before serving.

3 cups tomato juice
2 tablespoons tomato paste
4 minced scallions
Zest of ½ lemon
2 tablespoons fresh lemon juice
1 cup sour cream
2 teaspoons super-fine sugar
⅛ teaspoon thyme
½ teaspoon curry powder
Salt and freshly ground pepper to
   taste
   ❖   ❖   ❖
Fresh chives

Whisk together all of the ingredients except the chives in a large stainless steel or glass bowl. Chill. Ladle into chilled individual bowls and garnish with fresh chopped chives.
Serves 6.

Pork Loin
with Apricot-Rosemary Sauce

1 5-pound center-cut pork loin,
   boned and rolled (reserve the
   bones)
   ❖   ❖   ❖
2 tablespoons oil
2 tablespoons Italian olive oil
20 white peppercorns
1 bay leaf
1 large garlic clove, chopped
2 tablespoons apricot-flavored
   Brandy
¼ cup dry Vermouth
2 tablespoons fresh lemon juice
1 tablespoon crushed rosemary
   ❖   ❖   ❖
2 cups chicken stock
2 tablespoons arrowroot
2 teaspoons crushed rosemary
2 teaspoons minced garlic
3 tablespoons apricot purée (made
   from strained apricot jam)

Marinate pork in mixture of oils, spices, and flavorings for up to 24 hours. Remove meat from marinade and place on bones in roasting pan. Pour remaining marinade over meat and roast in a 350° oven for approximately 2 hours or until internal temperature reaches 180°. Remove meat to warm platter.

Measure ¼ cup of pork drippings into saucepan. Add chicken stock and skimmed pan juices. Blend in arrowroot, rosemary, and garlic. Add apricot purée and simmer 3 minutes. Strain and serve with meat.

Serves 8 to 12.

Strawberry Delight

1 cup all-purpose flour
½ cup chopped pecans
½ cup unsalted butter (1 stick), melted
¼ cup brown sugar, firmly packed

❖ ❖ ❖

1 10-ounce box frozen strawberries, thawed
1 cup sugar
2 teaspoons fresh lemon juice
2 egg whites
1 cup heavy cream, whipped
Fresh strawberries for garnish

Combine the flour, pecans, butter, and brown sugar in an 8-inch square pan. Bake for 20 minutes in a 350° oven. Cool. Stir occasionally. Line a 9-inch springform pan with waxed paper. Grease lightly. Press ⅔ of the crumb mixture in the bottom of the pan.

Combine strawberries, sugar, lemon juice, and egg whites in a large mixing bowl. Beat until stiff. Fold in whipped cream. Spoon into the prepared pan. Sprinkle remaining crumbs on top. Cover; freeze until firm. Let sit at room temperature for 10 minutes before slicing. Garnish with whole fresh strawberries. Beautiful and delicious.

Serves 9.

Chocolate Peanut Butter Torte

1 cup graham cracker crumbs (9 double crackers)
¼ cup brown sugar, firmly packed
¼ cup unsalted butter (½ stick), melted

❖ ❖ ❖

2 cups creamy peanut butter
2 cups sugar
2 8-ounce packages cream cheese
2 tablespoons butter, melted
2 teaspoons vanilla extract
1½ cups heavy cream, whipped

❖ ❖ ❖

4 ounces semi-sweet chocolate
3 tablespoons plus 2 teaspoons hot coffee

Combine crumbs, brown sugar, and ¼ cup butter. Press into a 9-inch springform pan. In the large bowl of electric mixer beat peanut butter, sugar, cream cheese, 2 tablespoons butter, and vanilla until smooth and creamy. Fold in whipped cream; spoon into crust. Refrigerate 6 hours.

Melt chocolate and coffee in a double boiler. Spread over filling. Refrigerate until firm.

Serves 16.

Misty Mountain Lodge

Stowe Hill Road, Box 114
Wilmington, Vermont 05363
(802) 464-3961

A farmhouse inn with nine guest rooms, Misty Mountain (built in 1803) is in a rural area near the Mount Snow Haystack Ski Area. It is the only inn in the Mount Snow valley owned and operated by a native Vermonter. Delicious home-cooked meals are served family style. The country breakfast is complemented by the homemade jams and jellies. The wide lawn and winding trails make for outdoor relaxation. The host loves music and plays the guitar and banjo to entertain the guests. Winter skiing and summer relaxation, lakes, tennis, and Marlboro music await every guest.

Hot Pepper Jelly

⅔ cup chopped bell pepper
⅔ cup chopped hot pepper
1½ cups vinegar
6 cups sugar

❖ ❖ ❖

1 6-ounce bottle Certo
Green food coloring

Place the bell pepper, hot pepper, and vinegar into a blender, chop fine and pour into a saucepan. Add sugar. Boil vigorously for 5 minutes, stirring often. Remove from heat, let stand for 5 minutes. Add the Certo. Add green food coloring (or use red at Christmas if desired). Place hot jelly into hot sterilized jars. Seal with wax. Delicious served with cream cheese on crackers. Makes a wonderful hors d'oeuvre.

Fills 4 to 6 8-ounce jars.

Ham Sauce

1 cup brown sugar, firmly packed
½ cup crushed pineapple with juice (or ¼ cup pineapple juice)
¼ cup pure maple syrup
1½ teaspoons dry mustard
¼ teaspoon cloves
1 heaping tablespoon Hot Pepper Jelly (see recipe for this)

❖ ❖ ❖

2 tablespoons cornstarch

Place all the ingredients except cornstarch in a saucepan. Heat the ingredients over low heat until the sugar has dissolved. In a separate container add enough water to cornstarch to make a light cream consistency. Stirring constantly, pour creamed cornstarch into the heating sauce. Continue heating and stirring until mixture thickens and clears. Remove from heat. Increasing or decreasing amount of cornstarch will change the consistency of sauce. Thick sauce may be put on the ham while cooking. Gravy consistency sauce may be poured over the ham on serving platter or onto each serving.

Makes 2¼ cups sauce.

Trail's End Lodge

Smith Road
Wilmington, Vermont 05363
(802) 464-2727

Just five miles from Mount Snow, the Trail's End Lodge is a secluded country inn offering warm hospitality and charm. Rooms are individually decorated and have private baths. Family suites have fireplaces. A dramatic lounge with a two-story fireplace and loft is a favorite of guests; the game room is also a popular place. Hearty country breakfasts and home-cooked dinners are served family-style. The inn offers an outdoor swimming pool, a clay tennis court, a fully stocked trout pond, and lovely English flower gardens.

Inn Chicken

2 cloves of garlic, minced
1 cup sour cream
2 tablespoons lemon juice
Salt to taste
½ teaspoon paprika
1 teaspoon Tabasco sauce
4 boneless chicken breasts
1 cup seasoned bread crumbs
½ cup butter, melted (1 stick)

Combine the garlic, sour cream, lemon juice, salt, paprika, and Tabasco. Marinate the chicken overnight in mixture. Coat the chicken breasts with breadcrumbs. Place in a greased baking dish. Pour melted butter over the chicken and bake in a 350° oven for 1 hour.

Serves 4.

Fillet of Sole Stuffed with Shrimp

3 cloves garlic, minced
3 small onions, finely chopped
¼ cup butter (½ stick)
1 green pepper, finely chopped
36 medium shrimp, cooked and chopped
1 cup bread cubes
3 tablespoons chopped parsley
¾ teaspoon salt
¼ teaspoon pepper
6 pounds fillet of sole
2 cups butter (4 sticks)

❖ ❖ ❖

3 egg yolks
1 tablespoon lemon juice
Sprinkle cayenne pepper
½ cup butter (1 stick)
Paprika

Cook the garlic and onions in ¼ cup of butter until brown. Add the green pepper and cook for 1 minute. Add the shrimp, bread cubes, parsley, salt, and pepper. Cook, stirring occasionally, for 5 minutes. Remove from heat. Place 2 tablespoons shrimp mixture on each fillet. Roll up and secure with a toothpick. Refrigerate for several hours. Melt 2 cups of butter in a large baking dish. Roll each fillet in butter. Bake in a 350° oven for 30 minutes.

To make the Hollandaise sauce, in a blender combine the egg yolks, lemon juice, and pepper. In a saucepan melt ½ cup of butter. Blend the yolk mixture on high for a few seconds then slowly add the butter through the opening in the top of the blender. Pour the Hollandaise over each fillet and sprinkle with paprika before serving.

Serves 6 to 8.

Apple Cake
with Cognac Cream

6 tablespoons Calvados
4 cups peeled, chopped apples

❖ ❖ ❖

2 eggs
1 cup oil
2 cups sugar
2 cups all-purpose flour
1 teaspoon salt
2 teaspoons baking soda
2 teaspoons cinnamon
1 teaspoon nutmeg
1 cup raisins
1 cup walnuts, chopped

❖ ❖ ❖

1 cup heavy cream
2 tablespoons sugar
2 tablespoons Cognac
Nutmeg

Grease and flour a 13x9-inch pan. Pour the Calvados over the chopped apples; set aside and stir occasionally. Beat together the eggs, oil, and sugar. Sift together the flour, salt, soda, and spices. Stir half of the flour mixture into the egg mixture. Mix the apples with the raisins and nuts and remaining flour mixture. Stir into the egg mixture. Pour into the pan. Bake in a 350° oven for approximately 1 hour.

Whip the cream with the sugar and Cognac. Slice the cake into squares. Serve warm with the whipped cream mixture. Sprinkle nutmeg on top.

Serves 12 to 16.

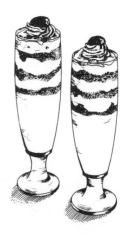

The White House: A Cross-Country Inn

Route 9
Wilmington, Vermont 05363
(802) 464-2136

The White House was built in 1914 by a New England lumber baron and had its own nine-hole golf course, private bowling alley, formal gardens, and sweeping staircases, one of which is a replica of the hidden staircase in the House of Seven Gables. Guests today enjoy spacious rooms, some which still have the original furnishings. In the lounge, which overlooks the ski trails and Mount Snow valley, guests can savor a hot drink or a favorite cocktail. In the evening they can enjoy fine dining, a bottle of wine from the wine cellar, and cozy up to one of the eight fireplaces. Also available at The White House spa are a sauna, whirlpool, steambath, and indoor pool.

Chocolate Almond Pie

3 cups blanched almonds
6 tablespoons sugar
¼ cup butter (½ stick)

❖ ❖ ❖

20 ounces semi-sweet chocolate
15 ounces miniature marshmallows
1 12-ounce can evaporated milk

❖ ❖ ❖

2 cups heavy cream
1 teaspoon almond extract

❖ ❖ ❖

Whipped cream

Using a food processor, pulsate the almonds, sugar, and butter until mealy. Divide the mixture in half and press into 2 8-inch pie plates, forming shells. Bake in a 350° oven for 8 to 10 minutes, until brown. Cool.

Prepare the filling by melting in a double boiler the chocolate and marshmallows, stirring until well-blended. Cool to room temperature, but not too cool. Whip heavy cream with almond extract, beating until stiff. Fold chocolate mixture into the cream. Fill the baked almond shells. Serve with whipped cream.

Serves 12 to 16.

Juniper Hill Inn

R.R. 1, Box 79 Juniper Hill Road
Windsor, Vermont 05089
(802) 674-5273

Atop Juniper Hill, the Juniper Hill Inn has a commanding view of Mount Ascutney and the valley below. The winding drive, lined with a fieldstone wall and tall, whispering pines, offers an ideal setting for walking. This three-story mansion has fifteen guestrooms, all with private baths. The library wing, with its elegant palladian window and oak stairway, leads to two special large guestrooms, one with a canopy bed ideal for honeymoons or anniversaries, the other with its own screened porch. Full country breakfasts are served daily. Breakfast in bed will be brought if arranged in advance, and candlelight dinners are served in the elegant dining room. Dining is also open to the public on Friday, Saturday, holidays, and between December 26 and January 1 by reservation.

Cornish Hens
with Blackberry Sauce

4 Cornish hens (2 pounds each)

❖ ❖ ❖

1 quart water
2 cups chopped onion
1 cup chopped celery
1 cup chopped carrots

❖ ❖ ❖

2 16-ounce cans blackberries
¼ cup Cointreau

Juniper Hill Inn

¼ cup blackberry jam
1 tablespoon and 1 teaspoon all-
   purpose flour
1 tablespoon and 1 teaspoon butter

Roast hens in a 400° oven for 1 hour, basting when needed. Combine giblets from hens, water, onion, celery, and carrots in medium saucepan. Bring to a boil, stirring well. Reduce heat; cover and simmer 20 to 25 minutes. Drain mixture, reserving 2 cups of stock. Discard giblets and vegetables.

Drain the blackberries, reserving 2 cups blackberry juice; set blackberries aside. Combine scrapings from roasting pan, reserved blackberry juice, Cointreau and stock in a medium saucepan. Bring to boil, and boil 15 minutes or until liquid is reduced by half. Make a paste by combining jam, flour, and butter; gradually add to liquid in pan, stirring well. Cook over medium heat, stirring constantly, until thickened. Stir in blackberries. Cut hens in half with poultry shears and serve with sauce. Duck is also good with this sauce.
Serves 8.

Juniper Hill Inn Stuffed Breast of Veal

5 pounds veal breast
½ pound lean pork, ground
½ pound lean beef, ground

   ❖   ❖   ❖

3 tablespoons butter
½ cup chopped shallots
1 pound spinach, parboiled,
   squeezed dry, and chopped
½ teaspoon dried thyme
½ teaspoon dried marjoram
1½ teaspoons salt
¼ teaspoon pepper
½ cup bread crumbs
1 egg, beaten

   ❖   ❖   ❖

1 large onion, chopped
2 carrots, chopped

   ❖   ❖   ❖

2 cups water

Remove and reserve the bones from the veal. Set aside. Place the ground meats in a medium bowl and mix well.

Melt butter in a small frypan over medium heat. Stir in the shallots, cook for 2 to 3 minutes until transparent. Add chopped spinach, stir; cook until it is dry and sticks slightly to the bottom of the pan. Remove from heat. Add the mixture to the ground meats. Add thyme, marjoram, salt, pepper, bread crumbs, and beaten egg. Mix until thoroughly combined. Spread the stuffing lightly over the veal, roll tightly and truss with cord. In a large roasting pan arrange the bones like a rack. Set the stuffed veal on the bones. Add onion and carrots to the pan. Cover with foil and roast in a 400° oven for 30 minutes. Remove foil and add water. Reduce heat to 350° and braise for 2 more hours.
Serves 6 to 8.

Krisha's Grilled Lamb

1 leg of lamb
2 cups red wine
1 teaspoon garlic powder
1 teaspoon oregano
1 teaspoon rosemary
½ teaspoon thyme
1 bay leaf

Debone and trim leg of lamb. Butterfly the meat at the thickest parts to lay flat. Mix the remaining ingredients and marinate the meat for 6 to 8 hours or overnight in the refrigerator. Grill about 20 to 30 minutes on each side or until desired doneness. Best if served medium rare. Baste with marinade if needed. Slice and serve.
Serves 16.

Moussaka

2 medium eggplants
Salt

   ❖   ❖   ❖

1 pound ground lamb or beef
1 cup chopped onion
¼ cup red wine
¼ cup water
2 tablespoons chopped parsley
1 tablespoon tomato paste
1 teaspoon salt
Dash pepper
3 tablespoons bread crumbs
2 eggs, beaten
¼ cup shredded Cheddar cheese
2 dashes cinnamon

   ❖   ❖   ❖

3 tablespoons butter
3 tablespoons all-purpose flour
1½ cups milk
½ teaspoon salt
Dash pepper
Dash nutmeg
Dash Tabasco sauce
1 egg, beaten
½ cup bread crumbs
¼ cup shredded Cheddar Cheese

Peel and slice eggplants in ½-inch thick slices. Sprinkle with salt and set aside. Lay eggplant on greased cookie sheets and bake in a 350° oven for 20 minutes.

In a frypan, brown meat and onion; drain off excess fat. Add wine, water, parsley, tomato paste, 1 teaspoon of salt, and pepper. Simmer until liquid is nearly absorbed. Cool; stir in bread crumbs, 2 eggs, ¼ cup cheese, and cinnamon.

In a saucepan melt butter; stir in flour. Add milk; cook and stir until thick and bubbly. Add ½ teaspoon salt, pepper, nutmeg, and Tabasco sauce. Mix a small amount of hot liquid with the remaining egg, then return it to the saucepan. Cook over low heat about 2 minutes, stirring constantly. Sprinkle the bottom of 12x7½-inch baking dish with bread crumbs. Place in layers ½ of the eggplant slices, the meat mixture, the remaining eggplant slices, and the milk sauce. Sprinkle the top with ¼ cup Cheddar cheese. Bake in a 350° oven for about 45 minutes. Serve hot.
Serves 6 to 8.

The Woodstock Inn

Fourteen the Green
Woodstock, Vermont 05091
(802) 457-1100

Built in 1969, the Woodstock Inn radiates the Colonial New England style, enhanced by up-to-date luxury. The inn is three stories on the front and four on the garden side. Its 120 guest rooms are air-conditioned and appointed with specially designed furniture and hand-made quilts. Other facilities include a coffee shop, dining room, lounges, gift shop, a complete indoor sports facility, and country club. Downhill and cross-country skiing nearby.

Vermont Herb Cheese Puffs

¼ cup milk
¼ cup water
1 tablespoon butter
½ cup all-purpose flour
2 eggs, beaten

❖ ❖ ❖

2½ cups grated cheese
Dash salt
Dash pepper
Dash thyme
Dash tarragon
Dash chervil
Dash basil
2 ounces white wine

In a saucepan bring the milk, water, and butter to a boil. Add the flour and heat; mix with a wooden spoon until the dough comes away from the sides of the pan. Mix in the eggs slowly.

Add the remaining ingredients to the dough, adding the wine last. Shape into 1-ounce balls and deep fry in 350° oil until golden brown.

Serves 10.

Baked Shrimp and Morels

8 fresh morels, halved lengthwise
1 pound fresh spinach, washed
12 to 15 shrimp, peeled and
    deveined
2 tomatoes, peeled, seeded and
    diced

❖ ❖ ❖

1 tablespoon diced shallots or
    leeks, blanched
1 sprig fresh tarragon, chopped
1 tablespoon butter
Juice of 1 lemon
1 cup heavy cream

❖ ❖ ❖

1 cup grated Vermont Cheddar
    cheese
Lemon wedges

The Woodstock Inn

Sauté separately the mushroom halves, spinach, shrimp and tomatoes; set aside and keep warm.

In a saucepan lightly sauté the diced leeks or shallots and tarragon with the butter until the shallots or leeks are limp. Add the lemon juice and cream. Reduce by ½ and reserve.

Layer the bottom of a ceramic casserole dish with the spinach and alternate on top the shrimp and morels. Top with the sauce. Sprinkle cheese over the entire mixture and bake under the broiler or in the oven to lightly brown the cheese. Top with sautéed tomatoes. Serve with lemon wedges.

Peter J. Wynia, Executive Chef.
Serves 4.

Curried Morels
with Crab Meat and Leeks

¾ cup small to medium-sized fresh
    morels
4 fresh wild leeks, blanched (or
    unblanched scallions)
½ cup Alaskan king crab meat
1 tablespoon pine nuts
½ tablespoon curry powder (or to
    taste)
Splash sweet Vermouth
¼ cup cream
¼ cup grated mild Vermont
    Cheddar cheese

Cut the morels in half lengthwise. Larger ones may be cut into ¼-inch ribbons. Trim the blanched wild leeks or scallions and slice the white part only. Sauté the leeks in butter. Add the crab meat, pine nuts and curry powder. Blend well and continue to sauté over medium heat. Add the sliced morels, Vermouth, and cream. Stir well and cook over medium heat for approximately 2 minutes. Top with grated cheese and continue cooking over low heat until the cheese melts and the sauce settles and firms, approximately 4 to 5 minutes.

Peter J. Wynia, Executive Chef.
Serves 4.

Morel Piccata

2 eggs
1 teaspoon oil
1 tablespoon chopped parsley
½ cup grated Parmesan cheese
10 to 12 large fresh morels

Mix the eggs, oil, parsley, and Parmesan cheese; let settle for 5 minutes.

Slice the morels in half lengthwise, dredge lightly in flour, and dip in the piccata batter. Sauté the battered morels in butter, turning once. Serve with veal scallopini or lamb.

Peter J. Wynia, Executive Chef.
Serves 4.

Sautéed Chicken Breasts
with Morels

4 chicken breasts, skinned and
    boned
Flour
½ cup butter (1 stick)
3 ounces fresh morels, sliced
1 cup blanched almond slices
6 tablespoons Apple Jack Brandy
    or Calvados
2 tablespoons tarragon vinegar
1 cup cream
Chopped parsley

Lightly dredge the chicken breasts in flour and sauté in butter until browned slightly on both sides. Add the morels and almonds. Sauté over low heat. Do not allow the chicken to brown further. Remove the chicken to a serving pan. Deglaze the pan with Brandy; add the vinegar and cream. Reduce the sauce to a smooth consistency; pour over the chicken. Sprinkle with parsley. Serve with rice and seasonal green vegetables.

Peter J. Wynia, Executive Chef.
Serves 4.

Virginia

Olive Mill: A Bed and Breakfast

General Delivery
Banco, Madison County, Virginia 22711
(703) 923-4664

Following the British bed and breakfast tradition, Olive Mill is not an inn, but a private home open for guests who wish to experience a comfortable and casual visit in an environment not easy to duplicate in this century. Set adjacent to an old mill, the Miller's House attests to the prosperity of the family-owned milling trade until the mid-twentieth century. Simple and foursquare, the house is of generous size and proportion. Roomy porches front and back offer chairs and a hammock for leisure. Breakfast is served after 8:30 A.M. in the dining room, with a fire in the fireplace in cool weather. Breakfasts are special. Heart-shaped Norwegian waffles and fresh-baked bread are featured. Two double-bedded rooms and a twin-bedded room are available. All rooms share baths in the main house. Children over twelve are welcome.

The river, woods, and mill invite exploration. Madison County offers plenty of activities. Hiking is excellent at White Oak Canyon, Old Rag Mountain, Hoover Camp, and Shenandoah National Park. Horseback riding, swimming, antiquing, shopping, wineries, auctions, and interesting craft fairs make this area famous. A swimming pool is now available in season on the premises.

Olive Mill Breakfast Bread

¾ cup butter (1½ sticks), softened
2 eggs
2 tablespoons brown sugar
2 tablespoons grated orange peel
❖ ❖ ❖
2¼ cups all-purpose flour
2 teaspoons baking powder
½ teaspoon baking soda
½ teaspoon salt
1 teaspoon cinnamon
❖ ❖ ❖
1 cup plain yogurt
1 teaspoon vanilla extract
❖ ❖ ❖
1 cup prunes, chopped (or other dried fruit)
½ cup chopped nuts

Mix the butter, eggs, sugar, and orange peel and set aside. Sift together the dry ingredients and add alternately with the yogurt. Add the vanilla. Grease 1 tube or 2 loaf pans. Pour a layer of batter on the bottom; sprinkle on half of the prunes and nuts. Add the remaining batter and top with the remaining prunes and nuts. Bake in a 350° oven for 50 to 60 minutes.

Makes 2 loaves, or 16 servings.

Elmo's Rest

Route 2, Box 198
Bedford, Virginia 24523
(703) 586-3707

Elmo's Rest is an 1890s farmhouse on a 250-acre fruit and cattle farm. Fishing and horseback riding are available No meals are provided, but apple "goodies" from the orchard are served and a fully equipped kitchen is available for guests' use. This farm is ideal for family vacations. It is five miles from Peaks of Otter and the Blue Ridge Parkway and near many historic and scenic attractions.

Apple Cider Salad

1 6-ounce package orange-flavored gelatin
4 cups apple cider
1 cup raisins
1 cup coarsely chopped apple
1 cup chopped celery
Juice and grated rind of 1 lemon

Dissolve the gelatin in 2 cups of hot cider. Stir in the raisins; cool. Add the remaining cider. Chill until slightly thickened.

Add the remaining ingredients and chill until set.

Serves 8.

429

Spiced Sparkling Cider Jelly

4 cups unpasteurized cider
3 whole cloves
2 cinnamon sticks
1 1¾-ounce box Sure-Jel
5 cups sugar

In a 6- to 8-quart saucepan combine the cider, cloves, cinnamon sticks, and Sure-Jel. Bring to a boil and stir in the sugar at once. Bring to a full rolling boil for 1 minute. Skim and ladle into prepared jelly glasses.

Fills about 6 8-ounce jars.

Johnson's Apple Crisp

4 to 5 large apples
1 cup all-purpose flour
1 cup sugar
1 teaspoon baking powder
1 teaspoon cinnamon
1 egg
⅓ cup butter

Peel and core the apples. Slice thin and arrange in the bottom of a greased dish. Mix the dry ingredients. Break the egg on the dry mixture and stir until crumbly. Sprinkle over the apples. Melt the butter and pour over the topping. Bake in a 350° oven until the apples are tender, approximately 35 to 40 minutes.

Serves 4 to 6.

Applesauce Pie

2 eggs
1 cup sugar
½ cup butter (1 stick), melted
1 cup applesauce
2 tablespoons all-purpose flour
½ teaspoon vanilla extract
2 tablespoons lemon juice (unless the applesauce is tart)

❖ ❖ ❖

1 9-inch pie shell

Mix all of the ingredients. Pour into a 9-inch pie shell and bake in a 350° oven for 45 minutes.

Serves 6.

The Boar's Head Inn and Sports Club

Post Office Box 5185
Charlottesville, Virginia 22905
(804) 296-2181

The head of a boar symbolized festive hospitality in Shakespeare's London. Today, guests at The Boar's Head Inn can enjoy this tradition of hospitality with a touch of country charm. A country estate atmosphere has been created here in the foothills of the Blue Ridge Mountains of Virginia. The inn contains one hundred and seventy five guest rooms and suites, twelve meeting rooms, a ballroom, shopping, offices, and a private sports club with extensive year-round resort facilities.

The Boar's Head Inn is also an appealing place for recalling the traditional celebration of Christmas that Virginia's first settlers brought to the colonial wilderness. Hearty enjoyment of feasting, gambols, and good fellowship permeates the celebration. Here guests find echoes of the tradition that Virginia has cherished from its start. In the early 1960s, John B. Rogan, President of The Boar's Head Inn, brought to the inn the first traditional celebration with the "bringing of the boar's head" ceremony. Since then, each year some new and special events have been added to this Merrie Old England Christmas Festival.

Boar's Head Seafood Salad

3 pounds cooked scallops
2 pounds cooked crabmeat
3 pounds cooked shrimp pieces
2 pounds celery, diced
1½ cups pickle relish
2 cups mayonnaise
4 teaspoons lemon juice
1 teaspoon salt
¼ teaspoon white pepper
1 tablespoon seafood seasoning

Mix the seafood, celery, relish, and mayonnaise together. Then add the lemon juice, salt, pepper, and seafood seasoning. Mix well; chill and serve.

Serves 40.

Cornish Game Hens

3 12-ounce Cornish hens
Salt and pepper to taste
½ cup butter (1 stick), melted
Beets and orange slices for garnish

Split the hens in half and place in a baking dish that is coated with butter. Season to taste. Bake in a 350° oven for about 45 minutes to 1 hour or until done. Baste frequently with the melted butter. Garnish the hens with freshly cooked beets and orange slices, if desired.

Serves 6.

Syllabub

1 part white wine
3 parts cream
Sugar to taste
Orange juice to taste
Nutmeg

Add the white wine to the cream, but not so much that the thickness of the cream is lost. Whip together to produce a thick, frothy texture, adding sugar to taste, and a little orange juice and nutmeg. Serve in a marmite cup and sprinkle nutmeg on top to garnish.

Boar's Head Pie

1½ pounds diced pork shoulder
3 cups water
½ cup raisins
½ cup prunes
2 teaspoons cinnamon
1 cup sliced apples
1½ teaspoons ginger
2 whole cloves
½ cup butter (1 stick)
½ cup all-purpose flour
Pastry for 1 8-inch 2-crust pie

Cook the meat in simmering water until tender. Add the raisins, prunes, cinnamon, apples, ginger, and cloves. In a saucepan melt the butter and stir in the flour. Add this mixture to the other ingredients. Cook slowly, stirring very gently, until the mixture thickens. Line an 8-inch square baking dish with pastry and fill with the meat mixture. Cover with the top crust and bake in a 350° oven for 45 minutes.

Makes 6 generous servings.

Swan Cake

The swan cake is meant to reproduce the image of the inn's resident swans swimming on the lake. The swan atop the cake is made by hand in sections out of puff pastry. The sections are held together by custard.

The cookies shaped like a boar's head are made from this recipe, with raisins for the eyes.

2½ cups all-purpose flour
1 teaspoon baking soda
½ teaspoon salt
1½ teaspoons ginger

❖ ❖ ❖

1 egg
1 cup maple syrup
1 cup sour cream
¼ cup melted butter

❖ ❖ ❖

2 cups confectioners' sugar
½ cup shortening
2 teaspoons cream
Blue food coloring

Mix all of the dry ingredients together. Mix the egg, syrup and sour cream and stir them into the dry ingredients. Beat until smooth; add the butter. Line an 8-inch square baking pan with waxed paper. Butter and flour the paper and pour in the batter. Bake in a 350° oven for about 30 minutes.

Cream the sugar and shortening. Slowly add the cream and stir until smooth. Add the food coloring drop by drop until the icing is the desired color. When the cake cools, decorate with blue icing.

Serves 9.

Plum Pudding

4 cups mincemeat
3 cups coarse dry bread crumbs
1 cup minced plums
1 teaspoon cinnamon
1½ teaspoons ginger
½ teaspoon nutmeg
¼ teaspoon salt

❖ ❖ ❖

6 eggs
1 cup milk

❖ ❖ ❖

1 cup Brandy
Additional Brandy to soak pudding
Hard sauce or Brandy sauce to top
**   pudding**

In a mixing bowl combine the mincemeat, bread crumbs, plums, spices and salt.

In a separate bowl beat the eggs until foamy; add the milk. Add to the dry mixture and stir well. Add the Brandy; mix well and pour into a buttered 3-quart pudding mold. Cover with a lid or foil. Place the mold on a rack in a large pan; then fill the pan with boiling water half-way up the side of the mold. Cover the large pan with foil or a lid and steam over low heat for 4 hours. Occasionally check the water to see if more boiling water needs to be added. Cool. Turn the pudding out of the mold and soak with Brandy. Serve topped with hard sauce or Brandy sauce.

Makes 1 pudding.

Rose Water Cookies

2 cups all-purpose flour
¾ teaspoon baking powder
¼ teaspoon salt
¾ cup sugar
⅔ cup shortening
2 eggs
4 teaspoons rose water

Sift the dry ingredients together into a mixing bowl. Add the shortening, eggs, and rose water and mix well. Roll the dough out very thinly on a flat surface and cut with a floured cookie cutter. Place the cookies on a greased cookie sheet and bake in a 400° oven for 8 to 10 minutes.

Makes 4 dozen cookies.

Spiced Walnuts

1½ cups walnut halves
½ cup sugar
¼ cup water
½ tablespoon grated orange rind
¼ teaspoon cinnamon
⅛ teaspoon ginger
⅛ teaspoon cloves
Pinch nutmeg

In a heavy skillet combine all of the ingredients. Bring to a boil over medium heat. Stir constantly until all of the liquids have evaporated and the walnuts are coated with sugar. Spread on a non-stick cookie sheet, separating the nuts and allowing them to cool.

Sugar Coated Lemon/Orange Rind

1 cup sugar
½ cup water
2 cups thinly sliced orange or
**   lemon rind**

In a saucepan dissolve the sugar in water over medium heat. Add the rinds and continue to cook over medium heat, stirring frequently. Cook until the rinds are completely coated. Spread over an ungreased pan and bake in a 250° oven for about 30 minutes. Stir at 5 minute intervals. Allow the rinds to cool, then serve.

Makes 2 cups.

Sleepy Hollow Farm: Bed and Breakfast

Route 3, Box 43
Gordonsville, Virginia 22942
(703) 832-5555

Sleepy Hollow Farm lies on a country road in Orange County, where colonial, northern, and southern troops once trod and where cattle, sheep, and horse farms now flourish. It is three miles north of Gordonsville on the former toll road, now Route 231. Indian projectiles and artifacts are often found along the stream that runs through the farm. The main house and the Chestnut Cottage out back, once a slave cabin, are furnished in antiques and family possessions. The farm house contains several fireplaces, woodstoves, porches and terraces. Wildlife, a pond, and delicious spring water are on the grounds. Sixteen guests can be accommodated in both houses, which are air-conditioned. Hearty country breakfasts begin each day in one of the several breakfast settings in the main house or on outside terraces. Children are welcome, but pets need an invitation. Horseback riding, hiking, canoeing, antiquing, historic sites, and good restaurants are nearby.

Impossible Pie

12 slices bacon crisply fried and crumbled
1 cup shredded Swiss cheese (Cheddar or Havarti can be used)
⅓ cup chopped onion
⅓ cup chopped green pepper
1 4-ounce can mushroom pieces
2 cups milk
1 cup baking mix
4 eggs
¼ teaspoon salt
⅛ teaspoon pepper

Sprinkle the bacon, cheese, onion, pepper and mushrooms in a lightly greased 10-inch pie plate. Beat the remaining ingredients until smooth (15 seconds in blender on high speed or 1 minute with hand beater). Pour into the pie plate. Bake in a 400° oven for about 30 minutes. Let stand about 5 minutes. Refrigerate leftovers.

Serves 6.

Note: If using a 9-inch pie plate decrease the milk to 1½ cups, the baking mix to ¾ cup and the eggs to 3.

Virginia Fried Apples

3 tablespoons butter
6 tart cooking apples, peeled and sliced
⅓ cup sugar
¼ teaspoon nutmeg
¼ teaspoon cinnamon

Melt the butter in a frying pan; add the apples and cook until slightly soft. Add the sugar and spices. Lower the heat and continue cooking until the apples are soft and glisten, about 15 minutes. Stir gently and occasionally while cooking.

Serves 6.

Shenandoah Springs Country Inn

Box 122
Haywood, Virginia 22722
(703) 923-4300

Guests of this pre-Civil War home enjoy cozily decorated bedrooms and waken to breakfast by a crackling fire. Added to this is the scenic view from the dining room of the rolling hills, the Shenandoah National Park, and the pastoral farmland. Guests relax on 1000 acres of forest land, meadows, shady lanes, and bridle trails. Springs Lake is great for fishing, canoeing, and ice skating in the winter; cross-country skiing on the inn's trails is a popular winter activity.

Egg Cheese Strata

1 pound sausage (ham, or bacon), cooked and crumbled
5 slices bread, lightly buttered and cubed
⅔ cup shredded sharp cheese
½ teaspoon salt
Dash pepper
5 eggs, beaten
2½ cups milk

In a 9x13-inch baking pan layer the sausage and the cubed bread. Sprinkle the cheese over all. Add the salt and pepper. Combine the eggs and milk, pour over the layered ingredients. Cover and refrigerate overnight.

Bake uncovered in a 325° oven for 30 minutes.

Serves 12.

Orange-Banana Treat

1 12-ounce can frozen orange juice
1 fully ripe banana
Sugar

Add the proper amount of water to the orange juice as directed on the label. Add the banana. Mix in a blender; may need to add sugar to taste. Refreshing! Serves 12.

Vine Cottage Inn

Post Office Box 918
Hot Springs, Virginia 24445
(703) 839-2422

Guests at Vine Cottage Inn are made to feel as relaxed and comfortable as they do in their homes. The inn's fifteen rooms offer a variety of accommodations, from a single room or comfortable double, to a multi-bedded "dorm-style" room, popular with golfers and skiers. Every morning from 8:00 to 9:30 A.M. a country continental breakfast is served. The items vary to suit the season but guests can always count on fresh rolls or a freshly-baked sweet bread.

The Vine Cottage Inn is located in a sportsman's and nature lover's paradise. The magnificent beauty of the Allegheny Mountains surrounds the inn, and a wide variety of outdoor attractions are available in the area.

Chili Con Carne

2 onions, chopped
2 tablespoons bacon drippings
1 tablespoon oil
4 cloves garlic, crushed

3 pounds lean ground beef
1 tablespoon tomato paste
1 35-ounce can Italian tomatoes
2 tablespoons Worcestershire sauce
2 tablespoons hot sauce
1 tablespoon salt
1 teaspoon pepper
1 teaspoon oregano
3 teaspoons celery salt
3 teaspoons coriander seeds
3 teaspoons coriander leaves
3 teaspoons cumin
1 teaspoon crushed red pepper
2 tablespoons chili powder
1 4-ounce can green chilis
1 35-ounce can kidney beans

In a large pot gently cook the onions in the bacon drippings and oil until soft. Add the garlic and beef. Cook quickly. Stir in the remaining ingredients except the kidney beans. Cover and cook over low heat for 2 hours, stirring occasionally. Stir in the kidney beans and cook for 1 more hour.
Serves 12 to 16.

Crab Mold

1 10½-ounce can condensed
mushroom soup
1 8-ounce package cream cheese
1 ¼-ounce package unflavored
gelatin
1 6-ounce can crab meat
1 cup mayonnaise
1 cup chopped celery
½ cup chopped onion

Heat the soup, cream cheese and gelatin. Beat with a whisk until smooth; do not boil. Allow to cool. Add the crab, mayonnaise, celery, and onion; mix well. Pour into a mold and chill for 6 to 24 hours.
Serves 6 to 8.

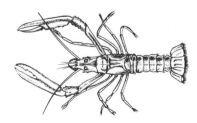

The Norris House Inn

108 Loudoun Street Northwest
Leesburg, Virginia 22075
(703) 777-1806

This house was lovingly restored to recapture Virginia's past charm. Built in the 1800s, it has seven bedrooms, two of which have private baths. The home has been decorated with many antiques and collectibles, with stencils a part of the wall decor. Guests are offered complementary wine, iced tea, or cider, depending on the season. In the two shared bathrooms they find hospitality baskets filled with special soaps, shampoo, and bubble bath. Breakfast includes fresh melon, lemon muffins, salmon quiche, country ham with raisins and honey, orange juice, and a special blend of coffee. The meal is served in a handsome dining room. Bedcovers are turned down and a pineapple-filled chocolate is left on the guest's pillow every evening.

Colonial Muffins

1½ cups all-purpose flour
¼ cup sugar
2 teaspoons baking powder
½ teaspoon salt
1 teaspoon cinnamon
1 teaspoon nutmeg
1 teaspoon mace
1 teaspoon allspice
1 teaspoon cloves
❖ ❖ ❖
½ cup apple juice or cider
2 eggs
½ cup butter (1 stick), melted
1 cup canned mincemeat
❖ ❖ ❖
⅔ cup sugar
⅓ cup rum

Combine all of the dry ingredients and blend well. In a separate bowl stir the apple juice or cider and eggs into the melted butter. Beat well. Stir the liquid ingredients into the dry mixture. Add the mincemeat and blend until moistened. Spoon into a greased muffin pan and add 1 teaspoon of sugar/rum mixture on top of batter. Bake in a 375° oven for 15 to 20 minutes.

Makes 1 dozen muffins.

Autumn Pancakes

2 cups unbleached flour
2½ cups sugar
2 teaspoons baking powder
1¼ teaspoons baking soda
½ tablespoon salt
1 teaspoon cinnamon
½ teaspoon ginger
½ teaspoon freshly grated nutmeg
1 teaspoon cloves
½ teaspoon mace

❖ ❖ ❖

3 eggs
2½ cups buttermilk
2½ tablespoons bacon drippings or oil
1½ cups shredded tart apples, firmly packed
1½ cups coarsely chopped pecans or walnuts

Combine the flour, sugar, baking powder, soda, salt, and spices. In a large bowl beat the eggs lightly; stir in the buttermilk and bacon drippings or oil. Add the flour mixture and blend just until the dry ingredients are moistened. The batter will be slightly lumpy. Stir in the apples and pecans and let stand for 20 minutes. Stirring lightly, pour ¼ cup batter onto a hot griddle or skillet for each pancake. As small bubbles appear on the top, turn and brown on the other side.

Serves 10.

Lemon Muffins

½ cup butter (1 stick), melted
1½ cups sugar
2 eggs
Grated zest of 2 lemons
Juice of 1 lemon
2¼ cups all-purpose flour

1 teaspoon baking powder
½ teaspoon salt
½ cup chopped pecans, toasted
½ cup half and half

❖ ❖ ❖

Juice of 1 lemon
Sugar as needed

Grease or spray muffin tins. In medium mixing bowl, cream butter and sugar. Beat eggs thoroughly and add to creamed mixture. Add lemon zest and juice, flour, baking powder, salt, nuts, and half and half; continuing to mix until well-blended. Fill each greased muffin cup approximately ⅔ full. Bake in a 375° oven for 10 to 20 minutes.

Combine the juice of one lemon and sugar to make the lemon glaze. Mix well until the sugar is completely dissolved. Remove the muffins from the oven and spoon the lemon glaze over each muffin while still hot.

Makes 18 muffins.

The Red Fox Inn and Tavern

Post Office Box 385
Middleburg, Virginia 22117
(703) 687-6301
(703) 471-4455 (D.C. Metro)

An inspired blend of period furnishings with modern conveniences makes a night's stay at the Red Fox Inn and Tavern a special occasion. The traditional character of the inn has been preserved with period-style furniture, area rugs, writing tables, original wooden mantel pieces, and hand-stenciled details. Guest rooms have been furnished with fabrics, furniture, wallcoverings, and accessories in the eighteenth century style. Each of the centrally air-conditioned bedrooms has a four-poster bed (most with canopies), private bath, direct-dial telephone, and color television. Some have fireplaces. Fresh cut flowers, cotton bathrobes, and bedside sweets are a few of the many extra touches that make an overnight visit at this historic country inn memorable. In the morning, guests may enjoy the paper with a continental breakfast in their rooms. Country breakfasts, hearty lunches, and elegant dinners are served in the main dining rooms. Room service is also available.

Black Bean and Sausage Soup

1 cup chopped carrots
1 cup chopped onions
1 cup chopped celery
⅛ cup minced garlic
Salt and pepper to taste
⅛ head chopped thyme
⅛ cup chopped fresh basil
⅛ head marjoram
Red wine
½ gallon chicken stock
10 ounces black beans
20 ounces cooked Italian sausage

Sauté the vegetables with the spices in butter or oil. Deglaze the pan with red wine; reduce by ⅔. Add the chicken stock, beans, and sausage. Cook slowly until tender.

Makes 1 gallon.

Highland Inn

Post Office Box 40
Monterey, Virginia 24465
(703) 468-2143

This three-story white Victorian clapboard hotel, now known as the Highland Inn, was known as the "Pride of the Mountains" when it was built as a resort hotel. Its outstanding architectural feature is an elaborate Eastlake-style, two-level porch. The Highland

Highland Inn

Inn is one of the few hotels of its size to continue operation. Henry Ford and Field Marshal Rommel have visited the Highland Inn in the past.

Chicken á la Bleu

Spinach soufflé
Chicken breast, boned
Blue cheese dressing

Use an individual prepared frozen spinach soufflé or make a spinach soufflé from your favorite recipe. Bake until slightly firm. Top with a precooked skinless chicken breast, browned in butter. Return to the oven to finish cooking the soufflé. Smother with chunky blue cheese dressing. We use our own house dressing. Warm and serve.

Serves 1.

Utterly Deadly Southern Pecan Pie

1 cup sugar
1½ cups corn syrup
4 eggs
¼ cup butter (½ stick)
1 teaspoon vanilla extract
1½ cup broken pecans
Pastry for 1 9-inch 1-crust pie

Boil the sugar and corn syrup together for 2 or 3 minutes. Lightly beat the eggs and pour the hot syrup into the eggs. Add the butter, vanilla, and pecans. Pour into the unbaked pie shell. Bake in a 350° oven for about 45 minutes or until set.

Serves 6.

The Inn at Montross

Post Office Box 908
Montross, Virginia 22520
(804) 493-9097

The Inn at Montross was built prior to 1683, and parts of the structure have been in continuous use for over 300 years. It offers six guest rooms, each with private bath and individual heat and air conditioning. The rooms are furnished with four-poster beds, some with canopies, and are decorated with a mix of reproduction and original antiques from the owner-innkeepers's personal collection. A small lounge with television is provided for guests' use, in addition to the living room on the main floor that is open to the public. The main floor also boasts a magnificent grand piano that guests (and occasionally guest artists) are invited to use. In addition, background music is played through one of the finest sound systems in the area. The two dining rooms are decorated in the colonial tradition and provide a charming atmosphere in which to dine at affordable prices. A complimentary continental breakfast of southern specialties from the inn's ovens is served. A full breakfast can also be provided. The dining room is open to the public for luncheons and dinner on specified days only.

Seafood Nomini
(Shrimp and Scallops in Sherry Sauce)

3 pounds shrimp (25 to 30 per pound), shelled and deveined
3 pounds bay scallops
12 ounces dry Sherry
1½ cups parsley leaves
3 cloves garlic
3 tablespoons chopped scallions
¾ teaspoon oregano
2¼ cups herbed bread crumbs
1½ teaspoons salt
¾ teaspoon cayenne pepper
1½ cups butter (3 sticks), melted

Divide the shrimp and bay scallops among 12 5-inch au gratin dishes; sprinkle each dish with 1 ounce of Sherry. Mince together, or chop with a steel blade in a food processor, the remaining ingredients except the butter. Sprinkle the mixture over the seafood. Drizzle melted butter over the seafood. Bake in a 400° oven for 12 minutes or until lightly browned.

Serves 12.

Fillet Montross
(Peppered Fillet of Beef in Red Wine Sauce)

Cracked black pepper
2 8-ounce beef fillet steaks
2 strips bacon
2 tablespoons oil
2 tablespoons butter

❖ ❖ ❖

½ red bell pepper
½ green bell pepper
½ cup dry red wine
½ cup heavy cream

Sprinkle the cracked black pepper generously on both sides of the steaks; press into the meat. Wrap each steak with one strip of bacon; secure with a toothpick. In a hot pan sauté the steaks in the oil and butter, 6 minutes per side for pink centers. Remove the toothpicks, set aside and keep warm. Seed the peppers; slice into julienne strips. Sauté the pepper strips in the steak drippings until softened but not browned. Remove from the pan. Add wine and deglaze the pan; add the cream and reduce until the sauce is thickened. Arrange the peppers on top of the steaks, alternating colors. Pour the sauce over the steaks; serve immediately.
Serves 2.

taining the charm and friendliness of bygone days. This inn has twelve guest rooms (including two suites), each with private bath and controlled temperature. Guests will find all they need for a relaxing getaway: a large family library, woodstove, leisurely breakfasts, and Wintergreen's 10,000 acres of space. However nearby is a rich tradition of American history, including Monticello, Ash Lawn, and the Woodrow Wilson Birthplace. A full breakfast is served each morning with the exception of Sunday, when a continental breakfast is available. Breakfast is included in the price of the room. Lunch and dinner are also served, but special arrangements and reservations are required.

Blue Ridge Chicken Breasts

½ cup water
3 tablespoons butter
1 cup herbed stuffing crumbs

❖ ❖ ❖

1½ pounds blue cheese
2 eggs, beaten
24 6-ounce chicken breasts with skin, boned
24 slices bacon
¼ cup butter (½ stick)

Bring the water and 3 tablespoons of butter to a boil; remove from heat and

stir in the stuffing crumbs. Cover and let sit for 5 minutes.

Crumble the blue cheese into a medium-size bowl. Mix in the eggs and prepared stuffing. To each chicken breast gently pull up one side of the skin, forming a pocket between the flesh and skin; using a rubber bowl scraper stuff approximately ⅓ cup of blue cheese filling into each breast. Tuck the skin and meat under, forming an even, round dome shape. Wrap each breast with a slice of bacon and secure with a toothpick. Place in a buttered pyrex or metal baking dish. Melt the remaining butter and brush the tops of the breasts lightly. Bake in a 350° oven for 35 to 40 minutes only.
Serves 24.

Spinach Rich Rice

2 10-ounce boxes frozen chopped spinach
12 cups spinach juice and water
1 tablespoon chicken base

❖ ❖ ❖

½ cup butter (1 stick)
1 large or 2 medium onions, diced
5 cups uncooked rice
10 fresh parsley sprigs
¾ cup heavy cream
½ cup butter (1 stick), softened
Salt and white pepper to taste

Thaw the spinach in a colander over a bowl. Press well to extract the juice from the spinach. Measure this juice

Trillium House: A Country Inn at Wintergreen

Post Office Box 280
Nellysford, Virginia 22958
(804) 325-9126

Trillium House is one of a few country inns in America designed and built to meet today's travel standards while re-

Trillium House

and add water to total 12 cups of liquid. Add the chicken base and heat in a stockpot or saucepan.

Melt ½ cup of butter in a large frypan or rondo that has a well-fitting lid. Add the onions and sauté for approximately 2 minutes. Add the rice and continue cooking, stirring for 3 to 4 minutes. The rice will become golden in color, but do not let it brown. Add the heated liquid. Stir once, cover, and cook for 17 to 20 minutes over medium heat, until all of the liquid is absorbed. Meanwhile, chop the parsley in a food processor, adding the thawed and pressed spinach, cream, and ½ cup of butter until well-blended. After the rice is cooked, remove from heat and stir in the spinach mixture. Salt and pepper to taste. The rice will take on a nice green color as you continue to blend in the spinach.

Serves 8.

Pumpkin Pound Cake

2 cups butter (4 sticks), melted
4 cups sugar
5 cups canned pumpkin
8 eggs, room temperature

❖ ❖ ❖

6 cups all-purpose flour
½ teaspoon salt
1 tablespoon plus 1 teaspoon
  baking powder
2 teaspoons baking soda
1 teaspoon fresh grated nutmeg
2 teaspoons cinnamon
2 teaspoons vanilla extract

❖ ❖ ❖

3 cups heavy whipping cream,
  chilled
¾ cup orange juice concentrate
2 tablespoons confectioners' sugar
1 cup chopped walnuts or pecans
  (optional)

Cream the butter and sugar. Add the pumpkin and beat until light and fluffy. Add the eggs one at a time, beating well after each addition. Combine the dry ingredients and slowly add to the creamed mixture. Add the vanilla and beat well. Pour into 2 greased and floured bundt or tube pans and bake for 1 hour and 15 minutes.

Whip the cream until stiff. Mix in the orange concentrate and sugar. Let the cakes cool in the pans for 25 to 30 minutes. Serve slices garnished with a dollop of orange cream sprinkled with walnuts.

Serves 24 to 30.

The Catlin-Abbott House on the Hill

A Bed and Breakfast Inn
2304 East Broad Street
Richmond, Virginia 23223
(804) 780-3746

Family heirlooms, fresh flowers, and working fireplaces await the guests of the Catlin-Abbott House. Situated in the historic Church Hill District, the house was built in 1845 for William Catlin by one of the finest brick masons in the country. Beautiful period furnishings, a spacious veranda overlooking the courtyard, a special honeymoon suite, and the innkeepers' hospitality make a stay at the Catlin-Abbott House memorable. Sherry and mints are placed at each bedside in the evening, and the bed covers are turned back, promising a restful night. Each morning a full breakfast featuring sausage and pancakes, fresh juice, and tea or coffee awaits each guest. Breakfast may be enjoyed in the privacy of one's own room or in the dining room. Many of Richmond's historical sites and extensive battlefield parks, as well as the famous plantations on the James River, are close by on Route 5.

The Catlin-Abbott House

The Catlin-Abbott House

Sausage-Cheese Bake

3 cups spoon-size shredded wheat
3 tablespoons butter, melted
1 cup shredded Swiss cheese
1 cup shredded Monterey Jack
  cheese
1½ pounds sausage, cooked,
  drained and crumbled

❖ ❖ ❖

1 10¾-ounce can mushroom soup
12 eggs
1½ cups milk
¼ cup white wine
1 medium onion, minced
1 tablespoon mustard

Lightly butter a 9x13-inch baking dish. Spread the spoon-size shredded wheat in dish. Drizzle with melted butter. Sprinkle with Swiss and Monterey Jack cheeses and the sausage.

In a medium bowl, beat together the soup, eggs, milk, wine, onion, and mustard. Pour over the layers in the dish. Cover with foil and refrigerate at least 6 or up to 24 hours. Let the casserole stand at room temperature for 30 minutes before baking. Bake covered in a 325° oven until set, about 1 hour. Let stand for 5 minutes before slicing into squares.

Serves 8 to 10.

Fran's Baked Chicken

4 chicken breasts, skinned and boned
¼ cup butter (½ stick)
1 medium onion, chopped
1 10¾-ounce can cream of chicken soup, undiluted
⅔ cup dry Sherry or white table wine
1 tablespoon parsley, chopped
1 teaspoon paprika
Pepper to taste
1 tablespoon lemon juice
Lemon slices and/or fresh parsley for garnish
Hot cooked rice

In a covered skillet lightly brown the chicken breasts in butter. Remove the chicken from the skillet and place in a medium-size baking dish. Add the onions to the butter remaining in the skillet and cook until tender, being careful not to brown. Add the soup, Sherry, seasonings, and lemon juice. Blend thoroughly and pour over the chicken. Bake in a 350° oven for about 1 hour or until the chicken is fork-tender. Garnish with lemon slices and/ or fresh parsley. Serve with hot cooked long grain rice.

Serves 4.

Round Hill Hall: Bed and Breakfast

Box 14, Route 1
Round Hill, Virginia 22141
(703) 338-9221

At Round Hill Hall, a twenty-room estate, the staff greets guests in *Gone With the Wind* costumes and urges newcomers to join in the fun. (There is a wonderful hat collection to delve into.) The innkeepers, with theatrical and musical backgrounds, plan many special events, which guests should inquire about when making reservations.

Ambrosia Pancakes

These are miniature pancakes topped with fresh orange sauce.

1 cup pancake mix
1 cup milk
1 egg
1 tablespoon melted shortening
½ cup flake coconut
1 teaspoon grated orange rind

❖ ❖ ❖

1½ cups syrup
2 medium oranges, peeled and diced

Combine the pancake mix, milk, egg, and shortening until just moistened. Stir in the coconut and rind. Bake on a hot griddle, using 1 tablespoon of batter for each pancake. Keep warm until ready to serve.

Combine the syrup and diced orange. Heat and serve warm with pancakes.

Serves 4.

Sweet and Sour Meatball Appetizer

"This recipe has always been a crowd pleaser, and easy to make since the meatballs don't have to be browned first. Just drop them in the sauce to cook. They can be made in advance and refrigerated or frozen."

1 15-ounce jar grape jelly
1 12-ounce jar chili sauce
½ teaspoon lemon juice

❖ ❖ ❖

2 pounds lean ground chuck
2 eggs
⅓ cup bread crumbs
Dash parsley
Dash nutmeg
Salt and pepper to taste

In a deep saucepan, combine the jelly, chili sauce, and lemon juice and bring to a boil. Mix the meat with the remaining ingredients in a large bowl. Shape into tiny bite-sized balls and drop in the hot sauce. Cook for 30 minutes, covering the pan during the last 10 minutes of cooking. Serve in a chafing dish.

Makes 20 to 30 meatballs.

Huevos Rancheros

1 small onion, minced
1 clove garlic, minced
2 tablespoons oil
1 16-ounce can whole tomatoes, drained and chopped
2 tablespoons tomato paste
2 tablespoons chopped green chiles
Dash ground coriander
Salt and pepper to taste
4 small corn tortillas (5 inches)
4 eggs
¼ cup fresh shelled peas (or frozen)
Fresh coriander sprigs for garnish

Combine the onion, garlic and oil in a 2-quart baking dish. Microwave on high, stirring once, for about 2 minutes. Stir in the tomatoes, tomato paste, chopped chiles, and seasonings. Cook in the microwave on high for 2 to

4 minutes stirring once until boiling and thickened. Remove from the microwave.

Sprinkle the tortillas with water and wrap in plastic wrap. Microwave on low for 45 seconds to 1 minute. Place the tortillas over the bottom of a 10-inch pie plate. Top with sauce. Break the eggs over the sauce. Pierce the yolks lightly with a fork to prevent bursting. Sprinkle with peas. Cover the dish with plastic wrap. Cook on high for 3 to 4 minutes until the eggs are barely set. Let stand covered for 3 to 5 minutes until yolks are almost set and whites are opaque. Garnish with coriander.

Serves 4.

Rosemont Farm Inn

Route 3, Box 240
Warrenton, Virginia 22186
(703) 347-5422

Rosemont is an ante-bellum manor house on twenty acres, one hour from Washington, D.C., in beautiful horse country. The original part of the house was built about 1850, the remainder in 1927. It is located in Casanova Hunt, one and one-half miles from Warrenton, which has two excellent restaurants and several quaint shops in which to browse. The innkeepers make guests feel at home, and the entire house is open to them. Guests also are free to roam the twenty acres. All the animals (two dogs, one cat, and numerous horses) are friendly and love attention.

Hot Buttered Rum

2 tablespoons brown sugar
1 teaspoon whole allspice
1 teaspoon whole cloves
¼ teaspoon salt
Dash nutmeg
1 cinnamon stick
2 quarts apple or pineapple juice
**   (or combination)**
1 cup rum

In a large saucepan combine the brown sugar, allspice, cloves, salt, nutmeg, cinnamon, and juices. Slowly bring the mixture to boiling. Reduce the heat, cover, and simmer for 2 minutes. Stir in the rum; return just to boiling. Remove from heat; pour through a strainer. Place a pat of butter in each of 8 mugs. Pour in the hot mixture.

Serves 8.

Monkey Bread

3 10-ounce cans buttermilk biscuits
¾ cup sugar
1 teaspoon cinnamon
Raisins
Chopped nuts
1 cup brown sugar, firmly packed
½ cup butter (1 stick)

Cut each biscuit into fourths (do one can at a time, separately). Put the sugar and cinnamon into a plastic bag; shake well. Shake the biscuit pieces from 1 can a few at a time in the cinnamon-sugar mixture and layer them in a well-greased tube pan. Sprinkle raisins and chopped nuts over the biscuits. Repeat with the second can; sprinkle with nuts and raisins. Repeat with the third can, top with nuts and raisins. Melt the brown sugar and butter; boil for 1 minute, no longer. Pour over the three layers of biscuits, nuts, and raisins. Bake in a 350° oven for 35 minutes or until done. Let stand for 15 minutes before turning out. Do not cut this creation. Just pull the biscuits apart with a fork and enjoy!

Serves 10 to 12.

Cherry Crisp

½ cup all-purpose flour
½ cup quick-cooking oats
½ cup brown sugar, firmly packed
¼ cup butter (½ stick), softened
1 16-ounce can cherry pie filling
½ teaspoon almond flavoring
¼ cup pecans, chopped

Combine the sifted flour, oats, and brown sugar. Cut in the softened butter with a pastry blender. Pat ½ of the mixture on the bottom and sides of a 9-inch pie pan to form a crust. Spread with the cherry pie filling to which the almond flavoring has been added. Add the chopped pecans to the remaining flour-oatmeal mixture; Spread evenly around the outer rim of the pie, leaving the center open. Bake in a 375° oven for 25 to 30 minutes. Let cool before serving.

Serves 6.

Channel House

2902 Oakes Avenue
Anacortes, Washington 98221
(206) 293-9382

Channel House

The Channel House was built in 1902 by an Italian count. Furnished throughout with turn-of-the-century antiques, the guest rooms are large and airy. The main floor has a library-music room and a formal living room, each with its own fireplace, as well as a tiled solarium filled with greenery. Fresh baked breads, fresh fruit, and special ground coffee are served for breakfast each morning. From the large outdoor hot tub behind the house guests have a panoramic view of the sunset over Puget Sound and the boats navigating the Guemes Channel. The Channel House is just minutes from the international ferry.

Tangy Cream Cheese

2 8-ounce packages cream cheese, softened
½ cup confectioners' sugar
2 tablespoons grated orange rind
2 tablespoons Cointreau
2 tablespoons frozen orange juice concentrate

Combine the ingredients thoroughly in a food processor. Cover and refrigerate overnight.

Makes 2½ to 3 cups.

Scones

2 cups biscuit mix
½ cup buttermilk
1 egg
1 to 2 tablespoons sugar
Handful currants (not raisins)

❖ ❖ ❖

1 egg, beaten

Combine the biscuit mix, buttermilk, 1 egg, sugar, and currants. Turn onto a floured board. Work the dough just a little (too much and you lose the lightness). Shape into a well-rounded lump the size of a grapefruit. Cut into 8 pie-shaped wedges. Place the wedges on an ungreased cookie sheet. Brush with beaten egg. Bake in a 425° oven for 10 minutes.

Makes 8 scones.

Apricot Raisin Jam

1 cup apricot preserves
1 teaspoon grated lemon peel
¼ cup golden raisins
½ cup coarsely chopped walnuts (optional)
12 maraschino cherries, sliced
2 tablespoons lemon juice

Blend the ingredients and store covered in the refrigerator.

Makes 3½ cups.

Ashford Mansion

Box G
Ashford, Washington 98304
(206) 569-2739

This Georgian-style house, listed in the National Register for Historic Places, was built by the Ashford family at the turn of the century. On Old Mountain Road, Ashford Mansion is six miles from Mount Rainier National Park entrance. The mansion is set against a background of giant evergreens and has a lower porch that extends three-quarters of the way around the house, a veranda on each end of the second floor, and a stream bubbling a few feet away. The outward appearance of the house has remained the same since 1903, and the interior has changed very little. Accommodations include the parlor with its fireplace, where guests can relax, sip a hot or cold drink, play the grand piano, or have a game of Checkers. There is also a regulation-size pool table. Guests awaken to the fragrance of muffins baked fresh every morning and served with other types of breads and an entree.

ASHFORD MANSION 1903

Crumpets

1 ¼-ounce package active dry yeast
½ teaspoon sugar
2 tablespoons warm water (110° to 115°)
  ❖ ❖ ❖
1 cup all-purpose flour
¼ teaspoon salt
1 tablespoon butter
½ cup milk
1 egg
  ❖ ❖ ❖
¼ cup clarified butter (½ stick)

In a small, shallow bowl, sprinkle the yeast and sugar over the warm water. Let stand for 2 or 3 minutes, then stir them together to dissolve the yeast completely. Set the bowl in a warm, draft-free place, such as an unlighted oven, for 4 or 5 minutes, or until the yeast bubbles and the mix almost doubles.

Sift the flour and salt into a large mixing bowl and cut 1 tablespoon of the butter into the flour and salt mixture. Make a well in the center. Pour in the yeast mixture and the milk, and drop in 1 egg. Beat vigorously with a large spoon until a smooth soft batter is formed. Drape a towel loosely over the bowl and set it aside in a warm, draft-free place for about 1 hour, or until the batter has doubled in volume.

With a pastry brush, coat the bottom of a heavy 10- to 12-inch skillet (a 12-inch teflon electric skillet works great) and the inside surfaces of flan rings with clarified butter. Arrange rings in the skillet and place the pan over moderate heat. Drop a small amount of batter in each ring. When the crumpets bubble and the bottoms are brown, remove the rings. Turn the crumpets and cook another minute or so to brown.

Serve with a pat of unsalted butter and your favorite jam (ricotta cheese if desired).

Makes 1 dozen crumpets.

Cliff House

5440 South Grigware Road
Freeland, Washington 98249
(206) 321-1566

Guests of Cliff House enjoy the delights of a beautifully landscaped grounds and designed building in a setting that allows them to watch ships bound for ports around the world. At this secluded retreat one can enjoy the lush fir forest, stunning sunsets over Admiralty Straights, beachcombing, sunbathing, a warm fireplace, and the steaming jacuzzi. The architecture is rugged, blending stone, wood, oriental carpets, and primitive and contemporary art. A continental breakfast is served. Nonsmokers are preferred. No children or pets.

❖ ❖ ❖ ❖ ❖ ❖

Buckeye Balls

½ cup butter (1 stick)
1½ cups peanut butter
1 pound confectioners' sugar
1 tablespoon vanilla extract
  ❖ ❖ ❖
1 12-ounce package chocolate chips
½ cake paraffin

Cream the butter and peanut butter together. Add the sugar and vanilla and thoroughly blend. Shape into small 1-inch balls and refrigerate on waxed paper for 30 minutes.

Melt the chocolate chips and paraffin together in a double boiler. With a toothpick dip the buckeye balls into the chocolate, covering all but a small circle on the top. Let cool on waxed paper. May be presented in small fluted candy cups. Guests love them!

Makes 40 balls.

The Flying L Ranch

Route 2, Box 28
Glenwood, Washington 98619
(509) 364-3488

The Flying L Ranch is a secluded inn and retreat in the peaceful, picturesque Glenwood Valley on the eastern slope of the Cascade Range. Just sixteen miles away, 12,276-foot Mount Adams dominates the northwestern skyline. The ranch, open year-round, can accommodate at least twenty people in its modern, electrically-heated rooms with private baths. Four more guests can sleep in a light-housekeeping cabin. The main house has a spacious living room for group gatherings. Nutritious, family-style breakfasts are served in the rustic cookhouse, and, with advance arrangement, full dinners can be prepared for groups. Guests are invited to walk, ride, or cross-country ski the nature trails. Rafting, swimming in the meadow lake, and horse rides are available.

Bran Bread or Muffins

1 cup all-purpose flour
⅓ cup brown sugar, firmly packed
2 teaspoons baking powder
½ teaspoon salt
¼ teaspoon baking soda

❖ ❖ ❖

1 egg
1 cup milk
3 tablespoons oil
1 cup bran
⅓ cup chunk-style peanut butter
2 tablespoons honey

In a medium bowl combine the dry ingredients. In a separate bowl beat the egg, milk, and oil. Add the bran and let it soak for 5 minutes. Add the peanut butter and honey. Combine the wet ingredients with the dry ingredients just until moistened. Bake in a greased loaf pan in a 400° oven for about 35 minutes, or a greased muffin pan for 20 to 25 minutes.

Makes 1 loaf or 12 to 15 muffins.

St. Mark's Eggs

8 slices bread, buttered on 1 side
8 slices sharp Cheddar cheese
10 eggs
4 cups milk
1 teaspoon salt
½ teaspoon white pepper
1 teaspoon dry mustard
4 slices bread

Place 8 slices of bread buttered side down in a 9x13-inch cake pan. Cover each slice of bread with a slice of cheese. Beat together the eggs, milk, salt, pepper, and mustard. Pour over the bread and cheese. Cube 4 more slices of bread and cover the other ingredients. Place in the refrigerator overnight. Bake in a 325° oven for about 1 hour.

Serves 8 to 10.

Huckleberry Hot Cakes

3 cups all-purpose flour
¾ cup uncooked oatmeal
¼ cup bran cereal
4 teaspoons baking powder
4 teaspoon baking soda
2 teaspoons salt (or less)
4 eggs, beaten
4 cups buttermilk or yogurt
4 tablespoons oil
1 cup fresh or frozen huckleberries

In a large bowl, mix the dry ingredients. Beat the eggs, then add the buttermilk and oil, mixing well. Stir the egg mixture into the flour mixture until just mixed. If it seems too thick, add more liquid. Just before frying on a hot griddle, gently fold in the berries.

Serves about 8.

Strawberry-Rhubarb Cream Pie

1½ cups shortening
3 cups unbleached flour
¾ cup water

❖ ❖ ❖

4 cups chopped rhubarb
½ cup strawberries
3 eggs, beaten
1½ cups sugar
2 tablespoons butter
¼ cup all-purpose flour
¾ teaspoon nutmeg

Blend the shortening into the flour. Add the water; mix. Press into 2 round balls, flattened on the top. Roll out the bottom crust on a floured pastry cloth. Fit into a 10-inch pie pan. In a large bowl mix the fruit and eggs. Combine the dry ingredients and add to the fruit mixture. Stir. Pour into the pastry shell. Top with 2 tablespoons of butter. Roll out and add the top crust. Cut gashes for steam to escape. Bake in a 400° oven for 1 hour. Cool. Enjoy a piece with a scoop of ice cream.

Serves 6.

Tuna Potato Casserole

3 7-ounce cans of tuna
1 3-ounce can sliced mushrooms
1 tablespoon Worcestershire sauce
½ teaspoon Tabasco sauce

❖ ❖ ❖

2 tablespoons vinegar
3 cups potatoes, cooked and diced

❖ ❖ ❖

¼ cup butter (½ stick)
¼ cup thinly sliced onion
¼ cup thinly sliced celery

❖ ❖ ❖

¼ cup all-purpose flour
1 teaspoon dry mustard
2 cups milk
1 cup mayonnaise

Combine the tuna, mushrooms, Worcestershire sauce, and Tabasco sauce; set aside. In a separate bowl, combine the vinegar and potatoes; set aside.

In a sauté pan melt the butter and simmer the onion and celery until tender. Add the flour and dry mustard, remove from heat. Gradually add the milk and mayonnaise and stir.

Place ½ of the potatoes in a large casserole. Top with ½ of the tuna mixture and half of the sauce mixture. Repeat the layers. Bake in a 350° oven for 30 minutes.

Serves 6.

Chile Con Carne

2 cups dry pinto beans
1 large onion, sliced
2 green peppers, chopped
1 fresh jalapeño, diced
2 pounds ground beef and sausage
(or 2 pounds cubed chuck
roast)
2 pounds (4 cups) canned tomatoes
1 8-ounce can tomato sauce
1½ tablespoons chile powder
1½ tablespoons cumin
1 bay leaf, crumbled
1 tablespoon sugar
⅛ teaspoon garlic powder
Dash cayenne
1 8-ounce can of mushrooms, sliced
Corn meal
Salt and pepper to taste (optional)

Rinse the beans; soak overnight in 2 quarts water. Cover and simmer until tender, about 1½ hours. Drain.

Brown the onion, green pepper, jalapeño, and meats. Drain. Add the remaining ingredients. Simmer for 1 hour and 30 minutes. Mix the beans and the sauce. Serve with brown rolls and a green salad.

Serves 10.

Caroline's Country Cottage

215 6th Street
Post Office Box 459
Langley, Washington 98260
(206) 221-8709

Caroline's Country Cottage provides any guest to Whidbey Island in Puget Sound a lovely retreat reminiscent of a fine country home. Situated on three scenic acres with a sweeping view of the village of Langley, the Cascades, and the Saratoga Passage, its decor of country elegance relaxes guests and makes them feel at home. Guests who rest in one of the inn's three country suites with private baths will find it a pleasant place to read and write, or they may stroll the country roads while gazing at mountains and sea. A full gourmet breakfast is served in the sun room or the scenic dining room. The charming living room or deck is the setting for a complimentary evening social hour.

Whidbey Island Overnight Brunch Casserole

3 tablespoons butter
½ cup sliced green onions
½ cup sliced mushrooms
½ cup chopped green pepper
½ zucchini, thinly sliced (or
chopped, slightly cooked
asparagus)
Chipped (thinly sliced) ham, beef,
or pastrami, cut up
12 eggs, beaten

❖ ❖ ❖

3 tablespoons butter
3 tablespoons flour
1½ to 2 cups milk
1 cup shredded cheese
1 teaspoon salt

❖ ❖ ❖

1½ cups bread crumbs
½ teaspoon paprika
3 tablespoons butter, melted

In 3 tablespoons of butter sauté the vegetables. Add the ham to the pan. Then add the eggs; softly scramble. Place in a greased 9x12-inch pan.

To make the cheese sauce, melt 3 tablespoons of butter. Blend in the flour and cook over low heat, stirring until smooth. Remove from heat. Stir in the milk. Bring to a boil, stirring con-

Caroline's Country Cottage

stantly. Boil briefly. Stir in the cheese and salt. Spread the sauce over the eggs.

Top with bread crumbs, paprika, and melted butter mixed together. Refrigerate overnight. Bake in a 350° oven for 30 to 40 minutes until heated through and bubbly. May easily be doubled.

Serves 6 to 8.

Fresh Fruit Dip

1 carton nondairy whipped topping (thawed)
1 carton sour cream (of the same size as topping)
⅓ cup brown sugar, firmly packed
⅓ cup orange liqueur
⅓ cup Grand Marnier

Fold together topping and sour cream. Whip in brown sugar. Stir in liqueurs. Dip is to be used with fresh ripe strawberries with the hulls left on. (Also good with other fruits. Use Amaretto to replace other liqueurs when serving fresh or canned peaches.)

Makes approximately 4 cups.

The Tudor Inn

1108 South Oak
Port Angeles, Washington 98362
(206) 452-3138

The Tudor Inn, constructed in 1910, has been restored to capture the charm of that era. The lounge and library, each with its own fireplace, invite guests to relax, whether reading, planning the next day's journey, or enjoying conversation with fellow travelers. The inn's five bedrooms overlook either the Olympic Mountains or the Strait of Juan de Fuca. Queen and king-size beds are available, as well as two large hallway bathrooms.

A full breakfast is served in the formal dining room, featuring farm-fresh eggs, homemade muffins or bread, and jams, juice, fruit in season, tea, and coffee. Upon request, a fresh pot of tea or coffee can be placed outside one's room each morning before breakfast.

Grilled Salmon Steak

2 pounds salmon steaks
1 cup dry Vermouth
⅔ cup butter, melted (or oil)
¼ cup lemon juice
2 tablespoons finely chopped onion
2 teaspoons salt
¼ teaspoon marjoram
¼ teaspoon pepper
¼ teaspoon thyme
Pinch sage

Place the salmon in a shallow pan. Combine the remaining ingredients and add to the salmon. Allow to sit about 4 hours, turning the steaks occasionally. Remove the steaks, reserve the sauce. Place the steaks on a grill 4 inches from the hot coals for about 8 minutes. Turn and cook the other side. Baste during cooking.

Serves 6.

The Shelburne Inn

Pacific Highway 103 and North 45th Street
Post Office Box 250
Seaview, Washington 98644
(206) 642-2442

The Shelburne Inn in Seaview is one of the few surviving Victorian hotels in southwest Washington. Due to its colorful past, the inn has been placed on

the National Register of Historic Places. In 1896 Charles Beaver chose the name *Shelburne* for the home and boardinghouse he built. Under the ownership of William Hoare in 1911, a team of horses was hired to pull the Shelburne across the street and join it to another building. A covered passageway was constructed between the buildings to create The Shelburne Inn.

All seventeen rooms are furnished with antiques, ten with private baths. A hearty breakfast is complimentary, as well as Sunday brunch in the inn's restaurant, The Shoalwater. Bounded on one side by the Pacific Ocean, on another by Willapa Bay, and yet another by the Columbia River, the peninsula hosts an abundance of fish and wildlife. Dramatic vistas are varied, and the ocean front has one of the cleanest and longest stretches of sandy beach in the Pacific Northwest.

Eggs and Shrimp

12 eggs
❖ ❖ ❖
½ cup butter (1 stick)
1 teaspoon dried chervil
1 teaspoon dried parsley
3 tablespoons Dijon mustard
1 pound fresh cocktail shrimp
1 cup heavy cream
2 cups grated Gruyère cheese

Place the eggs into slowly boiling water. Cover. Cook for 7 minutes. Remove from the water, crack the shells, and plunge into cold water. Peel and set aside.

Melt the butter in a large sauté pan over medium-high heat. Slice the eggs into the butter and swirl in the pan to coat well. Add the chervil, parsley, and mustard. Swirl gently again to combine. Add the shrimp and cream. Heat until the shrimp are hot and the mixture is slightly thickened. Divide evenly among 6 ramekins. Top each with cheese and brown under the broiler.

Serves 6.

Shelburne Porridge

2 cups steel-cut oats (available in
    health food stores and co-ops)
3 cups water
3 cups milk
1 teaspoon salt
½ cup raisins
2 tablespoons butter
2 tablespoons brown sugar (or to
    taste)
2 tablespoons Irish Whiskey
    (optional)

In a saucepan combine the oats, water,
milk, salt, and raisins. Heat just to a
boil, reduce heat and simmer for 15
minutes, or until the liquid is absorbed.
Remove from the heat, cover and let
stand for 10 minutes to set up. To
serve, spoon into 6 bowls and top with
1 teaspoon each of butter, brown
sugar, and Irish Whiskey.
    Makes 6 cups.

Avgolemono
(Greek Lemon Chicken Soup)

8 cups chicken stock
½ cup plus 1 tablespoon fresh
    lemon juice
½ cup shredded carrots
½ cup chopped onions
½ cup chopped celery
Freshly ground white pepper to
    taste
¼ cup butter, softened (½ stick)
¼ cup all-purpose flour
8 egg yolks, room temperature
1 cup cooked rice
1 cup cooked chicken, diced
Salt to taste

Combine the stock, lemon juice, carrots, onions, celery, and pepper in a
soup pot; bring to a boil over high
heat. Reduce the heat, cover partially,
and simmer until tender (about 20
minutes). Blend the butter and flour
until smooth; add into the hot soup a
little at a time, stirring well after each
addition. Simmer for 10 minutes, stirring frequently. Meanwhile, beat the
yolks in a mixer at high speed until
light and lemon-colored. Reduce the
speed and gradually mix in some of

the hot soup. Return the mixture to the
saucepan. Add the rice and chicken.
Cook until heated through. Season to
taste. Ladle into bowls; garnish with
lemon slices.
    Serves 8 to 10.

Poached Pepper Oysters

6 tablespoons butter
2 tablespoons minced garlic
2 tablespoons medium-grind
    pepper
36 oysters (may be varied,
    depending on the size of the
    oysters)
2 cups fish stock (or oyster liquor)
6 limes, juiced

    ❖   ❖   ❖

6 tablespoons butter

In a small sauté pan heat 6 tablespoons
of butter over medium-high heat. Add
the garlic and pepper. Sauté for approximately 1 minute. Add the oysters
and sauté for 30 seconds, turning occasionally. Add the fish stock and lime
juice. Bring to a boil. Remove the oysters and set aside on a warm platter.
Reduce the liquid in the pan for 30 seconds. Add an additional 6 tablespoons
of butter to the liquid. Mix until the
sauce thickens. Arrange the oysters on
plates and top with the sauce.
    Serves 6.

Pan-Fried Oysters

Flour
Salt and pepper to taste
36 oysters (use less if the oysters
    are large)
6 tablespoons butter, clarified

Mix the flour and seasonings. Coat the
oysters on each side. Set on a plate and
allow to sit until they begin to get
gummy or sticky. Heat the butter in a
pan over medium-high heat. Add the
oysters and fry until golden brown.
Turn and fry the other side until

brown. Remove from the pan and
serve with lemon wedges, tartar
sauce, and parsley.
    Serves 6.

Escargot with Hazelnut Butter

½ cup dry white wine
1 tablespoon Cognac
1 teaspoon thyme
2 bay leaves
4 dozen snails

    ❖   ❖   ❖

3 cups butter (6 sticks)
3 shallots, finely minced
2 cloves garlic, finely minced
½ cup finely chopped hazelnuts
¼ cup finely chopped parsley

Combine the wine, Cognac, thyme,
and bay leaves. Marinate the snails in
the wine mixture for at least 4 hours in
the refrigerator.
    Whip the butter with the shallots,
garlic, hazelnuts, and parsley until
well-blended; refrigerate.
    Sauté 6 snails per serving with 3
ounces of hazelnut butter over medium heat until foaming. Serve immediately with plenty of fresh French
bread.
    Serves 6 to 8.

Pumpkin Cheesecake

6 8-ounce packages cream cheese
    (room temperature)
2¾ cups sugar
8 eggs
1 1-pound 3-ounce can pumpkin
1 teaspoon ginger
1 teaspoon cinnamon
½ teaspoon cloves
¼ teaspoon nutmeg
½ teaspoon salt

Butter the bottom and sides of 2 8-inch
springform pans (3 inches deep). Preheat the oven to 350° and arrange
baking rack one-third up from the bot-

tom of oven. Beat the cream cheese in a mixer at medium speed until completely smooth, stopping occasionally to scrape the sides and bottom of the bowl with a rubber spatula. When smooth, beat in the sugar and mix well. Add the eggs, one at a time. Add the pumpkin and seasonings. Beat only until all of the ingredients are thoroughly mixed. Pour the batter into the prepared springform pans. Place the springforms inside larger pans; pour 1½ inches of hot water in the larger pans. Bake for 1½ hours, or until the top is a rich golden brown and feels dry to the touch. The cake should still be soft inside. Remove from the water bath and cool completely on a rack before removing the springform pan sides or refrigerating.

Serves 16.

Blakely Estates Bed and Breakfast

East 7710 Hodin Drive
Spokane, Washington 99212
(509) 926-9426

Blakely Estates Bed and Breakfast is nestled cozily on the banks of the Spokane River. This private setting offers its guests peace and quiet just fifteen minutes from downtown Spokane. Two bedrooms are available with a shared bath, and guests have their own private entrance and sitting room. After a day in the city, they are invited to relax in the outdoor hot tub overlooking the river. Fresh coffee and a full gourmet breakfast await guests as they prepare for another day.

Baked Eggs

10 eggs
½ cup all-purpose flour
1 teaspoon baking powder
½ teaspoon salt
½ cup butter (1 stick), melted
2 ounces green chiles, diced
2 cups cottage cheese
4 cups grated Jack cheese

Beat the eggs well. Mix the flour, baking powder, and salt into the melted butter; add to the eggs. Stir in the chiles. Add the cheeses and mix well. Bake in a greased pan in a 350° oven for 45 minutes to 1 hour or until the center is firm. Serve with Cheese Dill Sauce.

Serves 4 to 6.

Cheese Dill Sauce

⅓ cup butter
⅓ cup all-purpose flour
2½ cups milk
½ cup shredded Cheddar cheese
½ teaspoon salt
2 teaspoons dill

Melt the butter in a saucepan. Blend in the flour. Gradually add the milk. Cook until thick, stirring constantly. Remove from heat; stir in the Cheddar cheese, salt and dill. Cover until serving time.

Makes 4 cups.

Eggs in a Basket

1½ cups sifted all-purpose flour
⅓ cup grated Cheddar cheese
½ teaspoon salt
½ cup shortening
4 to 5 tablespoons cold water

❖ ❖ ❖

Eggs
Salt and pepper to taste

❖ ❖ ❖

Cheese Dill Sauce

Combine the flour, cheese, and salt. Cut the shortening into the flour mixture and add the cold water. On a floured surface roll out the dough to ⅛-inch thickness and cut circles to fit muffin pans. Fit each circle into an individual muffin cup. Let the pastry edge extend around each cup. Break an egg into each cup lined with pastry and season with salt and pepper. Cover each egg with another circle of dough. Bake in a 450° oven for 20 to 22 minutes.

Makes 12 to 15 baskets.

West Virginia

COOLFONT

Coolfont Re+Creation

Berkeley Springs, West Virginia 25411
(304) 258-4500
(Washington, D.C.: 1-800-424-1232, Toll Free)

When guests arrive at Coolfont, they see mountain vistas, two sparkling spring-fed lakes, and the beautiful treetop house and restaurant. Only later do they realize that hidden in the unspoiled landscape is a variety of lodging and recreational facilities. A lodge, chalets, vacation homes, a conference center, and the famous restaurant high in the trees exist alongside tennis, hiking, fishing, cross country skiing, swimming, and relaxing.

Fundamental to life at Coolfont is a wide variety of recreational, cultural, and healthful activities, from concerts, art classes, and films to family activities, nature hikes, and square dances.

Coolfont contains 1200 acres between Cacapon Mountain and Warm Springs Ridge near Berkeley Springs in the Eastern Panhandle of West Virginia.

Coolfont Lo-Cal House Dressing

3 1-pint containers cottage cheese
3 1-quart containers yogurt
1 cup skim milk
1½ 1¼-ounce packages Ranch Dressing mix

Mix well and refrigerate.
Makes 1 gallon.

Folkestone Bed and Breakfast

Route 2, Box 404
Berkeley Springs, West Virginia 25411
(304) 258-3743

In 1929, Captain L. H. Kirby commissioned an English-style residence to be built two miles east of the nation's first health spa, the town of Bath (Berkeley Springs), in the eastern panhandle of West Virginia. Its second owners named the eight-room house after their home in England, Folkestone. This home adjacent to the historic spa

has accommodated prominent guests who desired privacy. The surrounding ten acres of wooded grounds are rich with dogwood, azalea, oak, forsythia, and rhododendron. Bed and breakfast guest accommodations are on the second floor. Guests share the sitting room. The bathroom is large and sunny. There is no shower, but the original claw-foot tub offers bathing luxury today's smaller models do not. Breakfast, which is served in the dining room or, weather permitting, on the screened-in porch, includes juice and seasonal fresh fruit, homemade pastry or breads, the daily entree, and tea, coffee or milk.

Instead of Eggs Benedict

1 10½-ounce can cream of mushroom soup
½ cup white Chablis
1 teaspoon parsley
½ teaspoon garlic salt

❖ ❖ ❖

4 eggs
English muffins
Ham slices

Bring the soup, wine, and seasonings to a simmer. Poach 4 eggs in the mixture to the desired doneness. Serve on English muffins topped with slices of ham, and cover with sauce.
Serves 4.

447

Highlawn Inn

304 Market Street
Berkeley Springs, West Virginia 25411
(304) 258-5700

A delightful turn-of-the-century home, today Highlawn Inn welcomes its guests with warm hospitality and superb accommodations for bed and breakfast. The rooms are decorated with furniture and accessories from an earlier era. Day begins with a full country breakfast, featuring hot breads and specialties of the house, served in the Victorian dining room. A wealth of activities is available within a few miles, from the famed mineral baths just a few blocks away to the picturesque mountains nearby. Guests may choose to laze away their day reading, rocking, or dreaming on the spacious veranda or in front of a comforting fire.

Highlawn Inn

Lemon Curd

½ cup butter (1 stick)
1¼ cups sugar
3 whole lemons, quartered
3 eggs, beaten

Melt the butter in a double boiler. Add the sugar; squeeze the juice from the lemon quarters. Add the juice along with the quarted lemon rinds; Stir until the sugar is dissolved. Add the eggs and cook until the mixture thickens. Keeps several weeks in refrigerator.

Makes 1 pound.

Sunday Eggs

2 cups grated Swiss cheese (or Cheddar cheese)
¼ cup butter (½ stick)
1 cup heavy cream
½ teaspoon salt
Dash freshly ground pepper
½ tablespoon dry mustard
12 eggs, lightly beaten
Minced fresh parsley or parsley sprigs

Spread the cheese on the bottom of a buttered shallow baking dish. Dot with butter. Mix the cream and seasonings. Pour ½ of the cream over the cheese. Add the eggs and pour the remaining cream on top. Bake in a 325° oven for 30 minutes or until cooked to taste. Garnish with parsley.

Serves 6 to 8.

Valley View Farm

Route 1, Box 467
Mathias, West Virginia 26812
(304) 897-5229

Nestled in a small valley among hills and woodland, this cozy home offers neat, clean, and comfortable accommodations on a cattle and sheep farm. The innkeepers have been in the guest-house business many years. The bountiful country meals, with plenty of homemade breads, pies, and similar goodies, will be long-remembered. In addition to the good food, the area offers many scenic and recreational activities, ranging from touring country lanes and back roads to horseback riding, hiking, tennis, swimming, and lawn sports. Guest rooms for eight to ten people are available in the home, with shared bath facilities. A primitive separate cabin is also available in the backyard for ten people. Children are welcome and will enjoy the farm animals.

Twenty-Four-Hour Salad

1 head lettuce, broken into small pieces
1 cup chopped celery
1 7½-ounce can water chestnuts, thinly sliced
1 small red salad onion, thinly sliced
1 10-ounce package frozen peas

❖   ❖   ❖

1 pint mayonnaise
1 tablespoon sugar
Salt and pepper

❖   ❖   ❖

1 ½ to ¾ pound package grated Mozzarella cheese
Parmesan cheese

❖   ❖   ❖

5 or 6 slices bacon, cooked and crumbled
Tomatoes, sliced

Layer the vegetables in the order given in a 9x13-inch baking dish. Mix the mayonnaise with the sugar, salt, and pepper. Spread completely over the layers in the baking dish. Sprinkle with the cheeses. Cover with foil and refrigerate for 24 hours. When ready to serve, top with crumbled bacon and tomato slices.

Serves 10 to 12.

Rich Dinner Rolls

This recipe can be used for cinnamon buns and fancy coffee cake rings or even raised doughnuts.

½ cup warm water (110° to 115°)
2 ¼-ounce packages active dry
   yeast

❖   ❖   ❖

¾ cup lukewarm milk
½ cup sugar
1 teaspoon salt
5 cups sifted all-purpose flour
½ cup shortening, softened
2 eggs

Dissolve the yeast in the warm water. Pour the milk over the sugar and salt in a bowl. Stir until dissolved. Beat in 1 cup of flour, the shortening, eggs, and yeast mixture. Add the remaining flour to make a soft dough. Knead until the dough becomes smooth and elastic. Place in a lightly greased bowl; oil the top of the dough. Cover and allow the dough to rise in a warm place until doubled in bulk (about 1 or 1½ hours). Shape into rolls. Allow to double in bulk (30 or 40 minutes). Bake in a 375° oven until done. Brush with melted butter and serve hot. May be reheated.
   Makes 2 dozen rolls.

Crispy Venison Steak

Slice a venison ham or loin ¼-inch thick. Place on a block and tenderize well with steak hammer. Roll generously with flour. Melt enough solid shortening to cover the bottom of an iron skillet. Fry the venison quickly. Salt and pepper to taste or add onion or garlic powder if desired. Serve hot.

Pumpkin Cake Roll

⅔ cup pumpkin
3 eggs, beaten at high speed
   (5 minutes)
1 cup sugar
¾ cup all-purpose flour
1 teaspoon baking powder
2 teaspoons cinnamon
1 teaspoon ginger
¼ teaspoon nutmeg
½ teaspoon salt
1 teaspoon lemon juice
1 cup chopped nuts

❖   ❖   ❖

1 cup confectioners' sugar
¼ cup butter (½ stick)
6 ounces cream cheese (softened)
1 teaspoon vanilla extract

Combine the pumpkin and beaten eggs. Sift and mix the dry ingredients; add to the pumpkin mixture. Add the lemon juice. Pour into a waxed paper-lined jelly roll pan. Top with the chopped nuts. Bake in a 375° oven until golden brown. When done, place on a damp clean towel sprinkled with confectioners' sugar. Remove the paper, roll up, and cool for 1 hour. Unroll, and fill with the filling made by beating together the confectioners' sugar, butter, cream cheese, and vanilla. This cake freezes well.
   Serves 8.

Kilmarnock Farm

Route 1, Box 91
Orlando, West Virginia 26412
(304) 452-8319

Kilmarnock Farm is nestled in a secluded valley with sparkling brooks and grassy meadows surrounded by deep forests. Nearby is a 970-acre lake that provides some of the East's best musky fishing. Guests of Kilmarnock Farm are treated personally (only two bedrooms are available) and share the delicious country fare, served family style in the comfortable nineteenth century farmhouse. Breakfast and dinner are served; a lunch is packed. Special diets are catered upon request. No pets, please.

Marinade for Lamb Chops

¼ cup oil
¼ cup lemon juice
1 teaspoon garlic
1 teaspoon brown mustard
¼ cup soy sauce

Combine the ingredients. Marinate the lamb chops for 4 to 6 hours; place over medium-hot coals and grill until medium rare.
   Makes 1 cup of marinade.

Venison Bulgogi

4 tablespoons green onion
2½ teaspoons minced garlic
1½ teaspoons minced ginger root
2 tablespoons ground sesame seed
2 tablespoons sesame oil

❖   ❖   ❖

4½ tablespoons soy sauce
2½ tablespoons sugar
Dash pepper

❖   ❖   ❖

1½ pounds venison, thinly sliced

Brown the onion, garlic, ginger root, sesame seed, and sesame oil. Add the soy sauce, sugar, and pepper. Brown the venison, and add the onion mixture.
   Serves 3 to 4.

West Virginia Fruit Cup

A breakfast treat.

Bananas
Fresh blueberries
Summer apples
Orange pieces
Peach slices
Blackberries
Melon
Any other fruit in season
Orange juice or pink champagne

Combine the fruit; add orange juice or pink champagne and serve in pretty stemware. Very appetizing.

Cobblestone Inn Bed and Breakfast

103 Charles Street
Sistersville, West Virginia 25175
(304) 652-1206

The Cobblestone Inn, a late-Victorian house built as a private home about 1903, affords a breathtaking view of the Ohio River. Its spacious rooms, high ceilings, fireplaces, staircase, and ornate woodwork are typical of that era. The decor is English country with some antiques and original art work. A wide assortment of books and music tapes are available to guests, and there is a television in the front parlor. Breakfast may be served on the front porch if requested.

The Cobblestone Inn is a perfect setting for exploring the Mid-Ohio Valley. In the center of West Virginia's glass-making industry, Sistersville was a turn-of-the-century oil boom town. The wealth of that era gave Sistersville mansions, lovely Victorian homes, and brick, tree-lined streets and a heritage that is celebrated every September in the Oil and Gas Festival. Antique, glass, and craft shops are plentiful, as are places to dine.

Cobblestone's Sunshine Omelet

½ carrot, sliced
6 to 8 small broccoli spears
1 tablespoon butter
3 eggs, beaten
¼ cup cubed baked ham, heated (optional)
1 slice American cheese (or Velveeta)

Steam the carrots and broccoli spears until tender. Heat the butter in a pan over low heat. Pour the beaten eggs in the hot pan, cover and let the eggs partially set. Sprinkle ½ of the pan with carrots, broccoli, ham, and cheese. Fold over the eggs and cover the pan until the eggs are set. Serve on a warmed plate with biscuits or toast.
Serves 1.

Cafe Borgia

A winter treat.

1 12-ounce box instant hot cocoa mix (the type you add hot water to)
12 cups freshly perked coffee
Whipped cream
Grated orange peel

In a large mug, combine 1 packet of cocoa mix with 1 cup of hot coffee instead of hot water. Stir well. Garnish with whipped cream and a shake of grated orange peel. This is a quick, tasty, warming drink.
Serves 2.

Refrigerator Pastry for Pies

4 cups all-purpose flour
1 teaspoon salt
1 teaspoon baking powder
1¾ cups shortening
1 egg, beaten
½ cup cold water
1 tablespoon vinegar

Crumble the dry ingredients and shortening by hand or with an electric mixer on low speed. Add the egg, water and vinegar. Mix all together and store in the refrigerator. This will keep indefinitely. Roll out and bake according to the pie recipe being used.

This pastry is used with Berry Pie Filling. Makes a tender flaky crust. Makes 5 to 6 pie shells.

Berry Pie Filling

1½ cups sugar
½ cup all-purpose flour
3½ to 4 cups raspberries or blackberries

Combine the sugar and flour. Add to the berries. Stir well to dissolve the sugar. Pour into an unbaked pie shell. Cover with a top crust. Bake in a 350° oven for about 40 minutes until the crust is golden brown. Serve with a scoop of ice cream.
Serves 6.

Nine-and-One-Half Minute Can't Fail Fruitcake

2 eggs, slightly beaten
1 28-ounce jar mincemeat
1 15-ounce can sweetened condensed milk
1 cup walnuts, coarsely chopped
2 cups mixed candied fruit
2½ cups sifted all-purpose flour
1 teaspoon baking soda

Butter a 9-inch tube or springform pan. Line with waxed paper and butter again. Combine the eggs, mincemeat, milk, walnuts, and fruit. Fold in the dry ingredients; pour into the prepared pan. Bake in a 300° oven for 2 hours. Cool. Turn out, remove the paper. Decorate with walnuts and cherries. Freezes well.

Makes 6 individual loaves when using small loaf pans.

Silver Creek

Pinnacle Management Corporation
Post Office Box 150
Slatyfork, West Virginia 26291
(800) 624-2119 (Outside West Virginia)
(304) 572-4000 (Inside West Virginia)

Nestled in the snowy mountains of West Virginia, Silver Creek ski resort features well-groomed slopes, magnificent mountain views, luxurious lodging, service, and hospitality. This contemporary nine-story hotel houses 237 apartments, hotel rooms, and efficiencies, each offering majestic views. Sound-proof apartments feature the added comfort of climate control, direct-dial phones, color TV, and full kitchens with microwaves. All have fireplaces, clothes washers, and dryers, except hotel rooms and efficiencies. A full service restaurant and deli for snacks provide excellent food, and guests can relax in the Silver Bush Saloon each evening as they enjoy live entertainment during the ski season.

Olive Cheese Balls

    4 tablespoons butter, softened
    ½ pound Cheddar cheese, shredded
    1 cup all-purpose flour
    ¼ teaspoon salt
    Cayenne pepper to taste
    1 to 3 teaspoons water
    50 whole ripe black olives

Cream the butter and Cheddar cheese. Blend in the flour, salt and pepper. Add water until workable. Wrap each olive in dough and bake on an ungreased sheet in a 400° oven for 15 minutes.
Makes 45 to 50 cheese balls.

Hauhn Chicken with Apricot Brandy Sauce

    Pancake mix
    Beer
    Chicken breasts, boned and cut in
        strips
    Sliced almonds
        ❖ ❖ ❖
    ½ cup sugar
    3 pints fruit juice
    ½ cup chopped maraschino
        cherries
    ½ cup chopped apricots
    ½ cup chopped plums
    1 teaspoon cinnamon
        ❖ ❖ ❖
    1 tablespoon cornstarch
    1 cup apricot brandy

Mix pancake mix with beer to make a batter and dip strips of chicken breasts in the batter. Dip in sliced almonds and fry to a golden brown.

Melt the sugar to a light brown and add the fruit juice, fruits and cinnamon. Simmer for 30 minutes. Dissolve the cornstarch in a small amount of water and add, cooking until thick. Add the brandy and serve hot over the chicken.
Serves 4 to 6.

Baked Oysters Remick

    6 oysters
    White wine
    2 teaspoons butter
    Chicken stock
        ❖ ❖ ❖
    6 ounces thick mayonnaise
    3 ounces chili sauce
    1 ounce horseradish
        ❖ ❖ ❖
    6 ounces grated Swiss cheese

Poach the oysters in the wine, butter, and chicken stock until the oysters curl. Do not overcook. Drain and put back on the half shell.

Combine the mayonnaise, chili sauce, and horseradish to make a sauce; cover each oyster generously with sauce. Sprinkle each oyster with 1 ounce of Swiss cheese. Broil or bake at 400° until golden brown.
Serves 2.

Countryside

Box 57
Summit Point, West Virginia 25446
(304) 725-2614

The Countryside was the first bed and breakfast inn in the state of West Virginia. Situated in the quaint, rural village of Summit Point, it is close to many scenic and historic attractions, yet far enough away to be private and relaxing. Countryside is decorated with a cheery mixture of antiques, collectibles, quilts, baskets, and original artwork. Guests enjoy the rural quiet. A complimentary breakfast is served every morning and includes coffee, juice, and rolls. Also served is an afternoon tea. Books, magazines, menus and area information guides are available to guests.

A Small Bed and Breakfast Inn

Countryside

Countryside's Apple Cake

Since Countryside is located on the edge of an apple orchard, and their logo is an apple tree, an apple recipe is indeed appropriate.

4 cups unpeeled apples, chopped
      and cored
3 eggs, beaten
1 cup oil
          ❖   ❖   ❖
2 cups all-purpose flour
2 cups sugar
1 teaspoon salt
1½ teaspoons baking soda
1 teaspoon cinnamon
Cinnamon and sugar

Combine the apples, eggs, and oil in a mixing bowl. In another bowl combine the flour, sugar, salt, baking soda, and cinnamon. Stir the flour mixture into the apples, mixing well. Oil a sheet, tube, or 2 9-inch bread pans thoroughly. Coat the pan completely with the cinnamon-sugar mixture. Pour the batter into the pan. Bake in a 350° oven for 60 minutes.
    Serves 8.

Salmon Spread

1 16-ounce can salmon
2 8-ounce packages cream cheese
1 tablespoon lemon juice
2 drops liquid smoke

Combine the ingredients. Delicious on crackers.
    Makes 3 cups of spread.

Waldorf Whole Wheat Sandwiches

1 8-ounce package cream cheese,
      softened
1 tablespoon milk
2 teaspoons lemon juice
1 cup finely chopped apple
½ cup finely snipped pitted dates
¼ cup finely chopped walnuts
16 slices whole wheat bread
Butter or margarine, softened

Combine the cream cheese, milk, and lemon juice. Stir in the apple, dates and walnuts. Spread the bread with softened butter. On each of 8 slices of bread, spread ¼ cup of the filling mixture. Top with the remaining bread. The recipe may be reduced to half.
    Makes 8 sandwiches.

Drover's Inn

1001 Washington Pike
Wellsburg, West Virginia 26070
(304) 737-0188

Built in 1848, the Drover's Inn required three years of work by skilled craftsmen to construct the three-story, sixteen-room edifice. The open, winding staircase extends from the ground floor to the third floor. The rooms on the second floor still retain the numbers originally placed on the doors when the inn was built. A ladies' parlor on the same floor brings back nostalgic memories of bygone days. In early 1850 the inn was opened to travelers and drovers. At Drover's Inn they could obtain lodgings and food for themselves, and pasture for their livestock.

Summer Slaw

3 small heads cabbage (½ gallon)
2 cups vinegar
3 cups sugar
½ teaspoon salt
½ teaspoon turmeric
¼ cup mustard seeds
¼ cup celery seeds

Grate the cabbage. Mix the remaining ingredients in a saucepan. Bring to a simmer and cook long enough for the sugar to dissolve. Pour over the slaw. Allow the slaw to marinate overnight. The slaw will keep 1 week.
    Makes ¾ gallon of slaw.

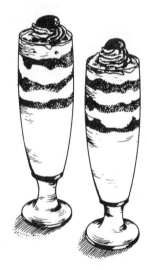

Wisconsin

The Gallery House

215 North Main Street
Alma, Wisconsin 54610
(608) 685-4975

The Gallery House Mercantile Building, built in 1861, was recently added
to the National Register of Historic
Places. Perched on the bluffs of the
Mississippi River at Lock and Dam
No. 4 on the Great River Road, it provides a beautiful view of the Mississippi valley. In Alma guests can see
homes and buildings carved into the
bluffs with stone retaining walls and
terraced gardens and stairways instead of streets. A deck on the side of
the building provides peaceful surroundings for a morning cup of coffee,
an afternoon chat, or an evening of
reminiscing. Breakfast is served in the
dining room at 8:00 A.M. with a variety of homemade delicacies. Each of
the three guest rooms has a double
bed, brass appointments, and is decorated in restful shades of yellow and
gold. Across the hall is the bath with its
claw foot tub and old brass plumbing
fixtures.

Frittata

⅓ pound sausage
½ cup chopped onion
½ teaspoon dry mustard
¼ teaspoon cumin
½ teaspoon thyme
½ teaspoon chili powder
3 small cooked potatoes, diced
3 eggs
⅓ pound cheese, grated

In an 8-inch skillet, brown the sausage
and onion. Add the spices and stir in
the potatoes. Beat the eggs and add to
the sausage mixture. Cook until the
eggs are firm. Cover with grated
cheese and heat until melted.
Serves 7.

Fruit Soup

½ cup minute tapioca
2 cups raisins, light or dark
1 cup pitted prunes
1 cup dried peaches or apricots
1 cinnamon stick
6 cups hot water

❖   ❖   ❖

4 cups apple juice

In a large saucepan, combine the tapioca, raisins, prunes, peaches or apricots, cinnamon stick, and water. Blend
the ingredients over medium heat. Reduce the heat and simmer until the tapioca is transparent, 30 to 35 minutes.
Soup will be thick and clear. Add apple
juice. Before serving, reheat to a simmer. Serve as is or with cream.
Serves 10 to 12.

The Parkside Bed and Breakfast

402 East North Street
Appleton, Wisconsin 54011
(414) 733-0200

Appleton's historic city park area,
once the neighborhood of magician
Harry Houdini and author Edna Fer-
ber, is the setting for this 1906 Richard-
son Romanesque-style home. A short
walk from the campus of Lawrence
University and the city's downtown
shops and restaurants, the Parkside offers convenience as well as gracious
hospitality. Decorative leaded glass is
prominent throughout the home, and
on sunlit days, its beveled panes cast
rainbow patches of light across the
first floor living and dining areas.
Guests are invited to breakfast beside
the dining room's curved glass window, or browse the bookshelves of the
formal living room. The breakfast
menu includes a variety of the freshest
seasonal fruits, warm breads, and Wisconsin cheese. The Parkside's accommodations feature ample space for
private relaxation. The bright and airy
third floor suite includes an informal
living room area, adjoined by a separate bedroom and bathroom with

The Parkside

Plum Gingerbread

A delicious version of this holiday favorite. It's rich and fragrant.

½ cup butter (1 stick), softened
½ cup sugar
½ cup molasses
2 eggs
2 cups all-purpose flour
1 tablespoon ground ginger
¾ teaspoon baking soda
¾ cup milk
½ cup raisins
½ cup currants

In a mixing bowl cream the butter and sugar. Add the molasses and eggs; beat well. Stir in the flour, ginger, and soda alternately with the milk. Blend well after each addition. Add the raisins and currants. Pour into a greased 9x13-inch pan. Bake in a 350° oven for 25 to 30 minutes.
Serves 16.

shower. Guests enjoy the treetop view of City Park from their windows and balcony. Those wishing to investigate the many activities of the area will find a current list of cultural, artistic, and sports events always available.

Poached Eggs with Chicken Livers

A special request for those who enjoy an elegant breakfast entree.

6 slices Swiss cheese
½ pound chicken livers, sautéed
6 eggs, poached
6 teaspoons half and half (or cream)
Parmesan cheese

Place a slice of Swiss cheese in the bottom of 6 greased custard cups. Add a layer of sautéed chicken livers. Slip a poached egg on top. Pour a teaspoon of light cream over each and sprinkle with Parmesan cheese. Slip under broiler for a minute.
Serves 6.

Vermont Johnnycake

Rich cornbread with a hint of maple. Wonderful in the fall or winter.

2 cups all-purpose flour
4½ teaspoons baking powder
¾ teaspoon salt
1 cup cornmeal
3 eggs, beaten
1 cup milk
½ cup maple syrup
¾ cup melted shortening or oil

Sift the flour, baking powder, and salt together; add cornmeal and mix well. Combine the eggs, milk, syrup, and melted shortening, and add to dry ingredients, stirring only enough to dampen flour. Pour into greased 9-inch square pan. Bake in a 400° oven for 30 minutes. Serve warm.
Serves 6 to 8.

The August Ringling Inn

821 Oak Street
Baraboo, Wisconsin 53913
(608) 356-3283

The August Ringling Inn, a lovely three-story turn-of-the-century home, was built by the Ringling Brothers of circus fame, for their parents, August and Salome Ringling, hence the name of the inn. Now owned by former sailors from San Francisco, The August Ringling Inn contains much of their maritime memorabilia. It is close to the town square and within walking distance of the Circus World Museum. Also close by are Devil's Lake and the Crane Foundation.

Eggs Poached in Chili Tomato Sauce

1½ pounds tomatoes

❖ ❖ ❖

1½ cups chicken stock

❖ ❖ ❖

1 large garlic clove, peeled
¼ cup safflower oil
1 large onion, coarsely chopped
1 4-ounce can green chiles (mild or medium hot), drained and chopped
¾ teaspoon salt
2 teaspoons tomato paste

❖ ❖ ❖

8 eggs

Prepare tomatoes by placing them on a baking sheet and set under the broiler. Roast them as you would peppers, turning with tongs until the skins blacken, about 10 minutes. Remove the skins and cut out stem ends. Place on a plate and set aside until ready to use. Discard any juice that drains from them.

In a saucepan heat the chicken stock. Keep hot until ready to use.

In a large skillet sauté the garlic in hot oil and discard. Turn off the heat and add onion, stir well to coat with oil. Wilt over low heat. Add the chiles, tomatoes, salt, and tomato paste. Stir and simmer for 10 minutes to blend the flavors and reduce the liquid a bit. When ready to cook the eggs, add the hot stock and bring to a simmer. Add the eggs, one at a time, by cracking each into a flat saucer and sliding it into the stock. Cover and continue to simmer for 6 to 8 minutes or until eggs are at the desired degree of firmness.

Serves 4.

The Best Ever Cinnamon Rolls

Thaw 2 frozen bread loaves and let rise. Roll out into rectangles. Cover liberally with melted butter, brown

sugar, cinnamon, walnuts. (Don't spare the goodies!) Roll up and slice. Place ½-inch apart or so on greased baking sheets to allow rolls to expand and rise. Add even more melted butter, brown sugar, and cinnamon if desired. Cover; let rise in a warm place. Bake in a 350° oven for 15 to 20 minutes, or until done. (Baking time depends on how many are on the pan.)

Makes 3 dozen.

Veal with Pine Nuts

This recipe serves 1; increase as needed.

5 ounces veal
Flour
4 to 5 tablespoons clarified butter
Salt and pepper to taste

❖ ❖ ❖

½ cup mushrooms
½ teaspoon minced shallots
½ teaspoon minced garlic
¼ teaspoon parsley
1 tablespoon pine nuts
2 tablespoons raspberry wine vinegar
Few drops lemon juice
½ teaspoon Dijon mustard
¼ cup Madeira
2 tablespoons cream
1 tablespoon finely chopped green onion

Cut veal into petite fillets and flour each fillet lightly. Sauté quickly in butter. Brown on both sides. Season to taste. Remove to a warming platter.

Add to the pan mushrooms, shallots, garlic, parsley, pine nuts, vinegar, and lemon juice. Add mustard, blend well. Deglaze with Madeira. Add cream; reduce heat until thickened. Add green onion; mix well. Pour the sauce over veal.

Serves 1.

The Old Rittenhouse Inn

Box 584
Bayfield, Wisconsin 54814

Old Rittenhouse Inn, a beautiful Victorian mansion built in 1890 by Civil War General Alen C. Fuller, has twenty-six rooms and twelve working fireplaces. Antique furnishings are used in the dining rooms and overnight guest rooms. Elegant Victorian dining is available nightly. The menu changes daily with such choices as fresh Lake Superior trout aux champagne, chicken cordon bleu with wild rice dressing, prime roast leg of lamb, crêpes de la mer, and scallops provencale. A choice of soup, salads, homemade breads, and a tempting array of desserts accompany each meal. It is open all year.

Strawberry Consommé

1 pint fresh strawberries
1⅔ cups cut rhubarb (or 1 16-ounce package frozen, thawed, and drained)
1 3-inch cinnamon stick
¾ to 1 cup sugar
2 cups water (use juice from frozen rhubarb plus water)

❖ ❖ ❖

½ cup Burgundy
½ cup soda water

❖ ❖ ❖

Sour cream

Set aside about 6 strawberries; cut up the remainder; put in a saucepan with rhubarb, cinnamon stick, sugar, and water. Bring to a boil, reduce heat, and simmer until rhubarb is tender, about 5 minutes. Pour into a strainer and press out the juice. There should be 3 cups rosy-pink juice. Add the Burgundy and soda water. Serve hot or chilled, garnish with remaining sliced berries and dollops of sour cream.

Variation: Chilled Crabapple Consommé (substitute 3 cups crabapple juice for strawberries and rhubarb. Serve chilled with a dollop of sour cream decorated with a sprig of fresh mint.)

Serves 4 to 6.

Onion-Dill Bread

1½ cups all-purpose flour
1 ¼-ounce package active dry yeast

❖ ❖ ❖

1 medium onion (or 6 green onions)
1 stalk fresh or dried dill (or 2
   tablespoons dried dillweed)
1¼ cups milk

❖ ❖ ❖

2 tablespoons sugar
1 teaspoon salt
2 tablespoons butter or margarine
1 egg
2 cups all-purpose flour

In a mixing bowl, combine 1½ cups of flour with yeast, set aside. Coarsely chop onion and dill (onion should measure about ½ cup). In a blender, combine milk, onion, and dill; whirl until blended. (If you do not have a blender, mince onion and dill; add to milk.)

In a saucepan, combine milk mixture, sugar, salt, and butter, cut into pieces. Heat, stirring constantly to melt butter, until just warm (110 to 115°). Add the milk mixture and egg to the dry mixture. Beat with an electric mixer 30 seconds on low, constantly scraping side of bowl. Beat at high speed 3 minutes. Gradually stir in remaining 2 cups of flour, adding additional flour if necessary to make a dough of medium stiffness.

Turn out on a floured board and knead about 10 minutes, adding a little flour if necessary to keep the dough from sticking. Put in a greased bowl,

turning dough to grease top. Cover and let rise until double in bulk, about ½ hour.

Punch down the dough and shape into a loaf. Place in a greased loaf pan. Cover and let the dough rise again until the loaf fills the pan. Bake in a 350° oven 35 to 40 minutes.

Makes 1 loaf.

Rittenhouse Cheese Pie

2½ cups graham cracker crumbs
½ cup butter (1 stick), melted
1 teaspoon cinnamon
⅓ cup sugar

❖ ❖ ❖

12-ounce carton cottage cheese
18 ounces cream cheese
1½ cups sugar
4 eggs, beaten
1 teaspoon vanilla extract (or
   almond extract)
1 tablespoon lemon peel (optional)
⅓ cup lemon juice

❖ ❖ ❖

½ pint heavy cream
1 pint sour cream
3 tablespoons sugar

Combine the graham cracker crumbs, melted butter, cinnamon, and ⅓ cup sugar for a crust. Pat into 2 9-inch pie pans. Bake in a 400° oven for 5 minutes. Cool.

Press the cottage cheese through a sieve and add cream cheese, 1½ cups sugar, eggs, vanilla, lemon peel if desired, and lemon juice. Whip until stiff, pour into prepared crust. Bake in a 350° oven for 45 minutes or until done. Cool.

Whip the cream until stiff. Fold in sour cream and 3 tablespoons sugar. Spread over tops of pies and chill before serving.

Makes 2 9-inch pies.

The Stagecoach Inn: Bed and Breakfast

W61 N520 Washington Avenue
Cedarsburg, Wisconsin 53012
(414) 375-0208
(414) 375-3035

The Stagecoach Inn, housed in a restored 1853 stone building, is on the National Register of Historic Places and is decorated totally with antiques, although the comfortable rooms have modern conveniences. Each room is decorated with wall stenciling and Laura Ashley comforters and has a private bath and central air. A continental breakfast of hot croissants, juice, cereal, coffee, and herbal tea is included. The Stagecoach Pub is on the first floor of the inn, and many special house drinks are available. The pub serves as a pleasant gathering room for guests, and to enhance the warm coffee house feeling of the pub, many games are played in the evenings. Also located on the first floor are two specialty shops. Beerntsen Candy Shops offers an excellent selection of handmade chocolates, nuts, and hard candies. Inn Books carries a complete line of adult and children's books. Because of the historic restoration of the building, smoking is not allowed.

Stagecoach Sachet

Combine equal parts of rosemary, peppermint, lemon balm, sage, and wintergreen. Add small quantities of lavender, woodruff, and marjoram.

Mix well and place into a sachet pocket.

Lavender-Apple Jelly

6 pounds apples
1½ cups fresh or dried lavender
flowers
3 cups sugar (or honey)

Cut the apples into quarters. Place in a large ketttle and add flowers. Bring to a boil, lower heat, and simmer until apples are tender. Turn the apples and flowers into a jelly bag. Let drip into a large bowl overnight. Pour 3 cups of the strained apple-lavender juice into a large kettle and add sugar. Bring to a boil, then pour into sterilized canning jars, cool and seal tightly. It's great!

Makes 4 8-ounce glasses.

Chamomile Tea

1 cup hot water
1 to 1½ teaspoons dried chamomile
flowers
Honey to taste

Pour hot water over the flowers and steep for at least 5 minutes. Strain and sweeten to taste.

Serves 1.

The Washington House Inn

Corner of Washington and Center
W62 N573 Washington Avenue
Cedarsburg, Wisconsin 53012
(414) 375-3550

The atmosphere of Victorian days comes alive in the Washington House Inn. A collection of antique furniture, a marble-trimmed fireplace and fresh cut flowers offer guests a warm reception, and the rooms are comfortable, yet elegant, featuring cozy down quilts and flowers. In the late afternoon guests relax in front of a cheery fire and socialize with others prior to dining at one of the excellent Cedarsburg restaurants. Each morning continental breakfast is served in the warmth of the gathering room. Homemade muffins, cakes, and breads are baked in the kitchen using recipes from an authentic turn-of-the-century Cedarsburg cookbook; fresh fruit, cereal, freshly squeezed juices, and a fine selection of tea and coffee are served as well. The Washington House is on the listing of National Register of Historic Places.

❖ ❖ ❖ ❖ ❖ ❖

The Washington House Inn

Cherry Buns

½ cup milk
¼ cup butter (½ stick)
2 tablespoons water
1 cup all-purpose flour
¼ cup sugar
½ teaspoon salt
1 ¼-ounce package active dry yeast
1 egg
½ cup to 2 cups all-purpose flour

❖ ❖ ❖

Cherry pie filling

Heat milk, butter, and water to 110°. In a large bowl mix 1 cup flour, sugar, salt, and yeast. Add the warm milk mixture; beat 2 minutes. Add the egg and ½ cup flour. Beat 2 minutes. By hand stir in enough flour to make a stiff dough. Knead 3 to 5 minutes until smooth. Place in a greased bowl, cover and let rise until double. Punch the dough down, let rest 10 minutes. Roll the dough to slightly less than ½-inch thick. Cut with a 2½-inch cutter. Place 2 inches apart on a greased baking sheet. Cover and let rise until light, about 45 minutes. Make a deep depression in buns, fill with cherry pie filling. Bake in a 375° oven about 15 minutes. Brush with melted butter.

Makes 18 buns.

Cherry Muffins

1 cup frozen or canned cherries, drained
2 cups all-purpose flour
4 teaspoons baking powder
¾ cup sugar
1 teaspoon salt
2 eggs
½ cup butter (1 stick), melted
1 cup milk

❖ ❖ ❖

¼ cup sugar
¼ to ½ teaspoon cinnamon

Cut cherries in ½. Combine the flour, baking powder, ¾ cup sugar, and salt in a mixing bowl. Stir in the cherries until well-blended. In a small bowl beat the eggs, add the butter and milk. Stir into the flour mixture, just to blend. Fill muffin cups ¾ full. Sprinkle lightly with ¼ cup sugar and cinnamon to taste. Bake in a 400° oven about 15 minutes.

Makes 12 muffins.

Chocolate Nut Bread

3 1-ounce squares unsweetened chocolate
½ cup butter (1 stick), softened

❖ ❖ ❖

3 cups all-purpose flour
1 teaspoon baking powder
½ teaspoon baking soda
1 teaspoon salt

❖ ❖ ❖

1 cup sugar
2 eggs, slightly beaten
1 cup milk
2 teaspoons vanilla extract

½ cup chopped nuts

❖ ❖ ❖

1 cup confectioners' sugar
Milk

In a small saucepan melt chocolate and butter over low heat, stirring until smooth. Remove from heat, cool. Mix the flour, baking powder, soda, and salt. In a large bowl, beat the sugar, eggs, 1 cup of milk, and vanilla with a wooden spoon until blended. Stir in the dry ingredients until blended. Add the cooled chocolate mixture, stir until smooth. Fold in nuts. Divide the batter into 3 small greased and floured loaf pans. Bake in a 350° oven for 40 to 45 minutes. Cool in the pans on a rack 5 minutes. Remove from the pans to cool completely.

Make a glaze by combining confectioners' sugar and a small amount of milk. Drizzle over the tops of the loaves.

Makes 3 small loaves.

Red, White and Blue Tart

¼ cup butter (½ stick), softened
2 tablespoons sugar
Dash salt
½ teaspoon grated lemon peel
½ teaspoon vanilla extract
1 egg yolk
¾ cup all-purpose flour
¼ cup ground almonds

❖ ❖ ❖

2 teaspoons currant jelly
½ cup all-purpose flour
3 tablespoons sugar
¼ cup butter (½ stick), softened
½ teaspoon grated lemon peel
½ teaspoon almond extract
1 3-ounce package cream cheese, softened
1 egg

❖ ❖ ❖

1 21-ounce can blueberry pie filling
1 21-ounce can cherry pie filling

In a medium bowl combine ¼ cup butter, 2 tablespoons sugar, and salt. Beat at medium speed until fluffy. Add ½ teaspoon grated lemon peel, vanilla, and egg yolk; beat until smooth. Stir in ¾ cup of flour and almonds, blend well. Press the pastry into the bottom and sides of 10-inch tart pan. Bake in a 375° oven for 10 minutes, cool.

Brush baked pastry with currant jelly. In a medium bowl combine ½ cup of flour, 3 tablespoons sugar, ¼ cup butter, ½ teaspoon grated lemon peel, almond extract, cream cheese, and egg. Beat 1 minute at medium speed. Pour the filling over pastry. Bake in a 375° oven for about 20 minutes or until the center is set. Cool.

Arrange the blueberry and cherry pie filling on top as desired.

Serves 12.

Eagle Harbor Inn and Cottages

Post Office Box 72B
Ephraim, Wisconsin 54211
(414) 854-2121

A place where the gentle amenities of life are still observed, Eagle Harbor Inn is removed from the cares of the workaday world. Lake and shore, cedars and birch all combine to create a setting for tranquil relaxation. Family-owned and operated, it is near one of the world's great fresh water lakes; yet it is close to all those things for which Door County is famous: quaint antique and craft shops, excellent restaurants, remarkable art galleries, scenic paths and remote places for sunning, swimming, picnicking, fishing, golfing, and cross country skiing.

Oatmeal Orange Muffins

1 cup rolled oats
½ cup orange juice
½ cup boiling water

❖ ❖ ❖

⅓ cup butter
½ cup brown sugar, firmly packed
½ cup white sugar
2 eggs, beaten
1 teaspoon vanilla extract

❖ ❖ ❖

1 cup flour
1 teaspoon baking powder
1 teaspoon baking soda
1 teaspoon salt
1 cup raisins
1 tablespoon grated orange rind

Soak oats in a large bowl with orange juice and boiling water for 15 minutes. In a large mixing bowl cream butter and sugars. Beat in the eggs, vanilla, and oats mixture.

Measure into a separate bowl the flour, baking powder, soda, and salt; stir raisins and rind into flour mixture. Add to the wet mixture, stirring just until moist. Fill greased muffin cups and bake in a 350° oven for 20 minutes.

Makes 14 large muffins.

Strictly Wonderful Stew

3 pounds cubed beef chuck
1 tablespoon shortening
3 cups beef broth
2 cloves garlic, chopped
1 bay leaf
1 tablespoon salt
Few grains cayenne pepper

❖ ❖ ❖

4 potatoes, cubed
2 green peppers
3 tablespoons butter
2 tablespoons all-purpose flour
1 tablespoon paprika

❖ ❖ ❖

Broiled tomatoes

Brown beef in shortening. Add the beef broth, garlic, bay leaf, salt, and cayenne pepper. Cover tightly and cook until the meat is tender. Cook slowly for 30 minutes. Add potatoes and cook for 5 minutes. Add peppers that are cut in broad rings and cook 5 more minutes. Mix butter with flour and paprika to make a smooth paste and stir into meat mixture. Cook 2 more minutes. Serve with broiled tomatoes.

Serves 8 to 10.

Apple Pie Bread

3 cups white all-purpose flour
1 cup sugar
4 teaspoons baking powder
1 teaspoon salt
½ teaspoon ground cardamon
1 teaspoon cinnamon
1 teaspoon ground cloves
1½ cups milk
1 egg, beaten
2 tablespoons oil
1½ cups green apples, unpeeled and diced

In a medium bowl, sift together dry ingredients. In large bowl, mix together milk, egg, and oil. Gradually stir in dry ingredients until well mixed. Fold in apples. Pour into a 9x5x3-inch greased loaf pan and bake in a 350° oven for 1 hour and 20 minutes or until toothpick inserted in center comes out clean.

Makes 1 loaf.

Blueberry Bread with Orange Glaze

2 tablespoons butter
¼ cup boiling water
½ cup orange juice
3 tablespoons grated orange rind
1 egg
1 cup sugar
2 cups sifted all-purpose flour
1 teaspoon baking powder
¼ teaspoon baking soda
½ teaspoon salt
1 cup blueberries

❖ ❖ ❖

2 tablespoons orange juice
1 tablespoon grated orange rind
2 tablespoons honey

Melt butter in boiling water in a small bowl. Add ½ cup orange juice and 3 tablespoons grated orange rind. Beat the egg with sugar until light and fluffy. Add sifted dry ingredients alternately with orange liquid until smooth. Fold in blueberries. Pour batter into a greased loaf pan. Bake in a 325° oven for 1 hour and 10 minutes. Cool 10 minutes and remove from pan onto a rack. Prepare a glaze by combining 2 tablespoons of orange juice, 1 tablespoon of grated orange rind, and honey. Pour over loaf.

Makes 1 loaf.

Cherry Bread

1 cup sugar
2 eggs, beaten
2 cups sifted all-purpose flour
1 cup milk

❖ ❖ ❖

1 cup sifted all-purpose flour
4 teaspoons baking powder
1 teaspoon salt
1 8-ounce jar maraschino cherries, drained and chopped
2 tablespoons butter, melted

Add the sugar to eggs in a mixing bowl; beat well. Mix in 2 cups of flour, adding alternately with the milk. Combine 1 cup of flour, baking powder, and salt; stir into batter. Add cherries and butter, mix well. Pour into a greased and floured loaf pan. Bake in a 350° oven for 1 hour.

Makes 1 loaf.

Chocolate Zucchini Bread

2½ cups all-purpose flour
½ cup cocoa
2½ teaspoons baking powder
1½ teaspoons baking soda
½ teaspoon salt
1 teaspoon cinnamon

❖   ❖   ❖

¾ cup butter (1½ sticks)
2 cups sugar

❖   ❖   ❖

3 eggs
2 teaspoons vanilla extract
2 cups grated zucchini
½ cup milk
1 cup nuts

Sift together the dry ingredients. In a mixing bowl cream together the butter and sugar. In a separate bowl, mix together the eggs, vanilla, zucchini, milk, and nuts. Alternate combining the wet and dry ingredients with the creamed mixture. Spread batter into 2 greased loaf pans. Bake in a 350° oven for 1 hour.
Makes 2 loaves.

Hobo Bread

1 cup raisins
2 teaspoons baking soda
1 cup boiling water

❖   ❖   ❖

1 cup sugar
¼ cup oil
1 egg
1¼ cups all-purpose flour
1 cup 40% bran flakes
Chopped nuts (optional)

Cook the raisins, soda and boiling water together. Cool. In a mixing bowl combine the sugar, oil, and egg together. Add the flour and bran flakes. Chopped nuts may be added, if desired. Add the cooled raisin mixture. Pour into greased tin cans and bake in a 350° oven for 50 minutes.
Makes 1 loaf.

Mandel Bread

3 eggs
1 cup oil
1 teaspoon lemon juice
1 teaspoon vanilla extract
3 cups all-purpose flour
1 cup sugar
1 teaspoon baking powder
1 cup mini-chocolate chips (optional)
1 cup chopped walnuts (optional)

In a mixing bowl combine the eggs, oil, and lemon juice; beat well. Add the remaining ingredients, including chocolate chips and walnuts if desired. Shape into long strips and place on a greased cookie sheet. Bake in a 350° oven for 40 to 50 minutes.
When golden brown, remove from the oven and cut at an angle while still hot. Return to the cookie sheet and toast each side under the broiler.
Makes 2 loaves.

Egg Pasta Dough

4 eggs
2 cups all-purpose flour
4 tablespoons cold water
2 cups all-purpose flour (approximately)

Break eggs into the center of 2 cups of flour. Add water; with wire whisk beat until very smooth. Add approximately 2 more cups of flour and work with your hands into a soft dough. If the dough seems sticky, add more flour. Turn dough onto a kneading surface and knead for at least 10 minutes. Put the dough back into the bowl, cover and let rest for 30 minutes. Roll the dough into desired thickness and shapes to make lasagna, fettuccine, etc., or use a pasta machine.
Serves 2.

Fettuccine Romana

12 ounces fettuccine
⅔ cup heavy cream
½ cup butter (1 stick), softened

⅔ cup grated Parmesan cheese
½ pound thinly sliced Prosciutto or boiled ham
¾ cup cooked green peas
½ teaspoon black pepper

Cook the fettuccine in boiling water until al dente. While the fettuccine is cooking, heat the cream. Drain the fettuccine and return to saucepan. Quickly add butter and cheese. Add hot cream, ham, and peas. Toss again. Add pepper and serve at once!
Serves 4.

Beef Burgundy with Rice

5 medium onions, thinly sliced
2 tablespoons shortening

❖   ❖   ❖

2 pounds beef chuck, cut into bite size cubes
2 tablespoons all-purpose flour
2 tablespoons thyme
2 tablespoons marjoram
½ cup beef bouillon
1 cup dry red wine

❖   ❖   ❖

½ pound fresh sliced mushrooms
4 cups hot cooked rice

In a heavy fry pan, cook onions in shortening until golden brown; remove onions from pan. Add beef cubes and brown well. Sprinkle beef with flour and seasonings. Stir in bouillon and wine. Simmer slowly for 3 hours or until meat is tender. If necessary add more bouillon and wine, (one part bouillon to 2 parts wine). Keep beef barely covered with liquid. Return onions to pan, add mushrooms. Cook 30 minutes. Serve over hot rice.
Serves 6 to 8.

Chinese Pepper Steak

2 pounds round steak, cut in long thin strips

⅓ cup soy sauce
1 teaspoon sugar

❖   ❖   ❖

¼ cup olive or peanut oil
2 cloves garlic
¾ teaspoon ginger
2 green peppers, cut in long thin
   strips

❖   ❖   ❖

1 tablespoon cornstarch
2 tablespoons soy sauce
½ cup water

❖   ❖   ❖

3 large tomatoes, quartered

❖   ❖   ❖

2 cups hot cooked rice

Marinate round steak overnight in ⅓ cup soy sauce and sugar.

In a frypan heat oil and sauté garlic, ginger, and green pepper for 3 minutes. Add the steak and marinade, and sauté 3 more minutes. Remove garlic. Blend together the cornstarch, 2 tablespoons soy sauce, and water and add to frypan. Add tomatoes and cook 10 more minutes. Serve over hot rice.

Serves 6 to 8.

Rick's Baked Mostaccioli

1 pound mostaccioli
6 quarts boiling water
1 teaspoon salt

❖   ❖   ❖

4 to 5 cups spaghetti sauce
1 pound grated Mozzarella cheese
½ cup grated Parmesan cheese

Cook the mostaccioli in boiling water with salt until al dente, then drain. Spread a portion of spaghetti sauce in the bottom of a 9x13-inch casserole. Layer ¼ of the mostaccioli, Mozzarella cheese, spaghetti sauce, and Parmesan cheese. Repeat this 2 or 3 times. Finish with a top layer of Parmesan cheese. Bake in a 350° oven for 30 to 45 minutes. Cut like lasagna.

Serves 4 to 5.

Shepherd's Pie

1 pound ground beef
1 onion, chopped
Salt and pepper to taste
1 clove garlic, minced

❖   ❖   ❖

4 large baking potatoes
½ cup milk
¼ cup butter (½ stick)
½ cup grated Cheddar cheese

❖   ❖   ❖

1 10-ounce package frozen mixed
   vegetables, thawed

Brown the ground beef in a frypan with onion, salt, pepper, and garlic. Drain and set aside.

In a saucepan boil the potatoes until tender. Add milk, butter, and cheese; mash. Place the ground beef mixture in the bottom of a 2-quart casserole dish. Add vegetables; top with potatoes. Bake in a 375° oven for 15 to 25 minutes until the top is light brown.

Serves 8 to 10.

Tam Tam

4 strips bacon, chopped
1 large onion, chopped

❖   ❖   ❖

4 pounds ground beef
2 29-ounce cans whole tomatoes,
   chopped
1 10¾-ounce can tomato soup
2 tablespoons sugar
2 tablespoons Worcestershire sauce
2 teaspoons salt
1 teaspoon pepper

❖   ❖   ❖

3 16-ounce cans red kidney beans

Sauté the bacon. Add the onion and cook until golden brown. In another deep pan brown the ground beef; drain. Add the bacon and onion that has not been drained. Add the tomatoes, soup, sugar, and seasonings. Simmer at least 1 hour.

Add the kidney beans and cook an additional 30 minutes. Serve with hot buttered bread as you would chili. Delicious in the winter.

Serves 10 to 12.

Fresh Apple Fritters

1⅓ cups all-purpose flour
2 tablespoons sugar
2 teaspoons baking powder
½ teaspoon salt
¼ teaspoon nutmeg

❖   ❖   ❖

⅔ cup milk
2 beaten eggs
1 tablespoon oil
3 cups chopped apples

❖   ❖   ❖

Cinnamon and sugar

Sift all dry ingredients. In a mixing bowl blend milk, eggs, and salad oil. Add dry ingredients all at once. Mix until moistened. Stir in apples. Drop by tablespoonfuls into deep fat heated to 375°. Fry until golden brown and puffy. Turn to fry other side. Frying time is about 3 to 4 minutes. Drain and roll in a mixture of cinnamon and sugar.

Makes 12 fritters.

French Doughnuts

5 tablespoons butter
½ cup sugar
1 egg, beaten
½ cup milk
1½ cups all-purpose flour
1 teaspoon salt
1 teaspoon nutmeg

❖   ❖   ❖

6 tablespoons butter, melted
¾ cup sugar
2 teaspoons cinnamon

In a mixing bowl cream 5 tablespoons of butter and ½ cup of sugar; add egg and mix well. Add milk to the mixture alternately with dry ingredients. Fill greased muffin cups to ½ full. Bake in a 350° oven for 20 to 25 minutes.

While the muffins are hot, roll first in melted butter and then in a mixture of ¾ cup of sugar and cinnamon.

Makes 12 doughnuts.

Jelly Doughnuts

3 eggs
6 egg yolks
1 cup sugar
½ cup butter (1 stick), melted
Grated rind of 1 orange
1 teaspoon salt
½ cup cream, warm
½ cup milk
2 cups all-purpose flour
2 ³/₅-ounce cakes compressed yeast
1 tablespoon milk, warm
Lard

❖ ❖ ❖

Confectioners' sugar
Jelly

In a mixing bowl beat eggs, yolks, and sugar. Add cooled melted butter and beat thoroughly. Add orange rind, salt, cream, and milk; beat well. Add flour gradually and continue to beat. Dissolve the yeast in 1 tablespoon of warm milk. Add to the batter and mix thoroughly. Beat dough about 15 minutes. Place dough in a greased bowl and let rise until double, about 2 hours. Punch down and roll out ¼-inch thick on a floured pastry cloth. Cover and let rise 40 minutes. Cut with a glass dipped in flour. Fry in hot lard until brown, then turn to brown other side. Drain and cool.

Roll doughnuts in confectioners' sugar, then make a slit and fill with jelly.

Makes 1½ dozen.

Potato Doughnuts

1 teaspoon salt
¼ teaspoon nutmeg
½ teaspoon cinnamon
¼ cup shortening
1 cup sugar
2 eggs
¾ cup unseasoned mashed
    potatoes, cold
3½ cups all-purpose flour
4 teaspoons baking powder
¾ cup milk

In a mixing bowl combine salt, nutmeg, cinnamon, shortening, sugar, and eggs with potatoes and mix well.

Add the flour and baking powder, gradually blending in the milk to make a dough. Roll out dough in ½-inch thick slices and cut with a doughnut cutter. Fry 2 minutes on each side. Dough can be refrigerated and used at your convenience.

Makes 2 dozen.

Ricotta Doughnuts

3 eggs
2 tablespoons sugar
4 teaspoons baking powder
1 pound ricotta cheese
1 cup all-purpose flour
¼ teaspoon salt

❖ ❖ ❖

Confectioners' sugar

Beat eggs until fluffy; add sugar, baking powder and cheese, mix well. Add flour and salt; stir well. Drop by teaspoonfuls into fat heated to 375°. Fry for 2 to 3 minutes. Remove from fat with a slotted spoon. Drain on paper towel. Sprinkle with confectioners' sugar. Serve warm.

Makes 1½ dozen.

Almond Macaroons

1 8-ounce can almond paste
1¼ cups sugar
2 egg whites

Cut almond paste in small pieces. Add sugar and egg whites. Mix until smooth. Place drops of the mixture the size of a quarter on waxed paper-lined baking sheets. Bake in a 325° oven for 30 minutes. After baking allow to cool, then wet back of paper to remove cookies.

Makes 2 dozen.

Angel Wings

½ teaspoon salt
6 egg yolks
6 tablespoons sugar
1 tablespoon rum

½ pint sour cream
2 cups cake flour

❖ ❖ ❖

Confectioners' sugar

In a mixing bowl add salt to egg yolks and beat until thick and lemon colored. Add sugar and rum; continue to beat. Add sour cream and cake flour alternately, mixing well after each addition. Knead on a cake-floured board until the dough blisters. Cut in ½, roll very thin and cut into strips 4 inches long. Slit each piece in the center and pull one end through slit. Fry in hot fat until lightly browned. Drain on a paper towel and sprinkle with confectioners' sugar.

Makes 2 dozen.

Cherry Bars

2 cups all-purpose flour
½ cup confectioners' sugar
1 cup butter (2 sticks)

❖ ❖ ❖

½ cup all-purpose flour
1½ cups sugar
1 teaspoon baking powder
Pinch salt
2 eggs, beaten
1 cup cherries, fresh or frozen
1 cup coconut
1 cup chopped nuts

Combine 2 cups of flour and confectioners' sugar, cut in the butter. Mix well and press into the bottom of a 9x13-inch cake pan. Bake in a 350° oven for 10 minutes. Combine ½ cup flour, sugar, baking powder, salt, and eggs and mix well. Stir in the cherries, coconut, and nuts. Spread over the top of crust. Bake for an additional 35 minutes. Cool completely, then slice crosswise into 6 strips. Cut each strip into 4 pieces.

Makes 2 dozen bars.

Date Bars

1 13-ounce package chopped pitted
    dates
1 cup brown sugar, firmly packed

1 cup water

❖   ❖   ❖

2 cups sifted all-purpose flour
1½ cups rolled oats
1 cup brown sugar, firmly packed
1 teaspoon baking soda
¼ teaspoon salt
¾ cup shortening

Place the dates, 1 cup of brown sugar, and water in a medium saucepan. Boil until thick, stirring occasionally. Set aside.

In a mixing bowl combine the flour, oats, 1 cup of brown sugar, soda, and salt. Stir to blend well. Cut in the shortening until the mixture resembles coarse crumbs. Pat ½ of this mixture into the bottom of a 9-inch square pan. Spread the date mixture in a layer over this. Layer the remaining oat mixture over the top. Bake in a 350° oven for 30 minutes.

When completely cooled, cut into 1½-inch strips one way. Divide the strips into 3 sections.

Makes 18 bars.

Italian Pastry Cookies

2 ³/₅-ounce cakes compressed yeast
½ cup lukewarm milk (85°)
2 teaspoons sugar
2 teaspoon vanilla extract
1 teaspoon almond extract
1 cup butter (2 sticks)
1 cup shortening
5 cups sifted all-purpose flour
2 egg, slightly beaten
Confectioners' sugar

Crumble the yeast in milk. Stir until dissolved. Add the sugar, vanilla, and almond extract.

In a mixing bowl cut butter and shortening into the flour until mixture resembles fine bread crumbs. Add the yeast mixture to flour mixture. Stir in eggs. Knead dough lightly in the bowl. Grease the top, cover, and let rise about 1 hour. Sprinkle confectioners' sugar on pastry cloth. Roll 1 teaspoon dough at a time into a rope about 8

inches long. Shape each dough rope into a figure 8 and place on an ungreased cookie sheet. Bake in a 375° oven for 15 minutes. Sprinkle with confectioners' sugar.

Makes 4 to 5 dozen.

Ruby Squares

1 cup all-purpose flour
1 teaspoon baking powder
¼ teaspoon salt
2 tablespoons butter
1 egg, beaten
1 tablespoon milk

❖   ❖   ❖

4 large apples, sliced
1 3-ounce package strawberry gelatin

❖   ❖   ❖

1 cup sugar
1 cup all-purpose flour
½ cup butter (1 stick)

Sift together 1 cup of flour, baking powder, and salt into a mixing bowl. Cut in 2 tablespoons of butter. Combine the egg and milk; add to dry ingredients. Mix well. Roll on a floured board into a large thin rectangle and press into the bottom and sides of a 7x11-inch pan. Fill with apple slices. Sprinkle gelatin powder on top.

Combine sugar and 1 cup of flour, cut in ½ cup of butter to make streusel topping. Sprinkle over gelatin powder. Bake in a 375° oven for 45 minutes.

Serves 12.

Amazin' Raisin Cake

3 cups all-purpose flour
2 cups sugar
1 cup mayonnaise
⅓ cup milk
2 eggs
2 teaspoons baking soda
½ teaspoon salt
1½ teaspoons cinnamon
½ teaspoon nutmeg
¼ teaspoon cloves

❖   ❖   ❖

3 cups chopped apples

1 cup seedless raisins
½ cup chopped walnuts

❖   ❖   ❖

Cream Cheese Frosting

In a large bowl combine the flour, sugar, mayonnaise, milk, eggs, soda, salt, and spices. Beat for 2 minutes at low speed, scraping bowl frequently (batter will be very thick). With a spoon stir in apples, raisins, and walnuts. Spoon the batter into 2 greased 9-inch round pans. Bake in a 350° oven for 45 minutes. Cool in pans for 10 minutes; then remove and finish cooling. Fill and frost with cream cheese frosting.

Makes 1 2-layer cake.

Cream Cheese Frosting

1 8-ounce package cream cheese, softened
1 1-pound box confectioners' sugar
½ cup butter (1 stick), softened
2 teaspoons vanilla extract

Cream together the cream cheese and sugar; add butter and vanilla. Blend together until smooth and of spreading consistency.

Frosts 1 cake.

Banana Split Delight

2 cups finely crushed vanilla wafers
⅓ cup butter, melted

❖   ❖   ❖

½ cup butter (1 stick), softened
2 eggs
1½ cups sifted confectioners' sugar

❖   ❖   ❖

¼ cup sugar
1 cup whipping cream
2 tablespoons cocoa

❖   ❖   ❖

1 cup chopped toasted almonds
2 ripe bananas, sliced
½ cup maraschino cherries

Combine the wafer crumbs and ⅓ cup melted butter. Press into an 8-inch square pan. Cream together ½ cup butter, eggs, and confectioners' sugar; beat well. Spread over the crumbs. Combine the sugar, whipping cream, and cocoa; whip until stiff. Fold in the almonds, bananas, and cherries. Pour topping over the filling. Chill 24 hours.

Serves 12.

Heath Candy Bar Cake

The easiest way to break the Heath bars is by placing them on a chopping board with the wrappers still on and rapping them with a hammer.

    2 cups all-purpose flour
    2 cups light brown sugar, firmly
        packed
    ½ cup butter (1 stick)
        ❖   ❖   ❖
    1 cup milk
    1 teaspoon baking soda
    1 teaspoon vanilla extract
        ❖   ❖   ❖
    6 Heath candy bars, broken in
        small pieces
    ½ cup chopped pecans

Combine flour and sugar in a mixing bowl, cut in butter. Set aside 1 cup of this mixture for topping. Add milk, soda, and vanilla into the mixing bowl; beat well. Pour into a greased 9x13-inch pan and sprinkle with the reserved topping, then candy bar pieces, and pecans. Bake in a 350° oven for 35 minutes.

Serves 12.

Regal Almond Cake

    1 cup butter (2 sticks)
    2 cups sugar
    2 teaspoons grated lemon rind
    1 teaspoon almond extract
    2 teaspoons vanilla extract
    4 egg yolks
    3¼ cups sifted cake flour
    4 teaspoons baking powder

    1½ cups milk
    4 egg whites
        ❖   ❖
    Almonds
    2 tablespoons sugar

Cream butter and 2 cups of sugar until light and fluffy. Add lemon rind, almond extract, vanilla, and egg yolks and beat until light and fluffy. Sift together cake flour and baking powder. Alternate mixing portions of flour and milk into cake batter, ending with milk. Beat egg whites until stiff; fold into cake batter. Grease a 10-inch tube pan with margarine, and generously sprinkle with almonds and 2 tablespoons sugar, then pour in batter. Bake in a 325° oven for 45 minutes.

Serves 12.

Strawberry Hill Bed and Breakfast

Route 1, Box 524-D
Green Lake, Wisconsin 54941
(414) 294-3450

Strawberry Hill is two miles from beautiful Green Lake and four miles from the American Baptist Conference Center. A full range of summer and winter recreation opportunities is available, including three golf courses within four miles. The nearby Fox

River is for both fishermen and boaters. Shoppers enjoy browsing in Berlin's famous fur and leather shops. The house is a large, comfortably furnished old farmhouse, fully air-conditioned. Four guest rooms, each with a view of Wisconsin's rolling farm lands, share two full baths. A hearty breakfast is served in the pleasant dining room, and guests are invited to relax in the paneled sitting room or enjoy a variety of table games and puzzles in the solar room. No pets or children under the age of twelve are welcome. No smoking is permitted.

Bauernfruhstuck— Farmer's Breakfast

    6 slices bacon, cut in small strips
    1 small green pepper, diced
    2 tablespoons minced onion
    3 large boiled potatoes, cubed
    Salt and pepper to taste
    6 eggs, unbeaten
    ½ cup grated cheese

In a large skillet fry the bacon over low heat only until lightly brown. Drain all but 3 tablespoons of fat. To the bacon and fat add the green pepper, onion, potatoes, salt, and pepper. Cook over medium heat about 5 minutes to turn potatoes golden. Stir frequently. Add the unbeaten eggs all at once; cook and stir over low heat until the eggs are set. Sprinkle cheese over potatoes and stir.

Serves 6.

Strawberry Daiquiri

This is the house specialty with which all breakfasts at Strawberry Hill begin.

    1 cup fresh strawberries
    2 tablespoons frozen limeade
        concentrate
    1 cup crushed ice
    1 to 2 1-ounce jiggers white rum
    2 tablespoons sugar

In a blender, combine the strawberries, limeade concentrate, crushed ice, rum, and sugar. Blend until smooth and thick.

Serves 2.

The Manor House

6536 3rd Avenue
Kenosha, Wisconsin 53140
(414) 658-0014

Listed in the National Register of Historic Places, the Manor House is a stately, sixty-year-old Georgian mansion overlooking Lake Michigan. Completely redecorated and refurnished with eighteenth century antiques and accessories, it boasts large, airy rooms, beautiful wood paneling, leaded glass windows, and a grand piano. Formal gardens, including a sunken lily pool with a fountain, and a gazebo, beckon summer guests for sunning or a leisurely stroll. Across the street, Kemper Center, a park and cultural activities facility, boasts tennis courts, a handicapped accessible fishing pier, and an art gallery where local artists work and exhibit. Swimming, charter fishing, boating, golfing and skiing are nearby. Gourmet lunches and dinners, or a box lunch for picnicking at Kemper Center are available at extra charge.

Quick Crescent Rolls

1 ¼-ounce package active dry yeast
1 cup warm water (110-115°)
¾ cup evaporated milk
⅓ cup sugar
1½ teaspoons salt
1 egg
1 cup all-purpose flour

¼ cup butter (½ stick), melted and cooled

❖ ❖ ❖

1 cup firm butter (2 sticks)
4 cups all-purpose flour

❖ ❖ ❖

1 egg
1 tablespoon water

In a large bowl let the yeast soften in 1 cup warm water. Add the evaporated milk, sugar, salt, 1 egg, and 1 cup of flour. Beat to a smooth batter. Add ¼ cup melted butter. In a large bowl or food processor cup, cut 1 cup firm butter into 4 cups of flour until mixture is the size of small lima beans. Pour the yeast batter over flour mixture and fold in until all the flour is moistened. Cover with plastic wrap and refrigerate 2 hours to 2 days.

Remove dough to a floured surface; knead 6 to 10 times to release the air bubbles. Divide into 4 parts. Roll each section into a 16-inch circle. Cut into 8 to 10 pie-shaped wedges. Roll each wedge toward the point; curve into crescent. Place on an ungreased baking sheet, allowing space for rising. Let rise in a draft-free place until almost double (2 to 4 hours). Brush lightly with 1 egg mixed with 1 tablespoon of water. Bake in a 325° oven for 25 to 35 minutes or until lightly browned.

Makes 2 dozen.

The Duke Guest House: Bed and Breakfast

618 Maiden Street
Mineral Point, Wisconsin 53565
(608) 987-2821

In colonial America the pineapple symbolized a hearty welcome and gracious hospitality, and the Duke House has appropriately adopted this symbol. Afternoon refreshments and cool drinks are served between 6:00 and 7:00 P.M. A full breakfast is served featuring coffeecake, muffins, tea biscuits and scones.

Cheese Coffee Cake

1 ¼-ounce package active dry yeast
¼ cup warm water (110 to 115°)

❖ ❖ ❖

½ cup scalded milk, cooled
2 teaspoons sugar
2 egg yolks, lightly beaten
1 teaspoon vanilla extract

❖ ❖ ❖

2½ cups all-purpose flour
½ teaspoon salt
½ cup margarine (1 stick)

❖ ❖ ❖

2 3-ounce packages cream cheese, softened
¾ cup sugar
1 teaspoon vanilla extract
1 teaspoon lemon juice
2 egg whites

❖ ❖ ❖

¾ cup all-purpose flour
¼ cup margarine (½ stick)
¼ cup sugar

Dissolve the yeast in warm water. Combine the milk, 2 teaspoons of sugar, egg yolks, yeast mixture, and 1 teaspoon of vanilla.

Place in a mixing bowl 2½ cups of flour and the salt. Cut in ½ cup of margarine to form fine crumbs. Add in the liquid mixture, mixing until smooth. Wrap the dough in waxed paper and refrigerate overnight.

About 2 hours before serving time take the dough out of the refrigerator. Roll the dough on a floured surface into 2 rectangles and place on 2 separate cookie sheets. Allow to stand for 1 hour.

Beat lightly the egg whites; brush the dough with the mixture. Combine the cream cheese, ¾ cup of sugar, 1 teaspoon of vanilla, and lemon juice; beat until smooth. Spread the mixture down the center of the crusts. Fold the crusts, ends first and then sides. Brush with the egg whites.

Make a streusel topping by combining ¾ cup of flour, ¼ cup of margarine, and ¼ cup of sugar. Sprinkle over the coffee cakes. Bake in a 375° oven for 30 minutes.

Serves 6 to 8.

Plum Bread

½ cup butter (1 stick), softened
1 cup sugar
½ teaspoon vanilla extract
2 eggs
1½ cups all-purpose flour
½ teaspoon salt
½ teaspoon cream of tartar
¼ teaspoon baking soda
⅓ cup plain yogurt
½ teaspoon grated lemon peel
1 cup diced plums
½ cup chopped walnuts

Cream together the butter, sugar, and vanilla until fluffy. Add the eggs one at a time; beat after each addition. Into a mixing bowl, sift the flour, salt, cream of tartar, and soda. Blend yogurt and lemon peel, add to creamed mixture, alternately with dry ingredients. Stir until well-blended. Add plums and walnuts; mix well. Pour into a greased loaf pan. Bake in a 350° oven for 50 to 55 minutes.

Makes 1 loaf.

Halfway House

Route 2, Box 80
Oxford, Wisconsin 53952
(608) 586-5489

Named Halfway House in the 1800s when it was a stage station on the old logging road from Portage to Stevens Point, the inn was remodeled in 1961. Surrounded by a large lawn, flower beds, and flowering trees, Halfway House is on a working farm with Herefords grazing the meadows, and wild

The Duke Guest House

game, deer, fox, badger, and many birds abounding.

The house is full of Wisconsin wildlife art and artifacts from Africa, as the innkeepers have traveled extensively through Canada, Mexico, Africa, Holland, Wales, and England. The Halfway House is close to lakes, golf courses, snowmobile trails, and downhill and cross country skiing. Its four bedrooms share one bath. Children and pets cannot be accommodated. Smoking is not permitted.

Corned Beef Egg Patties

1 12-ounce can corned beef
⅓ cup minced celery
2 tablespoons minced green onion
1 egg
½ teaspoon salt

❖ ❖ ❖

1 tablespoon oil

❖ ❖ ❖

4 eggs

❖ ❖ ❖

2 English muffins, split

In a bowl combine the corned beef, celery, green onion, 1 egg, and salt; mix well. Shape into four patties. In a skillet over low heat fry the patties in oil for 10 minutes; turning once. With a spoon make an indentation in each patty and break an egg into the hollow. Cover the skillet and cook 10 to 15 minutes until the eggs are done. Place on muffin halves.

Serves 4.

Festive Egg Squares

1 pound bulk pork sausage, cooked
and drained
4 ounces mushrooms, sliced
½ cup sliced green onions
2 medium tomatoes, chopped
2 cups shredded Mozzarella cheese

❖ ❖ ❖

1¼ cups buttermilk baking mix
12 eggs
1 cup milk
1½ teaspoons salt
½ teaspoon pepper
½ teaspoon oregano

Layer the sausage, mushrooms, green

onions, tomatoes, and cheese in a greased 13x9x2-inch baking dish. Beat together the remaining ingredients; pour over sausage mixture. Cook uncovered in a 350° oven until golden brown and set, about 30 minutes. Cut into 12 3-inch squares.

Serves 12.

Blueberry Buckle

2 cups all-purpose flour
½ teaspoon salt
3 teaspoons baking powder
½ cup shortening
½ cup sugar
1 egg, beaten
½ cup milk

❖ ❖ ❖

2 teaspoons lemon juice
2 cups fresh blueberries (or canned, well-drained)

❖ ❖ ❖

⅓ cup sugar
⅓ cup all-purpose flour
½ teaspoon cinnamon
¼ cup butter (½ stick)

Sift 2 cups of flour, measure and resift 3 times with salt and baking powder. Cream the shortening and ½ cup of sugar until soft and smooth. Add the egg and beat until light and fluffy. Add milk and dry ingredients, alternately in three portions, beating well after each. Line a 9-inch square cake pan with waxed paper and pour in the batter. Add lemon juice to the blueberries and scatter over the batter. Combine ⅓ cup of sugar, ⅓ cup of flour, and cinnamon. Add the butter and work together with fingers to a crumbly mass; sprinkle over the top of blueberries. Bake in a 350° oven for 1 hour or until the cake tests done. Serve slightly warm.

Serves 9.

The Renaissance Inn

414 Maple Drive
Sister Bay, Wisconsin 54234
(414) 854-5107

The Renaissance Inn is in a residential area, within walking distance of shops, galleries, boat docks, and the public beach. It has a parlor and five small bedrooms, all with private baths. Each room is decorated differently with European furniture and Renaissance art. The Renaissance features a five-course breakfast, which is included with the room. Evening meals feature seafoods such as oysters, clams, shrimp, and fresh fish of the day, as well as boiled gulf shrimp, steamed crab legs, and charbroiled prime rib.

Cheddar and Vegetable Omelet

¾ cup chopped fresh vegetables
2 tablespoons butter

❖ ❖ ❖

9 eggs
½ cup plain yogurt
½ cup milk
½ teaspoon salt
½ teaspoon basil

❖ ❖ ❖

6 ounces Cheddar cheese, grated

Sauté the vegetables in butter for a few minutes, then drain and place in a 9-inch pie pan. Whisk the eggs, yogurt, milk, salt, and basil in a blender. Pour over the vegetables and sprinkle with cheese. Bake in a 325° oven for 35 minutes. Let sit 5 minutes and serve.

Serves 4 to 6.

Clams Renaissance

75 fresh cherrystone clams (or canned chopped clams)
1 medium onion
4 cloves garlic
½ cup chopped green peppers

❖ ❖ ❖

1 cup dry bread crumbs
1 tablespoon ground basil
2 tablespoons seasoned salt
1 tablespoon Worcestershire sauce
¼ cup chopped parsley

❖ ❖ ❖

4 to 6 cooked bacon slices, crumbled

Drain and reserve the liquid from the clams. Finely grind the onion, clams, garlic, and green peppers.

Prepare a Velouté sauce (a classic white sauce using stock instead of milk) using the reserved clam liquid.

Combine the ground clams and vegetables with the bread crumbs and seasonings. Add in Velouté sauce to the desired moistness, mix well. Place in a 13x9-inch casserole. Top with bacon crumbs. Place in a 350° oven until thoroughly heated, about 15 minutes.

Serves 12 to 15.

Fruit 'n' Pudding

1 15¼-ounce can pineapple chunks, drain and reserve juice
1 3-ounce package vanilla instant pudding mix
1 16-ounce can fruit cocktail, drained

❖ ❖ ❖

2 medium bananas, sliced
½ cup fresh blueberries or strawberries

Add enough cold water to the reserved pineapple juice to make 1 cup, mix well with the pudding. Add the fruit cocktail and pineapple (may be done the night before). Before serving, add the fresh fruit.

Serves 4.

Wyoming

Paradise Guest Ranch

Post Office Box 790
Buffalo, Wyoming 82834
(307) 684-7876

The Paradise Guest Ranch is "roughing it" in luxury. The decor of the eighteen beautifully appointed log cabins is rustic and cozy, but with modern conveniences and a fireplace. The main lodge offers a dining room, recreation hall, enclosed whirlpool spa, and heated outdoor pool. There are no televisions, no video games, and no radios. Guests enjoy sing-a-longs, square dances, and chuckwagon dinners in the surroundings of a million acres of national forest. From one-day rides on horseback to the four-day pack trip at the wilderness fishing camp, guests enjoy adventure in the natural settings of the Big Horn National Forest. Youngsters and adults alike are welcome to join the ranch activities, including the ranch rodeo on Saturday afternoon.

Chicken Wings Appetizer

3 pounds chicken wings
⅓ cup soy sauce
2 tablespoons oil
2 tablespoons chili sauce
1 tablespoon Sherry
½ cup honey
2 tablespoons salt
½ teaspoon ginger
1 clove garlic
4 drops Tabasco

Prepare the chicken wings by removing tips; wash and dry. Combine all the ingredients in a 9x13-inch casserole dish. Marinate overnight. Bake uncovered in a 350° oven for 30 to 40 minutes.

Serves 21 to 24.

Apricot Bread

1½ cups dried apricots
Flour for dredging
2¾ cups all-purpose flour
5 teaspoons baking powder
½ teaspoon salt
½ teaspoon baking soda
¾ cup sugar
1 cup buttermilk
1 egg, beaten
1 tablespoon butter, melted
½ cup chopped pecans

Cook apricots according to directions on package; cut in thin strips and dredge in flour. Set aside. Sift dry ingredients together; Add buttermilk mixed with egg. Add butter; fold in pecans and apricots. Bake in a 9x5-inch greased loaf pan for 1 hour in a 350° oven.

Makes 1 loaf.

❖ ❖ ❖ ❖ ❖ ❖

Apple Fritters

1 cup all-purpose flour
1 teaspoon salt
1 teaspoon baking powder
2 teaspoons sugar
2 eggs, beaten
½ cup milk
1 teaspoon oil
1 teaspoon vanilla extract
4 medium cooking apples

❖ ❖ ❖

1½ cups sifted confectioners' sugar
⅛ teaspoon salt
3½ tablespoons milk
1 teaspoon vanilla extract
1 tablespoon butter

In a mixing bowl combine the flour, 1 teaspoon salt, baking powder, and sugar. In another bowl combine the eggs, ½ cup of milk, oil, and 1 teaspoon of vanilla. Add to the dry ingredients and mix well. Peel and slice each apple into 8 wedges. Dip into the batter and fry in hot oil (375°) until golden brown. Drain on paper towels.

Prepare a glaze by combining confectioners' sugar, ⅛ teaspoon of salt, 3½ tablespoons of milk, 1 teaspoon of vanilla, and butter. Coat the fritters with the glaze and serve hot.

Makes 8 fritters.

Jumbo Raisin Cookies

2 cups raisins
1 cup water

❖ ❖ ❖

1 cup shortening

2 cups sugar
3 eggs
1 teaspoon vanilla extract

❖   ❖   ❖

4 cups all-purpose flour
1 teaspoon soda
1½ teaspoons cinnamon
½ teaspoon nutmeg

❖   ❖   ❖

½ cup chopped nuts

Cook raisins and water for 5 minutes and drain, reserving liquid. Cream shortening, sugar, eggs, and vanilla. Add dry ingredients with ½ cup juice drained from raisins. Stir in the raisins and nuts. Bake in a 375° oven for 12 to 15 minutes.

Makes about 6 dozen.

South Fork Inn

Post Office Box 854
Buffalo, Wyoming 82834

The South Fork Inn is open year round, but only on Friday through Sunday in the winter. The inn is in the process of developing a cross country ski trail system that starts at its cabin doors. In the Bighorn Mountains summer is a beautiful time, ideal for fishing, hiking, horseback riding, and star gazing.

Spicy Orange Bran Muffins

1½ cups bran
1¾ cups buttermilk

❖   ❖   ❖

1¼ cups wheat flour
1 teaspoon baking powder
½ teaspoon baking soda
2 teaspoons cinnamon
½ cup raisins
2 tablespoons grated orange peel

❖   ❖   ❖

1 egg
¼ cup brown sugar, lightly packed
¼ cup corn oil
2 tablespoons molasses
2 tablespoons honey

Combine bran and buttermilk. Let stand for 5 to 10 minutes.

In a medium bowl combine flour, baking powder, soda, cinnamon, raisins, and orange peel. In a large bowl beat egg lightly. Stir in brown sugar, oil, molasses, and honey. Stir in bran. Add dry ingredients. Fill greased muffin cups ¾ full and bake in a 375° oven for 20 minutes. Serve warm.

This recipe doubles nicely.

Serves 12.

Chocolate Pecan Pie

½ cup semi-sweet chocolate chips
1 unbaked 9-inch pie shell
3 eggs
¾ cup dark corn syrup
½ cup sugar
¼ teaspoon salt
¼ cup butter (½ stick), melted
2 tablespoons vanilla extract
1 cup pecan halves

❖   ❖   ❖

Whipped cream
Chocolate sprinkles

Sprinkle chocolate chips on bottom of pie shell. Place in the freezer for 10 minutes.

To prepare pie filling whisk eggs, corn syrup, sugar, and salt until blended. Beat in butter and vanilla. Pour filling over chocolate chips. Arrange pecan halves in consecutive circles over filling. Bake in a 375° oven for 40 to 50 minutes, until set. Cool, then top with whipped cream and chocolate sprinkles.

Serves 6.

Hunter Peak Ranch

Box 1931
Painter Route
Cody, Wyoming 82414
(307) 587-3711
(307) 754-5878

The Hunter Peak Ranch is a small, family-owned and operated guest ranch in an unadvertised, non-commercialized area. It can handle up to thirty guests. Activities at the ranch include hiking, painting, photography, croquet, throwing horseshoes, as well as fishing in the streams, lakes, and Clarksfork River for mouth-watering trout, and swimming in Bear Creek. Rustic cabins and modern condo apartments are available as accommodations. Cabins are heated with wood; condos have steam heat. Facilities include a recreation room, library, and laundry facilities. In the Ole' Homestead House are the dining room and lodge room for conversation and dancing. Hunter Peak Ranch is known for big game hunting: elk, deer, bear, mountain sheep, moose, and mountain goat. Summer fishing pack trips are available.

Coronation Chicken

This dish is good served as a cold supper on a hot day or for a ladies' luncheon. The recipe came from a caterer in Scotland.

2 cups mayonnaise
1 10¾-ounce can cream of
**   mushroom soup**
5 pounds cooked chicken, chopped
2 avocados, chopped
1 16-ounce can sweet corn, drained
4 ribs celery, finely sliced
Salt and pepper
1 tablespoon curry powder

❖   ❖   ❖

4 cups rice
¼ cup Italian salad dressing
2 tablespoons chopped fresh herbs
¼ cup chopped green onions
¼ cup chopped green peppers

❖   ❖   ❖

1 small bunch green grapes

In a large mixing bowl combine the mayonnaise and soup, blend until smooth. Stir in chopped chicken, avocados, corn, celery, salt, pepper, and curry powder. Mix well. Chill.

Cook the rice until tender; rinse under cold water to cool. Combine with salad dressing, herbs, onions, and peppers. Place around the outer edges of a large serving platter. Mound the chicken mixture in the center. Garnish the chicken with grapes.

Serves 15.

Just Good Cookies

1 cup shortening
1 cup peanut butter (or less, to
**   taste)**
1 cup brown sugar, firmly packed
½ cup sugar
3 eggs
3 teaspoons vanilla extract
2 cups all-purpose flour
2 teaspoons baking powder
2 cups oatmeal
1 12-ounce package chocolate chips
Coconut, salted peanuts, and
**   raisins (optional)**

In a large mixing bowl cream together the shortening, peanut butter, brown sugar, and sugar. Add in eggs and vanilla extract, beat until light and fluffy.

Sift the flour and baking powder, add to the creamed mixture and blend well. Stir in oatmeal and chocolate chips, plus coconut, peanuts, or raisins if used.

Place on greased cookie sheets, making cookies any size desired. Bake in a 350° oven for 10 to 12 minutes.

Number of cookies depends on size made. Approximately 2 dozen.

Rhubarb Crisp

1 cup all-purpose flour
¾ cup uncooked oatmeal
1 cup brown sugar, firmly packed
½ cup margarine (1 stick), melted
1 tablespoon cinnamon

❖   ❖   ❖

4 to 5 cups diced rhubarb
**   (strawberries may be added)**

❖   ❖   ❖

1 cup sugar
1 tablespoon cornstarch
1 cup water
1 teaspoon vanilla extract

Combine in a mixing bowl the flour, oatmeal, brown sugar, margarine, and cinnamon. Press ½ of this mixture into a 9x13-inch pan. Cover with the rhubarb.

In a small mixing bowl place sugar and cornstarch. Stir in water and vanilla. Cook and stir until thick and clear. Pour over the rhubarb. Top with remaining crumb mixture. Bake in a 350° oven for 1 hour.

Serves 10 to 12.

Trout Creek Inn

Trout Creek
Cody, Wyoming 82414
(307) 587-6288

Like other deluxe motels, the Trout Creek Inn offers plush modern rooms with queen-size beds and color television. The location of the inn is ideal for the Yellowstone vacationer, as it is located between Cody and the national park. However, unlike at the normal motel, from the heated pool guests can see some of the most beautiful mountains in the world and even watch buffalo graze at the Trout Creek Buffalo Preserve. Horseback riding is offered; whether for an hour or a week, skilled, experienced guides will show guests the most beautiful country in the west.

Guacamole

3 to 4 avocados
1 large tomato
½ onion, coarsely chopped
Juice of 1½ lemons
Salt to taste

Peel the avocados and cut into ½-inch cubes. Cut up the tomato similarly, trying not to lose the juice. Add the onion and lemon juice. Mix well and salt to taste.

Serves 6.

Fried Trout

Split the trout in ½ lengthwise, leaving the bone on one side if desired. Cut into convenient pieces about 3 inches square. If fish is very large, you may fillet. Salt both sides, then dip into a prepared mixture of flour and egg whites to coat thoroughly; fry until brown, and serve with lime or lemon juice.

Serves 1.

Fried Cabbage

1 head cabbage
Salt to taste
Water to cover

❖ ❖ ❖

4 eggs

Shred the cabbage. Place in a saucepan with salt and water. Boil 3 to 5 minutes (depending on altitude; do not overcook). Drain well.

In a mixing bowl beat eggs. Add the cabbage and stir until well-blended. Deep fry by tablespoonfuls in hot oil.

Serves 10.

Hotel Higgins

The Paisley Shawl
Box 741
Glenrock, Wyoming 82637
(307) 436-9212

Built just after the turn of the century, in the days when Wyoming was roaring, today the Hotel Higgins still maintains its historical charm and offers sophisticated dining. From the original terrazzo in the entry to the antique Seth Thomas clock, shoe-shine stand, beautiful old piano, and victrola in the lobby, guests will find the elegance of the past restored in the present. A walk into the cozy bar will find the atmosphere as intoxicating as one's before and after dinner drinks. The chef, from the New York Culinary Institute, delights guests with gourmet dishes.

Chutney Pâté

This unusual pâté is a favorite at the Paisley Shawl.

1¼ pounds cheese, softened
1½ cups Major Grey's chutney, puréed
⅛ cup Brandy

Whip the ingredients together until very smooth. Chill at least 30 minutes. Serve with crackers or crudités.

Pike en Papillote with Caper Sauce

This recipe serves one; multiply according to the number of servings needed.

1 6 to 8-ounce fresh pike fillet
1 tablespoon wine
1 teaspoon fresh chopped dill
2 to 3 lemon slices
Salt and pepper to taste

❖ ❖ ❖

2 tablespoons chopped shallots
3 tablespoons butter
¼ cup lemon juice
1 cup chicken stock
Salt and pepper to taste

❖ ❖ ❖

2 to 3 tablespoons drained capers

Place the fillet on parchment paper, sprinkle with wine, and chopped dill, add the lemon slices, and salt and pepper to taste. Seal and bake to flaky tenderness in a 350° oven for approximately 12 minutes.

While the fish bakes, prepare the caper sauce. Sauté the shallots in butter, add the lemon juice, chicken stock, and seasonings. Cook until reduced by ½; then add the capers and simmer for 5 minutes. Serve on the side with Pike en Papillote.

Serves 1 to 2.

Poulet au Sauce Concombres

Prepare the cucumber sauce first and allow time for it to chill before preparing the chicken.

½ large cucumber
½ tablespoon Dijon mustard
½ tablespoon horseradish
½ tablespoon tarragon vinegar
2 tablespoons confectioners' sugar
½ cup whipped cream

❖ ❖ ❖

6 chicken breasts, halved
Flour
Oil
Salt and white pepper to taste
2 tablespoons tarragon leaves

Hotel Higgins

½ cup Dijon mustard
¾ cup Brandy
1¾ cups white wine

To prepare the cucumber sauce peel the cucumber, remove the seeds, and cut into chunks. Place in a blender along with ½ tablespoon Dijon mustard, horseradish, and vinegar; purée to a fine consistency. Remove to a bowl. Fold confectioners' sugar into the whipped cream, then fold whipped cream into cucumber mixture.

Prepare the chicken breasts by removing the skin, bones, fat, and sinew; butterfly and flour. Cover the bottom of a large sauté pan with oil; heat and add chicken. Sprinkle the top side lightly with salt and pepper and ½ of the tarragon leaves. Turn the breasts on the other side, sprinkle with the remaining tarragon leaves, and sauté until pale golden brown. Drain the grease from the pan, add ½ cup of Dijon mustard, Brandy, and white wine; simmer for 5 minutes until the sauce is slightly thickened. Serve with chilled cucumber sauce on the side.

Serves 6.

4-Bear Outfitters

R.R. 1, Box 110
1297 Lane 10
Powell, Wyoming 82435
(307) 754-3731

The 4-Bear Outfitters specializes in furnishing its guests with old-fashioned country hospitality, with gentle, trail-sure horses, licensed mountain guides, cozy sleeping quarters inside huge camp tents (or they will rig guests up to sleep under the stars), and mouth-watering, country-fresh cooking. Their season runs from June 1 through October 15, and they recommend that arrangements be made at least thirty days in advance of one's visit. 4-Bear Outfitters is the only outfitter in the nation who specializes in taking disabled people on wilderness trips to hunt, fish, or just have fun.

4-Bear Never Fail Bread

4 ¼-ounce packages active dry yeast
1½ cups warm water (110 to 115°)

❖   ❖   ❖

2 cups milk
½ cup lard
2 tablespoons salt
½ cup sugar
4 eggs
10 to 12 cups all-purpose flour

Place the yeast into a small bowl with water. Let stand until completely dissolved.

Scald the milk and lard in a saucepan, then pour into a large mixing bowl and allow to cool. Add the yeast, salt, sugar, eggs, and 2 cups of flour. Beat well with a wire whisk or mixer. Knead and beat in the remaining flour until smooth but not stiff. Let rise twice. Put into greased loaf pans. Bake in a 350° oven for 30 to 40 minutes, or until done.

Makes 3 to 4 loaves.

4-Bear Barbecue Burgers

This versatile recipe can be cooked on top of a camp stove, in an oven, or at home. It can be set back and kept warm until the last straggler has eaten.

5 pounds ground beef

❖   ❖   ❖

1 tablespoon Worcestershire sauce
½ cup brown sugar, firmly packed
½ cup vinegar
2½ cups ketchup
1 cup water
½ teaspoon salt
1 tablespoon liquid smoke

Shape ground beef into patties; overlap in a large Dutch oven.

Combine the remaining ingredients in a saucepan. Heat to boiling. Pour over the patties. Cook slowly until done.

Serves 8 to 12.

4-Bear's Best Corn

4 quarts corn
1 heaping tablespoon salt
1 quart water

Cut the corn off the cob; place in a large saucepan with salt and water. Simmer for 10 minutes, then serve. To freeze cool as quickly as possible and place in the freezer.

Makes 32 ½-cup servings.

4-Bear Mountain Man Marks
(Cattail Casserole)

1 pound fresh spring cattails
Salt

❖   ❖   ❖

Butter
3 cups grated Cheddar cheese
1½ cups cooked diced potatoes
Milk or cream
Paprika
Salt and pepper to taste

To prepare cattails cut stalks, clipping off top and bottom. Carefully wash in cool spring water. Then clip off the tough outer layer. Cut ivory-colored pieces into 1-inch slices; steam until tender. Remove cattails from steamer, dry on a towel, and salt lightly.

Place a small amount of butter in the bottom of a 2-quart casserole. Add cattails, cheese, and potatoes in layers. Pour a small amount of milk or cream over the top. Sprinkle with paprika, salt, and pepper. Heat in a 350° oven until thoroughly heated.

Serves 8.

4-Bear's Best-Ever Pie Crust

5 cups all-purpose flour
1 tablespoon salt
2 cups lard

❖ ❖ ❖

1 egg
⅔ cup water
1 tablespoon brown sugar
1½ tablespoons vinegar

Place the flour and salt into a large mixing bowl. Cut in ½ of the lard with a pastry blender until the mixture resembles cornmeal. Cut the remaining lard into the dough until it is pea sized.

In a small bowl beat egg into water; add brown sugar and vinegar. Add to dough, mix gently. Knead well, then let rest for a few minutes. Roll on a floured surface, rolling a little thicker than regular dough. Let the crust roll around the rolling pin to transfer to pie pan.

Makes pastry for 2 9-inch 2-crust pies.

Hotel Wolf

Post Office Box 1298
Saratoga, Wyoming 82331
(307) 326-5525

The Hotel Wolf, a three-story structure built for $6,000 in 1893, served as a stagecoach stop on the Walcott Junction stageline. During its early years, the hotel was the hub of the community and was noted for its fine food and convivial atmosphere. Early hotel registers contain names of the famous and the infamous. After extensive renovation, it is now possible to enjoy lunch, dinner, and one's favorite cocktail in the hotel's comfortable "turn of the century" Victorian atmosphere. Today the hotel rents rooms as they were in 1893, catering to sportsmen, travelers, and the general public. Of its seventeen rooms, six have private baths. The rooms are simple and quaint with cast iron beds and basic wooden dressers. The restaurant enjoys a reputation for excellence, as was true in its earliest days. The luncheon menu features a wide selection of sandwiches, as well as the "Wolf Burger," and a soup and salad bar. The dinner menu offers several steak cuts, prime rib, chicken, shrimp, and crab enhanced by the soup and salad bar.

Potage Basque Soup

4 10¾-ounce cans beef bouillon
4 10¾-ounce cans cold water
1 cup chopped cabbage
½ cup diced onion
3 unpeeled potatoes, chopped
1 clove garlic, sliced
1 tablespoon chopped parsley
½ cup barley
1 16-ounce can peeled tomatoes, chopped
6 slices bacon, chopped and lightly browned
Salt and white pepper to taste
2 cups cold water
¾ cup all-purpose flour

Bring the bouillon and 4 cans of water to a boil in a large pan or soup kettle. Add the cabbage, onion, potatoes, garlic, parsley, barley, and tomatoes. Simmer until the barley is cooked and vegetables are tender. Add the bacon, salt, and pepper, continue to simmer. Mix 2 cups of cold water and flour with a wire whisk until smooth. Slowly add flour mixture to soup mixture, stirring constantly. Cook until thickened. Adjust seasoning, if necessary.

Makes 3½ quarts.

Cheesecake

3 tablespoons butter
1 tablespoon sugar
1 cup graham cracker crumbs

❖ ❖ ❖

4 eggs
1 cup sugar
2 8-ounce packages cream cheese, softened
1 teaspoon vanilla extract

❖ ❖ ❖

½ cup sugar
½ teaspoon vanilla extract
1 16-ounce carton sour cream

Melt butter in an 8x2-inch round springform pan in a 300° oven. Add 1

Hotel Wolf

tablespoon of sugar to the crumbs, mix well; and pat down firmly into the bottom of the pan. Bake 10 minutes. Remove from the oven.

In a mixing bowl beat the eggs for 3 minutes; add 1 cup of sugar and beat for 2 more minutes. Add cream cheese slowly, then add 1 teaspoon of vanilla and continue to beat for 10 minutes. Pour into baked crust. Bake in a 325° oven for 50 to 60 minutes or until firmly set.

Add ½ cup of sugar and ½ teaspoon of vanilla to sour cream, mix well. Set this mixture aside and allow to reach room temperature while the cake bakes. Spread on the cake while it is still warm. Bake for an additional 10 to 12 minutes. Chill the cake. Remove from the pan and slice.

Serves 8 to 10.

Heck of a Hill Homestead

Post Office Box 105
Wilson, Wyoming 83014
(307) 733-2393

The Heck of a Hill Homestead is a resort on three acres adjacent to Teton National Forest. It offers a convenient location while providing a private setting. Moose, deer, and elk are frequently seen on the property. The home is styled and furnished in an elegant western fashion. A steam bath is available, and the guest bedrooms have separate bathrooms (each with shower and bath). A television satellite dish allows more than eighty channels for viewing. Fresh bread, milk, chicken, and rabbit are but a few of the delectable homemade or grown dishes served.

"Heck of a Muffin"

1 egg, beaten
¼ cup goat's milk
¼ cup safflower oil
¾ cup mashed ripe banana

❖ ❖ ❖

1 cup all-purpose unbleached flour
½ cup unprocessed bran
½ cup sugar
1 tablespoon nutritional yeast
2 teaspoons baking powder
½ teaspoon salt

❖ ❖ ❖

½ cup pecans

In a mixing bowl combine egg, milk, and oil. Stir in banana. Combine the dry ingredients; add to liquids, mixing just until moistened. Fold in pecans. Fill 12 medium-sized greased muffin cups ⅔ full. Bake in a 400° oven about 20 minutes. Delicious and healthful.

Makes 12 muffins.

Kahwa Moose

Wyoming spelling for mousse.

¼ cup sugar
4 tablespoons coffee liqueur

❖ ❖ ❖

¼ pound semi-sweet chocolate
2 tablespoons whipping cream

❖ ❖ ❖

2 egg whites, stiffly beaten
2 cups whipping cream, stiffly beaten

❖ ❖ ❖

Whipped cream for garnish

In a small saucepan over low heat cook sugar in the coffee liqueur until dissolved, but do not brown.

Melt the chocolate in a double boiler. Remove from the heat and stir in 2 tablespoons of cream. Add the coffee syrup, stirring until smooth. When the mixture is cool, fold in egg whites. Then very gently fold in 2 cups of whipped cream. Chill in parfait glasses at least 2 hours. Garnish with whipped cream.

Serves 8 to 10.

Index of Cities

Index of Foods